Forgotten Heroes
of American Education

The Great Tradition
of Teaching Teachers

A volume in
Readings in Educational Thought

Forgotten Heroes of American Education

The Great Tradition of Teaching Teachers

Edited by

J. Wesley Null

Diane Ravitch

INFORMATION AGE
PUBLISHING

Greenwich, Connecticut • www.infoagepub.com

Library of Congress Cataloging-in-Publication Data

Forgotten heroes of American education : the great tradition of teaching
teachers / edited by J. Wesley Null, Diane Ravitch.
    p. cm. – (Readings in educational thought)
  Includes bibliographical references and index.
  ISBN 1-59311-447-8 (pbk.) – ISBN 1-59311-448-6 (hardcover)
  1. Teachers–Training of–United States. 2. Education–United
States–Philosophy. 3. Educators–United States–Biography. I. Null, J.
Wesley, 1973- II. Ravitch, Diane. III. Series.
  LB1715.F56 2006
  370.71'173–dc22

                                                              2005029948

The editorial labors of Claudiu Cimpean, doctoral candidate at Baylor University,
were essential to the completion of this book. Thank you, Claudiu.

Cover photo was taken in Renner School (circa 1888), which is located in the
Dallas Heritage Village at Old City Park in Dallas, Texas; Photo was taken
by J. Wesley Null, summer 2005

Cover design assistant: Ted Filkins

For Teachers and Historians

CONTENTS

SECTION I
Selected Writings of William C. Bagley

SECTION II

Selected Writings of Charles DeGarmo

SECTION III
Selected Writings of David Felmley

SECTION IV
Selected Writings of William Torrey Harris

SECTION V
Selected Writings of Isaac Leon Kandel

SECTION VI
Selected Writings of Charles Alexander McMurry

SECTION VII
Selected Writings of William C. Ruediger

SECTION VIII
Selected Writings of Edward Austin Sheldon

SECTION IX
John Dewey's Forgotten Essays

FOREWORD

This book is titled *Forgotten Heroes of American Education* because it contains representative writings by significant educators who challenged mainstream thinking. The editors of this volume believe that the work of these thoughtful and important educators deserves to be remembered. They have been forgotten because in the great pedagogical battles of the twentieth century, they lost. They argued on behalf of a well-educated teaching profession, a coherent academic curriculum, and clearly defined standards. Time and again, they found themselves in conflict with the leaders of the education profession, who had fallen in love with romantic or political theories that diminished the value of teachers, curriculum, and standards. Time and again, they battled with their progressivist colleagues over the purpose and goals of elementary and secondary education. Because they lost the arguments, their role as leaders and thinkers was almost completely ignored by historians of education, who identified with the winners.

We think this was a grand mistake, for the ideas of men such as William Chandler Bagley and Isaac Kandel about curriculum, philosophy, teacher education, student discipline, educational ideals, and the purpose of schooling continue to be pertinent today, perhaps even more pertinent today than ever before. Today, we would call them traditionalists, for they understood the great tradition of education in which they worked. Yet they were by no means reactionaries or old fogies. They did not romanticize "the good old days." They had a clear understanding of what needed to be changed as well as what should be preserved. To their credit, they were never swept up by the fads and follies that periodically captivated their colleagues. It is for these reasons that this volume, written to honor their legacy, is called *Forgotten Heroes of American Education*.

Forgotten Heroes of American Education, pages xi–xv
Copyright © 2006 by Information Age Publishing
All rights of reproduction in any form reserved.

When I was a graduate student in the early 1970s, working towards a doctorate in the history of education at Teachers College, I never encountered the names or ideas of William Chandler Bagley or Isaac Kandel. Instead, I imbibed, along with other students of education, a partial history of our nation's educational efforts, based on the view that American education was and always would be American progressivism writ large. Two books shaped the general understanding of the history of education at that moment in time: *The Transformation of the School* and *The Wonderful World of Ellwood P. Cubberley*. Both were written by my mentor, Lawrence A. Cremin, who was then and now, even after his death, the leading scholar of American education in general and American progressivism in particular. When I started my graduate studies at Teachers College, Cremin was the chair of the department of humanities and social sciences; he later became President of Teachers College.

Cremin's *The Transformation of the School* (1961) was not only a wide-ranging intellectual history of progressivism, it was generally considered—not only at Teachers College but at schools of education across the land—the definitive account of the ideas that determined the evolution of American education. I had two copies of the book, both heavily underlined and dog-eared. In his 1965 book, *The Wonderful World of Ellwood P. Cubberley*, Cremin maintained that Cubberley had popularized a beautiful, inspiring myth about the rise and triumph of American education over all obstacles; the problem with this myth was that it was not true: New obstacles and challenges had arisen to supercede the old ones, and educators were left confused and puzzled since the story did not have the happy ending that Cubberley had led them to expect. Cremin concluded that historians of education had to acknowledge that society educates through many institutions, not just schools. He indicted Cubberley for his naïve estimation of the role of schools, but he did not point out that Cubberley's pedagogical assumptions were as much in need of criticism and revision as his political assumptions.

Cremin was a wonderful, wise, and generous mentor, and I will always be grateful to him for his guidance, his unfailing generosity, and his helpful criticism of my work. He was also a brilliant critic of progressive education. His *Transformation* contains some of the most trenchant critiques of progressive theory to be found anywhere. Yet the book nonetheless made clear that progressive education *was* the mainstream of American educational thought and that its critics were outside the mainstream. Of course, he was right. Outside the mainstream were all sorts of cranks and ideologues, as well as thoughtful and intelligent scholars like Arthur Bestor, Isaac Kandel, and William Chandler Bagley. It was not a good thing to be outside the mainstream. Some of the best and most clear-headed thinkers were ignored by Cremin, while the works of not only John Dewey but William Heard Kilpatrick, Harold Rugg, George Counts, and far lesser lights were magnified and glorified as pedagogical visionaries.

I did not think of myself as a rebel against the progressive consensus when I received my doctorate in 1975. I learned what everyone else learned. Dewey was the saint of pedagogy, the other icons of progressivism were his disciples, and Teachers College was the High Temple. Educators would lead the way to social justice and to the renewal of American life once the principles of the one true faith were fully understood and disseminated. It was only later, when I was writing *The Troubled Crusade,* that I began to think critically about the mainstream consensus, in part because I tend by habit to question whatever passes as conventional wisdom. While researching *The Troubled Crusade,* I began to read the writings of Bagley and Kandel, and I was greatly impressed. I found myself more in tune with what they were saying than with the writings of the progressive icons. I found myself enjoying their skill at exposing progressivist axioms as shibboleths. I found myself laughing as Kandel lacerated the arrogance and utopianism of progressive ideology. Slowly I realized that I was losing my belief in the first principles that I had absorbed as a graduate student.

Kandel and Bagley worried that the progressives, with their disdain for subject matter and curriculum, were undermining the schools' responsibility to foster a common culture. They feared that the younger generation would be deprived of knowledge of the history, art, literature, and science that provided the foundation for deep understanding of their culture and other cultures. They thought that civic life would be harmed if schools failed to instill high levels of civic knowledge. I found in their writings a confirmation of my own concerns about American schools in the 1980s and 1990s, my own vision of a generation of students who were being inducted by the mass media into a shoddy version of a commercialized common culture, but who were ignorant of American history, literature, foreign languages, science, and almost anything else that should be an integral part of an excellent education.

A decade later, I decided to write a book to express my counter-vision of the conventional wisdom. I thought I would focus on the ideas of Bagley and Kandel, and I would call it "The Lost Tradition of American Education." As it turned out, their ideas were not the whole book, but only a chapter (where I describe them as dissidents). The book eventually was published as *Left Back: A Century of Failed School Reforms.* It ended up as a counter-version of *The Transformation of the School,* an account of the twentieth century in which the progressives captured the mainstream with half-baked ideas that politicized the schools and undermined subject matter and student self-discipline.

I was very taken with Bagley and Kandel's insistence that good schools do not come about by magical transformation; that they are the result of good teaching, well-designed curriculum, excellent resources, and adequate public support; and that of all these factors, good teaching is chief above all. In opposition to their wise counsel, their progressive contemporaries were advising future teachers to use the schools to establish a new social order or to liberate their students from books and tests or to eliminate the schools and send the children to work in the community. It is hard to summarize in a few words why the battle went to the progressive crusaders instead of to their sensible adversaries (I spent most of *Left Back* trying to explain that outcome). One need only read the newspaper on any day to see that the hydra-headed beast of progressivist theory pops up again and again in American schools. One day, there is a story about a school that is eliminating books and tests; another day, there is a story about a school of education that is training teachers to be transformational change agents; on yet another day, a story about students who spend their time in the "real world," not in the classroom. As I write, the reform *du jour* has focused on the high school, and all of the putative solutions sound as though they were written by Kilpatrick, Rugg, or Counts.

Given this background, the reader can imagine my pleasure when one day I received a copy of a dissertation by Wesley Null, a young assistant professor of the history of education at Baylor University. The dissertation, soon to be published, was an appreciative biography of Bagley, who is one of my intellectual heroes (I contributed a chapter about Bagley to a book of essays written by historians titled *Forgotten Heroes of American History*). Null and I corresponded, aired our differences, and I soon realized that he shared many of my concerns. At present, Professor Null is writing a biography of Kandel, and I look forward to reading it, for he too is a forgotten hero of American education.

The only author that I consider a hero of American education who is not included in this collection (because, unlike the others, he was not a teacher of teachers) is W. E. B. DuBois. It was DuBois who took issue with Booker T. Washington when Washington was winning accolades from progressive educators and progressive Northern foundations for his emphasis on manual and vocational education for black students. In his writings, DuBois championed equal education, liberal education, academic education, and college education. This debate is well-known. Not so well-known is that DuBois responded to George Counts' famous question: Can the school build a new social order? While progressive educators were thrilled with this challenge to take responsibility for all of society, DuBois balked, knowing that schools did not have the capacity to do this and might neglect their fundamental responsibilities by trying to do what was far beyond their capacity. In 1935, he addressed a meeting of black teachers in Georgia and spoke directly about Counts' challenge, which was then hotly debated. He said:

Whenever a teachers' convention meets and tries to find out how it can cure the ills of society, there is simply one answer; the school has but one way to cure the ills of society and that is by making men intelligent. To make men intelligent, the school has again but one way, and that is, first and last, to teach them to read, write and count. And if the school fails to do that, and tries beyond that to do something for which a school is not adapted, it not only fails in its own function, but it fails in all other attempted functions. Because no school as such can organize industry, or settle the matter of wage and income, can found homes or furnish parents, can establish justice or make a civilized world.[1]

Of course, there is far more to education than reading, writing, and counting, and no one knew that better than W. E. B. DuBois. The point he was making, however, is that the *only* way that schools transform society is by making children more intelligent. This requires excellent teachers and excellent teaching. Nothing else can do the job. This is the work of the schools. This is what they do to uplift and change the social order, and this is what they do best.

The writers in this book believe in the importance of preparing excellent teachers for our schools. They do not believe in miracles. They know that the hard work necessary to improve schooling requires persistence, clear goals, and realistic methods. Those who have steadily advocated this vision of schooling should not have been forgotten. Wes Null and I hope that their ideas will re-enter the mainstream of American educational thought, where they belong.

—Diane Ravitch
Brooklyn, New York
July 2005

---

1. W. E. B. DuBois, cited in Kenneth James King, *Pan-Africanism and Education: A Study of Race, Philanthropy, and Education in the Southern States of America and East Africa* (Oxford, Eng.: Clarendon Press, 1971), p. 257.

ACKNOWLEDGMENTS

The research for this book was funded by a University Research Committee grant from Baylor University and a Teaching American History grant from the U.S. Department of Education.

WE MUST START OVER

A New Vision for the Profession of Teaching

The profession of teaching has been shattered. It has been shattered by bad philosophy. It has been shattered because we in the profession do not know our history. We do not know the ideas, traditions, and debates that have shaped our present practices. Our profession has been shattered by theory divorced from practical action. It has been shattered to the point that the profession has lost its soul. It has been shattered by higher education's obsession with money, power, and self-promotion. It has been shattered by the rejection of social and moral philosophy by our profession's hyper-specialized intellectual leaders. It has been shattered by higher education's emphasis on narrow research that does not relate to the social, moral, and political challenges that face the United States. The situation is grim. The hour is late. The clouds are dark. There is no time to waste.

Our current predicament, however, is not hopeless. The dominant philosophy that feeds the profession of teaching today is not the only option. There is an alternative. The time has arrived for a new vision. I want everyone who picks up this book to know that this volume—in no uncertain terms—supplies the best and most reliable foundation for this new vision. The profession of teaching will continue to decline unless its leaders—especially the profession's younger leaders—read and learn from the authors who produced the essays that are found in this volume.

Forgotten Heroes of American Education, pages xix–xxix

The purpose of this text is to draw attention to eight forgotten heroes of American education: William C. Bagley, Charles DeGarmo, David Felmley, William Torrey Harris, Isaac L. Kandel, Charles McMurry, William C. Ruediger, and Edward Austin Sheldon. Each was a powerful figure in the history of teaching. They are by no means the only forgotten members of our profession who held firm to the philosophy expressed in this book, but they are, however, some of the most essential. Due to the dominance of a certain doctrine of so-called "Progressive" educational theory during the 20th century, these thinkers have been marginalized from our profession. They have been marginalized from educational thought as well as practice. The fact that these individuals have been forgotten is a serious problem for our field, one that must be corrected.

To provide an alternative vision for the profession of teaching, we have reprinted primary source publications from these long lost educators. The only person included in this book who cannot be considered "forgotten" is John Dewey. He himself of course has not been forgotten, but certain of his essays have. We have included these forgotten works in a special chapter at the end of the book, entitled "Dewey's Forgotten Essays." We have drawn attention to Dewey's views on teacher training and his criticism of so-called "Progressive" educational philosophy.

We have introduced each author and selection with a bit of social and historical context, which helps readers to make sense of what the authors were doing with each piece of writing. These essays should be understood within their historical context, but they also are timeless in that they deal with eternal questions about curriculum, teaching, teacher education, democracy, educational philosophy, and the profession of teaching. By drawing upon these forgotten heroes, the profession of teaching once again can establish itself as a focused, powerful force in American culture. The authors included in this book provide the moral and intellectual substance that alone can revitalize the teaching profession and give the teachers of our nation the liberal and professional education they need and deserve.

The intended audience for this book includes: 1) practicing classroom teachers, 2) school administrators, 3) teacher educators who hold positions as university professors in schools of education and/or colleges of arts and sciences, 4) deans and other university administrators in schools, colleges, and departments of education, 5) college and university presidents, 6) legislators who are searching for an alternative vision for the profession of teaching, 7) historians of education, 8) curriculum specialists, 9) specialists in teacher training, and 10) members of the general public who are interested in teaching and teacher education. We believe these selections speak directly to everyone in this list. All Americans are concerned about education. Everyone has a stake in improving our schools and our democracy. This book is fundamentally about what good democratic education ought to be; consequently, it should be of interest to everyone who is interested in democracy and education.

Why am I so confident that this book is the only hope for the reconstruction of the teaching profession? I am convinced of this point for three main reasons, which I will describe in more detail below. First, this book is the only alternative to the failed Progressive educational philosophy that came to dominate the teaching profession in the 20th century. Second, this book recovers the only vision for the teaching profession that includes the what, the how, and the why dimensions of curriculum for teaching teachers. Third, and finally, this work restores the foundation of the teaching profession by realigning it with a moral and intellectual philosophy that has its roots in the work of Aristotle.

The very idea of Progressive education hinders our task of moving forward as teacher educators. When I use the term Progressive I mean to imply an approach to professional education that grows out of the efforts of psychologists such as Edward L. Thorndike and William Heard Kilpatrick from the early 20th century. These individuals believed that a "scientific" profession of teaching could be established, one that would exist separate from the various subject-matter disciplines of history, philosophy, mathematics, literature, and so forth. The Progressives' conception of "science," however, was flawed and incomplete. They accepted the label Progressive to separate themselves from the traditionalists who did not think that democratic education should be attempted in the first place. Progressives like Thorndike and Kilpatrick, to their credit, were deeply concerned about both democracy and education, but their conception of how democratic education should be realized was radically misconceived. The psychology they produced assumed that human nature could be fixed once and for all. They were wrong. Their vision failed because it was based on a flawed conception of human nature. Like the medical profession that claimed to fix the body, psychologists like Thorndike claimed they could fix human nature; in the process, they ignored the most essential aspect of human nature—the soul—and instead focused exclusively on behavior. That decision was a mistake, and our profession has paid dearly for it. The Kilpatrick and Thorndike vision also failed because the moral philosophy that feeds our profession cannot and should not be separated from the various intellectual disciplines—whether it be history, physics, government, mathematics, science, foreign languages, reading, writing, or philosophy—that teachers teach.

The individuals included in this book did not fall victim to the fractured vision of Progressives like Kilpatrick and Thorndike. They understood that disciplinary specialists have a responsibility to teach teachers, just like education faculty have a responsibility to teach teachers. Rather than obsessing with the production of theory, the heroes in this book focused the attention of their colleagues on the critically important third piece—the moral piece—of curriculum for teaching teachers. Despite the fact that Progressives like Kilpatrick talked endlessly about bringing together theory and practice, the tragic consequences of their philosophy produced an enormous gap between knowing and doing. Their actions were different from their words, and actions, as they say, speak louder than words. They produced a seemingly unbridgeable chasm between thought and action because they left nothing substantive to span the divide. Their contributions are notably weak in the realm of moral philosophy. To overcome this problem, what we need are people who integrate theory and practice *in practice*. That is what Progressives like Thorndike and Kilpatrick did not do.

The distinction between progressive in a historical sense and Progressive in a philosophical sense is worth considering at this point. William Bagley, for example, should be considered a "progressive" when our task is to understand his work within its historical context. He wrote and taught during what historians have termed the progressive era, and his work reflects the times in which he lived. When we are trying to be teachers rather than historians, however, our task is a moral, practical one, not a historical, modern scientific one. In that respect, Bagley was not a Progressive because he did not agree with Progressive moral and intellectual philosophy. He thought the Progressives' ideas culminated in nihilism, encouraged the rejection of subject-matter knowledge, abandoned the necessity for self-discipline, weakened academic standards, and inevitably lowered the status of classroom teachers. The consequences of Progressive educational philosophy are evident today. For one example, teachers are often referred to as "facilitators" rather than teachers. Which is the more honorable legacy for our profession, teachers or facilitators?

If the last fifty years of American educational history teaches us anything, it is that the Progressive vision for the teaching profession has failed. It has no future. Those who study to be teachers rarely learn that there is an alternative. They rarely encounter the ideas of traditionalists who had a substantive vision for the teaching profession. This volume gathers the leading proponents of this democratic traditionalist vision. None of these individuals allowed themselves to be reduced to a single, narrow label like traditionalist, nor did they belong to an organized group. Each of them, however, provides a new and different way to conceptualize the mission of the teaching profession. Their philosophy has long-term viability, which cannot be said of the Progressive theory that has reigned for decades, and that is undergoing severe revision today.

One example demonstrates the power of this Progressive legacy. In her book on the history of educational research, Ellen Lagemann, Dean of the

Harvard Graduate School of Education, argued that, in the history of our profession, Dewey "lost" and Thorndike "won."[1] I see this story in a different light. The reason the profession of teaching—as a whole—lost is because Thorndike and Dewey have been viewed as the only two options we have. In the broader picture of educational history and philosophy, however, Thorndike and Dewey belong in the same company. They both believed that the fields of philosophy, psychology, and pedagogy should have no connection to their European roots. They were both "functionalist" psychologists (a purely American strain) before they were behaviorists, which meant that they refused to entertain discussions of the mind or the soul. They both greatly overestimated the value of experimental psychology for teachers and teaching. They were both modernists. They both became fixated with the production of measurable results, a philosophy that reduced teachers to the status of technicians. Dewey is less guilty of this transformation than Thorndike, but, without any conception of the mind or the soul, they both reduced teaching to training, transformed teachers into mechanics at worst and facilitators at best, and disconnected the profession of teaching from its rightful historical and philosophical heritage, which stretches back to the Greek Sophists, Socrates, Plato, Aristotle, and many others.[2] From this broader perspective, the Thorndike-Kilpatrick-Dewey tradition won, and the philosophy found in the pages of this book lost.

But the thesis of this book is that the loss was only temporary, not permanent. Indeed, many of our greatest teachers have never lost or forgotten the lessons taught by the essays in this volume. The tradition of teaching and learning represented by Bagley, Kandel, DeGarmo, Sheldon, and others lives on in the work of all those teachers who understand that good teaching involves a mental or spiritual act that cannot be captured by statistical measurements. They also recognize that good teaching cannot be reduced to nothing but the product (or project) that is produced when a new teaching method is "tried out to see if it works." Good teachers also understand that they must always have an ideal of excellence in mind as they go about integrating subjects and students. Good teaching impacts the minds, hearts, and souls of students, and that dimension of teaching, learning, and curriculum was seriously neglected if not downright abandoned by the Dewey-Thorndike school of Progressivism. As a result, the ideal of teaching teachers has been abandoned by higher education,

---

1. Ellen Condliffe Lagemann, *An Elusive Science: The Troubling History of Education Research* (Chicago: University of Chicago Press, 2000), p. xi.
2. J. Wesley Null, *A Disciplined Progressive Educator: The Life and Career of William Chandler Bagley* (New York: Peter Lang, 2003), pp. 34–41.

whereas the tradition of hyper-specialization in the name of "science" and "professionalism" limps along without a clear aim in mind. The choice for our profession to make is not between Dewey and Thorndike, but rather between the democratic traditionalists found in the pages of this book and the failed vision that traces its roots back to Thorndike, Kilpatrick, and, yes, Dewey. Reading these essays makes evident that option number one is the wiser choice for us to make. This Bagley-Kandel-DeGarmo-Sheldon tradition alone has the potential to propel teaching to its proper status as a profession.

The second reason this book offers the best hope for the teaching profession is because these thinkers revive all three essential ingredients in any curriculum for teaching teachers. Their work integrates what to teach, how to teach, and why to teach. Contemporary discussions of teacher training—whether they take place in state legislatures, university seminar rooms, or think tanks far removed from classroom walls—are so polarized between sects of people who cling recklessly either to "what to teach" or "how to teach" that the results of these discussions are almost completely useless. We must do better, and with the help of the authors in this book, we can.

What to teach and how to teach are twin aspects of the same single activity. They only come together in the moral act of teaching in a classroom. As soon as curriculum for teacher training is reduced to a theoretical problem divorced from particular students in particular institutions, the heart of the curriculum that gives rise to good teachers is destroyed. The crucial piece of curriculum to remember in this respect is why to teach. Why to teach is a practical question that every prospective and practicing teacher must answer if he or she is to survive in our profession. Why to teach, moreover, leads teachers and teacher educators to address the critically important question of purpose. Purpose takes into account ideals, ends, and virtues. As many of the essays in this book make evident, subjects like history and physics are means to a greater end (for example, citizenship) that must be kept in mind if good teaching is to take place. Because of their obsession with money, power, and a narrow conception of purely intellectual prestige (as opposed to moral prestige), however, institutions of higher education have forgotten to teach their graduates, as well as their faculty, why to teach. Most institutions of higher education today have ceased to consider the question of purpose. This problem must be corrected if we are to have the teachers our nation desperately needs.

Third, the tradition that is found in this book is critical to the teaching profession because it realigns our field with the moral and intellectual philosophy of thinkers such as Plato, Aristotle, and Augustine. Most specifically, Aristotle is the thinker who influenced these eight educators most directly. His moral philosophy is evident in everything they wrote. It can be found more powerfully in some than it can in others, but, nonetheless, it is there.

When I talk with university faculty and prospective teachers about the writers included in this book, I am often asked, "Why are they important, and why should I care?". I respond that these educators matter because they recognized that teaching—as well as teaching teachers—is a moral problem, not an intellectual one. This distinction is critical.

Intellectual problems and moral problems differ not only in the subject-matter with which they deal, but also in the ends to which they are directed. The end of an intellectual problem is thinking about intellectual problems. The goal is to think and to produce new, more interesting questions for thinkers to ponder. The goal is to understand. That is it. One example of an intellectual question is "How do children learn?". Thinking about intellectual questions like this one leads to additional intellectual questions toward the end of understanding, in this example, "how children learn".

Moral problems as contrasted with intellectual problems, on the other hand, do not, cannot, and should not end in understanding. The end of a moral problem is a *decision* about what one *should do* within a particular social, moral, and political context. The goal is *to act* and *to do,* not to understand. Of course, understanding is one part of a moral problem, but it is *not the end* of a moral problem. The end of a moral problem is action, not contemplation. Action, moreover, takes place only after deliberation about the various decisions one can make in a particular political situation. The knowledge produced by intellectual conversations can and should be taken into account when a person engages in moral decision-making, but we must remember that the end of a moral problem is a decision for action and not contemplation. A good example of a moral question is "What should I *do* right now with these students in this classroom, with this man as my principal, with these objectives being forced upon me, with these students in front of me, with this school board, with this textbook, with these teaching materials at my disposal, with this parent-conference scheduled for 3rd period, and with this superintendent in charge of our district and the likelihood of his survival into next year?". The fundamental questions that teachers face every day are moral in nature, and the goal of a moral problem is to make a good decision while having a clear aim in mind when doing so.[3]

---

3. Joseph J. Schwab, "The Practical: A Language for Curriculum," *School Review* 78 (November 1969): 1–24.

The moral and intellectual philosophy that begins with these distinctions has its roots in Greek philosophy. It can be found most clearly and succinctly, however, in the social philosophy of Aristotle. Aristotle's works entitled *Nicomachean Ethics* and *Politics* form the foundation for much of what is found in this book, and the profession of teaching would be well-advised to read, reread, discuss, and use Aristotle's works in the months and years ahead.[4] Progressives from the early 20th century did everything they could to eradicate Aristotelian philosophy from the teaching profession. They thought the idea of discussing ends and purposes had become anachronistic, and they were largely successful at eliminating Aristotelian questions of purpose and action (as opposed to production) from discussions of curriculum and teaching. Discussing means, methods, and "functions" was sufficient to the Progressives.[5] In our current context, however, purpose is back. The Progressives were wrong to think that it could be eliminated. This book brings our field back to the only roots that will help us to rebuild—indeed thrive—in the 21st century when moral controversies are at the heart of every issue that Americans face.[6]

Some people may recoil at the idea of giving the title heroes to the people in this book. I disagree. We live in a time that rejects the idea of heroes. Without heroes, however, we never get heroism. Without heroes, we never get ideals and virtues. And without heroism and ideals, our nation will not prosper socially, culturally, politically, morally, or economically. Some people who produce history may tell us that there are no heroes in the past, only villains. They may tell us that the identification of heroes is somehow anti-egalitarian and oppressive. This philosophy seems fatally flawed to me. Every culture, every tradition, and every nation has heroes. The issue is not whether or not we identify heroes in our history and culture. We inevitably do. We can choose, for example, John Winthrop, Jonathan Edwards, George Whitefield, George Washington, Thomas Jefferson, Patrick Henry, Catharine Beecher, Chief Joseph, Frederick Douglass, Abraham Lincoln, Susan B. Anthony, Jane Addams, Martin

---

4. Alasdair MacIntyre, *After Virtue: A Study in Moral Theory* (Notre Dame, IN: Notre Dame University Press, 1980); For more on the rapid increase in attention to ethics in higher education, or what some scholars have termed the "ethics boom," see Michael Davis, *Ethics and the University* (London: Routledge, 1999); David Carr and Jan Steutel, Eds., *Virtue Ethics and Moral Education* (London: Routledge, 1999); and J. Mark Halstead and Terence H. McLaughlin, Eds., *Education in Morality* (London: Routledge, 1999).

5. Dewey, too, ceased to consider ends, ideals, and purposes, a change that took place in his thinking around 1900. The Dewey essays in this book, however, show him emphasizing ideals and ends, although, by 1910, his work differed in many respects from Aristotle's.

6. William A. Reid, *Curriculum as Institution and Practice: Essays in the Deliberative Tradition* (Mahwah, NJ: Lawrence Erlbaum Associates, 1999).

Luther King Jr., Malcolm X, Lyndon Johnson, Franklin Roosevelt, Eleanor Roosevelt, Ronald Reagan, Bill Clinton, none of the above, or all of the above, but we inevitably choose heroes. We need heroes to serve as models of excellence before us. Without heroes, we cannot get better at what we do. Civilizations, in fact, can be measured by the nature of the heroes they hold up as exemplars. In the end, we are forced to ask: Who should our heroes be? How should we remember them? And what should we do to keep alive the traditions they embodied?

One more question also should be addressed. If these individuals are so important, then why have they been forgotten? Why does nobody know about the ideas they advanced? The answer to these questions is complex. These heroes have been forgotten because they viewed teaching and teaching teachers as a calling, not merely a job. They have been forgotten because they believed that teaching teachers should be the heart of all institutions of higher education during a time when higher education had other ideas in mind when it came to purpose. They have been forgotten because they believed that the interaction between students and teachers was the heart of all educational institutions. They certainly respected—not to mention produced—a great deal of research, but, with regard to teaching and research within higher education, they thought teaching should trump the production of information. Yes, they advocated for better teaching, but they also campaigned tirelessly for *more teaching*. They expanded the audience for good teaching to a much wider citizenry than ever before in the history of education, American or otherwise. In the words of almost all of the founders of the American republic (e.g., George Washington, Thomas Jefferson, Noah Webster, and Benjamin Rush), their ideal was to *diffuse knowledge more generally* throughout the citizen body. Teaching teachers was the means to achieve this end. Because of the positions they took on these and other similar issues, however, they were labeled as being on the "wrong side" of a theoretic battle that should have been moral and practical in the first place.

The emphasis on more high-quality teaching for more young people, however, was not the trend within higher education during the times in which they lived. Research and the production of theoretic explanations was becoming the ideal, not the application of a well-conceived social philosophy of teaching. These heroes also have been forgotten because the audience for their work vanished beneath their feet. As the field of education was ripped into warring camps of theoretically-driven Progressives and Traditionalists, the moral middle ground where these eight educators dared to travel gave way to a hollow core where only the echoes of each other's lonely voices could be found.

Finally, these educators have been forgotten because all of them took on the seriously difficult task of raising the status of the teaching profession. This has been a thankless, if not dangerous, job since at least as early as the 18th century when Noah Webster challenged legislators and the American public when he wrote: "Education, in a great measure, forms the moral characters of men, and morals are the basis of government. Education should therefore be the first care of a legislature, not merely the institution of schools but the furnishing of them with the best teachers.... I am so fully persuaded of this that I shall almost adore that great man who shall change our practice and opinions and make it respectable for the first and best men to superintend the education of youth."[7] All of these teacher educators had read Webster, and all of them understood his point. Picking up the mantle that Webster laid at their feet, however, did not lead to popularity.

The story of the marginalization of teacher education took place in every state in the nation during the 20th century. This development occurred at the same time that morality was discarded by what were once Christian institutions of higher education.[8] The consequences are tragic, sad, and shameful. Much of higher education has abandoned our nation's teachers and children. Few institutions of higher education hold up 3rd grade teachers as their most distinguished alumni, and that is a serious problem for American democracy. Teachers nationwide should be furious about this situation. The questions to be asked are endless. Why, for example, is running a corporation an acceptable end to leaders within higher education, whereas dedicating one's life to teaching children to read is not? How often do those who, in always glowing rhetoric, proclaim that education is the greatest and noblest of all human callings encourage their own sons to enter the work of the public schools? Why do the words that leaders give teachers always differ so greatly from what these leaders do? Teachers and teacher educators should ask and expect substantive answers to these and other questions. The most important task that any institution of higher education does is teach teachers. Upon graduation, higher education then must support these teachers during their careers as they lead the children and youth of our nation.

One of the primary reasons we do not know the story that is found in this book is because historians within universities have written the history of higher education that we know, not the teachers and the teacher educators who did the difficult, practical work of teaching every day. The

---

7. Noah Webster, "On the Education of Youth in America" (1790), in Frederick Rudolph, Ed., *Essays on Education in the Early Republic* (Cambridge, MA: Harvard University Press, 1965), pp. 63–64.
8. Julie A. Reuben, *The Making of the Modern University: Intellectual Transformation and the Marginalization of Morality* (Chicago: University of Chicago Press, 1996).

time has come for this situation to change. The challenge in our current situation is for legislators and leaders within higher education to rededicate themselves—and their institutions—to the ideal of teaching teachers. I hope they have the will to do so.

I do not want to conclude this introduction without thanking Diane Ravitch for her advice, diligence, and support in the production of this book. She collaborated in every aspect of the work, she helped to write and edit the introductions, and she asked the right questions about who should be included, what should be included, and why. In the course of our conversations and work, I hope that we have begun to remember the great forgotten content that holds teachers and historians together. The soul of the teaching profession has been shattered, and the time has long passed for us to work together to make it whole again. That is the moral challenge of our age. Dare we find the courage to face it?

—J. Wesley Null
Waco, Texas
July 2005

Section 1

SELECTED WRITINGS OF WILLIAM C. BAGLEY

William Chandler Bagley (1874–1946) is a forgotten hero of American education. Time and again, in the course of a long career as a teacher of teachers, he stood up and debated those whose ideas were harmful to American education. He was a staunch defender of high academic standards, discipline in the classroom, clear thinking, and common-sense approaches to educating children. Because he had been a teacher, a principal, and superintendent before he became a professor of education, he understood the needs of children and the dynamics of the classroom, unlike many of his intellectual adversaries, who know only theory. Bagley was a kindly, softspoken man, known for his courtesy and civility, but he never hesitated to enter the arena to argue forcefully against flawed ideas. His greatest ambition was to be a teacher of teachers, which he was, but his destiny was to become the leading challenger of powerful ideas that gripped the elites of his profession. Thus, he became the most prominent critic of romantic child-centered education, wherein the child is supposed to decide what he wants to learn and do; the most prominent critic of the misuse of intelligence tests by psychologists who believed that intelligence was innate, fixed, unchangeable, and tied to racial and ethnic origins; and the most prominent critic of those psychologists who tried to undermine the academic curriculum by claiming that it had no value. Underlying Bagley's role as a critic was his steadfast belief in the importance of teachers,

Forgotten Heroes of American Education, pages 1–3

not as facilitators but as teachers who had the power to change children's lives and improve society.

Bagley was born on March 15, 1874, in Detroit, Michigan. He attended elementary school in Weymouth, Massachusetts, before his family returned to Detroit in 1887. Bagley graduated from Detroit's Capitol High School in 1891. He then attended Michigan Agricultural College from 1891 to 1895. He began his career as a teacher in the fall of 1895. He taught in a one-room school in the Upper Peninsula of Michigan near Garth and Rapid River. From this point forward, Bagley made the profession of teaching his calling. He continued to study by enrolling as a graduate student at the University of Chicago in 1896. He only attended graduate school at Chicago, however, for one summer. He completed his Master's degree, in psychology, at the University of Wisconsin in Madison in 1898. He then moved to Cornell University in Ithaca, New York, where he studied with nationally-prominent psychologist Edward Bradford Titchener. Bagley completed his Ph.D. degree in psychology at Cornell in 1901.

Despite his Cornell training as a researcher, Bagley remained committed to the teaching profession. In 1901, he took his new knowledge of psychology with him to St. Louis, Missouri. In St. Louis, he was an elementary school principal during the 1901–1902 school year. In 1902, he and his family moved across the country to Dillon, Montana. He taught teachers from 1902 to 1906 at Dillon's Montana State Normal School. He left Dillon in 1906 to accept a faculty position at the acclaimed Oswego State Normal School in Oswego, New York. Bagley remained at Oswego for only two years, however, before moving to the University of Illinois in 1908.

While at the University of Illinois from 1908 to 1917, Bagley worked to establish the university's first teacher training program for high school teachers. He and his colleagues were successful at creating the School of Education at the University of Illinois in 1916. Bagley soon left Illinois, however, to teach and conduct research at Teachers College, Columbia University. Teachers College offered Bagley a position that allowed him to focus his efforts on improving the nation's teacher training schools. He began his faculty appointment at Teachers College in 1918 after working for approximately two years at the Carnegie Foundation for the Advancement of Teaching. Bagley lived in the New York City area until his death on July 1, 1946.

For nearly fifty years, Bagley remained deeply committed to teaching teachers. He continued an American tradition in teacher education that began most prominently at Oswego in the 1860s with Edward Austin Sheldon. Bagley worked assiduously to continue this tradition by focusing all of his professional energies on the moral and intellectual task of teaching teachers. He was both a scholar who labored to understand the history and philosophy of education, as well as a practitioner who put these ideas into practice by helping to improve the nation's body of teachers.[1]

Bagley published dozens of books and hundreds of articles during his almost fifty year career. Examples of his books include *The Educative Process, Craftsmanship in Teaching, Determinism in Education,* and *Education and Emergent Man.*[2] The fact that Bagley has been narrowly caricatured by the profession of teaching for almost fifty years demonstrates the fact that very few people have taken the time to read and understand his work. Liberal arts, science, and education faculty members in the 21st century have much to learn from Bagley's example.

1. J. Wesley Null, *A Disciplined Progressive Educator: The Life and Career of William Chandler Bagley* (New York: Peter Lang, 2003).
2. William C. Bagley, *The Educative Process* (New York: Macmillan, 1905); William C. Bagley, *Craftsmanship in Teaching* (New York: Macmillan, 1911); William C. Bagley, *Determinism in Education* (Baltimore, MD: Warwick and York, 1925); and William C. Bagley, *Education and Emergent Man* (New York: T. Nelson and Sons, 1934).

Craftsmanship in Teaching
(1907)[1]

Between 1905 and 1911, Bagley delivered numerous lectures and commencement addresses at schools and colleges in Montana, Idaho, Utah, South Dakota, and New York. In 1911, he collected these addresses and published them as a book entitled Craftsmanship in Teaching. *These writings are unique in that Bagley had teachers and the general public—not other psychologists—in mind as his audience. During this time in his life, he wrote alternately for scholars of education and for a general public, especially teachers. Unlike his work on educational psychology, essays such as this one provide insight into Bagley's personal views and his personality.*

Bagley delivered this address, entitled "Craftsmanship in Teaching," to the graduating class of Oswego State Normal School in February of 1907. He had been teaching at Oswego for six months. With the notion of "craft," Bagley is emphasizing the artistry that he thought is involved in all good teaching. He was an energetic young man at the time, and, with his various addresses, books, and articles, he was fighting to establish social, political, and economic support for his profession.

Bagley's idealism as a teacher of teachers is evident in this paper. He discusses several "vows" that he argues teachers must make if they are to be successful at their craft. The teaching profession, he insists, is not truly comparable with professions such as medicine and law. Those professions, he holds, are less dependent on moral ideals, while the profession of teaching has an ethical ideal at its very core.

---

1. An address to the graduating class of the Oswego, New York, State Normal School, February, 1907.

Forgotten Heroes of American Education, pages 5–16

In the laboratory of life, each newcomer repeats the old experiments, and laughs
and weeps for himself. We will be explorers, though all the highways have their
guideposts and every bypath is mapped. Helen of Troy will not deter us, nor the wounds
of Caesar frighten, nor the voice of the king crying "Vanity!" from his throne dismay.
What wonder that the stars that once sang for joy are dumb and the
constellations go down in silence.

—Arthur Sherburne Hardy: *The Wind of Destiny.*

I

We tend, I think, to look upon the advice that we give to young people as
something that shall disillusionize them. The cynic of forty sneers at what
he terms the platitudes of commencement addresses. He knows life. He
has been behind the curtains. He has looked upon the other side of the
scenery,—the side that is just framework and bare canvas. He has seen the
ugly machinery that shifts the stage setting—the stage setting which
appears so impressive when viewed from the front. He has seen the rouge
on the cheeks that seem to blush with the bloom of youth and beauty and
innocence, and has caught the cold glint in the eyes that, from the
distance, seem to languish with tenderness and love. Why, he asks, should
we create an illusion that must thus be rudely dispelled? Why revamp and
refurbish the old platitudes and dole them out each succeeding year? Why
not tell these young people the truth and let them be prepared for the fate
that must come sooner or later?

But the cynic forgets that there are some people who never lose their
illusions,—some men and women who are always young,—and, whatever
may be the type of men and women that other callings and professions
desire to enroll in their service, this is the type that education needs. The
great problem of the teacher is to keep himself in this class, to keep himself
young, to preserve the very things that the cynic pleases to call the illusions
of his youth. And so much do I desire to impress these novitiates into our
calling with the necessity for preserving their ideals that I shall ask them
this evening to consider with me some things which would, I fear, strike the
cynic as most illusionary and impractical. The initiation ceremonies that
admitted the young man to the privileges and duties of knighthood
included the taking of certain vows, the making of certain pledges of
devotion and fidelity to the fundamental principles for which chivalry
stood. And I should like this evening to imagine that these graduates are
undergoing an analogous initiation into the privileges and duties of
schoolcraft, and that these vows which I shall enumerate, embody some of
the ideals that govern the work of that craft.

II

And the first of these vows I shall call, for want of a better term, the vow of "artistry,"—the pledge that the initiate takes to do the work that his hand finds to do in the best possible manner, without reference to the effort that it may cost or to the reward that it may or may not bring.

I call this the vow of artistry because it represents the essential attitude of the artist toward his work. The cynic tells us that ideals are illusions of youth, and yet, the other day I saw expressed in a middle-aged working-man a type of idealism that is not at all uncommon in this world. He was a house painter; his task was simply the prosaic job of painting a door; and yet, from the pains which he took with that work, an observer would have concluded that it was, to the painter, the most important task in the world. And that, after all, is the true test of craft artistry: to the true craftsman the work that he is doing must be the most important thing that can be done. One of the best teachers that I know is that kind of a craftsman in education. A student was once sent to observe his work. He was giving a lesson upon the "attribute complement" to an eighth-grade grammar class. I asked the student afterward what she had got from her visit. "Why," she replied, "that man taught as if the very greatest achievement in life would be to get his pupils to understand the attribute complement,—and when he had finished, they did understand it."

In a narrower sense, this vow of artistry carries with it an appreciation of the value of technique. From the very fact of their normal school training, these graduates already possess a certain measure of skill, a certain mastery of the technique of their craft. This initial mastery has been gained in actual contact with the problems of school work in their practice teaching. They have learned some of the rudiments; they have met and mastered some of the rougher, cruder difficulties. The finer skill, the delicate and intangible points of technique, they must acquire, as all beginners must acquire them, through the strenuous processes of self-discipline in the actual work of the years that are to come. This is a process that takes time, energy, constant and persistent application. All that this school or any school can do for its students in this respect is to start them upon the right track in the acquisition of skill. But do not make the mistake of assuming that this is a small and unimportant matter. If this school did nothing more than this, it would still repay tenfold the cost of its establishment and maintenance. Three fourths of the failures in a world that sometimes seems full of failures are due to nothing more nor less than a wrong start. In spite of the growth of professional training for teachers within the past fifty years, many of our lower schools are still filled with raw recruits, fresh from the high schools and even from the grades, who must learn every practical lesson of teaching through the medium of their own mistakes.

Even if this were all, the process would involve a tremendous and uncalled-for waste. But this is not all; for, out of this multitude of untrained teachers, only a small proportion ever recognize the mistakes that they make and try to correct them.

To you who are beginning the work of life, the mastery of technique may seem a comparatively unimportant matter. You recognize its necessity, of course, but you think of it as something of a mechanical nature,—an integral part of the day's work, but uninviting in itself,—something to be reduced as rapidly as possible to the plane of automatism and dismissed from the mind. I believe that you will outgrow this notion. As you go on with your work, as you increase in skill, ever and ever the fascination of its technique will take a stronger and stronger hold upon you. This is the great saving principle of our workaday life. This is the factor that keeps the toiler free from the deadening effects of mechanical routine. It is the factor that keeps the farmer at his plow, the artisan at his bench, the lawyer at his desk, the artist at his palette.

I once worked for a man who had accumulated a large fortune. At the age of seventy-five he divided this fortune among his children, intending to retire; but he could find pleasure and comfort only in the routine of business. In six months he was back in his office. He borrowed twenty-five thousand dollars on his past reputation and started in to have some fun. I was his only employee at the time, and I sat across the big double desk from him, writing his letters and keeping his accounts. He would sit for hours, planning for the establishment of some industry or running out the lines that would entangle some old adversary. I did not stay with him very long, but before I left, he had a half-dozen thriving industries on his hands, and when he died three years later he had accumulated another fortune of over a million dollars.

That is an example of what I mean by the fascination that the technique of one's craft may come to possess. It is the joy of doing well the work that you know how to do. The finer points of technique,—those little things that seem so trivial in themselves and yet which mean everything to skill and efficiency,—what pride the competent artisan or the master artist takes in these! How he delights to revel in the jargon of his craft! How he prides himself in possessing the knowledge and the technical skill that are denied the layman!

I am aware that I am somewhat unorthodox in urging this view of your work upon you. Teachers have been encouraged to believe that details are not only unimportant but stultifying,—that teaching ability is a function of personality, and not a product of a technique that must be acquired through the strenuous discipline of experience. One of the most skillful teachers of my acquaintance is a woman down in the grades. I have watched her work for days at a time, striving to learn its secret. I can find nothing there that is due to genius,—unless we accept George Eliot's definition of genius as an infinite capacity for receiving discipline. That teacher's success, by her own statement, is due to a mastery of technique, gained through successive years of growth checked by a rigid responsibility for results. She has found out by repeated trial how to do her work in the best way; she has discovered the attitude toward her pupils that will get the best work from them,—the clearest methods of presenting subject matter; the most effective ways in which to drill; how to use text-books and make study periods issue in something besides mischief; and, more than all else, how to do these things without losing sight of the true end of education. Very frequently I have taken visiting school men to see this teacher's work. Invariably after leaving her room they have turned to me with such expressions as these: "A born teacher!" "What interest!" "What a personality" "What a voice!"—everything, in fact, except this,—which would have been the truth: "What a tribute to years of effort and struggle and self-discipline!"

I have a theory which I have never exploited very seriously, but I will give it to you for what it is worth. It is this: elementary education especially needs a literary interpretation. It needs a literary artist who will portray to the public in the form of fiction the real life of the elementary school,—who will idealize the technique of teaching as Kipling idealized the technique of the marine engineer, as Balzac idealized the technique of the journalist, as Du Maurier and a hundred other novelists have idealized the technique of the artist. We need some one to exploit our shop-talk on the reading public, and to show up our work as you and I know it, not as you and I have been told by laymen that it ought to be,—a literature of the elementary school with the cant and the platitudes and the goody-goodyism left out, and in their place something of the virility, of the serious study, of the manful effort to solve difficult problems, of the real and vital achievements that are characteristic of thousands of elementary schools throughout the country to-day.

At first you will be fascinated by the novelty of your work. But that soon passes away. Then comes the struggle,—then comes the period, be it long or short, when you will work with your eyes upon the clock, when you will count the weeks, the days, the hours, the minutes that lie between you and vacation time. Then will be the need for all the strength and all the energy that you can summon to your aid. Fail here, and your fate is decided once and for all. If, in your work, you never get beyond this stage, you will never become the true craftsman. You will never taste the joy that is vouchsafed the expert, the efficient craftsman.

The length of this period varies with different individuals. Some teachers "find themselves" quickly. They seem to settle at once into the teaching attitude. With others, it is a long, uphill fight. But it is safe to say that if, at the end of three years, your eyes still habitually seek the clock,—if, at the end of that time, your chief reward is the check that comes at the end of every fourth week,—then your doom is sealed.

III

And the second vow that I should urge these graduates to take is the vow of fidelity to the spirit of their calling. We have heard a great deal in recent years about making education a profession. I do not like that term myself. Education is not a profession in the sense that medicine and law are professions. It is rather a craft, for its duty is to produce, to mold, to fashion, to transform a certain raw material into a useful product. And, like all crafts, education must possess the craft spirit. It must have a certain code of craft ethics; it must have certain standards of craft excellence and efficiency. And in these the normal school must instruct its students, and to these it should secure their pledge of loyalty and fidelity and devotion.

A true conception of this craft spirit in education is one of the most priceless possessions of the young teacher, for it will fortify him against every criticism to which his calling is subjected. It is revealing no secret to tell you that the teacher's work is not held in the highest regard by the vast majority of men and women in other walks of life. I shall not stop to inquire why this is so, but the fact cannot be doubted, and every now and again some incident of life, trifling perhaps in itself, will bring it to your notice; but most of all, perhaps you will be vexed and incensed by the very thing that is meant to put you at your ease—the patronizing attitude which your friends in other walks of life will assume toward you and toward your work.

When will the good public cease to insult the teacher's calling with empty flattery? When will men who would never for a moment encourage their own sons to enter the work of the public schools, cease to tell us that education is the greatest and noblest of all human callings? Education does not need these compliments. The teacher does not need them. If he is a master of his craft, he knows what education means,—he knows this far better than any layman can tell him. And what boots it to him, if, with all this cant and hypocrisy about the dignity and worth of his calling, he can sometimes hold his position only at the sacrifice of his self-respect?

But what is the relation of the craft spirit to these facts? Simply this: the true craftsman, by the very fact that he is a true craftsman, is immune to these influences. What does the true artist care for the plaudits or the sneers of the crowd? True, he seeks commendation and welcomes applause, for your real artist is usually extremely human; but he seeks this commendation from another source—from a source that metes it out less lavishly and yet with unconditioned candor. He seeks the commendation of his fellow workmen, the applause of "those who know, and always will know, and always will understand." He plays to the pit and not to the gallery, for he knows that when the pit really approves the gallery will often echo and reecho the applause, albeit it has not the slightest conception of what the whole thing is about.

What education stands in need of to-day is just this: a stimulating and pervasive craft spirit. If a human calling would win the world's respect, it must first respect itself; and the more thoroughly it respects itself, the greater will be the measure of homage that the world accords it. In one of the educational journals a few yeas ago, the editors ran a series of articles under the general caption, "Why I am a teacher." It reminded me of the spirited discussion that one of the Sunday papers started some years since on the world-old query, "Is marriage a failure?" And some of the articles were fully as sickening in their harrowing details as were some of the whining matrimonial confessions of the latter series. But the point that I wish to make is this: your true craftsman in education never stops to ask himself such questions. There are some men to whom schoolcraft is a mistress. They love it, and their devotion is no make-believe, fashioned out of sentiment, and donned for the purpose of hiding inefficiency or native indolence. They love it as some men love Art, and others Business, and others War. They do not stop to ask the reason why, to count the cost, or to care a fig what people think. They are properly jealous of their special knowledge, gained through years of special study; they are justly jealous of their special skill gained through years of discipline and training. They resent the interference of laymen in matters purely professional. They resent such interference as would a reputable physician, a reputable lawyer, a reputable engineer. They resent officious patronage and "fussy" meddling. They resent all these things manfully, vigorously. But your true craftsman will not whine. If the conditions under which he works do not suit him, he will fight for their betterment, but he will not whine.

IV

And yet this vow of fidelity and devotion to this spirit of schoolcraft would be an empty form without the two complementary vows that give it worth and meaning. These are the vow of poverty and the vow of service. It is through these that the true craft spirit must find its most vigorous expression and its only justification. The very corner stone of schoolcraft is service, and one fundamental lesson that the tyro in schoolcraft must learn, especially in this materialistic age, is that the value of service is not to be measured in dollars and cents. In this respect, teaching resembles art, music, literature, discovery, invention, and pure science; for, if all the workers in all of these branches of human activity got together and demanded of the world the real fruits of their self-sacrifice and labor, if they demanded all the riches and comforts and amenities of life that have flowed directly or indirectly from their efforts,—there would be little left for the rest of mankind. Each of these activities is represented by a craft spirit that recognizes this great truth. The artist or the scientist who has an itching palm, who prostitutes his craft for the sake of worldly gain, is quickly relegated to the oblivion that he deserves. He loses caste, and the caste of craft is more precious to your true craftsman than all the gold of the modern Midas.

You may think that this is all very well to talk about, but that it bears little agreement to the real conditions. Let me tell you that you are mistaken. Go ask Rontgen why he did not keep the X-rays a secret to be exploited for his own personal gain. Ask the shade of the great Helmholtz why he did not patent the ophthalmoscope. Go to the University of Wisconsin and ask Professor Babcock why he gave to the world without money and without price the Babcock test—an invention which is estimated to mean more than one million dollars every year to the farmers and dairymen of that state alone. Ask the men on the geological survey who laid bare the great gold deposits of Alaska why they did not leave a thankless and ill-paid service to acquire the wealth that lay at their feet. Because commercialized ideals govern the world that we know, we think that all men's eyes are jaundiced, and that all men's vision is circumscribed by the milled rim of the almighty dollar. But we are sadly, miserably mistaken.

Do you think that these ideals of service from which every taint of self-seeking and commercialism have been eliminated - do you think that these are mere figments of the impractical imagination? Go ask Perry Holden out in Iowa. Go ask Luther Burbank out in California. Go to any agricultural college in this broad land and ask the scientists who are doing more than all other forces combined to increase the wealth of the people. Go to the scientific departments at Washington where men of genius are toiling for a pittance. Ask them how much of the wealth for which they are responsible they propose to put into their own pockets. What will be their answer? They will tell *you* that all they ask is a living wage, a chance to work, and the just recognition of their services by those who know and appreciate and understand.

But let me hasten to add that these men claim no especial merit for their altruism and unselfishness. They do not pose before the world as philanthropists. They do not strut about and preen themselves as one who would say: "See what a noble man am I! See how I sacrifice myself for the welfare of society!" The attitude of cant and pose is entirely alien to the spirit of true service. Their delight is in doing, in serving, in producing.

But beyond this, they have the faults and frailties of their kind, save one, the sin of covetousness. And again, all that they ask of the world is a living wage, and the privilege to serve.

And that is all that the true craftsman in education asks. The man or woman with the itching palm has no place in the schoolroom,—no place in any craft whose keynote is service. It is true that the teacher does not receive to-day, in all parts of our country, a living wage; and it is equally true that society at large is the greatest sufferer because of its penurious policy in this regard. I should applaud and support every movement that has for its purpose the raising of teachers' salaries to the level of those paid in other branches of professional service. Society should do this for its own benefit and in its own defense, not as a matter of charity to the men and women who, among all public servants, should be the last to be accused of feeding gratuitously at the public crib. I should approve all honest efforts of school men and school women toward this much desired end. But whenever men and women enter schoolcraft because of the material rewards that it offers, the virtue will have gone out of our calling, just as the virtue went out of the Church when, during the Middle Ages, the Church attracted men not because of the opportunities that it offered for social service, but because of the opportunities that it offered for the acquisition of wealth and temporal power,—just as the virtue has gone out of certain other once-noble professions that have commercialized their standards and tarnished their ideals.

This is not to say that one condemns the man who devotes his life to the accumulation of property. The tremendous strides that our country has made in material civilization have been conditioned in part by this type of genius. Creative genius must always compel our admiration and our respect. It may create a world epic, a matchless symphony of tones or pigments, a scientific theory of tremendous grasp and limitless scope; or it may create a vast industrial system, a commercial enterprise of gigantic proportions, a powerful organization of capital. Genius is pretty much the same wherever we find it, and everywhere we of the common clay must recognize its worth.

The grave defect in our American life is not that we are hero worshipers, but rather that we worship but one type of hero; we recognize but one type of achievement; we see but one sort of genius. For two generations our youth have been led to believe that there is only one ambition that is worth while,—the ambition of property. Success at any price is the ideal that has been held up before our boys and girls. And to-day we are reaping the rewards of this distorted and unjust view of life.

I recently met a man who had lived for some years in the neighborhood of St. Paul and Minneapolis,—a section that is peopled, as you know, very largely by Scandinavian immigrants and their descendants. This man told me that he had been particularly impressed by the high idealism of the Norwegian people. His business brought him in contact with Norwegian immigrants in what are called the lower walks of life,—with workingmen and servant girls,—and he made it a point to ask each of these young men and young women the same question. "Tell me," he would say, "who are the great men of your country? Who are the men toward whom the youth of your land are led to look for inspiration? Who are the men whom your boys are led to imitate and emulate and admire?" And he said that he almost always received the same answer to this question: the great names of the Norwegian nation that had been burned upon the minds even of these working men and servant girls were just four in number: Ole Bull, Bjornson, Ibsen, Nansen. Over and over again he asked that same question; over and over again he received the same answer: Ole Bull, Bjornson, Ibsen, Nansen. A great musician, a great novelist, a great dramatist, a great scientist.

And I conjectured as I heard of this incident, What would be the answer if the youth of our land were asked that question: "Who are the great men of *your* country? What type of achievement have you been led to imitate and emulate and admire?" How many of our boys and girls have even heard of our great men in the world of culture,—unless, indeed, such men lived a half century ago and have got into the school readers by this time? How many of our boys and girls have ever heard of MacDowell, or James, or Whistler, or Sargent?

I have said that the teacher must take the vow of service. What does this imply except that the opportunity for service, the privilege of serving, should be the opportunity that one seeks, and that the achievements toward which one aspires should be the achievements of serving? The keynote of service lies in self-sacrifice,—in self-forgetfulness, rather—in merging one's own life in the lives of others. The attitude of the true teacher in this respect is very similar to the attitude of the true parent. In so far as the parent feels himself responsible for the character of his children, in so far as he holds himself culpable for their shortcomings and instrumental in shaping their virtues, he loses himself in his children. What we term parental affection is, I believe, in part an outgrowth of this feeling of responsibility. The situation is precisely the same with the teacher. It is when the teacher begins to feel himself responsible for the growth and development of his pupils that he begins to find himself in the work of teaching. It is then that the effective devotion to his pupils has its birth. The affection that comes prior to this is, I think, very likely to be of the sentimental and transitory sort.

In education, as in life, we play altogether too carelessly with the word "love." The test of true devotion is self-forgetfulness. Until the teacher reaches that point, he is conscious of two distinct elements in his work,—

himself and his pupils. When that time comes, his own *ego* drops from view, and he lives in and for his pupils. The young teacher's tendency is always to ask himself, "Do my pupils like me?" Let me say that this is beside the question. It is not, from his standpoint, a matter of the pupils liking their teacher, but of the teacher liking his pupils. That, I take it, must be constantly the point of view. If you ask the other question first, you will be tempted to gain your end by means that are almost certain to prove fatal,— to bribe and pet and cajole and flatter, to resort to the dangerous expedient of playing to the gallery; but the liking that you get in this way is not worth the price that you pay for it. I should caution young teachers against the short-sighted educational theories that are in the air to-day, and that definitely recommend this attitude. They may sound sweet, but they are soft and sticky in practice. Better be guided by instinct than by "half-baked" theory. I have no disposition to criticize the attempts that have been made to rationalize educational practice, but a great deal of contemporary theory starts at the wrong end. It has failed to go to the sources of actual experience for its data. I know a father and mother who have brought up ten children successfully, and I may say that you could learn more about managing boys and girls from observing their methods than from a half-dozen prominent books on educational theory that I could name.

And so I repeat that the true test of the teacher's fidelity to this vow of service is the degree in which he loses himself *in* his pupils,—the degree *in* which he lives and toils and sacrifices for them just for the pure joy that *it* brings him. Once you have tasted this joy, no carping sneer of the cynic can cause you to lose faith in your calling. Material rewards sink into insignificance. You no longer work with your eyes upon the clock. The hours are all too short for the work that you would do. You are as light-hearted and as happy as a child,—for you have lost yourself to find yourself, and you have found yourself to lose yourself.

V

And the final vow that I would have these graduates take is the vow of idealism,—the pledge of fidelity and devotion to certain fundamental principles of life which it is the business of education carefully to cherish and nourish and transmit untarnished to each succeeding generation. These but formulate in another way what the vows that I have already discussed mean by implication. One is the ideal of social service, upon which education must, in the last analysis, rest its case. The second is the ideal of science,—the pledge of devotion to that persistent unwearying search after truth, of loyalty to the great principles of unbiased observation and unprejudiced experiment, of willingness to accept the truth and be governed by it, no matter how disagreeable it may be, no matter how roughly it may trample down our pet doctrines and our preconceived theories. The nineteenth century left us a glorious heritage in the great discoveries and inventions that science has established. These must not be lost to posterity; but far better lose them than lose the spirit of free inquiry, the spirit of untrammeled investigation, the noble devotion to truth for its own sake that made these discoveries and inventions possible.

It is these ideals that education must perpetuate, and if education is successfully to perpetuate them, the teacher must himself be filled with a spirit of devotion to the things that they represent. Science has triumphed over superstition and fraud and error. It is the teacher's duty to see to it that this triumph is permanent, that mankind does not again fall back into the black pit of ignorance and superstition.

And so it is the teacher's province to hold aloft the torch, to stand against the materialistic tendencies that would reduce all human standards to the common denominator of the dollar, to insist at all times and at all places that this nation of ours was founded upon idealism, and that, whatever may be the prevailing tendencies of the time, its children shall still learn to live "among the sunlit peaks." And if the teacher is imbued with this idealism, although his work may take him very close to Mother Earth, he may still lift his head above the fog and look the morning sun squarely in the face.

Ideals versus Generalized Habits
(1904)

One of Bagley's earliest engagements in controversy occurred in 1904 when he questioned the findings of Edward L. Thorndike, who was then the most powerful figure in the field of educational psychology. Thorndike had conducted a series of experimental studies which undermined the legitimacy of requiring students to take subjects like Latin and algebra. Over many generations, educators had believed that these subjects, because they are abstract and require rigorous thinking, taught students the value of self-discipline, logical thinking, and good study habits. Thorndike aimed to demonstrate that there was no "transfer of training," that what is learned in one study cannot be "transferred" to other applications in school or in life, and that therefore students learn only Latin when they study Latin, not good habits or clear thinking. Progressive educators greeted Thorndike's findings with glee, convinced that he had utterly demolished the rationale for the academic curriculum. From his work, they took as their mantra the belief that "you study what you study, and you learn what you learn." The only thing that students gain from the study of a foreign language, for example, was the knowledge of that language, not the ability to learn other subjects or become a better student. Thus, it became reasonable to argue that students should study vocational and industrial subjects, which were considered to have a "real" function in their lives, rather than academic subjects whose value was allegedly disproved by Thorndike.

As Progressive educators celebrated this upheaval of traditional assumptions about the value of academic studies, Bagley issued the following criticism of Thorndike's work, setting himself against not only the leader of his own field, psychology, but the numerous and influential university professors who hailed Thorndike's attacks on the academic curriculum.

Forgotten Heroes of American Education, pages 17–22

Bagley identifies several dangers that will come to pass if educators in general and psychologists in particular do not listen to his warnings. He criticizes psychologists who were over generalizing the results of Thorndike's work, yet the attacks on the academic curriculum based upon Thorndike's claims continued for decades to come. Much of the criticism that Bagley levels not only in this essay, but also in his more public-oriented scholarship has its roots in his disagreements with Thorndike.

The doctrine of the "formal disciplines" seems to be doomed. For some time educational theory has looked upon it with not a little doubt, and very recently experimental evidence has spoken so strongly against its validity that even its best friends are beginning to waver in their loyalty.

A formal discipline attempts to cultivate what may be termed a "generalized habit." A simple habit is a specific response to a specific stimulus. A generalized habit would be a specific response common to a number of different stimuli. The doctrine of formal disciplines assumes that a specific habit may become generalized; that a habit gained in one line of work may be "carried over" to another line of work differing from the first in important specific characters.

A child may acquire, for example, the habit of producing neat papers in arithmetic. The doctrine of formal disciplines assumes that if this habit is once thoroughly established, it will function equally well in connection with language and drawing; that, functioning successfully here, it cannot fail to insure neatness of person and attire; and that the habit of neatness thus ingrained upon the child will surely be carried over into mature years. A very large part of the work of the school has been based entirely upon this and similar theories. That the study of mathematics trains general habits of reasoning, that nature study trains general habits of observation, that the languages train the memory, and that all branches, properly pursued, train general habits of industry are propositions that have everywhere been taken for granted

The present paper does not propose to review the evidence that has forced education to modify this doctrine. The most important experimental work has been done at Columbia University and will be found in a summarized form in Professor Thorndike's *Educational Psychology*. An excellent critique of the doctrine from a theoretical standpoint will be found in Professor O'Shea's *Education as Adjustment*. The conclusions that seem to follow from both these sources are (1) that improvement in a specific function (such, for example, as the memory for dates) has no appreciable effect upon improvement in another specific function (such as memory for faces); (2) that such mental functions as memory, reasoning, observation, etc., are always specific and never general; and (3) that a "general habit" is a psychological absurdity.

There can be *no* doubt of the validity of these conclusions. Education has no alternative but to accept them and modify its practice consistently with their teachings. And yet there is a certain compensating factor that has been quite neglected (and properly neglected) in the experimental investigations. This factor will not militate in the least against the general validity of the results, but it should be carefully considered in the application of these results to educational practice. A few illustrations may serve to indicate the nature of this factor and the manner in which it operates.

The writer believes that he has acquired a passable habit of industry in connection with his school work. He is fairly regular in his hours of rising and retiring; he goes to his classroom and laboratory at regular periods and accomplishes a fairly uniform allotment of work each day. This routine goes on day after day throughout the school year. Of course the daily tasks present some degree of individuality; new situations will arise which must be met and mastered. But, in general, the day's work is reduced to the plane of habit. The "work attitude" is assumed at a definite time and dropped at a definite time. It forms, as it were, a large ring of habit, within which are smaller rings, and within these and across them are the dots and chains of focalized effort.

But outside these rings of habit, within which the day's work is accomplished, persistent effort is distasteful and unsatisfactory. If the writer attempts to "carry over" his habit of industry from the class-room to the woodpile, nature rebels. His tendency at such times, he frankly confesses, is to "loaf," "soldier," and temporize. Whenever possible, he spends the summer months upon a farm. Here it is to his advantage,—hygienic and otherwise,—to take a serious part in the farm work; and yet his first tendency is antagonistic to industry. He does not crave inaction, but he dislikes the persistent effort that one identifies with work as distinguished from the temporary and ever-changing activity which, however strenuous it may be while it lasts, is closely akin to play. He finds that a downright hard day's work is a constant battle against nature—*at the outset.* Yet in a few days it becomes as much a matter of course as his school work has previously been. That is, a new habit of industry has been acquired through a period,—longer or shorter,—of strenuous, conscious effort.

Now it seems perfectly clear that, in this case at least, the habit of industry,—the ability to sustain a line of continued effort to a fairly remote end,—is not carried over from school life to farm life. And yet the writer is confident that something is carried over. The formation of the new habit of work is, he believes, much more economical of time and energy than it would be had not the habit of work already been developed in another field.

Will the habits of application that a student has acquired in the pursuit of a specific study be carried over to another study? Will the student who has, for example, mastered the elements of calculus be able to apply the habits that he has gained in this mastery to the study of psychology? Experiment and enlightened theory answer "No" to these fineries, and I believe that we have no choice but to agree with them. Yet I am convinced beyond all theoretical argument that students who come into my classes in psychology after completing thorough courses in the higher mathematics do far better work than those who have not had this "training." Something has been carried over from the one study to the other. It is certainly not the *habit* of study, nor are the points that mathematics and psychology have in common sufficient to account for this difference.

And what about the habit of cleanliness? At the Montana State Normal College, careful experiments have been undertaken to determine whether the habit of producing neat papers in arithmetic will function with reference to written-work in other studies. The experiments were carried on for three months in the intermediate grades and the results are almost startling in their failure to show the slightest improvement in language and spelling papers, although the improvement in the arithmetic papers was noticeable from the very first. The writer has a friend who is scrupulously neat in his personal attire and yet whose desk and study are samples of conspicuous confusion. He has another friend who is neat almost to the point of femininity in the details of his work and yet careless to the point of slovenliness in his attire. He has another who is neat in both cases and another who is careless in both cases. Yet if we run over the list of our acquaintances, we should probably agree that, in general, neatness in one department of life is accompanied by neatness in other departments. There are so many exceptions, however,—obvious even to casual observation,— that we could not say that the *habit* has been generalized. The phenomenon must be explained through some other factor.

What, then, shall we fall back upon as the connecting link between habits of different species and the same genus? Let me revert to the illustration cited in connection with the habit of industry. It is clear that the ability to persist on a given line of effort for a somewhat extended period of time is not carried over from my school work to my farm work. In each case, the habit of industry is specific. And yet I am tolerably certain that the specific habit in the second case is acquired the more readily because the specific habit in the first case has already been established. To my mind, the factor that connects and establishes a functional relation between these two specific habits is not a generalized *habit* of work, but a generalized *ideal* of work. That is, it is something that functions in the focus of consciousness and hence cannot be identified with habit, which always functions either marginally or sub-consciously. This ideal furnishes a motive and this motive holds me to conscious, persistent effort until the new habit has become effective, until the distracting influences no longer solicit passive attention. If I had acquired a specific habit of work in one field without at the same time acquiring a general ideal of work, my acquisition of a specific habit in another field would not, I believe, be materially benefited.

Similarly with the habit of mental application or study. The students who come to me from the mathematical courses have no generalized habit of study, but they have an ideal of study. They have penetrated pretty deeply into abstract problems and, along with their drudgery, they have experienced some delight of achievement, some of the pleasure that attaches to successful effort. Mathematics has perhaps given them nothing except this, but this is enough to hold them to their new task until a new specific habit of psychological study has been established. College instructors constantly complain that the students coming from the high schools are mature enough and "bright" enough, but that they have never acquired the habit of study. Is it not more nearly true to say that they have never acquired ideals of study? And is this not very largely because of the lack of a study "atmosphere," a study environment, that characterizes many of these secondary institutions?

Similarly, too, with the habit of cleanliness. Those who appear to carry this habit over from one department of life to another really carry over the ideal of cleanliness. Habit is a fixed and comparatively unvarying function. If one person carried it over from one phase of life to another, all persons who had acquired the habit would certainly do the same. An ideal, however, is an individual factor. One may be neat in one's work from other motives than a general ideal of neatness. Neat work may be essential to success; neat work may mean economy of effort; neat work may mean a thousand other things that have no relation whatsoever to neatness of dress and person.

The word "discipline" implies a mechanizing process,—the formation of an habitual reaction that shall function with little or no effort of attention *after it has once been firmly established*. But, in its initial stages, the process of habit-building must always be conscious,—focal. There must necessarily be effort,—struggle to hold oneself to the line,—struggle to resist the normal temptation to change, to do "something else." Gradually this struggle becomes less and less strenuous until finally the process is completely mechanized. This mechanizing, however, must be thoroughly specific in the narrowest sense of this narrow term; and if the line of work is changed, ever so slightly, a new habit must be formed. This means a re-focalization, a new period of conscious effort, and it is at this point that what we have termed the ideal has its sphere of activity.

Now why does this factor fail to appear in the experiments that have sounded the death-knell of the "formal disciplines?" Simply because it has been eliminated for the purpose of experiment. The problem under investigation *is* whether a habit can be carried over *as habit,* not re-focalized and made to function as idea or ideal. In the experiment on neatness it was distinctly understood that the children were to have no general instruction on neatness as an ideal. Neatness was exacted of them in arithmetic and the matter ended there. We take it that the Columbia experiments upon observation, accuracy, etc., were made under similar restrictions.

When the conclusions of these experiments reach the rank and file of teachers, they are almost certain to be interpreted without taking this factor into account. The teachers will ask why it is necessary to fix habits in school at the cost of so much time and energy if these habits are not to function as such in life. The experiments, on their face, can do no more than reiterate the question. It is surely well to have an answer ready for a question that is certain to come, especially when that question, if left unanswered, will operate to disintegrate the work of the school in a degree far beyond the remedial capacities of all the laboratory science in the universities. The passing of the doctrine of formal discipline does not detract in the least from the serious responsibility of the school to develop specific habits of cleanliness, industry and mental application in the particular and specific lines of work with which it is concerned; for, if the carrying over of a good habit from one occupation to another demands a process of judgment dependent upon an ideal, surely this ideal can be strengthened and sustained only by a cultivation of the specific habits that form its concrete expression. It would be futile to instill ideals of cleanliness and industry and honor in the schools, expecting them to be applied in later life, if, at the same time, the antitheses of these ideals—filth, and sloth, and vice—were tolerated in the daily experience of the pupils.

The School's Responsibility for Developing the Controls of Conduct
(1907)[1]

This selection from Bagley addresses the question of purpose directly. He asks and answers the question "What is education for?" As the title of the paper suggests, his answer stresses moral education as much as it does intellectual. He explains the sheer complexity of moral education in any age. He describes the problems caused by people who were over generalizing the results of the transfer of training studies published a few years earlier.

Bagley indicates his faith in the power of schools and schooling, but he also points out how many different institutions within our communities—for example homes and churches—have a responsibility to contribute to moral education. At one point in the essay, Bagley uses the phrase "social efficiency," by which he meant something deeper and richer than the same phrase meant only a few years later. When the term became redefined along narrowly occupational and economic lines during the mid 1910s, he stopped using it.

Bagley believed that schools were social institutions that should provide both liberal and professional education to all young people. At a philosophical level, this paper provides an interesting example of one man's idealism clashing with the new understanding of "science" that was redefining human nature, as well as social science in general, during this time period in American history.

---

1. A lecture delivered before the College of Education, The University of Chicago, November 21, 1907.

Not long ago I read a newspaper anecdote that will, I think, make clear the character of the problem that I wish to discuss with you. I do not know whether this anecdote is a record of an actual occurrence or merely a bit of imaginative space-filling. In either case, however, it will serve my purpose. It had reference to the long list of railroad accidents that was just then horrifying the country, and it told the story of a young telegraph operator who had been brought to trial on the charge of criminal negligence. It appeared from the evidence that a serious disaster had occurred as a direct result of this young man's failure to perform the duty that had been assigned him, and it further appeared that his failure was due to no other factor than that which, for want of a more definite term, we call "carelessness." The attorney for the defense sought to establish the young man's good character by the testimony of a number of men and women who had been the defendant's teachers when he was a boy at school. He called one of these teachers to the witness stand and asked him this question: "What kind of a boy was the defendant?" And the witness replied that he had been a very good boy—diligent in his studies, never mischievous, and always companionable with his fellow-pupils and popular with his instructors. As the witness gave his testimony, the face of the defendant brightened and his attorney smiled hopefully. But when the defense had completed the direct examination and the prosecuting attorney began the cross-questioning, the bright looks vanished and the smile was changed to a frown. For, after repeating the question of his colleague and receiving the same answer, the prosecuting attorney suddenly turned upon the witness and asked: "Was this young man a careless boy at school? Was he what you would call a careless pupil?" And the witness, after an awkward hesitation, finally admitted that the boy had been a little careless, but was, withal, a good boy and an exemplary pupil. "But," persisted the attorney, "what did you do to change him in this respect? Having recognized his carelessness, what did you do to break up his bad habits and replace them with better habits?" And the witness, reluctantly and with not a little confusion, was finally compelled to answer, "Nothing!"

Now, as I have intimated, this little anecdote may be purely imaginative, but it certainly raises a possible question with regard to the functions and responsibilities of education that cannot be brushed to one side as irrelevant and impractical. After all, what is education for? We have advanced far beyond the point where we thought of education as chiefly concerned with the acquisition of knowledge—with the cramming of the mind with facts and theories and laws and principles. We have got beyond the primitive conception of education as the process by means of which youth is endowed with certain "earmarks" of culture. We have left these inadequate conceptions behind, and have gradually come to the much broader view that education must fit the child for life and work and service and production in a complex social environment to the demands of which nature has very imperfectly adapted him. Social efficiency, formulated though it may be in diverse ways, is becoming the conscious aim of all educational effort.

As a result of this development, education is coming to its own as a human institution. As one writer has intimated, it has attained to its majority and is coming into its kingdom. And as in individuals, so in institutions, the first sign of approaching maturity is a hypertrophied self-consciousness. Like the adolescent youth, education is filled with a deep sense of its power, a yearning to know and test its function, an analytic impulse which leads it to unravel its mysteries, and to organize its efforts with foresight and intelligence toward the goal that it seeks to attain. And with these longings and strivings and yearnings, if I may continue the metaphor, is mingled now and then an undertone of foreboding, as if the task that lay before it were too stupendous for its powers; as if the problem that had been set it for solution—by far the most intricate and complicated that any human institution has yet attempted—were much too intricate and complicated for any human institution to solve. And so we find, now and then, an expression of pessimism, just as we find a marked tendency toward pessimism in individual adolescence—a tendency to distrust the power that education possesses, a temptation to repudiate nurture and hark back to nature, to discount the forces of the environment and magnify those of heredity, to take but a half-hearted hope in the school while we await, as patiently as we can, the arrival of the superman.

There can be no doubt that just such reflections upon the worth and efficiency of school training as that expressed by the prosecuting attorney of my anecdote contribute no small share to whatever pessimism one may feel. In what measure must the school hold itself responsible for the failure of its products to meet the demands imposed by social and industrial conditions? It would seem perfectly obvious that the effort of the teacher is quite without value unless, in some way or another, it modifies the conduct of his pupils. If those who come to me for instruction and training act in no way more effectively after they leave me than they would have acted had they never come under my influence, my work as a teacher must be adjudged a failure. Certainly if they act less effectively, my work is more than a failure—it is a catastrophe. And furthermore the fact that I could not foresee the results, the fact that I did my duty as I saw it, might mitigate the blame, but it could in no way mitigate the catastrophe. The pathetic lament of one of the greatest of our university presidents over the fact that so many of the men who figured prominently in the recent scandals of the business world were graduates of his own institution is a sad commentary on the failure of what we believe to be the most efficient training effectively to dominate or control conduct in really critical situations. And the terse criticism of my prosecuting attorney, whether the anecdote be fact or fiction, could find an easy sanction in the minds of thousands of business men who are looking to the schools for the raw material of efficient service.

Now it is clear that the responsibility of the school for the development of the controls of conduct must depend upon the degree in which the factors of control can be developed by the educative forces of the school. It is easy to make an offhand judgment in either direction. We can assume that the telegrapher's carelessness was due to a bad heredity, or to an inadequate home training, or to forces that operated after he left school. It would be hard to prove that all or even one of these factors could not be accounted sufficiently strong to counteract the results of school training. On the other hand, one might reasonably assert that the telegrapher's inefficiency was manifestly due to the lack of a certain set of habits which school work can and must develop, and that the admission of his teachers that these habits had been neglected is a sufficient evidence of their culpability.

It is a platitude to say that nine-tenths of human conduct is determined by the factor of habit. Educational theory has always recognized this basic truth, and, in a certain sense, it has always recognized the duty of the school to develop efficient habits. But even now educational theory is far from a due appreciation either of the wide scope or of the tremendous difficulty of the task. Indeed, until recently, educational methods, while assuming that habits were to be developed, seemed to have but a vague conception of what the development of a habit really means. One may cite the habits of speech as a convenient and definite illustration. It is only within a few years that futility of mere grammatical instruction in improving the efficiency of expression has been fully recognized. True, the study of formal grammar taught the pupil certain rules and principles that should have operated in the formation of efficient habits of expression—and doubtless did so operate in rare instances. But the kernel of habit—the purely automatic and unconscious character of its reaction—was very far from an effective recognition. When the futility of grammatical instruction was generally agreed upon, a reform movement took, as is usually the case, quite the opposite direction. It was grammar that was at fault, consequently there must be no grammar. Its place must be taken by language lessons, and since the essence of grammar is its logical coherence and organization, so the more incoherent and illogical the language lessons could be made, the greater would be the chance that they would correct the old defects. But this, quite naturally, was found to make matters worse instead of better. After all, the trouble did not lie in the mere matter of logical organization. That, in itself, was found to have rather a beneficial influence. The real difficulty lay in the comparative ease of mastering general principles and the extreme difficulty of applying these principles over and over again until the appropriate forms became thoroughly automatic. And so the next reform brought in a new factor. It attempted to provide a motive for application and repetition. The teacher of language turned to the content subjects for more interesting material, and attempted in various ways to inspire the pupil with a desire for correct expression. But this has been a long and tedious road to travel, and the results are still far from satisfactory.

I instance this specific habit of expression simply to press my point, and my point is this: If education finds it so difficult to build efficient habits in a comparatively simple field, dealing with very tangible and definite reactions, how much more difficult will be its task in the broader fields, such, for example, as that represented by the telegrapher's inadequacy in "habits of carefulness?"

And if the problem which seemed on its surface so simple has already proved so difficult what shall we say when we find that it is still further complicated by a much more important factor? Until recently it has been assumed that a habit, once established, would continue to operate in all situations of life wherever it might be needed. That this assumption failed to work out in practice did not seem to invalidate it in the least. Entire curricula were constructed under the guidance of the dogma that specific habits could be generalized indefinitely. The child might be disciplined into the most effective habits of promptness in the school, and yet fail to meet his first business engagement upon the stroke of the clock; the youth might be trained to reason with unerring certainty in his geometry, and yet fail to evince the slightest evidence of that ability in his later adjustments in business; the college student might win high honors in the study of the observational sciences, and yet find his trained observation incompetent to detect corruption in politics and chicanery in finance. These practical tests of the doctrine of formal discipline in its naive formulation have failed upon every hand, and yet the doctrine has died a hard death—in fact, it is still far from inanimate even in contemporary educational theory and practice. But experimental investigation has clearly revealed its inadequacy. We can hammer away at tardiness until our record is perfect, and yet we cannot be sure that our pupils will be any more prompt in meeting their out-of-school engagements than will the pupils of our neighbor, whose class record is the disgrace of the school. We may drill upon correct expression until not an erroneous form creeps into our recitations, and still not know whether the first words that our pupils utter when they go out upon the playground—much less into the walks of adult life—may not represent enough samples of false syntax to satisfy the demands of even the old grammarians. And even though the telegrapher's teachers might have drilled him into the most efficient habits of carefulness and attention in his school work, we could not assume that these would *necessarily* function, even the slightest degree, in his later work. In other words, the mere formation of a specific habit or of a set of specific habits is not in itself a conclusive proof that these habits will function in situations other than those in which they have been formed, or in closely parallel situations.

On the surface, all of this seems to justify nothing but the most hopeless sort of an outlook. Truly, if formal discipline is an impossible task—if habits are adequate only to the situations in which they have been formed—what we call general education must be in a very bad way. The school must restrict its function to matters of instruction, and even in these it must assume no value other than that which accrues intrinsically to the facts and principles learned. In this case, it is safe to predict that all training must become technical and vocational, and I think that I am safe in saying that there is at present a well-marked tendency toward this very end. The college and university reveal this tendency most clearly, but the high schools are coming to feel its influence. The traditional courses which were supposed to provide general culture and discipline are being replaced by courses that are more or less vocational in character.

Even in the elementary school, the rejection of the dogma of formal discipline is exerting a modifying influence. The methods that were formerly assumed to develop the stern virtues of accuracy and industry and duty and obedience have, in many cases, been discarded or greatly modified. Indeed, why subject the pupil to the hardships of a discipline not needed for immediate ends when the chances are so few that this discipline can be applied to remote ends? Why insist upon obedience, if the habits of obedience gained in the school cannot be generalized into the attitude of respect for law and authority, upon which every civilized government must depend for survival? True, hoodlumism is increasing at an alarming rate. True, the American child is becoming more and more a law unto himself and not infrequently a source of trial and tribulation to the adult members of society. The old-fashioned parent would have settled the difficulty in a trice, but should one inflict pain upon another merely to subserve the interests of one's own comfort, when science asserts that no remote end would be gained thereby and that irremediable injury might be caused? We could formerly justify heroic measures of discipline on the ground that our personal comfort was only an incident and that it was the remote end of civilizing the little savage that impelled us to take harsh measures. But now selfishness is the only excuse.

What is the responsibility of the school (or even of the home) for developing the controls of conduct? In the light of contemporary educational theory, one is forced to answer, Nil. Responsibility goes only with power, and power is plainly denied us—at least if the contemporary theory is valid.

But is it valid? and if not, what is its fallacy? After all, have we generalized too hastily? Have we discarded the dogma of formal discipline and repudiated the value of general training with insufficient consideration? Have we really accounted for every possible factor that might influence our judgment?

Personally, while I believe that those who still cling to the dogma in its original form cannot justify their position, I also believe that those who have entirely cast aside the idea of formal training have done so too hastily. In fact, there is now some basis for a reactionary movement in the experiments which seem to indicate that memory, for example, can be markedly improved by exercises of a very formal nature. But aside from this there is still another factor that has been neglected.

In order to make clear my own position upon this matter, let me refer to a type of conduct rather different from those just discussed. Why are you and I decent and peaceful and law-abiding—assuming, of course, that we are. Why do you and I refrain from doing unseemly things? If we were brought face to face with that question, I believe that most of us would answer that we do not do unseemly things because reason tells us not to. But this is probably far from the real truth. You and I and the rest of the men and women who live ordinarily decent lives do so very largely through the force of habit. Let us suppose that you are in a jewelry store and that you see a tray of beautiful and costly diamond rings lying upon the top of the showcase. The clerks are busy in another part of the store, and you examine these rings casually and yet admiringly. Let us suppose that you have long wished to possess a diamond ring the very counterpart of one that is right there within your reach. Why do you not slip the ring into your pocket? Let us assume that you would run absolutely no danger of detection in the theft. You tell me that your judgment tells you that this would be stealing; but judgment in your case and in mine, I hope, very seldom operates in a situation like this. As a matter of fact, you do not feel the slightest temptation to take the ring. Why? Simply because habits of honesty have been drilled into you from the earliest infancy. There is little judgment involved in the control of conduct in such a situation, because the demand for judgment is not present. In reality, there is no situation there. A situation might arise under the proper conditions. Nature tells you to appropriate the thing that pleases you. But civilized society tells you to respect the rights of others, and civilized society has been having the better of it for so long that the primitive, natural craving has been quite hushed. In short, if you and I had constantly to reason ourselves into being good, we should not be good very long. We are either good by habit or we go to the bad very quickly.

Now this, it will be agreed, approaches very close to what may be termed a general habit—to the very thing that formal discipline was supposed to engender. How has this habit been formed? Obviously not from specific experiences in that identical situation. You do not need to have suffered painful consequences for the theft of diamond rings in order to build up the habit of not appropriating diamond rings when you want them.

In order to envisage a possible solution of this problem, let us vary the conditions of the illustration. Let us assume that, instead of feeling no temptation to take the ring, one does feel the very slightest impulse. In other words, let us assume that habit is inadequate to the solution of the situation. Inherited impulse, left to itself, would solve the situation disastrously. What is it that checks and controls this impulse? Is it an intellectual judgment—this act is stealing; stealing is a sin; consequently I will inhibit the impulse? I venture to say that, if the judgment were of this bare intellectual type, it would exert not the slightest inhibiting force upon the impulse. What really determines conduct in such a situation is undoubtedly an *emotional wave*—an undefined and intangible, but thoroughly conscious, *feeling of repugnance* for the act itself. Let me ask if this is not a fair description of the controlling force in your own moments of temptation—if you ever have such moments. Impulse and emotion are so closely related as genetically not to be distinguishable; and unless one can oppose an inherited impulse with an idea that is just as powerfully colored with emotion, the impulse is bound to conquer. The idea alone, as a product of intellection, has not the weight of a feather in determining conduct in critical situations. It is the emotionalized idea—it is the *ideal*—that must hold the reins of conduct when instinct is battling for the control.

And this, it seems to me, is the explanation of the barrenness of our attempts to teach morality from the didactic standpoint. We see it coming out most clearly perhaps in that horrible example of pedagogical inefficiency that we call temperance physiology. In eight years of didactic instruction in temperance, the teacher usually accomplishes less in developing real controls of conduct, even in children whose plasticity and adaptability are the hope of the race, than an unlettered temperance reformer, with the fire of enthusiasm coursing through his veins, can accomplish in a single hour with adults who might reasonably be supposed to have every factor of control irrevocably fixed. This is the reason, also, that didactic ethics has so little influence in modifying the conduct of its students. This is why every attempt to read emotion out of religion has weakened the power of the church in controlling the conduct of its communicants. The power of an efficient incentive to action is always a direct function of the emotion that is back of it.

What term will most adequately describe the prime controls of conduct—the factors that govern adjustment in really critical situations? The term that I propose is this, "emotionalized prejudice." The adjective may be redundant, but I insert it in order that there may be no doubt as to the prime factor.

A man of science was once trying to persuade me that the trend of mental progress was toward the elimination of the emotions. As an illustration, he adduced his own clear-thinking logic engine of a mind, the workings of which, he assured me, had not the slightest emotional tinge. I could easily find it in my heart to pardon his egotism, for, with his next breath, he exclaimed passionately, "I am a priest of truth, and I worship the naked fact!" Not having with me the instruments of exact measurements with which emotions may be identified, I could not convince him that his mind was, at that moment, surcharged with a powerful affective process—but I convinced myself. And surely if the training that we give to students in science amounts to anything more than a mastery of technique and the assimilation of a few technical facts and principles, it must amount to this: the development of a prejudice, highly colored with positive emotional force, toward truth and veracity and impersonal observation and dispassionate judgment—*an emotional attitude against emotion, a prejudice against prejudice.* And similarly I should maintain that the student of mathematics should come from his study of algebra and geometry and calculus with a highly emotionalized prejudice toward that method of close, logical thinking that mathematics, above all other disciplines, represents.

It is true that not all students derive these prejudices from the pursuit of mathematics and science. Mastery of subject-matter does not involve this as a necessary consequence. But to some students, a long acquaintance with, and contemplation of, the methods by which some of man's greatest conquests over nature have been made possible give a profound sense of the worth and value of these methods—a feeling of respect and perhaps of reverence which supplies the emotional coloring essential to the modification of conduct in later adjustments. And I am certain that the efficiency of such a prejudice is a function, in part at least, of the time and effort that have been given to the mastery of the subject. After all, the things that appeal to us most strongly from the emotional aspect are the things that we have gained at the cost of effort and struggle; and the belief that the "tough" subjects of the curriculum have the greatest disciplinary value has a psychological basis in this fact.

I am here speaking of no vague, indefinite "mental power" or "mental faculty" that may be developed by the studies. The factor to which I refer may be intangible and elusive, but I maintain that it is thoroughly consistent with the accepted principles of modern psychology. The consciousness of power is often as important in gaining a victory as the possession of power. Indeed, it is the emotional force of a belief that renders the power itself dynamic rather than potential. The graduate of Cambridge may never use his mathematics in solving the situations of his later life, but it is possible that he has gained something from his mastery of mathematics that will help him more in solving a situation than he could be helped by any amount of instruction regarding the technique of that situation. The "something" that he has perhaps gained is a consciousness of conquest, or, if I may use a street phrase, the knowledge that he has been "up against" the "toughest" problems that the mind of man can devise and has come out a victor. Certainly his mastery of mathematics does not necessarily involve this feeling of confidence; but it *may* involve it, and, in case it does, there can be no doubt of its value in making his future adjustments more efficient.

This does not mean, of course, that one would decry the virtue of that technical and vocational education which aims to furnish specific facts and principles for the solution of specific situations. I assert simply this: that far more fundamental than the technical facts are the prejudices in favor of dogged persistence, unflinching application, relentless industry, and a determination to conquer, whatever the cost. These combined with technical knowledge and skill can spell nothing less than efficiency. Without technical knowledge, they might ultimately win, but the price of victory would be unnecessarily high and the chances of failure much greater. But technical knowledge alone without these other factors must spell disaster in every critical situation.

And I should not say that these prejudices which are so important cannot be engendered through the processes of education that give one technical knowledge and skill. I believe, however, that, as a rule, applied science is frequently less efficient, in this respect, than pure science, and applied mathematics than pure mathematics. Pure science and pure mathematics constantly emphasize the system and unity of the subject-matter. In a certain sense, the contemplation of a large system of knowledge has much in common with the contemplation of a great work of art. It is a unity in which every part is definitely related to every other part, in which there are no gaps, or lacunae, or jagged edges. And the emotional factor, I believe, is a function, in part, of this aesthetic quality— but I should not press this point.

But there still remains unanswered a question that was raised a little way back. Granting that emotionalized prejudices of a very effective sort may be engendered in the study of science and mathematics, what shall we say with regard to the generalization of specific habits such as those formed in the earlier stages of education? What is the value of disciplining the child into specific habits of promptness, or neatness, or accuracy? Will specific training give rise to emotionalized prejudices in favor of the virtues that the discipline represents? If it does, there can be no doubt that the effects of training may be generalized or carried over to situations other than those in which the training has been given.

Personally, I believe that we get most of our effective prejudices from just this source of early training, but it is, of course, true that the specific habits might be very adequately formed without at the same time engendering the corresponding prejudices. The indeterminate factor is the emotional factor. The discipline of the early home life is the great breeding ground of prejudices *because of the positive and profound emotional factors that operate.* (I mean by "positive" factors those that operate in favor of the virtues in question.) The most powerful prejudices upon which civilized society rests are engendered in the home—honesty, cleanliness, decency, self-denial. Except as these are taught by precept and example, and fortified by specific habits, and thoroughly imbued with positive emotional force, the social fabric must surely fall to pieces.

It is for these prejudices in particular that the home must be responsible. The school can do little to develop them unless the school takes over all of the educative functions of the home, and even then the weakness of the most important factor of all—the emotional factor—is apt to make the attempt abortive. But the school in turn must stand sponsor for certain prejudices that the home cannot always be depended upon to engender, and among these one must certainly include accuracy, promptness, industry, application, efficiency, order, respect for the rights and feelings of others, respect for authority, for truth, and for justice.

The important point is this: The specific habits which have reference to these various virtues are insufficient; *it is the prejudice in their favor that is the significant thing.* And this explains in part the failure of our older methods of teaching to develop efficient controls. We thought that the habit was the prime essential. We neglected the prejudice. And so we took the shortest road to the habit, forgetting that we might thereby be inducing a prejudice of quite the opposite kind—forgetting that *prejudices not only generalize habits, but sometimes negate them.* And so the net result has been very frequently to promote the very end that we sought to avoid. A prejudice against work and application and concentrated attention has often been engendered by the heart-rending, back-breaking grind of toil imposed upon the child of the farm. A prejudice against morality has been developed more than once, I believe, by the namby-pamby methods of the Sunday school. And I am more than tolerably certain that a prejudice against temperance has been promoted, in many cases, by the methods that we have taken to build temperate habits.

Again it is the emotional factor that must be considered, and this sometimes works in the most unexpected ways. Do we believe that imposing difficult tasks upon the pupil will develop in him that prejudice in favor of persistence and application and close, sustained attention, which is so necessary in meeting the situations of later life? How do we know that, instead of this, we are not developing its antithesis, and that he will not acquire a repugnance for these virtues? Do we believe that we can avoid the difficulty by catering to his interests? How do we know that we shall not develop a prejudice against all effort that is not bribed and all tasks that are not attractive? Or, do we wish to put the pupil into an habitual attitude of respect for authority? How can we be certain that we do not overshoot the mark, and make him a subservient tool, lacking in all initiative? Do we try to obviate this difficulty by leaving his inherited impulses to work themselves out without let or hindrance? How do we know that the liberty of childhood may not engender a prejudice in favor of license in manhood? Are these merely academic questions? Ask any principal of an elementary school who is face to face with the responsibility for governing five hundred children and who is endowed with both a brain and a heart. It is precisely these problems that such a man must attempt to solve at every turn of the day's work.

One can find no better example of the difficulty of solving these problems than is presented in the one department of education in which we have consciously attempted to develop an emotionalized prejudice, namely, the teaching of literature. From present indications, it would seem that our attempt to force upon the child an appreciation of art in any of its forms has been most barren in its results. The music hall still holds forth its allurements in spite of our costly experiment in public-school music. The variety stage draws with its blandishments those who have been carefully taught how to enjoy Shakespeare. All the garish distractions of our great cities prosper on the earnings, not of our unlettered immigrants, but of the products of our own public schools.

Have we not in this problem of developing prejudices both the most important and the most difficult problem of educational science? Is it not the crux of the whole question of moral education? Is it not the most significant factor in social improvement? Should it not receive adequate recognition in the present radical reconstructions to which the curricula of our high schools and colleges are being subjected?

Obviously enough, the key to the situation lies in the emotional factors; but here, unhappily, we need a key that will unlock the door. At the very outset, we confront a danger that will do much to defeat our purpose. I refer to the danger of sentimentalism. Our present conception of the emotional life is far too narrow and restricted to serve as a basis for fruitful investigation from the standpoint that I have proposed. In popular use, the word "emotion" is heavily freighted with associations that make it a veritable bugbear for scientific research. And no small source of the negative prejudices that we are now developing in education is this silly, sentimental recognition of the emotional factors so-called that is little less than disgusting to the serious and self-respecting student. If you wish to give a boy a first-class prejudice against nature, put him through the average course in nature-study that has for its object the development of a love for nature's beauty. What the true emotional nature of the boy craves is not something to love, but something to respect. Love is a word that ought always to be in our hearts, but seldom upon our lips, lest we cheapen the sentiment by constant reiteration. And the emotional factors to which we give the name "love" function in only a weakened form prior to puberty, and even after puberty, the less ado that we make about them in education, the more completely, I believe, will their ideal elements emerge from the background of instinct and become positive forces in the control of conduct. Just now we hear upon every side that the child must love his school, he must love his work, he must love his teacher, he must love literature, he must love art, he must love nature; but we never hear that he must respect anything, except (and this only by implication) his own whims and fancies. Now respect is just as thoroughly a sentiment as is love, and with the preadolescent child, it is based upon a far more powerful emotion. I might also add, although I may seem unorthodox, that the only kind of love worth having is the kind that grows out of respect.

Now this is far from saying that the teacher should not have a genuine affection for his pupils. Love of that type comes from the other side and is based upon parental instincts—paternal or maternal—that are fundamental. The person who does not feel the power of these instincts is abnormal, and certainly has no place among teachers.

And so the first step in the solution of our problem must be an investigation of the emotional forces that govern conduct—using the term emotion in the very broad sense that I have suggested. This will be no simple task, but the full investment of education with scientific dignity and worth must await its outcome. We must come to know in a fairly definite and concise form the number and sources of these great controls of conduct. Now we know them only in the vaguest fashion. We know that there are certain emotionalized ideas, like the principle of religious liberty, or the principle of equality under the law, which have dominated councils of war and stained battle fields; that there are certain emotionalized standards, like honesty and chastity and personal honor, which not infrequently determine the greatest and most critical of individual adjustments; that there are certain powerfully emotionalized abstractions, like truth, or faith, or service, which may map out the entire trend of a man's life and mark the clear path of his career; that there are certain profoundly emotionalized conceptions, like friendship, or motherhood, or divinity, which not only quite defy the words of a David or a Job to formulate, or the pigments of a Raphael to depict, but which still lie somewhere deeply imbedded in every human motive that makes for what we call the right. Of these, at present, we can say with certainty only this: that somewhere during that long period of human plasticity which we call childhood and youth, they are implanted in the heart, there to work out into action and bring forth fruit of their kind. Now perhaps the seeds are sown by precept and admonition; now by objective example and conscious imitation; now by long years of growth and training and discipline; now by a sudden flash of inspiration. Many, and these doubtless the most potent, come from the home, others from the social environment, others from religion, others from the *Zeitgeist,* others from literature and art and history and biography. But some must surely come from the school, and in all of them the influence of the school must be felt. Whether we will or no, we cannot escape the responsibility.

And even if the more accurate investigations are still to be made, the very recognition of the importance of these factors should have its effect upon the actual work of teaching. When the teacher asks himself not only what he wishes to impart in the way of knowledge and train in the way of habits, but also what sort of prejudices and what sort of standards and what sort of ideals he wishes to give his pupils, the very attitude of questioning will, I believe, modify his work in the direction of greater efficiency. We cannot all be teachers like Pestalozzi or Froebel or Arnold or Sheldon or Parker, but we can all appreciate the characteristic that made these men masters of their craft. We can know that they were great and influential, not merely because of the knowledge that they possessed, but far more fundamentally because of the ideals with which they were inspired, and that their influence was due to the facility and skill with which they could pass on this inspiration to their pupils. And knowing this, we too may be encouraged to strive for idealism to the end that our pupils may feel, however feebly, the uplift, and catch a glimpse, however fleeting, of the sunlit peaks.

Optimism in Teaching
(1908)[1]

The profession of teaching was a calling to Bagley. This point is evident in this essay on remaining positive when facing difficult challenges. He was 34 years old when he delivered this address, and was facing a lifetime of work on behalf of the teaching profession. He recognized the problems that lay ahead as he and others sought to turn teaching into a true profession. The enormity of these problems, Bagley acknowledges, often can lead to negativity on the part of teachers. To counter this tendency, however, he identifies several reasons why young men and women should enter his profession, despite the fact that it does not receive the material rewards that it deserves.

Although the month is March and not November, it is never unseasonable to count up the blessings for which it is well to be thankful. In fact, from the standpoint of education, the spring is perhaps the appropriate time to perform this very pleasant function. As if still further to emphasize the fact that education, like civilization, is an artificial thing, we have reversed the operations of Mother Nature: we sow our seed in the fall and cultivate our crops during the winter and reap our harvests in the spring. I may be pardoned, therefore, for making the theme of my discussion a brief review of the elements of growth and victory for which the educator of to-day may justly be grateful, with, perhaps, a few suggestions of what the next few years may reasonably be expected to bring forth.

---

1. An address before the Oswego, New York, County Council of Education, March 28, 1908.

Forgotten Heroes of American Education, pages 37–47

And this course is all the more necessary because, I believe, the teaching profession is unduly prone to pessimism. One might think at first glance that the contrary would be true. We are surrounded on every side by youth. Youth is the material with which we constantly deal. Youth is buoyant, hopeful, exuberant; and yet, with this material constantly surrounding us, we frequently find the task wearisome and apparently hopeless. The reason is not far to seek. Youth is not only buoyant, it is unsophisticated, it is inexperienced, in many important particulars it is crude. Some of its tastes must necessarily, in our judgment, hark back to the primitive, to the barbaric. Ours is continually the task to civilize, to sophisticate, to refine this raw material. But, unfortunately for us, the effort that we put forth does not always bring results that we can see and weigh and measure. The hopefulness of our material is overshadowed not infrequently by its crudeness. We take each generation as it comes to us. We strive to lift it to the plane that civilized society has reached. We do our best and pass it on, mindful of the many inadequacies, perhaps of the many failures, in our work. We turn to the new generation that takes its place. We hope for better materials, but we find no improvement.

And so you and I reflect in our occasional moments of pessimism on that generic situation which inheres in the very work that we do. The constantly accelerated progress of civilization lays constantly increasing burdens upon us. In some way or another we must accomplish the task. In some way or another we must lift the child to the level of society, and, as society is reaching a continually higher and higher level, so the distance through which the child must be raised is ever increased. We would like to think that all this progress in the race would come to mean that we should be able to take the child at a higher level; but you who deal with children know from experience the principle for which the biologist Weismann stands sponsor—the principle, namely, that acquired characteristics are not inherited; that whatever changes may be wrought during life in the brains and nerves and muscles of the present generation cannot be passed on to its successor save through the same laborious process of acquisition and training; that, however far the civilization of the race may progress, education, whose duty it is to conserve and transmit this civilization, must always begin with the "same old child."

This, I take it, is the deep-lying cause of the schoolmaster's pessimism. In our work we are constantly struggling against that same inertia which held the race in bondage for how many millenniums only the evolutionist can approximate a guess,—that inertia of the primitive, untutored mind which we to-day know as the mind of childhood, but which, for thousands of generations, was the only kind of a mind that man possessed. This inertia has been conquered at various times in the course of recorded history,—in Egypt and China and India, in Chaldea and Assyria, in Greece and Rome,—conquered only again to reassert itself and drive man back into barbarism. Now we of the Western world have conquered it, let us hope, for all time; for we of the Western world have discovered an effective method of holding it in abeyance, and this method is universal public education.

Let Germany close her public schools, and in two generations she will lapse back into the semi-darkness of medievalism; let her close both her public schools and her universities, and three generations will fetch her face to face with the Dark Ages; let her destroy her libraries and break into ruin all of her works of art, all of her existing triumphs of technical knowledge and skill, from which a few, self-tutored, might glean the wisdom that is every one's to-day, and Germany will soon become the home of a savage race, as it was in the days of Tacitus and Caesar. Let Italy close her public schools, and Italy will become the same discordant jumble of petty states that it was a century ago,—again to await, this time perhaps for centuries or millenniums, another Garibaldi and Victor Emmanuel to work her regeneration. Let Japan close her public schools, and Japan in two generations will be a barbaric kingdom of the Shoguns, shorn of every vestige of power and prestige,—the easy victim of the machinations of Western diplomats. Let our country cease in its work of education, and these United States must needs pass through the reverse stages of their growth until another race of savages shall roam through the unbroken forest, now and then to reach the shores of ocean and gaze through the centuries, eastward, to catch a glimpse of the new Columbus. Like the moving pictures of the kinetoscope when the reels are reversed, is the picture that imagination can unroll if we grant the possibility of a lapse from civilization to savagery.

And so when we take the broader view, we quickly see that, in spite of our pessimism, we are doing something in the world. We are part of that machine which civilization has invented and is slowly perfecting to preserve itself. We may be a very small part, but, so long as the responsibility for a single child rests upon us, we are not an unimportant part. Society must reckon with you and me perhaps in an infinitesimal degree, but it must reckon with the institution which we represent as it reckons with no other institution that it has reared to subserve its needs.

In a certain sense these statements are platitudes. We have repeated them over and over again until the words have lost their tremendous significance. And it behooves us now and again to revive the old substance in a new form,—to come afresh to a self-consciousness of our function. It is not good for any man to hold a debased and inferior opinion of himself or of his work, and in the field of schoolcraft it is easy to fall into this self-depreciating habit of thought. We cannot hope that the general public will ever come to view our work in the true perspective that I have very briefly outlined. It would probably not be wise to promulgate publicly so pronounced an affirmation of our function and of our worth. The popular mind must think in concrete details rather than in comprehensive principles, when the subject of thought is a specialized vocation. You and I have crude ideas, no doubt, of the lawyer's function, of the physician's function, of the clergyman's function. Not less crude are their ideas of our function. Even when they patronize us by saying that our work is the noblest that any man or woman would engage in, they have but a vague and shadowy perception of its real significance. I doubt not that, with the majority of those who thus pat us verbally upon the back, the words that they use are words only. They do not envy us our privileges,—unless it is our summer vacations,—nor do they encourage their sons to enter service in our craft. The popular mind—the nontechnical mind,—must work in the concrete;—it must have visible evidences of power and influence before it pays homage to a man or to an institution.

Throughout the German empire the traveler is brought constantly face to face with the memorials that have been erected by a grateful people to the genius of the Iron Chancellor. Bismarck richly deserves the tribute that is paid to his memory, but a man to be honored in this way must exert a tangible and an obvious influence.

And yet, in a broader sense, the preeminence of Germany is due in far greater measure to two men whose names are not so frequently to be found inscribed upon towers and monuments. In the very midst of the havoc and devastation wrought by the Napoleon wars,—at the very moment when the German people seemed hopelessly crushed and defeated,—an intellect more penetrating than that of Bismarck grasped the logic of the situation. With the inspiration that comes with true insight, the philosopher Fichte issued his famous Addresses to the German people. With clear-cut argument couched in white-hot words, he drove home the great principle that lies at the basis of United Germany and upon the results of which Bismarck and Von Moltke and the first Emperor erected the splendid structure that to-day commands the admiration of the world. Fichte told the German people that their only hope lay in universal, public education. And the kingdom of Prussia—impoverished, bankrupt, war-ridden, and war-devastated—heard the plea. A great scheme that comprehended such an education was already at hand. It had fallen almost stillborn from the only kind of a mind that could have produced it,—a mind that was suffused with an overwhelming love for humanity and incomparably rich with the practical experiences of a primary schoolmaster. It had fallen from the mind of Pestalozzi, the Swiss reformer, who thus stands with Fichte as one of the vital factors in the development of Germany's educational supremacy. The people's schools of Prussia, imbued with the enthusiasm of Fichte and Pestalozzi,[1] gave to Germany the tremendous advantage that enabled it so easily to overcome its hereditary foe, when, two generations later, the Franco-Prussian War was fought; for the *Volksschule* gave to Germany something that no other nation of that time possessed; namely, an educated proletariat, an intelligent common people. Bismarck knew this when he laid his cunning plans for the unification of German states that was to crown the brilliant series of victories beginning at Sedan and ending within the walls of Paris. William of Prussia knew it when, in the royal palace at Versailles, he accepted the crown that made him the first Emperor of United Germany. Von Moltke knew it when, at the capitulation of Paris, he was asked to whom the credit of the victory was due, and he replied, in the frank simplicity of the true soldier and the true hero, "The schoolmaster did it."

And yet Bismarck and Von Moltke and the Emperor are the heroes of Germany, and if Fichte and Pestalozzi are not forgotten, at least their memories are not cherished as are the memories of the more tangible and obvious heroes. Instinct lies deeply embedded in human nature and it is instinctive to think in the concrete. And so I repeat that we cannot expect the general public to share in the respect and veneration which you and I feel for our calling, for you and I are technicians in education, and we can see the process as a comprehensive whole. But our fellow men and women have their own interests and their own departments of technical knowledge and skill; they see the schoolhouse and the pupils' desks and the books and other various material symbols of our work,—they see these things and call them education; just as we see a freight train thundering across the viaduct or a steamer swinging out in the lake and call these things commerce. In both cases, the nontechnical mind associates the word with something concrete and tangible; in both cases, the technical mind associates the same word with an abstract process, comprehending a movement of vast proportions.

To compress such a movement—whether it be commerce or government or education—in a single conception requires a multitude of experiences involving actual adjustments with the materials involved; involving constant reflection upon hidden meanings, painful investigations into hidden causes, and mastery of a vast body of specialized knowledge which it takes years of study to digest and assimilate.

It is not every stevedore upon the docks, nor every stoker upon the steamers, nor every brakeman upon the railroads, who comprehends what commerce really means. It is not every banker's clerk who knows the meaning of business. It is not every petty holder of public office who knows

---

1. It should be added that the movement toward universal education in Germany owed much to the work of pre-Pestalozzian reformers,—especially Francke and Basedow.

what government really means. But this, at least, is true: in proportion as the worker knows the meaning of the work that he does,—in proportion as he sees it in its largest relations to society and to life,—his work is no longer the drudgery of routine toil. It becomes instead an intelligent process directed toward a definite goal. It has acquired that touch of artistry which, so far as human testimony goes, is the only pure and uncontaminated source of human happiness.

And the chief blessing for which you and I should be thankful to-day is that this larger view of our calling has been vouchsafed to us as it has been vouchsafed to no former generation of teachers. Education as the conventional prerogative of the rich,—as the garment which separated the higher from the lower classes of society,—this could scarcely be looked upon as a fascinating and uplifting ideal from which to derive hope and inspiration in the day's work; and yet this was the commonly accepted function of education for thousands of years, and the teachers who did the actual work of instruction could not but reflect in their attitude and bearing the servile character of the task that they performed. Education to fit the child to earn a better living, to command a higher wage,—this myopic view of the function of the school could do but little to make the work of teaching anything but drudgery; and yet it is this narrow and materialistic view that has dominated our educational system to within a comparatively few years.

So silently and yet so insistently have our craft ideals been transformed in the last two decades that you and I are scarcely aware that our point of view has been changed and that we are looking upon our work from a much higher point of vantage and in a light entirely new. And yet this is the change that has been wrought. That education, in its widest meaning, is the sole conservator and transmitter of civilization to successive generations found expression as far back as Aristotle and Plato, and has been vaguely voiced at intervals down through the centuries; but its complete establishment came only as an indirect issue of the great scientific discoveries of the nineteenth century, and its application to the problems of practical schoolcraft and its dissemination through the rank and file of teachers awaited the dawn of the twentieth century. To-day we see expressions and indications of the new outlook upon every hand, in the greatly increased professional zeal that animates the teacher's calling; in the widespread movement among all civilized countries to raise the standards of teachers, to eliminate those candidates for service who have not subjected themselves to the discipline of special preparation; in the increased endowments and appropriations for schools and seminaries that prepare teachers; and, perhaps most strikingly at the present moment, in that concerted movement to organize into institutions of formal education all of those branches of training which have, for years, been left to the chance operation of economic needs working through the crude and unorganized though often effective apprentice system. The contemporary fervor for industrial education is only one expression of this new view that, in the last analysis, the school must stand sponsor for the conservation and transmission of every valuable item of experience, every usable fact or principle, every tiniest perfected bit of technical skill, every significant ideal or prejudice, that the race has acquired at the cost of so much struggle and suffering and effort.

I repeat that this new vantage point from which to gain a comprehensive view of our calling has been attained only as an indirect result of the scientific investigations of the nineteenth century. We are wont to study the history of education from the work and writings of a few great reformers, and it is true that much that is valuable in our present educational system can be understood and appreciated only when viewed in the perspective of such sources. Aristotle and Quintilian, Abelard and St. Thomas Aquinas, Sturm and Philip Melanchthon, Comenius, Pestalozzi, Rousseau, Herbart, and Froebel still live in the schools of to-day. Their genius speaks to us through the organization of subject-matter, through the art of questioning, through the developmental methods of teaching, through the use of pictures, through objective instruction, and in a thousand other forms. But this dominant ideal of education to which I have referred and which is so rapidly transforming our outlook and vitalizing our organization and inspiring us to new efforts, is not to be drawn from these sources. The new histories of education must account for this new ideal, and to do this they must turn to the masters in science who made the middle part of the nineteenth century the period of the most profound changes that the history of human thought records.[2] With the illuminating principle of evolution came a new and generously rich conception of human growth and development. The panorama of evolution carried man back far beyond the limits of recorded human history and indicated an origin as lowly as the succeeding uplift has been sublime. The old depressing and fatalistic notion that the human race was on the downward path, and that the march of civilization must sooner or later end in a cul-de-sac (a view which found frequent expression in the French writers of the eighteenth century and which dominated the skepticism of the dark hours preceding the Revolution)— this fatalistic view met its deathblow in the principle of evolution. A vista of hope entirely undreamed of stretched out before the race. If the tremendous leverage of the untold millenniums of brute and savage ancestry could be

---

2. While the years from 1840 to 1870 mark the period of intellectual revolution, it should not be inferred that the education of this period reflected these fundamental changes of outlook. On the contrary, these years were in general marked by educational stagnation.

overcome, even in slight measure, by a few short centuries of intelligence and reason, what might not happen in a few more centuries of constantly increasing light? In short, the principle of evolution supplied the perspective that was necessary to an adequate evaluation of human progress.

But this inspiring outlook which was perhaps the most comprehensive result of Darwin's work had indirect consequences that were vitally significant to education. It is with mental and not with physical development that education is primarily concerned, and yet mental development is now known to depend fundamentally upon physical forces. The same decade that witnessed the publication of the *Origin of Species* also witnessed the birth of another great book, little known except to the specialist, and yet destined to achieve immortality. This book is the *Elements of Psychophysics,* the work of the German scientist Fechner. The intimate relation between mental life and physical and physiological forces was here first clearly demonstrated, and the way was open for a science of psychology which should cast aside the old and threadbare raiment of mystery and speculation and metaphysic, and stand forth naked and unashamed.

But all this was only preparatory to the epoch-making discoveries that have had so much to do with our present attitude toward education. The Darwinian hypothesis led to violent controversy, not only between the opponents and supporters of the theory, but also among the various camps of the evolutionists themselves. Among these controversies was that which concerned itself with the inheritance of acquired characteristics, and the outcome of that conflict has a direct significance to present educational theory. The principle, now almost conclusively established,[3] that the characteristics acquired by an organism during its lifetime are not transmitted by physical heredity to its offspring, must certainly stand as the basic principle of education; for everything that we identify as human as contrasted with that which is brutal must look to education for its preservation and support. It has been stated by competent authorities that, during the past ten thousand years, there has been no significant change in man's physical constitution. This simply means that Nature finished her work as far as man is concerned far beyond the remotest period that human history records; that, for all that we can say to-day, there must have existed in the very distant past human beings who were just as well adapted by nature to the lives that we are leading as we are to-day adapted; that what they lacked and what we possess is simply a mass of traditions, of habits, of ideals, and prejudices which have been slowly

---

3. The writer here accepts the conclusions of J. A. Thomson (*Heredity* New York, 1908, ch. vii).

accumulated through the ages and which are passed on from generation to generation by imitation and instruction and training and discipline; and that the child of to-day, left to his own devices and operated upon in no way by the products of civilization, would develop into a savage undistinguishable in all significant qualities from other savages.

The possibilities that follow from such a conception are almost overwhelming even at first glance, and yet the theory is borne out by adequate experiments. The transformation of the Japanese people through two generations of education in Western civilization is a complete upsetting of the old theory that as far as race is concerned, there is anything significantly important in blood, and confirms the view that all that is racially significant depends upon the influences that surround the young of the race during the formative years. The complete assimilation of foreign ingredients into our own national stock through the instrumentality of the public school is another demonstration that the factors which form the significant characteristics in the lower animals possess but a minimum of significance to man,—that color, race, stature, and even brain weight and the shape of the cranium, have very little to do with human worth or human efficiency save in extremely abnormal cases.

And so we have at last a fundamental principle with which to illumine the field of our work and from which to derive not only light but inspiration. Unite this with John Fiske's penetrating induction that the possibilities of progress through education are correlated directly with the length of the period of growth or immaturity,—that is, that the races having the longest growth before maturity are capable of the highest degree of civilization,—and we have a pair of principles the influence of which we see reflected all about us in the great activity for education and especially in the increased sense of pride and responsibility and respect for his calling that is animating the modern teacher.

And what will be the result of this new point of view? First and foremost, an increased general respect for the work. Until a profession respects itself, it cannot very well ask for the world's respect, and until it can respect itself on the basis of scientific principles indubitably established, its respect for itself will be little more than the irritating self-esteem of the goody-goody order which is so often associated with our craft.

With our own respect for our calling, based upon this incontrovertible principle, will come, sooner or later, increased compensation for the work and increased prestige in the community. I repeat that these things can only come after we have established a true craft spirit. If we are ashamed of our calling, if we regret openly and publicly that we are not lawyers or physicians or dentists or bricklayers or farmers or anything rather than teachers, the public will have little respect for the teacher's calling. As long as we criticize each other before laymen and make light of each other's honest efforts, the public will question our professional standing on the ground that we have no organized code of professional ethics,—a prerequisite for any profession.

I started out to tell you something that we ought to be thankful for,—something that ought to counteract in a measure the inevitable tendencies toward pessimism and discouragement. The hopeful thing about our present status is that we have an established principle upon which to work. A writer in a recent periodical stoutly maintained that education was in the position just now that medicine was in during the Middle Ages. The statement is hardly fair, either to medicine or to education. If one were to attempt a parallel, one might say that education stands to-day where medicine stood about the middle of the nineteenth century. The analogy might be more closely drawn by comparing our present conception of education with the conception of medicine just prior to the application of the experimental method to a solution of its problems. Education has still a long road to travel before it reaches the point of development that medicine has to-day attained. It has still to develop principles that are comparable to the doctrine of lymph therapy or to that latest triumph of investigation in the field of medicine,—the theory of opsonins,—which almost makes one believe that in a few years violent accident and old age will be the only sources of death in the human race. Education, we admit, has a long road to travel before it reaches so advanced a point of development. But there is no immediate cause for pessimism or despair. We need especially, now that the purpose of education is adequately defined, an adequate doctrine of educational values and a rich and vital infusion of the spirit of experimental science. For efficiency in the work of instruction and training, we need to know the influence of different types of experience in controlling human conduct,—we need to know just what degree of efficiency is exerted by our arithmetic and literature, our geography and history, our drawing and manual training, our Latin and Greek, our ethics and psychology. It is the lack of definite ideas and criteria in these fields that constitutes the greatest single source of waste in our educational system to-day.

And yet even here the outlook is extremely hopeful. The new movement toward industrial education is placing greater and greater emphasis upon those subjects of instruction and those types of methods whose efficiency can be tested and determined in an accurate fashion. The intimate relation between the classroom, on the one hand, and the machine shop, the experimental farm, the hospital ward and operating room, and the practice school, on the other hand, indicates a source of accurate knowledge with regard to the way in which our teachings really affect the conduct and adjustment of our pupils that cannot fail within a short time to serve as the basis for some illuminating principle of educational values.

This, I believe, will be the next great step in the development of our profession.

There has been no intention in what I have said to minimize the disadvantages and discouragements under which we are to-day doing our work. My only plea is for the hopeful and optimistic outlook which, I maintain, is richly justified by the progress that has already been made and by the virile character of the forces that are operating in the present situation.

On the whole, I can see no reason why I should not encourage young men to enter the service of school-craft. I cannot say to them that they will attain to great wealth, but I can safely promise them that, if they give to the work of preparation the same attention and time that they would give to their education and training for medicine or law or engineering, their services will be in large demand and their rewards not to be sneered at. Their incomes will not enable them to compete with the captains of industry, but they will permit as full an enjoyment of the comforts of life as it is good for any young man to command. But the ambitious teacher must pay the price to reap these rewards,—the price of time and energy and labor,—the price that he would have to pay for success in any other human calling. What I cannot promise him in education is the opportunity for wide popular adulation, but this, after all, is a matter of taste. Some men crave it and they should go into those vocations that will give it to them. Others are better satisfied with the discriminating recognition and praise of their own fellow-craftsmen.

The Ideal Teacher
(1908)[1]

In this commencement address that Bagley delivered at Oswego, he sought to inspire the young graduates to the nobility of their calling as they began their careers as classroom teachers. This lecture is a bit more autobiographical than the others, but, like other essays in his book entitled Craftsmanship in Teaching, *Bagley emphasizes the moral and spiritual aspects of the teaching profession. Note that Bagley's conception of the ideal teacher takes into account all of the great teachers from the past—for example Dante and Cicero and Shakespeare. To Bagley, the role of a teacher could never be reduced to simplistic mechanical techniques.*

I wish to discuss with you briefly a very commonplace and oft-repeated theme,—a theme that has been handled and handled until its once-glorious raiment is now quite threadbare; a theme so full of pitfalls and dangers for one who would attempt its discussion that I have hesitated long before making a choice. I know of no other theme that lends itself so readily to a superficial treatment—of no theme upon which one could find so easily at hand all of the proverbs and platitudes and maxims that one might desire. And so I cannot be expected to say anything upon this topic that has not been said before in a far better manner. But, after all, very few of our thoughts—even of those that we consider to be the most original and worth while—are really new to the world. Most of our thoughts have

---

1. An address to the graduating class of the Oswego, New York, State Normal School, February, 1908.

Forgotten Heroes of American Education, pages 49–58

been thought before. They are like dolls that are passed on from age to age to be dressed up and decorated to suit the taste or the fashion or the fancy of each succeeding generation. But even a new dress may add a touch of newness to an old doll; and a new phrase or a new setting may, for a moment, rejuvenate an old truth.

The topic that I wish to treat is this, "The Ideal Teacher." And I may as well start out by saying that the ideal teacher is and always must be a figment of the imagination. This is the essential feature of any ideal. The ideal man, for example, must possess an infinite number of superlative characteristics. We take this virtue from one, and that from another, and so on indefinitely until we have constructed in imagination a paragon, the counterpart of which could never exist on earth. He would have all the virtues of all the heroes; but he would lack all their defects and all their inadequacies. He would have the manners of a Chesterfield, the courage of a Winkelried, the imagination of a Dante, the eloquence of a Cicero, the wit of a Voltaire, the intuitions of a Shakespeare, the magnetism of a Napoleon, the patriotism of a Washington, the loyalty of a Bismarck, the humanity of a Lincoln, and a hundred other qualities, each the counterpart of some superlative quality, drawn from the historic figure that represented that quality in richest measure.

And so it is with the ideal teacher: he would combine, in the right proportion, all of the good qualities of all of the good teachers that we have ever known or heard of. The ideal teacher is and always must be a creature, not of flesh and blood, but of the imagination, a child of the brain. And perhaps it is well that this is true; for, if he existed in the flesh, it would not take very many of him to put the rest of us out of business. The relentless law of compensation, which rules that unusual growth in one direction must always be counterbalanced by deficient growth in another direction, is the saving principle of human society. That a man should be superlatively good in one single line of effort is the demand of modern life. It is a platitude to say that this is the age of the specialist. But specialism, while it always means a gain to society, also always means a loss to the individual. Darwin, at the age of forty, suddenly awoke to the fact that he was a man of one idea. Twenty years before, he had been a youth of the most varied and diverse interests. He had enjoyed music, he had found delight in the masterpieces of imaginative literature, he had felt a keen interest in the drama, in poetry, in the fine arts. But at forty Darwin quite by accident discovered that these things had not attracted him for years,— that every increment of his time and energy was concentrated in a constantly increasing measure upon the unraveling of that great problem to which he had set himself. And he lamented bitterly the loss of these other interests; he wondered why he had been so thoughtless as to let them slip from his grasp. It was the same old story of human progress; the sacrifice of the individual to the race. For Darwin's loss was the world's gain, and if he had not limited himself to one line of effort, and given himself up to that work to the exclusion of everything else, the world might still be waiting for the *Origin of Species,* and the revolution in human thought and human life which followed in the wake of that great book. Carlyle defined genius as an infinite capacity for taking pains. George Eliot characterized it as an infinite capacity for receiving discipline. But to make the definition complete, we need the formulation of Goethe, who identified genius with the power of concentration: "Who would be great must limit his ambitions; in concentration is shown the Master."

And so the great men of history, from the very fact of their genius, are apt not to correspond with what our ideal of greatness demands. Indeed, our ideal is often more nearly realized in men who fall far short of genius. When I studied chemistry, the instructor burned a bit of diamond to prove to us that the diamond was, after all, only carbon in an "allotropic" form. There seems to be a similar allotropy working in human nature. Some men seem to have all the constituents of genius, but they never reach very far above the plane of the commonplace. They are like the diamond,—except that they are more like the charcoal.

I wish to describe to you a teacher who was not a genius, and yet who possessed certain qualities that I should abstract and appropriate if I were to construct in my imagination an ideal teacher. I first met this man five years ago out in the mountain country. I can recall the occasion with the most vivid distinctness. It was a sparkling morning, in middle May. The valley was just beginning to green a little under the influence of the lengthening days, but on the surrounding mountains the snow line still hung low. I had just settled down to my morning's work when word was brought that a visitor wished to see me, and a moment later he was shown into the office. He was tall and straight, with square shoulders and a deep chest. His hair was gray, and a rather long white beard added to the effect of age, but detracted not an iota from the evidences of strength and vigor. He had the look of a Westerner,—of a man who had lived much of his life in the open. There was a rugged-ness about him, a sturdy strength that told of many a day's toil along the trail, and many a night's sleep under the stars.

In a few words he stated the purpose of his visit. He simply wished to do what half a hundred others in the course of the year had entered that office for the purpose of doing. He wished to enroll as a student in the college and to prepare himself for a teacher. This was not ordinarily a startling request, but hitherto it had been made only by those who were just starting out on the highroad of life. Here was a man advanced in years. He told me that he was sixty-five, and sixty-five in that country meant old age; for the region had but recently been settled, and most of the people were either young or middle-aged. The only old men in the country were the few surviving pioneers,—men who had come in away back in the early days of the mining fever, long before the advent of the railroad. They had trekked across the plains from Omaha, and up through the mountainous passes of the Oregon trail; or, a little later, they had come by steamboat from St. Louis up the twelve-hundred-mile stretch of the Missouri until their progress had been stopped by the Great Falls in the very foothills of the Rockies. What heroes were these graybeards of the mountains! What possibilities in knowing them, of listening to the recounting of tales of the early days,—of running fights with the Indians on the plains, of ambushments by desperadoes in the mountain passes, of the lurid life of the early mining camps, and the desperate deeds of the vigilantes! And here, before me, was a man of that type. You could read the main facts of his history in the very lines of his face. And this man—one of that small band whom the whole country united to honor—this man wanted to become a student,—to sit among adolescent boys and girls, listening to the lectures and discussions of instructors who were babes in arms when he was a man of middle life.

But there was no doubt of his determination. With the eagerness of a boy, he outlined his plan to me; and in doing this, he told me the story of his life,—just the barest facts to let me know that he was not a man to do things half-heartedly, or to drop a project until he had carried it through either to a successful issue, or to indisputable defeat.

And what a life that man had lived! He had been a youth of promise, keen of intelligence and quick of wit. He had spent two years at a college in the Middle West back in the early sixties. He had left his course uncompleted to enter the army, and he had followed the fortunes of war through the latter part of the great rebellion. At the close of the war he went West. He farmed in Kansas until the drought and the grasshoppers urged him on. He joined the first surveying party that picked out the line of the transcontinental railroad that was to follow the southern route along the old Santa Fe trail. He carried the chain and worked the transit across the Rockies, across the desert, across the Sierras, until, with his companions, he had—"led the iron stallions down to drink through the canyons to the waters of the West."

And when this task was accomplished, he followed the lure of the gold through the California placers; eastward again over the mountains to the booming Nevada camp, where the Comstock lode was already turning out the wealth that was to build a half-dozen colossal fortunes. He "prospected" through this country, with varying success, living the life of the camps,—rich in its experiences, vivid in its coloring, calling forth every item of energy and courage and hardihood that a man could command. Then word came by that mysterious wireless and keyless telegraphy of the mountains and the desert,—word that back to the eastward, ore deposits of untold wealth had been discovered. So eastward once more, with the stampede of the miners, he turned his face. He was successful at the outset in this new region. He quickly accumulated a fortune; he lost it and amassed another; lost that and still gained a third. Five successive fortunes he made successively, and successively he lost them. But during this time he had become a man of power and influence in the community. He married and raised a family and saw his children comfortably settled.

But when his last fortune was swept away, the old *Wanderlust* again claimed its own. Houses and lands and mortgages and mills and mines had slipped from his grasp. But it mattered little. He had only himself to care for, and, with pick and pan strapped to his saddlebow, he set his face westward. Along the ridges of the high Rockies, through Wyoming and Montana, he wandered, ever on the lookout for the glint of gold in the white quartz. Little by little he moved westward, picking up a sufficient living, until he found himself one winter shut in by the snows in a remote valley on the upper waters of the Gallatin River. He stopped one night at a lonely ranch house. In the course of the evening his host told him of a catastrophe that had befallen the widely scattered inhabitants of that remote valley. The teacher of the district school had fallen sick, and there was little likelihood of their getting another until spring.

That is a true catastrophe to the ranchers of the high valleys cut off from every line of communication with the outer world. For the opportunities of education are highly valued in that part of the West. They are reckoned with bread and horses and cattle and sheep, as among the necessities of life. The children were crying for school, and their parents could not satisfy that peculiar kind of hunger. But here was the relief. This wanderer who had arrived in their midst was a man of parts. He was lettered; he was educated. Would he do them the favor of teaching their children until the snow had melted away from the ridges, and his horse could pick the trail through the canons?

Now school-keeping was farthest from this man's thoughts. But the needs of little children were very near to his heart. He accepted the offer, and entered the log schoolhouse as the district schoolmaster, while a handful of pupils, numbering all the children of the community who could ride a broncho, came five, ten, and even fifteen miles daily, through the winter's snows and storms and cruel cold, to pick up the crumbs of learning that had lain so long untouched.

What happened in that lonely little school, far off on the Gallatin bench, I never rightly discovered. But when spring opened up, the master sold his horse and his pick and his rifle and the other implements of his trade. With the earnings of the winter he made his way to the school that the state had established for the training of teachers; and I count it as one of the privileges of my life that I was the first official of that school to listen to his story and to welcome him to the vocation that he had chosen to follow.

And yet, when I looked at his face, drawn into lines of strength by years of battle with the elements; when I looked at the clear blue eyes that told of a far cleaner life than is lived by one in a thousand of those that hold the frontiers of civilization; when I caught an expression about the mouth that told of an innate humanity far beyond the power of worldly losses or misfortunes to crush and subdue, I could not keep from my lips the words that gave substance to my thought; and the thought was this: that it were far better if we who were supposed to be competent to the task of education should sit reverently at the feet of this man, than that we should presume to instruct him. For knowledge may come from books, and even youth may possess it, but wisdom comes only from experience, and this man had that wisdom in far greater measure than we of books and laboratories and classrooms could ever hope to have it. He had lived years while we were living days.

I thought of a learned scholar who, through patient labor in amassing facts, had demonstrated the influence of the frontier in the development of our national ideals; who had pointed out how, at each successive stage of American history, the heroes of the frontier, pushing farther and farther into the wilderness, conquering first the low coastal plain of the Atlantic seaboard, then the forested foothills and ridges of the Appalachians, had finally penetrated into the Mississippi Valley, and, subduing that, had followed on westward to the prairies, and then to the great plains, and then clear across the great divide, the alkali deserts, and the Sierras, to California and the Pacific Coast; how these frontiersmen, at every stage of our history, had sent back wave after wave of strength and virility to keep alive the sturdy ideals of toil and effort and independence,—ideals that would counteract the mellowing and softening and degenerating influences of the hothouse civilization that grew up so rapidly in the successive regions that they left behind. Turner's theory that most of what is typical and unique in American institutions and ideals owes its existence to the backset of the frontier life found a living exemplar in the man who stood before me on that May morning.

But he would not be discouraged from his purpose. He had made up his mind to complete the course that the school offered; to take up the thread of his education at the point where he had dropped it more than forty years before. He had made up his mind, and it was easy to see that he was not a man to be deterred from a set purpose.

I shall not hide the fact that some of us were skeptical of the outcome. That a man of sixty-five should have a thirst for learning was not remarkable. But that a man whose life had been spent in scenes of excitement, who had been associated with deeds and events that stir the blood when we read of them to-day, a man who had lived almost every moment of his life in the open,—that such a man could settle down to the uneventful life of a student and a teacher, could shut himself up within the four walls of a classroom, could find anything to inspire and hold him in the dull presentation of facts or the dry elucidation of theories,—this seemed to be a miracle not to be expected in this realistic age. But, miracle or not, the thing actually happened. He remained nearly four years in the school, earning his living by work that he did in the intervals of study, and doing it so well that, when he graduated, he had not only his education and the diploma which stood for it, but also a bank account.

He lived in a little cabin by himself, for he wished to be where he would not disturb others when he sang or whistled over his work in the small hours of the night. But his meals he took at the college dormitory, where he presided at a table of young women students. Never was a man more popular with the ladies than this weather-beaten patriarch with the girls of his table. No matter how gloomy the day might be, one could always find sunshine from that quarter. No matter how grievous the troubles of work, there was always a bit of cheerful optimism from a man who had tasted almost every joy and sorrow that life had to offer. If one were in a blue funk of dejection because of failure in a class, he would lend the sympathy that came from his own rich experience in failures,—not only past but present, for some things that come easy at sixteen come hard at sixty-five, and this man who would accept no favors had to fight his way through "flunks" and "goose-eggs" like the younger members of the class. And even with it all so complete an embodiment of hope and courage and wholesome light-hearted-ness would be hard to find. He was an optimist because he had learned long since that anything but optimism is a crime; and learning this in early life, optimism had become a deeply seated and ineradicable prejudice in his mind. He could not have been gloomy if he had tried. And so this man fought his way through science and mathematics and philosophy, slowly but surely, just as he had fought inch by inch and link by link, across the Arizona desert years before. It was a much harder fight, for all the force of lifelong habit was against him from the start. And now came the human temptation to be off on the old trail, to saddle his horse and get a pick and a pan and make off across the western range to the golden land that always lies just under the sunset. How often that turbulent *Wanderlust* seized him, I can only conjecture. But I know the spirit of the wanderer was always strong within him. He could say, with Kipling's *Tramp Royal:*

> It's like a book, I think, this bloomin' world, Which you can read and care for just so long, But presently you feel that you will die unless you get the page you're reading done, An' turn another—likely not so good; But what you're after is to turn them all.

And I knew that he fought that temptation over and over again; for that little experience out on the Gallatin bench had only partially turned his life from the channels of wandering, although it had bereft him of the old desire to seek for gold. Often he outlined to me a well-formulated plan; perhaps he had to tell some one, lest the fever should take too strong a hold upon him, and force his surrender. His plan was this: He would teach a term here and there, gradually working his way westward, always toward the remote corners of the earth into which his roving instinct seemed unerringly to lead him. Alaska, Hawaii, and the Philippines seemed easy enough to access; surely, he thought, teachers must be needed in all those regions. And when he should have turned these pages, he might have mastered his vocation in a degree sufficient to warrant his attempting an alien soil. Then he would sail away into the South Seas, with New Zealand and Australia as a base. And gradually moving westward through English-speaking settlements and colonies he would finally complete the circuit of the globe.

And the full fruition of that plan might have formed a fitting climax to my tale, were I telling it for the sake of its romance; but my purpose demands a different conclusion. My hero is now principal of schools in a little city of the mountains,—a city so tiny that its name would be unknown to most of you. And I have heard vague rumors that he is rising rapidly in his profession and that the community he serves will not listen to anything but a permanent tenure of his office. All of which seems to indicate to me that he has abandoned, for the while at least, his intention to turn quite all the pages of the world's great book, and is content to live true to the ideal that was born in the log schoolhouse—the conviction that the true life is the life of service, and that the love of wandering and the lure of gold are only siren calls that lead one always toward, but never to, the promised land of dreams that seems to lie just over the western range where the pink sunset stands sharp against the purple shadows.

The ending of my story is prosaic, but everything in this world is prosaic, unless you view it either in the perspective of time or space, or in the contrasts that bring out the high lights and deepen the shadows.

But if I have left my hero happily married to his profession, the courtship and winning of which formed the theme of my tale, I may be permitted to indulge in a very little moralizing of a rather more explicit sort than I have yet attempted.

It is a simple matter to construct in imagination an ideal teacher. Mix with immortal youth and abounding health, a maximal degree of knowledge and a maximal degree of experience, add perfect tact, the spirit of true service, the most perfect patience, and the most steadfast persistence; place in the crucible of some good normal school; stir in twenty weeks of standard psychology, ten weeks of general method, and varying amounts of patent compounds known as special methods, all warranted pure and without drugs or poison; sweeten with a little music, toughen with fifteen weeks of logic, bring to a slow boil in the practice school, and, while still sizzling, turn loose on a cold world. The formula is simple and complete, but like many another good recipe, a competent cook might find it hard to follow when she is short of butter and must shamefully skimp on the eggs.

Now the man whose history I have recounted represents the most priceless qualities of this formula. In the first place he possessed that quality the key to which the philosophers of all ages have sought in vain,— he had solved the problem of eternal youth. At the age of sixty-five his enthusiasm was the enthusiasm of an adolescent. His energy was the energy of an adolescent. Despite his gray hair and white beard, his mind was perennially young. And that is the only type of mind that ought to be concerned with the work of education. I sometimes think that one of the advantages of a practice school lies in the fact that the teachers who have direct charge of the pupils—whatever may be their limitations—have at least the virtue of youth, the virtue of being young. If they could only learn from my hero the art of keeping young, of keeping the mind fresh and vigorous and open to whatever is good and true, no matter how novel a form it may take, they might, like him, preserve their youth indefinitely. And I think that his life gives us one clew to the secret,—to keep as close as we can to nature, for nature is always young; to sing and to whistle when we would rather weep; to cheer and comfort when we would rather crush and dishearten; often to dare something just for the sake of daring, for to be young is to dare; and always to wonder, for that is the prime symptom of youth, and when a man ceases to wonder, age and decrepitude are waiting for him around the next corner.

It is the privilege of the teaching craft to represent more adequately than any other calling the conditions for remaining young. There is time for living out-of-doors, which some of us, alas! do not do. And youth, with its high hope and lofty ambition, with its resolute daring and its naive wonder, surrounds us on every side. And yet how rapidly some of us age! How quickly life seems to lose its zest! How completely are we blind to the opportunities that are on every hand!

And closely related to this virtue of being always young, in fact growing out of it, the ideal teacher will have, as my hero had, the gift of gladness,— that joy of living which takes life for granted and proposes to make the most of every moment of consciousness that it brings.

And finally, to balance these qualities, to keep them in leash, the ideal teacher should possess that spirit of service, that conviction that the life of service is the only life worth while—that conviction for which my hero struggled so long and against such tremendous odds. The spirit of service must always be the cornerstone of the teaching craft. To know that any life which does not provide the opportunities for service is not worth the living, and that any life, however humble, that does provide these opportunities is rich beyond the reach of earthly rewards,—this is the first lesson that the tyro in schoolcraft must learn, be he sixteen or sixty-five.

And just as youth and hope and the gift of gladness are the eternal verities on one side of the picture, so the spirit of service, the spirit of sacrifice, is the eternal verity that forms their true complement; without whose compensation, hope were but idle dreaming, and laughter a hollow mockery. And self-denial, which is the keynote of service, is the great sobering, justifying, eternal factor that symbolizes humanity more perfectly than anything else. In the introduction to *Romola,* George Eliot pictures a spirit of the past who returns to earth four hundred years after his death, and looks down upon his native city of Florence. And I can conclude with no better words than those in which George Eliot voices her advice to that shade:

Go not down, good Spirit: for the changes are great and the speech of the Florentines would sound as a riddle in your ears. Or, if you go, mingle with no politicians on the marmi, or elsewhere; ask no questions about trade in Calimara; confuse yourself with no inquiries into scholarship, official or monastic. Only look at the sunlight and shadows on the grand walls that were built solidly and have endured in their grandeur; look at the faces of the little children, making another sunlight amid the shadows of age; look, if you will, into the churches and hear the same chants, see the same images as of old— the images of willing anguish for a great end, of beneficent love and ascending glory, see upturned living faces, and lips moving to the old prayers for help. These things have not changed. The sunlight and the shadows bring their old beauty and waken the old heart-strains at morning, noon, and even-tide; the little children are still the symbol of the eternal marriage between love and duty; and men still yearn for the reign of peace and righteousness—still own that life to be the best which is a conscious voluntary sacrifice.

Education and Utility

(1909)[1]

In discussions of education in the early 1900s, utility was all the rage. Bagley here uses an autobiographical approach to examine the many problems that were being created by educational theorists who were obsessed with making education "useful" and "practical." Bagley takes the time in this address to stop and think about the meaning of terms such as useful and practical to those who influence educational thought and practice. He also argues for what he thinks these terms should mean.

During this time in his life, Bagley was growing increasingly skeptical of the ideas of Progressive educators who valued utility above all else. Bagley remained committed to ideals and standards, which he thought were imminently useful and practical. He argues forcefully that curriculum must not be reduced to utilitarian concerns for material comfort, paths of least resistance, and merely economic understandings of vocational education.

I

I wish to discuss with you some phases of the problem that is perhaps foremost in the minds of the teaching public to-day: the problem, namely, of making education bear more directly and more effectively upon the work of practical, everyday life. I have no doubt that some of you feel, when this problem is suggested, very much as I felt when I first suggested to

---

1. An address before the Eastern Illinois Teachers' Association, October 15, 1909. Published as a Bulletin of the Eastern Illinois Normal School, October, 1909.

Forgotten Heroes of American Education, pages 59–72

myself the possibility of discussing it with you. You have doubtless heard some phases of this problem discussed at every meeting of this association for the past ten years—if you have been a member so long as that. Certain it is that we all grow weary of the reiteration of even the best of truths, but certain it is also that some problems are always before us, and until they are solved satisfactorily they will always stimulate men to devise means for their solution.

I should say at the outset, however, that I shall not attempt to justify to this audience the introduction of vocational subjects into the elementary and secondary curriculums. I shall take it for granted that you have already made up your minds upon this matter. I shall not take your time in an attempt to persuade you that agriculture ought to be taught in the rural schools, or manual training and domestic science in all schools. I am personally convinced of the value of such work and I shall take it for granted that you are likewise convinced.

My task to-day, then, is of another type. I wish to discuss with you some of the implications of this matter of utility in respect of the work that every elementary school is doing and always must do, no matter how much hand work or vocational material it may introduce. My problem, in other words, concerns the ordinary subject-matter of the curriculum,—reading and writing and arithmetic, geography and grammar and history,—those things which, like the poor, are always with us, but which we seem a little ashamed to talk about in public. Truly, from reading the educational journals and hearing educational discussion to-day, the layman might well infer that what we term the "useful" education and the education that is now offered by the average school are as far apart as the two poles. We are all familiar with the statement that the elementary curriculum is eminently adapted to produce clerks and accountants, but very poorly adapted to furnish recruits for any other department of life. The high school is criticized on the ground that it prepares for college and consequently for the professions, but that it is totally inadequate to the needs of the average citizen. Now it would be futile to deny that there is some truth in both these assertions, but I do not hesitate to affirm that both are grossly exaggerated, and that the curriculum of to-day, with all its imperfections, does not justify so sweeping a denunciation. I wish to point out some of the respects in which these charges are fallacious, and, in so doing, perhaps, to suggest some possible remedies for the defects that every one will acknowledge.

II

In the first place, let me make myself perfectly clear upon what I mean by the word "useful." What, after all, is the "useful" study in our schools? What do men find to be the useful thing in their lives? The most natural answer to this question is that the useful things are those that enable us to meet effectively the conditions of life,—or, to use a phrase that is perfectly clear to us all, the things that help us in getting a living. The vast majority of men and women in this world measure all values by this standard, for most of us are, to use the expressive slang of the day, "up against" this problem, and "up against" it so hard and so constantly that we interpret everything in the greatly foreshortened perspective of immediate necessity. Most of us in this room are confronting this problem of making a living. At any rate, I am confronting it, and consequently I may lay claim to some of the authority that comes from experience.

And since I have made this personal reference, may I violate the canons of good taste and make still another? I was face to face with this problem of getting a living a good many years ago, when the opportunity came to me to take a college course. I could see nothing ahead after that except another struggle with this same vital issue. So I decided to take a college course which would, in all probability, help me to solve the problem. Scientific agriculture was not developed in those days as it has been since that time, but a start had been made, and the various agricultural colleges were offering what seemed to be very practical courses. I had had some early experience on the farm, and I decided to become a scientific farmer. I took the course of four years and secured my degree. The course was as useful from the standpoint of practical agriculture as any that could have been devised at the time. But when I graduated, what did I find? The same old problem of getting a living still confronted me as I had expected that it would; and alas! I had got my education in a profession that demanded capital. I was a landless farmer. Times were hard and work of all kinds was very scarce. The farmers of those days were inclined to scoff at scientific agriculture. I could have worked for my board and a little more and I should have done so had I been able to find a job. But while I was looking for the place, a chance came to teach school, and I took the opportunity as a means of keeping the wolf from the door. I have been engaged in the work of teaching ever since. When I was able to buy land, I did so, and I have to-day a farm of which I am very proud. It does not pay large dividends, but I keep it up for the fun I get out of it,—and I like to think, also, that if I should lose my job as a teacher, I could go back to the farm and show the natives how to make money. This is doubtless an illusion, but it is a source of solid comfort just the same.

Now the point of this experience is simply this: I secured an education that seemed to me to promise the acme of utility. In one way, it has fulfilled that promise far beyond my wildest expectations, but that way was very different from the one that I had anticipated. The technical knowledge that I gained during those four strenuous years, I apply now only as a means of recreation. So far as enabling me directly to get a living, this technical knowledge does not pay one per cent on the investment of time and money. And yet I count the training that I got from its mastery as, perhaps, the most useful product of my education.

Now what was the secret of its utility? As I analyze my experience, I find it summed up very largely in two factors. In the first place, I studied a set of subjects for which I had at the outset very little taste. In studying agriculture, I had to master a certain amount of chemistry, physics, botany, and zoology, for each and every one of which I felt, at the outset, a distinct aversion and dislike. A mastery of these subjects was essential to a realization of the purpose that I had in mind. I was sure that I should never like them, and yet, as I kept at work, I gradually found myself losing that initial distaste. First one and then another opened out its vista of truth and revelation before me, and almost before I was aware of it, I was enthusiastic over science. It was a long time before I generalized that experience and drew its lesson, but the lesson, once learned, has helped me more even in the specific task of getting a living than anything else that came out of my school training. That experience taught me not only the necessity for doing disagreeable tasks,—for attacking them hopefully and cheerfully,—but it also taught me that disagreeable tasks, if attacked in the right way, and persisted in with patience, often become attractive in themselves. Over and over again in meeting the situations of real life, I have been confronted with tasks that were initially distasteful. Sometimes I have surrendered before them; but sometimes, too, that lesson has come back to me, and has inspired me to struggle on, and at no time has it disappointed me by the outcome. I repeat that there is no technical knowledge that I have gained that compares for a moment with that ideal of patience and persistence. When it comes to real, downright utility, measured by this inexorable standard of getting a living, let me commend to you the ideal of persistent effort. All the knowledge that we can learn or teach will come to very little if this element is lacking.

Now this is very far from saying that the pursuit of really useful knowledge may not give this ideal just as effectively as the pursuit of knowledge that will never be used. My point is simply this: that beyond the immediate utility of the facts that we teach,—indeed, basic and fundamental to this utility,—is the utility of the ideals and standards that are derived from our school work. Whatever we teach, these essential factors can be made to stand out in our work, and if our pupils acquire these we shall have done the basic and important thing in helping them to solve the problems of real life,—and if our pupils do not acquire these, it will make little difference how intrinsically valuable may be the content of our instruction. I feel like emphasizing this matter to-day, because there is in the air a notion that utility depends entirely upon the content of the curriculum. Certainly the curriculum must be improved from this standpoint, but we are just now losing sight of the other equally important factor,—that, after all, while both are essential, it is the spirit of teaching rather than the content of teaching that is basic and fundamental.

Nor have I much sympathy with that extreme view of this matter which asserts that we must go out of our way to provide distasteful tasks for the pupil in order to develop this ideal of persistence. I believe that such a policy will always tend to defeat its own purpose. I know a teacher who holds this belief. He goes out of his way to make tasks difficult. He refuses to help pupils over hard places. He does not believe in careful assignments of lessons, because, he maintains, the pupil ought to learn to overcome difficulties for himself, and how can he learn unless real difficulties are presented?

The great trouble with this teacher is that his policy does not work out in practice. A small minority of his pupils are strengthened by it; the majority are weakened. He is right when he says that a pupil gains strength only by overcoming difficulties, but he neglects a very important qualification of this rule, namely, that a pupil gains no strength out of obstacles that he fails to overcome. It is the conquest that comes after effort,—this is the factor that gives one strength and confidence. But when defeat follows defeat and failure follows failure, it is weakness that is being engendered—not strength. And that is the trouble with this teacher's pupils. The majority leave him with all confidence in their own ability shaken out of them and some of them never recover from the experience.

And so while I insist strenuously that the most useful lesson we can teach our pupils is how to do disagreeable tasks cheerfully and willingly, please do not understand me to mean that we should go out of our way to provide disagreeable tasks. After all, I rejoice that my own children are learning how to read and write and cipher much more easily, much more quickly, and withal much more pleasantly than I learned those useful arts. The more quickly they get to the plane that their elders have reached, the more quickly they can get beyond this plane and on to the next level.

To argue against improved methods in teaching on the ground that they make things too easy for the pupil is, to my mind, a grievous error. It is as fallacious as to argue that the introduction of machinery is a curse because it has diminished in some measure the necessity for human drudgery. But if machinery left mankind to rest upon its oars, if it discouraged further progress and further effortful achievement, it *would* be a curse: and if the easier and quicker methods of instruction simply bring my children to my own level and then fail to stimulate them to get beyond my level, then they are a curse and not a blessing.

I do not decry that educational policy of to-day which insists that school work should be made as simple and attractive as possible. I do decry that misinterpretation of this policy which looks at the matter from the other side, and asserts so vehemently that the child should never be asked or urged to do something that is not easy and attractive. It is only because there is so much in the world to be done that, for the sake of economizing time and strength, we should raise the child as quickly and as rapidly and as pleasantly as possible to the plane that the race has reached. But among all the lessons of race experience that we must teach him there is none so fundamental and important as the lesson of achievement itself,—the supreme lesson wrung from human experience,—the lesson, namely, that every advance that the world has made, every step that it has taken forward, every increment that has been added to the sum total of progress has been attained at the price of self-sacrifice and effort and struggle,—at the price of doing things that one does not want to do. And unless a man is willing to pay that price, he is bound to be the worst kind of a social parasite, for he is simply living on the experience of others, and adding to this capital nothing of his own.

It is sometimes said that universal education is essential in order that the great mass of humanity may live in greater comfort and enjoy the luxuries that in the past have been vouchsafed only to the few. Personally I think that this is all right so far as it goes, but it fails to reach an ultimate goal. Material comfort is justified only because it enables mankind to live more effectively on the lower planes of life and give greater strength and greater energy to the solution of new problems upon the higher planes of life. The end of life can never be adequately formulated in terms of comfort and ease, not even in terms of culture and intellectual enjoyment; the end of life is achievement, and no matter how far we go, achievement is possible only to those who are willing to pay the price. When the race stops investing its capital of experience in further achievement, when it settles down to take life easily, it will not take it very long to eat up its capital and revert to the plane of the brute.

III

But I am getting away from my text. You will remember that I said that the most useful thing that we can teach the child is to attack strenuously and resolutely any problem that confronts him whether it pleases him or not, and I wanted to be certain that you did not misinterpret me to mean that we should, for this reason, make our school tasks unnecessarily difficult and laborious. After all, while our attitude should always be one of interesting our pupils, their attitude should always be one of effortful attention,—of willingness to do the task that we think it best for them to do. You see, it is a double-headed policy, and how to carry it out is a perplexing problem. Of so much I am certain, however, at the outset: if the pupil takes the attitude that we are there to interest and entertain him, we shall make a sorry fiasco of the whole matter, and inasmuch as this very tendency is in the air at the present time, I feel justified in at least referring to its danger. Now if this ideal of persistent effort is the most useful thing that can come out of education, what is the next most useful? Again, as I analyze what I obtained from my own education, it seems to me that, next to learning that disagreeable tasks are often well worth doing, the factor that has helped me most in getting a living has been the method of solving the situations that confronted me. After all, if we simply have the ideal of resolute and aggressive and persistent attack, we may struggle indefinitely without much result. All problems of life involve certain common factors. The essential difference between the educated and the uneducated man, if we grant each an equal measure of pluck, persistence, and endurance, lies in the superior ability of the educated man to analyze his problem effectively and to proceed intelligently rather than blindly to its solution. I maintain that education should give a man this ideal of attacking any problem; furthermore I maintain that the education of the present day, in spite of the anathemas that are hurled against it, is doing this in richer measure than it has ever been done before. But there is no reason why we should not do it in still greater measure.

I once knew two men who were in the business of raising fruit for commercial purposes. Each had a large orchard which he operated according to conventional methods and which netted him a comfortable income. One of these men was a man of narrow education: the other a man of liberal education, although his training had not been directed in any way toward the problems of horticulture. The orchards had borne exceptionally well for several years, but one season, when the fruit looked especially promising, a period of wet, muggy weather came along just before the picking season, and one morning both these men went out into their orchards to find the fruit very badly "specked." Now the conventional thing to do in such cases was well known to both men. Each had picked up a good deal of technical information about caring for fruit, and each did the same thing in meeting this situation. He got out his spraying outfit, prepared some Bordeaux mixture, and set vigorously at work with his pumps. So far as persistence and enterprise went, both men stood on an equal footing. But it happened that this was an unusual and not a conventional situation. The spraying did not alleviate the condition. The corruption spread through the trees like wildfire, and seemed to thrive on copper sulphate rather than succumb to its corrosive influence.

Now this was where the difference in training showed itself. The orchardist who worked by rule of thumb, when he found that his rule did not work, gave up the fight and spent his time sitting on his front porch bemoaning his luck. The other set diligently at work to analyze the situation. His education had not taught him anything about the characteristics of parasitic fungi, for parasitic fungi were not very well understood when he was in school. But his education had left with him a general method of procedure for just such cases, and that method he at once applied. It had taught him how to find the information that he needed, provided that such information was available. It had taught him that human experience is crystallized in books, and that, when a discovery is made in any field of science,—no matter how specialized the field and no matter how trivial the finding,—the discovery is recorded in printer's ink and placed at the disposal of those who have the intelligence to find it and apply it. And so he set out to read up on the subject,—to see what other men had learned about this peculiar kind of apple rot. He obtained all that had been written about it and began to master it. He told his friend about this material and suggested that the latter follow the same course, but the man of narrow education soon found himself utterly at sea in a maze of technical terms. The terms were new to the other too, but he took down his dictionary and worked them out. He knew how to use indices and tables of contents and various other devices that facilitate the gathering of information, and while his uneducated friend was storming over the pedantry of men who use big words, the other was making rapid progress through the material. In a short time he learned everything that had been found out about this specific disease. He learned that its spores are encased in a gelatinous sac which resisted the entrance of the chemicals. He found how the spores were reproduced, how they wintered, how they germinated in the following season; and, although he did not save much of his crop that year, he did better the next. Nor were the evidences of his superiority limited to this very useful result. He found that, after all, very little was known about this disease, so he set himself to find out more about it. To do this, he started where other investigators had left off, and then he applied a principle he had learned from his education; namely, that the only valid methods of obtaining new truths are the methods of close observation and controlled experiment.

Now I maintain that the education which was given that man was effective in a degree that ought to make his experience an object lesson for us who teach. What he had found most useful at a very critical juncture of his business life was, primarily, not the technical knowledge that he had gained either in school or in actual experience. His superiority lay in the fact that he knew how to get hold of knowledge when he needed it, how to master it once he had obtained it, how to apply it once he had mastered it, and finally how to go about to discover facts that had been undetected by previous investigators. I care not whether he got this knowledge in the elementary school or in the high school or in the college. He might have secured it in any one of the three types of institution, but he had to learn it somewhere, and I shall go further and say that the average man has to learn it in some school and under an explicit and conscious method of instruction.

But perhaps you would maintain that this statement of the case, while in general true, does not help us out in practice. After all, how are we to impress pupils with this ideal of persistence and with these ideals of getting and applying information, and with this ideal of investigation? I maintain that these important useful ideals may be effectively impressed almost from the very outset of school life. The teaching of every subject affords innumerable opportunities to force home their lessons. In fact, it must be a very gradual process—a process in which the concrete instances are numerous and rich and impressive. From these concrete instances, the general truth may in time emerge. Certainly the chances that it will emerge are greatly multiplied if we ourselves recognize its worth and importance, and lead our pupils to see in each concrete case the operation of the general principle. After all, the chief reason why so much of our education miscarries, why so few pupils gain the strength and the power that we expect all to gain, lies in the inability of the average individual to draw a general conclusion from concrete cases—to see the general in the particular. We have insisted so strenuously upon concrete instruction that we have perhaps failed also to insist that fact without law is blind, and that observation without induction is stupidity gone to seed.

Let me give a concrete instance of what I mean. Not long ago, I visited an eighth-grade class during a geography period. It was at the time when the discovery of the Pole had just set the whole civilized world by the ears, and the teacher was doing something that many good teachers do on occasions of this sort: she was turning the vivid interest of the moment to educative purposes. The pupils had read Peary's account of his trip and they were discussing its details in class. Now that exercise was vastly more than an interesting information lesson, for Peary's achievement became, under the skillful touch of that teacher, a type of all human achievement. I wish that I could reproduce that lesson for you—how vividly she pictured the situation that confronted the explorer,—the bitter cold, the shifting ice, the treacherous open leads, the lack of game or other sources of food supply, the long marches on scant rations, the short hours and the uncomfortable conditions of sleep; and how from these that fundamental lesson of pluck and endurance and courage came forth naturally without preaching the moral or indulging in sentimental "goody-goodyism." And then the other and equally important part of the lesson,—how pluck and courage in themselves could never have solved the problem; how knowledge was essential, and how that knowledge had been gained: some of it from the experience of early explorers,—how to avoid the dreaded scurvy, how to build a ship that could withstand the tremendous pressure of the floes; and some from the Eskimos,—how to live in that barren region, and how to travel with dogs and sledges;—and some, too, from Peary's own early experiences,—how he had struggled for twenty years to reach the goal, and had added this experience to that until finally the prize was his. We may differ as to the value of Peary's deed, but that it stands as a type of what success in any undertaking means, no one can deny. And this was the lesson that these eighth-grade pupils were absorbing,—the world-old lesson before which all others fade into insignificance,—the lesson, namely, that achievement can be gained only by those who are willing to pay the price.

And I imagine that when that class is studying the continent of Africa in their geography work, they will learn something more than the names of rivers and mountains and boundaries and products,—I imagine that they will link these facts with the names and deeds of the men who gave them to the world. And when they study history, it will be vastly more than a bare recital of dates and events,—it will be alive with these great lessons of struggle and triumph,—for history, after all, is only the record of human achievement. And if those pupils do not find these same lessons coming out of their own little conquests,—if the problems of arithmetic do not furnish an opportunity to conquer the pressure ridges of partial payments or the Polar night of bank discount, or if the intricacies of formal grammar do not resolve themselves into the North Pole of correct expression,—I have misjudged that teacher's capacities; for the great triumph of teaching is to get our pupils to see the fundamental and the eternal in things that are seemingly trivial and transitory. We are fond of dividing school studies into the cultural and the practical, into the humanities and the sciences. Believe me, there is no study worth the teaching that is not practical at basis, and there is no practical study that has not its human interest and its humanizing influence—if only we go to some pains to search them out.

V

I have said that the most useful thing that education can do is to imbue the pupil with the ideal of effortful achievement which will lead him to do cheerfully and effectively the disagreeable tasks that fall to his lot. I have said that the next most useful thing that it can do is to give him a general method of solving the problems that he meets. Is there any other useful outcome of a general nature that we may rank in importance with these two? I believe that there is, and I can perhaps tell you what I mean by another reference to a concrete case. I know a man who lacks this third factor, although he possesses the other two in a very generous measure. He is full of ambition, persistence, and courage. He is master of the rational method of solving the problems that beset him. He does his work intelligently and effectively. And yet he has failed to make a good living. Why? Simply because of his standard of what constitutes a good living. Measured by my standard, he is doing excellently well. Measured by his own standard, he is a miserable failure. He is depressed and gloomy and out of harmony with the world, simply because he has no other standard for a good living than a financial one. He is by profession a civil engineer. His work is much more remunerative than is that of many other callings. He has it in him to attain to professional distinction in that work. But to this opportunity he is blind. In the great industrial center in which he works, he is constantly irritated by the evidences of wealth and luxury beyond what he himself enjoys. The millionaire captain of industry is his hero, and because he is not numbered among this class, he looks at the world through the bluest kind of spectacles.

Now, to my mind that man's education failed somewhere, and its failure lay in the fact that it did not develop in him ideals of success that would have made him immune to these irritating factors. We have often heard it said that education should rid the mind of the incubus of superstition, and one very important effect of universal education is that it does offer to all men an explanation of the phenomena that formerly weighted down the mind with fear and dread, and opened an easy ingress to the forces of superstition and fraud and error. Education has accomplished this function, I think, passably well with respect to the more obvious sources of superstition. Necromancy and magic, demonism and witchcraft, have long since been relegated to the limbo of exposed fraud. Their conquest has been one of the most significant advances that man has made above the savage. The truths of science have at last triumphed, and, as education has diffused these truths among the masses, the triumph has become almost universal.

But there are other forms of superstition besides those I have mentioned,—other instances of a false perspective, of distorted values, of inadequate standards. If belief in witchcraft or in magic is bad because it falls short of an adequate interpretation of nature,—if it is false because it is inconsistent with human experience,—then the worship of Mammon that my engineer friend represents is tenfold worse than witchcraft, measured by the same standards. If there is any lesson that human history teaches with compelling force, it *is* surely this: Every race which has yielded to the demon of individualism and the lust for gold and self-gratification has gone down the swift and certain road to national decay. Every race that, through unusual material prosperity, has lost its grip on the eternal verities of self-sacrifice and self-denial has left the lesson of its downfall written large upon the pages of history. I repeat that if superstition consists in believing something that is inconsistent with rational human experience, then our present worship of the golden calf is by far the most dangerous form of superstition that has ever befuddled the human intellect.

But, you ask, what can education do to alleviate a condition of this sort? How may the weak influence of the school make itself felt in an environment that has crystallized on every hand this unfortunate standard? Individualism is in the air. It is the dominant spirit of the times. It is reenforced upon every side by the unmistakable evidences of national prosperity. It is easy to preach the simple life, but who will live it unless he has to? It is easy to say that man should have social and not individual standards of success and achievement, but what effect will your puerile assertion have upon the situation that confronts us?

Yes; it is easier to be a pessimist than an optimist. It is far easier to lie back and let things run their course than it is to strike out into midstream and make what must be for the pioneer a fatal effort to stem the current. But is the situation absolutely hopeless? If the forces of education can lift the Japanese people from barbarism to enlightenment in two generations; if education can in a single century transform Germany from the weakest to the strongest power on the continent of Europe; if five short years of a certain type of education can change the course of destiny in China;—are we warranted in our assumption that we hold a weak weapon in this fight against Mammon?

I have intimated that the attitude of my engineer friend toward life is the result of twisted ideals. A good many young men are going out into life with a similar defect in their education. They gain their ideals not from the great wellsprings of human experience as represented in history and literature, in religion and art, but from the environment around them, and consequently they become victims of this superstition from the outset. As a trainer of teachers, I hold it to be one important part of my duty to fortify my students as strongly as I can against this false standard of which my engineer friend is the victim. It is just as much a part of my duty to give my students effective and consistent standards of what a good living consists in as it is to give them the technical knowledge and skill that will enable them to make a good living. If my students who are to become teachers have standards of living and standards of success that are inconsistent with the great ideal of social service for which teaching stands, then I have fallen far short of success in my work. If they are constantly irritated by the evidences of luxury beyond their means, if this irritation sours their dispositions and checks their spontaneity, their efficiency as teachers is greatly lessened or perhaps entirely negated. And if my engineer friend places worldly emoluments upon a higher plane than professional efficiency, I dread for the safety of the bridges that he builds. His education as an engineer should have fortified him against just such a contingency. It should have left him with the ideal of craftsmanship supreme in his life. And if his technical education failed to do this, his general education ought, at least, to have given him a bias in the right direction.

I believe that all forms of vocational and professional education are not so strong in this respect as they should be. Again you say to me, What can education do when the spirit of the times speaks so strongly on the other side? But what is education for if it is not to preserve midst the chaos and confusion of troublous times the great truths that the race has wrung from its experience? How different might have been the fate of Rome, if Rome had possessed an educational system touching every child in the Empire, and if, during the years that witnessed her decay and downfall, those schools could have kept steadily, persistently at work, impressing upon every member of each successive generation the virtues that made the old Romans strong and virile—the virtues that enabled them to lay the foundations of an empire that crumbled in ruins once these truths were forgotten. Is it not the specific task of education to represent in each generation the human experiences that have been tried and tested and found to work,—to represent these in the face of opposition if need be,— to be faithful to the trusteeship of the most priceless legacy that the past has left to the present and to the future? If this is not our function in the scheme of things, then what is our function? Is it to stand with bated breath to catch the first whisper that will usher in the next change? Is it to surrender all initiative and simply allow ourselves to be tossed hither and yon by the waves and cross-waves of a fickle public opinion? Is it to cower in dread of a criticism that is not only unjust but often ill-advised of the real conditions under which we are doing our work?

I take it that none of us is ready to answer these questions in the affirmative. Deep down in our hearts we know that we have a useful work to do, and we know that we are doing it passably well. We also know our defects and shortcomings at least as well as one who has never faced our problems and tried to solve them. And it is from this latter type that most of the drastic criticism, especially of the elementary and secondary school, emanates. I confess that my gorge rises within me when I read or hear the invectives that are being hurled against teaching as a profession (and against the work of the elementary and secondary school in particular) by men who know nothing of this work at first hand. This is the greatest handicap under which the profession of teaching labors. In every other important field of human activity a man must present his credentials before he takes his seat at the council table, and even then he must sit and listen respectfully to his elders for a while before he ventures a criticism or even a suggestion. This plan may have its defects. It may keep things on too conservative a basis; but it avoids the danger into which we as a profession have fallen,—the danger of "half-baked" theories and unmatured policies.

To-day the only man that can get a respectable hearing at our great national educational meetings is the man who has something new and bizarre to propose. And the more startling the proposal, the greater is the measure of adulation that he receives. The result of this is a continual straining for effect, an enormous annual crop of fads and fancies, which, though most of them are happily short-lived, keep us in a state of continual turmoil and confusion.

Now, it goes without saying that there are many ways of making education hit the mark of utility in addition to those that I have mentioned. The teachers down in the lower grades who are teaching little children the arts of reading and writing and computation are doing vastly more in a practical direction than they are ever given credit for doing; for reading and writing and the manipulation of numbers are, next to oral speech itself, the prime necessities in the social and industrial world. These arts are being taught to-day better than they have ever been taught before,—and the technique of their teaching is undergoing constant refinement and improvement.

The school can do and is doing other useful things. Some schools are training their pupils to be well mannered and courteous and considerate of the rights of others. They are teaching children one of the most, basic and fundamental laws of human life; namely, that there are some things that a gentleman cannot do and some things that society will not stand. How many a painful experience in solving this very problem of getting a living could be avoided if one had only learned this lesson passing well! What a pity it is that some schools that stand to-day for what we call educational progress are failing in just this particular—are sending out into the world an annual crop of boys and girls who must learn the great lesson of self-control and a proper respect for the rights of others in the bitter school of experience,—a school in which the rod will never be spared, but whose chastening scourge comes sometimes, alas, too late!

There is no feature of school life which has not its almost infinite possibilities of utility. But after all, are not the basic and fundamental things these ideals that I have named? And should not we who teach stand for idealism in its widest sense? Should we not ourselves subscribe an undying fidelity to those great ideals for which teaching must stand,—to the ideal of social service which lies at the basis of our craft, to the ideals of effort and discipline that make a nation great and its children strong, to the ideal of science that dissipates the black night of ignorance and superstition, to the ideal of culture that humanizes mankind?

The Scientific Spirit
in Education
(1910)[1]

The St. Louis Society of Pedagogy was a powerful group of thinkers and teachers who were deeply knowledgeable about the major philosophical traditions that were influencing educational theory and practice. William Torrey Harris launched the Society in 1870 when he was superintendent of the St. Louis Public Schools. During his service as an elementary school principal in St. Louis during the 1901–1902 academic year, Bagley came to know the Society well. Like all members of the Society, Bagley was engaged in the question of what science might mean for the practice of education.

In this lecture, delivered in 1910, Bagley explains his view of science in education. The fact that he included the word spirit in the title of the paper indicates that he was reluctant to separate science from ethics. He called upon science when he was seeking to influence scholars, but he was unwilling to separate "science" from social and moral concerns. However, during the 1920s and 1930s, Bagley became increasingly skeptical of his earlier understanding of science. He began to consider the possibility that modern science would not be able to "fix" all of the thorny problems of educational policy and practice. As his skepticism toward the scientific interpretation of education grew, so too did his reliance on the social and moral aspects of his philosophy of education.

---

1. An address delivered before the St. Louis Society of Pedagogy, April 16, 1910.

I know that I do not need to plead with this audience for a recognition of the scientific spirit in the solution of educational problems. The long life and the enviable record of this Society of Pedagogy testify in themselves to that spirit of free inquiry, to the calm and dispassionate search for the truth which lies at the basis of the scientific method. You have gathered here, fortnight after fortnight, to discuss educational problems in the light of your experience. You have reported your experience and listened to the results that others have gleaned in the course of their daily work. And experience is the corner stone of science.

Some of the most stimulating and clarifying discussions of educational problems that I have ever heard have been made in the sessions of this Society. You have been scientific in your attitude toward education, and I may add that I first learned the lessons of the real science of education in the St. Louis schools, and under the inspiration that was furnished by the men who were members of this Society. What I knew of the science of education before I came to this city ten years ago, was gleaned largely from books. It was deductive, *a priori*, in its nature. What I learned here was the induction from actual experience.

My very first introduction to my colleagues among the school men of this city was a lesson in the science of education. I had brought with me a letter to one of your principals. He was in the office down on Locust Street the first Saturday that I spent in the city. I presented my letter to him, and, with that true Southern hospitality which has always characterized your corps, he took me immediately under his wing and carried me out to luncheon with him.

We sat for hours in a little restaurant down on Sixth Street,—he was my teacher and I was his pupil. And gradually, as the afternoon wore on, I realized that I had met a master craftsman in the art of education. At first I talked glibly enough of what I intended to do, and he listened sympathetically and helpfully, with a little quizzical smile in his eyes as I outlined my ambitious plans. And when I had run the gamut of my dreams, he took his turn, and, in true Socratic fashion, yet without making me feel in the least that I was only a dreamer after all, he refashioned my theories. One by one the little card houses that I had built up were deftly, smoothly, gently, but completely demolished. I did not know the A B C of schoolcraft —but he did not tell me that I did not. He went at the task of instruction from the positive point of view. He proved to me, by reminiscence and example, how different are actual and ideal conditions. And finally he wound up with a single question that opened a new world to me. "What," he asked, "is the dominant characteristic of the child's mind?" I thought at first that I was on safe ground—for had I not taken a course in child study, and had I not measured some hundreds of school children while working out a university thesis? So I began with my list. But, at each characteristic that I mentioned he shook his head. "No," he said, "no; that is not right." And when finally I had exhausted my list, he said to me, "The dominant characteristic of the child's mind is its *seriousness*. The child is the most *serious* creature in the world."

The answer staggered me for a moment. Like ninety-nine per cent of the adult population of this globe, the seriousness of the child had never appealed to me. In spite of the theoretical basis of my training, that single, dominant element of child life had escaped me. I had gained my notion of the child from books, and, I also fear, from the Sunday supplements. To me, deep down in my heart, the child was an animated joke. I was immersed in unscientific preconceptions. But the master craftsman had gained his conception of child life from intimate, empirical acquaintance with the genus boy. He had gleaned from his experience that fundamental truth: "The child is the most serious creature in the world."

Sometime I hope that I may make some fitting acknowledgment of the debt of gratitude that I owe to that man. The opportunities that I had to talk with him were all too few, but I did make a memorable visit to his school, and studied at first hand the great work that he was doing for the pupils of the Columbia district. He died the next year, and I shall never forget the words that stood beneath his picture that night in one of the daily papers: "Charles Howard: Architect of Character."

II

The essence of the scientific spirit is to view experience without prejudice, and that was the lesson that I learned from the school system of St. Louis. The difference between the ideal child and the real child,—the difference between what fancy pictures a schoolroom to be and what actual first-hand acquaintance shows that it is, the difference between a preconceived notion and an actual stubborn fact of experience,—these were among the lessons that I learned in these schools. But, at the same time, there was no crass materialism accompanying this teaching. There was no loss of the broader point of view. A fact is a fact, and we cannot get around it,—and this is what scientific method has insisted upon from its inception. But always beyond the fact is its significance, its meaning. That the St. Louis schools have for the last fifty years stood for the larger view; that they have never, so far as I know, exploited the new and the bizarre simply because it was new and strange,—this is due, I believe, to the insight and inspiration of the man[1] who first fashioned the framework of this system, and breathed

---

1. Dr. W. T. Harris.

into it as a system the vitalizing element of idealism. Personally, I have not always been in sympathy with the teachings of the Hegelian philosophy,—I have not always understood them,—but no man could witness the silent, steady, unchecked growth of the St. Louis schools without being firmly and indelibly impressed with the dynamic value of a richly conceived and rigidly wrought system of fundamental principles. The cause of education has suffered much from the failure of educators to break loose from the shackles of the past. But it has, in some places, suffered still more from the tendency of the human mind to confuse fundamental principles with the shackles of tradition. The rage for the new and the untried, simply because it is new and untried,—this has been, and is to-day, the rock upon which real educational progress is most likely to be wrecked. This is a rock, I believe, that St. Louis has so far escaped, and I have no doubt that its escape has been due, in large measure, to the careful, rigid, laborious, and yet illuminating manner in which that great captain charted out its course.

III

Fundamentally, there is, I believe, no discrepancy, no inconsistency, between the scientific spirit in education and what may be called the philosophical spirit. As I have suggested, there are always two dangers that must be avoided: the danger, in the first place, of thinking of the old as essentially bad; and, on the other hand, the danger of thinking of the new and strange and unknown as essentially bad; the danger of confusing a sound conservatism with a blind worship of established custom; and the danger of confusing a sound radicalism with the blind worship of the new and the bizarre.

Let me give you an example of what I mean. There is a rather bitter controversy at present between two factions of science teachers. One faction insists that physics and chemistry and biology should be taught in the high school from the economic point of view,—that the economic applications of these sciences to great human arts, such as engineering and agriculture, should be emphasized at every point,—that a great deal of the material now taught in these sciences is both useless and unattractive to the average high-school pupil. The other faction maintains that such a course would mean the destruction of science as an integral part of the secondary culture course,—that science to be cultural must be pure science,—must be viewed apart from its economic applications,—apart from its relations to the bread-and-butter problem.

Now many of the advocates of the first point of view—many of the people that would emphasize the economic side—are animated by the spirit of change and unrest which dominates our latter-day civilization.

They wish to follow the popular demand. "Down with scholasticism!" is their cry; "Down with this blind worship of custom and tradition! Let us do the thing that gives the greatest immediate benefit to our pupils. Let us discard the elements in our courses that are hard and dry and barren of practical results." Now these men, I believe, are basing their argument upon the fallacy of immediate expediency. The old is bad, the new is good. That is their argument. They have no sheet anchor out to windward. They are willing to drift with the gale.

Many of the advocates of the second point of view—many of the people who hold to the old line, pure-science teaching—are, on the other hand, animated by a spirit of irrational conservatism. "Down with radicalism!" they shout; "Down with the innovators! Things that are hard and dry are good mental discipline. They made our fathers strong. They can make our children strong. What was good enough for the great minds of the past is good enough for us."

Now these men, I believe, have gone to the other extreme. They have confused custom and tradition with fundamental and eternal principles. They have thought that, just because a thing is old, it is good, just as their antagonists have thought that just because a thing is new it is good. In both cases, obviously, the scientific spirit is lacking. The most fundamental of all principles is the principle of truth. And yet these men who are teachers of science are—both classes of them—ruled themselves by dogma. And meantime the sciences are in danger of losing their place in secondary education. The rich promise that was held out a generation ago has not been fulfilled. Within the last decade, the enrollment in the science courses has not increased in proportion to the total enrollment, while the enrollment in Latin (which fifteen years ago was about to be cast upon the educational scrap heap) has grown by leaps and bounds.

Now this is a type of a great many controversies in education. We talk and theorize, but very seldom do we try to find out the actual facts in the case by any adequate tests. It was the lack of such tests that led us at the University of Illinois to enter upon a series of impartial investigations to see whether we could not take some of these mooted questions out of the realm of eternal controversy, and provide some definite solutions. We chose among others this controversy between the economic scientists and the pure scientists. We took a high-school class and divided it into two sections. We tried to place in each section an equal number of bright and mediocre and dull pupils, so that the conditions would be equalized. Then we chose an excellent teacher, a man who could approach the problem with an open mind, without prejudice or favor. During the present year he has been teaching these parallel sections. In one section he has emphasized economic applications; in the other he has taught the class upon the customary pure-science basis. He has kept a careful record of his work, and at stated intervals he has given both sections the same tests. We propose to carry on this investigation year after year with different classes, different teachers, and in different schools. We are not in a hurry to reach conclusions.

Now I said that the safeguard in all work of this sort is to keep our grip firm and fast on the eternal truths. In this work that I mention we are not trying to prove that either pure science or applied science interests our pupils the more or helps them the more in meeting immediate economic situations. We do not propose to measure the success of either method by its effect upon the bread-winning power of the pupil. What we believe that science teaching should insure is a grip on the scientific method and an illuminating insight into the forces of nature, and we are simply attempting to see whether the economic applications will make this grip firmer or weaker, and this insight clearer or more obscure. I trust that this point is plain, for it illustrates what I have just said regarding the danger of following a popular demand. We need no experiment to prove that economic science is more useful in the narrow sense than is pure science. What we wish to determine is whether a judicious mixture of the two sorts of teaching will or will not enable us to realize this rich cultural value much more effectively than a traditional purely cultural course.

Now that illustrates what I think is the real and important application of the scientific spirit to the solution of educational problems. You will readily see that it does not do away necessarily with our ideals. It is not necessarily materialistic. It is not necessarily idealistic. Either side may utilize it. It is a quite impersonal factor. But it does promise to take some of our educational problems out of the field of useless and wasteful controversy, and it does promise to get men of conflicting views together,—for, in the case that I have just cited, if we prove that the right admixture of methods may enable us to realize both a cultural and a utilitarian value, there is no reason why the culturists and the utilitarians should not get together, cease their quarreling, take off their coats, and go to work. Few people will deny that bread and butter is a rather essential thing in this life of ours; very few will deny that material prosperity in temperate amounts is good for all of us; and very few also will deny that far more fundamental than bread and butter—far more important than material prosperity—are the great fundamental and eternal truths which man has wrought out of his experience and which are most effectively crystallized in the creations of pure art, the masterpieces of pure literature, and the discoveries of pure science.

Certainly if we of the twentieth century can agree upon any one thing, it is this: That life without toil is a crime, and that any one who enjoys leisure and comfort and the luxuries of living without paying the price of toil is a social parasite. I believe that it is an important function of public education to impress upon each generation the highest ideals of living as well as the arts that are essential to the making of a livelihood, but I wish to protest against the doctrine that these two factors stand over against one another as the positive and negative poles of human existence. In other words, I protest against the notion that the study of the practical everyday problems of human life is without what we are pleased to call a culture value,—that in the proper study of those problems one is not able to see the operation of fundamental and eternal principles.

I shall readily agree that there is always a grave danger that the trivial and temporary objects of everyday life may be viewed and studied without reference to these fundamental principles. But this danger is certainly no greater than that the permanent and eternal truths be studied without reference to the actual, concrete, workaday world in which we live. I have seen exercises in manual training that had for their purpose the perfection of the pupil in some little art of joinery for which he would, in all probability, have not the slightest use in his later life. But even if he should find use for it, the process was not being taught in the proper way. He was being made conscious only of the little trivial thing, and no part of his instruction was directed toward the much more important, fundamental lesson,—the lesson, namely, that "a little thing may be perfect, but that perfection itself is not a little thing."

I say that I have witnessed such an exercise in the very practical field of manual training. I may add that I went through several such exercises myself, and emerged with a disgust that always recurs to me when I am told that every boy will respond to the stimulus of the hammer and the jack plane. But I should hasten to add that I have also seen what we call the humanities so taught that the pupil has emerged from them with a supreme contempt for the life of labor and a feeling of disgust at the petty and trivial problems of human life which every one must face. I have seen art and literature *so* taught as to leave their students not with the high purpose to mold their lives in accordance with the high ideals that art and literature represent, not the firm resolution to do what they could to relieve the ugliness of the world where they found it ugly, or to do what they could to ennoble life when they found it vile; but rather with an attitude of calm superiority, as if they were in some way privileged to the delights of aesthetic enjoyment, leaving the baser born to do the world's drudgery.

I have seen the principles of agriculture so taught as to leave with the student the impression that he could raise more corn than his neighbor and sell it at a higher price if he mastered the principles of nitrification— and all without one single reference to the basic principle of conservation upon which the welfare of the human race for all time to come must inevitably depend,—without a single reference to the moral iniquity of waste and sloth and ignorance. But I have also seen men who have mastered the scientific method,—the method of controlled observation, and unprejudiced induction and inference,—in the laboratories of pure science; and who have gained so overweening and hypertrophied a regard for this method that they have considered it too holy to be contaminated by application to practical problems,—who have sneered contemptuously when some adventurer has proposed, for example, to subject the teaching of science itself to the searchlight of scientific method.

I trust that these examples have made my point clear, for it is certainly simple enough. If vocational education means simply that the arts and skills of industrial life are to be transmitted safely from generation to generation, a minimum of educational machinery is all that is necessary, and we do not need to worry much about it. If vocational education means simply this, it need not trouble us much; for economic conditions will sooner or later provide for an effective means of transmission, just as economic conditions will sooner or later perfect, through a blind and empirical process of elimination, the most effective methods of agriculture, as in the case of China and other overpopulated nations of the Orient.

But I take it that we mean by vocational education something more than this, just as we mean by cultural education something more than a veneer of language, history, pure science, and the fine arts. In the former case, the practical problems of life are to be lifted to the plane of fundamental principles; in the latter case, fundamental principles are to be brought down to the plane of present, everyday life. I can see no discrepancy here. To my mind there is no cultural subject that has not its practical outcome, and there is no practical subject that has not its humanizing influence if only we go to some pains to seek it out. I do not object to a subject of instruction that promises to put dollars into the pockets of those that study it. I do object to the mode of teaching that subject which fails to use this effective economic appeal in stimulating a glimpse of the broader vision. I do not object to the subject that appeals to the pupil's curiosity because it informs him of the wonderful deeds that men have done in the past. I do object to that mode of teaching this subject which simply arouses interest in a spectacular deed, and then fails to use this interest in the interpretation of present problems. I do not contend that in either case there must be an explicit pointing of morals and drawing of lessons. But I do contend that the teacher who is in charge of the process should always have this purpose in the forefront of his consciousness, and—now by direct comparison, now by indirection and suggestion—guide his pupils to the goal desired.

I hope that through careful tests we shall some day be able to demonstrate that there is much that is good and valuable on both sides of every controverted educational question. After all, in this complex and intricate task of teaching to which you and I are devoting our lives, there is too much at stake to permit us for a moment to be dogmatic,—to permit us for a moment to hold ourselves in any other attitude save one of openness and reception to the truth when the truth shall have been demonstrated. Neither your ideas nor mine, nor those of any man or group of men, living or dead, are important enough to stand in the way of the best possible accomplishment of that great task to which we have set our hands.

IV

But I did not propose this morning to talk to you about science as a part of our educational curriculum, but rather about the scientific spirit and the scientific method as effective instruments for the solution of our own peculiar educational problems. I have tried to give you reasons for believing that an adoption of this policy does not necessarily commit us to materialism or to a narrowly economic point of view. I have attempted to show that the scientific method may be applied to the solution of our problems while we still retain our faith in ideals; and that, unless we do retain that faith, our investigations will be without point or meaning.

This problem of vocational education to which I have just referred is one that is likely to remain unsolved until we have made a searching investigation of its factors in the light of scientific method. Some people profess not to be worried by the difficulty of finding time in our elementary and secondary schools for the introduction of the newer subjects making for increased vocational efficiency. They would cut the Gordian knot with one single operation by eliminating enough of the older subjects to make room for the new. I confess that this solution does not appeal to me. Fundamentally the core of the elementary curriculum must, I believe, always be the arts that are essential to every one who lives the social life. In other words, the language arts and the number arts are, and always must be, the fundamentals of elementary education. I do not believe that specialized vocational education should ever be introduced at the expense of thorough training in the subjects that already hold their place in the curriculum. And yet we are confronted by the economic necessity of solving in some way this vocational problem. How are we to do it?

It is here that the scientific method may perhaps come to our aid. The obvious avenue of attack upon this problem is to determine whether we cannot save time and energy, not by the drastic operation of eliminating old subjects, but rather by improving our technique of teaching, so that the waste may be reduced, and the time thus saved given to these new subjects that are so vociferously demanding admission. In Cleveland, for example, the method of teaching spelling has been subjected to a rigid scientific treatment, and, as a result, spelling is being taught to-day vastly better than ever before and with a much smaller expenditure of time and energy. It has been due, very largely, to the application of a few well-known principles which the science of psychology has furnished.

Now that is vastly better than saying that spelling is a subject that takes too much time in our schools and consequently ought forthwith to be eliminated. In all of our school work enough time is undoubtedly wasted to provide ample opportunity for training the child thoroughly in some vocation if we wish to vocationalize him, and I do not think that this would hurt him, even if he does not follow the vocation in later life.

To-day we are attempting to detect these sources of waste in technique. The problems of habit building or memorizing are already well on the way to solution. Careful tests have shown the value of doing memory work in a certain definite way—learning by unit wholes rather than by fragments, for example. Experiments have been conducted to determine the best length of time to give to drill processes, such as spelling, and penmanship, and the fundamental tables of arithmetic. It is already clearly demonstrated that brief periods of intense concentration are more economical than longer periods during which the monotony of repetition exhausts the mind to a point where it can no longer work effectively. We are also beginning to see from these tests that a systematic method of attacking such a problem as the memorizing of the tables will do much to save time and promote efficiency. We are finding that it is extremely profitable to instruct children in the technique of learning,—to start them out in the right way by careful example, so that much of the time and energy that was formerly dissipated, may now be conserved.

And there is a suggestion, also, that in the average school, the vast possibilities of the child's latent energy are only imperfectly realized. A friend of mine stumbled accidentally upon this fact by introducing a new method of grading. He divided his pupils into three groups or streams. The group that progressed the fastest was made up of those who averaged 85 per cent and over in their work. A middle group averaged between 75 per cent and 85 per cent in their work, and a third, slow group was made up of those who averaged below 75 per cent. At the end of the first month, he found that a certain proportion of his pupils, who had formerly hovered around the passing grade of 70, began to forge ahead. Many of them easily went into the fastest stream, but they were still satisfied with the minimum standing for that group. In other words, whether we like to admit it or not, most men and women and boys and girls are content with the passing grades, both in school and in life. So common is the phenomenon that we think of the matter fatalistically. But supply a stimulus, raise the standard, and you will find some of these individuals forging up to the next level.

Professor James's doctrine of latent energies bids fair to furnish the solution of a vast number of perplexing educational problems. Certain it is that our pupils of to-day are not overburdened with work. They are sometimes irritated by too many tasks, sometimes dulled by dead routine, sometimes exhilarated to the point of mental *ennui* by spectacular appeals to immediate interest. But they are seldom overworked, or even worked to within a healthful degree of the fatigue point.

Elementary education has often been accused of transacting its business in small coin,—of dealing with and emphasizing trivialities,—and yet every time that the scientific method touches the field of education, it reveals the fundamental significance of little things. Whether the third-grade pupil should memorize the multiplication tables in the form, "8 times 9 equals 72" or simply "*8-g's—72*" seems a matter of insignificance in contrast with the larger problems that beset us. And yet scientific investigation tells us clearly and unequivocally that any useless addition to a formula to be memorized increases the time for reducing the formula to memory, and interferes significantly with its recall and application. It may seem a matter of trivial importance whether the pupil increases the subtrahend number or decreases the minuend number when he subtracts digits that involve taking or borrowing; and yet investigation proves that to increase the subtrahend number is by far the simpler process, and eliminates both a source of waste and a source of error, which, in the aggregate, may assume a significance to mental economy that is well worth considering.

In fact, if we are ever to solve the broader, bigger, more attractive problems,—like the problem of vocational education, or the problem of retardation,—we must first find a solution for some of the smaller and seemingly trivial questions the very existence of which the lay public may be quite unaware, but which you and I know to mean an untold total of waste and inefficiency in the work that we are trying to do.

And one reason why the scientific attitude toward educational problems appeals to me is simply because this attitude carries with it a respect for these seemingly trivial and commonplace problems; for just as the greatest triumph of the teaching art is to get our pupils to see in those things of life that are fleeting and transitory the operation of fundamental and eternal principles, so the glory of the scientific method lies in its power to reveal the significance of the commonplace and to teach us that no slightest detail of our daily work is necessarily devoid of inspiration; that every slightest detail of school method and school management has a meaning and a significance that it is worth our while to ponder.

The Future of the Training of Teachers
(1913)

As Bagley points out in the opening line of this address, he delivered it at the 50th anniversary celebration of the founding of Oswego State Normal School in Oswego, New York. All normal schools were created for the single purpose of preparing teachers for public school service. Oswego was one of the most powerful normal schools in the nation at the time. Bagley taught on the faculty at Oswego State Normal from 1906 to 1908. When he gave this address, he was returning to a faculty that he knew well. He was well-read in the philosophical literature that gave rise to Oswego. He also had a deep respect for Edward Austin Sheldon, the founder of the institution.

The thrust of this paper is the point that the public must increase its support for professional schools that train teachers. Bagley questions the peculiar fact that political leaders often use glowing rhetoric to demonstrate how "important" education is; yet, they provide little or no support and even fewer resources for professional schools that train teachers. Bagley often wondered why the faith that Americans have in education did not transfer to increased support—social, political, and economic—for institutions that train teachers. Why does the rhetoric about the "importance" of education in America not translate into social, political, and economic standing for the people who teach American schoolchildren every day?, Bagley wondered. Why does this rhetorical advocacy not translate into support for higher education faculty who teach teachers? Why is there such a disconnect between language and action when it comes to education in general and teaching teachers in particular?

As he did on many other occasions, Bagley supports a curriculum for teaching teachers that includes scholastic and professional dimensions. Throughout his career, although not specifically in this selection, he voiced support for practice teaching

Forgotten Heroes of American Education, pages 85–89

85

experiences within laboratory school settings. Finally, Bagley acknowledges in this
paper that the most significant results of teaching are spiritual in nature, which
means that they are not conducive to simplistic measurement techniques.

The Fiftieth Anniversary of the founding of this School is an occasion which should stimulate us not only to reminiscences of the past but also to a forecast of the future. This School represents an educational movement of fundamental significance. Drawing its early inspiration in part from the ideals and visions of the greatest figure of modern education—the Swiss schoolmaster, Pestalozzi—it has always stood for a thoroughgoing professionalizing of the work of elementary education. So thoroughly have Pestalozzi's ideals of a universal elementary education been assimilated into the fabric of our present-day life that we are prone to forget that this movement is a product of a single century. We take the free and compulsory education of the elementary school for granted; it is an accomplished fact in our civilization; and quite naturally we find it difficult to imagine a period of time when conditions were otherwise.

As a matter of fact, we have not yet begun to appreciate the basic significance of the movement. The new problems of social organization that so penetrating and pervasive an influence is bringing about are quite beyond our present appreciation. Certain tendencies that characterize the educational doctrine of to-day indicate that we are dimly aware of impending crises; the fervor for industrial and vocational education, for example, indicates a recognition of weaknesses in our present system that were unsuspected by the early advocates of universal education.

There are two functions of civilized society the importance of which can never be overemphasized. They have been named and described in various ways. The economist calls one of them production, the other conservation. In this country, our energies have been going very largely into production, and only recently has the significance of conservation been clearly recognized. We have seen our soil in grave danger of impoverishment through overcropping; we have seen our forests stripped of their timber, and the soil left unprotected to be swept by the rains and carried away through the rivers into the sea; we have seen our deposits of coal and iron and petroleum shrinking at an alarming rate. On every hand the lack of foresight and wisdom and a reasonable frugality has been evident to anyone who saw an inch beyond the superficial, and yet we have produced, produced, produced; until, in tangible wealth, we are the richest people that the world has ever known. To-day we are awakening to the crime against posterity that our intemperate demand for immediate prosperity has involved.

But neither production nor conservation is limited to material things. Indeed, the most important "commodity" of all is something that is immaterial and subjective in its nature, namely, human experience. To "manufacture" a superior article of experience—superior in the sense that it is more accurate and trustworthy—is the function of scientific research. To conserve this and whatever other valuable increments human experience may furnish is the primary function of education, and by conservation we mean transmitting this experience faithfully from generation to generation to the end that the race may never have to relearn the lessons of the past through the same blind, stumbling process.

Of the problems that confront education to-day, there is none so significant as that which is concerned with the training of teachers; and this is tantamount to saying that there is no problem so significant to social welfare and progress. And with all our zeal and fervor for education in general, this prerequisite of any successful educational system seems to be the last to claim its share of public attention. This School has been rendering the most important type of social service for fifty years; other Normal Schools have been rendering similar service; and yet the Normal Schools of to-day are the most inadequately supported and the least appreciated of all our educational institutions. A magnificent building is being erected to house this School. We rejoice in this evidence of the State's liberality. But let us not deceive ourselves. Good buildings and luxurious material equipment can never make a school great. It takes men and women to do that, and while in the future, as in the past, you will be able to enroll a few men and women of the highest type in the work of training teachers, you will not, until the public attitude has been transformed, attract to this service as many representatives of this type as the work demands. Normal School work must come into its own. Service in the Normal Schools must come to be looked upon as the highest type of professional service. The remuneration that it offers must be large enough to enable men and women to take advantage of every reasonable opportunity for growth and development. Economic pressure and worry must be eased. Arrangements must be made for such leaves of absence— sabbatical or otherwise—as university professors are generally allowed. And above all, the position of Normal School teacher must carry with it the recognition that is given to hard-earned efficiency in other fields of social service. This recognition is the reward that most men and women seek— despite the assertions of those cynics who insist that material rewards are the only incentives that really impel.

If the Normal Schools are to render a maximum of service to the community, they must be much more largely attended than at the present time. The number of new teachers demanded every year by the schools of the United States is not less than one hundred thousand, and probably more. To supply this demand, all of the Normal Schools of the country— public and private, state, county, and city—furnish annually only about eighteen thousand trained teachers, or a number only just about large enough to supply the new positions which open up each year because of the increase in population and the differentiation of teaching service. This takes no account of the teachers who leave the service each year, and this number is probably not less than one in every five of the teaching population.

A situation of this sort constitutes a veritable menace to the cause of popular education. Only so long as schools are well taught and ably managed can we expect them to do efficient work. Nay, the truth is better expressed by the converse statement: only when the schools are well taught and ably managed can we expect them not to do positive harm. Today in this country, lawlessness and disrespect for authority are increasing at a most alarming rate. Who shall say that the public school situation has not been a factor in this undesirable type of degeneration? When you place at least half of the children of the country in charge of immature girls, themselves just out of the High Schools; when the only kind of professional training that you give these embryonic teachers is a week of institute work; when you let these institutes be honeycombed by superficial, bizarre, irresponsible, and spectacular educational doctrines that could not stand the test of sober reflection for a single instant; and when you send these teachers back to their schools saturated with fallacies about child training that would not work successfully even in Utopia itself; can you wonder that we are rearing generation after generation of young people whose only law is the caprice of the moment?

A careful preparation, both scholastic and professional, is the only remedy for this situation. So long as the average teacher remains only about four years in the profession, every effort must be made to secure a maximum of initial efficiency. The Normal School can insure a goodly measure of such efficiency; but the Normal School at the present time is touching only a very small proportion of the candidates for teaching service. How can its influence be extended? There is one answer to this question that must be brought home with compelling force to the American people. Service in the public schools must be placed on the same footing as service in the army or the navy, and those who are by nature qualified to become teachers *must receive their training at public expense*. Like the cadets at Annapolis and West Point, the Normal School student should be paid a living salary while undergoing the process of preparation for the work that he proposes to enter. Not to admit this is to imply that war is a more important and fundamental type of public service than education. To expect intending teachers in large numbers to prepare at their own expense for a poorly paid profession is to expect the impossible. If the standards are raised and the salaries raised proportionately, great benefit will accrue to the schools, but a large number of young men and women would be debarred from the service because of the increased cost of preparation and training. We say to our young men: "If you have mental and physical ability, you can prepare yourself for the army or for the navy at public expense. The entire cost of your training will be borne by the government." We say to our intending teachers: "If you wish to prepare yourself for teaching at your own expense, do so; if you do not care to undergo the expense, we shall let you teach with poor training or without any training whatsoever. After you have made a little money, you may use it to purchase a trousseau or to prepare yourself for a real profession. You may do this at the expense, not of the public treasury, but of the nation's children."

When will the people of this country awaken to the gross iniquity of this system of providing teachers for the public schools?

Some Handicaps to Education in a Democracy
(1916)[1]

Bagley was invited to deliver this lecture at the 25th anniversary celebration of the appointment of Paul Henry Hanus (1855–1941) as professor of education at Harvard University. When he arrived in 1891, Hanus began to lay the groundwork for the creation of the school of education at Harvard.

Bagley emphasizes several themes in this paper that resonate with contemporary problems in American education. For example, he makes the point that teachers always face the challenge of interesting the American public in scholastic endeavors while living in a culture that prizes flashy, immediate, and material rewards to the exclusion of almost everything else. He also argues that democracy is handicapped because of its inability to think long-term. This problem must be counterbalanced, Bagley affirms, by an increasing emphasis on education in general and good teacher training in particular.

The first and most serious weakness in American education to Bagley was the fact that teaching was not viewed as a serious career. Bagley thought the only way to address this problem was for universities like Harvard to do exactly what they had done when they created the position for Paul Henry Hanus in 1891. Teaching must be made a respectable profession, Bagley argues, and universities like Harvard were the institutions responsible for making this happen.

This selection also shows that Bagley was beginning to voice his opposition to Progressives like William Heard Kilpatrick. Bagley asserts that educators should re-emphasize duty within educational theory (as well as practice) during a time when

---

1. A paper read at a meeting of the Harvard Teachers' Association, Boston, March 11, 1916.

Forgotten Heroes of American Education, pages 91–103

the trend was to relax standards and follow paths of least resistance. Kilpatrick and other followers of John Dewey, during this time, began to emphasize vocational training, romantic-inspired teaching, and an exclusively "project"-based curriculum, all of which, Bagley thought, were in danger of being overemphasized.

Bagley ends the address by making the point, which he made often, that the profession of teaching must continue to build social and political support. He was striving to create leaders for the profession of teaching who were well-read in social and political thought, who dedicated themselves to teaching teachers, and who were able to communicate with the general public about the profession of teaching in general and its relationship to American democracy in particular.

I am very glad indeed to have the privilege of being present at this celebration of the twenty-fifth anniversary of Professor Hanus's appointment. It is my pleasure to convey to Professor Hanus, to the Harvard Teachers' Association, and to the Harvard Division of Education the greetings and the congratulations of the school of education of the University of Illinois. The establishment of the chair of education at Harvard University was a most important event in that it stamped with the approval of our oldest and best known university the movement for the higher study of the educational problem. We in the Middle West rejoice with you on this occasion, in part because the work that you have done has been an important factor in making our work possible. We rejoice in the record that the Division of Education in Harvard University has made; in the capable and competent leadership of Professor Hanus; and in the good results that this leadership has achieved. We wish Professor Hanus abounding health and many more years of efficient service.

The relation of education to national life is a topic that is especially pertinent to this time and this occasion. Under our decentralized system of public-school administration, local and sectional needs are bound to have an undue influence in the determination of educational policies; the educational needs of the nation, as a whole, have no official channel through which to seek satisfaction. It is all the more important, then, that unofficial and indirect agencies, represented by organizations such as yours, shall do what they can to integrate and unify the educational activities of the country, as a whole. We can for the time being and for the purposes of our discussion, erase the lines that bound our small, almost autonomous units of school administration, and view the educational problem not as it concerns Boston alone, or Chicago alone, or Massachusetts alone, or Illinois alone; but rather as it concerns the nation as a nation.

And this effort at integration is, I believe, peculiarly significant, peculiarly necessary, at the present stage of our national development. We have talked glibly of our national destiny, but hitherto it has often been the charm of the phrase itself rather than its deeper meaning that has fascinated us. To-day we are in a position, dimly perhaps, and yet somewhat effectively, to appreciate what this destiny really involves. Through no act of aggression or conquest upon its own part, our country finds itself likely within a short time to be in a position of world supremacy. Whatever may be the outcome of the great war, it can spell little less than economic exhaustion for the nations that are involved. Their industrial forces will be decimated, their treasuries impoverished, their intellectual and political leadership inevitably weakened; while our wealth and strength have been relatively augmented through their misfortune, our resources have been relatively conserved, and our dominant and oncoming generations have escaped the terrible sacrifice of vigorous manhood which it has been their misfortune to sustain.

It is not in the hearts of our people to rejoice because they may profit by the misfortune of others. It is true that we have been in the past a "lucky" nation; we have had at hand an unusual, perhaps an unprecedented, advantage—a continent favored above all others in its varied and generous resources. But the price had to be paid for the development of these resources—the price of effort and sacrifice and toil. Our fathers paid this price, and it is not in the hearts of our people to-day to forget this fact, or to accept in the spirit of exultation the advantages and opportunities that seem now to be ours by what in large measure are the mere accidents of fate. I believe that it is in the hearts of our people rather to view the immediate future in the light of a grave responsibility involving duties and obligations more serious, more exacting, than any that they have hitherto been impelled to assume. But however this may be, the fact remains that the immediate future involves problems of stupendous magnitude that the people *as a nation* must face and try to solve. And this fact lays upon the agencies of education the heaviest of responsibilities and renders imperative the formulation of educational policies primarily in terms of our national life rather than in terms of sectional, local, class and individual demands and interests.

It is well, then, that we should consider rather carefully the handicaps which education has to overcome if it is adequately to discharge these serious responsibilities. Many of these handicaps are inherent in the very nature of democracy itself, and the task of overcoming or mitigating them is rendered doubly difficult by the necessity not only of preserving intact but of strengthening as far as possible, the ideals of democracy. Other handicaps are imposed, not by the nature of democracy as such, but by the peculiar expression of our democracy in the institutions of local self-government and in the ideals of local initiative and local autonomy, especially in matters pertaining to education. These ideals, too, are deeply rooted in the institutions and prejudices of our people, and are far too precious and fundamental to be imperiled by radical changes. The task in both cases must be to gain educational efficiency on a national scale and still preserve and strengthen both democracy and democracy's expression in local self-government.

The one way in which this problem may be solved is not an easy way, nor can the solution be effected overnight. It will involve the truly democratic means of insuring progress—an appeal to the people through argument and reason and debate, an appeal to the national consciousness which is already taking a new form under the stimulus of our international relationships, and which is already beginning to sense the heavy responsibility that we, as a nation, must assume. This collective intelligence, this collective aspiration, must be directed toward the problem of education as a national asset. Something akin to the educational revival that swept over New England and the Middle West eighty years ago is what is demanded now—something similar in intensity, similar in the devotion and consecration of its advocates, and differing from its prototype in that it is working upon another plane and for a somewhat different purpose—differing too in that it will not have to contend against the apathy of the people as did the work of Horace Mann, but, on the contrary, may utilize the tremendous capital of popular interest in public education that is now so general throughout the land.

But even with this advantage, the task will be far from simple. Our people are interested in their schools, but here as elsewhere a wide popular interest is much more readily caught by that which promises immediate and showy results than by fundamental policies which look far into the future. This is obviously only one form of the general handicap under which democracy labors. I mean that it is difficult for democracy to look ahead. The immediate problem is easily apprehended by the collective mind, but in collective thinking that pushes its termini far into the future and collective action that is dominated by a remote goal and which may involve present sacrifice for the sake of attaining this goal—it is in such thinking and such action that democracy is weak.

And so the intense interest of the people in their schools can be exploited, and is being exploited, not only by the educational charlatan with his plausible cure-alls, but also by the doctrinaire reformer who sincerely believes that he has at last found the royal road to learning. Our teachers and school administrators themselves are often caught by these proposals. Through glittering promises of immediate results, a new educational procedure may sweep across the country, affecting millions of boys and girls before its alleged virtues have been clearly demonstrated. I have young men and young women in my classes who in the eight years of their elementary-school life learned and unlearned successively four different systems of handwriting, each one guaranteed to be the final word in the pedagogy of penmanship. The discussions of our teachers' institutes and teachers' associations not infrequently reflect the amateurish kind of educational thinking that one might excuse among laymen, but which certainly ought not to characterize a truly professional group.

And this may suggest one of the weaknesses of the present educational situation which must be removed or alleviated if our schools are effectively to discharge their increasingly heavy responsibilities—a weakness, too, that expresses all too clearly the fundamental difficulty of a democracy to think far into the future. I refer to the fact that teaching in this country is not a career. Educational work to-day offers careers of various types—careers in administration, careers in scholarship, careers even in politics if we consider typical the experience of a president and three governors whose life work has been in the field of education. But education affords no career in the basic educational activity—namely, class-room teaching. Unusual success here meets with no unusual sanction, with no unusual recognition or reward. Even in the normal schools, where the art of teaching is supposed to be a matter of deep concern, the best teacher is not infrequently withdrawn from the classroom to spend his precious time and his precious talents in cajoling legislatures and making out study-lists—and all because of the notion that the highest salary must be paid to the man who does this administrative work. In our universities, it would seem at first glance that the teacher comes into at least a little corner of his kingdom—but the satisfaction that one might take in this apparent fact quickly disappears when one discovers that the fact is only apparent and not real; for the sanctions and rewards go not to teaching as such, but to the productive scholarship which crystallizes in printer's ink, and to administrative talent. Indeed, I know of universities where in the eyes of most of the students and of some of the professors themselves, the man who sits at a roll-top desk and dictates to a stenographer occupies a position far in advance of the man who, day after day and year after year, does with a skill that only infinite pains can perfect, the primary work for which the university exists. And in the public-school service, promotion and advancement beyond a certain limit, and a very low limit at that, now necessarily take the teacher from the classroom and give him work to do which, important though it is, can not be thought of as anything more than supplementary to the actual work of teaching.

It is my firm conviction that education in this country can not serve our people with a maximal measure of efficiency until the people themselves decree that effective sanctions, recognitions and rewards shall accrue to unusual success in teaching as such. The people themselves must catch something of the far-seeing wisdom of that monarch who declared that his first concern as a monarch should be, not his army nor his navy nor his courts of justice, but the welfare of the teachers of his people's schools. It was easy for an autocrat thus to initiate a policy that was destined to give to his people that passion for learning that has been the dominant element in their national strength. But it would be hard for democracy to initiate a similar policy, for the results would not be immediate, nor could the proposal be supported by the kind of spectacular evidence that the public has been led to expect from promoters of educational reforms.

But some effective means of solving this problem must be found. The current proposals for increasing the efficiency of the schools are emphasizing primarily the need of curriculum readjustments and reorganizations. Many readjustments and reorganizations are certainly needed. The materials of the elementary and secondary programs deserve the overhauling to which they are just now being subjected. Educational values must be carefully tested. The outcomes of subject-matter must be formulated in terms of conduct and character. The current skepticism regarding the value of traditional educational materials is a wholesome sign, and its effects will be beneficial—unless, indeed, it becomes in its turn dogmatic and unreasonable, and seeks to escape the burden of evidence that the proponents of fundamental changes must always assume—unless, in other words, from the valid premise that much in the past work of education has been weak and inefficient, it jumps to the unwarranted conclusion that nothing in the past is worthy of perpetuation. There is, then, abundant justification for these present efforts to reorganize the school program; but our enthusiasm here must not blind us to the fundamental fact that educational efficiency involves a teaching problem as well as a curriculum problem, and that no legerdemain of subjects, courses and curriculums can cover up the evils of poor teaching.

Nor can we who teach seek to hide our inefficiency under the convenient blanket of a maladjusted curriculum. The curriculum is doubtless at fault in many respects, but other teachers have been able to extract from the same materials, and indeed from materials much less adequate than ours, rich elements of educational value. The great problem of teaching is one of adaptation. It is a double adaptation: the cultural elements that the race has wrought out of its experience must be fitted to the needs and capacities of our boys and girls, and the immature minds of these boys and girls must be stimulated and trained and disciplined to the point where the quintessence of race experience may be incorporated into the experience of the individual. It is a double problem and a difficult problem, but it is the fundamental problem of the teacher, and its responsibilities are not to be escaped merely by finding fault with the materials. We can not jump out of our skins, as an old teacher of mine was wont to say; and while we can not deny that the crystallized experience of the race leaves much to be desired and much for the present and the future to achieve, it would be the height of folly to throw overboard that which has already been accomplished. Those who devoutly wish that the human species could awake some fine morning entirely oblivious to its past, cut off by some miracle from its stores of skills, traditions and ideals, and ready for a fresh start, forget one very important fact—the fact, namely, that there are some things from which no miracle could relieve us. It is conceivable that the arts, the skills, the traditions and the ideals might be sloughed off—but the fundamental instincts and impulses would still remain; and to tame, refine and sublimate these anew, the same old roads would have to be retraversed, the same old mistakes made, the same old blind alleys followed up to their cul-de-sacs of disappointment and despair. No; the problem of educational reform is one of evolution, not one of revolution. It must proceed slowly, gradually, scientifically. We must try, but we must also test. And above all we must test in segregated areas and under standardized conditions.

And this suggests another need which must be made clear to the people in this new educational revival. It is the need for experimental schools where new proposals may be tested, and where improved methods of solving the educational problem may be worked out. We have had experimental schools for some time—schools that have been experimental in name but scarcely in fact, for they have commonly started with a theory to exploit, and the "dice have been loaded" from the outset. I am reminded of a visit that was once made to a school of this type. The visitor had been told that marvelous results were obtained without recourse to that method of teaching that we call drill. The visitor went through the various rooms with the principal and noted that the work in the formal subjects was unusually good. He engaged one of the teachers in conversation while the principal went on an errand to the office. "How do you obtain these results without drill?" the visitor asked the teacher. "We don't," replied the teacher; "Drill! I should say that we *did* drill—but *he* doesn't know it."

I do not mean to imply that all so-called experimental schools have deceived themselves and the public in this way; nor should I dogmatically affirm that good results might not be obtained through an application of the theories that this particular school was exploiting; I simply maintain that such schools are not experimental schools and should not be called by this name. But we do need real experimental schools—experimental schools in which the dice are not loaded—experimental schools that are dominated by only one ideal, and that is the ideal of truth. And these experiment stations should, I believe, be established and maintained by the people in the interests of the people's schools, just as the people have established and maintained their elaborate system of agricultural experiment stations. This is an educational function that the federal government might easily assume without imperiling in the slightest measure the principle of state and local autonomy in educational administration.

But again some of the difficulties which educational progress must overcome in a democracy appear as handicaps. The economic waste that poor methods of agriculture entail is easily seen, and the public purse opens readily at the behest of a proposal which will eliminate this waste. The economic and social waste which inadequate methods of teaching and inadequate plans for school organization entail is not so readily discernible. But the waste is there, none the less, and frequently in appalling amounts. If a system of educational experiment stations could keep even one inadequate but plausible proposal from sweeping through the country before its real merits had been tested, it would repay in the actual saving of the people's money vastly more than it would cost. There are, of course, some proposals that can be tested only on a large scale and during an extended period of time. These at the outset must be subjected to rigid theoretical analysis, discussion and debate, with the burden of evidence on the side of their proponents. But there are innumerable smaller problems that the segregated experimental school might well solve in a short time and with a measure of accuracy that would eliminate further discussion.

Probably the most serious difficulty that must be surmounted if our schools are adequately to do their part in preparing the country for its new responsibilities is suggested by this fact that public interest is more readily aroused by and public funds more readily available for educational plans that promise economic betterment than by and for those plans in which the economic factor is not dominant. In one respect this condition is a distinct asset, for our educational system is still sadly deficient in its provisions for vocational and industrial training, and vocational education must certainly play a large part in any comprehensive scheme for national development. But the basic need of democracy, after all, is a high level of general intelligence, and it is general or liberal education that must be depended upon to meet this need.

If the present situation reveals the future, the time has almost arrived when our people must, whether they will or no, play the leading role in the family of nations. Upon what our people think, and upon the way in which they act, upon their policies and their practises, will depend in very large measure the progress and welfare of humanity in the decades that are to come. It will not be a world dominion in the sense of an actual government of subject peoples, but it will in all probability be a position of leadership and of inevitable responsibility in something that must sooner or later approach a world union. With our position, our power, our wealth, and our strength, that responsibility can in self-respect be neither evaded nor avoided. Adequately to discharge that responsibility will be the supreme test of democracy, and this test will demand first of all a measure of collective intelligence the like of which Plato may have dreamed of, but which has not been realized or even approached in any republic of the past or the present. And this will demand something akin to collective effort, something very close to sacrifice, something that can be adequately motived by nothing less virile than the keenest sense of duty.

There is a notion abroad in our land just now that duty, sacrifice and effort are ideals that have outlived their usefulness and are now ready for the scrap heap. That is a dangerous notion. In a period of great material prosperity the last policy for a nation to adopt is one that sanctions the lines of least resistance. Now, if at any time, the virile ideals must be kept alive. It is true of the nation as it is of the individual that real freedom, the only kind of freedom that does not sink one in hopeless individualism, is not the kind that comes as a gift, but the kind that comes as a conquest— the freedom that has been bought at the price of sacrifice and effort. And real freedom must be won anew by each generation and by each individual. There is nothing more heavily fraught with peril than the notion that this payment can be escaped or that the spiritual capital that the past has accumulated can support the spiritual life of the present and the future. We must in truth stand upon the shoulders of those who have gone before; but we must *stand*, not recline; and, standing, we too must pay the price, perhaps in coinage from another mint, but ultimately the same price. We are wont to think of the periods of national adversity as constituting the severest test of a people's character. I am not at all certain that the real test does not come in periods of prosperity, for it is during these periods that simplicity and rigor may easily give way to the degenerating forces of luxury and ease. And perhaps the first task of educational statesmanship in a period such as we now seem to be entering is to stand four-square against the softening tendencies which are certain to be infused into educational policies. Already in our educational philosophy, we

   . . . call too loud on Freedom to cloak our weariness,

and the doctrines of freedom, interest and spontaneity, indispensable ingredients as they are of an effective educational theory, must be supplemented and complemented by the more virile virtues of duty and effort and sacrifice. To keep these alive and active under circumstances which would promote their rapid decay is the first condition of national welfare; it is the first problem for education to solve at the present critical juncture. The need of these ideals will not be apparent, their need will not be immediate, but no nation that has allowed these virtues to decay has failed sooner or later to pay the penalty.

But if the need is neither immediate nor apparent, it is none the less real and fundamental. It lies in this new responsibility which our nation must assume and in this imperative necessity for the highest possible measure of general intelligence among all of those who have a voice or a vote in guiding the destinies of this democracy. If ever a country should adopt the policy of an iron education, it is our country and this is the time. In the new order, there can be no substitute for the informed mind and the disciplined will. Our boys and girls must be brought to see that their education is something more than a mere means of gratifying individual ambitions or of securing an advantage in the social and economic orders. Their education and their attitude toward it must have a broader reference and a deeper meaning. The narrower ideals of patriotism should give way to ideals more comprehensive, but the same force that makes patriotism a tower of collective strength may well be enlisted in the service of education. If war should be declared to-morrow, and if the call to arms should be sounded, our boys would flock to the recruiting offices and our girls would wish to volunteer as nurses, each deeming life itself a very trifling gift to offer to one's country. To the duty of courage, every normal youth will make a quick response. But the new ideals of patriotism will involve another duty—the *duty of intelligence;* and to be faithful to this duty also demands sacrifices—sacrifices less spectacular than those of the battlefield, but sacrifices that still make their hard demands upon the individual. Our boys must come to see that, for them to be ignorant when they might know, for them to lack the basis of sound judgment and intelligent opinion when they might have this basis at the cost of effort, is just as likely to imperil their country's welfare as would their failure to do their duty on the field of battle. In the new order, culpable ignorance and mental sloth will take their place alongside physical cowardice.

It is well that our people are concerned over the problem of national preparedness. We doubtless need armies and armaments. But the kind of preparedness that we need most of all is the kind that education alone can furnish, the kind that will prepare our people not only against the crises of war, but also against the sometimes more significant crises of peace. The time is opportune, I believe, to turn the national consciousness toward a consideration of these educational foundations of an effective democracy.

From other countries, less fortunate than we have been thus far, there are some basic lessons to be learned, and lessons which it would be folly for us to overlook. I quote from an editorial in a recent issue of the London *Journal of Education:*

The problem of the influence of education on national character seems to be in the air at present, as well it may be. The influence of national character on education might be quite as fruitful a theme but let that pass for the moment. What is more important is the meaning that we are to assign to the word "character." In England, its definition is singularly restricted. The word suggests the great public schools, which declare their aim to be the formation of character; and when we come to consider what the word means as used by their spokesmen, we find that it connotes mainly two things, *esprit de corps* and individuality. Of the other virtues, many are tacitly dropped from the connotation. Character in the public schools does not include industry. Neither boys nor masters really think any the worse of a boy because he does not work hard at his lessons. Nor does it include discipline, except the discipline of the playground. The public-school boy does not learn to do dull work cheerfully and thoroughly. It is, indeed, the weakness of Englishmen generally that they shrink from dull work. It was ever so with the Englishman; he is always ready for the great adventure, but not always ready to do sentry-go on lonely islands ... To turn out boys with pleasant manners, generous hearts and good animal spirits is not enough; we want boys and girls with trained intelligence, who have been made to use their brains and taught that not to use them is a sin ... Every boy and girl who grows up mindless, ignorant or intellectually undisciplined, is so much dead weight hanging around the neck of the community, and ought to be made to feel it. When we discuss character and education, therefore, let us give the fullest possible meaning to each word.

These are stinging criticisms administered to the English schools by the leading English journal of education. I quote them, not because I believe them to be altogether fair to the schools (the great secondary schools that have done so much for English civilization), but because they point compellingly to precisely the type of danger that our current American educational doctrines involve. Some day it will be *our* fate to meet a crisis. When that time comes shall we too call in vain for "boys and girls who have been made to use their brains and taught that not to use them is a sin"?

A clear perception of the duty of intelligence made general among our people will solve this problem, and I can think of nothing else that will. And it will do something else; it will provide the first and fundamental condition of educational efficiency. It is the attitude of our boys and girls toward their work that is the all-important factor. There are adolescent pupils in our high schools, and young men and young women in our state-supported colleges and universities, who look upon their educational opportunities and privileges simply and solely as rights, never stopping to consider that each right involves a correlative duty, never stopping to consider that the taxes which support these schools and colleges come from the people, and that the acceptance of the opportunities involves an obligation to make the most of them. It is wrong to permit this complacent attitude to continue—wrong to the boys and girls themselves, wrong to society for the protection, welfare and progress of which the schools have been established, wrong to the schools the efficiency of which is materially reduced by this attitude. And it is not only wrong, but unnecessary. Our boys and girls will respond to the call of duty just as soon as this call is clearly made. The adolescent is a natural altruist. One of the grave errors in our current educational theories is to assume that we must always make clear to boys and girls just how the tasks that we ask them to do are to be useful to them individually and personally. We can easily cultivate this individualistic attitude, and our current doctrines deliberately encourage it. The skepticism regarding educational values which is so wholesome a symptom of the desire for advancement may easily become a cloak for unworthy motives. It is well that our boys and girls should ask occasionally, "What good will this study do *me?*" and we should be ready with the answer. But to make the skeptical attitude a habit will be fatal, and it will be equally fatal not at every point to encourage a complementary question, "What is the use of this study or this task, not to me personally and individually, but to me as a citizen and to the state and the nation whose responsibilities I too must bear in the measure of my strength and my ability?"

I have said that it is difficult for a democracy to look ahead. Democratic progress has almost always been slow and laborious and experimental. Its blunders have been numerous and some of them have been costly. But the blundering process can not be altogether dispensed with. The grave danger lies in the temptation to glorify it as a species of democratic virtue. This is in effect a repudiation of intelligence, for it is the very essence of intelligence to subordinate the immediate to the remote, to look ahead, to anticipate, to adjust means to ends. If the collective intelligence of the democratic group is to do this effectively, there must be not only a high measure of general intelligence among the people, but also a goodly number of common elements in their culture. Without these common elements of culture anything approaching social solidarity will be very hard to insure. But this necessity, in turn, lays its demands upon the individual during the period of his formal education, and these demands can be met effectively only under the stimulus of the ideal of duty.

Difficult though it is, the only hope of solving the problem lies, as I have said, in an appeal to the people. The educational public has been accused of failure to take the people into its confidence. Many of the proposals that we have made to the public have not revealed what we clearly think and sincerely believe. Our arguments have often been superficial and not thoroughgoing. All too often they have appealed to unworthy motives and desires—to the desire to escape effort, to the primitive interest in the novel, the bizarre, the spectacular. These appeals may captivate some of our people, but to use them simply because they will insure a following is to be recreant to our professional trust. As I write these words I have before me a letter from a layman whom I do not know personally, but who has been keenly interested as a citizen in educational problems, and whose interest has led him frequently to attend the meetings of teachers' organizations. It has been the shallowness of the discussions and the superficial character of the appeals that have impressed him most. But he has recently noted an improvement. He says:

> Surface digging, I hope, is gone and with it the superficial things in education. We are asking, fairly howling, for the "heavy stuff." No educator need fear to speak the truth and talk candidly.

And if the truth is candidly and frankly told, it will sound something like this: That bricks can not be made without straw, nor can mental growth be achieved without individual effort and individual sacrifice; that accuracy and thoroughness are fundamental; that system and order and sequence are essential to mental mastery; and that, while education through indirection may be a possibility, its possibility should be demonstrated by a rigorous test before it is accepted as the central doctrine in the government of the people's schools.

The Distinction Between Academic and Professional Subjects
(1918)

This essay of Bagley's explains his views on curriculum for teaching teachers. At the heart of the problem that he is addressing is the tendency of disciplinary specialists to reject any moral content in their specialties. Bagley is putting forth a vision of "profession" for the profession of teaching that is deeply moral in its outlook. He wants normal schools, teachers colleges, and schools of education within universities to focus on the purpose for which they were created: to teach teachers. He also expects support for these institutions from the general public, from all leaders within higher education, and from state legislators.

The main problem that Bagley faced with realizing the ideals that he sets forth in this article was that higher education in general was marginalizing moral ends like teaching teachers. Following the secularization of formerly Christian institutions like Harvard and Yale, all of higher education began to pursue research, economically lucrative professions, and a purely intellectual form of prestige. The ideal that was set up for all institutions of higher education, consequently, was research and intellectual power, not teaching and moral influence. In the 1940s and 1950s, normal schools and teachers colleges followed this pattern of marginalizing teaching (as well as teaching teachers), which is why Bagley's curricular vision for teacher education found few adherents. He sought to unify the academic and professional aspects of teacher training curriculum by emphasizing institutional purpose. He also did this by emphasizing laboratory training schools where the act of teaching children and youth took place every day. All normal schools and teachers colleges, well into the 1950s, had training schools that existed for the sole purpose of teaching teachers.

Forgotten Heroes of American Education, pages 105–111

With the move toward research and purely intellectual endeavors within higher education, however, training schools were eliminated nationwide.

During the early 21st century, however, the public in general and political leaders in particular are recognizing that the overemphasis on research within higher education has created problems. The time has come for a revitalization of Bagley's philosophy of curriculum for teaching teachers.

In many, if not most, of our institutions for the preparation of teachers a sharp distinction is made between the academic and the professional courses. This distinction is inevitable in all cases where professional preparation consists chiefly in providing a few courses in psychology, educational theory, and the history of education as a supplement to the typical subject-matter courses of the secondary or collegiate programs. The inadequacy of this type of so-called "professional" training is now pretty generally recognized, and yet this inadequate type of program is still characteristic of many normal schools, as well as of practically all the liberal-arts colleges that make an explicit effort to prepare teachers for elementary or high-school service.

I am myself thoroughly convinced that the sooner we abandon the unfortunate distinction between the academic and the professional the better it will be for the welfare and ultimate success of our cause. That a house divided against itself cannot stand is as true of professional education as it is of government. Until we can concentrate all the work of our normal schools upon the purpose for which the normal school exists our efforts are bound to be abortive, and we cannot expect those who have been skeptical of the serious value of our work to undergo a change of mind and of heart, and to join with us in our efforts to place the professional training of teachers upon a basis that is consistent with the fundamental significance of the public service that the graduates of our schools are called upon to render.

When I say, however, that the work of the normal schools and teachers' colleges should be professionalized thruout, I do not mean this in a narrow sense. I should not eliminate the distinction between the academic and the professional by eliminating entirely, as some normal schools have attempted to do, the subject-matter courses, and limiting the training of teachers to a thin pabulum of psychology, history of education, general method, special methods, and practice teaching. Nor should I assume, as other normal schools have assumed, that the so-called academic training can be adequately looked after by preliminary courses taken in the high school or even in the junior college. The normal school of the future will lay much greater emphasis upon subject-matter courses than it has done in the past and relatively less emphasis upon detached and formal courses in psychology and educational theory.

What I have in mind then is rather a fundamental reorganization of all our work with the professional end constantly in view. Everything that goes into the teacher-training curriculum should be admitted solely upon the basis of its relation to the equipment of the successful teacher. It must include scholarship of a very high order, but a unique quality of scholarship. Not only must the teacher know his subject, but, as we have said so often in defending the normal school from its critics, he must know how to adapt his subject to the capacities and needs of those whom he is to teach. I have in mind, for example, the organization of the work in Latin in one of the middle western normal schools which is doing good work in preparing high-school teachers. The students who are preparing to teach Latin take advanced courses in this subject in the normal school. While these courses are of the same grade as courses that the students might have taken in a liberal-arts college, they are selected and taught with reference to the light that will throw upon the high-school teacher's problem. These courses furnish the students with a new, fresh, vigorous, and virile view of the subject-matter illuminated from every source of light that they can profit by thru their maturity and advanced training.

I know of another normal-school instructor in mathematics whose course in arithmetic, requiring as prerequisites strong courses in collegiate mathematics, is itself a course of real university grade, demanding I am sure, the same quality of mental effort that a course in calculus would demand. At the same time it is distinctly a professional course, laying very large emphasis upon the very materials that a teacher in the primary grades will need; but it is very far from a primary course.

I think that the point of view that one needs to have in the construction of these advanced courses in elementary subjects has sometimes been handicapped by our inadequate conception of the elementary materials. We look upon them as simple and rudimentary, and as given to little children they must be simple and rudimentary. The very fact indeed that they are basic and fundamental means that their roots strike deeper and ramify more widely than anything else that we teach. There is, however, in this case at least, a vast difference between what is common and what is commonplace. The fact that the earth is round is a fact of common knowledge, but it is very far from a commonplace fact; its establishment was very far from a commonplace achievement. The method of long division which we teach in our lower grades seems to be a simple and rudimentary device, and yet keen mathematicians struggled for generations with cumbrous cancellation methods before the present simple and relatively facile method was devised.

When I say then that the subject-matter courses should be professionalized I do not mean that they should be deprived of meat and substance, nor that they should be limited to the rudimentary content that the prospective teacher is to pass on to his future pupils. Nor do I mean that advanced courses bearing other names but which will throw light upon the elementary and secondary materials are to be abandoned. I simply mean that these latter courses are to be selected primarily because of this light, and I do mean emphatically that the question as to whether they will or will not be "recognized" by institutions that have other purposes ought not to enter at all into the discussion.

Subject-matter courses organized upon the principle that has been suggested will do much to break down the unfortunate dualism between the academic and the professional. In the first place, it is inconceivable that an instructor who is unfamiliar with the problem of teaching his subject on the lower levels will be competent to organize such courses. Instead of holding a proud aloofness from the elementary- and high-school classes, the subject-matter instructor will be compelled by the very nature of his work to keep in the closest possible contact with the training school. He will have to know what his students are doing in the training school, what problems they are trying to solve, and how his course can help them in the solution of these problems. He will, I hope, be looked upon as a member of the training department, with a seat in its cabinet and a voice and a vote in determining its policies.

In the second place the application of this principle of organization will do away very largely with the need of separate and often quite detached courses in "special methods." Subject-matter and method will develop together instead of in separate and water-tight compartments.

In the third place, these professionalized subject-matter courses, together with the constant contact of instructors and students with the work of the training school, will make it possible to reorganize in a fundamental and thoro-going way what we now call the professional work. The traditional organization of this work, starting with abstract theory and culminating in concrete practice, is the most tragic example that I know of an educational institution refusing to take its own medicine, absolutely declining the challenge to practice what it preaches. It is an actual fact that professional schools of medicine and especially of law are today infinitely better exemplars of the very educational theory which we consider sound than are our own training institutions.

I have said that we should reorganize our professional work so that its general procedure will be from practice to theory, from cases to principles, from the concrete to the abstract, rather than the reverse. We shall have, I think, an introductory "orienting" course in very simple, very concrete theory—a brief course to serve as a propaedeutic to these substantial subject-matter courses which will be closely interwoven with laboratory work in the training school. Along with these we shall have brief but succinct and practical courses in the technique of teaching and management, in school hygiene, and in other subjects which can be made to bear directly upon the work that the student is doing. As the student's participation in the actual work of teaching comes to deal with the more difficult types of teaching and to involve larger and larger responsibilities for the progress of the pupils, his work in educational theory will increase in scope and intensity. There will be a place here for summarizing courses where he will consider as a whole the problems of some particular field, such as primary teaching, intermediate-grade teaching, upper-grade or junior high school teaching, or high-school teaching. These will be essentially curriculum courses, aiming to furnish a unified point of view regarding a particular field of teaching service. Finally, at the culmination of his normal-school residence, he will study general educational theory and the organization of school systems, and in three-year and four-year curricula perhaps he will have a substantial course in the history of education designed to bring together and systematize a great many things that he has learned in his earlier courses.

The plan of organization that I have so roughly sketcht would do much, I am convinced, to insure an adequate equipment for the teacher. I may be permitted by way of summary to set forth very briefly what I consider to be the essential elements in a teacher's equipment, and how I believe that the suggested organization will furnish these elements. In the first place, the teacher must have scholarship of a high grade but of a unique quality. This the professionalized subject-matter courses should furnish. In the second place, a teacher must have a knowledge of the needs and capacities of the pupils whom he is to instruct. Here our primary dependence must be placed upon his actual contact with these pupils in the training school, with a definite responsibility from the earliest possible moment for a part of their care and culture. In the light of this intimate acquaintance he will be ready for whatever instruction in psychology may still further extend and rationalize his knowledge.

A third important item in the teacher's equipment may be included under the head of technical skills. This is the strictly habit side of the teacher's art, and its mastery involves primarily the study of good models, with careful supervision from the very moment that the student begins his actual teaching, helped out by a study of the rules and precepts of teaching. For these models we must depend primarily upon the normal-school instructors themselves, and it is evident that their technique of teaching should illustrate in a positive way all the recognized proprieties of the art.

A fourth item in the teacher's equipment, for want of a better term, I shall refer to as teaching insight and resourcefulness. This finds expression in such capacities and abilities as the following:

1. Aptness in and fertility of illustration.
2. Clearness and lucidity in explanation and illustration.
3. Keen sensitiveness to evidences of misunderstanding and misinterpretation upon the part of pupils and students.
4. Dexterity and alertness in devising problems and framing questions that will focus the attention upon just the right points.
5. A sense of humor that will relieve tense or wearisome situations.
6. Ability to suspend judgment and yet avoid chronic neutrality.
7. The intellectual humility that means a bias toward a reasoned support of each point presented.
8. Ability to create an attitude in the class which is favorable to industry and application, and which takes good work and adequate results as matters if course.
9. Sensitiveness to evidences of inattention and lack of aggressive effort upon the part of pupils.
10. Ability to develop interests in pupils that will be more than merely transitory and will carry over to other subjects and other phases of life.
11. A sense of proportion that insures the emphasis of salient topics and distinguishes clearly between the fundamental and the accessory; partly dependent upon—
12. A clear perception of ends.

It is the possession of these abilities that makes the teacher an artist in his work, and it is with respect to the development of these abilities that our teacher-training work now is notably defective. The study of theory will not help much here. Practice under sympathetic supervision will be the factor upon which the greatest reliance must be placed, and this again must be helped by the study of models. There is perhaps no better way to induct the student-teacher into a mastery of these elements than for the supervisor to say to him, when the student has failed at some point in his own practice: "Watch the way in which Mr. So and So handles this type of teaching."

A final item in the teacher's equipment is a real and dynamic professional attitude—an attitude, not only surcharged with enthusiasm for the service that he is to enter, but also intelligent as to its needs and problems, and competent to evaluate proposals for its improvement. It is here especially that the integrating and summarizing courses that will come toward the conclusion of the curriculum must find their principal justification. However, dependence must not be placed upon these alone. Each of the courses that the student takes, each of the instructors with whom he comes in contact, each element, indeed, in the life of the school, must contribute as much as it can to this important end.

Education and Our Democracy
(1918)

Bagley wrote this selection after serving on a Commission on Education and Our Democracy, which was formed by the National Education Association during World War I. Bagley discusses the problems with America's education system, which had become obvious following the administration of tests to thousands of young men who had been drafted into the armed services. Many of these new recruits were shown to have poor reading, writing, and mathematics skills. They also had been shown not to know much about American history and government. During this time, many political figures and educators were discussing what should be done to make sure that future recruits were better educated.

Bagley explains his views on the role that the federal government should play in educational policy. He rejects the claim that the federal government's role was being overemphasized, and makes the point that the traditions of American political theory in this country will never allow education to be, as he puts it, "Prussianized." He does, however, argue in favor of additional involvement in education by the federal government.

Because of the crisis that America was facing during the war, Bagley also makes the point that the time for talk about improving education had ceased and that the time for action had arrived. Once again, he argues that increased attention to quality teacher training was the only route to the improvement of American education. We always talk about the need for better education, Bagley asserts, yet we neglect the education of the most vital person in any school, the teacher. He wonders out loud why America is the only nation in the world that neglects the problem of quality teacher training.

Forgotten Heroes of American Education, pages 113–117

It has been the conviction, shared by all of the members of the commission, that the present crisis has brought to those responsible for public education both unprecedented responsibilities and unprecedented opportunities. Two great facts have stood out sharp and clear in all of our discussions: The first is the marvelous awakening of the national consciousness, the sweeping away of the old divisions between sections of the country and groups of the population, and the birth of a new, fresh, and vigorous sense of national unity. The second great fact is the rapid growth and development of a new and persuasive and comprehensive meaning for the word democracy.

The first of these great movements—the development of the new nationalism—has created almost overnight an educational need of which we have hitherto been only dimly conscious. It is the imperative need of educational efficiency upon a national scale, and the parallel requirement of programs and policies that are framed with the needs of the nation primarily in mind. We have become suddenly aware that it does make a difference whether all of the people of the country can think together and act together. We have become suddenly aware that educational backwardness and intellectual stagnation in any part of the country may handicap the progress and imperil the safety of the nation as a whole. With seven hundred thousand illiterate young men subject to the draft, the welfare of the schools in every locality and the adequacy of the education provided for every type of child have become matters of national concern. When we of the educational world are astounded to learn that there have been hundreds of communities in this country where boys and girls have grown to manhood and womanhood in utter ignorance of American ideals and institutions, ignorant of the very language of our country, and even nurtured upon alien ideals brought to them through the medium of an alien tongue, it is pretty clear that we have been thinking of education and planning for education too exclusively in the terms of our circumscribed local units. And when we find entire contingents of our United States Army unable to understand commands given to them in the language of their country, unable in some cases to understand any language save that of our principal enemy, it is pretty clear that the doctrine of local autonomy in education needs some very radical modification.

But it is not alone the revelations of the draft and the discovery of centers of active enemy propaganda in various sections of the country that point to the imperative need of a national aim in education. Again almost overnight the position of our country with reference to other nations has been radically transformed. From a sequestered and in many ways self-sufficient people we have suddenly assumed a position of prime significance in a new family of nations. Whatever may have been the insufficiencies of our educational system under the older order, they concerned ourselves alone. Whether we will or no, that day of complacency has past, never to return. It will make a difference now, not only to ourselves, but to the free peoples who have fought for us and with us, whether 30 or 50 or 100 per cent of our schools are efficient. Our people constitute the richest and strongest of the great democracies. In the coming federation of free nations they must bear a responsibility for the preservation and strengthening of the democratic ideal—a responsibility commensurate with their strength and their wealth. Upon the way in which our people think and feel and act from this time forth will depend conditions and issues that reach far beyond our own borders and comprehend vastly more than our own happiness and welfare and progress. When we were an isolated and self-sufficient people we could temporize with the educational problem. We could lament the shameful neglect of our rural and village schools, which enroll more than one-half of the nation's children, and take it out in lamenting. We could regret that we were not able to solve this great problem which lies closer to the root and source of our national life than any other problem in the realm of education. The time for regrets and lamentations is past; the time for action has come.

We have temporized with the problem of preparing teachers until we have the unenviable reputation of giving less attention to the problem than any other great nation, and no problem is fraught with greater significance to the welfare of our schools and to the responsibilities that they represent. We have temporized with the health problem and the problem of adult illiteracy. We have temporized with the problem of furnishing educational stimulus and direction to the great masses of our boys and girls who leave school and enter bread-winning employment before their habits have been formed and their ideals of life and conduct firmly established.

And it is only fair to say that we have temporized because we have had to temporize. Our system of school support has been such that we have had to depend almost entirely upon local revenues; our system of school administration has been such that we have had to depend almost entirely upon local initiative. As a result our programs and policies have been framed to meet the local needs and fit the local purse. If a community wished to have good schools and could pay the price, it usually had good schools. If a community was indifferent to education, it had, in general, the privilege of neglecting its schools. If a community was poor but ambitious, it did the best that it could with its slender resources. And because in general our thickly settled communities are rich and our sparsely settled communities are poor the most glaring inequities of education have prevailed.

But all this represents in reality an unnecessary situation. While it is true that there are marked inequalities among various sections of the country in respect to per capita wealth, it is also true that the country as a whole is very far from poor. We can have something akin to an equality of educational opportunity if our people only say the word. We can have a good school in every locality, and mature, well-prepared and permanently employed teachers in every school. If our people say the word, we can within a decade solve the rural-school problem. We can put into our rural and village schools two hundred thousand teachers who can, who will, do for rural America and for the nation as a whole what the village dominies have done for Scotland, and what the rural schoolmasters have done for Denmark and Norway; two hundred thousand teachers who will make these rural schools of ours, these lonely outposts of culture, what they should be, strategic centers of national life and national idealism. For outposts tho they may be in one sense, in another and a deeper sense these little schools, of all of our educational institutions, are closest to what is formative and virile and abiding in our national life.

And if the people only say the word, the next decade may easily see the great problem of adolescent education well on the road toward a satisfactory solution. If England in this most critical hour of her history can deliberately decide to advance the limit of compulsory continuation schooling to the age of eighteen, if France, struggling so bravely to defend not only herself but the entire world against a ruthless aggression, can even in the midst of that struggle plan to keep her boys under educational direction until the age of twenty, shall we, living in comparative security and abundance, confess that we are unequal to the task? I repeat that if our people will only say the word we can within a decade attain to a high measure of educational efficiency on a nation-wide scale. It is the judgment of your commission that we should urge our people to say that word and say it quickly. After all, it means only an extension of a principle that they have long since firmly established as a basis for the free schools of a democracy—the principle, namely, that it is just and equitable to tax the entire wealth of a community for the education of all of the community's children. Commerce and industry have long since been nationalized. Of all our collective enterprises education alone remains hampered and constrained by the narrow confines of an obsolete conception. But now with this new national awakening we find that state boundaries can be easily and quickly transcended. The golden hour of American education has struck. The opportunity is here and the need is compelling to employ the resources of the nation for the education of the nation's children. We have a national problem to solve that transcends all state and local problems. We have international obligations to discharge which will call for the very highest level of enlightened intelligence in the body politic. And we have in the nation something that neither the states nor the local communities have developed in like measure, namely, a system and policy of taxation which distributes the burden of collective enterprises in the most equitable fashion that the mind of man has yet been able to devise.

It is but natural that there are those among our people who will look askance at a change in our educational system which makes the national treasury an important source of school revenues. There are sincere and well-informed men and women in this audience who have grave fears that federal cooperation in the support of public schools will mean federal control and the domination of a hidebound bureaucracy. I have even heard expressed a fear that national support for education will Prussianize our great democracy.

The members of this commission respect these doubts and fears. But they also believe, not only that every worthy feature of local school control may be perpetuated, but that local initiative may be healthfully stimulated and local interest in and responsibility for education greatly augmented by the kind of federal cooperation that they propose. Personally I do not share the fear that the nationalization of our schools will Prussianize our people. In the first place, I do not think that anything could Prussianize our people. Prussianism is only superficially a form of organization; fundamentally it is a disease, a moral lesion which has cut away every sentiment of decency and humanity, which has eaten from the social mind the spiritual and moral values of life, which has glorified the material and left the brute supreme. Germany has not needed even a federal system of education to spread this disease among her people. Her unit of school control, like ours, is the state, and not the nation.

France has the most highly centralized and nationalized educational system in the world. Has the nationalization of her schools Prussianized France? England is nationalizing her schools today. Will England's new schools Prussianize the English people? We have nationalized our railroads and many of our industries. We have nationalized our Army. Do we find in our national life today anything that smacks of the Hun?

It is the conviction of this commission that the nation may participate in the support of education without involving the dangers of bureaucracy and autocratic control. It is further the conviction of the commission that these dangers, if they exist, may be the more readily avoided if the initiative in promoting this principle of national support is taken by the National Education Association. We may be very sure that this movement is coming. Some individual or organization is bound, some have already essayed, to take the leadership. This responsibility falls naturally to our Association. Shall we accept the plain challenge, or shall we lie back and let someone else do the work? It is the belief of the commission that you will have but one answer to that question.

The Status of the Classroom Teacher
(1918)

The title of this essay highlights the campaign that Bagley waged on behalf of classroom teachers for almost 50 years. If he was concerned about anything, it was raising the status of the people who dedicate their lives to classroom teaching. He reiterates common themes from much of his work when he wonders why Americans place so much faith in education, yet, through their actions, define the profession of teaching as something less than a worthy vocation. What must be done to improve American education for the long-term, Bagley declares, is the establishment of institutions that make teaching children and youth an end in and of itself and not a means to some other supposedly more important end (e.g., school administration, business, research, or law).

Bagley recognizes that teaching is a calling that is supported by social and moral principles, not merely an applied science that can be treated mechanically. He compares the profession of teaching with fine arts such as singing and painting, rather than with applied sciences like engineering and agriculture. He concludes by affirming that the only route to the improved status of classroom teachers is through the continued establishment and support of professional schools for teachers throughout the landscape of higher education. These professional schools, moreover, should make teaching teachers their most supported and well-respected task.

From the point of view of the internal organization of the American educational system the most unsatisfactory situation today is that which is represented by the anomalous status—or perhaps better, the lack of status—of the classroom teacher. In spite of the fundamental educational axiom that

Forgotten Heroes of American Education, pages 119–123

the critical and vital element in every school is the teacher, in spite of the unction with which the work of the teacher is lauded and the tremendous responsibility of the teacher emphasized, it still remains true that the actual work of teaching in this country neither offers the opportunities nor provides the conditions of a real career. Educational work, it is true, affords opportunities for careers of various types—for careers in administration, careers in scholarship, careers even in politics—but the basic act of education which is represented by the work of the classroom teacher affords no such opportunities. Here unusual success brings no unusual recognitions or rewards except as it may actually lead one away from the work of teaching into administrative and supervisory activities.

Our conception of what constitutes promotion in educational work is in itself a sad commentary upon the unprofessional status of our calling. In general the line of promotion is from rural school to graded elementary school, from lower grades to higher grades, from elementary school to high school, from high school to administration or perhaps to college teaching. And even in college and university work the effective sanctions and recognitions attach not to teaching as such, but either to the kind of productive scholarship that finds expression in printer's ink, or again to administration. It is not too much to say that the current policy of promotion in educational work is actually backward—from the most exacting tasks to those which, while still difficult enough, really make smaller demands upon the individual.

THE "FACTORY" PLAN OF SCHOOL ADMINISTRATION

In common with many of you in this audience I have tried to think out plans by means of which the status of the classroom teacher in the scheme of public education might be effectively recognized—plans thru which effective rewards and sanctions might come to attach to the actual work of teaching. I think that, upon the whole, you and I have been animated in these plans and hopes by purely unselfish motives. We find certain satisfactions in our work—satisfactions that often overtop any material rewards of which we can conceive—but this, after all, does not solve the problem. The great majority of our public-school teachers are transient, immature, and untrained. They do not look upon teaching as a permanent career. They do not prepare themselves adequately for it. They do not remain in the service long enough to acquire anything more than an amateur's conception of its problems, its methods, its technique, and its responsibilities. Those who enter it as a permanent calling are continually tempted to seek promotion that takes them away from the actual, vital contact with pupils and students. The great, and just now the very momentous problem of getting the next generation ready for its serious responsibilities is being accomplished more and more upon the factory plan. I mean by this very frankly that the status of the classroom teacher is becoming more and more akin to that of the "hands" in a factory, working under foremen and superintendents who assume the real responsibility. More and more frequently too these foremen and superintendents in our schools are being recruited from a group which has never served an apprenticeship in the actual work of teaching boys and girls.

Schools, however, cannot be operated on the factory plan except at the peril of the vital and fundamental function that they must discharge. We are wont to think of teaching as an applied-science. It is the fashion to believe that general principles analogous to those that govern the processes of agriculture and engineering can be worked out and reduced to simple rules that anyone can apply under competent direction, and the plain corollary of this thesis is that the teacher may be considered as an artisan, analogous in every essential way to the carpenter and the bricklayer and the plumber who take the plans and specifications worked out by the architect and the construction engineer and realize them in actual material production.

I have all sympathy with the scientific study of educational problems up to this point, but here I balk. Teaching is only in part an applied science. The analogy with agriculture and engineering is mischievously misleading, once it has been carried beyond a relatively narrow range of application. The alliance of teaching is rather with the fine arts than with the applied sciences. The effective teacher must be an artist rather than an artisan.

ADMINISTRATION V. EDUCATIONAL POLICY

A final suggestion, thoroughly practicable, is designed primarily to offset the insidious tendency that I have noted—the tendency to operate the modern public school on the factory plan. There is a very great difficulty to overcome here. In so far as administrative matters are concerned, there must be in every large educational institution, or system of institutions, a hierarchy of authority and responsibility. Administratively we must have our foremen and our superintendents; but this is not at all inconsistent with delegating to the teachers as such a large measure of collective responsibility for what may be called the educational policies of the school or the school system. This distinction between purely administrative matters on the one hand and educational policies on the other has been worked out most admirably in certain of the colleges and universities that are supported at public expense. The lay boards of trustees are responsible to the people for the proper expenditure of the people's money, but these boards, if they are intelligent, depend almost entirely upon professional judgment for educational policies. In the colleges that I refer to these educational policies are always initiated by the faculties, which comprise usually only the mature and permanent teachers. The president of the institution, while administratively the agent of the board, is educationally not the autocratic boss but rather the cooperating leader of the faculty.

I believe that a similar plan is thoroughly practicable in a high school or in a complete school system, assuming in each case that the teaching staff is mature, permanent, and well trained. Educational policies concerning the course of study, the adoption of textbooks, the adjustment of the program, the provisions for exceptional pupils of all types, and similar matters may well be determined either by the teaching staff acting as a unit, or by a representative "senate" of teachers elected by the teachers themselves. That the administrative and supervisory officers will exercise a leadership is both inevitable and proper, but leadership in these educational matters should be entirely without the authority of coercion or even the suggestion of such authority. The recommendations of the teachers must, of course, be subject to the approval of the board representing the people, but they should not be subject to an individual administrative veto.

ADEQUATE PREPARATION OF TEACHERS

It should go without saying that the permanent betterment of the classroom teacher's status is absolutely dependent upon far better facilities for the professional preparation of teachers. It is, after all, the dead weight of the transient, immature, and untrained majority of our teaching population that forms the heaviest handicap to educational efficiency and progress. With more than half of the nation's children under teachers who have had absolutely no adequate preparation for their serious responsibilities, teachers who themselves are scarcely more than boys and girls at work, there can be little hope of an essentially modified conception of the teacher's service. As a nation we give less attention to the preparation of teachers than does any other country of equal standing. Until this condition is corrected fundamentally we are hopelessly handicapped.

I sincerely trust that the classroom teachers as a group will aid and abet in every possible way the movement that is already on foot to raise the status of our normal schools and city training schools. This is part and parcel of our cause. Personally I am strongly in favor of federal cooperation in the support of these schools. I believe that the national government should do for these schools the same effective and stimulating service that it has done for the state agricultural colleges. I think indeed that the measure of cooperation should be even closer with the normal schools. At the present time the teachers of our public schools as a group are recruited from an economic level of the population that cannot afford to send its children to distant schools for an extended term of preparation for the work of teaching. This, I take it, is at basis the fundamental cause of our low professional standards. There is but one way out of this dilemma, and that is to place the preparation of public-school teachers upon the same basis that we have placed the training of officers for the army and navy; namely, to select candidates for the service upon a rigorous basis of merit and then to pay them a living wage so that they can afford to prepare for teaching in a way and to an extent consistent with the responsibilities that they are to assume. For the government to cooperate with the states in doing this would be to recognize in a most effective way the much-talked-of dependence of the nation's welfare upon the public school and the significance of the teacher's service to the nation's life.

The present time is peculiarly opportune to project an extended national, perhaps even an international, movement looking toward an appropriate status of the classroom teacher. Such a movement planned and projected now and launched full tilt immediately after the war would be thoroughly in harmony with the great democratic movement which has already gained momentum in industry and politics both here and abroad. And this larger movement itself is thoroughly in harmony with the spirit and purpose of the great cause for which we are fighting.

The Nation's Debt to the Normal Schools
(1921)[1]

Bagley delivered this address soon after he began his appointment as a professor of education at Teachers College, Columbia University. His role at Teachers College was to focus on the field of teacher training, which meant that he served as the nation's leading expert on normal schools and teachers colleges. These were the institutions that made teaching teachers their purpose at the time. His audience for the address consisted of the most prominent normal school and teachers college faculty and administrators from across the country, as well as members of the United States Congress.

This selection again emphasizes the central role that teacher training plays in Bagley's educational philosophy. In fact, he argues that the future of American democracy rests with the professional schools that are charged with the purpose of teaching teachers. He mentions other well-known educational thinkers, for example Charles DeGarmo and Charles McMurry, who also recognized the centrality of teacher training to American democracy.

This essay includes some of Bagley's most inspirational rhetoric. He speaks of the "silent service" of teaching, by which he also meant the silent, thankless task of teaching teachers. He also draws upon the well-known image of "an educational ladder with its base in the gutter and its tip in the University." He argues that professional schools for teaching teachers are the most critical rung in this ladder, in that they take the diffusion of knowledge throughout the population as their purpose.

---

1. Address at a dinner given by the National Council of Normal-School Presidents and Principals to members of Congress, Feb. 24, 1921.

Forgotten Heroes of American Education, pages 125–131

Reading this selection today raises questions about the extent to which American higher education in the early 21st century has abandoned the ideal of providing an educational ladder that all young Americans can climb.

Any sincere effort to evaluate the service of the American normal school to the Nation must take account of the conditions under which this institution first developed. It came into being in answer to the demand for universal common-school education. It was part and parcel of the movement toward democracy at the time when the dependence of democracy upon universal education was just beginning to be clearly grasped. It came particularly when the futility of providing universal education without first providing competent and devoted teachers had become painfully apparent. The first normal schools in a very real sense were missionary schools. They had their roots in the real needs of the people,—of the great masses of the "common people," whom, Lincoln said, the Lord must have loved because he made so many of them. The normal schools were democratic in their origin and democratic to the core—and democratic they have always remained.

Our attention is often called to the defects and shortcomings of our present-day public schools. Not often do we stop to think how stupendous a task it is to bring the rudiments of learning to every boy and girl in the land, nor for how relatively short a time this task has been attempted. The universal elementary school is essentially the product of the nineteenth century. Beginnings there were much earlier, but these were only beginnings. The greatest progress in Colonial times was made in New England, but even here it was only a crude beginning of mass education. There were academies and colleges scattered through the Colonies, but these in general were distinctly for the classes and not for the masses.

Until well on in the nineteenth century, there were two distinct types of schools even in the states that did the most for education. The private and endowed schools and colleges served those who could afford their advantages. Separate from them were the rude forerunners of our present school system,—the public or common schools.

Even as schools for beginners, these were often shunned by parents who could afford the private school or the private teacher. The stigma of poverty and charity in many cases attached to them. Indeed, they were often known as jumper schools or ragged schools. Between them and the higher institutions there was no connection. The grading system was unknown. The public high school was still far in the future. Reading, writing, and a little arithmetic made up the pabulum to which the children were limited. The teachers frequently were of the itinerant type of schoolmaster,—men themselves of very rudimentary learning; sometimes miserable failures even in the unskilled labor of the farm or the shop; bitten deep with the bug of innate laziness: all too often besotted with chronic drunkenness. The textbooks were few in number and pitiable in their limitations even when measured by the standards of that early day. The buildings at best were mere shacks, the equipment a few rude benches—and a plentiful supply of birches.

Such were the beginnings of our public-school system in the first quarter of the nineteenth century. Such indeed were the beginnings of mass education, of democratic education, almost everywhere.

From these crude beginnings to our present public-school system seems to be a far cry—but it is the achievement of less than a century. Not out of the private schools and academies and colleges of these early days, but out of the ragged common school has grown what may in time be the finest development in our American life. We have indeed the promise of it now: the pattern and the form and in some ways the substance and the fulfillment,—a great and pervasive system of public education, open to all and free to all,—the true spirit of which Huxley caught and crystallized in his famous phrase, "An educational ladder with its base in the gutter and its tip in the University." A short century ago only the first segment of that ladder had been constructed: it rested even then in the gutter; but its tip was very far from the University. But there were men who saw beyond the gutter; there were forces among the common people themselves that impelled them to look upward; and the ladder grew.

It is not my purpose to tell the story of that growth. Nor could I tell it in the way that it should be told. Some day it will be recounted as one of the great chronicles of our people—as one of the epics of American democracy; comparable, I am sure, to the greatest of the other epics,—the epic of the frontier and the gradual conquest of the wilderness. And the two are not without their parallels. For if the pioneers of the great West toiled on the physical frontier of democracy, the schoolmaster and the schoolmistress toiled on the spiritual frontier. The conquest of a material wilderness was the achievement of the one; the conquest of a spiritual wilderness the achievement of the other. The work of the one is now all but finished; but the work of the other has only just begun.

When the epic of this growth has been written, we may be very sure that the American normal school will have a place of high honor. It was in 1839 that the first normal school was established in Massachusetts. With an appropriateness that may not have been fully conscious to its founders, it was located at Lexington. In the same year another Massachusetts school was established and in the following year a third,—the famous school at Bridgewater. Other states followed quickly and by the close of the second quarter of the nineteenth century, the American normal school was an established institution.

And by this time, too, the new leaven had begun to work a miracle of transformation in American education. Stalwart men had been back of the movement which resulted in the normal schools,—men like Horace Mann and James G. Carter and Henry Barnard,—the Daniel Boones and Simon Kentons and Davy Crocketts of the educational frontier. And their task, in many ways, was no less arduous than that of the pathfinders of the forests and the plains. If they did not have the stubborn forces of nature to combat, they had something that was equally stubborn,—the opposition of conservative classes entrenched behind vested privilege, and the inert apathy of the masses of the people themselves. Indeed, the pioneers of the West had at least one real advantage. They could "go after" the wilderness with an axe. Much as the educational pioneers might have longed on occasion to use this effective instrument of civilization, they were confined to other methods—to argument, and persuasion, and the slow but ultimately certain influence of fact and reason. Little by little the sources of opposition were broken down; little by little the people were aroused to a new sense of responsibility for their children. It was a hard uphill fight, exacting from those who were engaged in it a full measure of heroic devotion.

If you ask what has brought about this transformation I can tell you that the American normal school has been the most important factor in the change. It was the Swiss schoolmaster, Pestalozzi, who first developed the methods of objective teaching that were ultimately to make the memorizing of meaningless words a relic of educational barbarism. It was the Oswego Normal School in New York State under the leadership of Edward A. Sheldon that introduced the humane and intelligent spirit of Pestalozzi to American schools. During the sixties and seventies there spread from Oswego as a center one of the most remarkable waves of educational reform that has ever swept the country. It was Herbart who proclaimed on the basis of sound theory a workable plan for making school tasks interesting instead of irksome. It was students from the Illinois Normal University,—especially DeGarmo and the McMurrys,—who went to Europe and brought back the message of Herbart. It was Francis W. Parker of the Cook County Normal School in Illinois who went up and down the country in the eighties and the nineties showing the absurdity of building education around anything less vital and less important than the actual living child himself.

If the schooling of your children has been more humanely governed, more intelligently directed, more mindful of children's needs and children's capacities than was your own schooling, you have the American normal school to thank in large part for the fact. If your own schooling was better than that of your father and your grand-father, a share of your indebtedness accrues to the normal school.

I could recount other types of service that the normal schools have rendered to the Nation. I could tell something of the men that they sent into the Army during the Civil War and the Great War. I could remind you that the commander-in-chief of the American forces in France was a product of the normal school al Kirksville, Missouri,—now one of the Missouri State Teachers colleges. I could tell you of the men who have gone from the normal schools into university work, there to win distinction as scholars or administrators. I could tell of those who have succeeded in business, in industry, in law, in medicine, and in politics.

The record is a proud one, but I prefer to emphasize what I may call the silent service of these schools,—the great work that they have done in the field that means most to the Nation's life and the Nation's growth, the field of common-school education. It is this silent service that does not get into the newspapers. Even the people who live in the towns where the normal schools are located may know nothing of it. It is an influence that spreads imperceptibly. It is not like the mountain torrent that foams noisily through the canyon—nor yet like the river that spreads itself proudly and complacently over the plains—nor yet like the rollers of the sea that thunder upon the beach. Rather it is like the deep subterranean waters that percolate through the rocks and through the soil—hidden from sight, and yet in their aggregate volume far surpassing the streams and the rivers and rivaling even the sea itself—silent and imperceptible, and yet the source of the living springs.

It is this type of deep but impalpable influence that truly educative forces always exert. It is this type of influence that the normal schools have exerted and are exerting. It is an influence that penetrates to the very heart of the Nation's life for the most fundamental and pervasive of all national influences are those that touch and quicken the Nation's children. Every factor that determines the texture of the lower schools is a force that must be reckoned with: the administrator who organizes their work; the framer of the course of study who determines what subjects are to be taught and learned; the textbook writer who builds out the framework with substance. But after all this has been counted up, it is the teacher who gives to it all the breath of life, and who, for this reason, wields the most potent and abiding influence. It is because the normal schools reach into the lower schools through the living personality of the teacher rather than through plans of organization or courses of study or printed books or other impersonal things—it is because of this that their influence is so profound.

If, with the meagre support that the normal schools have received, and if with the limitations of their service which have kept them from turning into the public schools more than a mere fraction of the teachers that these schools need,—if, with these handicaps, they have still wielded so profound and lasting an influence, one may well ask how much greater would be their service and their influence if they could be properly supported and given by the people the commission that they have so clearly earned—the commission, namely, of preparing all of the teachers who now enter the public school service immature and unprepared.

We have traveled far since the first uncertain steps were taken toward universal education. The old ragged and pauper schools became the common schools. The common schools extended outward and upward; gradually they became the schools not only of the common people but of all the people. For a time, the private secondary schools with their aristocratic traditions checked the upward growth of the common schools,—but only for a time. The people's high school appeared—at first a puny institution dangling in the air, joined neither with the common school below nor with the college above. But it had its roots in the same soil that had nourished the common school. Gradually it found its nexus with the common school which now by contrast became the elementary school. The grading system was developed and the first two segments of the educational ladder were complete. And then came further growth. The people's colleges appeared,—the state universities of the West and the land-grant colleges, both stimulated by generous Federal aid. These, too, were democratic in their origin. Soon they came to reach down to the high school, and the high school, reaching upward, touched the rungs of the third segment. The dream had come true—an educational ladder still with its base in the gutter but with its tip now in the university and in the professional school. Nothing like this had ever been achieved before in the whole history of mankind.

And as the different segments of the ladder have gradually taken their proper places, the whole scheme has appealed more and more to the imagination of the American people. They are proud of their schools,—and especially of their high schools and their public colleges. They have provided for these institutions magnificent buildings and costly equipment. They have sent their children to them in increasing numbers. The public high schools of our country now enroll more students than do the similar institutions of all other countries combined. Their enrollment since 1890 has grown ten times as fast as the general population. It has doubled within ten years. We are now probably sending more boys and girls to college than are all other countries combined. The enrollment in our colleges has practically doubled within five years. The ladder is more than an ornament. Every rung is crowded with ambitious youth.

But while our people are proud of their schools it is still the material side and to some extent the superficial side of the problem that has most strongly caught and held their attention. Buildings and equipment, laboratories, gymnasiums, and play grounds—all these are important—but they do not constitute a school. They are only the shell without the soul—and the soul of every real school is the living teacher.

To the most important part of the educational problem, then, the American people have given relatively the least attention. I have tried to tell you what the normal schools of the past accomplished; the signal service that they rendered to the Nation in spreading the gospel of universal education; the miracle of transformation that they wrought in the spirit and methods of the lower schools; the stabilizing elements that they alone have given to the teaching profession. And yet they have touched relatively few of the persons now engaged in the public-school service. All of the teachers that they have graduated in the eighty years of their existence would not lie sufficient in number to provide every classroom today with a trained teacher. Of the three hundred thousand teachers in our rural and village schools, only a bare handful have come directly under the stimulus of the normal school. If you are seeking an explanation of the twenty-five per cent of "near illiteracy" found by the military draft, you will find it here. Three-fourths of our elementary-school teachers are classified as untrained. We may be proud of the educational ladder, but we have to confess that it wobbles in spots—and that some segments are hardly worth the climbing.

What the normal schools need,—what they richly deserve, what they have most assuredly earned,—is a type of public recognition and support that they have never received. And they have never received this recognition and support because, as I have said, their service has been a silent service. But I do not urge recognition and support for these institutions merely as a reward for their past achievements. I do not urge it merely in justice to normal-school teachers who are giving themselves without stint to a difficult and ill-rewarded service. I urge it primarily in justice to twenty million boys and girls who can profit by the teachers that these schools are competent to train as they can profit by no other advantage that we can give them. Society cannot guarantee to every boy and every girl a devoted and intelligent mother or a wise and provident father, but society *can* guarantee to every child a good school and a competent teacher. The first step in giving every boy and every girl a competent teacher is to extend and expand and strengthen the institutions that have already demonstrated beyond question their ability to furnish these desirable products. These institutions are the normal schools. They and they alone can make the educational ladder well worth climbing. They and they alone can put substance into the form and pattern. They and they alone can make our public-school system what many enthusiastic but misinformed citizens think that it is today,—the finest thing in American life.

Projects and Purposes
in Teaching and in Learning
(1921)

This essay is one of Bagley's clearest responses to the publication of William Heard Kilpatrick's "The Project Method." This article of Kilpatrick's was widely influential among Progressive teachers when it was published in Teachers College Record *in 1918. Kilpatrick's basic idea with "The Project Method" was that students should learn what they wanted to learn through creating projects or solving problems, rather than what was specified in a logically designed curriculum. Bagley criticizes Kilpatrick's overemphasis on "projects" in educational theory and practice and describes the problems that this overemphasis creates. He recognizes the merits of the theory, but also warns that it could do irreparable damage to American education. He rejects the revolutionary rhetoric that many Progressives were using as they spread their ideas. The pragmatists who were advocating the "project method", he warned, were stripping American educational theory of the ideals that he thought were critical to student success.*

The project method represents a synthesis of movements and tendencies in educational theory that have been gathering momentum for several years—some of them indeed for several decades. It represents an attempt to formulate these tendencies and movements in a single and unified pattern of educational procedure. As such, it already ranks as a constructive achievement of the first magnitude. It is quite within the realm of possibility that it may work a complete transformation in school life, and a correspondingly profound transformation in the attitudes, standards, and methods of thinking and of acting in the coming generations. It represents

Forgotten Heroes of American Education, pages 133–140

133

something more than a method of teaching in the narrower sense of this term. It means a new point of view toward the whole problem of education. It may mean not only the reorganization of educational materials which it already promises, but the development of materials that have not as yet been utilized in education. It may mean not only the radical changes in educational ideals and objectives which have been so influential in bringing about its development, but also the genesis and projection of new aims and new ideals. In a very real sense we are standing today at the parting of the ways. There is a deep and well-nigh universal conviction that a different world lies ahead,—a civilization that may be as different spiritually from the existing order as our civilization is different materially and economically from that of two centuries ago. And the harbingers of the new order, its patterns and its promises, are probably nearer the surface in educational theory and practice than they are in any other department of human activity.

The present topic is approached, then, in an attitude that is about as far removed from dogmatism and "cocksureness" as it could possibly be. What we have specifically to ask concerning the project method may in the near future be recognized as quite beside the question. We are bound today to judge each new proposal by the standards with which we are familiar. But the development and acceptance of other standards may easily make our judgments of absolutely no consequence.

The most significant feature of the project method is its emphasis upon the element of purpose, and especially the basic importance that it attaches to the purpose of the learner. It recognizes the dynamic effect of a strongly felt desire in releasing the energy that is essential in learning, and it aims to capitalize this factor in the interest of education. It would seek in the experience of the child for dominant purposes which may be turned to educational ends. In the realization of such purposes, it maintains, the teacher will be able to bring to the child many if not most of the skills and the information that he will need in his later life. Coming to the child and assimilated by him in this natural context, the skills and the information will be acquired with a minimum of difficulty, it is assumed, because there will be no divided effort. It is also assumed that skills and information absorbed in this natural context will be retained longer than they would be if they were acquired in and for themselves, or without reference to a dominant purpose. A third assumption is that acquired in a matrix of application, that is, as instruments in the solution of real problems, the various items of skill and information will have a greater "transfer potency", because they have been learned from the outset as instruments in the solution of problems rather than as abstract entities, they will be readily applied to new and somewhat different problems.

These claims are referred to as assumptions because their validity has not as yet been established by thoroughgoing experimentation. It is possible, of course, that they do not need experimental substantiation. In so far as the greater economy of this "purposeful" learning is concerned, there can be little question; the statement, indeed, is almost, if not quite, axiomatic. It is my opinion, however, that the second and the third assumptions should be experimentally tested. There is some indirect evidence that information gained primarily to solve an immediate problem is *not* so long retained nor so easily recalled as is information that is mastered with the intent to make its mastery permanent. I have abundant experiences of my own that confirm this conclusion. Over and over again I have "worked up" information for some specific and immediate purpose only to find it necessary to work it up again on the next occasion. In fact, the validity of the principle of "learning with intent to remember" has been fairly well established by experimental evidence. It has also found expression in common-sense maxims. Dean Pound of the Harvard Law School, for example, has been quoted as advising the law student to read each case as if all printed record of it were to be forever destroyed immediately afterward. Such learning might be identified with "purposeful" learning, but obviously the meaning here would be quite different from that which the project method implies. Psychologically, learning with the intent to master permanently comes very close to learning for its own sake.

All this does not mean that the emphasis upon children's purposes and upon immediate purposes is futile. This emphasis in any case is clearly justified in the earlier stages of education and on occasion throughout the entire course of education. To say that such purposes have a place in education is one thing, however; to maintain, as is implied in some discussions of the project method, that all learning should take its cue from such purposes is quite another thing. And it is against the latter contention that I should advance the strong probability that information mastered for a temporary and specific purpose is not so well retained as is information gained in another way.

Let me pass now to the third assumption; namely, that the "transfer potency" of skill and information is increased by the acquisition of such skill and information in a project setting, or as instruments in the realization of an immediate purpose. There is little doubt, of course, that a clear recognition of the worth of a skill or of a principle will increase the probabilities of its application to a wide range of situations. In so far as the project gives a basis for a keen appreciation of the value of what is learned, it will certainly increase transfer potency. The element of purpose is doubtless an important factor here; and yet it is conceivable that the absorption of the learner in the immediate purpose and his desire to realize that purpose may actually blind him to the intrinsic virtues of the instruments that he finds useful toward that end, and consequently work against transfer rather than in the direction of transfer. What we know about the psychology of transfer is little enough, but such as it is, it suggests strongly the importance of lifting procedures and principles out of the matrix of their application,—out of their relationships to specific and immediate purposes,—and viewing them for a while as detached entities, taking care always that their applications to concrete problems be abundantly illustrated. Project teaching would have a very important place at both ends of the series: first, in introducing the pupil to the procedure or the principle in such a way that he would be impressed with its value, and then, after some acquaintance with it, in and for itself, bringing it back into a functional or purposive setting.

I should like to dwell a little longer on this tendency of the immediate purpose to overshadow the instruments used in its realization. The failure to recognize this tendency has, I think, been the cause of the failure of the project method generally to secure the results that formal and systematic teaching, with all of its evils and all of the wastage involved in divided attention, often succeeded in securing. Good teachers who have used the project method and testified to its virtues have often added the reservation that, as they expressed it, "You must still have some drill." Now to say that you "must still have some drill" is only another way of saying that you must take a procedure out of its purpose-context and give it a little time and attention in its own right, as an abstract entity if you please. Until further evidence is at hand, I should strongly recommend that, where geography and history and other content subjects are taught by the project method, this treatment be accompanied or followed by such systematic courses as will provide for coherent organization and for an acquaintance on the part of the pupil with facts and principles as such rather than as instruments for solving impelling problems.

And this leads to another difficulty which is not easy to straighten out. The project method, as I have suggested, lays a heavy emphasis upon the "instrumental" value of knowledge. The natural inference, indeed, from much of the project literature is that knowledge is valuable only to the extent to which it enables its possessor to solve the problems that he meets in life. Now of course, if we give the term "problem" a sufficiently elastic meaning, this is true enough; but the elasticity of meanings is confusing. The psychologist may tell us that conscious life is just one problem after another, and so make the two terms quite synonymous. But most people use the term problem in a much more restricted sense, and when they are told that the sole and only purpose of knowledge is to help people to solve their problems, they are likely to limit their conception of the function of knowledge in just the same narrow way. Unless they can see how a fact or a principle will help them out of some difficulty, they are almost certain to conclude that its value is *nil.*

Now to intensify the skepticism of the unthinking adult or the immature child regarding race experience is to incur a risk that ought not to be incurred unless there is a compensating gain. Continually to emphasize the instrumental values of knowledge to the exclusion of all others is to incur this risk. The prime function of education on the elementary level, and to a large extent on the secondary level, is to place the child in possession of his spiritual heritage,—the heritage of skill, knowledge, standard, and ideal which represents the gains that the race has made. Only a small fraction of this heritage is instrumental in the narrow meaning of the term. Only a small fraction of it is made up of items of skill and items of information which one deliberately uses in solving what most people call problems. We are certainly not willing to say that the great bulk of it is consequently of no value whatsoever. And if it has not this direct instrumental value, what value has it?

I should answer this question by suggesting that knowledge or race experience furnishes an equipment for life over and above the tools or instruments that it supplies,—something that is perhaps even more fundamental than tools or instruments. It furnishes foundations, backgrounds, perspectives, points of view, attitudes, tastes, and a host of other things that determine conduct in a very real fashion, and yet through devious channels that are likely to defy analysis and to escape the scrutiny of one who is looking only for direct and visible applications.

Within the past four months some tens of thousands of people have read Mr. Wells's *Outline of History.* I doubt very much whether one in a hundred of these interested readers has deliberately applied his newly gained or refreshed knowledge of human history to any specific life situation; but it would be futile to deny that the book has already had a marked influence in determining points of view and mental backgrounds. If its vogue continues until a substantial proportion of thinking people have read it, no one can safely deny that it may *have* a profound effect upon the course of human destiny.

Now one does not ordinarily go to a book like that of Mr. Wells to solve problems or to realize immediate purposes. One doubtless has a motive for everything that one does consciously, but the motive for the same act may vary among different individuals and at different times in the same individual; and generally speaking the result is not often much affected by the specific variety of motive that happens to impel one to the act. What one does when one reads well-written history is to live vicariously, to live in imagination, some of the epoch-making experiences through which the race has lived.

It has frequently been remarked that it is difficult to teach history by the project method, or rather to devise projects through which the essential "sweep" of historical movements can be brought to the learner. This difficulty I am sure is inherent in the unique educational value of history. It is not an instrumental subject as are arithmetic, grammar, and to a large extent the sciences. Generally speaking one cannot very profitably read history backward or in segments chosen in haphazard order, any more than one can profitably read Hamlet backward or in similarly disconnected fragments.

It is because the project method with its almost exclusive emphasis upon instrumental values breaks up the continuity and organization of subject-matter that it is inadequate, I believe, for the effective treatment of those subjects, the soul and substance of which are continuity and coherent organization. History is one of these subjects, and probably the most significant from this point of view. But, as I have suggested, there is place for logical organization and systematic treatment in practically all of the content subjects.

I am of course aware of the possibility of extending the project method in theory to cover these cases. It has been suggested that the learner, after dealing with materials brought to him in a problem or project setting, will ultimately come to the point where he *desires* a logical, coherent, systematic treatment of these materials, and where in consequence a real project setting is provided by this large purpose. I have no doubt that such a motive will arise spontaneously in some individuals. Doubtless it can be suggested to others by clever teachers in such a way that the learners themselves will accept it as their own purpose. It may be necessary and wise thus, either to wait until children spontaneously generate these larger purposes or to manoeuvre until they are ready to accept as their own a large purpose which the teacher has projected. The question involves a fundamental tenet in the theory which lies back of the project method, and which I have not considered up to this point. It is a tenet that strikes far more deeply than any of the questions of retention, recall, or transfer to which I have referred. Indeed if this particular tenet is valid, practically all of the objections to and limitations of the project method which I have suggested become matters of very small consequence.

Stated baldly, the question at issue is this: Is it ever justifiable to impose one's own purposes upon others? It is conceded by all, I think, that the individual's purposes must be thwarted when they run counter to the welfare of others. Beyond this area of agreement, however, there is in educational theory a much disputed territory, and in this territory many of the fundamental issues raised by the project method must be fought out.

Personally I have large sympathy with the idea of freedom from the enthrallment of purposes handed down by tradition or imposed by authority. I am quite clear that one important line of progress is in the direction of such freedom. I am fairly clear, too, that another, and I trust, a parallel line of progress demands, if not common purposes, certainly a community of culture, that is, ideas, standards, ideals, and attitudes that are common to all. Between these two demands, educational theory must effect at all times a working adjustment.

I do not believe that such an adjustment needs to involve a compromise of principles. In the specific question at issue, for example, I am inclined to the belief that, if provision is made for giving children scope and opportunity to work out many of their spontaneous purposes, there can well be some measure of controlled and directed activity to take care of the types of learning which our adult judgment deems essential and which the child may not happen to hit upon independently. Until further evidence is available, I should say that it is better that he should be encouraged to accept this control as a matter of course, than that we should attempt to delude him into the belief that he is making a free choice when in reality the choice is made by someone else.

The justification of control and direction lies in the very nature of childhood itself. As John Fiske taught us forty years ago, the essential meaning of immaturity lies in the plasticity which it permits, and in the necessity that it imposes for the care and culture of the young by the adults of the species. Of the innate tendencies, none surpasses in its significance that which makes the child's mind receptive and his nerve connections plastic *irrespective of his conscious purposes*. The consciousness of purpose, indeed, is a late development biologically. There are many reasons for inferring that it ripens relatively late in the individual. There may be dangers of premature exercise here, as there certainly are elsewhere in the development of young children. Be that as it may, the dependence of the child upon the adult for control and guidance is clear and indisputable. This is the basis from which we can safely work. We can ask ourselves when and to what extent the child's own purposes shall begin to replace the guidance and control which nature has so providentially necessitated. This point of view, I think, shifts the emphasis in educational theory. Instead of decrying adult control as a necessary evil, we see it now as an essential virtue through the agency of which, and *primarily through the agency of which*, human progress has been made possible. The great educational problem is to use it wisely but not to abuse it; to recognize where it should stop but not to abandon it entirely even in theory.

I have tried to point out what in my opinion are some of the theoretical dangers and difficulties of the project method. I have taken the emphasis of the learner's purposes as the most significant characteristic of the project method. I have pointed out that, to teach subject-matter exclusively in the context of immediate purposes may tend to reduce the revival value and the transfer value of what is learned; but that these dangers, if they exist, can doubtless be counteracted by complementing project teaching with an organized and systematic treatment of the same materials. A second danger to which I have referred is that the almost exclusive emphasis upon the instrumental values of knowledge which this method encourages tends to blind one to other values that are equally significant and, perhaps, in the general education of the elementary and secondary school, much more important. This would seem to speak rather strongly against a wide use of the project method in the present stage of its development in connection with certain subjects such as history and literature in which the instrumental values are vastly less important than are the interpretive and inspirational values. A third danger which I have mentioned is that an over-emphasis of purpose may blind us to the fact that nature has provided, and apparently quite wisely, for learning of a non-purposive sort; and that such over-emphasis may also lead to the assumption that the imposition of adult purposes is always an evil, when, as a matter of fact, its very possibility has been one of the most important factors in human evolution.

My treatment of this topic has been frankly theoretical. I cannot close without reiterating my conviction that the development of the project method constitutes an educational achievement of the very first magnitude. It is not at all unlikely that many if not most of the dangers which I have pointed out can either be shown not to be dangers at all, or at any rate can be counteracted by modifications which will not take from the method any of its acknowledged virtues. I have aimed at what seems to me to be the central doctrine which the method involves. Against any proposal that promises to revolutionize both education and life so completely as does the reorganization of education on a project basis every possible argument that may suggest its points of weakness ought to be brought into the open, not to destroy the proposal, nor to disparage its virtues, nor to discourage those who are committed to its extension, but simply and solely to test its validity from every possible direction before it has become crystallized in a fixed and permanent form.

Preparing Teachers
for the Urban Service
(1922)[1]

In this short paper, Bagley provides his views on an issue that is at the heart of American education today: the preparation of teachers for service in urban schools. As his thoughts indicate, this is not a new issue for democratic education.

Bagley addresses such issues as curriculum for teaching teachers, the purpose of education, and, in his view, the critically important role of practice teaching experiences for teachers-in-training. As was his custom, Bagley identifies teaching with the fine arts rather than with applied sciences such as engineering and medicine. He further argues that the most essential element to be developed in the souls of future teachers is the commitment to transmitting the spiritual heritage of mankind to each succeeding generation of young people.

The hypotheses which in my opinion should govern the development of curricula for the professional education of urban teachers do not differ fundamentally from those that apply to the professional education of other teachers. I may briefly summarize these hypotheses, then, before attempting to point out whatever adjustments or variations the urban situation involves. The hypotheses, I should say, are not to be looked upon as firmly established principles. They represent in part provisional principles fairly consistent with the facts as I know them, but of course are subject to revi-

---

1. A paper read before the City Training School Section, N. E. A., Chicago, February 27, 1922.

Forgotten Heroes of American Education, pages 141–144

sion in the light of facts which I may not have taken into consideration. In part, too, they represent what I may call "articles of faith," which follow as corollaries from my personal convictions regarding the function of education in a democracy, and the relation of the teacher to the effective discharge of this function. I may be permitted then to state these hypotheses in the form of a series of beliefs or convictions:

1. I believe that the prime function of education is to conserve and extend upon as nearly a universal scale as possible what is best thought of as the spiritual heritage of mankind—the skills, the traditions, the ideas, the ideals, and the standards of conduct that have been wrought out of the experience of the race. I believe that practically all of the children of all of the people can, under the proper guidance, build into their own experience the most precious elements of this heritage. I consequently conclude that the two outstanding functions of the professional education of teachers are: first, to insure that the prospective teacher himself has come into this heritage, that he knows what it means, and that he appreciates keenly what it has cost in terms of human effort, suffering, and sacrifice; and, secondly, that he be sensitized to the difficulties that the learner encounters in its mastery, and given an initial skill in the fine art of adapting its various elements to the widely varying capacities which every group of pupils or students is likely to represent.

2. I believe that, while teaching resembles in many important ways the artisan trades, and in other ways the applied sciences, its important resemblances are not with the skilled trades like plumbing, carpentry, and bricklaying, or with such applied sciences as medicine, engineering, and agriculture, but with the fine arts. In emphasizing this analogy I recognize that any work finely done, any work into which the worker reads his own hopes and dreams and ideals, may be artistic work in the truest sense of the term. But I also recognize that certain types of work not only present possibilities for fine workmanship but make demands for fine workmanship that other occupations do not present or make in the same degree. I believe that teaching is one of these occupations, and I base this belief on the fact that it is the personal and human element in teaching that has always been recognized as the most fundamental. Without vision the nation will perish—but without sympathy, insight, and infinite patience on the part of the teachers of a nation the children of the people will not be able collectively to grasp the meaning of the vision and let it lead them onward.

Consistently with these provisional principles and convictions, I believe that the professional education of teachers for the people's schools should aim to select as far as possible those recruits whose personal qualifications for their important work are the most promising. Here the urban professional schools for teachers have a great advantage.

These prospective teachers should live in an atmosphere surcharged with the professional ideals until devotion to their work has become ingrained as second nature. Here the urban professional schools for teachers meet a serious handicap in the fact that they do not have their students under their control through the whole day or the whole week. They must, then, attempt to compensate for this condition in other ways.

From the instructional standpoint, the prime task of the professional school is to equip the student with what we have called in the past a knowledge of his subjects. But this should be a quite different type of instruction and study than institutions of general education represent. It should in all of its phases be shot through and through with the professional purpose. This means that in connection with practically every topic studied, its history, its significance to human progress, and the problem of adapting it to the comprehension of the learning mind and of different types of learning minds should be considered. Far from being narrow and circumscribed, the treatment should be far broader and far more comprehensive than that which instruction for so-called general purposes involves. Viewed in this light, the materials of elemental or fundamental education may be made as liberalizing in their influence as the so-called higher or liberal studies. The latter, in themselves, will not be neglected, but they will be selected and taught with especial reference to the light that they throw either upon the more elemental materials, or upon the broader problems that the teacher must participate in solving as a member of a profession charged with the framing of constructive policies in its own field.

Along with this broad and comprehensive study of subject-matter should go, I believe, a series of very carefully graded and supervised contacts with the work of the lower schools. This phase of the work should be more than mere observation; from the outset it should involve actual responsibilities for some type of actual service with children and under the direction of master teachers of children. It should culminate in a period of responsible teaching under fairly normal classroom conditions. The urban teachers' colleges have a very distinct advantage over other professional schools in the facilities that they can command for this close and constant correlation of theory and practice.

As to "theory of education" itself, I am personally of the opinion that, while it should not be minimized in importance it should be so organized in the beginning as to explain and rationalize successful practice rather than to lay down a set of dicta or dogmas from which, it is assumed, effective precepts of practice can be derived *a priori*. I should try to furnish the student at the outset with a bird's eye view of the field of education, dealing chiefly with facts, but also presenting as concretely as possible the outstanding variations of opinion regarding disputed questions of theory. My aim would be to lead the student gradually to accumulate his facts and questions, dispose of them specifically and provisionally as he goes on, and come finally toward the close of his pre-service education to a fundamental and thoroughgoing study of educational principles. I believe that if we proceed in the opposite way, starting with recondite theory and finally reaching practice, we are almost certain to indoctrinate the student with regard to complicated problems about which no one can afford to be "cocksure," and what is far worse give him at the outset the conviction that there is just one way of practicing his art and thus permanently seal his mind against other ways which may be as good or better.

With regard to the scientific study of his problems I should certainly utilize every tested principle that the science of education has developed. This would be done all along the line, and with the rapid development of educational science, these tested principles will come to form an important point of his curriculum. I should still aim, however, to keep the science of education the handmaiden of the art of teaching. I should especially safeguard the best interests of the cause of education by training every teacher to distinguish clearly between fact and hypothesis, a distinction always important in scientific inquiry, but especially fundamental in the field of educational science. The method that educational science has developed and used is predominantly the statistical method, which is peculiarly likely to result in artifacts as well as in actual facts.

It is clear that a program of this sort can not be made maximally effective unless the time devoted to pre-service education is extended. The urban professional schools are in a position to initiate this extension. Steps have already been taken in many cities to provide through extramural or in-service courses for the further education of teachers. This is one of the most important movements in the whole field of education, for it expresses, I am sure, a quite new standard of professional service—the ideal, namely, that the teacher must always be a learner. It would, however, in my opinion, be a very serious mistake to think of in-service education as a substitute for extended pre-service education. It should rather be looked upon as a complement to pre-service education. It will accomplish its best results when it works upon the most thorough basis that pre-service education can provide. In-service education, indeed, should be regarded as a continuous process, the aim of which is to keep the teacher growing in his work as long as he remains a teacher. To think of it merely as a means of making up the deficiencies of pre-service education is, to my mind, to blind one's self to its real significance and its richest promise.

The Army Tests and the Pro-Nordic Propaganda
(1924)

Compared to some of Bagley's other writings, quite a bit more social and historical context must be taken into account to understand this one. When he wrote this article, Bagley was in the middle of a battle to determine how the nation's newly developed intelligence tests should be interpreted and used. Psychologists such as Lewis Terman had used their new tests to sort and place recruits for the army in the Great War.

Bagley's focus in this paper is a book entitled A Study of American Intelligence, *which was published by psychologist Carl C. Brigham in 1923. Brigham, who had helped to develop IQ tests during the war, drew specious conclusions based on the results of those tests. By ranking the scores of racial and ethnic groups, Brigham claimed to have discovered "proof" of the superiority of certain strains of "Nordic stock." Bagley was outraged by Brigham's study. He openly labels Brigham with such terms as inhumane, anti-democratic, and racist. Bagley uses the same data as Brigham to discredit Brigham's claims. At a time when racism was rampant in the United States and elsewhere, Bagley showed remarkable courage in combatting dangerously flawed ideas. In an article published in 1930 in the* Psychological Review, *Brigham recanted. He admitted that he had been wrong in making precisely the claims that Bagley criticizes in this article.*

Some of the views that Bagley includes in his "rational equalitarian" position, however, will strike us as inappropriate and wrong today. But his positions must be understood within the context in which he was writing. He rejects interracial marriage and notes a "possibility" that "certain of the white strains" may be more successful, but he was also attacking deeply racist views during a time that was much different from our own.

Forgotten Heroes of American Education, pages 145–158

Bagley argues repeatedly that differences in intelligence are the result of limited educational opportunity, not innate intelligence. He is making a case for increasing educational opportunity for all young Americans, not only certain races. Some children had access to good teachers, Bagley asserts, which is the primary reason why they had success in life in general and on intelligence tests in particular. Bagley sought to focus psychologists and educational policymakers on the task of identifying those common principles of humanity that hold Americans together, rather than emphasizing the differences that rip them apart. To Bagley, good teaching—and specifically good teacher training—was at the heart of the task of uniting Americans with common social and political ideals.

The book[1] under consideration in this article is an interesting expression of the mental attitude which the present writer has characterized as "educational determinism."[2] The type of thinking that it represents and the unmistakable trend of its argument abundantly justify the criticisms that I directed two years ago against the deterministic school of psychology. Inasmuch as I was accused at that time of "attacking a straw man,"[3] and particularly of emphasizing grotesque misinterpretations of the results of intelligence tests as seen by lay students of the problem, I may be permitted now to claim a full confirmation of my forebodings in this work of a recognized psychologist.

This is not to say, however, that Professor Brigham's work is barren of merit, or that the message that it conveys is not, from certain points of view, salutary and timely. He deals primarily with the implications of the Army intelligence tests as they affect the problem of immigration. Even from the point of view of the "rational equalitarian" (if I may so characterize the position that, in a very inadequate way, I have been trying to represent), the dangers of unrestricted immigration are unquestioned and the undesirable quality of much of our recent immigration is conceded. But one may believe all this without claiming for the Army tests a validity as accurate indices of native intelligence which they do not possess; and one may certainly believe all this without identifying one's self with that "parlor" cult of ku-kluxism of which our radical pro-Nordic propagandists constitute the mother-klan. To recognize unrestricted immigration as an

1. Carl C. Brigham: *A Study of American Intelligence.* Princeton: Princeton University Press, 1923.
2. "Educational Determinism; or Democracy and the I. Q.," in *Educational Administration and Supervision*, May, 1922; also *School and Society*, May 8, 1922.
3. For example, by Dr. L. M. Terman in *Journal of Educational Research*, June, 1922.

evil is one thing; to fan the fires of race-prejudice with alleged scientific findings is quite another.

Part I of Professor Brigham's book shows the author at his best when he is describing with admirable clearness and in non-technical terms the two group-examinations,—Alpha and Beta, given respectively to the literate and illiterate soldiers—and the individual examinations based on the Stanford-Binet tests. Much less clearly this section of the book discusses the reliability of the Army tests as measures of native intelligence. Part II very briefly sets forth the contrasts in intelligence-levels between the officers and the enlisted men, and between the whites and the negroes. It then proceeds to treat in detail the test-findings for the several groups of the foreign-born draft. Following this is a discussion of the race-hypothesis, the most important part of which (indeed, the key-section of the entire book) is a table that purports to reveal the relative proportions of Nordic, Alpine, and Mediterranean stock among the nationalities represented in the foreign-born draft. Section X contains supporting evidence drawn from studies of other types—chiefly quotations from pro-Nordic writers. The section devoted to conclusions presents as its most important feature a graph that is alleged to show the distribution of native intelligence among the following racial groups as revealed by the Army tests: "Total Nordic"; "Combined Alpine and Mediterranean"; and "Negro." A large measure of overlapping is revealed, the coincidence of the surfaces being fairly close in the case of the two groups last-named; but the Nordics are represented as by far the supreme racial stock. The final paragraphs are an appeal to the American people to put into effect rigorous policies of selective immigration and eugenic practices.

Professor Brigham's argument is built around three basic assumptions: (1) that the Army tests are trustworthy measures of native intelligence: (2) that the median scores made by national groups on the Army tests reveal true differences in national levels of native intelligence; and (3) that the proportion of Nordic blood in the foreign-born population can be identified on the basis of nationality-groups. I shall consider each of these assumptions in some measure of detail.

I

Professor Brigham's principal defense of the Army tests as a true measure of native intelligence is based upon the fact that the scores correlate highly with schooling. "The best proof of the test series comes from a study of the relation between the intelligence ratings and education," he says (p. 62); and he cites in support of his statement the correlation, 0.75, between Alpha scores and "school grade completed," and the correlation, 0.67, between Beta scores and "school grade completed." His assumption is that native intelligence will determine the amount of schooling that one receives—apparently to such an extent as to render negligible all other factors, including opportunity and stimulus for schooling. Unfortunately his treatment of this crucial question is brief and (from the educationist's point of view) inexcusably amateurish. He refers to the facts of school elimination (as shown by the Army data) in support of his contention that "school grade completed" is a measure of intelligence. He is apparently unfamiliar with the careful and extended studies that have been made of retardation, elimination, and persistence in school attendance, and which show very clearly that a veritable multitude of factors cooperate in determining whether an American child will have twelve, ten, eight, seven, six, or fewer years of schooling. He is apparently equally unfamiliar with the wide variations in school opportunity offered by American communities. Only under the condition that all of the individuals compared had had essentially equal opportunities for schooling could one conclude that native intelligence alone is reflected by differences in the Army scores.

Professor Brigham does not tell us how those who framed the Army tests attempted to account for differences in schooling and thus validate the tests as measures of native intelligence before they applied them on a wide scale in the training camps.[4] There are, however, certain comparisons between the scores made on the tests by officers and the scores made by enlisted men which the Army report cites as conclusive evidence that differences in the scores were not fundamentally affected by differences in schooling. These findings Professor Brigham quotes (p. 64) as the "crucial test" of the assumption that the Army scores actually reveal the levels of native intelligence reflected in the military draft.

Unfortunately for Professor Brigham's hypothesis, this "crucial test," when analyzed, loses entirely its "crucial" character. The facts that he cites are these: While most of the officers tested were highly educated, 660 officers were found who had not progressed beyond the eighth grade of the elementary school; and, while most of the enlisted men had had relatively brief schooling, about 14,000 reported varying degrees of education beyond the eighth-grade level. Here, then, are two groups; one apparently a group of naturally bright men who with limited education have demonstrated sufficient intelligence to win commissions; the other apparently a group of dull men who, in spite of a generous educational equipment, were none the less handicapped in intelligence. The Army

---

4. I have referred briefly to this attempted validation in an article entitled "Do Good Schools Pay?" *Journal of the National Education Association*, June, 1923.

report lays great emphasis upon the fact that the scores made by each of these groups, when distributed on a frequency surface, show practically identical curves with slight superiority for the officer-group; hence the conclusion, "It is evident then that the examination is measuring other qualities, in which officers stand above recruits, to a greater extent than it is measuring education."[5]

At first glance, this evidence seems overwhelming; but when one examines the data carefully, the contention that they validate the Army tests as measures of innate intelligence is very far from convincing. If selection for a commission is proof positive of greatly superior intelligence, and if the tests measure intelligence unaffected by differences in school opportunity, then the scores of these two groups, instead of showing practically an identical distribution, should reveal a marked superiority of the officer-group. From this point of view, then the "crucial test" proves far too much. Education apparently has lifted a dull group to the level of intelligence represented by a naturally bright group. This is by long odds a greater recognition than the environmentalist has heretofore gained from the determinist.

But this is not all. The curves published in the Army report (p. 779) and copied by Professor Brigham in his book (p. 65) would tell a different story if drawn in another way. When one goes back to the original data from which the curves were drawn, one finds that the differences between these two groups in schooling are far less significant than either the Army report or Professor Brigham's discussion leads one to suspect. An overwhelming majority of the officers (almost seventy per cent.) *had completed the eighth grade,* while nearly half of the enlisted men *had been limited to ninth-grade and tenth-grade education.* Thus instead of a striking contrast between a relatively uneducated group of officers and a highly educated group of officers and a highly educated group of enlisted men, we have merely an interesting comparison between two groups that in the mass differed very little in respect of intelligence and are now seen to have differed very little in schooling. There is an abundance of evidence that one year's or two years' difference in schooling may make no difference whatsoever in the amount of education actually acquired. The number of days constituting the average "school year" in 1900 varied from 70.5 in North Carolina to 191 in Rhode Island, hence the actual time in school represented by those who reported eight years' schooling may have varied from 564 days to 1,528 days,[6] or from *3.1 school years* of thirty-six weeks each to 9 school years of thirty-six weeks each—all passing muster as "eight years of schooling

---

5. *Memoir XV,* of the National Academy of Sciences, p. 778.
6. See *Report* of U.S. Commissioner of Education for 1900.

completed"! Furthermore, it has been found, even in a state like New York where the rural and urban schools are in session approximately the same number of days each year, that eight years' schooling in the one-room rural schools insures no greater gain in educational achievement for the average pupil in typical subjects than seven years' schooling or even less will insure in urban schools.[7] In every way, the fallacy of taking a mere statement of "grade of school completed" as an adequate index of schooling is obvious.

Why the Army report failed to set forth more trustworthy comparisons relative to the probable influence exerted by schooling upon the Army scores is to my mind incomprehensible. I have shown in earlier studies[8] that the variations among the median scores made by state contingents of troops on the Alpha tests resemble almost perfectly the variations among these states in school efficiency, and that this resemblance is uniformly closer for the years when the drafted men were in school than for any other years. By using measures of present-day intelligence-levels and efficiency (levels other than the Army scores) I have been able to demonstrate that good schools have by far the best claim to a causal influence in determining all the resemblances disclosed. In other words, however reliable the Army tests may be as measures of differences in native intelligence when applied to groups that are homogeneous with respect to educational opportunities, they have no reliability whatsoever as measures of intelligence-levels when applied to groups so large and so heterogeneous educationally as were the state contingents of recruits in the drafted army. When applied to such groups, the tests become in an outstanding fashion measures of educational opportunity.

II

Professor Brigham's primary concern is not with state groups, but with national groups. It is to be inferred, then, that the wide difference in median scores upon which he lays so heavy an emphasis reflect equally wide differences in educational opportunity and can be adequately explained by reference to this factor. I shall now consider the facts that abundantly confirm this inference.

Professor Brigham compares sixteen nationalities represented in the foreign-born draft. These men had been resident in the United States for varying periods of time. Some of them took the Alpha tests and some the

---

7. See *Rural School Survey of New York State*, Ithaca, 1922, ch. ix.
8. *Journal of the National Education Association*, June, 1923; also a supplementary note in *School and Society*, Nov. 3, 1923.

Beta tests, while from both groups a few were given individual examinations. On a scale combining all three types of tests, Professor Brigham gives the median scores of those who had lived in the United States over twenty years; of those who had been residents between 16 and 20 years; between 11 and 15 years; between 6 and 10 years; and between 0 and 5 years. He finds (p. 89) that "from 0 to 20 years of residence, the average rises steadily and the variability becomes less and less." It is clear, then, that the foreign-born recruits who had been in the country the longest made, as a group, the highest scores. But it is also clear that most of those who had been residents for sixteen years or more had attended American schools (remembering that the draft affected only those between the ages of 21 and 31). It would be reasonable to conclude, then, that the superior scores of the longer-residence groups were due in part to American schooling. While Professor Brigham does not refer to the probable attendance of these longer-residence recruits in American schools, he does recognize the possibility of an "educational" factor. This, however, he completely rules out by reference to the fact that the differences hold as well for those who took the Beta tests as for those who took the Alpha tests. Because he believes that the Beta tests could have been affected in no possible way by schooling, he contends that the findings justify only one conclusion—namely, that the recent immigrant-groups are of inferior *native* intelligence.

The argument that Beta-test scores are unaffected by schooling is, of course, inadmissible. As Professor Brigham himself points out, there is a correlation of 0.67 between Beta scores and "school grade completed"; and any unprejudiced person who examines the Beta materials must admit that school training would be a factor in determining median scores if two groups, one entirely without school training and the other with reasonably good school education, were subjected to the tests. This is precisely what happened in the army. Large numbers of recruits who had had good schooling in non-English speaking countries took the Beta tests, along with large numbers of native-born and foreign-born illiterates who had had little or no schooling. Recent immigration has come most largely from countries where school facilities are relatively meager—most recently from countries that are very backward educationally; hence the gradual decrease in the Beta scores as we reach the more recently arrived immigrant-groups can be explained with a thoroughgoing consistency by reference to the educational factor.

I now pass to Professor Brigham's discussion of the national levels of intelligence as reflected by the Army scores. On his combined scale, the principal nations represented in the foreign-born draft rank as follows: England, Scotland, Holland, Germany, Denmark, Canada, Sweden, Norway, Belgium, Ireland, Austria, Turkey, Greece, Russia, Italy, Poland.

More than three fourths of the cases considered by Professor Brigham fall in the "late-arrival" groups and could have been affected little if at all by American education; hence if education had any influence upon the scores, this influence must be traced to the schools (and, of course, to the elementary schools) provided in the countries from which the soldiers came. Taking my data from the Report of the United States Commissioner of Education for 1912 (which gives the ratio of elementary-school enrollment to total population in foreign countries for the year 1910 or thereabouts), and checking the figures (in some cases with slight changes) by data contained in the *Statesmen's Yearbook,* I find between the above "intelligence" ranking and the "school" ranking of the same countries, a correlation of 0.84. In this computation I placed Turkey at the foot of the list in school facilities because no school data for Turkey were available. The fairer way would be to omit Turkey. If this is done and if the proportion of "A" and "B" men is made the basis of the intelligence-ranking, the correlation of "intelligence" with elementary-school facilities reaches the very impressive magnitude of 0.91. This is a shade higher than the corresponding figure for the twenty-six American states that have populations sufficiently stable to permit comparisons to be drawn between present levels of intelligence and school conditions a generation ago.

I have already demonstrated that differences found among the median scores of contingents of recruits from American states can be amply explained in terms of the educational facilities afforded by these states. I submit that the same explanation will hold with even greater force for the differences found among the various nationalities represented by the foreign-born draft. This is not to say that there are not in both cases real differences in the group-levels of native intelligence. These differences, however, have yet to be demonstrated. Personally I believe that they exist, but that, when large groups are considered, they become practically negligible. It is certainly clear from my earlier findings that, if all of the American states had had in 1900 school systems as efficient as were those of Massachusetts, Connecticut, and California at that time, the level of native-born American "intelligence" as revealed by the Army tests would have been substantially higher and the differences among the states far less in magnitude. It is an equally safe inference that, if all of the nations contributing to recent American immigration had had a generation ago elementary schools equal to those of England, Scotland, Holland, and Germany, the "intelligence" differences found by the Army tests and emphasized by Professor Brigham would have been reduced to a negligible minimum.

III

Let us now consider the basis of Professor Brigham's claim that the Nordic race represents the highest levels of native intelligence, and the correlative confirmation of Mr. Madison Grant's contention[9] that the long-headed blonds are beyond doubt the Chosen People and should proceed forthwith to realize to the full their manifest destiny.

Professor Brigham here depends upon arguments that are even more questionable than those which he advances in the earlier sections of his book. He constructs (p. 159) a table which purports to show the relative proportions of Nordic, Alpine, and Mediterranean stock in each of the important national groups. Sweden stands first with one hundred per cent of Nordic blood; Norway follows with ninety per cent; then come Denmark, Holland, and Scotland with eighty-five per cent, each; England, eighty per cent; British North America and Belgium, sixty per cent; Wales and Germany, forty per cent; France and Ireland, thirty per cent; Poland and Spain, ten; Italy, Russia, and Portugal, five per cent; Greece, Rumania, and Turkey, no per cent. (Inasmuch as Alpines and Mediterraneans are lumped together in his conclusions, we need not trouble ourselves with the relative proportions of these two strains.) This table, Professor Brigham says, was worked out "in collaboration with students of this subject" and is "only an approximation to the truth." He does not hesitate, however, to draw some very important and sweeping generalizations from this "approximation."

As to the relative intelligence of the three groups as thus distributed among the different nationalities, Professor Brigham finds that 12.3 per cent of the English-speaking Nordics were "A" and "B" men; 8.1 per cent of all Nordics; 5.7 per cent of non-English speaking Nordics; 3.8 per cent of Alpines; and 2.5 per cent of Mediterraneans. A high correlation between "Nordicism" and "intelligence" is thus apparently established. In spite of clear evidence of the operation of a language factor (note the difference between "English-speaking Nordics" and "all Nordics"!) Professor Brigham concludes that "the underlying cause of the nativity differences ... is race, and not language." (p. 174.) The educational factor he does not mention in this connection, for he has already demonstrated to his own satisfaction that education is a result and not a cause of intelligence; hence, even if one were to contend that the superior schools of the non-English speaking Nordics made a significant difference, Professor Brigham would rule out the contention *instanter*. In fact he says (p. 194):

---

9. Madison Grant: *The Passing of the Great Race.* New York, 1916.

If intelligence counts for anything in the competition among human beings, it is natural to expect that individuals of superior intelligence will adjust themselves more easily to their physical and social environment, and that they will endow their children not only with material goods, but with the ability to adjust themselves to the same or a more complex environment.... In the same way, our educational institutions are themselves a part of our own race heritage.

Now if Professor Brigham had followed his analysis of the Army report a little further, he would have found evidence that would either annihilate his assumption that "intelligence" is not affected by schooling or completely reverse his conclusions regarding the alleged supremacy of the Nordic stock. For example:

1. While no one can seriously doubt the general superiority of the whites over the negroes in native intelligence, the Army tests show clearly the tremendous influence of good schools in stimulating the growth of intelligence and the corresponding handicap imposed by poor schools. On pages 724–725 of the Army report will be found tables that distribute by states the scores made by literate negroes on Army Alpha. After computing the medians one finds that the literate negroes from Illinois not only surpassed the literate negroes from the South but also achieved a median score above the median scores of the literate whites from nine Southern states; that the literate negroes from New York surpassed the literate whites from five Southern states; that the literate negroes from Pennsylvania surpassed the literate whites from two Southern states; while for all Northern negroes reported, the median Alpha score surpasses the median Alpha score for the whites of Mississippi, Kentucky, and Arkansas.

   In view of the fact that the Southern whites, according to Professor Brigham's method of determining Nordicism, represent about the purest Nordic stock in the country, two alternatives are open: either (a) he must grant that schooling *did* affect the intelligence-ratings, or (b) his theory of Nordic superiority is knocked into a cocked hat.

2. Massachusetts and Connecticut have been literally overswept by a Mediterranean tide. In Massachusetts, for example, nearly one third of the present population is both foreign-born and heavily Mediterranean; and more than another third represents the second and third generations of similar immigrant stock. An analogous condition exists in Connecticut. And yet Massachusetts and Connecticut stand right up in the front rank among the forty-eight states on the Alpha tests as well as on every other measure of intelligence and efficiency that I have been able to apply. They are surpassed only by the far-western states and on some counts not even by these. What hap-

pens to the claim of an inevitable Nordic superiority in the light of such a comparison?

3. If the Nordic stock is so far and away superior in native intelligence and if (as Professor Brigham infers) superior native intelligence will inevitably provide good schools as part of the "heritage" that it passes on to its children, how comes it that the states in which the white population shows the highest proportions of Nordic blood have both the poorest schools and the lowest white "intelligence" as measured by Army Alpha, by adult white literacy, by the distribution of public libraries, by the proportion of leaders produced, and by every other standard that has been suggested?

4. If Professor Brigham will compute (using his own interesting formulae) the per cent of Nordic blood in the white populations of the several states and then correlate "Nordicism" as thus determined with white intelligence as indicated by Army Alpha (or any like measure) he will obtain a very respectable *negative* correlation (around –.50). In other words, if Professor Brigham's assumptions and methods are valid, the actual facts revealed by the Army tests prove just the reverse of the contention that he has set forth. Truly one may understand how William James felt when he wrote, a quarter of a century ago, "If the Anglo-Saxon race would drop its sniveling cant it would have a good deal less of a 'burden' to carry."[10]

If we pass to Europe, we might ask Professor Brigham to explain why the most stable and promising nation on the Continent to-day is Czecho-Slovakia—a country the dominant peoples of which are listed by Mr. Madison Grant[11] as true Alpines, closely akin to the Poles whom Professor Brigham apparently regards as the last word in Alpine inferiority.

I have no doubt that the pro-Nordic enthusiasts have plausible explanations for all of these apparent inconsistencies. The Irish, Italian, Hungarian, Greek, Portuguese, and French-Canadian elements in Massachusetts and Connecticut may be Nordics in disguise. The tall, long-headed, blue-eyed whites that people the southern Appalachian uplands may, for aught I know, be transformed overnight into stubby Alpines or swarthy Mediterraneans, and thus save the "Great Race" from the stigma of illiteracy and low Alpha scores. The negroes who came north, and whose children trained in Northern schools made as a group better Alpha scores than many of the Southern whites, may have been pale negroes with strong admixtures of real Nordic blood. And Czecho-Slovakia, now that it has

10. Henry James (ed.): *The Letters of William James.* Boston, 1920, vol. ii, p. 88.
11. Madison Grant: *The Passing of the Great Race.* New York, 1916, p. 128.

achieved a highly distinguished place among the nations, may suddenly be revealed as a Nordic island, surrounded on all sides by Alpine seas of Croats, Wends, Serbs, and Magyars. The collective imagination of our pro-Nordic writers has already demonstrated its agility; what it may be able to do when pressed I cannot venture to predict.

In the meantime, those of us whose imaginations are cribbed and confined by a prejudice in favor of facts will find in good schools and an effective educational stimulus an explanation for these phenomena that is reasonable, hopeful, and humane. Massachusetts and Connecticut have kept up the ideal of good schools, and while they have been overswept by a Mediterranean tide, and while they have sent to the Western states innumerable scions of their original Nordic stock, they still maintain a high rank among our most intelligent commonwealths. Can any one doubt that they will retain their leadership if only they keep alive their faith in good schools? The Nordics in the Southern states, even when playing the role of a dominant race, have discovered that without good schools both for their own children and for the children of the subject race, they are hopelessly handicapped in competition with the "Mediterraneans" of New York and New England and the "Alpines" of the Middle West. And as for Czecho-Slovakia, the clear explanation of her present status is to be found in a tradition of mass-education which dates from the era of Comenius and which, long before the outbreak of the Great War, had given to Moravia, Bohemia, and Silesia a literacy rating unsurpassed on the Continent.

IV

Professor Brigham's study appears, then, as a most questionable and biased interpretation of certain facts that can be far more reasonably interpreted in quite another way. Because he has not adequately set forth this alternative interpretation, and particularly because he makes no mention of the mass of evidence that supports it, his efforts must be regarded as either misinformed or prejudiced. Furthermore, of his two basic assumptions—the validity of the Army tests as measures of native intelligence-levels especially when applied to large heterogeneous groups, and the alleged percentile distributions of racial stock in national groups—the first has been proved to be a fallacy, and for the second not an iota of respectable evidence has been presented. Finally, from the ethical point of view, his conclusions, even if backed by evidence far more convincing than that which he sets forth, suggest no possible solution short of measures which, if put into effect, would quickly entail an inter-racial war. Into such a maelstrom, pro-Nordic propagandism is certainly heading.

Against this drab picture, I may be permitted to project the constructive program of the rational equalitarian. Because it is rational this program does not quarrel with facts; hence it does not deny racial differences in intelligence-levels. It recognizes a high degree of probability that the Negro race will never produce so large a proportion of highly gifted persons as will the white race. It recognizes a possibility that certain of the white strains may be more prolific in talent and genius than certain others; but it also holds that, in the present state of knowledge, invidious distinctions cannot safely be drawn among Nordics, Alpines, and Mediteraneans in this regard. It holds furthermore that the level of effective intelligence in any group of whatever race can be substantially raised through education. In support of this tenet it cites the investigations which prove beyond cavil that schooling exerts a positive and powerful influence in stimulating the growth of native intelligence.[12]

Resting his case upon these facts and assumptions, the rational equalitarian proposes: (1) a vast extension of educational facilities and a far-reaching refinement of educational materials and methods; and (2) among other objectives, the direction of educational agencies toward (a) the establishment of the ideal of race-purity in all major races, and (b) a voluntary acceptance of eugenic practices to the end that, *in all races,* the reproduction of less worthy stock may be reduced. He holds that coercion can never accomplish the ends that eugenics seeks but that appropriate education may lead to the desired practices. He holds especially that to seek these ends through either the annihilation or the subjugation of certain races would sound the death-knell of any race that undertook it— just as the thoroughly analogous effort on the part of a certain well-known nation has apparently sounded that nation's death-knell. He holds, then, that whether his proposals will work or not (and the clear indications are that they will work), they constitute the one and only hope of humanity.

The rational equalitarian, as we have said, does not quarrel with facts. Recognizing racial *differences* for what they are, he builds his program upon the far more numerous *resemblances* that now exist, and upon the already demonstrated possibility of multiplying such resemblances. Instead of emphasizing the forces that pull men apart, he would emphasize the forces that draw men together. Instead of intensifying biological differentiation, he would stimulate cultural integration. He believes that diverse racial stocks can learn to live together and to work together without necessitating a blend of blood, and that undesirable blends of blood can be prevented through education. His program, as compared with that of the radical

---

12. For example, Cyril Burt: *Mental and Scholastic Tests,* London, 1921; O. Bishop: "What is Measured by Intelligence Tests?" *Journal of Educational Research,* Jan. 1924.

hereditarian, promises to do all that the latter would do in promoting human evolution. It differs from the program of the hereditarian in being more nearly consistent with the observed facts, in being clearly in harmony with the ideals of humanity and democracy that have been winnowed and refined through the ages, and above all in being workable. The hereditarian's solution of the problem is intolerant of the facts that do not support it; it is openly inhumane and blatantly anti-democratic; and to make it work would involve an upheaval beside which the late war would look like an afternoon tea.

What is Professionalized Subject-Matter?: A Statement and Brief Development of Thesis
(1928)

Bagley addresses in this work one of the most troublesome of all philosophical problems related to curriculum for teaching teachers. He refuses to allow the profession of teaching to be separated from the various subject-area specialties. He battled this problem with a conception of "profession" that was different from what was being advocated by many of his colleagues.

"Professionalized subject-matter" is a phrase that Bagley uses in much of his writing. In this essay, he defines it carefully in order to counter the numerous misunderstandings of his ideas that were prevalent in the profession. With his philosophy of professionalized subject-matter, Bagley is, in short, trying to hold together the moral and the intellectual dimensions of curriculum for teaching teachers. His vision never took off, however, because the overwhelming majority of specialists in the intellectual disciplines wanted nothing to do with teachers (including the task of teaching teachers), and Progressive educators wanted to focus exclusively on process-based theories divorced from the subject-matter fields. Only when ideal ends—for example civic virtue, deliberation, and principles of teaching—are taken into account can these two pieces of curriculum be held together.

I regret very much that an ungainly term has become associated with the idea or conception that I have been asked to discuss with you this evening. To speak of the *professionalization* of subject-matter is almost to invite resentment that subject-matter or anything else should be treated by so inhumane a process,—whatever the process may be. I must assure you at the outset, then, that I have no dark designs on subject-matter, and no intention to treat it harshly or cruelly. On the contrary, what I mean by professionalizing subject-matter in the normal schools and teachers colleges might quite justly be thought of as a really serious attempt to humanize knowledge, to reveal its true meaning, to show how it has evolved out of human experiences and how it has helped men and women to solve their problems, and especially to show how it can be built into the experience of each oncoming generation. As I conceive of it, indeed, the whole purpose of professionalizing subject-matter is to make sure that knowledge will throb with life and meaning, and that it will enrich in the largest possible measure the lives of just as many people as possible.

In reflecting upon this problem and discussing it with my students and other friends over a long period of years, I have become more and more firmly convinced that the most important function of the professional school for teachers is to do this very thing: to enable the teacher to make knowledge really live in the experiences of boys and girls. I have become more and more firmly convinced, too, that in discharging this transcendent function, the professional school must place its chief dependence upon its subject-matter instructors.

It is at this point that the rub has come. In the development of professional education for teachers a sharp distinction has been made between a teacher's equipment in subject-matter and his equipment in the art or technique of teaching. The subject-matter equipment has generally been taken care of by instructors and departments that we have designated as "academic," while the theory and art of teaching have been taken care of by instructors and departments that we have called "professional." By our very terminology, then, we have implied that the subject-matter equipment is not part of the teacher's professional equipment. Further than this, the dualism between subject-matter and method has left the subject-matter specialists generally speaking with little sympathy for the all-important task of making subject-matter live in the experiences of boys and girls. That, they have assumed, is not their problem, but rather the problem of the professional departments,—the instructors in educational theory, psychology, and "method," and the supervisors of student-teaching.

The result of this division, in my judgment, has not been at all happy. In the first place, it has led to bickerings and jealousies among faculty groups. In many of our professional schools for teachers, there is either open hostility or at best an armed truce between the subject-matter departments and the so-called professional departments. Much more serious than this, however, is the power and influence that the so-called professional groups practically monopolize in determining the work of the lower schools. This is not their fault. A monopoly has simply been handed over to them. By refusing themselves to professionalize their courses, the subject-matter specialists have voluntarily surrendered their potential influence. My colleague, Dr. Evenden, has a very effective name for the courses which the professional departments offer to bridge the gap between mastery of subject-matter and the actual work of teaching boys and girls,—such courses as the psychology of elementary-school subjects, the teaching of the common branches, and the like. He calls them "George" courses, meaning that the subject-matter specialists have been content to "let George do it."

The same general problem is met even more acutely in the liberal-arts colleges and universities that attempt to prepare teachers. The subject-matter specialists in these institutions usually take a most contemptuous attitude toward the professors of education to whom by default the problem of adapting subject-matter to the needs and capacities of elementary and high-school pupils has been left. In recent numbers of both *The American Mercury* and *Harper's Magazine* there have appeared bitter attacks upon the professors of education. They have been accused of practically all of the sins on the calendar, and the righteous indignation of their academic colleagues has descended upon them. A few professors of education have resented these articles,—but not for long. And why not? Simply because they have been too busy doing necessary work that their critics have declined to do on the ground apparently that it might soil their hands or spot their lily-white reputations. And back of these criticisms, too, is a quite obvious suspicion on the part of the critics that "George," with all of his obvious faults and imperfections, is after all exerting a tremendous influence. He is, and it is an influence that he and his group ought not to monopolize; it is an influence that ought to be shared by his academic colleagues, or at least by a certain proportion of them who would prepare themselves to undertake the responsibilities. As a matter of fact in our country to-day the policies and practices of the lower schools are being determined in large part by professors of education,—and chiefly because these men and women alone have regarded the work of the lower schools as worth studying. They are of course not competent alone to solve the problems, and they should have especially the cooperation of their colleagues in the various fields of human scholarship and culture. Lacking this cooperation "George" is doing the best that he can with a huge task,— and I do not hesitate to say that in some cases I think that he is doing more harm than good.

As I see it, the influence both of the educational theorist and of the so-called educational scientist very distinctly needs the balance that the subject-matter specialist might well provide if he interested himself in the difficult art of teaching boys and girls. I do not mean by this that "George" should be dispensed with entirely. There is a place for the out-and-out student of education. But when we turn the entire field of elementary and secondary education over to him, we are giving him too large an order. We need only to glance at our prodigious professional literature to see how confused we are. And we need only to look at what is happening particularly in elementary education to find how our confusion is affecting the teaching of boys and girls. For some reason or another "George" is uncannily adept in the fine art of messing things up. Now it is perhaps true that things need messing up in education as a first step in making them better; but I have serious doubts that some of our recent efforts have carried us or will carry us very far forward.

Let me give a few examples of what I mean. For the past few years "George" has been busily engaged in what he has liked to call "curriculum reconstruction." In this obviously important work he has found it necessary to introduce a host of new terms ostensibly to cover important ideas. As a matter of fact, many of these terms either merely cover up our ignorance or are substitutes for much better terms that have, for one reason or another, become unpopular in our professional circles. The current vogue of such terms as "activities," "objectives," and "attitudes" illustrates what I mean by the introduction of words that merely cover up our ignorance; and the substitution of the term "social control" for the much more virile and significant term "discipline" indicates the lengths to which we go in trying to avoid even the barest suggestion of anything unpleasant in the processes of education. By far the most serious charge against "George" is that he is partly and I think pretty largely responsible for the very serious softening of the educational fiber that has been going on for the past two or three decades. Having protested in season and out of season against these softening tendencies I believe that I may justly claim a personal alibi in connection with this charge.

Now one hope that I have had in urging a greater emphasis upon subject-matter in the professional education of teachers is that the subject-matter specialist, working as he does in a much more limited field than that of the educationist, and concerned as he is with much more definite and tangible materials, will counteract looseness and softness toward which, for some inexplicable reason, the educationist almost always tends. But the subject-matter specialist cannot exert a corrective influence as long as he holds himself aloof from the lower schools and their problems. He may sneer at the educationist and proclaim in his own classes the utter futility of "George" and all of his works; but that will get him nowhere.

"George" may be all that is said about him, but he is right there on the job, and the man who is on the job is the man who wields the influence.

The problem has become, then, one of getting the subject-matter specialist on this job, at least to the extent of having him reflect in some of his courses the point of view of the teacher in the lower schools, with some concern regarding what elements among his own materials can be profitably taught to boys and girls and how such elements may be made to vibrate with life and meaning. If even so much as this could be done, I have contended, we could dispense with some of the courses in educational theory some of which, as we all know, are extremely thin, and in many of which there is a great deal of overlapping.

I confess that I have been surprised that this proposal has met with so much opposition from the very people who would seem at first glance most likely to support it,—namely, the subject-matter specialists themselves. Many of them have asked very testily how I could propose that subject-matter and method could be taught at the same time. This attitude merely shows how deep-lying is the dualism that we have allowed to develop in connection with the professional education of teachers. As long as people hold this view, we may be certain what ought to be the finest of all fine arts will remain very largely a trade, and that its technique, which ought to grow out of the substance with which teaching deals, will remain a mere bag of tricks.

Just as surprising is the criticism that has come to my attention from Dr. Bachman of the General Education Board, who—I am told—has characterized my proposal as the most dangerous notion now abroad in American education. If so, I should say that it must be fairly perilous. Just why Dr. Bachman should oppose my efforts to put more substance into the professional education of teachers and dispense with some of the froth I am unable to see.

The topic assigned to me on the program is "Twenty Years' Progress in the Professionalization of Subject-Matter." I have not said very much as yet about progress, and both my time and your patience are now exhausted. I should not leave you with the impression, however, that no progress has been made.

The first extended study of the problem was published in 1922,—E. D. Randolph's "The Professional Treatment of Subject-Matter" (Baltimore: Warwick and York). Since that time there have been several monographs dealing with the problems of professional treatment in specific subject-matter fields. A substantial beginning has also been made in the construction of textbooks for professional content courses of collegiate grade. These have been prepared by subject-matter specialists who are also close students of education and both familiar with and sympathetic toward the problem of teaching in the lower schools.

Beyond all this, however, and perhaps more important than anything else, is the greatly increased recognition of the problem in two institutions that prepare many of the instructors for the normal schools and undergraduate teachers' colleges. I refer particularly to the George Peabody College for Teachers and to the Teachers College of Columbia University.

At Peabody, an effort is being made to discover in the several subject-matter courses the important contributions that they may make to the work of the teacher and to bring these contributions into high relief in the organization and conduct of the courses. A member of the college staff has been relieved of other duties and assigned to study the various courses offered and the way in which they are taught. All of this is for the purpose of making these courses maximally helpful to teachers in the lower schools.

At Teachers College our subject-matter departments are much more important than they were ten years ago,—more important, indeed, than they have been since they were known as "secondary" departments, at a time when the College was predominantly an undergraduate institution and prepared many teachers for the high schools.

In recent years, Teachers College has become almost exclusively a graduate school, and its graduate students are preparing chiefly for supervision, for normal-school and teachers' college service, and for administrative posts. When this change in student-personnel became apparent, there was a general conviction among the members of the staff that the subject-matter departments of the College would be superfluous, that the courses offered in the College would be exclusively technical and professional, and that whatever subject-matter work our students wished to have could be provided in other colleges of the University.

It was very soon discovered, however, that this would not solve the problem. It was found that, even for graduate students preparing for elementary-school supervision or for normal-school instructorships, advanced courses in education alone did not suffice. It was found, too, that the purely academic subject-matter courses offered elsewhere in the University would not entirely answer the purpose. In short, there was a real need for what I have termed professional-content courses—this time on the graduate level. Our recent development has been distinctly toward the development of such courses. Today the group in Teachers College which has the largest enrollment of major students for the Master's degree is the English group.

These facts I advance as significant of the fundamental importance of the type of work which the professional treatment of subject-matter represents. They offer further testimony to my main contention,—namely, that the most unfortunate fallacy in the professional education of teachers is the assumption that only technique and educational theory are "professional,"—and that to equip the teacher with substantial materials for teaching is a task that has nothing professional about it.

It is time that this dualism, which has done untold harm to education, should be thoroughly resolved. I repeat that the fine art of teaching is something more than a mere bag of tricks. The notion of a "general method" of teaching which will be indiscriminately applicable to all materials is just as much of a delusion and a snare now when the "project method" or the "contract plan" or the "mastery formula" is the fashion as it was when the "five formal steps" were regarded as the universal panacea for all of our educational ills. Each of these and other theories of teaching has its place, but it is a place that must always be determined by the closest consideration of the subject-matter to be taught. Techniques which are merely "fastened on" to subject-matter instead of growing out of the very nature and function of subject-matter have not helped us much in the past nor will they help us much in the future. Only the "teacher-scholar" can resolve this fatal dualism. Unless our professional schools for teachers can develop these teacher-scholars and give them a position of significance in their organization, the professional school as such, I believe, will soon disappear. The preparation of teachers will become a minor function of the liberal-arts colleges, taken care of exclusively by detached departments of education, which will essay to solve the most intricate and important of all human problems on a necessarily superficial basis.

I believe that the time is peculiarly opportune for a much more extended attack on this problem than we have been able to make in the past. The lengthening of the curricula for elementary-school teachers is making it possible to give to these teachers a much richer equipment. We can insure both a broader outlook and a firmer and more dependable foundation. What may this mean to the lower schools? It will mean very little if the teacher regards the so-called academic courses as not having any relationship to the work of teaching on the lower levels; it will mean very little if the teacher in his exposure to these courses has gained the notion that what he calls culture is a thing apart from his daily work. In the professional education of physicians and engineers, it may be legitimate and wise to distinguish sharply between the vocational and the cultural but not in the education of teachers; for what we call culture is not only a part of the teacher's professional equipment,—it is altogether the most important part. If, then, the broader outlook and the firmer foundation made possible by our longer curricula can be directed definitely toward enriching the lives of children,—if these developments can be made to mean a wider extension of culture among the masses of the people,—a forward step of large magnitude will have been taken. My very firm conviction is that this cannot be left to chance. I recently interviewed a number of young women just finishing their first half-year teaching in the elementary school. They had all taken courses in the so-called professional and academic subjects in preparation for their work. I tried to learn from each the types of courses that they had drawn upon in their teaching. With but one exception the testimony of the teachers was that the only helpful courses were those that had been taught in very close connection with the elementary-school problem,—most of them "George" courses accompanied by observation and participation, but also a few subject-matter courses where a specific effort had been made to show what could be done with materials in the lower schools. All the rest of their preparatory work was detached and isolated. They frankly said that they were doing nothing with it.

One teacher, however, was the exception, a young woman of unusual intelligence and deeply interested in teaching. She answered my first question by saying that she did not know of any course that she had taken that she did not draw upon in one way or another in her teaching,—and she gave me clear-cut illustrations one after another even showing how she had drawn on her Latin to tell some fascinating stories about words to fifth-graders, and on her French for some interesting folk-lore that was not available in English. That teacher's "culture" was more than a personal adornment, and she was using it for something besides getting relief from the "humdrum" work of teaching children. She was using it to illuminate the lives of children,—and because she could use it in this way the work itself was very far from humdrum.

Now this teacher had an unusual capacity for "transferring" her training from one field to another. The others did not, but their experiences proved clearly enough that they could transfer and transfer effectively when illustrative connections are made and clearly demonstrated in the preparatory work. What they were carrying over most frequently were the "George" courses,—and by no means all of these. This means that, in general, their tendency was to carry over only the most superficial elements in their training. The most substantial and fundamental phases of their training remained things quite apart. It is this unnecessary wastage that I believe the point of view that I have set forth will do something to correct.

The Profession of Teaching in the United States (1929)[1]

Bagley delivered this paper to the International Institute at Teachers College, Columbia University, at the request of his good friend and colleague, Isaac Kandel. He begins the paper with a brief history of the profession of teaching in the United States. He discusses the impact of the establishment of professional schools for teaching teachers at private universities like Chicago, Columbia, Stanford, and Yale, as well as at public universities like Wisconsin, California (Berkeley), and Illinois, where he helped to establish the School of Education in the 1910s. He also provides a brief history of the development of normal schools and teachers colleges.

This essay, one of Bagley's longest in this collection, proves that many, if not all, of the challenges that face the task of teaching teachers today have been with us for decades. He makes plain some of his views on such troublesome dualisms as theory versus practice, elementary teaching versus high school teaching, administration versus teaching, teaching versus research, and education as an industry versus education as a moral enterprise. He concludes the article on a positive note by proclaiming his hope that his profession would be successful at meeting the challenges that lay ahead.

The development of American education has been beset from the outset by handicaps and obstacles, many of which undoubtedly confront our fel-

---

1. A lecture given December 18, 1928, in the course, "American Education," offered especially for foreign students by the International Institute of Teachers College.

Forgotten Heroes of American Education, pages 167–179

low-workers in other countries, but some of which are indigenous, so to speak, to our own soil, growing out of our own peculiar traditions and *mores*: our deep-seated and thoroughly dynamic ideals of local self-government; the diverse standards of our conglomerate population; the sharply contrasting needs and interests of our urban and rural people; our fondness for quantity-production and our delight in numerical magnitudes; our distrust of the expert; our zeal in making laws and our zest in breaking them; and a host of other factors and forces, many of which work in quite opposite directions, but all of which have cooperated to make extremely difficult the development of an educational system which would be constructively effective on a nation-wide basis.

And yet these unique factors in our problem, even though they have constituted serious handicaps to educational effort, have also been, perhaps for that very reason, a stimulating challenge, the continued response to which has resulted in progress of a most substantial sort, with promises for the future that should give hope and inspiration to those in other countries who are facing problems similar in difficulty although in many instances quite different in kind.

The advancement in the status of the teacher's calling, while the most recent of the large developments in American education, is in some respects the most significant and promises for the future the most far-reaching results. It is also, I believe, a development quite unprecedented in the history of education and, so far as I know, it is unparalleled in other countries.

In reviewing the handicaps that have beset this development, it goes without saying that many of them are not at all peculiar to our country. Something akin to contempt for the work of teaching, especially in the lower schools, has found expression, I suppose, in all ages and in all climes. It was the Englishman, Bernard Shaw, who coined the famous epigram, "Those who can, do; those who can not, teach." The immortal Boswell, in a ponderous effort to explain why Samuel Johnson was so complete and pitiable a failure as a teacher of youth, ventured the following sage reflection:

> The art of communicating instruction, of whatever kind, is much to be valued; and I have ever thought that those who devote themselves to this employment, and do their duty with diligence and success, are entitled to very high respect from the community, as Johnson himself often maintained. Yet I am of the opinion that the greatest abilities are not only not required in this office, but render a man less fit for it.

While this patronizing attitude of thinly veiled contempt for the work of teaching is no new thing and not at all confined to our own country, I believe that it has constituted a far more serious handicap to the development of our profession here than it has elsewhere.

In the first place, until recently, the teaching personnel of our public schools has been transient and unstable. Twenty years ago, the average period of service of the public-school teacher was not more than four years, which meant that tens of thousands of teachers remained only one, two or three years in the service. The occupation was distinctly recognized in most communities as temporary, and those who from force of circumstances were compelled to make it a life work were naturally regarded with something akin to pity. For the able and ambitious, teaching was openly taken up as a stepping-stone to what both the teacher and the public thought of as worthier callings. One of the early university professors of education, in whose classes I sat thirty years ago, laughingly referred to public-school teachers as a group made up chiefly of immature women and feeble men.

Along with this condition, of course, went the parallel fact that the teachers as a whole were pitifully unprepared for their work. Twenty years ago, more than a majority of the public-school teachers had had no education beyond the high school, and more than ten thousand were limited in their education to what the elementary school provided.

Although every state maintained professional schools for teachers, not one in four of those employed in the public schools was a product of such an institution. As short a time ago as 1916, Judd and Parker asserted in an official bulletin of the Bureau of Education that the United States gave less attention to the training of teachers than did any other civilized nation. With brief tenure and lack of training quite naturally went meager compensation, and in a country where occupations won public regard in direct proportion to the material rewards that they provided, this condition was in itself a sufficient stigma to the teacher's calling.

Closely related to the handicaps which transiency, instability, low training standards and meager preparation placed in the way of professional development was the unequal competition with other occupations for talented recruits. This was most serious, of course, in connection with the problem of drawing able men into the profession. Not only did the vast development of business and industry multiply the opportunities for building huge individual fortunes, but the spectacular achievements of our captains of industry, finance and organization caught the public imagination, bringing to successful efforts in those fields a measure of renown and popular adulation beside which even the material rewards were of quite subordinate value.

There are one or two incidents in my own life that may give a concrete setting to the conditions to which I have referred. Some forty years ago I was a schoolboy in the city of Detroit. As cities went, even in those days,

Detroit was an unpretentious, rather conservative urban center, surpassed in wealth, population and promise by nearly a score of American cities. One day in the early nineties, while walking along one of the streets of the city, I saw a little group gathered around a queer-looking conveyance drawn up alongside the curb. I joined the crowd, and found that the object of their interest was what we then called a horseless carriage. A young man was rather frantically engaged in overhauling the machinery, every now and again making a desperate effort to get the clumsy contraption to show some signs of life. As long as I watched, his efforts were rewarded only by a wheezy cough from the crude engine, echoed, of course, by the jeers of the crowd. That jeering crowd little dreamed that the scene which they were witnessing for the first time would be reenacted within the next thirty years on ten thousand city streets and country roads by hundreds of thousands of exasperated drivers of self-propelled vehicles; still less did they dream that the evolution of that clumsy, horseless carriage would cause their city to outdistance all but three of its competitors in population and wealth and make it the world center for the most highly organized branch of modern industry; least of all did they dream that the young man who was struggling so desperately to conjure a vital spark in that newfangled internal-combustion engine was in all likelihood the man who, within three decades, would be recognized and acclaimed as the type and symbol of American genius at its own unique best.

It is not at all to be wondered at that the marvelous expansion of American industry, with its overwhelming rewards of wealth and fame for successful effort, should have cast a shadow over fields of endeavor less spectacular, less appealing to the concrete imagination of the public, less obviously creative of new values. It is small wonder that, with competition of this sort, the latter fields were unable to attract so large a share of superior talent as has been the case in many other countries. The relative paucity of our national contributions to pure science, to literature, music and the other fine arts, and to statesmanship of the first order may be explained at least in part by this factor. Obviously an occupation so modestly rewarded as teaching and one that offers so few opportunities for renown would have, under these conditions, a relatively low place in public esteem.

The effect of all this upon the morale of the teaching group may be readily inferred. Those who remained for any length of time in the profession acquired, in many cases, an inferiority complex of large dimensions. They openly regretted that they had not taken up another occupation. Just as openly, they advised young people against teaching as a career and commiserated one another over their hard lot. About eight years ago in visiting the college in Michigan where I spent my undergraduate days, I called on one of the two or three of my former instructors who still survived. He asked me what I had been doing over the years and where I was located. I told him that I had been teaching and was still engaged in that occupation. Then he asked me where I had come from when I entered college. He shook his head sadly when I told him, and then, with a sincere sigh of pity, he said, "And just think what you might have become if you had only gone back to Detroit and entered the automobile business." I left his office and my old college with a deep sense of my failure to reflect any worthy credit on my *alma mater.*

I could multiply concrete examples of this sort from my own experience and that of my friends, but enough has been said to indicate one of the most serious obstacles that the development of a real profession of teaching has confronted in our country. With what I have said regarding the instability, inadequate training and transiency of the great rank and file of teachers, this may give us a sufficient background against which to project the advances that our profession has made.

To-day, many of the conditions to which I have referred are radically different from what they were fifteen, ten, even five years ago. The period of service of the average teacher has been extended from four or five years to at least eight or nine years. The level of training has advanced to a much higher plane—where fifteen years ago the median public-school teacher had no more than a high-school education at most, today it is probable that 60 per cent of these teachers have had two years or more in advance of high-school graduation. In several states the proportion is nearly 100 per cent. The number of college graduates in the public-school service has also shown a remarkable increase. The enrolment in our normal schools and teachers' colleges has doubled in the past five years, and the output of these professional schools is now so large that, for the first time in our history, there is an actual surplus of trained teachers in most of the cities and in some of the states.

This condition has led to significant advances in the standards of our professional schools. Many of the former two-year normal schools have advanced the requirements for elementary-school teachers to three years and some are now on a full four-year basis. Paralleling these advances there has been a really remarkable development within the profession, some of the outstanding trends of which I shall mention a little later. In public esteem, too, the teacher's calling has made significant advances.

Like most profound changes, these developments have been brought about in part by conscious and deliberate purposing, and in part by the fortunate operation of forces and factors that are largely beyond either individual or social control. Let us consider first these latter, impersonal factors.

Primarily, of course, one must recognize the unprecedented material prosperity of our country. This has made possible both a wider extension of educational opportunity and a keener demand for better schools and better teachers. As a result, the level of teachers' salaries has advanced significantly, and is still advancing in spite of a tendency toward the stabilization of wage and salary levels in other occupations. Teaching can now compete with other callings on terms much more nearly equal than have prevailed heretofore.

This, however, does not tell the whole story, for the contrasts with the spectacular rewards of business and industry still persist. Yet for some reason the influence of this contrast is less noticeable to-day than it was only a few years ago. This may be due to a recognition on the part of the public that these huge material rewards in the very nature of things can go to only a very few of the most capable or the most fortunate, while the rank and file must necessarily fare much more modestly.

Back of all this, however, is another set of facts, the full significance of which we are probably not yet in a position to grasp. The leaven of the Industrial Revolution, which has been responsible for so many fundamental social changes, is still working, and working in a more thoroughgoing fashion in our country than anywhere else. The report of the American Federation of Labor, recently published, reveals the astounding fact that, in spite of the vast development of American industry in the present decade, the number of persons actually engaged in manufacturing has decreased by approximately a million since 1920. In other words, the improvement of automatic machinery has not only kept pace with the expansion of industry; it has sent a million workers to seek other means of earning a living. In this country, too, much more than in other countries, the influence of the Industrial Revolution has profoundly affected agriculture. Power-driven machinery has apparently replaced no fewer than 800,000 farm workers since 1920.

As a mere layman in economics, it would be presumptuous of me to attempt an interpretation of these facts. I can not escape the conclusion, however, that they are related in a very direct way to the opportunities that our profession has recently enjoyed to augment its numbers, advance its standards and stabilize its service. If I am right in my inferences, these developments in invention and industrial organization are actually driving men and women out of industry and farming into the white-collar occupations. Not only have the traditional professions grown in numbers— there are 250,000 more professional workers now than in 1920, according to the Federation's report—but a veritable multitude of other white-collar occupations are advancing toward a professional status in the sense that specific and often prolonged courses of education are willingly undertaken by those seeking either employment or advancement. Banks, department stores, the great hotel syndicates, insurance companies and public service corporations are developing elaborate schools for the training of their personnel. In at least one of the big insurance companies the vice-president in charge of education is one of the highest paid and most highly respected of the executives. With this emphasis upon specialized training, there has naturally been a corresponding emphasis upon an extended and thoroughgoing general education which shall serve as a background for the specialized courses; hence another reason why the high-school enrolment has trebled in fifteen years and why the college enrolment has doubled in ten years.

May I say parenthetically that it is of the utmost significance to education that this recent turn of the Industrial Revolution has not only reduced the proportion of workers needed in industry and farming, but has also increased the numbers needed in the white-collar occupations? The development of type-setting machinery, for example, made it possible for one operator to do the work of four compositors, and thus reduced the demand for the old-time printer, but the economy and efficiency of the new process greatly multiplied the demand for writers, editors, illustrators and advertising specialists. In fact, every department of automatic machines for mass-production has opened new fields of useful employment almost all of which have meant a stepping-up of the intellectual level of the work involved. Within the past decade this change has been going on with unprecedented acceleration; hence the heavy demands now made upon the schools and colleges are something more than a mere reflex of our economic prosperity; in a very real sense, they are the expression of a tremendously enlarged need on the part of millions of people for a type of instruction and discipline that will mean for them a genuine intellectual advance. Hence the recent controversy in our field regarding the possibilities of raising through education the mass-levels of effective intelligence is concerned with something more than a merely academic question. Upon the issue that this controversy involves hangs the future of our industrialized civilization.

I have suggested that the recent development of our profession has been conditioned in part by impersonal forces, largely-economic in character, which have operated to expand the field of our service, to increase the demands made upon us and to give us more and better recruits. The net result has been an almost complete transformation of the conditions under which we have been working. May I impress particularly the fact that, so far as its outward manifestations are concerned, this transformation has come very suddenly—almost overnight, so to speak? Many of our fellow-workers are still rubbing their eyes and wondering whether it is not all a dream. Others are still, in a manner of speaking, fast asleep—working on programs which reflect needs that seemed genuine enough a few years ago, but which can now be seen as based upon quite erroneous assumptions regarding the trends of contemporary civilization;

programs, for example, that would keep the farm boys on the farms to compete with gasoline engines and combined harvesters; and programs for premature vocational training based on the theory that the white-collar occupations are overcrowded when they are apparently the only occupations that have not been seriously overcrowded in the past few years and are to-day the occupations in which there are evidences of the greatest expansion.

It need hardly be said that the situation which confronts us is fairly unique to our own country. Other nations undoubtedly need heavier emphasis upon agricultural and trade education and less emphasis upon intellectual education. Be that as it may, it is clear enough that some of our own students of education have made some rather bad guesses during the past two decades and that some of them are still repeating their stereotyped pleas even though the need for their particular variety of reform no longer exists. On the other hand, it is equally true that the progress of our profession has been influenced in a very powerful positive fashion by the students of education. While they have undoubtedly made mistakes in some of their efforts to define social problems and to construct programs that would work toward the solution of these problems, they have played an important part in laying the foundations upon which a real and great profession of teaching is even now arising.

For upward of thirty years, a steadily increasing number of men and women have been devoting their lives to the serious study of the educational problem. The pioneers of this group were a few scattering school executives who conceived of their duties as comprehending something beyond the machinery of organization and the routine of administration, and who set a splendid example of constructive leadership and truly creative effort. One of these men was William Torrey Harris, who infused into the city school system of St. Louis a vigorous new life and who later served with distinction as the federal commissioner of education. Another was Francis W. Parker, who, as head of the schools of Quincy, Massachusetts, was the founder in America of what we now call the progressive school of educational theory; another was William H. Maxwell, the first superintendent of the schools of Greater New York. A fourth was Calvin Kendall, for many years superintendent of schools in Indianapolis and during the latter part of his life commissioner of education for the State of New Jersey.

Among the early colleagues and companions of these executives were the first professors of education in the colleges and universities. The real development of these departments of education may be dated from about 1890. Two years before, Clark University had been founded under the leadership of Stanley Hall, and during the following decade Clark was a nursery of educational ideals and enthusiasms. Then came the development of Teachers College under James E. Russell, and at the University of Chicago the pioneer work of John Dewey. From Clark and Columbia and Chicago men and women in increasing numbers went out to other colleges and universities either to establish or to remodel on a true university basis the departments of education. State universities, like those of Wisconsin, Iowa, Minnesota, California and Illinois, became in their turn centers of instruction, research and inspiration directed toward the problems of teaching and learning, of administration and supervision in the public schools. Private and endowed institutions like Peabody, Stanford, Yale and Harvard assumed their share of the great task.

The influence of this development of the university study of education upon the profession of teaching has been profound. In the first place, it has provided for the professional education of teachers a substantial body of knowledge. The recency of this development is exemplified by the fact that many of the men who have done the pioneer work are still in their prime. Some of them indeed have already addressed you in this course, and others will address you. Dr. Thorndike spoke to you last week of the work that has been done here and at other centers in the strictly scientific study of education, but with the modesty of the true scientist, he did not tell you of the mighty part that he has played in it.

A second influence of the university study of education has been a new access of self-respect on the part of the teaching personnel. The inferiority complex, to which I referred as one of the handicaps to our professional development, is gradually but certainly giving place to a sense of professional pride and dignity, tempered as it should be and as I hope it always will be, by a keen sense of the complexities of our problem and of the serious responsibilities which one must assume who would do even the humblest work in the field of teaching.

A third influence is one of the most significant of all. The university study of education has played a most important part in integrating the teaching profession. As Dean Russell told you a few weeks ago, something akin to the old-world caste distinction between the education of the masses and the education of the classes has persisted even in our unit system which otherwise so closely articulates the elementary and secondary schools. With us, the distinction has been one primarily of training and material rewards. The elementary-school teacher has represented a narrower and briefer training than the high-school teacher and even now receives in most of our school systems a distinctly lower salary. It has been a popular belief, shared by many members of the profession itself, that the work of teaching increases in difficulty, dignity and importance as one goes up the age scale. The university study of education has probably done more than anything else to reveal the fallacy of this popular belief, and to correct the injustice that has been done to the younger children in our schools by a deliberate policy which uses the lower grades as the testing ground for the immature and inexperienced teachers, the permanent abode of the weak and the indolent, and the final resting-place of the old and decrepit. To-day there is a growing conviction that no phase or field of teaching can lay valid claim to being more difficult or more important than any other phase. Discriminations and distinctions as to salaries are breaking down, as, for example, in the gradual extension of the single-salary schedule which does away with all distinctions except those that are based upon training, experience and meritorious service.

This general movement has been a powerful force in integrating our profession vertically, so to speak. Other forces have been operating to integrate the profession horizontally or geographically. Chief among these are our educational organizations. Foreign students sometimes wonder why, with our lack of any centralized educational authority in the nation as a whole, with the lack even of highly centralized state systems, our schools all over the country are in fundamental ways very much alike, dominated by the same aims and ideals, following fairly similar programs of study, governed by essentially uniform standards. The answer is simple. While our school systems are essentially local, the teaching profession is essentially national. For seventy years the educational leaders of the nation have met annually to discuss their common problems, but it has been only within the past twenty years that the state and national organizations have really represented the profession as a whole. Today these organizations are made up of, and controlled very largely by, the rank and file of elementary and secondary teachers. The National Education Association has grown in active membership from 10,000 to 200,000 in a single decade. Its policies are now determined by a representative assembly made up largely of delegates elected by the state associations. Many of the latter, in turn, are controlled by similar representative assemblies elected by district and local associations. The total enrolment in all of these organizations aggregates nearly three quarters of a million, which means that three out of every four members of our profession can have a vote and a voice in determining where our profession will go and how it will get there—in formulating our collective ideals and devising the means of realizing them through collective action. To this end the national association employs a headquarters staff with a personnel of more than one hundred men and women, including expert research workers, editors, legislative agents, publicity agents and specialists in the major educational fields. Several of the state organizations have similar staffs, and practically all of them employ full-time secretaries and publish official journals. May I emphasize the fact that this development has taken place almost entirely within a single decade?

One of the striking characteristics of this and other phases of our professional development has been the clear-cut tendency toward a thoroughgoing democracy. Not only are the distinctions between the elementary-school service and the high-school service being obliterated, but the equally unfortunate distinctions between the classroom teacher and the executive and supervisory officials are being minimized. In our professional organizations, as in our classes in education, all the workers in our field can meet on a common footing.

This tendency, which has been abetted by many of the administrators themselves, merits an especial emphasis in a discussion of the profession of teaching in the United States. It is distinctly a conscious effort to counteract in education some of the admitted evils that elaborate organization has brought about in business and industry. In the latter fields, the magnification of the executive and supervisory officers in contrast with those who do the first-hand work has perhaps been inevitable. Quite naturally, as our school systems expanded, a similar hierarchy of administrative authority was established, and the distinctions involved in this administrative hierarchy became in effect professional distinctions. To be transferred from the first-hand work of teaching boys and girls to an executive or administrative post was generally, and still is in many places, looked upon as a professional promotion. Under these conditions a large city school system became quite analogous to a great factory with its board of directors, its superintendent, managers, foremen, bosses and "hands." In school work, the classroom teachers were the "hands."

Now whatever may be the advantages or the dangers of such a hierarchy in business and industry, it works veritable mischief when applied to education. A simple contrast will, I think, make this clear.

If I buy an automobile I am not particularly concerned, except from a humanitarian point of view, with the workmen who have actually put it together. I can be reasonably certain that a few highly competent engineers designed the car, that a few others devised elaborate machinery for making and testing the various parts, and that a competent hierarchy of executives, superintendents, managers, foremen and bosses formed a responsible overhead for supervising its construction. The factory hands who operated the automatic machinery, screwed up the nuts, clinched the cotter-pins and sprayed on the paint and varnish: these may have been morons or they may have been near-geniuses; they may have had no interest whatsoever in their work beyond their pay-checks or they may have been true craftsmen with a fine pride in good workmanship; they may have been human automata going through their motions with as little real understanding of what it all meant as the machines that they operated, or they may have been men of keen insight, seeing their work in clear relation to the completed product. To me, merely as a purchaser of an automobile, it would make little difference. I can trust the machinery of production and testing under the supervision of the overhead. In fact, I can be fairly certain that if any one of the factory-hands were a near-genius and tremendously interested in his work for its own sake and able to see his work clearly in its relation to the completed product, he would very quickly be taken from the ranks and promoted to the overhead.

So much if I should buy an automobile.

When I send my children to school, however, my attitude toward the person who does the actual, first-hand work of their education is almost completely reversed. It is true that I would wish plans and specifications of that education to be well drawn by highly competent students of the problem; I would like the text-books to be authoritative and well-written; I would like the tests to be objective and accurate; I would like an organization that would guarantee a healthful school environment. But above all I would want for my children a real teacher. No virtues of the "overhead" could compensate for a teacher who had no interest in his work, who saw nothing beyond his pay-check, who found no joy and felt no pride in doing his work as well as it could be done irrespective of the material rewards that it brought, who had no vision of what it meant and no understanding of what his efforts contributed to the completed product.

One of the prominent objectives of our profession at the present time is to give to those who do the actual first-hand work of teaching an adequate recognition. Within the past ten years there has been a distinct tendency toward the participation of classroom teachers in the construction of educational policies and programs. In some school systems, councils elected by the teachers have a recognized function in the government of the schools. Probably the most characteristic expression of this tendency, however, is found in the work that is now going on all over the country in the revision and construction of curricula by groups of classroom teachers.

While practices such as these tend to dignify the actual first-hand work of teaching, they have, I think, an even deeper significance. They represent a quite new type of control for public education—and a type of control which has vast possibilities for the future. It goes without saying that some of the results will be disappointing. There must necessarily be groping and stumbling and blundering; but in the end the progress that is made is likely to be both substantial and enduring.

And this I take it is the fundamental justification of democracy as a mode of social control. Autocratic leadership gets results more quickly; and, under extremely competent leadership, the results may mean genuine progress. But dependence upon autocratic leadership suffers under two handicaps. In the first place, a really competent leader may not appear for years or even generations. In the second place, progress which is made possible only by a dictatorship is not likely to be sustained when the strong hand loses its grip. Given a reasonably high level of trained intelligence, the democratic group will be able to carry on even if competent leadership does not appear; and although its progress may be slow, it is much more likely to be certain and sustained.

I have attempted to present in general outline the development of the profession of teaching in the United States. I have called attention to some of the typical handicaps that this development has encountered; to the economic forces which have transformed in a striking fashion some of these handicaps; to the contributions that the students of education have made to our professional development; and to some of the factors that have worked toward professional solidarity and integration. I have probably set forth certain of the characteristics of our profession as though they were full-fledged achievements rather than ideals and aspirations many of which are still far from realization. My aim has been, however, to portray substantial trends, in the future fruition of which some of our dreams may come true. Certain it is that the present situation is full of promise. Whether this great army of teachers, now numbering in all branches of education upward of a million men and women, can think together and work together toward the fulfillment of this promise is another question. There are, of course, social forces and economic factors that will constitute handicaps in the future as similar forces and factors have been handicaps in the past. But personally I am optimistic; the transformation that I have myself witnessed in thirty years is so thoroughgoing that I can not but believe that another generation will carry us much further on the road to better things. It is literally true that through our profession every significant unit in our vast population can be touched and quickened. It is within our power as an organized and responsible group to make the American school the greatest single constructive force in American life. I have every faith that our profession will prove neither recreant nor inadequate to its great trust and its great opportunity.

The Teacher's Contribution to Modern Progress

(1929)[1]

When he delivered this commencement address at Colorado State Teachers College in 1929, Bagley was the nation's leading voice on teacher education. He was relentless in his advocacy for raising the status of classroom teachers. He boldly asserts in the address that elementary schools are the most important institutions in all of American democracy. His commitments to democracy, the profession of teaching, and the craft of teaching teachers are evident throughout his comments.

Bagley challenges the criticisms of democracy that had gained notoriety following World War I. He argues for the ideal of universal education, which, as he points out, only can be accomplished through well-supported, well designed, powerful institutions for teaching teachers. He concludes the address by expressing his hope that the institutions of higher education that dedicate themselves to teaching teachers would one day be recognized for the essential role they play in American democracy.

It is a privilege for me to be present on this important occasion. It is a privilege to congratulate these students upon the successful completion of their work in this school. If I may consider myself as representing, in a very humble way, the great profession of teaching, I am very proud indeed to

---

1. This is the address given by Dr. William Chandler Bagley at the thirty-ninth commencement exercise at Colorado State Teachers College. In it Dr. Bagley emphasizes the need for the teacher recognizing the implications of teaching people to live in a democracy and to work for democracy's betterment.

---

welcome to our profession these young people who have prepared themselves to enter its service.

There are many themes that one could appropriately discuss on an occasion of this sort. The theme that I have chosen is an old one, and yet I think it is one to which we can frequently return without exhausting its possibilities. My theme is the significance of the work of the teacher to democracy and to the progress of democratic civilization.

I choose this subject primarily because most of these graduates will serve as teachers in the most important of all our educational institutions— namely, the elementary school. And a goodly proportion of the others will serve in the next most important institution—the high school. The elementary school is of prime significance, not only because it lays the foundation for all that is to follow, but also because, among all of our educational institutions, it is the one that in the largest measure touches and quickens "all the children of all the people." In our country, too, the high school is very rapidly becoming an institution of universal education, and the high school teachers are coming to share with the elementary school teachers this fundamental responsibility. In a country like ours, where all of the people have an equal voice in determining where our nation will go and how it will get there, it would seem that the primacy of the schools that bring light to the great masses of the people could scarcely be questioned.

And yet at the present time, the value of mass-education is being very seriously questioned and in quite reputable quarters. There are those who maintain that the democratic ideal is wrong, and that the effort to bring the great masses of the people to the point where they can participate intelligently in the determination of a nation's destiny is nothing less than futile. Fairly typical of this point of view is the following statement made a few years ago by a college president:

> It may be a wise course to treat the people like children and let them play at governing themselves, but would it not probably be as wise to recognize the truth? The play goes on until a problem arises and then we call for a leader. What we mean, of course, is a ruler. The ruler thus called rules autocratically, during the period of difficulty, and then lets us play again.

> The melting-pot figure has been incorrectly interpreted. There is no alchemy in the melting-pot. Some apparently thought that, if we put gold and silver and copper and iron into the pot, the product of the furnace would be gold. We find that we did not get rid of an ounce of iron. In fact, we find after a few generations more iron and less gold.

Not many years ago a well-known psychologist, then a professor in our oldest and most famous university, basing his arguments on the alleged stupidity of the average citizen, set forth an elaborate plan for saving civilization from the unintelligent rule of the masses. He would divide society into three groups: a superior group of leaders who would govern the nation; an inferior group of followers who would do the heavy work and the routine work; and an intermediate group made up of those springing from the lowest group who might be granted a twenty-year period of probation to determine whether they could qualify for the highest group. Intermarriage between the lowest and highest groups he would strictly prohibit. Education, according to his plan, would be free to all but not compulsory.

I mention these points of view to indicate how seriously democracy is being questioned by persons who are very far from unintelligent and very far from insincere. I could add to the list equally frank and radical statements from other sources. A recent report of one of the great foundations, for example, includes an incisive indictment of the American public school on the ground that, in its efforts to educate everybody, it is seriously neglecting the most promising members of each generation, and in view of this neglect it is making us a nation characterized by mediocrity in all of the important phases of civilization.

One would be rash, indeed, to deny that criticisms such as these have a certain measure of justification. One would be foolishly blind not to recognize the tremendously difficult problems that democracy involves. On the other hand, one may recognize the shortcomings and deficiencies of the democratic social order and yet work steadfastly toward the solution of its complicated problems without throwing overboard the democratic ideal.

The solid fact that most of the critics of democracy overlook is the complete dependence of democratic institutions upon the enlightenment of the great masses of the people. Popular government in illiterate and backward nations has always been either a farce or a failure. The conditions that exist today in such widely separated countries as Mexico, China, and Russia sufficiently illustrate this basic truth. The hopeful fact is that the government of the people by the people becomes stable and effective in precise proportion to the advance that is made toward an effective education of the masses.

Some illuminating contrasts are afforded by the experience of European peoples during the critical years that have passed since the close of the World War. Throughout this period every nation of Europe has been subjected to stresses and strains, the seriousness of which, we, in our more fortunate position, can scarcely appreciate. Some of these nations have broken under the strain; others have been saved at least for the time by surrendering constitutional and parliamentary government and submitting to the iron rule of a dictator; still others have so far weathered every storm; they have preserved their constitutional governments and their democratic institutions.

It is a notable fact that these European nations have withstood the stress and strain of the post-war years almost precisely in proportion to the attention that they had given in the pre-war years to universal elementary education. Indeed, no nation that had developed during the generation preceding the war a reasonably efficient system of elementary schools for the masses of the people has so far succumbed either to Bolshevism on the one hand or the rule of dictator on the other hand. Practically every nation that neglected mass-education before the war has been forced to surrender constitutional and parliamentary government at one time or another during the critical post-war years. These nations have fallen in almost the precise order of their illiteracy: Russia, Spain, Greece, Italy, Portugal, Poland, Yugoslavia.

It is important in this connection to emphasize the fact that it is mass-education that is the bulwark of democratic civilization—not the education of privileged classes or the "education of leaders." Russia did not neglect the education of her leaders. Her pre-war universities were highly organized and highly efficient. Her secondary school enrolled in 1913 more pupils than did the secondary schools of any other nation except the United States. What Russia neglected was the education of her masses, and with 60 or 70% of illiteracy to contend against, even Russia's highly educated leaders failed to save her in her critical hour. Italy did not neglect the education of her leaders. In many ways she represented high standards of civilized culture. But Italy had not succeeded prior to the war in bringing elementary education to all of her people, and with 80% of illiteracy as a handicap she found democratic government inadequate in a crisis. It was a dictator, a man of remarkable strength and vision, but nonetheless an autocratic ruler—who took the reins of government into his own hands and saved Italy from the fate of Russia. And it was the virtual abandonment of popular government that saved Greece, Spain, Portugal, and Poland from disaster.

But when we turn to the enlightened nations of Europe, we find an entirely different situation. England and France have passed through crisis after crisis with constitutional government often threatened but never seriously in jeopardy. Germany and Austria underwent revolutionary changes in government, but the revolutions were peaceful and not violent, and the highly literate populations of these countries quickly adjusted themselves to the new conditions. One of the most inspiring examples of what universal education can do for a nation is furnished by Czechoslovakia. In the three provinces that form the principal part of Czechoslovakia—Bohemia, Moravia, and Silesia—the level of mass-education was exceptionally high long before the war. Illiteracy was practically non-existent. Czechoslovakia today is one of the most prosperous and promising nations of Europe. It is not merely from sentimental reasons that this vigorous young republic recognizes as its chief national hero the gentle Moravian bishop who, far back in the seventeenth century, established a firm belief in elementary education for all the people. It is fairly safe to say that a nation that has had a Comenius will not need a Mussolini.

Nor are other sharp contrasts between the enlightened and unenlightened nations without their lessons. Three years ago, for example, Poland was shaken by a revolution, brief but bloody enough while it lasted. At almost the same time, England underwent the most serious industrial crisis in her history—culminating in a great general strike involving millions of workers—without the firing of a single shot and with a measure of self control on the part of her masses that commanded the admiration of the world. No one in his senses could maintain that this remarkable record of order and social stability would have been possible even in England if it had not been for the faithful work of the universal elementary school during the past two generations.

It is, of course, unsafe to generalize even from parallels that are so close and consistent as those just described. And yet with regard to some things we may face the future with a fair degree of confidence. Some of our fellow-countrymen are apprehensive over the possibility that Russian communism, achieved by revolutionary methods, will spread to western Europe and to America. But every indication today points to the probability that enlightened nations will not tolerate changes in the social order that involve violence. Universal education may not as yet be a safeguard against international wars, but it seems to be a most effective safeguard against internal revolutions. Insofar as I can learn, no nation that has adopted a thoroughgoing system of universal elementary education has so far had either a civil war or even internal dissensions causing serious bloodshed since the leaven of the universal school has had a chance to work. France had its latest violent internal disturbance more than a generation ago at the close of the Franco-Prussian war, and at a time when more than 25% of her people were still illiterate. Our own civil war occurred nearly two generations ago when educational facilities for the whites were woefully meager in the southern states, and when the percent of illiteracy in the country as a whole was not inconsiderable. The South American Republics are notoriously subject to revolutions, but in a quite noteworthy fashion the three that have established thoroughgoing educational systems—Argentina, Uruguay, and Chile—have had stable governments ever since their schools became effective. What has been happening in Mexico during the past year has never yet happened in a country that has embraced the universal school. Revolution runs riot today only among illiterate peoples, and whatever perils of violence the Russian propaganda may involve it is fairly clear that they threaten directly only the backward nations of Asia and southeastern Europe.

I said at the outset that my theme would be the contribution of the teacher to modern progress. The teacher whose contribution to the progress I have discussed is not the college professor, nor the teacher of the talented children of each generation, but rather the teacher who does the basic work of universal education in the elementary school of this and other civilized countries. If what I have said is true, the contribution that this teacher makes to progress is central and fundamental. We are likely to think of the teacher's work in the elementary school as largely concerned with routine tasks. Children must be taught to read and write and cipher; they must be instructed in the basic facts of geography and history; they must, if possible, be introduced to some of the great masters and masterpieces of literature and art; they must be trained in the habits of work, in habits of order, in habits of decent and healthful living.

Born as we are into a civilized society and taking for granted the arts and amenities of civilization, it is hard for us to appreciate in full measure what the sum of these seemingly trivial conquests really means. It is only when we take the larger view—when we contrast the conditions that exist today with the conditions that prevailed before the advent of the universal school, or when we compare backward nations with enlightened nations— that the full meaning of the teacher's work is brought home to us. Then and only then can we see beyond the interlacing threads to the broader fabric which every conscious teacher of children is helping in a quite indispensable way to weave. It is a fabric that will not resist change, but will rather evaluate proposed changes and choose intelligently those to which it will give its support. It is a fabric the strength and durability of which depend, not upon a few supporting strands, but upon the strength and durability of each component thread.

This is only another way of saying that the universal school has operated, after all, in really a striking way to realize some of the most significant ideals of democracy. What it seems to guarantee is a reasonable measure of social order, a reasonable measure of patience in discussion and deliberation, a reasonable measure of adaptability to changes that are either desired or inevitable. It is not that the education of the masses can or should enable democracy to dispense with leadership; it is rather that the education of the masses can ensure the continuance of order and of orderly institutions even if leadership is not forthcoming.

And this seems to be a fairly significant service. What the future needs is a self-perpetuating, self-governing, self-controlled democracy, and it is a folly to dream that this can be achieved without paying the price. The alternatives are already clear enough: either class domination by proletariat, achieved as in Russia by the terrorism of violence, or a dictatorship made possible by the appearance of a powerful leader. The first is not a pleasant prospect to contemplate. The second might be effective if the times could always be counted upon to produce the right men. Both history and biology combine to convince us that this is a false hope. We need but look across the sea to note the contrast: England, France, and Germany are competent to pass safely through desperate crises because their masses are literate and disciplined.

Those who are intrusted with the education of the great unselected groups of children in the mass schools have, then, a unique as well as a fundamental responsibility. You who are about to assume this responsibility will not find it an easy burden, and at times you may be tempted to doubt its importance. In all probability, when you face your first class next fall you will find it a fairly typical cross-section of the community that you serve. Some children will come from well-to-do homes, some from middle-class homes, some from the homes of the poorer groups. A few of these children will be rather dull, a few will be bright, many will be "betwixt and between". If you are like most other good teachers, you will become deeply interested in some of these children. You will doubtless dwell in imagination on what they may become in later life. Like the fond parent, you will see among your pupils the future Edison, the future Lindbergh, and the future Hoover. It is always well to have these possibilities in mind, and to be on the lookout for genius or talent that you may help to develop. But as you go with your work, you will doubtless conclude that, in the very nature of things, Edisons and Lindberghs and Hoovers are fairly rare, and that most of the children who come under your instruction are likely to be just ordinary folk—representative of the great mass of "common people", whom Lincoln said the Lord must have loved because he has made so many of them. And it is then that you may be tempted to believe that teaching in the elementary school is not a very important job after all.

It is just here that you will make a serious mistake. Upon what you and your fellow-workers can accomplish with this unselected group—with these children who will be the butchers and bakers and candlestick-makers of the next generation, the factory workers, the artisans, the shopkeepers, the salespeople, the farmers and farm-hands, the clerks, stenographers, bookkeepers—upon what you and your fellow-workers in the public schools can do for the children who will become the great rank-and-file of the next generation, the whole future of democracy and democratic civilization depends. Every little bit that you can do to help them think straighter, to judge more wisely, to live more healthfully means a new step forward.

And if a serious responsibility lies upon the teachers of the mass-schools, a doubly serious responsibility lies upon the institutions that prepare these teachers. Someday the debt that modern progress owes to our normal schools and teachers colleges will, I am sure, be fittingly recognized. Take the country as a whole, these institutions have not as yet the measure of public respect and support that they richly deserve. They have, however, made marked advances during the past 10 years, and are in a position today to render even greater service than they rendered in the past.

I congratulate these graduates upon having had the privilege of living and working in one of the most famous of these teachers' colleges. As they go out into the wider field of professional service, they will carry with them, I am sure, the ideals which this institution has so clearly reflected. They will have toward their work the true professional attitude. They will know that, whatever others may think, the teachers' task is not sinecure. They will know, too, that, wherever their work may lie—whether in the kindergarten or the first grade or the fifth grade or the high school—they will find problems that will challenge every ability that the human mind possesses to think clearly and judge wisely and act resolutely. They will appreciate what William Lyon Phelps meant when he said, "Nothing is too minute or trivial that concerns the great work of teaching."

Wherever they go, they may be sure that their work will be important. In teaching, there are no "humble posts."

Teaching as a Fine Art
(1930)

In this commentary, Bagley makes the point that teaching should be viewed as a fine art such as music, rather than an applied science like medicine. He made this claim in much of his writing, but only in this short essay does he make this point his only focus. His ideal figure for American public school classrooms was the artist-teacher, whose qualifications, as well as virtues, he makes explicit in this piece. He valued the role of modern science in making teaching better, but he also understood that good teachers draw upon poetry as much as they do psychology. At the heart of his argument is that teaching, unlike other sciences, cannot ignore the subject of moral character.

I suggest that the scientific attitude may well be regarded as a most desirable part of the equipment of the artist-teacher. It is in no sense inconsistent with other essential items in this equipment. Among the latter I would list: (1) a thoroughgoing mastery of the materials that one teaches; (2) a keen appreciation of the significance of these materials to human life; (3) an ardent desire to have others know and appreciate these materials; (4) a sympathetic understanding of the difficulties which the learner will encounter in mastering the materials; and (5) a command of the technics by which these difficulties may best be overcome.

Regarding the last-named desideratum, it is reasonable to believe that many if not most of these technics will be gained in part from the observation of master-teachers and in part from the discipline of experience. The technology of education will, I think, help the teacher somewhat here although will not alone solve the problem. An acquaintance with the general patterns or methods of teaching should be

Forgotten Heroes of American Education, pages 189–192

helpful, but this help is supplementary rather than central. I am inclined to think that the technology of education will be of largest service in what may be called the extra-teaching activities, as caring for the health of the learners and measuring their progress, and such duties as may devolve upon the teacher in determining what subjectmatter to teach.

Far more significant to the artist-teacher than the technics, however, are the qualities of appreciation and sympathy and devotion which come primarily neither from his instruction in the materials and technologies of his art nor from his specific training during the apprenticeship stage of his career, but rather from the forces, no less real but far more subtle, that we refer to as insights and intuitions and inspirations. Like all true artists, the artist-teacher is a sensitive soul,—sensitive to the finer and more humanly significant elements in the subjectmatter that he teaches, sensitive as well to the finer and nobler elements in those who come to him for instruction and inspiration and guidance. All of the fundamental analogies here hark back to the fine arts and to the attitudes and responses of the creative artists in these fields. In a beautiful tribute to one of his teachers, George E. Woodberry, a recent writer[1] in *The Nation* sums up the essential factors:

> Mr. Woodberry's magic was *sui generis*. He was a great teacher ... because he was an authentic poet ... [But] had Mr. Woodberry never written a line of verse, he would be proved poet by his teaching. The proof lay not only in his tenderness and his rare understanding of the raw boys before him, but in the way in which he poured out himself and the best that was in him without stint or limit. Within his scope Mr. Woodberry had much to give, and only a poet could have given with such lavishness.

It is the germinal roots of these qualities that we who train teachers must try to discover and to develop in our students. Our technologies and our experiments, I am sure, will help us here; but we must not be led astray by a premature solution; and, what is even more important, we must not infer that, because our scientific methods may not as yet suggest a solution, we are justified in neglecting the problem or in assuming that the problem does not exist.

It has come to me with increasing force in the past few months that we ourselves have not been fully cognizant of the magnitude and intricacy of the task that we have assumed. We envy the physical sciences and the technologies based upon them; we envy almost as much the biological sciences and their technologies. What we have not sufficiently recognized is that their data are vastly simpler than ours, and that advancement with

---

1. Kellock, H.: "Woodberry—A Great Teacher," *The Nation,* January 29, 1930.

them is far easier than with us. It was with no small measure of consolation and encouragement that I read the following pronouncement by Henry Fairfield Osborn, one of the most distinguished of American scientists in the biological field:

> Marvelous as are (the) recent discoveries in astronomy, they are becoming comprehensible because of the uniformity of the laws and principles revealed to man through centuries of research. In brief, physics, astronomy, and chemistry are alike coming within the field of exact science capable of measurement, calculation, prediction, and prophecy.

What a contrast is presented in the biological sciences, ancient and modern! With a wide circle of astronomic friends and with the most intense admiration for the achievements of astronomy and pure mathematics, I yet believe that their problems are not nearly so difficult or so baffling as our problem. In anatomy, in physiology, in pathology, in heredity we have not yet reached even the threshold of exactitude. With increasing energy, refinement, and ingenuity, we know all the organs revealed in comparative and human anatomy, in both their grosser and their finer structure. We know also the history of the rise of many of these organs in the course of past time and what their functions and relations are, but there is always the Great Beyond of the unknown, and perhaps unknowable, which is summed up in the word life.

Of all incomprehensible things in the universe Man stands in the front rank, and of all incomprehensible things in Man the supreme difficulty centers in human intelligence, human memory, human aspirations, human powers of discovery, research, and conquest of obstacles .... [2]

It is literally true that we have today more definite and dependable knowledge about stars that are thousands of light years distant, and about atoms that no human eye can ever see, than we have about the human mind that has made these discoveries and given us this knowledge.

What Dr. Osborn says, in effect, is that the task of the physical scientist is a simpler task than that of the biologist, and that the task of the biologist, difficult as it is, is a simpler task than that of the psychologist. The same comparisons hold, I maintain, with reference to the technologies based upon these three groups of sciences. Insofar as dependable guidance from fundamental laws and principles is available, the task of the engineer is a simpler task than that of the physician, and the task of the physician, difficult as it is, is a simpler task than that of the teacher.

---

2. Henry Fairfield Osborn's Foreword to *The Brain from Ape to Man,* by Frederick Tilney: Paul B. Hoebner. Inc., New York, 1928.

Fortunately, under the conception of teaching as a fine art, we can still carry on, encouraging in every possible way the objective study of our problems, grateful for every positive gain that our technology can record, and yet firm in the faith that a mastery of our materials combined with sympathy and insight and a sincere devotion both to our ideals and to the best interests of those who come to us for instruction and guidance may carry us forward, even though we are dealing with the most intricate of human problems and even though the human mind, which it is our particular task to feed and form, is still the "most incomprehensible thing in the universe."

The Upward Expansion of Mass Education

Its Causes and Some of the Problems That It Has Raised
(1930)

In addition to his achievements as a philosophical thinker on teacher education, Bagley was an accomplished historian. The following is an important essay for historians as well as for philosophers of education. Bagley explains the serious challenges that faced the expansion of universal education. He touches upon the social, political, and economic dimensions of this uniquely American task.

This historical essay provides further evidence of Bagley's commitment to the ideal of liberal education for all Americans. Through his work as a scholar as well as a teacher of teachers, he advanced the cause of universal liberal education in both theoretic and practical ways. Among other points, Bagley explains the critical role that professors of education have to play in advancing democratic education toward the ideal of liberal education for all.

By this time in his career, Bagley had become deeply critical of the Progressive school of educational theory. He makes his criticisms of these thinkers evident in this work. At one point in the essay, he lists seven points that are prevalent in the Progressives' problematic theories, all of which he asserts are destructive when taken to their extremes. Instead of blaming the problems of American education on 19th century formalism as the Progressives did, Bagley lays the blame at the feet of "moral slackness," which he thought was pervasive in American culture. He also blames an educational theory that condones rather than attacks this problem. This tolerance of "half-learning," he thought, led to low-quality work in schools as well as other

Forgotten Heroes of American Education, pages 193–205
Copyright © 2006 by Information Age Publishing
All rights of reproduction in any form reserved.

institutions across the landscape of American society. The challenge for democratic education, Bagley recognizes, is the difficulty of finding a balance—in both thought and action—between equity and excellence.

The most significant problems that confront higher education in the United States have their roots in an ideal of educational democracy that is uniquely American. The famous characterization of our school system as an educational ladder with its base in the gutter and its tip in the university was perhaps an adequate formulation of this ideal in Huxley's time, but it will scarcely suffice to-day. In certain other countries, very poor children who show outstanding ability find it possible to climb an educational ladder of equal or greater height. An English boy, indeed, if highly competent, has his financial path made even easier than it is for an American boy of comparable talent. Surely the English situation reflects educational democracy of a fairly definite sort. The American ideal of democratic education doubtless had its origin in a desire to place all able and ambitious youth on the same economic footing in respect of opportunities for getting an education, but it has come in the past few decades to have a far less restricted meaning. It embodies a much more literal interpretation of "equality." The earlier notion at least implied that educational opportunities should be provided for all who were both eager and able to embrace them. Here the responsibility was clearly upon the individual who accepted the opportunities offered. The clear tendency to-day is to provide education for all on all educational levels and to hold the educational system responsible on every level for making these opportunities attractive, pleasant, and profitable to all.

Very emphatically, this is a distinction with a difference, and obviously such a change is fraught with possible consequences of serious moment, not only to education but to the character and fiber of the national life. It is the purpose of the present paper to trace the evolution of this change and to set forth some of the problems that it presents, particularly in the field of higher education.

The outstanding development in American education during the past generation has been the remarkable growth in the enrollment of the high schools and colleges. The ratio of high school enrollment to the total population was more than quadrupled in the thirty-year period between 1896 and 1926. In many American communities to-day secondary education is as nearly universal as was elementary education a generation ago. In 1900, for example, in a typical mid-western city, only one-eighth of the children of ninth grade age were enrolled in ninth grade classes; seven-eighths of these children were either retarded in the lower grades or had dropped out of school. In 1928 the proportions were exactly reversed;

seven-eighths were in the ninth grade, only one-eighth had dropped out or were retarded. In California—from this point of view undoubtedly the most progressive American state—an overwhelming majority of the children of high school age are now attending high school.

In spite of the lessened emphasis upon college preparation as a function of secondary education, the expansion of the higher institutions has followed close upon the heels of the high schools' growth. The ratio of college enrollment to the total population was twice doubled between 1906 and 1926, and during the past decade the colleges and universities have been hard pressed to find quarters and instructors for the students who have flocked to them in ever increasing numbers.

While exact comparisons with other countries are difficult because of varying definitions of elementary, secondary, and higher education, certain statements may be made with a fair degree of confidence. In our high schools, public and private, the aggregate enrollment is not far below the combined enrollment in the secondary schools of Europe. In our institutions of collegiate and university grade, the aggregate enrollment is approximately equal to the total number of students on the level of higher education in all other countries. Indeed it is not very far from the truth to say that in the United States more persons above the age of fourteen are in regular full time attendance at school or college than in all other countries combined.[1] It is clear, then, that the situation which the secondary and higher institutions are facing to-day is not only unique in the history of education but quite unparalleled elsewhere in the contemporary world.

---

1. These statements are based in part upon official government reports and in part upon data (chiefly summarized from such reports) published in *Europa* (volume for 1927) and in *The Statesman's Yearbook* (volume for 1929). In most of the other countries, of course, the secondary school enrollment includes a substantial proportion of pupils who in our country would be classed as elementary, and a certain proportion, too, who with us would fall in the college group. The following ratios, based upon the combined enrollments in secondary and higher institutions for the midyears of the present decade, constitute, I believe, comparisons that do not exaggerate the relative position of the United States in this regard:

Ratio of secondary and higher enrollments to total population

United States	44,184 to the million of population
Germany	13,605 to the million of population
England, Scotland, Wales	10,593 to the million of population
Italy	9,482 to the million of population
France	5,700 to the million of population

Some of the smaller European nations—Czechoslovakia, Holland, Denmark, Switzerland, and Finland, for example—show higher ratios than any of the European countries named; in no case, however, does the ratio approximate that of the United States.

The fact to be given first consideration is that the growth of the high schools and colleges constitutes at basis an upward expansion of mass education, and consequently has involved a radical change in the character both of the secondary school and of the college. Historically these have been essentially selective institutions. If those who sought instruction in them were not adapted by nature and nurture to the curricula provided and the methods of teaching employed, they were quickly eliminated. Generally speaking there was no thought of obligation on the part of the institutions themselves to adjust their curricula and their methods to the needs and limitations of an unselected group.

Slowly but surely the forces that were making for the growth of the public high schools and later for the growth of the tax-supported colleges and universities forced the selective function into the background and compelled the institutions to assume some measure of responsibility for adjusting their requirements to an increasingly heterogeneous group of pupils and students. A brave showing of "numbers" became increasingly necessary in appeals for public funds—and large numbers are not often consistent with rigorous standards of selection and retention. This need was felt especially in the tax-supported colleges and universities, but it was not without its effect upon the endowed institutions, practically all of which depended for their support in part upon student fees. On the secondary level there was a growing pressure to attract to the high schools as large a proportion as possible of the elementary school graduates and to keep as many of these as possible through the four years. On the elementary level there was an even more powerful pressure to pass pupils through the successive grades "on schedule" and to keep pupils from leaving school prior to the completion of the eighth grade work. It was in the first decade of the present century that "retardation" and "elimination" became the bugaboos of public school administration.

On the side of the curriculum, there came in close succession in the colleges and universities the elective principle and the diversified programs of study; in the secondary school, the differentiation of curricula, the provision of vocational courses, and to some extent the principle of free election; in both types of institution a marked relaxation of the standards governing entrance and graduation.

One of the most important developments had its origin in the need of more skillful teaching for the increasingly heterogeneous groups that crowded into the high schools. The college-trained teacher who had himself passed through the older type of secondary school found the older type of secondary teaching quite inadequate to the task presented by the unselected pupil-groups;—or, if he did not make this discovery himself, the public school administrator made it for him. From school superintendents and high school principals there came to the colleges an increasingly insistent demand that prospective high-school teachers be given some instruction in the theory and art of teaching as part of their college work. This demand (reinforced in many instances by new requirements for obtaining teachers' certificates) the colleges reluctantly answered by appointing professors of "pedagogy," who came a little later to be called professors of "education." While a few chairs of this sort were established somewhat earlier, the movement had its real start in the decade between 1890 and 1900, at the time when the public high schools were rapidly losing their selective function and taking on the characteristics of unselective "mass" schools.

From the outset, the professors of education represented in the colleges and universities the interests of the lower schools and particularly of the new type of high school. This is only to say that the professors of education represented the principle of non-selective education as against the principle of selective education. The latter principle still continued to dominate the colleges and universities; the professors of education in a very real sense were educational democrats living in an academic aristocracy; and their lot was far from happy.

There were, however, compensations. In the period of growth and expansion which was just opening, the professors of education—the educational "generalists"—were in a most strategic position to assume leadership. As a matter of fact the leadership of the great upward movement of mass education was forced upon them. The lower schools looked to them for guidance. More and more, the important posts in public school administration came to be filled by their students. In increasing numbers, public school teachers enrolled in their classes, especially during the summer sessions which developed so remarkably in the second decade of the present century. Beginning about 1910, these professional students of education were called upon with increasing frequency to direct "surveys" of public school systems and to make recommendations as to policies and programs. Beginning soon after 1920, they guided, either directly or indirectly, the far reaching movement in elementary and secondary education which has gone under the name "curriculum-reconstruction."

It has come about, then, that the persons most influential in American education to-day are neither the scholars in the specialized academic fields nor the school and college administrators, but rather the "educational generalists"—the professors of education and more recently the directors of educational research both in the universities and in state and city school systems. Like the growth that has brought him into existence the educational generalist is uniquely American. And because that growth was in essence a vast upward expansion of mass education, it has been his particular function to rationalize and justify the changes in educational organization, administration, and policy that were necessary in making this expansion possible.

Leaving for the moment the work and influence of the educational generalist, it will be profitable to inquire a little further into the underlying causes of the movement that brought him into being and into power. This is especially important because some of these causes were quite unrecognized by him or by any one else at the time.

The upward expansion of mass education is usually attributed to the rapidly increasing wealth which permitted the release of young people from wage-earning work in larger proportions than had been possible in the past and in larger proportions than is possible to-day in other countries.

There is no doubt that the increasing wealth has been an indispensable factor in bringing about the situation, but in itself it seems to be only a partial explanation of the phenomena in question. As a matter of fact, the forces that have operated to increase wealth have had the effect of stimulating educational expansion in a degree that is over and above the opportunities that the margin of wealth has created. In other words, the forces behind our material prosperity have not only made possible educational expansion; in a fundamental and far reaching sense, they have necessitated educational expansion. The machine has not only released large numbers of men and women from routine work; it has impelled— even necessitated—tens of thousands of young people to prepare themselves for the non-routine occupations—for the kind of work that cannot be done by the machine.

Within the past generation, the Industrial Revolution has taken quite a new turn through the remarkable development of automatically controlled machinery. The fundamental import of this development, however, has only recently been clearly discernible. It is now reported that the number of workers in manufacturing has decreased by at least a million within the decade in spite of a very great increase in production. This means a need upon the part of the displaced workers to adjust themselves to other occupations, and the difficulty of making such an adjustment explains why, in the midst of a material prosperity unprecedented in history, we have had in this country a serious problem of unemployment. The situation is complicated, too, by the decreased need for farm labor which has been due, in part at least, to the increased use of power-driven and automatically controlled machinery in agriculture.

What has clearly happened, then, has been a sharp reduction in the opportunities to earn a livelihood on the routine occupational levels. Compensating for this in part, although only in part, there has been an increase in occupational opportunities on what may be called the "stepped-up" levels where intelligent adaptation rather than routine skill is the important factor. Thus, while the number of routine workers has sharply decreased during the decade, the older professions have increased their numbers, and—what is more significant—many occupations, especially those concerned with business, have moved distinctly toward the professional or semi-professional level in the sense that those seeking employment must meet certain educational standards, both general and specific in character. The larger banks, the great public service corporations, the hotel syndicates, the insurance companies, and the big department stores now have elaborate provisions for training their personnel; and in almost every case those who would seek such training find it distinctly to their advantage to have a good background of general education. Here, too, the curve of growth seems to be distinctly upward. A great engineering corporation reports that ten years ago ninety per cent of its employees were routine and clerical workers; to-day one half of its personnel is made up of highly educated technologists and executives. One of the largest public service corporations in the country, already employing many college graduates in technological and executive posts, plans within the coming decade to double its personnel on the higher level and to reduce substantially the number and proportion of its routine workers.

The upward expansion of American education, then, has been not merely a reflex of material prosperity; beyond this, it has been a response to a fundamental economic need or demand. The complaint that too many young people are attending high school and college is beside the point,—as even more emphatically is the contention that a goodly proportion of these young people should be in overalls or aprons doing the routine work of the world. It is entirely conceivable that some of these young people are better adapted to hewing wood and drawing water than to the work involved in the white-collar jobs. But this again is beside the question. Hewing wood and drawing water can be done and are being done very much more effectively and economically by mechanical slaves.

How far can the influence of these fundamental economic forces be extended? On the side of the machine, the limits seem to be fairly remote. The engineers promise mechanical contrivances that will do any purely repetitive work, however complicated, with a minimum of human control. The sources of power, if not inexhaustible, are still abundant and many of them as yet are untouched. Approximately seventy per cent of the mechanical horse-power generated in the world to-day is generated and used in the United States. Every man, woman, and child in our country has working for him or her the potential equivalent of at least thirty-five slaves. The ratio could undoubtedly be increased substantially within the next two decades.

The vital question, then, concerns the man rather the machine. Educationally, perhaps, the most important problem is this: How far can the human types that have heretofore done the routine work be fitted for the stepped-up occupational levels? Failure here would seem to necessitate a deliberate slowing down, halting, or even reversal of the forces that are now operating to extend the reign of the machine. I am told that certain industries, even now, have machinery at hand (or at least designed) which would enable them to increase their output and at the same time effect a substantial reduction in the number of workers employed. These improvements, however, are held in abeyance because of the effect that their introduction would have upon the labor market. A gradual adjustment is necessary, and in the long run this must mean an adjustment upward from the routine levels to the stepped-up levels. The most significant question is whether education can mediate this end. The hours of labor—especially of routine labor—will undoubtedly be shortened, and this will take up some of the slack in unemployment; but it cannot entirely solve the problem. The increase in leisure which is clearly predictable already constitutes an important educational problem; but in the last analysis it is not an enlarged leisure that is important but rather an enlarged opportunity; and it is an enlarged opportunity that occupations of the higher grades provide.

If this analysis of the economic forces underlying educational expansion is measurably correct, it would seem to follow that the policies that have accompanied and facilitated educational expansion will need revision. I have suggested that one function of the educational theorist or "generalist" has been to rationalize and otherwise justify a relaxation of standards. In doing this, he has been, I am sure, thoroughly sincere. Many policies that are in effect loosening and softening in an unfortunate sense make an immediate appeal because they can be readily contrasted with stupid, meaningless, and even brutal practices which, it is assumed, have very largely governed education in the past, and some of which are incontestably far from uncommon to-day. It is clearly not to the discredit of the educational theorist that his proposals, in general, have been directed toward an educational regime that would be increasingly more humane, sympathetic, and regardful of individual rights and needs; nor is it difficult to confuse essential rigor with lack of sympathy. With the best of intentions, then, educational theory in the United States has tended in many ways and (in the circumstances) almost inevitably toward a weakening of the educational fiber. It is a stiffening of this fiber that is now in order.

A brief statement of some outstanding policies that reflect this progressive loosening of standards may not be out of place at this point:

1. In both the lower and the higher schools, the elimination of comprehensive examinations covering large units of work.
2. The elimination in many cases of promotional examinations of any sort and the passing of pupils through the elementary and high school grades and into college on the basis of an accumulation of term or semester credits.
3. On the secondary and higher levels, the abandonment of coherent curricula that might be made to reflect some measure of educational continuity and integrity, and the substitution of elective programs comprising a bewildering offering of necessarily short-unit courses.
4. On the elementary level, especially, the evaluation of individual achievement in terms of standards that reflect mass-achievement under average conditions; standards which may and probably do represent lower levels even of mass-achievement than are attainable; a process which may easily operate to standardize mediocrity at an unnecessarily low level.
5. An increasing dependence upon personal charm and an ingratiating manner on the part of the teacher to insure order and industry on the part of the pupils and students, and a fairly deliberate discrediting of such impersonal factors as effortful achievement for its own sake, pride in good workmanship for its own sake, and an ingrained respect for law and order.

Along with these developments, some of which have been in evidence for thirty years or more, there has been on the part of educational theory a rationalized justification of the paths of least resistance in learning. There has been an official and authoritative denunciation of drills, of reviews, and even of systematic and sustained effort on the part of the learner. Most revealing of all, however, has been the denial by educational theory of the possibilities of anything akin to a general discipline. This denial has been predicated upon a number of psychological experiments concerned with the "transfer of training." The actual results of these experiments, while warranting a marked modification of the doctrine of formal discipline in its older and quite naive form, do not by any means justify the out-and-out denial of disciplinary possibilities that characterizes contemporary educational theory.

The increasing vogue and influence of the so-called "Progressive" school of educational theory are symptomatic, in part at least, of the same general tendencies. The tenets advanced by the more radical wing of this school are especially significant because of the appeal that they make to many members of the lay public who are interested in educational reform.

The general position of this more radical wing may be summarized as follows:

1. Education is primarily a process of natural growth,—a growth that must proceed from an inner urge and not from an external compulsion; hence:—

2. The initiative in the learning process must always come from the learner.

3. The continuance of the learning process must be justified at each step by the learner's own recognition of its value in meeting his immediately felt needs or in solving immediate problems that appeal to him as worth solving. A clear implication of the theory is that the learner is to be condoned for avoiding tasks for which he does not feel an immediate yearning or from which he cannot anticipate a pleasurable thrill.

4. Imposed tasks and prescribed programs of study not only violate the inherent right of the learner to make free choices; they are in themselves either futile or negative as educational means.

5. The chief problem of teaching is not to teach in the sense of imparting instruction or directing the mastery of skills, but to watch for the appearance of desirable interests, purposes, and "felt needs" on the part of the learner and, if they appear, to suggest sources from which the learner may, if he wishes, get help in realizing them.

6. Systematic mastery through persistent application to a series of extended and integrated learning activities is justified only if the learner undertakes the arduous task of his own free will and then only if he sees clearly the end to be gained and the relation of the means to the end.

7. Moral controls are to be attained by a similar process. In general the growth must be from within. Imposed commands, even precepts and cautions, while admitted by the theory as necessary now and then to prevent immediate disaster, are at best necessary evils. The essential condition of all growth is freedom.

We are not concerned just now with either the inherent worth or the inherent validity of these tenets. Regardless of such questions, it is incontestable that these statements constitute a consistent summary of American educational theory followed to its logical conclusion. It is obvious also that a theory which yields logical conclusions of this sort fits admirably the demand for educational expansion. While it would seem from the theory that the responsibility for effort is placed upon the learner, in actual practice the learner is, in a quite real sense, relieved of responsibilities. The educational system—and particularly the teacher—must shoulder the entire load.

An attempt to realize the possibilities inherent in the upward expansion of American education will be a much better use of time and energy than will reactionary proposals looking toward a stemming of the tide. One may be justified in occasional pessimistic reflections anent the prominence of non-intellectual activities in college life and the prostitution of college opportunities to such personal ambitions as the itch to improve one's social status or the urge to make influential acquaintances. In so far, however, as these phenomena are anything more than surface currents, they lend emphasis to a far more fundamental defect: namely, the lack of thoroughness, system, and rigor which has come to characterize American education from the kindergarten to the university. The weakness of American education does not lie in the formalism which one group of reformers will always exaggerate; nor in the "dead wood" which another group would excise from the curriculum, usually with the aid of a butcher's cleaver; nor yet in the "regimentation" which still another group would break up—with dynamite if necessary. As a matter of fact, our schools have far less formalism, dead wood, and regimentation than have the schools of any other comparable nation. The real weakness of American education lies in what Professor Morrison has aptly termed "half-learning," and in the mental sloth and moral slackness which half-learning encourages. Such moral slackness may have nothing to do with conventional morality, of course, but it is none the less an unfortunate trait for education to propagate on a nation-wide scale. It is not at all impossible that this trait is responsible in part for the complacent attitude of the easy-going average citizen toward such unsavory phenomena as our unparalleled ratios of serious crime, the mounting divorce rates, and the wide prevalence of corruption in public office.

The flabbiness and superficiality of American education are due in part to the lack of adequately prepared teachers, not only in the elementary school but on the secondary and higher levels as well—a condition almost inevitable in view of the rapid growth of the high schools and colleges. With the slowing-down of the growth (which is already in evidence) this weakness in some measure will gradually be remedied; but only partially, unless a change of a more fundamental type is effected, for the influence of ill-prepared teachers is compounded, as we have seen, by an educational theory which,—with the very best of intentions,—has in reality condoned and sanctioned loose standards.

The large problem which American education faces may be simply stated: Can our schools and colleges "level up" rather than down? Can we realize the praiseworthy democratic ideal of equal educational opportunity for all without committing the American people to a standardized—an institutionalized—mediocrity? Can we maintain secondary schools that are quite unselective and higher institutions far less selective than those of other countries and still compete with other countries in the development of talent that will be competent to the higher realms of intellectual activity? Finally, throughout the range of school and college life, can we make the education of all an effective stimulus to intellectual and volitional growth upon the part of all?

The interesting experiments that have been undertaken in some of the colleges and universities to solve certain phases of this problem are well known and need not detain us here. They seem to be directed toward the provision of special opportunities for students of exceptional ability, promise, and ambition; but at the same time they recognize, at least by implication, the practical necessity of keeping the college doors still open to a relatively unselected group. One or more of these experiments may point the way toward a substantial advance in standards for those who are competent to meet highly rigorous requirements.

The more serious question, however, is whether a general stiffening of standards from the lowest to the highest levels of education is not only practicable but absolutely essential to even a modest realization of the possibilities inherent in the present situation. This does not mean, of course, that all should be expected to meet the same standards; such a hope would be so futile as to be foolish. It might well mean, however, a readjustment through which every individual would feel an increased stimulus to effort and hence to the intellectual growth that effort alone can bring about. This general forward movement along the entire educational front would in the end help the colleges far more than local advances in its own sector, important as the latter may prove to be.

There is sufficient evidence to warrant the conviction that not only the more competent groups but the average groups as well are working well below their capacities. In short, even for the masses, the standards are far below what might well be demanded without seriously affecting the retention of pupils and students. It is significant in this connection that achievement tests in the "fundamentals" standardized on the basis of the average attainments of our elementary school pupils have to be revised upward when used in classes of the same grade in Canadian schools; and one who compares the elementary schools of our country with those of western Europe cannot escape the conclusion that our results fall far short of what equally unselected groups in other countries find it possible to achieve in the way of accurate knowledge, adequate skills, and even dependable and dynamic ideals and attitudes.

The plain fact is that the relaxation of standards which made the upward expansion of education possible has been carried far beyond the measure essential to insure this end. Further than this, educational theory, which doubtless rendered a beneficial service in encouraging these relaxations, gave to the process so much momentum that loose standards have come in many quarters to be looked upon as virtues. This is clearly seen in the complete discrediting of the disciplinary ideal. There can be no doubt that the ideal needed revision, but the revision was carried so far as, in effect, to throw the baby out with the bath. A problem of the immediate future should be to rescue the infant and restore him to his proper place in both school and college; in fact, we are in a position now to see that an educational family without him is Hamlet with Hamlet omitted. He is essential—and I am confident that he will be healthier and stronger for the scrubbing that the reformers have given him. In any event, the indicated task of the educational theorist for the immediate future is to develop a New Discipline that will be able to compete successfully with the New Freedom.

What Does the Dominant American Theory of Education Imply for the Redirection of the Professional Education of Teachers?

(1933)

By 1933, Bagley had become a well-known critic of the Progressive school of educational theory. The sudden reversal that many Progressives made in their theories during the early years of the Depression made Bagley even more critical of their philosophy. He deplores the fact that these individuals were exerting significant influence on educational policy. This brief statement is an example of Bagley's frequent criticism of Progressive educational theory during the 1930s. He laments specifically the impact that these ideas were having on curriculum for teaching teachers, his specialty.

The question that I have been asked to discuss grows out of a movement in education that has been gathering a good bit of acceleration in recent years—the movement to synthesize the subjectmatter in the various fields of knowledge and to make new groupings of educational materials. It has been exemplified by the organization of such courses as general science and general mathematics for the early years of the secondary school, and by the so-called fusion courses in the social studies. On the level of higher

Forgotten Heroes of American Education, pages 207–210
Copyright © 2006 by Information Age Publishing

education, there has been a multiplication of survey courses, of which the best known type aims to cover the entire field of the natural sciences.

Going much further toward breaking down subjectmatter boundaries has been the theory that all of the necessary skills, facts, and principles should and could be learned as they are needed in the solution of problems. A variant of this theory is that which would take a center of interest, such as a poem that the pupils like, and follow out the "leads" suggested by the poem, thereby picking up painlessly various items of information. Still another is represented by the plan upon which a famous experimental school was operated nearly a generation ago. The work of one grade for an entire year, for example, was centered about the grocery store. I recall a visit that I made to this school almost twenty years ago. In one of the classrooms the pupils were working at something that looked to me like an arithmetic lesson. I remarked upon it to the principal, speaking of it as a class in arithmetic. He fired up at once: "I would have you know, sir, that arithmetic is not taught in this school." In theory, neither arithmetic nor any other subject was taught.

All of these theories and many of the practises based upon them are very far from new, but in all probability they have never had so wide a vogue as they have today in American education, except in Russia where the work of the Soviet schools from the beginning was organized very largely on the basis of "complexes" or projects in which subjectmatter divisions as such seem to have been entirely eliminated. It is interesting to note that last August the Central Committee of the Communist Party directed the commissars of education in the several republics to "liquidate" what the decree refers to as "these perversions of the laboratory method" and to provide "systematic and sequential" instruction based on textbooks. Thus the most extensive and pervasive attempt ever made to replace logical organization with so-called psychological organization has reached what some persons will regard as, in more than one sense of the term, its logical conclusion.

In our country, however, the tendency is increasingly toward the system that the Soviets have abandoned after a ten-year trial. There is, indeed, in the very rapid extension of the so-called activity program a suggestion that our schools will go even further than did the Soviet schools. In a city of a half-million population the superintendent directed his teachers to organize an activity program. When asked why he did this he replied frankly that he had had to yield to political pressure. If this sort of thing keeps up we may expect to find our political platforms bristling with such words as psychological and logical organization, unit plans, activity programs, and the child-centered school. I am not at all certain, indeed, that it will be only the boundaries between subjects that will disappear. A prominent woman in our profession was heard to remark apropos of a proposal for organizing an activity program that she hoped that it would not be necessary to use the program as a series of pegs upon which to hang subjectmatter. For all I know the American schools ten years hence may have no subjectmatter whatsoever in the curriculum.

However this may be, the training institutions cannot neglect the task of preparing teachers for the type of curriculum that seems now to be extending so rapidly—provided that a reversal of policy does not come here as in Russia. Most of the normal schools and teachers colleges have not been at all unmindful of this necessity. Their training schools have quite generally exemplified the theories and practises that are regarded as the most progressive and up-to-date. So far as I am informed, too, the courses in education tend to emphasize, and to provide a rationalized justification for the doctrines that constitute our dominant educational theory. So far as the normal schools and teachers colleges are concerned, then, the weakness seems to lie in the subjectmatter fields. Because these are still departmentalized or compartmentalized, the student is not prepared to teach in schools where subject boundaries are disregarded. This, at least, is the conviction of some students of the problem, and these persons wish to see the courses on the collegiate level modified to fit the pattern which is now the vogue in the elementary schools. Some of those who hold to the theory that learning tasks should not be imposed upon children but should rather grow out of interests aroused by their activities would consistently apply the same theory to the collegiate level. They would abandon the systematically organized courses and imposed assignments. Thus the student having learned in the way in which (according to the theory) children should learn will be able to adjust himself or herself to the elementary-school situation without difficulty.

Strangely enough, however, some of those who advocate this theory for the elementary school protest against anything like it in the training of teachers. Under the activity program, they say, the teacher must have a command of subjectmatter that is much more extensive than is needed when one teaches logically organized subjects. "Where can you tell where the mind of the child will lead you?" was the answer given to one of my students appointed to a position in an up-to-date school when she asked for a copy of the course of study. And if one cannot predict where the learner's interests will lead, one must in consequence be prepared for anything. The preparation of the teacher, then, must be very thorough and very broad, and systematic courses are deemed (by this group) essential to this end.

In a way I am disqualified to suggest steps toward a solution of the problem because, while I believe that the activity program has an important place in the kindergarten and the primary grades, I am convinced that it has a quite limited place after that, except for subnormal learners and for those who remain so volitionally immature that they can work only at the behest of immediate interest. For prospective kindergarten-primary teachers and teachers of subnormal classes, I should say that the best preparation would be extensive contacts with the activity program in the laboratory school. The training institutions, however, will need apparently to reckon with the possible extension of the activity program throughout the elementary and high school, and this will demand, I think, a type of training that reflects on the college level at least some features of the activity program itself. The solution that Dr. Alexander and Dr. Stratemeyer are trying in New College combines thorogoing and systematic courses in subjectmatter, paralleled by a series of seminars which operate in some measure on an activity basis, and this may prove to be an effective compromise.

There still remains for consideration the type of preparation that will best meet the needs of those who will teach the courses which combine materials from related subject fields. Here I would suggest professional-content courses similar to that which Dr. W. L. Schaaf has prepared for teachers of junior high-school mathematics. This is a course on the collegiate level dealing with the actual materials of the junior high-school course, with related materials of a much more advanced type, and treating also the problem of adapting materials to the needs and capacities of junior high-school pupils. For teachers of the so-called fusion course in the social studies, one might expect that well-organized professional content courses in history, government, geography, and economics would suffice, but this does not seem to be the case, and I am inclined to think that a course similar in purpose and organization to that of Dr. Schaaf will be necessary if the fusion movement is extended.

If any teachers should be carefully prepared it is the teachers of the American schools as operated under our dominant educational theory. The whole tendency of this theory is to increase the complexity of the processes of teaching and learning, sometimes to the point of confusion.

The Ideal Preparation of a Teacher of Secondary Mathematics from the Point of View of an Educationist
(1933)[1]

This selection describes Bagley's ideas on the specific task of preparing secondary teachers of mathematics. Readers should note that this paper is on secondary teachers of mathematics, not on elementary teachers, which Bagley regarded as a quite different task.

Bagley's goal with using terms such as "professional background courses" and "professional content courses" is to avoid the simplistic, destructive distinction between "what to teach" and "how to teach." They are one and the same to Bagley. Separating them is deeply harmful to the profession of teaching. His point with this discussion is to provide a vision for teaching teachers that is richer and deeper than much of what passed for teacher training curriculum during his time.

Bagley's substantive views about teacher education were not accepted by either of the two major educational constituencies. On one hand, the academic specialists cared only about establishing their disciplines on purely intellectual grounds and cared not at all about the moral content of their subjects. On the other hand, Progressives like William Heard Kilpatrick, who dominated the teaching profession, rejected traditional liberal education, a position that was anathema to Bagley.

---

1. Read before the annual meeting of *The National Council of Teachers of Mathematics at Minneapolis* on February 25, 1933.

Forgotten Heroes of American Education, pages 211–216

Rejecting both extremes, Bagley found himself nearly alone in the middle of the road, trying to advance a commonsense moral vision for the profession of teaching. Having few allies, he could not win the fight. And yet, from the vantage point of the present, it is clear that Bagley's prescriptions were far more sound than those advanced by the Progressives who took control of the teaching profession.

It would scarcely be profitable, I think, to place too strict a construction on the term "ideal" as used in the title of this paper. In fact I have been so continuously confronted with the handicapping conditions that must be met in preparing teachers that I should hardly know what to do or to say if these conditions were suddenly removed. For example, there is always the matter of the time that can be given to preparation; there is always the type of person whom we may expect to make the preparation; there are always large gaps in our knowledge as to the best ways in which to select and organize materials; and in the preparation of a high-school teacher there is the practical need of providing training that will enable him to teach in at least two fields of specialization.

We shall start, then, by assuming certain conditions: (1) a four-year program following high-school graduation; (2) a group of students who reflect the top quarter of the high-school graduating class in respect of scholarship, who in the high school have completed at least three years of secondary mathematics with a measure of success which indicates that they are mathematically-minded, and who are genuinely interested in the problem of teaching high-school boys and girls; (3) a teachers' college well equipped with mathematical materials, including instruments suited to demonstrate the various applications of mathematics, and well equipped too with laboratory schools of secondary grade; (4) a well trained staff all of the members of which satisfy the standards of scholarship demanded of teachers in the best institutions of collegiate grade, all of whom are interested in the problems of mathematics teaching in the lower schools, and at least half of whom are equipped with the training in educational theory, educational psychology, and educational measurements that is essential to a relatively expert treatment of the problems involved in adapting mathematical instruction to learners on the lower levels and to learners of varying abilities. At least one member of the staff should have a special interest in and knowledge of the history of mathematics as such and the history of mathematics as an educational discipline. We shall also take it for granted that the student will have one field of specialization in addition to mathematics.

Under these conditions, I should divide the four years' work somewhat as follows: (1) To the two fields of specialization I should expect that the student would give approximately half of his time. Assuming that this half would be divided equally between the two fields of specialization, mathematics would have approximately the equivalent of thirty semester hours. I shall refer to courses in the two fields of specialization as *professional content courses*. They will include the equipment directly needed in the secondary teaching of the subject and the equipment indirectly needed. By the latter I mean the additional courses in the specific field that are necessary to give to the teacher a thoroughly firm grasp of his teaching materials. The specific content of such courses in mathematics would be determined primarily by the mathematics staff.

(2) Approximately forty semester hours would be given to what I shall call *professional background courses*. I mean by these courses—outside of his two fields of specialization—hours that add desirable elements to his equipment as a teacher. This is on the assumption that wide horizons and a rich culture are fundamental in the professional equipment of every teacher. It is to be noted that I call these not cultural courses but professional background courses because I wish to emphasize my belief that the educational equipment of every teacher, and especially of every teacher in the elementary and secondary schools, should not be that of the narrow specialist, but rather that of the teacher-scholar who knows his own subject in its broader relationships and in its broader applications. In short, instead of multiplying what we are calling *integrated courses* crossing many subject-matter lines, I should prefer to safeguard the essential unity within the field but to have the teacher so well equipped that he can point out to the learner the relationships between his field and the fields of his colleagues. This will effect the end that the integrationists have in mind, I believe, and at the same time prevent the catastrophe that befalls the learner when the fusion courses become confusion courses.

These background courses should be quite distinct from the courses offered for specializing students. I should hope, for example, that teachers of history, teachers of English, teachers of art, primary teachers, intermediate-grade teachers, and all other teachers not specializing in mathematics would have a course offered by the mathematics staff dealing with the materials of college mathematics for the non-specializing student. Many of these background courses will be of the survey variety. All teachers except those specializing in the natural sciences should have a survey course in the physical sciences. I think of this as covering a year and a half or nine semester hours and including a survey of astronomy, physics, chemistry, and geology. This would be in addition to a full year of biology, which I should require of all teachers. Science teachers, of course, would have much more elaborate courses in each of the physical and biological sciences.

Perhaps I can make my conception of the professional content and professional background courses a little clearer by reference to the equipment that I should expect each to give. In the fields of his specialization, the student should make the acquaintance not only of the treatise-literature of his field; he should also know the monographic literature, both in some important corner of present-day research and through the classic monographs in his field; he should know the principal technical journals reporting discoveries first-hand and furnishing authoritative reviews of additions to the literature of his field; even as a student he should be encouraged to subscribe for one or more of these journals but whether he subscribes or not he should be encouraged to read them religiously as they come from the press. In his junior and senior years, the acquaintance with the periodical literature of his field should extend to the journals of at least one non-English-speaking country. To this end I have long recommended that in every four-year curriculum for the preparation of teachers two years of foreign-language study be required. If the student already has a reading mastery, say, of French, then the two years should be spent in gaining a reading mastery of German or of any other language in which important contributions to his field are published.

Let us now take the non-specializing student. What will the professional-background courses in subjects that he will not teach do for him in such concrete terms as those just used with respect to the specializing student? I would wish such courses to give to the non-specializing student something more than a speaking acquaintance with the major fields of scholarly endeavor, but quite obviously the acquaintance cannot go so deep as the acquaintance of the specializing student must go. Reduced to such terms as I have just used with reference to the latter, I should say that for each of the major fields of knowledge, the non-specializing student should have read and assimilated one or more books representing the less technical treatise-literature of the field; should know the names and something of the contributions of those who to-day speak with the most highly respected authority in the field as well as the names and contributions of the outstanding scholars of the past; should have a reasonable understanding of the methods of investigation used in making new discoveries in the field; and should know in what relatively non-technical journals such discoveries are likely to be reported.

My suggestion is that, between the professional content courses on the one hand and the professional background courses on the other, the prospective teacher should have a fairly thorough acquaintance with two fields of specialization (in both of which he has had good basic work on the secondary level) and something more than a speaking acquaintance with other major fields of human endeavor. The program would be organized on the basis of prescriptions rather than on the elective plan, but provisions should be made for adjustment to individual needs, especially in the matter of insuring contacts with major fields in which the student may be especially deficient. It is assumed that his basic interests will be in his fields of specialization.

New College for Teachers, an undergraduate subdivision of Teachers College, Columbia University, starts with three innovations which may well be considered as worth a trial in other professional schools. One of these is a series of seminars which it is hoped will integrate the work done in separate subject-matter courses; a second innovation is the requirement of a period of study and travel in Europe, presumably during one of the summers; and the third is a similar period devoted to actual employment in an occupation other than teaching—factory work, social-center work, work in department stores, work on a farm or in the transportation service. These requirements will aim to provide another type of background for the teacher's professional work—something that will supplement or complement his classroom and laboratory experiences.

So far the discussion has concerned what may be called the substantive equipment of the teacher. Woven intimately with this, especially in the professional-content courses, will be the most useful materials now usually taught in separate courses in education. My own theory, from which there are many dissenters, is that the number of these detached courses can be and should be markedly reduced on the ground that the teacher's needs can be more adequately met if the problem of selecting subject-matter for the lower schools, the problem of adapting these materials to the capacities of the younger learners, and the problem of relating one's own subject to other subjects are considered in the subject-matter courses of the professional school rather than in the so-called professional courses. The older terminology itself is absurd, for if any courses are truly professional for the prospective teacher it is those that provide him with his stock in trade. There are rules of teaching and standards of good practice in teaching that can be applied to practically all subject-matter fields, but it is best I think for the prospective teacher to get his initial acquaintance with these in his own field and in the observation of the work done by competent teachers in his own and other fields, and come later to a brief course which treats these rules and standards in the light of educational theory. The quite opposite policy still governs pretty generally in our professional schools for teachers and in the liberal-arts colleges which prepare teachers. The student receives his substantive materials in so-called academic courses, often with little reference to the professional use that he will make of them; while he receives instruction in generalized teaching procedures from educational generalists some of whom have at most only a speaking acquaintance with his own subject field and many of whom have a distinctly doctrinaire attitude.

For the four-year undergraduate professional school, and for teachers of such subjects as mathematics, history, English, and the like, I should limit the detached courses in education to not more than ten or possibly twelve semester hours exclusive of the student's contacts with the laboratory schools. In so far as the latter are concerned with the teaching problems in his fields of specialization, they should be regarded as part and parcel of his professional-content work, and the supervision of his student-teaching should be looked after in large part by representatives of the subject-matter staff. In the laboratory high schools and on the upper levels of the laboratory elementary schools, critic teachers should be closely affiliated with the corresponding subject-matter groups in the college.

The contacts of the prospective teacher with the laboratory schools should begin very early in his course of pre-service training. They should include systematic observation of the best teaching, and if possible observation of teaching procedures that represent the best from the standpoint of each distinct school of educational theory. These observations should be closely related to the professional-content courses as well as to the courses in education. They should be in part replaced and in part supplemented by definite assignments of responsible duties in one of the laboratory schools, and they should culminate in a brief period—say nine weeks—of fairly complete responsibility for the conduct of a class through one or more units of work.

I use the term laboratory school in place of practice school or training school because I wish to emphasize my conviction that the student-teacher in a professional school is not to be regarded as an apprentice or a cadet, but rather as a student. It is not to be expected that this initial practice of his art will give him all of the skills and insights that he will need. It is rather to be hoped that his contacts with the laboratory schools will give point and meaning to his courses in subject-matter and in educational theory, familiarize him with the standards of good practice, and furnish a start in the acquisition of skills and insights.

It goes without saying, of course, that no schedule of courses, activities, and other stated requirements will work automatically to produce an efficient teacher. One may even say that a faulty curriculum carried out by scholarly and inspiring instructors would probably produce a better teacher than an ideal program administered by instructors who had no interest in their task and who did their work in a listless and perfunctory way.

The professional program for prospective teachers, then, is something more than its curriculum offerings or requirements. It includes the life of the school itself, which should provide many opportunities for informal contacts between instructors and students, and also the teaching which goes on in the classrooms. Enthusiasm for one's work and devotion to the interests of the learner are qualities of the artist teacher for which there are no substitutes—and these qualities are not taught to the novice, they are rather caught from his instructors if his instructors exemplify them in a striking way.

The ideal preparation of the teacher, then, would include the privilege of working with such instructors.

Modern Educational Theories and Practical Considerations
(1933)

This is one of Bagley's most colorful lectures. It shows plainly his courage in confronting the powerful Progressive consensus favored by his colleagues. Bagley recognizes that Progressivism had become the new conventional wisdom, and he does not hesitate to challenge its assumptions. He jokes a bit with his Progressive colleagues at the outset, before criticizing them. He acknowledges that Progressive ideas have a clear role to play in educational thought and practice, specifically at the early elementary grades. He repeats his earlier warnings, however, that the over generalization of these ideas was dangerous to American democracy.

Bagley argues that the weak assumptions that under gird much of Progressive education are weakening the social fiber that holds America together. Bagley concludes the address with his famous "I still maintain that I would rather be right than Progressive" statement, which was one approach that he took in battling the dogmatism that he saw promulgated by many of his colleagues. He always used the term Progressive, rather than progressive, when referring to his romantic-minded colleagues. He did this to make the point that just because someone chose not to label himself with the title "Progressive" did not mean that his ideas did not lead to real progress. Progress that had no direction or end, to Bagley, was useless and devoid of content.

The French naturalist, Cuvier, was once asked to pass judgment on the following definition, "A crab is a small red fish that walks backward." Cuvier

Forgotten Heroes of American Education, pages 217–224
Copyright © 2006 by Information Age Publishing
All rights of reproduction in any form reserved.

replied, "The definition is entirely correct, except at three points: The crab is not a fish, it is not red, and it does not walk backward." I am reminded of this incident by the wording of my topic on this morning's program, "Modern Educational Theory and Practical Considerations." If I were disposed to be facetious I might paraphrase Cuvier and say regarding this topic, "Modern educational theory is not modern; it is not practical; and above all it is not educational."

I hasten to add, of course, that the statement is intended to be in the nature of satire and for this reason is slightly exaggerated; but if I understand aright the meaning of our dominant educational theory, my paraphrase of Cuvier's retort does a minimum of injustice to its subject—and this minimum is in the interest of truth and clear thinking.

The most salient characteristics of American educational theory have been summed up in four sentences by an Australian educator who spent several months in a nationwide study of American Schools: (1) "An experience which is not of immediate value to the child has no place in the schoolroom." (2) "All schoolroom situations should arise from the learner's felt need of the moment." (3) "The training (or disciplinary) value of a subject can no longer be used as a criterion in curriculum making." (4) "The walls between subjects must be broken down completely in order that the school work may be properly 'motivated'". These are the ideals that the Australian visitor found to dominate the thinking of many of the teachers and educational leaders whom he interviewed. They can be expressed in such terms as pupil-initiative in place of teacher-planning; pupil experiences not only as a basis for race-experience but as more significant than race-experience; immediate interest as more significant than adult needs; and freedom as a means of education rather than the attainment of freedom as an aim of education. That these are the ideals toward which school practice is being directed is shown clearly by the wide vogue of "activity programs" and "interest-unit plans." It is shown in the stigma that increasingly attaches to the systematic and orderly direction and pursuit of learning. A recent inquiry sent to the members of the National Society for the Study of Education, which is fairly representative of the leadership of our profession, indicates that two thirds of this membership are sympathetic toward these and related doctrines. More than one state department of education has virtually given to these and similar tenets an official sanction. And so an issue that has been a source of controversy for centuries seems likely to be settled now by official fiat.

In my opinion, American educational theory as I have defined it has an important but a quite limited field of application. Carried beyond this field, its results, I am confident, will be little short of disastrous. To be concrete, let me take the so-called activity programs. These, I believe, should dominate the earlier stages of education. I have held for many years, too, that throughout the elementary and secondary schools there should be abundant opportunities for the learner to follow the learning "leads" that his interests suggest. Fifteen years ago I called such opportunities "free-project periods." Next I called them "free-activity periods." Now I shall have to call them, I suppose, "free-areas-of-interest periods," and there will doubtless be another name for them next year— but they all mean the same thing.

Now, to recognize a limited place for free activities is one thing; to maintain that all learnings should be of this type is quite another; and it is the latter tenet that comes inevitably as a corollary from the fundamental premises of our dominant theory. This is nothing more or less than a downright negation of one of the most important human characteristics; the ability, namely, to work systematically and persistently in the face of immediate desire, interest or impulse. It is this capacity that has enabled mankind to climb upward from the plane of the savage and the brute. As Graham Wallas pointed out long ago, this ability has been a *sine qua non* of social evolution as contrasted with biological evolution. To attempt to nullify this factor, whether by official fiat or otherwise, suggests Huxley's famous epigram, "What has been ordained among the prehistoric Protozoa can not be altered by act of Parliament."

It is because this capacity for sustained effort is normally weak in young children that I believe our current theory to have a legitimate place in the earlier stages of education. I shall grant, too, that there are some unfortunates who never get beyond this stage; volitionally they never grow up, and for them activity programs and other appeals to immediate interest may be needed indefinitely. For normal children in the later pre-adolescent years, however, and throughout adolescence, the assumption that they can not and should not learn unless they have an immediate yearning for learning is not only an affront to their intelligence, it is a gratuitous denial of their grit, their courage—in short, their will-power. An educational theory which encourages the belief that there is no difference between the work attitude and the play attitude not only flies in the face of the plainest facts of experience, it is also charged with social dynamite. Of course many workers find their work fascinating, more fascinating sometimes than play, and most fascinating perhaps when, by effort and struggle, they have reached a high plane of endeavor. But to identify work and play under the same psychological rubric is fatal. I would maintain, furthermore, that the higher-order interests are attained in no other way than through an initial period of struggle—of effort to do initially uninteresting and sometimes distasteful things. An educational theory which says, not merely in effect but in so many words, "If you do not have an immediate interest in a task you are justified in evading it"—such a theory is about as debilitating in its probable influence as can be conceived. And yet it is just such a theory which has been weakening the fiber of American education for a generation and which is now being preached and, so far as possible, applied, in a most extreme form on a nation-wide front.

Our contemporary American educational theory of course is not new. Its most characteristic tenets were set forth in the seventeenth century by a group of European educators who, even at that remote day, very modestly dubbed themselves the "Progressives." The theory was given wide currency and effective expression by Rousseau. In the nineties of the last century it came out in sharp relief in a battle royal between the advocates of interest and the advocates of effort, and it was his classic attempt to integrate these opposing doctrines which first brought Mr. Dewey into prominence as an educational leader. It seemed at the time that Dewey's integration would solve the problem by combining on a higher level the valid and valuable elements in each doctrine. But the actual theory which came to dominate education and determine its ideals swung so far away from this solution that to-day the doctrine of interest is in sole possession of the field, and in a form far more extreme and sinister than ever before. Mr. Dewey's integration succeeded admirably in recognizing effort as an outcome of interest, but the basic fact that the interests which grow out of effort are unquestionably the highest and the worthiest of all interests has long been obscured. It is my contention that an educational theory which does not recognize this second factor is a limited theory and entirely inadequate; as a *sole* guide to practise, it is quite inadequate.

Let us follow some of these inadequacies a little further. Our dominant educational theory has not only rejected the notion of mental discipline, it has distinctly encouraged the correlative assumption that those who are subjected to the type of learning formerly supposed to discipline the mind are actually harmed thereby. Hence many young people who have been thoroughly competent to the more exacting studies have been sanctioned by educational theory in following the lines of least resistance. How far from the truth are these implications of our theory is suggested by an investigation reported two years ago by H. L. Kriner. The need of selecting carefully the candidates for admission to teacher-training institutions impelled Mr. Kriner to try to find something in a student's high-school record that would indicate whether he or she would make an efficient teacher. To this end, he asked superintendents of the most progressive of the smaller school systems in Pennsylvania to give him the names of their best teachers and their poorest teachers. Mr. Kriner then went back to the high-school records of these teachers. His discoveries are fairly disconcerting. The best single index of one's probable efficiency as a teacher, whether in the elementary or in the secondary school, is the successful completion of more than two years of high-school Latin. Next comes the successful completion of more than two years of high-school mathematics. Next, the successful completion of more than two years of natural science. If, however, the prospective teacher has taken more than two years of the social studies he is a poor risk. I am not claiming from this evidence any positive disciplinary influence for the hard subjects as compared with the easy subjects. I am merely giving evidence that the pursuit of the former does not necessarily have disastrous results. Some day, of course, our profession will have the courage to admit that in completely discarding the ideal of mental discipline, it proved itself to be extremely gullible—in fact, it was taken in by what the underworld would call "phoney" evidence.

Another vagary of current educational theory is the appealing notion that creative abilities are inevitably crushed or at least fettered by the disciplinary type of education; while the free type of education develops these abilities. Our good friends apparently have forgotten their history; perhaps because it was not taught to them through an activity program. Late in the sixth and early in the fifth centuries, B.C., Athenian education was severely disciplinary in the best sense of that much abused and now quite outmoded term. Less rigorous on the physical side than the education of Sparta, it nevertheless laid great emphasis upon the development of strength and physical vigor and manly courage and endurance. On the intellectual side, it emphasized the study of what were even then the great classics of Greek literature—the majestic hexameters of the Homeric cycle, the great songs and the choruses from the great tragedies. On the ethical aide, it included respect for elders, devotion to duty and especially devotion to the duties of citizenship. Unlike other systems of education in the ancient world, Athenian education was vital and meaningful rather than stupidly verbal. The classical masterpieces were learned by heart, but their meaning and significance were explained carefully by the teacher. In all history, perhaps, no body of educational practises has so well integrated the rights of the individual with the welfare and progress of society. It was a balanced, high-minded education, consciously designed to produce men who would be worthy of the name, "free," and competent to the serious duties of responsible citizenship in a social order in which collective action was determined by the collective will of the free citizens.

It was this disciplinary regimen, according to Aristophanes, which made possible the victory of the Greeks over the Persians and brought to a close the Persian wars. I do not maintain that Aristophanes was right, but I do maintain that this disciplinary regimen, if our current theory is right, should have entirely unfitted the Athenians for what followed. You will remember that, partly as a result of her leadership in the wars against Persia, partly through the tribute of new colonies and partly because of her growing commerce, Athens became rich beyond the dreams of avarice. Quite literally it was a golden opportunity that spread out before her. What was she to do with her opportunity? Well, what she did do with it she simply could not have done if our American educational theory were valid. She entered upon a period of creative productivity in sculpture, architecture, poetry, drama, and philosophy that has not only been unsurpassed in the world's history but never even approximated in its glory. More men of undying fame wrought their immortal achievements during the brief Age of Pericles than during any similar period in all history. Nay, one may go even further and say that more creative work of the very highest order was done during those thirty years than has been done in the two thousand years that have since elapsed.

Well, something apparently is wrong with our theory, and something else may be wrong if the sequel of Athens' rise to such grand heights tells the truth. In periods of great prosperity, standards tend to relax, abundance breeds not only leisure but luxury and idleness and the gratification of individual desire. Gradually the fiber of Athenian character softened—and, as almost always happens under such circumstances, the forces of education, instead of counteracting this tendency, were themselves weakened and actually compounded the evils. Thus we find fairly early in the age of Pericles the texture of education undergoing fundamental modifications. As we should say to-day, the curriculum was brought up to date to meet the changing character of the new civilization. The great poems and songs were replaced by contemporary literature in a much lighter vein; in many instances religion and the older moral values were ridiculed; less emphasis was given to respect for elders and for the law; duty to the state was derided as an outworn virtue. There were changes, too, in the methods of teaching. In the olden times, the teachers had explained the masterpieces while the boys listened; now teachers and pupils formed discussion groups and talked things over—the beginning, I take it, of the socialized recitation and the child-centered school. Most symptomatic of all, however, were the changes that were made in the aims and practices of physical education. The ideals of rugged strength and manly courage and endurance were abandoned in favor of beauty and grace—a calamitous change, for it was undoubtedly a factor in bringing about the perversions and depravities which played so important a role in the political collapse and the tragic moral degeneration of that wonderful city-state.

I am not personally concerned with the practicability of our dominant American educational theory, but I do challenge its validity as a theory when applied beyond the limits that I have already named. I make this challenge on the following grounds:

Its tenets regarding child-freedom are inconsistent with the plain biological implications of the greatly extended period of human immaturity which has clearly been a fundamental factor in human evolution and which derives its significance from the inescapable need of the human offspring for responsible support, control, direction, training, discipline and instruction on the part of the adult. To assume that children can grow normally without having this need met is to assume that natural laws can be transcended at the behest of human doctrinaires. Normal children crave direction and control.

The tenets of the theory imply that freedom is a gift. In the history of the race, true freedom—whether freedom from personal thralldom or freedom from fear, fraud, want, superstition and error—true freedom has never been a gift but always a conquest. In one way or another each generation must make this conquest for itself if it would be truly free.

The tenets of the theory obviously lack virility. I do not mean that they are feminine; I mean rather that they are effeminate. They are weak in their very nature and enfeebling in their influence.

We come finally to one of the most amazing phenomenon in the history of educational theory. As Dr. Kandel has recently pointed out the group that has been urging most insistently pupil-freedom and the planless curriculum, the group that has held to a theory which deifies the individual and his free choices, is now the group that is most ardently advocating a planned economic order, a central control of the industry and an abandonment of *laissez-faire.*

They can not find words that are strong enough when it comes to condemning individualism in the body politic; yet for a generation they have taught that education should follow the course dictated by the learner's individual interest. They protest against the profit motive in business and industry; but for a generation they have contended that every child should ask of every learning exercise, "What is there in it for me?" They protest against the sordidness of contemporary civilization, when the only criterion of truth that their basic philosophy has recognized is the test of narrow practicality, "Will it work?"

To judge by the closing of banks and the closing of schools, the present plight of our country is not matched in the civilized world. England and Canada have hard times, but the banks do not fail; and as for schools, Turkey, with all her poverty, opened in a single province 150 new schools last year and will open 150 more this year.

To-day the Progressives are shocked to look out on American society well-nigh wrecked on the rocks of individualism. But do they look back on their own teachings over the past two decades! Twenty years ago it was I who was declaiming against the evils of an excessive individualism. Just twenty years ago in addressing this department at the Philadelphia meeting

I warned you of the dangers in an educational theory that even then threatened to compound rather than correct these evils—a theory that even then, as I have proved by duly documented evidence, was softening the fiber of American education. I have repeated the warning at intervals ever since. I have been both pitied by my friends and condemned by my enemies for persisting in this attitude, and whatever professional reputation I may once have had has dwindled with every reference that I have made to this problem. But even though my profession may persist in the pleasant pastime of chasing butterflies, I still maintain that I would rather be right than Progressive.

Some Master Teachers
I Have Known
(1936)[1]

Bagley wrote this paper to honor the teachers who influenced his life. Because he spent his career working to develop solid programs for teaching teachers, Bagley's reflections on his days as a student are essential to understanding his thoughts on education in general and good teaching in particular. He wanted all young Americans to experience memorable teachers, like those he came to know as a young man. In addition to providing autobiographical information on Bagley's life, this work illustrates how his understanding of the "master teacher" was influenced by the teachers he experienced.

I do not believe that there can be any generic definition or description of the master teacher. There are hundreds, perhaps thousands, who in one way or another at some points in their lives deserve this designation. Before writing this paper I thought carefully over those whose teaching was aimed in part at me during my school, college, and university days. There were five, I think, whom I should rank as master teachers, and several who closely approached that rank. I shall describe each of the five briefly, and because this paper will be published, I shall read their names into the record.

---

1. Prepared for a meeting of the American Association of Teachers Colleges, February 21, 1936. Read before a luncheon meeting of the National Society of College Teachers of Education, St. Louis, February 24, 1936.

Forgotten Heroes of American Education, pages 225–234

These five teachers were all men. I had some very good women teachers. At least I thought they were good, altho at this distance, and recalling that I have always had a profound admiration for the ladies, I am not certain that I remember them pleasantly because as teachers they were good or merely good-looking. I hasten to add, however, that one of the best of my women teachers was very plain—a fact that we forgot in the excellence of her work.

My first teacher of the masculine persuasion was principal of an elementary school that I attended in Worcester, Massachusetts, almost a half century ago. His name was William H. Bartlett. He was a man of portly proportions and easy, graceful carriage, always well groomed and clean-shaven, wearing only a mustache in a day when bushy beards were the "mode" and when even those who were not long-bearded shaved as a rule only once a week.

This was before the days when principals gave all their time to administration and supervision. Mr. Bartlett taught for perhaps half of the school day in the ninth-grade room. (In Massachusetts at that time the elementary-school period was nine years in duration, and led to the high school which had four-year programs for the plain "garden variety" of pupils, but which required five years for those destined to go to college.) In teaching, Mr. Bartlett sat comfortably at his desk, asking questions and giving instruction in an exceptionally well-controlled voice, with an easy assurance of the mastery of his subject.

If I recall aright, Mr. Bartlett was a graduate of West Point; at least he had been a colonel (on the Union side, of course) in the Confederate War. Discipline was no problem in that school. We simply took it for granted that we should be orderly and industrious. We were in a brand-new school building and I recall that Mr. Bartlett got the boys together and spoke in a very reasonable way about the importance of keeping the building in good shape and quite frankly about the careful use of the toilets and the disreputability of defacing them in any way.

Of Mr. Bartlett's pet aversions, one was carelessness in articulation and enunciation. The new school building had a most spacious attic not divided into rooms. At periodic intervals he would take the ninth-grade boys to this attic. They would stand in line at one end of the attic; he would stand at the other end. He would recite to us verses and stanzas of poems; we would, in chorus and individually, give them back to him, and woe betide the lad who could not make himself distinctly heard at the other side of the room. His favorite poem was "Sheridan's Ride," and as we repeated it in unison I am inclined to think that no person within two blocks could have been unaware of the fact that Winchester was twenty miles away. Why the girls were not subjected to a similar process of training in vocal control I do not know.

At the close of the year the boys in the class (and maybe the girls, altho I believe that the latter made a similar gift to Mr. Bartlett's assistant teacher in the ninth grade) purchased a framed picture depicting in gorgeous colors the assault of the Union forces on Port Royal. Mr. Bartlett had told us, I remember, that he had taken part in this battle. It was a cheap "chromo," but I have a distinct image of Mr. Bartlett when the picture was presented holding it at arm's length with real or feigned enthusiasm, "Now that *is* a picture!"

I am not quite sure why Mr. Bartlett has remained in my memory as a formative force. Perhaps it was because he was the first man teacher that I had. I have very vivid recollections of the time when I went from the instruction of women teachers to the instruction of a man for at least half-time. Heretofore I had been addressed by my given name, which was always contracted to the diminutive, "Willie." But when we entered Mr. Bartlett's classroom, the boys were called by their last names (I was no longer "Willie," I was Bagley); each girl was "Miss Smith," or "Miss Jones," or "Miss Brown," as the case might be. My chest-girth extended about a foot that night. And it was in the following week, I think, that the short trousers of the boy gave place to the long trousers of the young man. Those were red-letter events.

I attended high school in Detroit. I do not recall any of my teachers there as outstanding, although I was impressed by the principal of the school—a refined and scholarly gentleman, whose place in public secondary education ended within the decade, for within that period the American high school began in a marked measure its transition from a selective to a non-selective institution. Mass-education began its upward expansion, and scholarly gentlemen of the intellectually aristocratic type gave place to those who could plan secondary education for "all the children of all the people."

In 1891 I entered the Michigan Agricultural College, now known as the Michigan State College. At that time, except for one or two daughters of members of the faculty, this was exclusively a men's college, (and I may say parenthetically that, in my judgment, coeducation at the college level is an unwise policy). My college was the oldest of its kind, having been opened in 1857, five years before the enactment of the Morrill act which endowed the so-called "land-grant" colleges. From the outset it had enlisted the services of exceptionally competent teachers and scholars. One of its early professors was still teaching when I was a student. This was Roscoe C. Kedzie, who was in charge of the work in chemistry and director of the chemical laboratory, one of the first laboratories of chemistry to be founded in the United States, and the very first, I think, to have a building all its own.

Kedzie was a teacher of the first magnitude. He was well past seventy when I first knew him. He had a magnificent head with his high brow fringed with snow-white hair. He stood erect behind the wide demonstration desk, lecturing in a clear well-organized discourse that I have never heard surpassed in a college or university classroom. He was independent and absolutely fearless. At a time long before the general recognition and popular condemnation of "racketeering" in business and industry, he publicly assailed the fraudulent claims of manufacturers of commercial fertilizers. I recall particularly his ridicule of the arguments of agents of lightning-rod manufacturers and his specific instructions regarding the home-made construction of equally effective lightning-rods from cheap iron pipes.

Kedzie was a schoolmaster of the old school, exact and exacting, and yet he had and frequently expressed the sense of humor which seems to me to be essential to most master teachers. As an old man he was a bit palsied, and his hand shook a trifle in his demonstrations. I recall that we all sat with our nerves on edge when, in holding a test-tube in which he had demonstrated the making of nitro-glycerin, he said casually, "Now gentlemen, if I should drop this test-tube—!" And what a sigh of relief went up when that test-tube was finally returned to its niche in the case!

I have never understood just why this little college of agriculture and the mechanic arts attracted and held so many teachers of high scholarship and unusual effectiveness. I believe that I am in a position to speak advisedly for I attended courses in four universities of high standing after leaving my Alma Mater. I venture the hypothesis that my college had been established in one sense as a protest against the then prevailing tradition, which was intellectually aristocratic and severely classical. It had gone so far toward the other extreme that not only were Latin and Greek absent from the curriculum, but, also (except for the students in engineering) modern foreign languages. It was establishing a new tradition—the tradition of the natural sciences—and fundamental, quite naturally, was the apotheosis of labor. Another of the early agricultural colleges—now the University of Illinois—had as its motto the phrase, "Learning and Labor," and I recall that a high-hatted instructor with his Ph.D. from Harvard construed this to mean (with reference to the ability of the students who came to his classes), "Learning *with* Labor."

In the law which established the Michigan Agricultural College, the labor *motif* was reflected in a provision which required each student to work on the farm two and one half hours every day except Saturday and Sunday. The sessions of the College extended through the Summer months, the "long vacation" coming in the Winter. The work delegated to the students was quite largely of a purely routine nature—raking leaves, shelling corn, hoeing potatoes, and the like. When I entered the College, however, it happened that a master teacher was in charge of the students' labor. He believed that it would be in keeping with the law to make this compulsory labor of real educational value. He developed a series of what we should now call projects, but which were then referred to as students' experiments. The first project which was assigned to me was to determine the most favorable depth at which to cultivate potatoes. I was to plant two adjoining plots of potatoes, and in the hours of farm-labor I was to operate a hand cultivator, with a deep adjustment of teeth on one plot and a shallow adjustment of the teeth on the other plot. At the harvest in the late Summer I was to compare the results of the two types of cultivation. The results were conclusively in favor of shallow cultivation, although at the time we had no measures of statistical significance. The experiment was described and the results published in an official bulletin of the Agricultural Experiment Station. A second project in the following year was aimed to determine whether a certain method of treating oat seed before sowing would prevent the germination of a serious fungus infection known as smut of oats. This was distinctly in the nature of an educational project for it necessitated a goodly amount of reading beyond the ground covered in classwork. This was another lesson for me in scientific method because the results of the experiment were inconclusive and I learned that the collection of trustworthy principles often involved the following-up of many false leads and "blind alleys" before dependable generalizations could be made. The then young man who directed these investigations (and who was also a superb classroom teacher) was Perry G. Holden.

A third master teacher in this little Michigan college at the time of my attendance was Howard Edwards, who later became President of the Rhode Island State College. I may be permitted to quote from an address that I gave at a meeting of the alumni of the Rhode Island State College shortly after the death of President Edwards.[2]

It was nearly forty years ago that I first became acquainted with Dr. Edwards. In 1890, I believe, he became professor of English in what was then called the Michigan Agricultural College. (This institution, by the way, is the oldest of the group of land-grant colleges. The Michigan College was founded in 1857, or five years before Lincoln signed the famous Morrill act which led to establishment of similar colleges in every state of the Union.) I entered the Michigan Agricultural College as a freshman in 1891. In the freshman class were 130 other boys, most of them from the back-country farms of a state many parts of which at that time still reflected the sturdy pioneer conditions which have made the American frontier a factor of the first magnitude in the development of American civilization.

---

2. Reprinted with courteous permission from the *Journal of Education*, June 23, 1930.

Both because of his personal qualities and because of the subject that he taught, Dr. Edwards was an ideal teacher for this group of raw boys. He was a gentleman in the finest sense of the word—a man who gracefully and instinctively did the right thing in the right way. Some of our instructors rather tended toward what he called a cult of crudity, assuming perhaps that refinements of speech and manner were somehow out of place in a farmers' college.

Not so Howard Edwards. Indeed the quality which above all other qualities endeared him to us was his high-minded integrity. He hated pose and cant and smugness and hypocrisy with a righteous hatred. I am very sure that many of us came for the first time in his classes to be sensitive to these vices—and there is, I think, no more significant function of a liberal education than to sensitize the student to vices that are the more insidious in that they so often parade in the garb of virtue.

Cut from the same cloth as this unshakable integrity were the kindly sympathy and broad tolerance of our beloved teacher. These found a fascinating expression in a quizzical smile and a twinkle of the eyes that it would be impossible to describe.

It was in the classroom and through his teaching that Edwards exerted the most lasting influence upon the students at Michigan. He was a past master of the rare art of making the subject of instruction tingle with life. He introduced us to the great masterpieces of literature and revealed why they were masterpieces. To many of us the world of books had never before been opened. Others were wont to scoff at all forms of art as unworthy of the attention of what we call today "real red-blooded he-men." For still others the liking for literature had been destroyed by the type of treatment accorded to the subject in the high schools.

Nearly everyone who enrolled in Dr. Edwards' classes saw literature in a new light. *Hamlet, Macbeth,* and *King Lear* became living and throbbing realities. The England of Swift and Dryden, Pope and Defoe became a real England peopled by men and women who worked and played, and lived and loved.

Then there was *Paradise Lost.* Frequently teachers objected to the inclusion of *Paradise Lost* in the required reading of high school or college on the ground that the average pupil or student cannot appreciate it. Howard Edwards taught *Paradise Lost* in such a way that the farm boys of Michigan rose to the majestic measures of Milton's great epic.

Dr. Edwards did not ask beforehand whether we wanted to read *Paradise Lost.* He probably thought that everyone should read, if possible, the greatest epic poem in the English language, and I am sure that he conceived it to be his primary duty as a teacher to make our reading of it as profitable as possible. I do not recall that we liked *Paradise Lost* at the outset, but under the stimulus of masterful teaching the light dawned. And that, I think, is the acid test of good teaching.

There was an artistry in Edwards' class work that I have many times tried to analyze in the hope that I could help other teachers to acquire it. But I have been unable to make such an analysis. The lessons themselves are what I remember—not the arts that the teacher employed to drive these lessons home. Only a few bits of his effective teaching technics can I recall.

It has been said of another great teacher that every class exercise was, for his students, a series of exciting adventures and hairbreadth escapes. Edwards had a similar capacity for capitalizing the dramatic possibilities of the teacher's art. Lines or verses that did not impress many of us on first reading he would have us work over and play with until suddenly their beauty or their grandeur or the nobility of their underlying thought burst upon us. Some things that we deemed pretty good he would deal with in similar fashion until we saw clearly that what we thought to be glittering gold was after all only tinsel, and that we had been worshiping at a false shrine. Frequently, too, he would take men and women then in the public eye and relate them to the types that the masters had portrayed.

Edwards did more than capitalize the dramatic possibilities of his classroom teaching. He made his assignments in such a way that the element of adventure was carried over into our out-of-class preparation. I recall a typical assignment. "Alexander's Feast" was among the poems to be read for the next class exercise. "In this poem," said Edwards, "there are three of the most beautiful verses in the English language. See whether you can find them." It would have been hard to miss them, but I doubt very much whether, without that suggestion, we should have caught the full effect of that marvelous alliteration of the liquid consonants:

> "War," he sung, "is toil and trouble;
> Honor, but an empty bubble;
> Never ending, still beginning,
> Fighting still, and still destroying:
> If the world be worth the winning,
> Think, O think it worth enjoying."

Edwards had a way, too, of calling attention to our crudities of speech in a way that was effective in correcting them without at the same time embarrassing us. I recall an occasion when, as a cadet officer in charge of the "awkward squad," I had just given a piece of my mind to a student who had persisted in holding his rifle in a wrong angle. My language may have been picturesque, and I probably used a few provincialisms which I was certain the student in question would understand, even if these words and phrases failed of elegance by a fairly wide margin—and perhaps even of strict propriety.

Dr. Edwards was walking across the parade ground and had just passed behind me as I finished my invective. Happening to look around, I saw him with that quizzical smile and the twinkle in his eye. The next day he took occasion in class to read us a good-natured but tolerant lecture about the needless use of certain words and phrases. He did not mention the occasion that led to the caution, but rather let his remarks come out quite naturally in the class discussion. Nevertheless, I got the point.

Among our instructors Dr. Edwards was one of the few who had students in their homes at frequent intervals. A red-letter event in our class history was the banquet he gave for us just before we graduated. There was a printed menu and—vastly more important—the speaking program was announced in verse, with an appropriate stanza for each of the student-speakers. We looked upon it as a tremendous honor that our professor of literature should have written poetry about us.

My first graduate work was undertaken at the University of Wisconsin in 1897. Here I found excellent teachers in Dr. J. W. Stearns and Dr. Joseph Jastrow, but it was a young Professor of Education who in some ways impressed me most, M. Vincent O'Shea. He was an excellent classroom teacher of the "developmental" type. Outside the fields of the history and philosophy of education, professional literature was very meager at that time, and O'Shea's principal work was in "child study" as developed by G. Stanley Hall. If the substance was a bit "thin" it was not O'Shea's fault, and many virtues of the man and his method were compensation in full. He was a strikingly handsome man, always immaculately groomed, with a graceful carriage and an excellent speaking voice. He was, I think, the most nearly perfect gentleman I have ever known. He developed rather remarkably in the years that followed, and his contributions to educational progress were numerous and far more substantial than they were credited with being in certain quarters.

The final teacher on my list was different—almost radically different—from any of the others. He was E. B. Titchener, of Cornell, who was my major professor in the work that I did toward the Doctor's degree. Titchener was at that time a young Englishman, a graduate of Oxford, who upon the advice of Thomas H. Huxley, had gone to Leipzig to study in the psychological laboratory which Wilhelm Wundt had opened in 1879. Titchener was convinced that the study of mind could be placed upon the basis of an exact science, and he conceived of the psychological laboratory as quite analogous to the laboratory of physics. Of course the young graduate students were quickly indoctrinated, and we had the habit of referring to philosophers who wrote about the nature of the mind as "arm-chair" psychologists. We were "laboratory men," real dyed-in-the-wool scientists.

Titchener was a disciplinist of the martinet type. In his seminar and in his class in German psychology—the only course that he taught by any except the lecture-method—he was unmerciful to those who made errors, or displeased him. The seminar was attended by a few students whose major subject was philosophy. Two of these students got into a heated discussion over a book that had recently appeared in their field—F. H. Bradley's "Appearance and Reality." Titchener stood it for a minute or two for he had a contempt for philosophy; finally he interrupted them roughly stating that scientific psychology had a far better use to make of its time. I recalled this incident a year or so ago when the distinguished astronomer and physicist, Sir James Jeans, published his "New Background of Science." Almost at the outset was a long quotation from Bradley's "Appearance and Reality." Physics, which psychology was emulating forty years ago, appears today to be leaving the laboratory occasionally and returning to metaphysics for some of its basic assumptions.

But if we did not get from Titchener an enduring system of psychology, we did get from him a clear notion of what the scientific method involves and of what scholarship in any field means. These lessons were enforced with rigor in all our work. Keeping up with our literature—reading the technical journals religiously as they come out—meticulous care in drawing conclusions from incomplete data—keeping personal prejudice from affecting research: all these and other characteristics of the scientific method became ideals which were dominant in the minds of most of his students.

It mattered nothing to Titchener that his psychology had no practical applications. He drew a sharp distinction between structural psychology and functional psychology, and he was a structuralist. His aim was to analyze consciousness and describe its parts. He was a "pure" scientist, and those who tried to find uses for facts were quite a bit below the pure scientist in importance and repute.

Rigid and formal as he was in lecture-room and laboratory, he had his students at his home more frequently than any of my college and university instructors. I was an assistant in Cornell's first summer session, and he asked me to come over every night after dinner, usually with student guests—men, for one of his evening's entertainments was the serving of beer, and while this in those days was a perfectly proper thing for a college professor in that part of the country to do, it was perfectly improper to ask a real lady to join the party.

Titchener had few friends among his colleagues. Indeed he had already broken with the newly organized American Psychological Association. He kept up a professional friendship with Stanley Hall and Stanford, of Clark University, but except for these with no other workers in psychology save his own graduates.

I began this paper with the statement that, in my judgment, one cannot give a description of traits that will fit all master teachers. I close with an additional limitation to the discussion of the subject—namely, that traits in teachers which appeal to one person may not appeal in the same way to others. Some of my fellow-students in college and university would not give the same degree of recognition that I have given to the men whom I have named. On the other hand, there are factors other than the actual efficiency of a teacher which may lead most students to regard him favorably or unfavorably and to take either kindly or unkindly to his instructions. One of these is a tradition that often grows up around him. In the first year the student learns from upper classmen that one, so-and-so, is a great teacher and that another, so-and-so, is quite the contrary. The student is likely to be greatly influenced by these traditions, altho, whether positive or negative, the traditions may be most unjust to the teacher concerned. I know instances of teachers who had acquired unfavorable traditions in one institution and who quite reversed their reputation when they moved to another community or another institution. I believe that a study of such cases would reveal dearly that much of a teacher's ability to rise to the role of master teacher depends upon adventitious factors which may either stimulate or depress him. This may not be true of the greatest geniuses in teaching like Mark Hopkins or William Rainey Harper, but these, I think, are only the exception that proves the rule. On the higher levels of instruction, too, the teacher's standing in his particular field of scholarship is likely to lead the student to a species of hero-worship that will blind him to the fact that a famous scholar may be a quite mediocre teacher. My own acquaintance with teachers and scholars, however, leads me to the conclusion that, in general, great scholars are also great teachers, sometimes having the ability to make clear to the average mind the contributions to human knowledge that have been made in their own specialized fields. I refer here to some (not all) of the great scholars. There are men and women who have made research investigations of outstanding value but who have no interest in illuminating either the duller intellects or the more competent minds in fields other than their own.

Are the Essentialists the True Progressives? (1938)[1]

This lecture by Bagley was never published. Essentialism was a movement that began in Atlantic City in March of 1938 when Bagley and some of his like-minded colleagues joined together to argue for the ideas they thought must be present in any educational theory. The Essentialists argued in favor of teachers teaching an organized curriculum to all students, the necessity for a reasonable degree of system in the organization of curriculum, sound teacher education, and the desirability for teachers to teach a body of core democratic principles to each generation of young Americans. These ideas were in opposition to Progressives such as John Dewey and William Heard Kilpatrick. As Bagley mentions below, Dewey and Kilpatrick reacted emotionally to the claims of the Essentialists. The debate that ensued between Dewey and Kilpatrick on one hand and Bagley and the Essentialists on the other attracted nationwide attention and was covered in Time, Newsweek, *and the* New York Times.

Bagley apparently intended to publish this article; he sent the manuscript to Educational Administration and Supervision, *which typeset the paper and readied it for publication. Bagley did not, however, return the galley proofs to the journal. Instead, he placed the typeset manuscript in his personal files.*

We have chosen to reproduce the paper here because of the insight that it provides into the controversy that followed the founding of Essentialism. One of the primary

---

1. An address prepared for the Educational Administration Conference, Teachers College, Columbia University, August 2, 1938; unpublished address, Hoover Institution Archives, Stanford University, William W. Brickman Collection, Box 51.

Forgotten Heroes of American Education, pages 235–243

reasons that Bagley may have chosen not to publish this address is that the work contains rhetoric that is quite a bit more heated than what is found in his other writings. He strongly criticizes Kilpatrick, Dewey, and others for their comments following the founding of Essentialism. Despite his claims to the contrary, Bagley's discussion in this essay makes clear that controversies over educational theory at Teachers College in the 1930s were deeply personal in nature.

Unfamiliar words and familiar words in an unfamiliar context are likely to attract attention, sometime quite beyond the expectation, and not infrequently to the embarrassment, of those who first use them. The term "essentials" is certainly familiar enough in educational discussions, and yet when a small group, meeting at Atlantic City last February, happened to call themselves "The Essentialist Committee for the Advancement of American Education," the mere name itself caused a commotion even before anything was said as to what the Essentialists believed or what they proposed. The Committee was really microscopic in size as committees go in our profession; it held no open meetings; and yet, even before it met, it had attracted attention. There seemed to be magic in the name—something akin to black magic, perhaps. And when, finally, one member of the group yielded to the importunities of the newspaper reporters and released some fragments from a set of theses which had been prepared primarily for discussion rather than for immediate publication, it was apparently the name of the Committee rather than anything in the fragments printed in the news reports that gave the term "Essentialists" a nation-wide currency overnight.

In as much as the press-release was made up largely of some theses that I had hastily prepared on the morning of the first meeting, I have believed it a duty to my profession to publish the statements as I originally framed them, adding a final section in the way of a provisional completion of my own Essentialist platform. This has recently been issued in pamphlet form.[2] In view of the fact that it is available to anyone who cares to read it, I shall not repeat its statements at this time. I shall rather take the opportunity to use the quite savage denunciations provoked by the term, "Essentialist," as the text of a little homily on the now clearly demonstrated need in American education for the type of impersonal and dispassionate discussion which the Essentialist group represents, whatever may be its tenets and whatever may be its shortcomings; for however obscure the

---

2. "An Essentialist's Platform for the Advancement of American Education," *Educational Administration and Supervision*, April, 1938, pp. 241ff. Reprints are available at 20 cents a copy from the publishers, Warwick and York, Baltimore.

members of the Essentialist committee may be in the educational world, they have never tried to obscure basic issues by that easy and tempting device—the appeal to prejudice.

Not so their critics. There was, for example, no discernible clarification of the intricate problems of American education when John J. de Boer, a leader in the American Federation of Teachers, referred in an editorial article in the official journal of the Chicago Teachers Union to the Essentialists as "educational Bourbons" who "are still catching up on their outside reading in Adam Smith and William T. Harris," and whose efforts in the judgment of Mr. de Boer, are restricted to "beating tom-toms" for the "comma-splice" and "the date of the Battle of Brandywine," in a futile effort to maintain "the vested interests in education and society."[3]

Nor did it augur well for clear thinking in American education when J. A. Sexson, Superintendent of the Pasadena schools and the retiring president of the American Association of School Administrators, charged the Essentialists with seizing what he alleged to be a period of social and economic reactionism in order to promote a return to the good old educational order represented by the dunce-cap and the hickory stick.

Mr. de Boer and Mr. Sexson are leaders respectively of two groups that are often thought of as mutually antagonistic; yet they apparently not only see eye to eye when it comes to the Essentialists, but are also willing to use the same time-dishonored methods in attacking what they consider to be a common foe.

Far more disquieting, however, was the prompt response of the two most prominent contemporary leaders in educational theory—the two men for whom, in spite of differences in opinion, I have a regard, both personally and professionally, that is very close to veneration. In a widely publicized statement made at the Atlantic City dinner meeting of the honor society, Kappa Delta Pi, Mr. Dewey characterized Essentialism as an imitation of religious fundamentalism and, by clear implication, identified its motives with those of the political and social reactionaries.

Mr. Kilpatrick, according to press reports, made similar charges on the same day: "The Essentialists represent the same sort of reactionary trend that always springs up when a doctrine is gaining headway." He added by way of comment on one of the theses that happened to be quoted correctly in the newspapers: "As for the statement that American children do not show up so well as foreign ones on standardized tests, in so far as it is true, it is a criticism of the traditional methods which are still largely in use in

---

3. Boer, J. J.: "Teachers are People." *Chicago Union Teacher,* April, 1938, p. 4.

this country despite the advance of progressivism."[4] I shall refer later to this comment.

I quote these statements because the leaders whom I have named are adherents of a school of educational theory which has enthroned the development of clear thinking as a primary aim of education. Yet these men, as Mr. Kandel has pointed out,[5] used on this occasion the propagandist appeals to prejudice recognized by students of propaganda as those best calculated to becloud thinking and obscure real issues— including the most reprehensible device of all, known in logic as the *argumentum ad hominem*, translated by Clyde Miller into current American vernacular as the "name-calling" device.[6] When the mere mention of a word like "Essentialist" arouses an emotional response that obscures the real issue among highly educated and responsible leaders who profess to see in clarity of thought the salvation of humanity, can we wonder that the ubiquitous "man in the street" goes haywire, one group when the word "Communism" is the stimulus; another group when "Fascism" is flashed upon the screen; another when "Economic Royalist" is mentioned; and still others when "Fundamentalism," "Pacifism," "Capitalism," or any one of a long list of similar terms, charged with emotional dynamite, pops into the picture?

May I now refer briefly, first, to specific instances of this impulse to becloud issues by an unwarranted and unjust imputation of absurd meanings and inferences which, like the "flowers that bloom in the Spring," have nothing to do with the case? Take, for example, Mr. de Boer's sarcastic reference to the "comma-splice" and "the date of the Battle of Brandywine" as among the alleged essentials of the Essentialists. What the Essentialist theses emphasized primarily was the weakness of the lower schools in failing to bring increasingly large proportions of pupils to an easily attainable level of facility in the basic art of reading. This glaring defect, Mr. de Boer does not question. He does not even ask for evidence supporting the charge. Apparently Mr. de Boer accepts it as an unpleasant fact and merely tries to cover it up by encouraging his readers to believe that ability to read is no more essential than the ability to recall dates (the more unimportant the better for the propagandist critic) or trifling conventionalities in punctuation. By the way of summary Mr. de Boer combines this device with that of "name calling": "The panoplied custodians of the racial heritage are confusing essentials with comfortable old habits."

---

4. The statements attributed to Mr. Dewey and Mr. Kilpatrick are based upon quotations from then current press reports reprinted by Kandel, I. L.: "Propaganda Analysis Illustrated." *School and Society*, March 19, 1938, p. 375.
5. In the article, "Propaganda Analysis Illustrated," referred to in the preceding footnote.
6. *Propaganda Analysis*, New York, November, 1937.

The unjust imputation of meanings is more than matched by those techniques of propaganda which employ an unjust and unworthy imputation of motives. The insinuation that the Essentialists are exploiting for personal or selfish ends a general tendency to reaction against all reform—a reaction alleged to be widely prevalent at the present time—is one case in point. The charge that the Essentialists are stupidly wedded to an outmoded economic and social order is another. This latter blanket accusation, long shopworn and tawdry from unbridled use, is explicit in the statements of Mr. de Boer and Mr. Sexson and implicit in the pronouncement attributed in the press reports to Mr. Dewey.

It is well to pause momentarily to consider this particular type of propagandist appeal which I may characterize as the effort to brand one's opponents with the stigma of a blind adherence to the "status quo." It is another species of "name-calling." If anyone is at all interested, I may say that there are some rather radical departures from the political, social, and economic "status quos" that I should be glad to support. In proof of this I may say that I have voted both for Mr. Franklin Roosevelt and for Mr. Norman Thomas—at different elections I hasten to add. On the other hand, I have a violent prejudice in favor of retaining at any cost and at any sacrifice certain other ingredients of existing "status quos" in our national life. Those who assail "status quo" indiscriminately and out of hand may not recognize that the very fact that they can indulge in this passionate denunciation rests upon those parts of the political "status quo" which constitute the guarantee of the Bill of Rights—freedom of speech, freedom of the press, freedom of assembly, freedom of religion. These, I am glad to concede, are among the primary essentials of the educational Essentialists, and are so listed in the theses to which I have referred. And may I add that the fundamental theories embraced by those who have assailed the Essentialists, if carried out consistently, would give us no room in the school to teach the Bill of Rights in the way in which it can be taught most effectively; namely, through a systematic and sequential reliving vicariously of the momentous and dramatic chain of events through the sacrifice and agony of which its guarantees were established and enthroned? I am forced to conclude that the only intelligible explanation of the instantaneous condemnation of the Essentialists is that their critics have a mind-set against recognizing any educational essentials whatsoever and that this attitude is inherent in their basic theories.

I have spoken of the unjust imputation of wrong meanings and of unworthy motives as methods of preventing clear thinking. A third method, often used quite innocently, is to deny dogmatically the truth of statements or the validity of inferences made by one's opponents. A favorite defense of the dominant school of educational theory is, in effect, that the theory has not been and is not now reflected in any appreciable degree in school practice, and consequently that no shortcomings of American education can be charged against the theory. Mr. Sexson uses this argument in his efforts to prove that the Essentialists are merely a set of busybody mischiefmakers who have set up a man of straw to attack for the delectation of a public "fed up" on reform-movements. It may not be at all significant that the "fan mail" which has come to my desk as a result of the unexpected and unwanted publicity at the time of the Atlantic City meeting does not bear out Mr. Sexson's contention that our dominant theory has had but a negligible influence on practice. Strangely enough, too, my letters have come predominantly not from antiquated schoolteachers wishing to be secure in their "comfortable old habits," but from parents who are sincerely concerned regarding what their children learn, and especially what they fail to learn, at school. Nor may it be significant that a substantial proportion of these letters—nearly one-half— have come from a single section of a single State—the southern part of the great State of California. It may be that the man of straw has no more a substantial embodiment in the vicinity of Hollywood than elsewhere. And it may be, of course, that the educational climate of southern California merely chanced to be quite unusual at the time these letters were written.

Similar in its import, but upon a somewhat different plane, is the remark attributed in the press reports to Mr. Kilpatrick, and which I have already quoted. Commenting on the statement in the theses that American school children make, age for age, substantially lower scores on our achievement tests than do children of other English-speaking countries, Mr. Kilpatrick is reported to have said, "In so far as this is true, it is a criticism of the traditional methods which are still largely in use in this country despite the advance of progressivism."

It will be a surprise to teachers in England, Scotland, Canada, and Australia to learn that they have gone further than the United States in abandoning the formal methods of instruction (for that, I take it, is what Mr. Kilpatrick means by "traditional methods"). And, of course, as a matter of plain fact they have not. American schools have reflected the theories advocated by our critics far more extensively and pervasively than have the schools of any other country—with one possible exception which need not concern us now, since in that country, the Soviet Union, after twelve years of consistent application the theories were completely abandoned as hopelessly weak and ineffective. These theories have gained scarcely a foothold in the English-speaking countries referred to in the theses, and they have received even less recognition in such enlightened countries as France, Holland, Switzerland, Sweden, Norway, and Denmark. They did get a foothold in Germany during the period of the short-lived Republic— a fact that has been advanced (erroneously, I believe) as a partial explanation of the Republic's short life.

The extent to which these theories have influenced American schools need not be entirely a matter of conjecture. In 1931 a study[7] was reported which was based on a survey of actual classroom procedures on a nation-wide sampling of American schools. If the results are to be trusted, such informal procedures as are represented by projects, activities, and the "socialized recitation" at that time were twice as frequently in evidence in the town and city elementary schools as was the typical "traditional" formal recitation based upon a class assignment to a single textbook. This inquiry was made and published under the auspices of the National Society for the Study of Education.

I am not here concerned with the relative efficiency of formal and informal methods of teaching. Informal methods have, of course, a highly important place. My sole concern at the present time turns upon a question of fact, not upon a question of values. What I want to emphasize is that it does not promote clear thinking to distort a situation by ignoring, even unintentionally, evidence that is a matter of reputable record. If the findings of the study referred to did not please our critics, the study could have been repeated, for the manner of conducting it was clearly described. If there were fallacies in the techniques employed or in the interpretation of the data, these could have been pointed out. Did our critics take this trouble? No. This study, sponsored and published by an organization of the highest reputation for careful and responsible research in our field, has been completely ignored, and statements made in direct contradiction to its findings have been given wide publicity. Again I insist that such a course of action does not permit, much less promote, clear thinking on issues that may be of critical significance to the American people.

I could cite many similar instances. Over and over again in educational controversy, I have been meticulous in assembling and citing factual evidence in support of the positions that I have taken. Over and over again these positions have been denounced without the slightest attempt to pit fact against fact or even to mention the evidence that I have advanced, much less to question its validity or its pertinence to the question at issue. This was true even in a controversy in which I was engaged with the psychologists sixteen years ago regarding the interpretation of the intelligence tests. The evidence that I submitted was ignored and I was merely laughed out of court. It is not because subsequent investigations abundantly justified my contentions and proved the psychologists to have been sadly in error—it is not because of this that I recall the episode, but

---

7. Bagley, W. C.: "The Textbook and Methods of Teaching." *Thirtieth Yearbook* of the National Society for the Study of Education, Part II. Bloomington, Illinois, 1931, ch. 11.

rather to illustrate a method of answering arguments that is tragically inimical to progress.

Not many years ago, in a published doctor's dissertation in the field of educational theory, I was condemned for taking a certain position with which the author of the dissertation violently disagreed. I had supported my position as usual with an abundance of duly documented evidence. Upon inquiry I was told that this was not necessary except when one criticizes an important person. I wondered why I was apparently important enough to be personally denounced and yet so unimportant that my evidence could not be fairly examined. I am still wondering.

I have frankly and deliberately used this occasion to discuss what I regard as superficial, misleading, unjustified, and profitless criticisms of the Essentialists as a result of the publicity given the name at the Atlantic City meeting. I do this because the issues at stake are vastly too significant to be beclouded by the type of appeal to which these criticisms have been limited, and I do it because the group represented by the critics has for years brooked no opposition. As Mr. Kandel[8] has said, this school of educational doctrine represents "the crystallization of a theory or philosophy into a gospel, infallible, unassailable, beyond criticism except on pain of being dubbed a heretic and treated as such even at a sacrifice of decency."

Nor do I present any apologies for referring to persons by name. I have no personal animus toward any one of them or toward anyone else. In forty years of controversy I have never imputed insincerity or self-seeking to those with whom I have happened to disagree. But on the other hand I have never hesitated to call a spade a spade and to name names—not call names. While, in the warfare of ideas, one with perfect safety may worry the humble and defenseless cargo-boats that chance to get within range, I prefer a bolder strategy. If a militant course seems necessary as in the present instance, I will at least throw down the gauntlet to the battleships and high-powered armored cruisers, foolhardy though such a course may be. For after all, in the warfare of ideas, persons and personal resentments and personal ambitions are not important. As my friend, the late Livingston C. Lord, so often quoted, "Not who is right but what is true" is the important thing. Or, as Mr. Thorndike said in one of his early books, "For the common good it is indifferent *who* is at the top, *which* men are achieving most. The important thing for the common good ... is that the top should be high, that much should be achieved."[9]

8. In the communication to *School and Society* cited above.
9. Thorndike, E. L., *Educational Psychology—Briefer Course*. New York, 1914, p. 399.

I was asked by your chairman to speak on the topic, "Are the Essentialists the True Progressives?" I have already referred to my own Essentialist program now in print, from which, if you wish, you can easily obtain your own answer to this question. Today I have limited my efforts to one criterion of what I regard as true progressivism—namely, the determination to live consistently as far as is humanly possible with the ideals of clear thinking, including an unwillingness to be swayed by prejudices or by the temptation to ignore facts that do not happen to fit one's preconceived theories. If by this criterion I have not proved the Essentialists to be the real Progressives, I have at least convicted the outstanding critics of Essentialism from their own words and deeds of a sad deficiency in these basic elements of a true progressivism.

Teachers' Rights, Academic Freedom, and the Teaching of Controversial Issues
(1938)[1]

The 1930s was a tumultuous decade at Teachers College. The Great Depression caused Progressive educators to rethink their views. They retreated from the romantic individualism that they had customarily advocated and instead embraced Social Reconstructionism and collectivism. Some Progressives at the college, such as George S. Counts, openly endorsed indoctrination in the classroom to hasten the age of collectivism. Progressive educators debated the ethics of indoctrination and the question of the teachers' responsibility for advancing their own political views. In this essay, Bagley weighs in to the discussion with a typically balanced discussion of the rights and duties of teachers.

When one speaks of the teacher's "rights" or of the "rights" of any other individual or group, one should try to make clear, at least to one's self, the way in which the term "rights" is used. Its meaning is obviously bound up with the meanings of many other terms, such as "freedom," "liberty," "justice." As a word, it suggests the contrasting moral concepts, right and

---

1. Prepared for the course, "Foundations of Education" (Education 200Fa), Teachers College, Columbia University, May, 1938. This course is conducted by a faculty "panel," comprising-usually four or five instructors.

Forgotten Heroes of American Education, pages 245–250

245

wrong. It is associated at different times with specifying adjectives; for example, "legal" rights, "civil" rights, "religious" rights, "property" rights, "marital" rights, and a host of others. Because in each of these usages, the meaning is frequently overlaid with feeling and emotion, even passion, it is especially necessary in a rational discussion to get below the surface and strive to see the basic implications of the term. Most important, perhaps, are the questions, What are the sources of rights? By whom or by what are they granted? What are their claims for recognition by others than the persons or groups by or for whom they are claimed as rights?

I shall take the liberty of giving my own answers to these questions, not because I assume any merit for the worth or validity of these answers, but because I have been asked to discuss problems which I cannot discuss intelligibly without letting you know where I stand—without setting forth as clearly, albeit as briefly, as I can the premises upon which I shall base my statements. Parenthetically I may say, as an anticipatory corollary of my own premises, that you have a "right" to know the premises upon which any speaker bases his claims for your attention, and the speaker has a corresponding "duty" to make these clear, especially when, as in the present instance, his statement must be determined by his own personal acceptance of certain standards or values.

My five fundamental theses, then, are as follows:

1. What we call "human rights" are, almost always, social in their origin.
2. Each right is balanced by a corresponding duty.
3. Might does not make *right,* but (with exceptions that I shall later specify) might very distinctly makes *rights*—and, as contemporary world events only too clearly demonstrate, might can *unmake* rights.
4. The concepts "right" and "rights" are not necessarily synonymous. Some rights may be right, and some rights may be wrong. A judgment, in either case, must depend upon one's accepted criterion or standard of right and wrong; hence, I must define the standard which I personally apply in making such decisions.
5. Very briefly stated, this criterion is, in my case, social welfare and social progress. What I believe to be right is what I conceive to promote social welfare and social progress. What I deem to be wrong is what I deem to be inconsistent with social welfare, or what, in my judgment, retards social progress. This is my interpretation of the famous "categorical imperative" of Immanuel Kant: "So act that the maxim of thy will may always at the same time hold good as a principle of universal legislation."

TEACHERS' RIGHTS

After this extended introduction, reminiscent perhaps of the introduction to the *Knickerbocker History of New York,* we come to the very specific question of teachers' rights and especially the question of freedom of teaching.

The notions of "rights" and "freedom" here are clearly related to certain ideals of outstanding significance that have been relatively recent developments of social evolution. These are the ideals reflected in the terms "freedom of speech," "freedom of the press," "freedom of assembly," and "freedom of religion," and to the first two of these, "freedom of teaching" bears the relation of a variety to a species. To this group should also be added the right of free inquiry or investigation. These rights illustrate clearly both the social origin of rights and their social justification. They originated, probably, as specific expressions of the more general concept, individual liberty, and thus they are among the outstanding contributions of Anglo-Saxon civilization to human progress. They have a justification, however, that is remotely suggestive of natural rights. Both biological and social evolution depend upon the appearance of mutations or changes that give to an organism or an institution an advantage over preceding organisms or institutions and consequently increase the chances that it will survive and perpetuate its kind. In social evolution, criticism of existing institutions, proposals for changes, and criticisms of such proposals must be free and unrepressed if the basic conditions of progress are to be met. In the light of our knowledge of evolution, then, freedom of speech, freedom of the press, and freedom of assembly have a far wider significance than they have historically as expressions of an individualistic doctrine of freedom or even as attributes of an emotionalized ideal of democracy. The suppression of these rights in the totalitarian states is a tragedy, not merely because it imperils democracy as a traditional institution which we have come to revere, but because it imperils human progress, it threatens to handicap and delay social evolution, it threatens even to start a retrograde process which could easily sweep away material as well as spiritual gains, and recovery from which might entail a repetition of the long struggle and sacrifice which have lifted mankind to its present plane.

Freedom of teaching and particularly freedom of inquiry and research are, as I have suggested, important ingredients in this fundamental ideal. Freedom of teaching, however, stands not in quite the same case as do freedom of inquiry, freedom of speech, and freedom of the press. The teacher in the lower schools especially is in a privileged position, and here a sensitized conscience must decide whether or not he takes an unfair advantage of his privileges. In a university, the dangers are not nearly so great as in the lower schools. If, for example, I make false statements in this class, I have here three colleagues who should and will correct me. Or if in another class where I am the sole instructor, I set forth my own particular and somewhat peculiar variety of educational theory, I can be certain that in their next class the chances are ninety-nine to one that my students will get a far more appealing statement of a rival theory. My conscience, then, is delightfully easy. My comfort is enhanced by the fact that you and my other students are mature men and women, and yet young enough to have come up through our American schools, an avowed objective of which in recent years has been to educate pupils and students to think for themselves, to seek reasons, to discount personalities. In short, you are by this time well-seasoned skeptics. So my conscience is further eased.

But if I were teaching in the elementary school—in the sixth grade, let us say—my position would be different. In such a situation, I believe, my conscience ought to keep me from deliberately "loading the dice" in favor of my own point of view. In this case my pupils are immature, and the ideals and habits of independent thinking are still in the making. Furthermore, my pupils are impressionable, and compensating instruction from other teachers may not be available. In addition, accepting the importance of leading the learner to think for himself, my conscience would dictate that in matters with which my teaching is concerned I should set forth whatever conflicting points of view are reflected among intelligent people. I should present fairly all the evidence that I could marshal for each, encouraging each learner to come to his own conclusion, to accept his own allegiance, or to decline any allegiance.

In a great deal of the teaching in the lower schools, the danger of indoctrination is negligible. The fundamental facts of arithmetic, the skills that must be developed in reading and the other language arts, the wide range of activities in health education do not involve many controversial issues, except in the selection of materials. It has been said by some critics that the teaching of such topics as interest, stocks and bonds, taxes, and insurance in arithmetic has predisposed the present generation toward a perpetuation of the present economic order. Even if the existing order is bad, however, I fail to see how a mere ignorance of its workings will contribute to its reform.

In the social studies, as such, and in the teaching of biology in the high school, the situation is obviously different, and here the teacher's conscience may encounter the necessity of making some rather fine ethical judgments. This is especially true when one is likely to run counter to the political and religious doctrines that characterize the homes of one's pupils. How far should the teacher refrain from teachings that might lead the immature learner to reject or even seriously question these doctrines? Is there anything to guide in these decisions that is more worthy and dignified than the practical expediency of acting in such a way that one may hold one's job?

I believe that there is. It is the same standard of social welfare and progress upon which, I have maintained, all ethical judgments should be based. If I merely assert dogmatically my right to teach what I believe to be true, freedom of teaching becomes merely a shibboleth. Such an assertion implies that freedom is an absolute, and all varieties of human freedom, as we have seen, are strictly relative. In the position that I have taken here, the only thing that partakes of the character of an absolute is the ultimate criterion, social welfare and social progress. Sometimes to live honestly and consistently with this standard necessitates the sacrifice of one's job, the sacrifice, it may be, of life itself, if by such a sacrifice one is convinced that the fundamental cause will be furthered or that failure to make the sacrifice would set progress back. Sacrifice is certainly not an end in itself.

The essential limitations upon freedom of teaching from this broad social point of view have been stated by Mr. Kilpatrick more clearly and more helpfully, I think, than by anyone else. It is a splendid example of the well-known standard of thinking that he has so successfully advocated: namely, that decisions must, insofar as possible, consider the total configuration of a given situation. To quote:[2]

1. In "adult education" and in the institutions of higher education teaching should be quite free of all interference except for the requirement of good taste and standards of scholarship. [This requirement is obviously justified by the social criterion.]

2. In the secondary school the like freedom and the like restrictions should hold. But the further limitation should be added of a decent respect for the feelings of the community and particularly of the parents directly concerned.

   What constitutes a decent respect will vary with differing topics, and with different communities. By and large, the more backward the community the greater will be the need to exercise consideration, partly because the school has a duty to help educate the community generally and to anger the people is likely to thwart this process ...

3. In the elementary school the same provisions hold except that the demand for respect for local and parental opinion is somewhat stronger.

---

2. Kilpatrick, W. H. "Freedom in Teaching." *Educational Administration and Supervision*, pp. 113f., Vol. 20, February, 1934. Quoted by courteous permission of Mr. Kilpatrick and of the publishers, Warwick and York.

4. In the out-of-school expression of opinion the same provisions still hold except that the demand for consideration of local and parental opinion is much less strong in the matter of out-of-school expression than is the case with classroom teaching, and especially is this so in large communities and for teachers of older pupils.

In respect to this out-of-school expression the teacher of course retains all his legal rights to freedom of speech and the like, but in consideration of his peculiar influence on his pupils he should use these rights with due regard to their entire educational influence ... [Note the emphasis on the *total* situation.]

Mr. Kilpatrick's suggested limitations on freedom of teaching are in no sense to be thought of as relieving the teacher of responsibility for resenting and resisting an invasion of his rights. There are occasions, when, with or without support or the prospect of support, one must stand firm—alone, if necessary, with one's back against the wall. That is the acid test both of conscience and of courage. It was a nineteenth century teacher, Horace Bushnell, who gave this heroic advice to his students: "First, be perfectly honest and sincere in formulating your own standards and principles of action; second, never swerve in conduct from your honest convictions; third, if, between these two, you go over Niagara,—go!" It is because in great crises men and women have kept faith with their ideals and have willingly paid the price and gone over Niagara—it is because of this that our civil liberties are today the most precious elements in our human heritage. They are conquests and not gifts, and as conquests these men and women have enthroned them. They must be just as bravely defended if they are to remain enthroned.

Basic Problems
in Teacher Education
(1939)[1]

When he was recruited to Teachers College in 1917, Bagley's purpose was to focus on teacher education. To concentrate on teacher education during the 1920s and 1930s meant to devote one's attention to the nation's normal schools, which provided the overwhelming majority of teachers for public school service at the time. When he delivered this paper in 1938, Bagley was only one year away from retirement. He takes the opportunity to reflect on the successes that he and others had experienced during the previous twenty-one years. Bagley ends the address by discussing the future of professional schools for teaching teachers. He pays careful attention to the specific problems, possibilities, and principles that leaders of these institutions needed to consider in the decades ahead.

It was in the school year, 1917–18, that a group of courses dealing specifically with the problems of professional schools for teachers was first organized in a very modest way at Teachers College. These offerings have consequently now just completed their twenty-first year. Because they have, so to speak, come of age and furthermore because nearly all the work represented by this group of courses has been taken over by other groups beginning this year, it has occurred to me that a brief review of what has happened during the past twenty-two years may be in order at this time.

---

1. An address delivered in Milbank Chapel, Teachers College, before the student body of the summer session, 1938.

In 1916, the year preceding the organization of these courses, an official bulletin of the United States Bureau of Education, prepared by Charles H. Judd and S. C. Parker, said that, taken as a whole, the United States gave less attention to the preparation of teachers than did any other comparable country. The notable advances that had been made in the preceding fifty years in elementary education and since the turn of the century in secondary education had been only in part paralleled by advanced standards for the preparation of teachers, especially teachers for the elementary schools. It is true that state normal schools, or something equivalent to them, had been provided in each of the states, yet a majority of the teachers in the elementary schools were not only not graduates of the normal schools but had had no education whatever beyond the high school. Tens of thousands, indeed, had entered the teaching service before completing a four-year high-school program, and the proportion of those who had not progressed beyond the elementary schools in which they taught was deplorably large.

The normal schools themselves as a group were low-grade institutions, although a majority were on the collegiate basis in the sense that high-school graduation was a condition of admission. Except in a few city training schools, there was practically no effort to select the better high-school graduates for admission, and usually anyone admitted could, if he or she remained for one or two years, be graduated with a diploma that was in most states a license to teach.

Because of the brief residence requirements the programs of instruction and training in the normal schools were necessarily narrow in range and limited in content. Furthermore, the instructional staffs, while in general made up of devoted and often skillful teachers, did not compare in educational attainments with the teaching-staffs of the high schools of the larger cities. The salary-schedules were uniformly below and often far below the schedules of other tax-supported institutions of collegiate grade. Compared with the latter, the normal-school buildings and their equipment in the way of libraries and laboratories were sadly deficient. Even the more important laboratories of a teachers' professional school— namely, the training schools—were poorly housed, poorly equipped, and inadequately staffed. In many cases, practically all of the instruction of pupils in the training school was done by student-teachers and all too often under very meager supervision.

This, in brief, was the condition of the professional schools for teachers in 1917 when the specific problems of these schools first became a serious subject of university study, research, and instruction, with the inauguration of the group of courses at Teachers College. I would not even intimate that the state normal schools were not at that time rendering a very valuable service since their first establishment in Massachusetts now just one hundred years ago. But they were from the outset very seriously limited and handicapped in their service by meager financial budgets and by a strange apathy upon the part of the public toward them and their work. This attitude was reflected both in begrudging financial support and in the persistent practice of keeping the teaching profession open to untrained and short-term teachers. It is a curious and regrettable fact that the strategic importance of the institutions preparing teachers for the lower schools has been so long in catching the imagination of the American people.

From the outset the work of our group at Teachers College has been centered upon the problems involved in raising the standards of the undergraduate professional schools for teachers to, or at least toward, a plane that would be consistent with the significance of the fundamental social service for which these schools prepare. More specifically we emphasized the following needs:

1. A longer period of residence in the professional school.
2. A recognition of broad scholarship and rich culture as essential ingredients in the *professional* equipment of all teachers whatever may be the age-level of the pupils and students whom they instruct.
3. A thoroughgoing integration of the courses and activities of the professional school, with the laboratory schools for: observation, participation, and responsible student-teaching as the center or focus.
4. The organization of the life of the students during their residence in the professional schools in a manner that will contribute as far as possible to the development of the personal and social qualities which are also to be listed among the significant ingredients of professional equipment.
5. The recognition of critic-teachers as co-ordinate in rank and salary with other instructors who have met comparable standards of education and experience.
6. The upgrading of the educational standards of the instructors of professional schools for teachers including critic-teachers at least to a plane comparable with the educational standards represented by the instructors in other tax-supported institutions of collegiate grade.
7. The upgrading of buildings and of such equipment as libraries, laboratories, and gymnasiums at least to the plane represented by other tax-supported institutions of collegiate grade.
8. Adequate provisions for the housing and equipment of laboratory schools.

I shall not attempt at this time to discuss the various ways in which these and related problems have been studied in the development of our work over the past twenty-two years. It should be said, however, that we began in many ways quite at the beginning. One of the advantages in bringing any field of human endeavor into the program of a university is that the traditions and ideals of a university have their roots in the importance of dependable knowledge. Knowledge already in existence must be collected, classified, organized, and made available. Knowledge desired but not in existence must be gained in so far as possible through research, discovery, and experimentation. Of the specific field of the professional education of teachers it may be said that dependable and helpful knowledge was notable by its scarcity twenty years ago; hence a most important phase of our work has been in the realm of research. Through the efforts of graduate students happily available in increasing numbers, gratifying progress has been made toward meeting this need. Students and instructors in other graduate schools have in more recent years added their contributions to the specialized literature of our field. Of significance, too, has been the fruitful source of important data represented by the surveys of the professional schools for teachers. Many of these surveys have been directed by members of our own staff and participated in by our students. The use of uniform check-lists has facilitated the collection of data concerning the students attending the professional schools, the communities from which they come, the types of homes that they represent, their attitude toward the profession of education; data of an analogous type regarding the instructors, with especial reference to the educational standards that they represent; data regarding the laboratory schools and their enrollment; data regarding the curricular patterns, requirements, and offerings, regarding administrative policies and practices, regarding buildings and equipment, and a wide variety of additional information. All this has been of basic importance in understanding the situation, locating and defining critical problems, and furnishing, so to speak, a base-line from which progress can be measured.

We are still, of course, only a little way from the beginning, but we now have from several extended investigations, undertaken and conducted consistently with accepted standards of research, the nucleus of a body of specialized and dependable knowledge that can be used in constructing programs toward the solution of many of the problems that I have listed. The published results of research studies are already represented by nearly one hundred doctors' dissertations; reports of state-wide surveys of the professional education of teachers in eleven states, representing all sections of the country; similar reports from a large number of city surveys; the reports of the National Survey of the Education of Teachers directed by Professor Evenden and participated in by other members of our group;

and several studies of the education of teachers in other countries. In addition hundreds of research reports have been published in the professional journals and several thousand studies representing students' term papers and reports are available in typed or mimeographed form.

During the twenty-two years under survey, the educational situation in the country as a whole has witnessed important changes and developments which have modified in many significant ways the character of our problems. Early in the 1920's a movement was initiated toward extending the residence-requirements of the professional schools. This gathered momentum a few years later when several of the schools, especially in the industrial states, found for the first time that many of their two-year graduates could not be placed as teachers in the town and city elementary schools. This apparent surplus of teachers trained according to the accepted standards was in evidence at least two years before the financial crisis of 1929. It cannot therefore be attributed to the depression. The actual causes are interesting and important, but the limitations of time preclude their consideration here. Suffice it to say that the teaching profession was even then becoming stabilized; teachers, in spite of the general prosperity of the country, were remaining longer in service; and larger numbers of young people were willing to undertake a longer preparation as the price of admission to the service.

When the depression was fully upon us in the early 1930's, this momentum was, of course, greatly increased. Of the public-school teachers it could emphatically be said that few died and none resigned. Teaching, long the Cinderella of the professions, seemed ready to reap the rewards symbolized by the glass slipper. Teachers were never so popular—especially among their relatives and their impecunious friends.

Under these conditions, it was inevitable that the professional schools should increase their residence requirements. For the first time, too, a more rigorous selection of entrants became possible on almost a nation-wide scale. The professional schools, too, could find, even with their low salaries, a much larger proportion of highly educated instructors than had ever before been available. All in all, it seemed clearly demonstrated that adversity even on the scale of a national calamity has its uses; and there was an abundant confirmation of the striking fact that Professor Edgar W. Knight was the first to call attention to in 1931—namely, that in the history of American education, every major economic depression has been the starting point of a major educational advance.

It is obvious that the problem of the professional education of teachers has been in many ways transformed by these developments. I do not regard the fundamental changes as merely temporary. As I have suggested, some of them were clearly in evidence before 1929, and similar educational advances in the past, for example, those initiated in the depressions following the panics of 1839, 1873, and 1893, far from being retarded or suppressed by economic recovery, were actually extended and accelerated.

The most important problems of the immediate future, as I conceive of them, I shall now very briefly formulate:

It is clearly possible to advance at once on a nation-wide front to a full four-year program of post-high-school education for all public-school teachers. In at least nine states today this is the legal minimum. In other states, while temporary licenses may be granted under exceptional circumstances on the basis of lower qualifications, the four-year standard is essentially in effect. Others with legal two-year minima license relatively few teachers who are not college graduates, and in several of these the full four-year standard is planned to begin as early as 1940.

The policy of selective admission to the professional schools should be adopted on a nation-wide scale. It is true that, in spite of a large number of extended and carefully conducted investigations, there is still a great deal of uncertainty as to the criteria that can be best employed in selecting high-school graduates for admission to the professional schools. There is certainly no single criterion, such as the Intelligence Quotient, or high-school scholarship standard, or personality ratings that will keep out all who are destined to fail lamentably in teaching or to include all who may render outstanding service. In any case, there should be a combination of criteria. On the basis of the studies with which I am familiar I make bold to suggest humbly and quite provisionally the following: a) select from those who are in the upper two-thirds of their high-school graduating classes; b) select on a rigorous basis of physical and especially mental health; c) use discriminately some of the available teaching-aptitude tests; d) in general, give the preference to those who, in high school, have completed successfully more than two years of Latin or mathematics or natural science or preferably two of these in combination; e) select on the basis of personal interviews with each candidate, if possible, and where not possible try to secure objective and disinterested personality ratings from high-school teachers and principals; f) accept only those who show a real interest in the profession of teaching as a life work.

The most important question next to selective admission is that of curricular offerings and requirements during the four years of college work. Here two important tendencies are to be noted: a) provide at least two years of general education of the liberal-arts type, limiting the specific study of teaching problems and of science, theory, and history of education to the senior-college years; and b) "professionalize" the work from the outset, providing, as all would agree, for breadth of scholarship and wide culture, but holding throughout to the desirable equipment of the teacher as the integrating center of all courses and activities in the classroom.

This is a question of fundamental importance, for, in my judgment, upon its answer turns the question as to whether we shall have in the future real professional schools for teachers, or whether teachers will be prepared in colleges, the main purposes of which are to provide a general liberal-arts education, caring for the needs of prospective teachers as far as possible through detached courses in education and student-teaching. The latter is now distinctly the trend in many parts of the country.

Undoubtedly this solution of the problem has many advantages. Among other things, it would postpone vocational choice until the beginning of the senior-college, and so simplify the problem of selective admission. It would, however, be a real handicap to the development of professional idealism which is far from an unimportant consideration. The success of many of our professional schools here has been noteworthy. Certain of the older normal schools, notably Oswego and Bridgewater, rendered a fundamental service to American education by sending out successive groups of teachers, relatively undereducated as judged by prevailing standards, but thoroughly imbued with dynamic ideals and a pervasive faith in the cause which they went forth to serve. And it is beyond question that the remarkable influence of our own Teachers College would have been impossible if this institution had not been dominated by a single purpose, and through its independence in a position to carry out without dictation from the University the policies and programs that it deemed to meet best the fundamental needs presented by its field of service.

One may be optimistic, however. It is possible that the two plans now in conflict may in the near future be integrated on a higher plane. I refer to the possibility, not at all either remote or impossible, that the standard of education for teachers may be advanced still another year to the level of the Master's degree. Under this condition, admission to the professional schools could well be advanced to the beginning of the junior-college year, and they could provide a program of three more additional years broadly conceived but closely integrated around the professional needs of the teacher.

Time does not permit me to discuss other outstanding problems in our field that are presenting themselves for solution as a result of recent developments and changes. Much could be said of the bearing of the present movement relative to "general education" upon the education of teachers; of the problem of preparing in the professional school teachers who can adjust themselves to the kaleidoscopic and confusing, not to say confused, changes that are taking place in the curricula of the lower schools; the problems involved in making parts of the teacher's professional equipment the important results of two movements that have recently gained great importance in the study of a truly effective educational guidance; and the problems bound to come increasingly in connection with the marked development of two relatively new fields of educational endeavor—namely, the junior college and adult education.

Personally, I am looking toward to the future of our field with a hope and a confidence quite beyond the hope and confidence that I held twenty-one years ago. I have strong faith that the time is not far distant when the Cinderella of the professions will become the Queen of the professions.

Latin from an Educationist's Point of View
(1941)[1]

The idea of a professor of education advocating the study of Latin would strike most people as odd today. Bagley, however, was the type of education professor who saw no conflict between his arguments for universal education and his advocacy for increased attention to the teaching of Latin. This article, which Bagley delivered to the New York Classical Club in 1941, outlines his thoughts on how, when, and why Latin was marginalized from the public school curriculum. He combines his conventional historical approach with political support for the Latin professors who were his audience.

I suffer under a serious handicap in this discussion because, of the four participants, I am the only one who is a layman in the field represented by this program. Unfortunately, I do not have a background of basic education and training in the classical languages and literatures. I am deeply regretful of this deficiency. It has been a severe handicap to me throughout my professional life. Indeed, a keen awareness of this deficiency long since convinced me that the attitude toward the classics of many of my fellow-workers in the professional study of education was shortsighted and, in some of its consequences, little less than tragic.

There have been reasons, of course, for this attitude. The specialized study of education on the university level had its first real beginning in the

---

1. Prepared for a forum meeting of the New York Classical Club, March 15, 1941.

last decade of the Nineteenth Century. This same decade also saw the first faint beginnings of the transformation of the American high school from a selective institution to a non-selective institution—the first faint foreshadowings of universal secondary education. The professor of education owed his job in large part to a demand from the high schools that the colleges and universities furnish them with teachers who could do more than merely pass on to a group of selected learners the materials that they themselves had mastered and by the same methods that had been used with them. The new demand was for teachers who could adapt their materials and their methods of instruction to minds of varying abilities.

With the continuance and acceleration of this movement in the first and second decades of the present century, the professor of education became in many ways the arch-protagonist of the non-selective high school, and, by the same token, the arch-antagonist of policies and programs that kept significant proportions of youth out of the high schools. The principal barriers were the requirements in what I have frequently referred to as the studies that are exact and exacting, to the mastery of which only a certain proportion of the members of each generation are mentally competent. These studies typically are Latin (and to some extent modern foreign languages), mathematics, and the physical sciences. The upward expansion of mass-education into the high schools would have been impossible without a relaxation of standards, especially of the standards imposed by these exact and exacting disciplines. To the professor of education, as the representative of this movement in the colleges and universities, fell the task of justifying or rationalizing this relaxation of standards—although he did not so bluntly define his function.

It is clear that a frontal attack on Latin was to the professor of education the line of least resistance. Indeed, opposition to Latin as a requirement in secondary education long antedated the movement toward the universal high school. As far back as the Seventeenth Century, a group of European educators, who, even in that remote day, called themselves the Progressives, contended against the "tyranny of the Latin" and urged with eloquence its replacement by instruction in the mother-tongue and in the "real" studies. This was at a time, it should be noted, when Latin was very far from a "dead" language. In fact, as far as the world of scholarship was concerned, it was the chief recording agency and the chief method of communication. It was a highly efficient Esperanto, which transcended national boundaries and enabled the scholars of all nationalities—Englishmen, Frenchmen, Germans, Czechs, Italians, and Spaniards—to converse and confer and discuss their problems through the spoken, written, and printed words of a common tongue. In this sense, Latin remained a language very much alive until the middle of the Eighteenth Century, when chauvinistic pressures compelled scholars in all fields, and especially students of the natural sciences, to publish the results of their investigations in the vernaculars. It is fairly clear now that, if Latin had continued to be the Esperanto of the world of scholarship, the advantages would have offset any handicaps to the democratic popularization of science that might have been entailed. For example, the candidate for the doctorate today must pass qualifying examinations in French and German. Even then, he is likely to confine his later efforts to keep up with investigations reported in these languages to the reading of abstracts and summaries published in English, and these may make no reference to the findings that he most needs. Even if he reads his French and German journals and monographs faithfully, he will often regret that he cannot read Italian, Spanish, the Scandinavian languages, Czech, and Russian— and in another generation, perhaps, Turkish, Arabic, and Chinese. If Latin had been continued as the common language of scientific and other types of scholarly investigation, all this would be avoided—and the popularization of increasingly involved technical discoveries through scientific accounts in the vernacular would serve the democratic purpose passing well, for to the layman a technical monograph in his own language is just as unreadable as it would be if printed in Latin.

But to get back to my subject. I have said that the opposition to Latin long antedated the effort to place the American high school on a non-selective basis. Indeed, in the high schools of some of the larger cities, even college-preparatory curricula were offered without the Latin requirement in the late 'eighties of the Nineteenth Century, if not earlier. When I entered the Detroit High School in 1889, there were at least three four-year programs in which Latin did not appear, and from two of these graduates could enter certain colleges of the state university without examination. And yet, within the past year, I have read and heard tirades against the way in which the Latin requirement keeps pupils out of the high schools, and usually with Latin are bracketed algebra, geometry, and physics, the last of which is required in very few secondary schools, while even algebra and geometry are rapidly disappearing from the required lists.

Since early in the first decade of the century, the chief weapons of the antagonists of Latin and of the other exact and exacting studies have been the investigations anent the "transfer of training," which, it is alleged, have completely demolished the theory of mental discipline, and left without support or justification even the offering, to say nothing of the requirement, of any subject of study that cannot clearly prove that the learnings involved can be applied directly and overtly to immediate life problems. During the past few years, the term "functional" has acquired an increasing vogue and is today the word that you must use if you are discussing educational values. Be sure to use it as a verb, "Does this subject function?" Only don't use the term "subject," except as an object of ridicule or invection. If you say, "Does this experience function?" you will be, I think, right up to the minute, although I cannot be sure, for only a short time ago you should have said, "Does this activity function?" And what you should say tomorrow, I do not know, but I can at least caution you to be careful. The literature of education is a remarkable reservoir of source materials for the study of semantics. An Australian educator, who made extensive observations of American schools a few years ago, when the curriculum-revision movement was at its height, commented in his report on the skillful way in which American educators use words. As one example, he cited the numerous references that had been made by those he interviewed to our "fluid" and "adjustable" curriculum in contrast with what they called the old "static" curriculum. He pointed out that if they had contrasted an "unstable" curriculum with a "stable" curriculum the intellectual meaning would have been the same, but the emotional effect on the listener exactly the opposite.

The reaction against the theory of mental discipline long since stepped over the bounds of reason into the realm of emotion and feeling. Those who have read without prejudice the records of the investigations from the psychological laboratories regarding the transfer of training know that the findings of these investigations, taken as a whole, far from invalidating the doctrine of mental discipline, actually support a reasonable faith in its tenets. They do not justify a blind faith, and they clearly indicate that, if disciplinary values are to be realized, a great deal will depend upon (1) the ability of the learner and (2) the skill and insight of the teacher, and especially the teacher's mastery of his subject and of its method and his keen appreciation of their significance and their worth.

I am personally convinced that the study of Latin, by the right type of learner and under the right type of teacher, can yield significant values in terms of mental discipline. There is impressive objective evidence that those who study Latin to the point of reasonable mastery acquire a mental equipment that gives them a distinct advantage over those who miss this discipline. Nor do I believe that this advantage can be explained by the hypothesis that, since only the naturally competent learners master Latin, their superiority can be attributed to their superior genes rather than to the discipline they have undergone. In this, as in other phases of the nature-nurture problem, the hypothesis justified by the evidence now available is that both favorable genes and the right kind of training are essential.

I shall make two references as to the very probable significance of Latin as a discipline. I have called attention on various occasions to H. L. Kriner's study, published in 1931, which attempted to find whether anything in the high-school record of an applicant for admission to a teachers college will indicate whether he will later become a successful teacher in the elementary or high school. Without going into the details of the study, I shall simply summarize his findings, which can be stated categorically as follows:

In so far as the high-school record of an applicant for admission to a teachers college is concerned, the best single predictive index of his future success as a teacher is whether he has successfully completed more than two years of high-school Latin; the second best index is the successful completion of more than two years of high-school mathematics; the third, the successful completion of more than two years of natural science. If, however, the candidate has taken more than two years of the social studies in high school, he is a poor risk.

Doubtless most, if not all, of you are familiar with Kriner's study. I mention it here because in the current number of *School and Society* there is a brief report of a study by Omar C. Held, of the University of Pittsburgh, based on a comparison of students' ratings on the psychological examination given to all freshmen with the amount of Latin taken in high school. There is no significant difference in psychological rating between those who have had no Latin and those who have had only one year of Latin. Two years of Latin give a significant, although not an impressive, difference. Three and four years apparently give to the Latin students a long lead over those who have taken no Latin in high school.

Held makes no claim for a disciplinary effect of Latin. He merely says his results indicate that "the more capable students tend to take up a study and continue it beyond one semester or one year." The question arises, however: How many of these students would have attained the same rank if they had not subjected themselves to the discipline of Latin for two years or more? And the best answer to the question in the light of existing evidence is that native competence is essential, but that native ability alone is not enough. The latent powers are undoubtedly given or withheld by nature, but without appropriate stimulation they will remain latent. And in so far as existing evidence is concerned, it seems probable that the most favorable stimulating agent among the school studies is Latin.

I have spoken rather strongly of the possibilities for mental discipline that I believe to be inherent in the study of Latin because it has been the fashion now for more than a generation to condemn out of hand these claims, and the condemnation has been particularly influential because it has been made in the magic name of science. I yield to no one in my respect for the methods of scientific inquiry or in my admiration for what these methods have accomplished. My own education on the higher level, both undergraduate and graduate, was almost exclusively in the natural sciences. I think that I speak advisedly, too, on the subject that I have been discussing. It is just forty years since the first significant experimental studies on the transfer of training were published. I read the report when it appeared, and I have studied carefully a goodly proportion of the more than one hundred published investigations of the transfer problem that have since appeared. One of the earliest investigations was made by three of my own students and published thirty-six years ago. Another, one of the most extensive of them all, was the basis of a doctor's dissertation made under my sponsorship ten years later. In 1904, I published a theory of transfer which I still hold and which fits the findings of eighty per cent of the reported studies.

On the relations of nurture and nature in determining intelligence I also speak, I think, advisedly. I was catapulted into the midst of this controversy just nineteen years ago. I was in it up to my neck and with my back against the wall for six years, and, because I emerged alive, I have naturally felt impelled to keep up with it ever since.

My own training in the natural sciences taught me above everything else a respect for facts and for reasoned inferences based on facts. In my judgment, many of my fellow-workers, who think of themselves as scientific psychologists and as educational scientists, do not always look facts squarely in the face. They work on the basis of established systems of psychology that they have accepted and on systems of educational theory, derived deductively from their psychological premises. If the observed facts do not fit these systems, the tendency is not to recognize the facts. This is what Karl S. Lashley referred to when he said that the discreditment of mental discipline has been due far more to the wide vogue of a mechanistic psychology, which had no explanation for transfer, than to any convincing experimental evidence. The weapons of the mechanistic psychologies in their attacks on mental discipline have been half-truths—and, as some one has said, a half-truth is like a half-brick; it carries farther.

If I were to offer any counsel to the classicists, it would be to reassert themselves and take the offensive, carrying the battle into the camp of their antagonists. The mechanistic psychologies, upon the tenets of which the negative interpretations of the transfer facts were primarily based, have been increasingly discredited since 1928, but they still cramp and crib and confine many discussions of educational values. The psychologists today are divided among fifty-seven different varieties of psychological theory. For more than a decade they have been quarreling among themselves, not infrequently to the extent of calling each other unpleasant names. In Kipling's phrase, they have been like "islands shouting lies to each other across seas of misunderstanding." Education should not have to wait until this still adolescent science comes to responsible maturity, if it ever does. Education can and should declare its independence and formulate its own theories as a basis for interpreting the observed facts in its own field.

In this paper I have emphasized chiefly the potentialities of the study of Latin as an apparently unique and certainly a powerful agency of mental discipline, the claims of which have been unjustly and contemptuously read out of court. I have spoken from the point of view of a psychologist— a renegade psychologist, it is true, long since drummed out of the psychologists' camp for his heterodoxy, but one who takes a certain pride in this heterodoxy, since he would rather be right than respectable. Others will speak, I am sure, of the equally incontestable functional values of the study of Latin from the point of view of its direct applicability to life problems, such as the effective use of the mother-tongue, as Professor Carr has I think abundantly proved in a summary of pertinent investigations shortly to be published. And there are other values, as well, some of which are forcefully set forth in the article by Karl P. Harrington, "Why Latin?" in *School and Society,* March 15th. I can only say that if the classicists wish to launch an offensive, they can start something that will not need to end in negotiated peace.

A Realistic Attitude Toward the Teachers College Problem

(1946)

This short work is another example of Bagley's campaign to awaken his profession. He challenges his colleagues to do something about the changes that were taking place in teachers colleges following World War II. He thought the move to de-emphasize teaching teachers was destructive to the profession of teaching. He published this article only five months before his death on July 1st, 1946. The column demonstrates his commitment to fighting for his profession to the very end.

Two contributions to the discussion of the problem of the professional education of teachers, appearing in this number of our journal, are especially significant in that they represent a reasoned acceptance of the present situation as more or less inevitable—and really not so bad after all. They both take what one of the papers refers to as a "realistic" attitude toward the problem.

Dr. Trailer's analysis of the differences between students entering teachers colleges and students entering "four-year colleges" (chiefly, it would seem, liberal-arts colleges) confirms evidence of long standing that the former are, in the average of cases, below the latter in intellectual capacity. While the differences that he reports have been consistent over a period of 10 years and are statistically significant, they are not, in his judgment, statistically very "impressive."

Forgotten Heroes of American Education, pages 267–269
Copyright © 2006 by Information Age Publishing
All rights of reproduction in any form reserved.

On the whole, apparently, the teachers colleges are a bit below the junior colleges in their power to attract the more competent high-school graduates. This would seem to make them the least selective of all higher institutions. The junior colleges, of course, by their generally accepted nature and purpose, should be relatively nonselective. Is such a status for the teachers colleges satisfactory to the profession of education? If the public were fully aware of the situation, would the public regard it as "unimpressive"?

A plain inference from the evidence presented is that half the recruits for the teaching service are drawn from a population that represents at best the lower 40 per cent of the high-school graduates who enter higher institutions. By implication it may be assumed that some, perhaps many, of the other professions draw their recruits predominantly from the higher 40 per cent of the high-school graduates. The conclusion is hardly inescapable that teaching on the lower educational levels is to be regarded as, at best, a semiprofession.

Dr. Snedden's letter is actually a plea for the acceptance of this semiprofessional status. Indeed, Dr. Snedden would favor a return to the normal school of the 1900's and 1910's—an essentially nonselective two-year institution, training for the elementary-school service girls who would enter the work of teaching (chiefly in their home communities) at age 20 or thereabouts, remain at most five years, and then gladly resign, marry, and "become mothers and full-time home-makers." (Of those who would not marry, or who would marry and wish to continue in the teaching service, Dr. Snedden says nothing, although he seems to imply that even these would be no worse off than many "nurses, secretaries, etc.," who are doomed to a similar semiprofessional status.)

In the judgment of the present writer, it is well to have these "realistic" contentions set forth so clearly. Personally, he is not as yet persuaded that he should give up the fight (in which he enlisted nearly 50 years ago) for a recognition of teaching on all educational levels as worthy of a true professional status, and of professional-education requirements and opportunities consistent with such a status. He makes bold to quote from an article that he contributed to the January, 1946, number of the *NEA Journal*:

> The inescapable conclusion is that teaching in the elementary and secondary schools is still far from the attractive calling that it should be if the education of "all the children of all the people" is basic to the welfare of democracy.

Leading public citizens often give lip-service to the importance of teaching in the public schools. Not so frequently do they encourage their children, and particularly their sons, to make public-school teaching a professional career. This is the acid test.

More attractive financial rewards will doubtless do something to correct this condition, but these, even if provided, will not alone solve the problem. The basic solution lies ... within the profession itself. At any rate, this has been true of other professions. *Generally speaking, the public rates professions as professions rate themselves.* The profession of education needs to develop a far keener sensitiveness to conditions that are inimical to its professional status in the eyes of the general public.

Other occupational groups have learned to command the public respect that they have clearly earned—groups whose services to the public are certainly no more fundamental than are the services of teachers. Can the educational profession do as much?

Section 2

SELECTED WRITINGS OF CHARLES DEGARMO

Charles DeGarmo (1849–1934) is a forgotten hero of American education. He has been forgotten because the ideals that he believed in were discarded by early 20th century Progressive educational thinkers such as John Dewey and William Heard Kilpatrick. DeGarmo's ambition was to become a leader in American education, and he achieved this goal during his lifetime. Beginning in the 1880s, DeGarmo became a powerful advocate of Herbartian educational theory, which was based upon the ideas of German educator and philosopher Johann Friedrich Herbart. Herbartian educational theory combined moral and intellectual training with sound pedagogy and teacher education. Herbartians like DeGarmo also emphasized the transmission of cultural traditions from one generation to the next, academic excellence for all teachers and children, and the necessity for all teachers to become well-schooled in the subject-areas they teach, as well as the traditional fields of psychology, ethics, and philosophy.

DeGarmo was born on January 17, 1849, in Muckwonago, Wisconsin. He grew up the son of Wisconsin farmers. At the age of 16, he served in the 149th Illinois Voluntary Army, but he never engaged in a Civil War battle. The money he was paid by the U.S. Government for his military service provided DeGarmo with the funds he needed to enroll at Illinois State Normal University in Normal, Illinois. He completed his undergraduate degree at Illinois State in 1873. He served as a teacher and school principal in Illinois schools before returning to Normal in 1883,

Forgotten Heroes of American Education, pages 271–272

when he became the head of the grammar department at the school's teacher training school.

In the early 1880s, DeGarmo began to look to Germany for opportunities to further his education. He sold his Illinois farm in 1883 and used the money to pay for three years of study at the University of Halle, a powerful center of pedagogical theory at the time. While a graduate student at Halle, DeGarmo became fascinated with Herbart's educational theory and earned his Ph.D. degree with a study of Herbart in 1886.

Upon his return to the U.S. in 1886, DeGarmo joined with Charles and Frank McMurry to popularize Herbart's ideas. DeGarmo was a professor of modern languages at Illinois State Normal University from 1886 to 1890. He moved to the University of Illinois as professor of pedagogy in 1890, and a year later he accepted a position as the Fourth President of Swarthmore College. After an eight-year term as President of Swarthmore, DeGarmo took a position as professor of the science and art of education at Cornell University. He served in this capacity from 1898 to 1914, when he retired from Cornell and moved to Florida. DeGarmo continued to write until his death in 1934.[1]

DeGarmo produced scores of articles and dozens of books during his prolific career. His books include *The Essentials of Method, An Introduction to the Pedagogy of Herbart* (with Christian Ufer), and *Interest and Education.*[2] DeGarmo is another example of an educational theorist and teacher educator from the past whose pre-Progressive educational philosophy has much relevance to 21st century educational thought and practice. DeGarmo's work speaks directly to contemporary questions about the nature of the curriculum and the most appropriate ways to prepare teachers.

---

1. Garraty, John A., and Mark C. Carnes, Eds., *American National Biography* 6 (New York: Oxford University Press, 1999): 344–345.
2. Charles DeGarmo, *The Essentials of Method* (Boston: D.C. Heath, 1892); Christian Ufer and Charles DeGarmo, *An Introduction to the Pedagogy of Herbart* (Boston: D.C. Heath, 1894); and Charles DeGarmo, *Interest and Education* (New York: Macmillan, 1902).

Social Aspects
of Moral Education
(1907)

DeGarmo provides an extended philosophical discussion of moral education in this essay. He emphasizes the social dimension of moral education in order to counteract the individualistic tendencies that he saw prevalent in American social and political thought. The acceptance of individual rights, he reminds his readers, also demands a duty to act on one's social responsibilities. He cites many philosophers—including the ancient Greeks, Thomas Hobbes, and Jean-Jacques Rousseau—to make this point. He is particularly critical of the influence of Rousseau, whose ideas, to DeGarmo, produced a "non-social" type of individual, by which he meant someone who did not recognize the social responsibilities that citizenship requires.

Like Bagley, who had been his student at Cornell University, DeGarmo emphasizes the significance of teacher training to the cultivation of social ideals in the minds and hearts of young Americans. In a section entitled "The Need of Higher Education for Teachers," DeGarmo makes a compelling case for moral and philosophical education for teachers. He believed that teachers were the crucial link that transmitted a nation's spiritual ideals from one generation to the next. This only could be done, DeGarmo asserts, if teachers are well-educated and well-trained to perform their jobs well.

In a democratic age and country the natural tendency is to exalt the importance of the individual. One may even declare that this is an habitual mode of thought with democratic peoples. This natural tendency is still further emphasized by our recent methods of child study, whereby the eyes of

Forgotten Heroes of American Education, pages 273–294

teachers are turned to individual peculiarities of body and mind. Without doubt this tendency will be wholly beneficial provided we hold steadily before ourselves the true ends for which the individualization is made. To see the social aspects of moral training we need to distinguish somewhat sharply between two types of individuality, which I call the social and the non-social.

TYPES OF NON-SOCIAL INDIVIDUALITY

A non-social individual is one that is, on the one hand, so absorbed in his subjective self that he is prone to overlook a large part of his duties to others and, on the other, to miss many of the best things of life, because he does not appreciate the opportunities that cooperation opens to him. There are several types of this form of non-social individuality. One is the emotional type, in which feeling is so exalted as to lose its connection with insight and action; the self is submerged in emotion. Another is the aesthetic type, in which beauty of form, harmony of color, concord of sound, self-poise of conduct, count for more than those forms of thought and action that make for efficiency in the accomplishment of actual work. Still another type of the non-social individual is seen in the man whose intellectual effort ends with analysis. Such a man is the logician, the man of introspective insight, the man whose mind has plenty of light, but no heat. In the popular imagination the college graduate is often pictured as such a character. This is also a common view of what a philosopher is; namely, a man who can make a thought-analysis of the cosmos, but who cannot manage with efficiency even the minor details of his own physical surroundings. Still another type of non-social individuality is seen in the man of strong, resolute action, such as the pioneer must be, who takes his fortune and his life in his hand, and who, plunging into the wilderness, tries to promote the one and to preserve the other by means of his axe and his rifle. He is the man who has no neighbors, whose life is lived out in solitary communion with nature. These types are all non-social because they make little or nothing of cooperation among men for the accomplishment of ends desired by all.

In the moral world he is the non-social individual who emphasizes but little, or in only a few directions, ethical relations to his fellows. Thus, for instance, one man may feel he has done his whole duty to society when he has subscribed a given amount to public or private charities; another when he has paid his assessments for the maintenance of the church; another when his heart is overflowing with good will for his neighbors to the extent of allowing them to do what they have a mind to, provided they do not hinder him in his enterprises; another thinks he has fulfilled his whole social function when he votes on election day, or when for a price he helps consume the things provided at a church sociable, or when he pays his taxes. Others conceive that they have kept the whole moral law when they have observed the negative commandments.

EUROPEAN INFLUENCES PRODUCING NON-SOCIAL TYPES OF CHARACTER

There are many historical reasons, besides the natural democratic tendencies of the age, that explain why our current educational theories concerning the individual are so largely non-social in character. As we know, during the Middle Ages, social organization was confined to a few broad lines, which though at first the means for promoting and preserving liberty, finally became the means for destroying it. Thus, in the religious and political realm, the church had become supreme, and had presumed to relieve men of the necessity of thinking. The natural rights of a man to his own thoughts and the freedom of expressing them were destroyed, the attempt being made to regulate the spiritual life of mankind by the authority of the church. In the economic life the feudal system, with its robber barons controlling the land, and its accompanying vassalage of the lower classes, became, through the rise of cities and the general growth of industrial life, a source of the greatest tyranny, though at first it was a condition of survival for the lower classes. Absolute monarchy, which in the earlier, more military phases of national life was a condition for the survival of the nation, became afterwards a keenly felt oppression. It is not strange, therefore, that with the revival of learning men should strive to emancipate themselves from the rule of spiritual authority, from the economic slavery of the feudal system, and from the caprices of absolutism.

The collision between the new spirit of independence and the old tyrannical institutions occurred at many points, as, for instance, in the Reformation and the wars that followed it; in the Puritan Revolution in England, and the French Revolution in France.

It is not strange, moreover, that this new movement should become embodied in the theories of the seventeenth and the eighteenth centuries. These are well represented by the doctrines of Hobbes, of Mandeville, and of Rousseau. Hobbes declared: (1) that man is by nature selfish, and non-social, (2) that for the sake of preserving his life and property he must give up some of his non-social rights and instincts, and (3) that the law as promulgated by the sovereign is the rule that must regulate his social conduct. This philosophy broke down in practice with the death of Charles the First. Mandeville, the precursor of Adam Smith, declared, first of all, with Hobbes, that man is by nature selfish and non-social, but (2) that the welfare of society depends upon the activity of the struggle among individuals to accomplish selfish ends. (3) That is therefore the most perfect society in which each individual strives the hardest to attain his selfish ends. This doctrine is the forerunner of the theory of supply and demand, and free competition in the economic world. Rousseau, the philosopher of the French Revolution, declared, first of all, that, contrary to the opinion of Hobbes and Mandeville, man is good and social by nature, but (2) that he has been perverted by history, his social nature being warped and destroyed, and that (3) society must first destroy itself in order to reconstruct itself in accordance with the primitive social nature of man.

AMERICAN REALIZATION
OF EUROPEAN NON-SOCIAL IDEALS

"All is good," declares Rousseau, in the *Emile,* "as it comes from the hand of the Creator; everything is perverted in the hands of man. Let us, therefore, live alone; let the boy and the girl be brought up by themselves, wholly isolated from society, which in all its influences is deteriorating."

It was impossible to realize in Europe this demand of eighteenth-century philosophy, but its realization became a necessity in the new world. In Europe men could not live alone; in America they were compelled to do so. We shall find, therefore, in the pioneer history of our country an accentuation of all those influences of the old world that led toward social disintegration. The strong natural desire for adventure, and the natural longing to exploit the possibilities of wealth opened by the discovery of a new continent, were greatly emphasized by the European conflicts of which mention has been made. Both religious and political influences in England tended toward the exodus to this country of the strong individuals who had revolted against the systems of political and religious authority in that land. Thus there came to our shores the Puritan, the Quaker, the nonconformist in general, the political offender, and the man of strong individualistic, democratic tendencies. It was quite out of the question to establish in the wilderness the social system of the highly developed European state. The pioneers scattered through the forests and over the plains, dwelling together in small communities only where it was necessary to secure themselves against the incursions of the Indians. In this life of isolation every type of non-social individuality found a fertile soil. The morose could remain by themselves, the man of individual opinions always found a scope for them, the recluse need not be disturbed by his neighbors, the man of strong will and independent daring could dwell alone in the virgin forests in his bark hut or his log cabin. Professor Turner, of the University of Wisconsin, has pointed out to us how for four hundred years these primitive non-social tendencies have been perpetuated through the influence of the constantly extending and widening frontier.[1] He has shown that in our history, both in civic and economic respects, our prevailing ideals of character have been determined vastly more by the energetic frontier than by the far more distant European civilization, which only in recent years has begun to have a powerful effect upon American ideals.

Taking into consideration the influence of these historic forces it is not strange that at the close of the nineteenth century, when the conditions of material, intellectual, social and political life have vastly changed, our doctrines of education should still be permeated by the spirit of the eighteenth century. The philosophy of Rousseau, of Mandeville, and to some extent of Hobbes still dominates American ideals of education. There has come to be, therefore, a sharp antithesis between the conditions of life as they now exist, and the non-social theories of individuality, which have by the exigencies of pioneer development been perpetuated to this day. It is, therefore, necessary for the teacher to take a survey of the real situation, in order to see where we are, both in fact and theory, and if possible to bring fact and theory again into concord.

THE PRESENT SITUATION ARISING FROM THE DISAPPEARANCE OF THE FRONTIER AND FROM THE GROWTH OF CITIES

When we attempt to study our present situation, two important facts come at once to view. The first is that there is no longer in America a true frontier. The last of our public lands available for agriculture have been taken up. The career of the huntsman is found only in the pages of literature, that of the herder has become a steady occupation in a few portions of the country, while robber farming is rapidly ceasing to be profitable. The other fact of momentous importance is the enormous growth of urban life. Our statistics show that, taking the country as a whole, nearly one-third of our people now live in cities having a population of more than eight thousand. If we take the country east of the Allegheny Mountains we shall find that fully half of the people in that section live in cities or their suburbs. The whole country is a network of railroads and trolley lines, binding all together into a cooperative whole. Even in the

---

1. F. J. Turner, "The Significance of the Frontier in American History," *Annual Report of American Historical Association*, 1893, pp. 199–227.

Mississippi valley there is a constant exodus from the country to the city, where most of the leaders of thought are to be found. Every village that is supplied with coal and water, and one or more of the raw materials for manufacture, has its tall chimneys and its regulated hours of labor. A whole set of new problems has arisen, quite insoluble under our old conditions of non-social life. In the early days every running stream furnished an abundant supply of pure water, or, lacking this, the pioneer could strike a crystal fount by digging a hole in the ground. Now almost every running stream is polluted with filth, and the well is more frequently a sink of corruption than a fountain of living water. Evidently only cooperation on a large scale can keep our urban communities supplied with pure water. A coordinate problem is that of draining these cities so as to preserve health and to avoid the contamination of the water sources. Beyond this, where large bodies of people live close together the earth itself is no longer a fit medium for moving about from place to place. The streets must be paved. The light of the stars and of the moon at night no longer suffices for the needs of men. The free, independent life of the frontier can no longer exist for the unfortunate or the indolent in the cities. The problem of the slums arises. The highway is no longer a free way, but certain groups of men must be entrusted with the rights of common carrier, else the railroad and the trolley line are no longer possibilities. All these vast enterprises of water supply, drainage, paving, light, the control of the slums, transportation, must either be undertaken by the community, acting in its corporate capacity, or must be granted in the form of franchises to private corporations. There thus arises the opportunity for robbing the community to satisfy the greed of corporations and politicians. It is said that in the city of Chicago more money is realized from the tax on dogs than from that on street railways.

It is evident that a new type of citizenship is needed to deal with all these problems. The non-social aspect of character is perhaps natural under pioneer conditions where each may do substantially as he pleases without seriously interfering with his neighbor, but in a highly developed state of civilization these forms of independence, which in a new country are right and beneficial, become a source of infinite corruption, and of vast personal hardship to the individual. Here again we see the need for a readjustment of our theory and practice in education to our new social and economic conditions.

We need, perhaps, first of all, to get a somewhat adequate ideal of what constitutes a character that is truly moral from the social standpoint. If, on the one hand, the non-social individual is defined as one who is so absorbed in his subjective self that he is prone to overlook both his duties and his opportunities, we may perhaps define a social individual as one who is constantly alive to all his duties toward his fellows, and keenly sensible of the social advantages that come to every man through the development of the cooperative spirit.

SOCIAL VERSUS SOCIALISTIC CONCEPTIONS

At this point we may well distinguish between a *social* and a *socialistic* organization of society. Nearly all socialistic schemes have this characteristic in common, that they would reproduce in the industrial world and for industrial purposes the same type of social institution that we see in the ancient world, in the domains of religion, and the state.[2] They would prevent any man from suffering hunger, by putting the industrial activity of every man under state surveillance. Their organizations are always vast, unwieldy, and highly mechanical—witness Bellamy's military state. The day is long since past when such organizations of society are necessary for its survival or for the survival of the individual. They belong to the type of society where the presence of external dangers, either of warlike incursion or of famine, compelled men to give up most of the things which, next to bare existence, they chiefly desired. It is highly improbable that the human race, after outgrowing these primitive forms and becoming so highly civilized and so firmly Christianized that the most serious of the dangers which formerly produced these organizations no longer exist, will be content of their own free volition to return to those forms of social organization that in the end have proved the greatest obstacles to liberty and progress. If this is true even among the warlike nations of Europe, how much truer must it ever remain in a powerful, yet isolated nation like our own.

A true social organization, on the other hand, permitting the agencies of production to remain in private hands, and eschewing all artificial schemes of distribution, is marked by its freedom of association, by its permission of individual initiative in every department of life, and by its division of authority between large and small bodies. It is permeated by the Anglo-Saxon idea of local control of local affairs. We have, it is true, a great nation, which is a powerful unit, but we have, on the other hand, our local political organizations, which in the affairs that concern them chiefly are practically autonomous. So in all the great organizations of religious life. We are a Christian people, but we are divided into many denominations,

---

2. "What is characteristic of socialism is the joint ownership by all the members of the community of the instrument and means of production, which carries with it the consequence that the division of the produce among the body of owners must be a public act according to rules laid down by the community."—J. S. Mill, *Socialism*.

and each denomination is separated into its own self-governing churches. All the business of the country is managed more and more in the same way. We have great accumulations of capital, controlled as to its general policy by corporations, but managed in its details by small groups of men. Every city has the possibility of perfect elasticity in the management of its affairs. If one group proves recreant to its trust, another composed of honest men can be substituted in its stead. Instead of one vast, dead, immovable organization, that can be changed only by revolution, we have an elastic system, sensitive to every determined phase of popular opinion, and changeable without violent outbreaks at any time or in any place. We have, in short, a system that is undergoing constant evolution. This is what I call a *social* as opposed to a *socialistic* organization of the various activities of men.

FUNDAMENTAL DIFFERENCES BETWEEN SOCIAL AND NON-SOCIAL TYPES OF CHARACTER

It is necessary to make a somewhat more fundamental analysis of the differences to be observed in the two types of character, the social and the non-social. As has already been intimated, the non-social individual centers all his thoughts and activity in himself. He contracts his individuality. The social individual, on the contrary, expands his personality. Professor James, in his chapter on "The Self" has well described these two types: "All narrow people," he says, "intrench their me. They retract it from the region of what they cannot securely possess. People who don't resemble them, or who treat them with indifference, people over whom they gain no influence, are people on whose existence, however meritorious it may intrinsically be, they look with chill negation, if not with positive hate. Who will not be mine, I will exclude from existence altogether—that is, as far as I can make it so—such people shall be made as if they were not. Thus may a certain absoluteness and definiteness in the outline of my me, console me for the smallness of its content. Sympathetic people, on the contrary, proceed by the entirely opposite way of expansion and inclusion."[3]

Readiness to participate in group activity is an index of the social character, whereas the inclination to avoid such participation by centering all activity in the self, or what the self can actually dominate, is the characteristic of the non-social individual. An illustration of this difference may be seen in the differing conceptions that people have of what constitutes a neighbor. Remembering that in answer to the question of the lawyer, "Who is my neighbor?" Jesus replied with the parable of the Good

---

3. James, *Psychology*, p. 189.

Samaritan, many have restricted the idea of neighborliness to that of benevolence. He is considered a true neighbor who would rescue the perishing, who would nourish the wounded, who would give of his substance to others less fortunate than himself.

However self-centered a man may be with respect to cooperation with others in group activities for common ends, he is considered a good neighbor if he has the quality of benevolence toward the unfortunate; but there is another and a better conception of the neighbor, which, including all that the old contains, greatly expands the range of neighborly action. Holding this idea of group activity before us, we can see that not he alone who is willing to give alms is the true neighbor, but he who is willing to work with his fellows in groups for common purposes: for example, to establish and maintain a good school, to protect the sanctity of the home, to have a good water supply and a good drainage system in the city, to have the streets properly lighted and paved, to forbid offensive sights, sounds, and smells in public highways, to protect the interests of the public against rapacious corporations and politicians, and to shut up the evil doer and let the innocent go abroad rather than, as in olden times, to shut up the innocent, such as the women and children and scholars, that the evil-minded might walk abroad.[4] A good neighbor is willing to combine with any group of men to have good roads in the country, to see that the conditions of health everywhere prevail, that churches are supported, that the amenities of social life may prevail in the country as well as in the city, so that the benumbing routine of unvarying drudgery so often found in the country may have its social relief. He is willing to vote with that party, or that section of a party, that insists that not only shall the flag be honored by the children, but that the civic liberties and rights pertaining to it receive due attention; that the community shall no longer be dominated by a boss, because the citizens are too indolent, or too selfish, or too cowardly, or too indifferent, or too much isolated in their feelings, to combine together for good government. Such a man, in brief, is anxious that the affairs of the community, county, state, and nation shall reflect the common honesty, and that they shall be conducted with economy and efficiency for the common good.

Another characteristic of social, as opposed to non-social individuality, which is observed in nations quite as much as in persons, is seen in the fact that the non-social are relatively analytic in their habits of thought and inclined to passivity rather than activity with respect to all the important things that go to make up the life of an individual or of a nation. Readiness

---

4. See Patten, "Economics for the Public School," *Annals of the American Academy of Social and Political Science,* January 1895.

of participation in group activity implies a synthetic rather than an analytic phase of character. The one type of character tends towards mere contemplation, as is seen in the man whose instincts are all esthetic. His self is satisfied in the enjoyment that comes from contemplating the various forms of art. He may indeed reflect upon their meaning, analyzing the motives of a painting or a statue, but his mental activity stops with himself. It is not associated with the arousing of the motor activities, for it does not stimulate him to do anything. In the same way we find the contemplative, analytic type of character in every department of life. We have the man who sits at home to tell how battles are won and lost. The politician who can analyze the condition of the country, but who does nothing to change it; the analytic moralist who can tell precisely what the evils of the liquor traffic are, but whose soul is never animated by an irrepressible desire to do something about it; the man who can analyze the sermon of the preacher, telling precisely what its content is and what its strong and its weak points are, but who never thinks of attempting to carry its maxims into actual practice. These types are all non-social because they are purely analytic and passive. There is a little flurry of introspective brain activity, but it does not pass over into motor impulse, which is the invariable index of the social or sympathetic character. With the latter, conviction leads to action, and perception of the desirability of doing something leads to the attempt to do it. If one type of character is passive, the other is active; if one is contemplative and analytic, the other is synthetic and executive; if one is self-centered and contracted, the other is cooperative and expanded. Professor Patten says on these points: "Social reasoning depends on the content given to the self. Only as the feeling of identity is expanded can the organism, the material world, society, and the universe become real to men. Should their attitude become strictly skeptical (or non-social) all these would become unreal; trains of sensorial ideas would alone remain. It is the synthetic self that is the basis of society. To the analytic self non-social individualism is the only logical system. It regards the social forces as unreal. The synthetic self is the active self; the analytic self is due to our passive states."[5]

Many examples could be cited from history where it is evident that the disintegrating non-social spirit of the people has prevented unity. The Greeks were, as we know, a people who were animated, not only in their daily occupations, but in their religion as well, by the aesthetic ideals, which are essentially non-social in their tendencies, being purely personal

---

5. "Relation of Sociology to Psychology," *Annals of the American Academy of Political and Social Science*, p. II, Philadelphia. See also for more expanded discussion, "The Theory of Social Forces," by the same author.

and contemplative in character. With them the good man was the sage, because he was the man who had analytic insight enough to distinguish the good from the bad, and who understood that the bad, constantly pursued by an individual, leads to his unhappiness, if not to his ultimate destruction. It was an axiom with them that he who truly knows the good is sure to do it, because otherwise he would have to repudiate his own deepest insight. This is the prevailing theme of the Grecian systems of morality, that of the Cyrenaics no less than of the Cynics. Even Plato resigned the direction of his state to his sages. Greece did indeed develop the subjective individuality of its citizens; it did indeed become great in the products of art, but it did not become great in those forms of industrial and political activity in which the social spirit is an essential element. Small though the country was, it was a series of discordant states, each ready to pounce upon the other with slight provocation. There was no sense of national unity. The Greek language itself, even, did not serve to produce political harmony.

In our own times the German nation furnishes a striking example of the unfortunate results of the non-social spirit. True German unity remained a dream of the philosopher for a thousand years. The country was divided into a countless number of petty principalities, each intent upon preserving its non-social individuality. It took the tremendous upheaval of the Napoleonic wars to crush out enough of these petty powers to make the ultimate union of 1870 possible. It is one of the marvels of history that only toward the close of the nineteenth century has the social spirit become sufficiently dominant in Germany to unite that great people of a common tongue into a nation.

MOTIVES FOR SOCIAL ORGANIZATION

If we inquire what the motives are that tend toward the growth of social unity and social organization in the varying phases of industrial and of religious national life, we shall find them in large degree in the Contrast between what Professor Patten calls a "pain economy" and a "pleasure" or social economy.[6] There are two classes of interests that stimulate men to social activity, the one negative, the other positive. Under the natural separating tendencies of the primitive environment it is common danger more than anything else that induces men to combine for common purposes. This fact is clearly revealed in the history of the American

---

6. "The Theory of Social Forces," *Annals of the American Academy of Political and Social Science,* Philadelphia.

colonies; each colony jealous of every other, desiring to stand upon its own feet, was induced only by the most alarming dangers of Indian warfare to unite with the others for common defense. We know the history of the colonial times and that of the period after the Revolution. We know the unsuccessful attempt to live under the Articles of Confederation, where mere external union was attempted; we are aware of the conflicting views of the representatives of the colonies in the Constitutional Convention; we are painfully conscious, moreover, of the doctrine of states' rights or state sovereignty, and how it arose, and how it was perpetuated almost to our own day. We cannot forget that it was only the lash of a tremendous civil war, and the growth of a nation outside of the original colonies that have at last brought us to a true national unity. It has been the fear of evil that has brought men together into social organizations in the past. There is, however, another basis for social unity gradually established by progress in civilization, and especially those phases of civilization that enable dense populations to maintain a high standard of life. This basis is not negative, but positive, not the fear of evil, but the opportunity for good. This is the true social spirit. According to this idea men combine for mutual good, and for promoting in positive ways, through group activity, the welfare of the whole. These groups, moreover, are manifold and flexible. Under the old pain economy, the danger of war or the imminence of famine was about the only motive for social cooperation, but under the affirmative social impulse the cooperative groups are as numerous, as flexible, and as changeable as the varying needs of the community. A society is organized for every social, philanthropic, political, economic end seen to be desirable by any given group of people. These social forces come to the front when the country is so advanced in standard of living and density of population that what may be called the pleasure or true social economy is possible. In such communities political or religious despotisms, together with military organizations, are no longer the conditions of survival. Our nation has no real fear of foreign invasion for two reasons, first, because it is strong enough to repel one should it be made, and, second, because there is no good reason, nor is there likely to be one, why such an invasion should be made. We are absolutely freed from the fear of those evils which made the early forms of institutions so formidable and so destructive to the true interests of men as soon as the danger of subjugation by foreign nations was removed. Being no longer dominated by the fear of evil, we are free to look about us and to enter into every form of social cooperation that promises to enhance our material, our civil, or our spiritual interests.

THREE SOCIAL FUNCTIONS OF THE SCHOOL

Having come to a definite conclusion as to what the social ideals, as represented in our educational literature, really are, and, on the other hand, what they should be when we take into consideration the natural conditions of social life as they now exist, the important question arises. What can the schools do to develop social as opposed to non-social individualism? Taking our analysis as a guide to what is desirable, it would seem that there are three prime requisites for accomplishing this end. They are the formation of right social ideals, the cultivation of adequate social disposition, and the formation of efficient social habits. The intellectual apprehension of the ideal is not sufficient to enable a human being to live up to it. Nor, on the other hand, is a kindly disposition without firm conviction enough to secure the best results; nor are ideal and disposition to conform to it of themselves sufficient. There must be the ingrained habit of moving toward an ideal conceived and desired. Each of these topics requires a much more thorough exposition than the limits of the present article permit.

THE STUDIES AS SOURCES OF SOCIAL IDEALS

Looking at the question in a broad way, it is upon the school studies that we must to a large degree depend for the revelation of social ideals. Every subject has its social side; each, in other words, has some relation to man and his activities. History records his will in action, literature shows ideally his struggle for and against ethical principles, science furnishes him the means whereby he can advance in civilization, linguistics teaches him how to use his thought most effectively for accomplishing the purposes for which he labors. It was a favorite conception with Herbart that the chief function of instruction is to furnish a moral revelation of the world to the child, but this morality so revealed is necessarily of a social character, for every one of the studies, in so far as it is moral at all in its influence, points to that phase of morality that we call social, for it reveals the actual and the ideal relations between man and man, community and community, nation and nation.

This conception of education is radically different from that which arises from regarding the function of education as the development of the individual in his non-social character. When viewed from this standpoint it is almost inevitable that the studies should be valued largely for their gymnastic worth, rather than for the ideals they contain. Our doctrine of formal discipline, whereby the mind is supposed to be educated by doing work, without much regard to what the thought and meaning of the work are, is the natural consequence of non-social theories of individualism. The function of education, according to this theory, is to drill the mind; but when we view moral education in its social aspects, we see that drilling is not the sole function of education. The standpoint changes, and the individual finds his relation to the rest of the world, instead of trying to subordinate all things to himself. Changing our point of view with respect to the studies from the non-social to the social aspect is almost as radical in its results as was the change adopted by Copernicus when he ceased to think of the earth as the center of the solar system, and regarded the sun as the center. The same elements of the problem were present, but the solution was very different. Whether we adopt the non-social or the social theory of education the same branches of learning are to be considered, but the whole situation is vastly different in the two cases. In the first the studies are material chiefly for drill, with information as a secondary purpose; under the social aspect the studies are regarded primarily as the means for a world-revelation to the child—*eine Weltanschauung*, as the Germans say.

Each of these studies has its own peculiar function in this ethical revelation, since each contains a different aspect from the others, or else exhibits the same thing from a different standpoint. Geography is, perhaps, the most universal of all elementary studies for giving a child social ideals. It shows him the various forms of government in the world; it informs him to some extent of the principal religions; it enables him to understand the conditions for plant and animal life in the various parts of the globe and their influence upon the life of man. The study of the climatic conditions in the arctic regions makes it clear why the Esquimaux live as they do; whereas a study of the conditions of life in the torrid zone explains in a large measure the development of uncivilized and of civilized life in the tropics. When we come to the temperate regions, in addition to this study of natural conditions, a detailed examination of the factors of industrial life, such as lumbering, mining, manufacture, farming, transportation, postal and telegraph systems, newspapers, etc., enables the child to grasp in some degree the reasons for the rapid advance in civilization everywhere found in these regions of the globe.

NEED OF HIGHER EDUCATION FOR TEACHERS

Similar considerations hold for all the departments of instruction. It is very evident that we shall not make a great deal of progress in the development of social ideals unless our teachers and our authors are alive to the need and the opportunity of teaching these ideals through the studies. So long as our teachers have only the inadequate conceptions of the purposes of education that are obtained through elementary training we shall not make a great deal of advance in the development of social ideals. We find here the reason for the utilization of the methods of higher education in the training of teachers. The great temptation in this work is to spend all the time in drilling upon elementary subjects, so that the teacher shall be thoroughly well qualified to do the detailed work in grammar and arithmetic and the other common-school studies. The ultimate results, however, under such a system of training teachers are sure to be disappointing. The teacher, always shortsighted with respect to the function of the school studies, becomes more and more so under the benumbing influence of daily routine with immature minds. We say the teacher dries up, meaning by this that the mind confines itself almost entirely to routine trains of thought. The only hope for the teacher so prepared is subsequent investigation into new realms of study under the leadership of school principals and superintendents who have had the advantages of liberal education. The essential difference between elementary and higher education lies in this, that elementary education deals necessarily with non-related fragments of knowledge, whereas higher education always takes a comparative view of any subject of study. Thus the study of botany is not merely the study of facts regarding plants, but it is, first of all, a study of the function of the parts of a plant. The whole plant is examined from the standpoint of the leaf, the blossom, the fruit, because every one of these has a vital function in carrying on the life of the whole. Furthermore, the study of the plant leads us at once to the comparative study of the environment of the plant—the air, its moisture and temperature; and the earth, its temperature and chemical qualities. A thorough study of the plant, moreover, involves its relation to its altitude above the ocean and to the latitude in which it grows; its influence upon man, if it has one, is also taken into consideration. This is especially true of all those plants whose products enter into the commerce of the world. Then, from the standpoint of botany, under the methods of higher education, we get a view of physical geography in several of its elements, of chemistry, of physics, of the industrial, and even social life of man. The same is true with every subject. In the history of art we read the history of civilization from the standpoint of the aesthetic. When we study the civil government of the United States we study the history of modern democracy as manifested in our own country. When we study political history we study the development of civilization as revealed in national activities. When we take up political science we make a similar study of the same thing from the standpoint of government. When we take up economics by the comparative methods of higher education we are studying history and religion and politics and education in the light of man's industrial development. Each one of these studies, then, pursued by the methods of higher education, gives a revelation of the chief factors of civilization. We stand on different peaks, but we see the same mountain range. It is not necessary that the teacher should know all these subjects in this way. It is, perhaps, sufficient to know thoroughly one study, or one group of studies, like science, or history, or literature, or linguistics. If the teacher once has the view from any one of these standpoints, it will be possible to utilize the common-school studies for the development of social ideals in the children.

THE DEVELOPMENT OF SOCIAL DISPOSITION

Intimately associated with the development of ideals is that of the corresponding development of social disposition. Discussion of this topic in Herbart circles always appears under the title of INTEREST. What is the great function of interest in the school? Not amusement, not even the desirable end of claiming the attention of the children during the recitation, but it is rather the development of an abiding hospitality for those phases of moral conduct that involve the happiness or unhappiness, the welfare or detriment of other members of the social group to which the individual belongs.

Reformers tell us that it does but little good to remonstrate with the inhabitants of the slums for living upon so low a plane. It is not even sufficient to tell them that there are better ways and to demonstrate to them that a higher life is within their reach. A disposition to live in accordance with the new light must in some way be established, else the reformer loses his breath. Even the construction of better buildings with the conveniences of life does not always suffice to effect the purpose desired. It is said that in one row of new tenement houses bath tubs were supplied for all the inhabitants. After a time the inspector found that one man had used his bath tub as a potato bin, another as a coal bin, another had salted a pig in his. These people had not yet acquired a desire for cleanly bodies; they had not even learned to keep their faces clean. The economist recognizes that desire is the one motive power that will lead men out of their misery. It is not sufficient to inform the intellect that better things are just ahead; there must be implanted in the bosom of the man a desire to reach them. Not only must he have a pious wish for better things, but that desire must pass over into the work he does. Every movement of the spade, every movement of the trowel must be animated by the interest that is transferred from the longed for end to the means for reaching it. To the teacher the work of the sculptor as he chisels from the shapeless marble the shapely form should be the type of all school activity. The sculptor sees in imagination the perfect statue, and every stroke of the hammer carries with it the force of the ideal. There is no indifference in his work; the interest in the end is transferred to the means for reaching it. The difference between work and drudgery, as Dr. Dewey tells us, lies right here:[7] When the end alone is desired, and the means for reaching it are only a hated routine, then we have drudgery, as in the case of the man who goes mechanically to his day's labor, without interest or pride in its stages, looking only to the reward that is to come at its close. That is drudgery. It is an intolerable thing in the schoolroom. But when the interest in the end is transferred to the means for reaching it, when the end is ever an advancing and broadening and brightening one and each day's labor makes the end of labor more attractive, then we have true work. The chief reason why children are so little interested in the routine of the school is that its revelations of social life are so few and so faint.

We find in this idea of a world-revelation of the ideals of social life the deepest meaning of interest in school studies. There are numerous secondary reasons why children should be interested in their studies that are in themselves perfectly valid, but they are not the most fundamental. A generous mind of the old Greek type, seeing clearly the meaning of civilization and the enormous cost of every advance, would doubtless be fired with the desire not to retard but to further this progress, but the majority of minds are not primarily generous in the sense that the comprehension of a noble ideal is sufficient to inflame the soul with zeal for its preservation and propagation. The acquisition of such a disposition is the work of years. It needs all the noble enthusiasm of the teacher and all the zeal that can come from an early-founded and long-developed interest in the subject-matter of education.

THE DEVELOPMENT OF SOCIAL HABITS

Not only must the school be a social institution in the development of ideals and the cultivation of hospitality and even enthusiasm for them, but it must be a social institution also in the development of efficient social habits. Some of the most important phases of this side of moral education have been developed by Dr. Harris. He shows the significance of cultivating the social habits of regularity, punctuality, silence and industry.

There is also another aspect of school discipline, in the narrower sense of the term, that demands a word of explanation. In the matter of punishments for school offenses the personality of the teacher should remain in the background and the social nature of the school should come

---

7. *Interest as Related to Will,* Dr. John Dewey, Second Supplement to *Herbart Yearbook* for 1895.

to the front. The idea should not be tolerated for a moment that offenses are committed against the teacher; they are not personal but social; they are against the good order and efficiency of the school itself. Every child should see clearly and feel keenly the truth of the social relations. School offenses or offenses against the school as a whole should, so far as possible, meet with social punishments. The objection to corporal punishment lies mainly in the fact that it is for the most part non-social in character. It is likely to be taken individually, and does not usually affect the pupil's standing in the eyes of his fellows, except perhaps to awaken sympathy for him as against the teacher. Social punishments, however, when made really effective, are usually much more keenly felt than physical ones. A boy will willingly endure almost any amount of physical suffering to make himself a hero in the eyes of his mates, but any diminution of his standing with them is felt more acutely than the sharpest biting of the rod. The boy in school is not far removed in his social feelings from the Indian, who for the sake of appearing heroic before the tribe patiently endures the bitterest physical agony. To be true to its social mission the school must in its punishments adopt the social as opposed to individualistic or non-social principles of government.

THE IMPORTANCE OF MOTOR EFFICIENCY

The true measure of a social habit is the degree of efficiency with which the student moves to the accomplishment of a social end. The man of affairs is always the man of ready action, both in mind and body. His thoughts are always at command, for he can focus them in an instant in any desired direction. He is always ready, moreover, to exert an amount of motor activity that is sufficient to accomplish the purpose desired; whether this activity is manifested in the word of command, in the written message, or in the use of tools, he can always concentrate the energies of his mind into adequate motor channels. The school cannot be an effective social institution, therefore, that does not in all its activities encourage and develop the mental and motor efficiency of the pupils in its charge. The development of such motor powers is one of the most fundamental reasons for the introduction of manual training, cooking schools, and other forms of industrial activity in our educational system. Another means for the development of motor efficiency is at hand in every school, and yet is usually but feebly utilized, and that refers to the play in which the children find their recreation.

THE SOCIAL FUNCTION OF PLAY

The kindergartner has learned how to make the early plays of children of great importance in the development of the best type of social character, but the elementary schools, regarding play as something foreign to education, have taken little thought of how the play of the pupils in the primary and grammar schools may be made an educational instrument for social advance. Play in any form develops motor activity, but it does not necessarily develop the social instincts. It may be so purely individualistic and non-social as rather to retard than advance social ideals. A new element, therefore, a social one, should be introduced into the plays for the schools, and a new thoughtfulness on this subject should be awakened in our teachers. For the most part the plays of children are still essentially in their non-social stage. Boys still play tag and marbles and other individualistic games, where the group idea scarcely appears. At present, however, they are fascinated, both small and great, by the social games of the college, chiefly by football, basketball, and baseball, but they attempt to play these games by professional rules. To the latter there are many objections, the chief of which arise from limitations of number and of space. A small school cannot furnish two nines or two elevens, the members of which are upon an equality in age and strength; nor is it likely, especially in cities, that grounds of regulation size can be provided. Moreover, in a large city school the numbers are so great that most of the pupils must be excluded from the games if professional rules are adhered to. For this class of games teachers need, therefore, to devise rules for adapting them to smaller or to larger groups and to smaller spaces. Change the rules somewhat and football can be played without special clothing by groups of three, four, five, six, eight, nine, eleven, or more upon a side, and that within contracted grounds. The main point is the equalization of the groups. Effect this result and group games will receive a tremendous impetus. A school in New York has, for example, devised a set of rules whereby thirty or forty boys may play upon a side in the game of football. The changes are chiefly two in character—first, that the ball can be moved from place to place only by punting or passing, never by carrying, and, second, that a touchdown is made only by punting the ball beneath the bar. This plan enables the groups to change from day to day, so that the school may be divided by choosing up, as in some of the older social games. In this form no objection is made by the parents to the game, because undue roughness is eliminated and special clothing is not required. Again, in baseball professional rules are not well adapted to children, for the group character of the play is largely neutralized by the fact that so much depends upon the pitcher. Basketball can be played out of doors in almost any available space; the baskets may be hung on poles, or between poles, or they may be placed upon or in the ground. These three games, which the schools are borrowing from the college, are merely types of social games which can easily be adapted to the needs of children.

The advantages of group games over individualistic ones are chiefly two—first, a strong individual insists upon being the whole game where it is the individual alone that counts, but in the group game he forgets himself in organizing and directing the group. Alone he can do but little, yet as a group director he may be able to win the game. On the other hand, the weaker boys, who are not allowed to be leaders and who are individually helpless, suddenly become powerful and essential as soon as a group is organized. In this way two of the most important lessons for the future man are learned—group direction and group cooperation. This fact, coupled with the other fact, that motor efficiency is highly developed by games, makes it apparent that play should be much more thoroughly utilized for the social development of children than it has ever been in the past.

VALUE OF THE RECITATION IN DEVELOPING EFFICIENCY

But one other phase of the development of efficiency need be urged in the present paper. A sharp distinction has already been made between what is called the analytic and the synthetic character. The development of analytic habits of mind without the accompanying development of practical efficiency in the use of the knowledge gained leads on the one hand to the aesthetic type of character and on the other to the analytic; it produces the man who sees clearly enough into moral and other practical relations, but whose mental activity is not accompanied by motor efficiency. One of the chief opportunities of the school to develop what has been called the synthetic man lies in the proper use of the recitation. The mere acquisition of facts does not produce the practical man. Even keen mental analysis is not sufficient. Insight must be accompanied by action; and this action, so far as it is distinct from motor activity proper, such as is seen in manual training, is developed especially in that phase of method which we call *application*. It is easily appreciated in such studies as grammar and arithmetic and linguistics, but not so clearly in geography and science and history. The acquisition of a grammatical principle is followed by its application in the parsing and analysis of extracts from the literary masterpieces. The comprehension of a principle in mathematics is properly followed by its persistent application to a large group of problems. This tends to make the mind efficient for the practical application of what it knows; mental alertness is developed, and the capacity to focus knowledge so as to be effective is a continual growth in the pupil. In history this practical application of facts learned will have to do largely with causal relations and with comparisons. The mind is strengthened in its practical capacity by tracing out in detail the causes, for example, that led to Burgoyne's invasion and his ultimate defeat. This practical efficiency is equally promoted by tracing out the effects of the invasion upon subsequent events. The mind is strengthened, furthermore, by the constant drill that leads to organization of knowledge. It is made facile by skillful questioning, that requires the pupil to focus all his resources, now upon this point, now upon that.

When the school has learned to use the subject-matter of instruction for the development of social ideals through a revelation to the child of the essential stages of civilization, when it has awakened a permanent vital interest, a warm hospitality for these ideals, and when it has, through its organization of class, its methods of school discipline, its utilization of play, and its conduct of the recitation, transformed these ideals and interests into habits, then the school has become a social institution.

THESES

1. There are two types of individuality, the social and the non-social. Only the former is moral from the social standpoint.

2. Non-social individuality, both in theory and practice, was developed in Europe during the seventeenth and eighteenth centuries; it has, on account of peculiar pioneer and frontier conditions, been perpetuated in the United States, at least in theory, until the present time.

3. The growth of cities and the disappearance of the frontier have made non-social individualism detrimental to our further progress; non-social should therefore give place to social individualism.

4. Social character is shown by its readiness to participate in group activity for the common good, and also by its practical efficiency, both mental and motor, as opposed to aesthetic and analytic types of character, which in themselves are essentially non-social.

5. The leading motive for group activity has, in the past, been the fear of evil, such as danger from enemies; it must in the future be much more the hope of good, such as the desire for good government, good conditions of health and comfort, good importunities for economic welfare. In this way *negative* must give way to *positive* motives for social cooperation.

6. The school must become a social institution, having as its chief functions (1) the unfolding of social ideals, (2) the development of social disposition, and (3) the formation of social habits.

(a) Social ideals are to be developed chiefly through the school studies.
(b) Social disposition must be cultivated through the awakening of an abiding *interest* in the social ideals.
(c) Social habits are to be formed by the conduct of the school with respect to regularity, punctuality, silence and industry, also with respect to punishments and to play. The practical efficiency of intellect, so necessary to the social man, is to be developed by rational methods of conducting the recitation.

Section 3

SELECTED WRITINGS OF DAVID FELMLEY

David Felmley (1857–1930) is a forgotten hero of American education. He strived to become an influential teacher of teachers, and he certainly achieved this goal. He served as President of Illinois State Teachers College for thirty years. Because of the time he spent engaged in the practical work of teaching teachers, Felmley did not produce a great deal of scholarship. He deserves to be remembered as a hero, however, because of what he did, rather than what he wrote. He is representative of the thousands of teacher educators from across the nation whose efforts have been neglected by historians of education. Individuals like Felmley have been hidden from history because all they did with their lives was "train teachers." The institutions they established and nurtured for this purpose, moreover, were outside the mainstream of elite institutions of higher education. Yet, what Felmley and many others like him did was provide teachers for the children of our nation. This great tradition of teaching teachers, which Felmley clearly represents, has been marginalized to such an extent that entire institutions—not just individuals—are often completely omitted from histories of higher education. Yet it is educators like Felmley who were the true builders of the teaching profession.

Felmley was born on April 24, 1857, in Somerville, New Jersey. He was a student at Blackburn University from 1873–1876, prior to enrolling at the University of Michigan in 1876. He attended the University of Michigan off

Forgotten Heroes of American Education, pages 295–296

and on for the next five years, completing his Bachelor of Arts degree in 1881. He was awarded LL.D. and L.H.D. awards from the University of Illinois in 1905 and 1906, respectively. Felmley served as a classroom teacher and high school administrator during the 1880s. He began his career as a teacher educator in 1890 when he became chair of the mathematics department at Illinois State Normal School.

From that point forward, Felmley dedicated his career to teaching teachers. During his tenure at Illinois State, which became one of the most well-known normal schools in the west, Felmley's career flourished. He became the sixth president of the institution in 1900, a position he held until 1930.[1] He died on January 24, 1930, only one month after a building on the campus was named in his honor.

Despite the considerable amount of time that Felmley dedicated to administrative tasks, he nonetheless found time to publish scholarship. He published books such as *Mathematics for the Eighth School Year* and *The Culture Epochs*.[2] Felmley's work supplies contemporary teacher educators with a pre-Progressive vision of curriculum for teacher training. His commitment to high-quality teacher education and his belief in the moral dimension of teacher education serve to remind us of what we have lost and must seek to recover.

---

1. *Who Was Who in America: A Companion Volume to Who's Who in America* Volume I, 1897–1942 (Chicago: A. N. Marquis Company, 1943), p. 390.
2. David Felmley, *The Culture Epochs* (Bloomington, IL: Public School Publishing Company, 1896); and David Felmley, *Mathematics for the Eighth School Year* (Bloomington, IL: Pantagraph, 1905).

The Reorganization of the Normal-School Curriculum
(1914)

No institutions within higher education have been more misunderstood than the normal schools. They have been caricatured by people who have never taken the time to study the curriculum that was taught inside them. The highly significant role that normal schools and teachers colleges played in educating American teachers in the 20th century has been misunderstood primarily because university historians, viewing the world from the prism of their elite status, disdained institutions that "merely" prepared teachers for the schools.

This essay by Felmley begins the task of writing a history of American higher education from the perspective of teachers. Historians of higher education have frequently described normal schools as intellectual backwaters that only taught methods of teaching. Felmley's extensive discussion of curriculum for teacher training obliterates this damaging myth for good. Anyone who claims that normal schools and teachers colleges only taught "how to teach" simply has not studied the curriculum that was taught at these institutions. Narrow caricatures of what normal schools and teachers colleges were all about are just flat wrong.

The spiritual dimension of teacher training curriculum, which Felmley emphasizes strongly, is almost gone from public institutions that train teachers today. To Felmley, moral education for teachers was just as important, if not more important, than intellectual training. He also places great emphasis on laboratory training schools, which served as the classroom-focused institutions where dualisms such as theory and practice, subjects and students, and the school and society were brought together in a practical way.

Felmley's work touches upon all of the challenges that face the practical task of teaching teachers today: low social and political support for the work, the

Forgotten Heroes of American Education, pages 297–305

theory–practice dichotomy, the transient nature of the teaching population, and the diversity of the roles that teachers fill once they graduate and begin their careers as classroom teachers.

The normal schools of the several states were established for the sole purpose of training teachers for the common schools. They are an integral part of the public-school system, and must develop with that system.

Our normal schools now are in the stage of rebuilding—a rebuilding pressed upon us by the rapid changes in the public schools. Fifty years ago the public schools taught little beyond the common branches. The curriculum of the normal schools contained these branches and some courses in mental philosophy, school economy, and methods of teaching.

At this time secondary education in the East was to be had in the private academy; in the West chiefly in the preparatory departments of the denominational colleges. Both of these looked to the colleges for their instructors.

In the decade after the war between the states, the greatest decade in our history in the founding of normal schools, the common schools in the towns and cities of the West were rapidly adding "other branches" to their program. Algebra and geometry, rhetoric, civil government, general history, physics, and other natural sciences, sometimes foreign languages, were thus introduced—at first without any separate high-school organization to take care of these higher studies. The high schools were thus a gradual outgrowth of the common schools, and were everywhere held by the courts a part of the common-school system. The normal schools of this section accordingly placed short courses in these subjects in their curriculums, along with the common branches and courses in psychology and education. The graduates of these normal schools found ready employment everywhere in the public schools, quite as often to instruct in these higher subjects as to teach in elementary grades.

In the East, the public high schools began rather as full-fledged institutions closely imitating the private academies which they largely displaced. From the beginning they sought college men and women as instructors. Accordingly, the normal schools of that section have usually continued as they began, chiefly as girls' schools fronting the elementary school; while in most states of the West they have constantly enrolled a large number of young men destined to be high-school teachers, principals, and superintendents, and have provided a curriculum adapted to their needs. The normal schools of forty years ago seem to have attached an exaggerated importance to method. They seem to have held the doctrine, not professedly but none the less really, that if one were a teacher he could teach anything from the multiplication table to Hebrew.

Knowledge of the subject was of secondary importance—that is, previous knowledge of the subject. The value of extended scholarship was recognized somewhat, but the ideal was not the learned scholar and specialist but the teacher, full of enthusiasm, resourceful in plying incentives, and skilled in the manipulation of methods and devices. The normal-school curriculum—usually three years in length—was the same for all students, whether they were to teach in town or country, in primary grades, or in the high school.

With the development of public high schools with four-year courses, during the last quarter of the nineteenth century, and the consequent influx of their graduates into the normal schools, these institutions gradually adjusted themselves to the new conditions. Fifteen years ago the curriculum had generally assumed a standard form—a two-year program containing studies in psychology, principles and methods of teaching, school management, the philosophy and sometimes the history of education, abundant practice teaching, some music and drawing, with review courses in the common branches intended to organize the material and teach the special method of each. In the western schools there was still maintained, along with this new curriculum, the older three-year or four-year course for non-high-school graduates. Since that date, vast changes have come about in the programs of the common schools. Music and drawing have been extended from the larger cities into every village school; nature study, manual training, the household arts, agricultural and industrial art, specific education for business life, physical education, with definite school instruction and practice, all have obtained a permanent footing in our high schools and to a large extent in the elementary schools. Then, too, we have come to recognize that the equipment of the individual teacher is not to be found chiefly in the mastery of psychology or general method or of the general rules of class management, important as these things are; but that his chief resource is his comprehensive and detailed knowledge of the subject-matter that he is to teach and an appreciation of its educational value. Hence, in the high school and grammar grades is needed a richer scholarship; in the lower grades a minute knowledge of all the arithmetic, geography, history, science, hygiene, poetry, stories, music, drawing, industrial art, sewing, plays and games to be used in these grades, a comprehension of their educational purpose, and a copious stock of the devices essential to skilful teaching of these subjects. We no longer assume that every teacher instructed in general principles will have the wit to apply them successfully in any sort of position. We have talked for some years of lengthening the standard two-year normal-school curriculum to three or even to four years, so that all teachers may be fully equipped to meet these new demands. This is, to my mind, wholly impracticable at the present time. Most of our teachers are young women who will not remain in the work longer than five years. They will leave to marry or to enter platform work, business life, or other activities for which they have developed special taste and aptitude. Young men will continue to make teaching a stepping-stone to other callings. Two years is as long a period of special professional preparation as we may justly require of people whose teaching career is likely to be so short. It is not good economy on the part of the state to provide them at this stage with instruction for a longer period. The normal schools should provide additional advanced courses in summer schools, in extension work, as well as in the regular school year for such experienced teachers as have decided to prepare themselves for long service in the higher walks of the profession, but should not require this work of the rank and file of normal-school graduates. We must then meet these new demands by differentiating our normal-school curricula according to the intended destination of the teacher in training.

In discussing this reorganization there are three chief questions to be considered:

1. What are the various kinds of school work for which teachers are to be prepared, and what subjects are to be included in due amount in the special curriculum leading to each of these destinations?
2. What is the character of the preparation that normal students have received before entering the normal school?
3. What is the length of time that society, with its present support of public education, may decently demand of the normal student in the way of professional preparation?

The different kinds of teachers for which particular preparation should be made now include in most of our states the following:

1. Teachers of the kindergarten and the first two primary grades.
2. Teachers of intermediate grades.
3. Teachers of grammar grades, including departmental teachers in upper grades.
4. High-school teachers of English and its expression, literature, mathematics, natural science, history and the social sciences, and foreign languages.
5. Special teachers of music, of art and design, of the household arts, of commercial branches, of physical education, of agriculture, of manual training and the trades.
6. Teachers for country schools.
7. Superintendents, principals, and supervisors.

Special programs should be provided for all of these types of teachers. Each program should contain the following elements:

1. A knowledge of psychology and general principles and methods of teaching and management based thereon, it being understood that all upper-grade teachers should include in their curriculum a special study of the psychology of adolescence.

2. A thorogoing knowledge of the subject-matter, the special method and teaching devices to be used within the particular fields in which the teacher is to work.

3. Certain school arts—drawing, singing, reading, speaking—in which all teachers should be fairly proficient.

4. Studies in political and social economy, in science, in history and literature that will keep the student in touch with the world about him, will reveal in increasing measure the function of the school in our civilization, and will nourish the deepening interest of teachers in the social problems of our time.

We should not forget that normal students are men and women who are to play a part, and a large part, in the world of men and women, and their normal-school preparation should not be bounded by the horizons of their childhood and youth.

The public kindergarten, outside a few of our larger cities and communities in which German influence has been strong, has not developed much strength as a feature of our school system. But the spirit of the kindergarten, its recognition of the doctrine of self-activity, of the play and the social and constructive instincts in children, has profoundly affected the primary schools, and every primary teacher should be permeated with this spirit. Accordingly, a teacher of these grades should be familiar with kindergarten theory and practice, should be equipped with rote songs and games and stories and folklore and children's poetry. She should know enough of the natural phenomena about her to be interested in it, to love plants and birds, and to be able to interpret nature to young children. She should be skilled in the beginnings of industrial art and whatever else should find a place in the life of the elementary school.

For the teachers of intermediate grades and for teachers of upper grades there should be provided separate programs, with a common core of studies in education, hygiene, music and drawing, physical training, and English, but separate practice teaching, and separate studies of the specific material in the various branches, peculiar to the grades in hand. Such upper-grade teachers as show special strength in geography, history, mathematics, English, or other elementary-school branches should be afforded opportunity for a long and thorough course in one or more of these as specialties, in order that these teachers may equip themselves for departmental work.

In some states, it is assumed that the work of the normal school should stop at this point, and that the training of high-school teachers, special teachers, and supervisors should be turned over to other institutions. I do not believe this to be wise educational policy, for the unity, harmony, and efficiency of the public-school system are not promoted by training supervisors, special teachers, and high-school teachers in one kind of institution and elementary teachers in another. The supervisors should be trained in a professional atmosphere where the same ideals are set up, the same philosophy expounded, the same principles and methods taught as are taught to the teachers who are to work under their leadership. High-school teachers should have a broad understanding of the needs of children, and of the principles, content, and method of elementary instruction. To train them in a separate school, with different standards and ideals, results in a serious break in spirit, in method, and in the character of work as the child passes to the high school. The special teachers will be more efficient if they study their specialties in vital relation to the other branches of the public-school curriculum. Teaching is a profession calling for a high degree of devotion, patriotism, and altruistic endeavor. This spirit of consecration is not easily developed in a school whose chief interests are economic or industrial, or whose chief aim is mere personal culture.

The organization of the normal school, its program, its incidental culture and social life, its close personal relations between students and teachers, its modes of class instruction, which are sure to be imitated by the young teacher, its less expensive appointments, the simpler and plainer style of living, its absence of social distinctions based upon wealth or membership in exclusive societies—all of these conditions tend to produce a type of teacher that readily adjusts himself to high-school conditions.

Not only will special teachers of music, art, domestic science, and other special branches prove more efficient when they study their specialties in vital relation to the other branches of the public-school curriculum, but elementary teachers themselves should be trained in the same environment as the often better-paid high-school teachers and special teachers. It is vital to the dignity and self-respect of the elementary school. This separate training begets exclusive educational castes. Our schools are already suffering from the presence of this cleavage between the professional aristocracy of the high schools and the commonality of the grades.

For these and other reasons that occur to every thoughtful student of the normal-school problem, we believe that the normal-school system of every state should provide somewhere for the training of high-school teachers, special teachers, and supervisors. Where there is but a single normal school, as in Indiana, Iowa, or North Carolina, the one school should provide them all. In states where there has been developed one parent school or teachers' college with other tributary schools of smaller attendance and resources, as in Kansas, Colorado, Michigan, and New York, the teachers' college may undertake the greater part of this higher work. In states containing several schools of approximately equal rank and strength, the work may properly be distributed among them to the best advantage, as in Wisconsin.

Wherever the preparation of special teachers is undertaken, there must be adequate equipment for this work. The two-year programs that we are now providing for high-school graduates preparing to enter these special fields must necessarily devote somewhat more than half the time to the special subject-matter and method of the department; but it is to be expected that the present strong demand for these teachers will soon be satisfied, and that three-year and ultimately four-year programs of study will be provided, which shall provide a generous amount of liberal culture along with the special knowledge required of these teachers. Even with our present short programs, we should provide the same general courses in English and in education as are taken by other normal-school students, and usually in the same classes.

For reasons already stated, I believe most of our normal schools are destined to become teachers' colleges and to maintain four-year programs beyond the high school. They will continue to grant a normal-school diploma for the completion of two-year programs in elementary or special education, and teachers' college diplomas with degrees in education to graduates of the full four-year program provided for high-school teachers and supervisors. In the junior college should be provided the courses in English and expression, music and drawing, physiology and hygiene, and physical training that nearly all high-school graduates need. We should include here also work in psychology and principles and methods of teaching, in order to make these students early conscious of the problems of the normal school. Half of the time should be spent upon strong courses in special lines of high-school work. In most of our states there are village high schools, unable to secure full college graduates as teachers, which for some time to come will welcome young men and women from the junior college. Practice teaching should be provided in the second year for these students who expect to leave to teach at this stage. A junior college diploma of the same rank as a normal-school diploma may properly be granted to such students.

In the senior college are found at least four classes of students for whom appropriate courses must be provided:

1. A group preparing to teach particular subjects in superior high schools. For these must be provided two-year senior-college courses in their special lines, and appropriate courses in the problems of high-school administration and teaching.

2. A group of elementary teachers—normal-school graduates—who desire to become supervisors, principals, or normal-school teachers. For these must be provided long courses in the history of education, in psychology and ethics, in school administration, with elective advanced courses in other subjects.

3. A group of college graduates from other institutions that feel the need of the special professional instruction, spirit, and life that the normal school affords.

4. In most of our states the normal school must continue to make provision for students who, in native capacity and sympathies, undoubtedly possess marked fitness for teaching, but who have been deprived of proper educational opportunities in their teens. Such students are now too old to enter a high school to obtain their preliminary academic culture. The normal school must open its doors to these people and provide for them a generous academic culture. Because of their maturity and the singleness of purpose with which these students pursue their studies, it is by no means necessary to hold them for four years or the equivalent of a high-school course. I think it is best, for this type of people, to offer two programs of study. For such as are ready to spend several years at the normal school, there should be provided a preparatory program equivalent to a four-year high-school course, but actually covered by three years of time, this program to be completed before the student enters upon any of the standard normal-school or teachers' college programs.

For such students of this type as may wish to begin to teach in the rural schools, there should be provided a two-year program of studies, including a review of the common branches, studies in elementary agriculture and household arts, music, elementary art, and primary methods, together with the discussions of the problems of country life and of the organization, management, and teaching of the country school. Beyond this should extend a supplementary program for such of these country-school teachers as will re-enter the normal school with a view to graduation.

A thoroughly organized and adequate training-school is essential to the efficiency of a normal school. The elementary training-school should accommodate classes in every grade sufficient in number to give at least 180 hours of practice to each student, and opportunity for practice should include every sort of special work undertaken in the normal school. A kindergarten, a high school, and, in most cases, one or more convenient rural schools should be included in the training-school system, and the buildings and equipment and teaching should be of such quality as to make the school truly a model school, for we cannot maintain the patronage and support of parents on any other basis.

It must be remembered that in the first few months of teaching we acquire our teaching habits—the way we prepare our lessons, our modes of assignment, of questioning, reacting upon the students' work our entire system of classroom technic. The question is, Shall students fall into habits more or less unconsciously, or shall they consciously set up ideals of practice and be held to these ideals by close supervision and thoroughgoing sympathetic criticism?

Where the training-school is closely connected with the normal school, where the normal-school departments write its course of study and give continuous attention to its work, where the normal-school instructors have themselves had experience as public-school teachers and see the children beyond the inchoate teachers on the benches before them, the training-school imparts to the work of the whole institution a vigor and vitality that can be obtained in no other way.

The scheme presented in this paper is, I suspect, more comprehensive than most normal schools are ready or willing, at present, to undertake; yet it does present what to the writer are the proper lines, not to say the necessary lines, of development of the American normal school in the twentieth century.

Section 4

SELECTED WRITINGS OF WILLIAM TORREY HARRIS

William Torrey Harris (1835–1909) is a forgotten hero of American education. After the death of Horace Mann and until the ascendancy of John Dewey, Harris was the nation's leading thinker on education, teaching, and curriculum. He was a relentless champion of free public education as the foundation of a democratic society. He insisted upon high-quality liberal education for all children. In his educational philosophy, students learned about the great achievements of human civilization. The key to good education, he believed, was a process of "self-alienation," in which the student entered into the lives of other eras and cultures distant from his own, thus to return to his own times with a new critical perspective. Harris's philosophy stood in sharp contrast to the Progressives' demand for relevance and personal experience.

By the time of his death in 1909, Harris had become an internationally-prominent philosopher. He was much more than a philosopher, however. He belonged to an era when philosophers of his type did not spend all of their time in contemplation. He also was one of the nation's best-known superintendents, having built the St. Louis, Missouri, public school system into one of the most successful in the nation. He also served as U.S. Commissioner of Education longer than anyone else in American history.

Harris has been forgotten because the Progressive writers who came to dominate American education in the early decades of the 20th century did not like his philosophy. They painted Harris as behind the times, out of touch, and "traditional." Rereading Harris's work today, however, reveals that his thoughts are much more enduring than many of the ideas espoused by Progressives. Harris's numerous essays provide early 21st century teachers and teacher educators with a long-lasting, solid foundation for their efforts.

Harris was born on September 10, 1835, in North Killingly, Connecticut. He attended elementary school in Providence, Rhode Island. After elementary school, he was a student at various new England academies, including Woodstock Academy in Connecticut and Phillips Academy in Andover, Massachusetts. He began work toward his undergraduate degree at Yale University in 1854, but left the school before completing his third year.

Harris moved to St. Louis, Missouri, in 1857. During that year, he taught shorthand at a phonographic institute and also served as a private tutor. The next year, 1858, he began teaching full-time in the St. Louis public schools. From 1858 to 1867, he continued his work as a teacher before becoming a principal and then an assistant superintendent. He accepted the superintendency of the school system in 1867, a position he held until 1880. During Harris's tenure as superintendent, the St. Louis public school system achieved a national reputation for its quality. He introduced new subjects into the curriculum—for example art, music, science, and manual arts. He also added a kindergarten school, which was the first public kindergarten in the United States.

Harris resigned his superintendent position in 1880 and moved to Concord, Massachusetts. In Concord, he sought to establish the Concord School of Philosophy. He worked on this project for nine years, but ultimately was unsuccessful at gaining popular attention. In 1889, Harris was appointed U.S. Commissioner of Education. He served in this capacity until 1906. He died on November 5, 1909, in Providence, Rhode Island.[1]

Harris was a prolific writer on philosophy and education. The thirteen annual reports that he produced during his tenure as superintendent of the St. Louis public schools attracted international attention for their brilliant, thoughtful discussion of educational policy. A bibliography of his works, if compiled, would stretch to nearly 500 titles. These works are a well-spring of knowledge for anyone who is interested in combining the ideals of philosophy, democracy, and education.

Harris was the founder of the *Journal of Speculative Philosophy,* the first philosophy journal ever to be published in the U.S. He also founded the St. Louis Society of Philosophy. Both of these venues helped Harris to spread the Hegelian philosophy that he studied throughout his lifetime. By the

---

1. Garraty, John A., and Jerome L. Sternstein, *Encyclopedia of American Biography,* 2nd ed. (New York: Harper Collins, 1996), pp. 513–514.

beginning of the 20th century, Harris was generally regarded as the nation's leading authority on Hegel.[2]

Examples of Harris's many books include *The Theory of American Education, Hegel's Logic, The Spiritual Sense of Dante's Divine Comedy,* and *Psychologic Foundations of Education.*[3] Harris has much to teach 21st century teacher educators as well as educators in general. It is remarkable to realize that this man was a teacher, a superintendent, and a philosopher. The fact that the profession of teaching has all but forgotten his contributions is a serious error that merits correction.

---

2. John F. Ohles, Editor, *Biographical Dictionary of American Educators* 2 (Westport, CT: Greenwood, Press, 1978), pp. 604–605.

3. William Torrey Harris, *The Theory of American Education* (Washington: J. H. Holmes, 1871); William Torrey Harris, *Hegel's Logic* (Chicago: S. C. Griggs, 1890); William Torrey Harris, *The Spiritual Sense of Dante's Divine Comedy* (Boston: Houghton Mifflin, 1896); and William Torrey Harris, *Psychologic Foundations of Education* (New York: D. Appleton and Company, 1898).

The Science of Education
(1879)

William Torrey Harris had a deep understanding of the history and philosophy of education. In this essay, he explains how education prepares children for life in a free society. Through cultivation and development of the individual, children gain the self-knowledge and self-discipline they must have in order to join civilized society and live lives of responsible, ethical, and mature action. Every field needs to investigate critically its moral and intellectual foundations. Harris succeeds at this task with his rich discussion of pedagogical philosophy.

§ 1. Pedagogics is not a complete, independent science by itself. It borrows the results of other sciences [*e.g.*, it presupposes the science of Rights, treating of the institutions of the family and civil society, as well as of the State; it presupposes the science of anthropology, in which is treated the relations of the human mind to nature. Nature conditions the development of the individual human being. But the history of the individual and the history of the race presents a continual emancipation from nature, and a continual growth into freedom, *i.e.*, into ability to know himself and to realize himself in the world by making the matter and forces of the world his instruments and tools. Anthropology shows us how man as a natural being—*i.e.*, as having a body—is limited. There is climate, involving heat and cold and moisture, the seasons of the year, etc.; there is organic growth, involving birth, growth, reproduction, and decay; there is face, involving the limitations of heredity; there is the telluric life of the planet and the circulation of the forces of the solar system, whence arise the processes of sleeping, waking, dreaming, and kindred phenomena; there is the emotional nature of man, involving his feelings, passions, instincts, and

Forgotten Heroes of American Education, pages 311–320

311

desires; then there are the five senses, and their conditions. Then, there is the science of phenomenology, treating of the steps by which mind rises from the stage of mere feeling and sense-perception to that of self-consciousness, *i.e.*, to a recognition of mind as true substance, and of matter as mere phenomenon created by Mind (God). Then, there is psychology, including the treatment of the stages of activity of mind, as so-called "faculties" of the mind, *e.g.*, attention, sense-perception, imagination, conception, understanding, judgment, reason, and the like. Psychology is generally made (by English writers) to include, also, what is here called anthropology and phenomenology. After psychology, there is the science of ethics, or of morals and customs; then, the Science of Rights, already mentioned; then, Theology, or the Science of Religion, and, after all these, there is Philosophy, or the Science of Science. Now, it is clear that the Science of Education treats of the process of development, by and through which man, as a merely natural being, becomes spirit, or self-conscious mind; hence, it presupposes all the sciences named, and will be defective if it ignores nature, or mind, or any stage or process of either, especially Anthropology, Phenomenology, Psychology, Ethics, Rights, Esthetics, or Science of Art and Literature, Religion, or Philosophy].

§ 2. The scope of pedagogics being so broad and its presuppositions so vast, its limits are not well defined, and its treatises are very apt to lack logical sequence and conclusion; and, indeed, frequently to be mere collections of unjustified and unexplained assumptions, dogmatically set forth. Hence the low repute of pedagogical literature as a whole.

§ 3. Moreover, education furnishes a special vocation, that of teaching. (All vocations are specializing—being cut off, as it were, from the total life of man. The "division of labor" requires that each individual shall concentrate his endeavors and be a *part* of the whole).

§ 4. Pedagogics, as a special science, belongs to the collection of sciences (already described, in commenting on § 1) included under the philosophy of Spirit or Mind, and more particularly to that part of it which relates to the will (ethics and science of rights, rather to the part relating to the intellect and feeling, as anthropology, phenomenology, psychology, aesthetics, and religion. "Theoretical" relates to the *intellect*, "practical" relates to the *will*, in this philosophy). The province of practical philosophy is the investigation of the nature of freedom, and the process of securing it by self-emancipation from nature. Pedagogics involves the conscious exertion of influence on the part of the will of the teacher upon the will of the pupil, with a purpose in view—that of inducing the pupil to form certain prescribed habits, and adopt prescribed views and inclinations. The entire science of mind (as above shown), is presupposed by the science of education, and must be kept constantly in view as a guiding light. The institution of the *family* (treated in practical philosophy) is the starting-point of education, and without this institution properly realized, education would find no solid foundation. The right to be educated on the part of children, and the duty to educate on the part of parents, are reciprocal; and there is no family life so poor and rudimentary that it does not furnish the most important elements of education—no matter what the subsequent influence of the school, the vocation, and the state.

§ 5. Pedagogics as science, distinguished from the same as an art: the former containing the abstract general treatment, and the latter taking into consideration all the conditions of concrete individuality, *e.g.,* the peculiarities of the teacher and the pupil, and all the local circumstances, and the power of adaptation known as "tact."

§ 6. The special conditions and peculiarities, considered in education as an art, may be formulated and reduced to system, but they should not be introduced as a part of the *science of* education.

§ 7. Pedagogics has three parts: first, it considers the idea and nature of education, and arrives at its true definition; second, it presents and describes the special provinces into which the entire field of education is divided; third, it considers the historical evolution of education by the human race, and the individual systems of education that have arisen, flourished, and decayed, and their special functions in the life of man.

§ 8. The scope of the first part is easy to define. The history of pedagogics, of course, contains all the ideas or definitions of the nature of education; but it must not for that reason be substituted for the scientific investigation of the nature of education, which alone should constitute this first part (and the history of education be reserved for the third part).

§ 9. The second part includes a discussion of the threefold nature of man as body, intellect, and will. The difficulty in this part of the science is very great, because of its dependence upon other sciences (*e.g.,* upon physiology, anthropology, etc.), and because of the temptation to go into details (*e.g.,* in the practical department, to consider the endless varieties of schools for arts and trades).

§ 10. The third part contains the exposition of the various national standpoints furnished (in the history of the world) for the bases of particular systems of education. In each of these systems will be found the general idea underlying all education, but it will be found existing under special modifications, which have arisen through its application to the physical, intellectual, and ethical conditions of the people. But we can deduce the essential features of the different systems that may appear in history, for there are only a limited number of systems possible. Each lower form finds itself complemented in some higher form, and its function and purpose then become manifest. The systems of "national" education (*i.e.,* Asiatic systems, in which the individuality of each person is swallowed up in the substantiality of the national idea—just as the individual waves get lost in the ocean on whose surface they arise) find their complete explanation in the systems of education that arise in Christianity (the preservation of human life being the object of the nation, it follows that when realized abstractly or exclusively, it absorbs and annuls the mental independence of its subjects, and thus contradicts itself by destroying the essence of what it undertakes to preserve, *i.e.,* life (soul, mind); but within Christianity the principle of the state is found so modified that it is consistent with the infinite, untrammelled development of the individual, intellectually and morally, and thus not only life is saved, but spiritual, free life is attainable for each and for all).

§11. The history of pedagogy ends with the present system as the latest one. As science sees the future ideally contained in the present, it is bound to comprehend the latest system as a realization (though imperfect) of the ideal system of education. Hence, the system, as scientifically treated in the first part of our work, is the system with which the third part of our work ends.

§ 12. The nature of education, its form, its limits, are now to be investigated. (§§13–50.)

§ 13. The nature of education determined by the nature of Mind or Spirit, whose activity is always devoted to realizing for itself what it is potentially—to becoming conscious of its possibilities, and to getting them under the control of its will. Mind is potentially free. Education is the means by which man seeks to realize in man his possibilities (to develop the possibilities of the race in each individual). Hence, education has freedom for its object.

§ 14. Man is the only being capable of education, in the sense above defined, because he is the only conscious being. He must know himself ideally, and then realize his ideal self, in order to become actually free. The animals not the plants may be *trained,* or *cultivated,* but, as devoid of self-consciousness (even the highest animals not getting above impressions, not reaching ideas, not seizing general or abstract thoughts), they are not realized for *themselves,* but only for us. (That is, they do not know their ideal as we do.)

§ 15. Education, taken in its widest compass, is the education of the human race by Divine Providence.

§ 16. In a narrower sense, education is applied to the shaping of the individual, so that his caprice and arbitrariness shall give place to rational habits and views, in harmony with nature and ethical customs. He must not abuse nature, nor slight the ethical code of his people, nor despise the gifts of Providence (whether for weal or woe), unless he is willing to be crushed in the collision with these more substantial elements.

§ 17. In the narrowest, but most usual application of the term, we understand by "education" the influence of the individual upon the individual, exerted with the object of developing his powers in a conscious and methodical manner, either generally or in special directions, the educator being relatively mature, and exercising authority over the relatively immature pupil. Without authority on the one hand and obedience on the other, education would lack its ethical basis—a neglect of the will-training could not be compensated for by any amount of knowledge or smartness.

§ 18. The general province of education includes the development of the individual into the theoretical and practical reason immanent in him. The definition which limits education to the development of the individual into ethical customs (obedience to morality, social conventionalities, and the laws of the state—Hegel's definition is here referred to: "The object of education is to make men ethical") is not comprehensive enough, because it ignores the side of the *intellect,* and takes note only of the *will.* The individual should not only be man in general (as he is through the adoption of moral and ethical forms—which are *general forms,* customs, or laws, and thus the forms imposed by the *will* of the *race),* but he should also be a self-conscious subject, a particular individual (man, through his intellect, exists for himself as an individual, while through his general habits and customs he loses his individuality and spontaneity).

§ 19. Education has a definite object in view and it proceeds by grades of progress toward it. The systematic tendency is essential to all education, properly so called.

§ 20. Division of labor has become requisite in the higher spheres of teaching. The growing multiplicity of branches of knowledge creates the necessity for the specialist as teacher. With this tendency to specialties it becomes more and more difficult to preserve what is so essential to the pupil—his rounded human culture and symmetry of development. The citizen of modern civilization sometimes appears to be an artificial product by the side of the versatility of the savage man.

§ 21. From this necessity of the division of labor in modern times there arises the demand for two kinds of educational institutions—those devoted to general education (common schools, colleges, etc.), and special schools (for agriculture, medicine, mechanic arts, etc.).

§ 22. The infinite possibility of culture for the individual leaves, of course, his actual accomplishment a mere approximation to a complete education. Born idiots are excluded from the possibility of education, because the lack of universal ideas in their consciousness precludes to that class of unfortunates anything beyond a mere mechanical training.

§ 23. Spirit, or mind, makes its own nature; it *is* what it produces—a self-result. From this follows the *form* of education. It commences with (1) undeveloped mind—that of the infant—wherein nearly all is potential, and but little is actualized; (2) its first stage of development is self-estrangement—it is absorbed in the observation of objects around it; (3) but it discovers laws and principles (universality) in external nature, and finally identifies them with reason—it comes to recognize itself in nature—to recognize conscious mind as the creator and preserver of the external world—and thus becomes at home in nature. Education does not create, but it emancipates.

§ 24. This process of self-estrangement and its removal belongs to all culture. The mind must fix its attention upon what is foreign to it, and penetrate its disguise. It will discover its own substance under the seeming alien being. Wonder is the accompaniment of this stage of estrangement. The love of travel and adventure arises from this basis.

§ 25. Labor is distinguished from play: The former concentrates its energies on some object, with the purpose of making it conform to its will and purpose; play occupies itself with its object according to its caprice and arbitrariness, and has no care for the results or products of its activity; work is prescribed by authority, while play is necessarily spontaneous.

§ 26. Work and Play: the distinction between them. In play the child feels that he has entire control over the object with which he is dealing, both in respect to its existence and the object for which it exists. His arbitrary will may change both with perfect impunity, since all depends upon his caprice; he exercises his powers in play according to his natural proclivities, and therein finds scope to develope his own individuality. In work, on the contrary, he must have respect for the object with which he deals. It must be held sacred against his caprice, must not be destroyed nor injured in any way, and its object must likewise be respected. His own personal inclinations must be entirely subordinated, and the business that he is at work upon must be carried forward in accordance with its own ends and aims, and without reference to his own feelings in the matter.

Thus work teaches the pupil the lesson of self-sacrifice (the right of superiority which the general interest possesses over the particular), while play develops his personal idiosyncrasy.

§ 27. Without play, the child would become more and more a machine, and lose all freshness and spontaneity—all originality. Without work, he would develop into a monster of caprice and arbitrariness.

From the fact that man must learn to combine with man, in order that the individual may avail himself of the experience and labors of his fellow-men, self-sacrifice for the sake of combination is the great lesson of life. But as this should be *voluntary* self-sacrifice, education must train the child equally in the two directions of spontaneity and obedience. The educated man finds recreation in change of work.

§28. Education seeks to assimilate its object—to make what was alien and strange to the pupil into something familiar and habitual to him. [The pupil is to attack, one after the other, the foreign realms in the world of nature and man, and conquer them for his own, so that he can be "at home" in them. It is the necessary condition of all growth, all culture, that one widens his own individuality by this conquest of new provinces alien to him. By this the individual transcends the narrow limits of particularity and becomes generic—the individual becomes the species. A good definition of education is this: it is the process by which the individual man elevates himself to the species.]

§ 29. (1) Therefore, the first requirement in education is that the pupil shall acquire the habit of subordinating his likes and dislikes to the attainment of a rational object.

It is necessary that he shall acquire this indifference to his own pleasure, even by employing his powers on that which does not appeal to his interest in the remotest degree.

§ 30. Habit soon makes us familiar with those subjects which seemed so remote from our personal interest, and they become agreeable to us. The objects, too, assume a new interest upon nearer approach, as being useful or injurious to us. That is useful which serves us as a means for the realization of a rational purpose; injurious, if it hinders such realization. It happens that objects are useful in one sense and injurious in another, and *vice versa.* Education must make the pupil capable of deciding on the usefulness of an object, by reference to its effect on his permanent vocation in life.

§ 31. But *good and evil* are the ethical distinctions which furnish the absolute standard to which to refer the question of the usefulness of objects and actions.

§ 32. (2) Habit is (a) *passive,* or (b) *active.* The passive habit is that which gives us the power to retain our equipoise of mind in the midst of a world of changes (pleasure and pain, grief and joy, etc). The active habit gives us skill, presence of mind, tact in emergencies, etc.

§ 33. (3) Education deals altogether with the formation of habits. For it aims to make some condition or form of activity into a second nature for the pupil. But this involves, also, the breaking up of previous habits. This power to break up habits, as well as to form them, is necessary to the freedom of the individual.

§ 34. Education deals with these complementary relations (antitheses): (a) authority and obedience; (b) rationality *(general* forms) and individuality; (c) work and play; (d) habit (general custom) and spontaneity. The development and reconciliation of these opposite sides in the pupil's character, so that they become his second nature, removes the phase of constraint which at first accompanies the formal inculcation of rules, and the performance of prescribed tasks. The freedom of the pupil is the ultimate object to be kept in view, but a too early use of freedom may work injury to the pupil. To remove a pupil from all temptation would be to remove possibilities of growth in strength to resist it; on the other hand, to expose him needlessly to temptation is fiendish.

§ 35. Deformities of character in the pupil should be carefully traced back to their origin, so that they may be explained by their history. Only by comprehending the historic growth of an organic defect are we able to prescribe the best remedies.

§ 36. If the negative behavior of the pupil (his bad behavior) results from ignorance due to his own neglect, or to his willfulness, it should be met directly by an act of authority on the part of the teacher (and without an appeal to reason). An appeal should be made to the understanding of the pupil only when he is somewhat mature, or shows by his repetition of the offence that his proclivity is deep-seated, and requires an array of all good influences to reinforce his feeble resolutions to amend.

§ 37. Reproof, accompanied by threats of punishment, is apt to degenerate into scolding.

§ 38. After the failure of other means, punishment should be resorted to. Inasmuch as the punishment should be for the purpose of making the pupil realize that it is the consequence of his deed returning on himself, it should always be administered for some particular act of his, and this should be specified. The "overt act" is the only thing which a man can be held accountable for in a court of justice; although it is true that the harboring of evil thoughts or intentions is a sin, yet it is not a crime until realized in an overt act.

§ 40. Punishment should be regulated, not by abstract rules, but in view of the particular case and its attending circumstances.

§ 41. Sex and age of pupil should be regarded in prescribing the mode and degree of punishment. Corporal punishment is best for pupils who are very immature in mind; when they are more developed they may be punished by any imposed restraint upon their free wills which will isolate them from the ordinary routine followed by their fellow-pupils. (Deprivation of the right to do as others do is a wholesome species of punishment for those old or mature enough to feel its effects, for it tends to secure respect for the regular tasks by elevating them to the rank of rights and privileges.) For young men and women, the punishment should be of a kind that is based on a sense of honor.

§ 42. (1) Corporal punishment should be properly administered by means of the rod, subduing willful defiance by the application of force.

§ 43. (2) Isolation makes the pupil realize a sense of his dependence upon human society, and upon the expression of this dependence by cooperation in the common tasks. Pupils should not be shut up in a darkroom, nor removed from the personal supervision of the teacher. (To shut up two or more in a room without supervision is not isolation, but association; only it is association for mischief, and not for study.)

§ 44. (3) Punishment based on the sense of honor may or may not be based on isolation. It implies a state of maturity on the part of the pupil. Through his offence the pupil has destroyed his equality with his fellows, and has in reality, in his inmost nature, isolated himself from them. Corporal punishment is external, but it may be accompanied with a keen sense of dishonor. Isolation, also, may, to a pupil who is sensitive to honor, be a severe blow to self-respect. But a punishment founded entirely on the sense of honor would be wholly internal, and have no external discomfort attached to it.

§ 45. The necessity of carefully adapting the punishment to the age and maturity of the pupil, renders it the most difficult part of the teacher's duties. It is essential that the air and manner of the teacher who punishes should be that of one who acts from a sense of painful duty, and not from any delight in being the cause of suffering. Not personal likes and dislikes, but the rational necessity which is over teacher and pupil alike, causes the infliction of pain on the pupil.

§ 46. Punishment is the final topic to be considered under the head of "Form of Education."

In the act of punishment the teacher abandons the legitimate province of education, which seeks to make the pupil rational or obedient to what is reasonable, as a habit, and from his own free will. The pupil is punished in order that he may be *made* to conform to the rational, by the application of constraint. Another will is substituted for the pupil's, and good behavior is produced, but not by the pupil's free act. While education finds a negative limit in punishment, it finds a positive limit in the accomplishment of its legitimate object, which is the emancipation of the pupil from the state of imbecility, as regards mental and moral self-control, into the ability to direct himself rationally. When the pupil has acquired the discipline which enables him to direct his studies properly, and to control his inclinations in such a manner as to pursue his work regularly, the teacher is no longer needed for him—he becomes his own teacher.

There may be two extreme views on this subject—the one tending towards the negative extreme of requiring the teacher to do everything for the pupil, substituting his will for that of the pupil, and the other view tending to the positive extreme, and leaving everything to the pupil, even before his will is trained into habits of self-control, or his mind provided with the necessary elementary branches requisite for the prosecution of further study.

§ 47. (1) The subjective limit of education (on the negative side) is to be found in the individuality of the pupil—the limit to his natural capacity.

§ 48. (2) The objective limit to education lies in the amount of time that the person may devote to his training. It, therefore, depends largely upon wealth, or other fortunate circumstances.

§ 49. (3) The absolute limit of education is the positive limit (see § 46), beyond which the youth passes into freedom from the school, as a necessary instrumentality for further culture.

§ 50. The pre-arranged pattern-making work of the school is now done, but self-education may and should go on indefinitely, and will go on if the education of the school has really arrived at its "absolute" limit—*i.e.,* has fitted the pupil for self-education. Emancipation from the school does not emancipate one from learning through his fellow-men.

University and School Extension
(1890)

This article by Harris makes the point that universities have a responsibility to connect to their local communities in practical ways. Harris praises several extension efforts that were underway during the late 19th century at some of our nation's most prominent institutions of higher education. These schools were being criticized as "ivory tower" institutions that had no concern for the social and moral problems that surrounded them.

Harris is describing the ways in which these institutions were countering this criticism. The efforts that Harris describes are thoroughly consistent with the notion of the diffusion of knowledge, which was discussed widely by American founders such as Thomas Jefferson, Noah Webster, and Benjamin Rush. Democratic education, to Harris and all three of these founders, required that knowledge be diffused generally throughout the American population, rather than bottled up or controlled by a narrow band of specialists. If Harris is arguing for anything in this paper, he is making a case for the more general diffusion of knowledge, both moral and intellectual.

Some years ago, the great universities of England commenced a movement known as "University Extension," with the express purpose of connecting those famous seats of learning more directly with the people. Lectures and courses of study have been laid out, and in numerous towns there are groups of students pursuing lines of reading and investigations under the direction of professors and fellows in the universities.

Forgotten Heroes of American Education, pages 321–330

The practical advantage of this is the hold which it gives those great institutions upon the thoughts and opinions of all classes of people. It is a conservative influence in an entirely good sense of that word. The institutions where the broadest and soundest views of the world are elaborated, can by the aid of this university extension scheme mould the thoughts and opinions of the people. But they are to mould not by mere dogmatic teaching of cut-and-dried doctrines. They will arouse and challenge investigation of grounds and reasons. They will teach the people how to think for themselves, and that too on sufficient premises.

Here in this country, we need university extension for all the reasons that exist in England, and for this additional reason: we wish to draw an increasing number of youth to complete their school courses in our colleges and universities. The extension movement will bring college professors into direct relations with large numbers of earnest and aspiring youth, and the result will be the happy one of inducing an increase of attendance on institutions of higher education, besides giving them far greater influence on the thinking and acting of the masses of the people who do not go beyond an elementary school course.

The graduate of a college or university is accustomed to celebrate two events of his life. He keeps a yearly feast in memory of his birth—the first great event of his life was his advent on this planet; the second was his education at the college. He ever holds in honor and reverence the mother who gave him birth and subsequent nurture; he likewise holds in honor his spiritual mother—his Alma Mater, and celebrates on all fitting occasions his spiritual new birth or palingenesia.

As natural beings, as animals, we live but do not know our living. Only as educated beings do we live a conscious life in the high sense of the word. Only by education do we go out beyond ourselves as mere individuals and enter in our heritage of the life of the race.

The uneducated consciousness of the mere animal does not enable him to take up the experience of his fellow-animals and appropriate its lessons in the form of moral and scientific ideas. Only to a small extent does he avail himself of the lives of others. Only the species lives on while the individual metamorphosis of life and death takes place. But the animal capable of education can go beyond his individual experience and avail himself of the lives of all. For the educated there is vicarious experience. He may live over in himself the lives of all others as well as his own life. In fact, each lives for all and all live for each on the plane of educated being. On this plane the individual may be said to ascend into the species, and we can no longer say of him what we say of the mere animal—the species lives and the individual dies. For individual immortality belongs to the being that can think ideas. Because ideas embody the life experience of the race and make possible this vicarious life of each in all. The religious mystery of vicarious atonement, is, we may see, adumbrated in this the deepest fact of our spiritual existence. The mistakes and errors of each and every man, as well as his achievements and successes, all go into common fund of experience of the race, and are converted into ideas that govern our lives through education. The human race lives and dies for the individual man. All the observation of the facts of the universe, all thinking into the causes of those facts by this process, is rendered available for each man. He may reinforce his feeble individual might by the aggregate feeling and seeing and thinking of all men now living and of all that have lived.

No wonder that the college graduate loves to celebrate the great event of his life, his spiritual new birth. Not to say that all education is obtained at college, for civilization itself is one vast process of education, going on for each individual that participates in it from the cradle to the grave. But the college-educated man remembers his narrow intellectual horizon and the closeness of his mental atmosphere in the days before his academic course of study; and he remembers well the growth and transformation that began there through the benign influences of that "cherishing mother." He then saw great men; men of lofty character, of deep learning, and of world-wide reputation. He came into contact with them in the lecture-room and at the religious services in the chapel and to some extent in social life. He had entered a community, and now lived in a brotherhood of students like himself, forming a great family all animated by one purpose; that of mental and spiritual growth. The student learns not merely from books and professors, but from his fellow students, learning to know himself by seeing his image reflected, magnified, and enlarged as it were in the spectacle of an entire class or the entire college. Each student measures his actual realization by the side of the ideal held up by his fellows, and he does much to rid himself of his eccentricities and provincialisms, his low motives, his philistinism, by the help of his college-mates, gaining more perhaps through their friendly jibes and sarcasm than through their advice and counsel.

While he is shaping his conduct of life in harmony with the student ideals, he is at the same time undergoing a mighty change in his aspirations. Above his class he sees advanced classes performing with ease daily tasks in the study of language, mathematics, and science, that seem to his undisciplined powers little short of miracles. The freshman looks up to the seniors as intellectual giants. One year of college growth causes a vast abyss of achievement and power to yawn between the present and the former stadium of growth.

Perhaps the greatest lesson that we learn in college education is this knowledge of our possibilities. If one year's growth through the study of certain subjects, under the direction of tutors and professors, can so lift us above ourselves, we infer that we are in a great measure the masters of our fortune. Learning, or the industry that acquires it, is a sort of talisman which may lift us out of our "low-vaulted past," and place us on heights of directive power. There is a promise and potency in the study of these branches which are learned in the college, a promise and potency to enlighten us and produce in us a sort of metamorphosis out of ourselves— out of ourselves as puny individuals, into our great self as the race.

This is what the second great event of our lives; namely, our new birth from our Alma Mater, meant to us, and still means. Our first birth gave us life, feeling, and locomotion—gave us individualism; and all of these are good things.

Our second birth gave us community with all fellow-men through thought; it secured for us our heritage in the wisdom of the race. It gave us personality in the place of mere individuality, using the word "personality" in a technical sense to signify a higher potency than individuality—in short, an individuality that combines with other individualities, namely its fellow-men, and reinforces its single might by the might of all.

This glance at the high place held by college or university education piques us to inquire next into the make-up of the course of study. What is the peculiarity of this course, and in how far does it contribute to the power of the student? We need not further discuss the advantages of association with a large body of fellow-students, all inspired with the one high purpose of overcoming the difficulties of comprehending human learning by means of industry. For even the poorest and unworthiest of students, the veriest shirk, is industrious, and cannot advance with his class unless he works much. Nor is it necessary to dwell upon the educative value of the spectacle of high character and deep learning that the student beholds in the college faculty, or of the spectacle of increased power gained by classes after one, two, or three years of college residence. These statements of education are obvious enough. But one interest concentrates on the function of the course of study in producing the mental emancipation of youth. What is a liberal course of study? This question is a very important one for those who advocate university extension. For the youth in his home far distant from the university may be aroused to industry on the lines of intellectual mastery. He may not gain the stimulus of direct personal contact and the self-knowledge that comes from seeing the growth of one's equals, but he may still gain what is not the least of the three educative results of the university—he may master the course of study which gives him the most insight into the world of nature and the world of human civilization.

The university extension scheme may lay out courses of study and hold several examination tests that will be sufficient to stimulate the aspiration and guide the labors of vast multitudes of youths and adults who have been debarred from the privilege of college residence.

At the very beginning of our inquiry we see that it will not do to suppose that the what one studies is indifferent, and that the mere fact of continued and persevering study on any lines haphazard, is all sufficient to make a university education. For no amount of study on the phase of primary education, or even of secondary education, will ever give one a university education.

Higher instruction differs from lower instruction chiefly in this; lower instruction concerns to a greater extent the mere inventory of things and events, and has less to do with inquiring into the unity of those things and events. Higher instruction deals more with the relation of things and events. It investigates the dependence of one phase upon another, and it deals especially with the practical relation of all species of knowledge to *man* as individual and as social whole. This latter kind of instruction, it is evident, is ethical; and we may say, therefore, that it is a characteristic of higher education that it should be ethical, and build up in the mind of the student a habit of thinking on the human relations of all departments of inquiry. In the lower instruction the ethical is taught by precept and practice. In higher education the mind of the student is directed towards the ethical unity that pervades the worlds of man and nature as their regulative principles. The youth is emancipated from mere blind authority of custom and made free by insight into the immanent necessity of ethical principles. Hence it is evident that philosophical investigation must constitute a leading feature of the method of higher instruction.

Not a mere inventory, not a collection or heap of mere information is demanded of the university students; not even the systematization of the facts and events inventoried, the mere classification and arrangement such as is done by secondary instruction, will suffice for the university. It demands profound reflection; it insists that the pupil shall see each branch in the light of the whole. It directs him to the unity underlying and making possible the classifications and systems as well as the inventory of the details themselves. It seeks as its highest aim in its instruction to give insight to the mind of the student.

Let us look at the idea of insight for a moment, and try to see for ourselves why the curriculum or course of study laid out by the university for its own work and for the preparatory work in the secondary school has taken the present form.

The general principle which determines the character of insight giving studies is this: They must be of such a kind that they lead the individual out of his immediate surroundings, and assimilate him with the atmosphere and surroundings of an early historical age of the people to which he belongs. Each stage of culture is a product of two factors: the activity of present social forces, and that of the previous stage of culture. Every stage of culture goes down into succeeding ones in human history as a silent factor, still exercising a determining influence upon them, but in an ever-weakening degree. The education of the child first proceeds to take him out of himself and bathe him in the rare atmosphere of the childhood of his race. Even the nursery tales that greet his dawning consciousness, and later the fairy stories and mythological fiction that delight his youth, are simply the transfigured history of the deeds of his race. With the education of the school begins a serious assimilation of the classics of his people, wherein he becomes by degrees conscious of the elements of his complex being. He finds one after another the threads that compose his civilization—threads that weave the tissue of his own nature as a product of civilization. The Chinese child reads Confucius and Mencius and sees the universal type and model on which the Chinese every-day world is formed. The Hindoo child listens to the stories of the Hitopadesa, and learns the Vedas and Puranas, and becomes conscious of the ideal principles of his caste-system. The Turk reads his Koran and learns to recognize the ordinances which direct and control his relations to his fellow-men and to himself.

Pursuing a similar course, and necessarily limited in its choice of the subject-matter of elementary education, our own school takes the pupils to Greece and Rome through the two dead languages, Latin and Greek; for the evolution of the civilization in which we live and move and have our being, issued through Greece and Rome on its way to us. Each one of our institutions traces its genesis in the necessities that arose in the histories of those people. The organism of the state, the invention of the forms in which man may live in a civil community and enjoy municipal and personal rights—these trace their descent in a direct line from Rome, and were indigenous to the people that spoke Latin. In our civil and political forms we live Roman life to-day. Even the vocabulary of the portion of our language that expresses these phases of our civilization, is of Latin derivation. To ferret out and make clear to ourselves this part of our being is to assimilate the Roman civilization. As the pupil penetrates the atmosphere of Rome, gradually becoming familiar from day to day with the modes of expression—the thinking and feeling of the Romans—he unconsciously ascends to one of his own fountains, and acquires a certain faculty of clear thinking and seeing in regards to his political and social existence. He acquires the power of insight into his surrounding conditions. Similarly with other phases, our scientific and aesthetic forms came from beyond Rome; they speak the language of their Greek home to this very day, just as much as Jurisprudence and Legislation pronounce their edicts in Roman words. Religion points to Nature as the radiating center of Christian doing.

This insight of which we speak cannot be obtained except through study, exactly equivalent to the Latin and Greek studies which are required in our higher schools.

To assimilate the antecedent stage of our civilized existence, we must come into immediate contact with it as such contact as we find by learning the language of the ancient people who founded it. Language is the clothing of the inmost spiritual self of a people, and we must don the garb in which they thought and spoke, in order to fully realize in ourselves these embryonic stages of our civilization. What we have lived through we know adequately; and when we have lived over Roman life in our dispositions and feelings, and then realized the forms of its imagination; as it embodied them in its art and poetry, and finally have seized it in the abstract conceptions of the intellect, and grasped its highest syntheses in the ideas of reason—then we know it, and we know ourselves in so far as we embody it in our institutions.

The present spirit and methods of scientific investigation bear me witness that to know an individual we must study it in its history. It is a part of a process; we need to find its presuppositions in order to make it intelligible. Only in the perspective of its history can we see it so as to comprehend it as a whole.

If a man is not educated up to a consciousness of what he presupposes; if he does not learn the wide-reaching relations that go out from him on all sides, linking him to the system of nature and to the vast complex of human history and society, he does not know himself, and is in so far a mere animal. Such existence as we live unconsciously, is to us a fate, and not an element of freedom.

When the scholar learns his presuppositions, and sees the evolution afar off of the elements that have come down to him and entered his being— elements that form his life and make the conditions which surround him and furnish the instrumentalities which he must wield, then he begins to know how much his being involves, and in the consciousness of this, he begins to be somebody in real earnest. He begins to find himself. His empty consciousness fills with substance. He recognizes his personal wealth in the possession of the world and the patrimony of the race.

Now this essential function of education to culture man into consciousness of his spiritual patrimony, to give him an insight into the civilization whose vital air he breathes, is attempted in our higher schools and colleges. There are many other threads to this education; notably those of mathematics and natural science. But the pith and core of a culture that emancipates us is classic study.

Measuring our fellow-men by power of intellect, we rank those the highest who can withdraw themselves out of their finitude and littleness, out of their feelings and prejudices, up into the region of the pure intellect, the region of unbiased judgment, so as to survey a subject in all its bearings. The thinker must be able to penetrate purely into the atmosphere of a subject until he feels it throughout, and his vision and sentiments are no longer merely his own personal impressions, but he feels and thinks his subject in its entire compass, and comprehends it.

This power of self-alienation hinges on the power to withdraw out of one's own immediateness into his generic existence—to withdraw to a standpoint whence he can see all his presuppositions, the complex of his surroundings, and take them into account. This power is attained through classical culture. The measure of this power of self-alienation is the measure of the mental power of man. We all call the man who cannot withdraw from the narrow circle of his every-day feelings and ideas a weak man, and say that he possesses no insight.

Our colleges and universities, in order to make this self-alienation more complete, have generally preserved a semi-monastic character in their organization. Their pupils are, for the most part, isolated from their families, and live in an artificial society of their own. The student life (wherein the family and civil society that have in modern times unfolded into independent and complex systems, are united into a sort of monastic institution through a dormitory system, and the organization of classes and secret societies and like) is a sort of embryonic civilization, and creates an atmosphere that reminds the historical student of the prevailing state of society in early ages.

In the university-extension scheme it is evident that we cannot have these accessories of self-estrangement; the Greek letter societies, the caps and gowns, the semi-monastic life of the college dormitory; but what is more essential, we can have the training in the classic languages—a sufficient amount of such training to give each person an insight into his spiritual embryology.

It must be admitted that the function of the university in our day is not precisely the same as that of its infancy. The art of printing has produced the change. The advent of the daily newspaper is perhaps the most significant circumstance of the present century. Its influence is as potent to change our educational systems, as the discovery of printing itself was in the fifteenth century.

Before the invention of printing information could not be circulated except orally, and except in a very limited degree. A very wealthy man could afford to buy only a dozen books; the man in moderate circumstances and the poor man could not own any unless he made them himself. At the university one could hear the most valuable books read by the bachelors of arts—slowly and distinctly, so that each student could write for himself a copy of what he wished to preserve. Collecting in groups, the enthusiastic learners could discuss the contents and meaning of the writings, and these discussions did most for the quickening of the intellects of the students at the old universities. Their minds being prepared by those dialectic exercises, they would come to the lectures of the masters with keen appetites for their expositions and explanations. Such intellectual feasts as were spread at the universities—no wonder that they attracted immense crowds of eager, awakened men. The lectures on Law at Bologna, drew 20,000 students to that university. Thirty thousand flocked to Paris five hundred years ago—by 7,000 a greater number than attended the twenty-six academies of the university system of all France in 1881. Oxford University attracted as many people in the time of Roger Bacon, as the twenty-five largest German universities together assemble today.

But we must remember that there were no test examinations in those days. Probably the greater part of those called masters could not pass the examination for matriculation, were they to present themselves now at Harvard or Yale, Johns Hopkins or Columbia. However this may be, it is certain that there were some very great scholars in the subjects which they professed to study. Their learning was limited to essential works of genius, and many of them knew thoroughly the entire works of Aristotle and Plato.

After the invention of printing the attendance in universities diminished. Oxford had 15,000 about the year 1400; 5,000 in 1500, and only 2,600 in 1880.

The university revived learning; the printed book makes learning accessible to the many, and finally, when it gets translated out of Latin into the language of each people, the book makes the wisdom of the race accessible to all. While knowledge was preserved only in manuscripts, and distributed orally at the university, it was necessary that there should be a common speech at the university—a learned language that all could understand, whatever his native dialect, and in which every scholar should write his discoveries.

The Latin language contained all the wit and wisdom extant at that time. But while it proved a great advantage to the scholar, it prevented the common people who knew no Latin from reading the books which had begun to abound in the community. The translation made of the Bible opened up the greatest world treasury to all who could read their native tongue, and led the way to further books in the mother-tongue of each of the northern nations of Europe.

The invention of the art of printing changed the function of the higher schools of Europe; it did not destroy them or render them superfluous. Examinations came into vogue, and classification and grading were perfected. The course of study became more and more disciplinary, and mere information studies were allowed subordinate places.

It is supposed that the study of classics, Latin and Greek, is retained in one system of higher education because of a blind conservatism which continues the good old way, after all reasons for its existence have vanished. I think that this is a serious mistake.

It is true that the necessity of a common language as the medium of instruction justified the use of Latin at the university of the middle ages. Now, however, it is to be justified on the ground of embryology, as I have already indicated. We study Latin, not because it is the most perfect, or the most flexible, or the most anything, but because it is the expression of that phase of civilization that enters our own as the most important determining factor, giving us the forms of our institutions and our laws, our methods of science and our literary forms. That Greek is the primitive expression of that nation which gave us the forms of art and science, is a sufficient reason why we are required to study it for a time, in order to understand that strand in our civilization.

The university (and in this paper I have used the word university as synonymous with college, notwithstanding their original difference of meaning, for I notice that the program of the university-extension movement does not include theology, medicine, and jurisprudence in its curriculum, but limits itself thus far to the academic or college course in the arts)—the university, I say, in our time, has most need of extension. In the age of the newspaper and the universal common school, people all receive primary education, and very many go on, in adult years, to acquire secondary education; very few, however, of the merely "self-educated" now get what may be called a higher education. There is a lack of philosophic insight—of that insight which sees the true moving principle of things. Consequently we have as the highest product of the self-educated multitude mere iconoclasm—mere negative activity, and but little constructive effort. The university extension will, when it is fairly inaugurated, give better occupation to this negative phase of culture, by directing it to the study of the origin of institutions, and to the more humanizing work of interpreting literature, art, and history.

With the multiplication of public high schools, there has come about in this country a tendency to neglect the college or university. Secondary instruction seems to many of our leaders in education to be more practical than higher education. But, if my opinion is well founded, this claim for secondary instruction must be held to be an error. The most practical of all instruction is that which finds the unity of all branches of knowledge, and teaches their human application. Ethics is certainly the most practical of all branches of human learning.

All friends of a sounder education will therefore bid God-speed to this movement for university extension, and all will hope that through it the university standards of thinking and investigating will become known as ideals, and that once well established it will have the effect of increasing the percentage of youth who complete their education in the university itself.

Educational Values
(1896)

As Harris mentions in his brief introductory note to this article, he originally wrote the essay as part of a superintendent's report in 1873. At the time, he was superintendent of schools in St. Louis, Missouri. The work includes his response to the criticisms that were being leveled against "traditional" education. He surveys the entire realm of knowledge and then connects this expansive discussion of knowledge to curriculum. He addresses curriculum at the elementary, high school, and college levels.

His goal was to coordinate the various levels of curriculum in order to avoid overlap, but he also sought to defend classical languages and literature in the curriculum at all levels. He criticizes the explosion of the public school curriculum in many communities, changes that were allowing dozens of new subjects into the public schools. To counteract this inadvisable explosion, Harris provides a well-designed, coherent, logically-conceived curriculum that he hoped would serve as a model for elementary schools, high schools, and colleges throughout the nation. The basis for his philosophy was a conception known as the five "windows on the soul," which he explores at some length in the work. He argues that these five windows on the soul—or, in some sense, subject-matter areas—should serve as the foundation upon which any school curriculum should be built. He also compares public and private schools before arguing—as one might suspect from a public school superintendent—in favor of public schools. Finally, Harris challenges higher education institutions (e.g. colleges and universities) to work with public schools to break down the barriers that exist between these two types of institutions. He thought destroying these barriers was essential if the ideal of a rich liberal education for all American youth was to be achieved.

Forgotten Heroes of American Education, pages 331–353

[The following article on educational values I reprint from the report of the St. Louis schools for the year 1872–73. It contains a somewhat fuller discussion of some of the points relative to the educative value of the several studies in elementary and secondary schools, and in this way may be useful in explaining points that are left obscure in the report of the subcommittee on correlation of studies.]

The educator is called upon especially to scrutinize the character of his elementary work. He must see from afar the effects of the trifling things with which he makes his beginnings. It is the feeling of this duty that has in late years drawn so much attention to Froebel's theories of the kindergarten and to primary education generally. It is all essential that the foundation should be sufficient for the superstructure. Of late, therefore, much thought has been expended on the question of adapting the course of study in the common schools to the actual demands upon the citizen in after life. The same zeal which has challenged the methods and subjects of the common schools has with still more emphasis challenged the higher education in our colleges and universities. It has demanded the substitution of more practical studies for the traditional disciplinary course. It has asked for more science and less Latin or Greek and for a radical extension of the elective system of making up a course of study for each individual. Much has been accomplished by this movement toward gaining its points. Meanwhile a vigorous reaction has set in, and the old finds its defenders and apologists. The discussion widens its scope and extends to many other phases not originally called into question, not only the proper course of study for the public schools, but their right to exist on appropriations from the public treasury; especially with reference to the public high school the discussion is a warm one. Teachers and directors of public-school systems have become suddenly aware that there may be an "irrepressible conflict" between the system of public and that of private instruction. It is somewhat startling to learn that there are two systems firmly established in our land confronting each other with radically different theories as to a proper course of study. Such hostility could not but develop sooner or later into an open contest. Now the general attention is directed to education as an element of national and social strength, we can no longer avoid a discussion of these differences and of the theories on which they are based. The peaceful victories of industry at Paris, London, and Vienna and the colossal victories of Prussian arms at Sadowa and Sedan have aroused statesmen and political economists to the study of public education as essential to national strength in productive industry and in the field of battle as well. What this education should be, how far it should be carried, whether compulsory or not, whether there should be different courses of education, adapted to the supposed destinies of the pupils—these and other kindred questions must be discussed in the light of fundamental principles. On the one hand it is contended, in the interest of productive industry, that the public schools, being for the masses who are destined to fill the ranks of common laborers, should give a semitechnical-education and avoid the purely disciplinary studies. The latter should be reserved for private academies and preparatory schools founded by private enterprise and open to such of the community as can afford to patronize them. The higher education in this country conducted in its colleges and universities should, according to this view, have no organic relation whatever to the public school system, but only to the system of preparatory schools and academies supported by private wealth. That the effect of such a state of affairs is to injure the cause of education in general, who can doubt, when he reflects that such isolation must have the effect of arraying the supporters of public schools and those who have received the primary education given in them against the supporters of higher education and against the class of citizens who have received it? For it will result that those who receive a higher education will have been, during their whole course in a system of schools founded on a basis different from the public schools, having a different course of study and supported in a radically different manner. That the graduates of higher institutions should under those circumstances be in sympathy with public school education is impossible. The public schools would necessarily be the schools of a caste—of the proletariat—the class whose chief organ is the hand, and whose brains are educated solely to serve the hand better. The very persons themselves are called "hands" very appropriately.

In this country, with its boundless possibilities, living as we do largely upon our hopes, conscious of a rapid development in the past and of great prospects in the future, with a national history whose biographical side is the story of "self-made" men, aspiration is the leading characteristic of the people, and the poorest immigrant here soon kindles with its impulse, and while he endeavors by thrift to accumulate a fortune, he prepares for its perpetuity by educating his children.

There is nothing more favorable to the character of the foreigner newly arrived on our shores than this, that he is everywhere eager to avail himself of the school privileges. To the self-respect born of aspiration, what greater shock can be offered than the establishment of caste schools—public schools founded especially for the industrial class, to the end that its children being born from "hands" shall be "hands" still, and shall not mingle with the children of the wealthy, nor with those of the liberally educated. Such discrimination leads the laborer to refuse all school education unless he can afford to pay for it in the private school.

The complete degradation of the public school results. On the one hand those who have received higher education have been nurtured in an atmosphere of contempt for the free schools of the laboring classes. On the other hand the laboring classes themselves despise the symbol of their inferiority and the institution designed to make their inferiority hereditary.

But it may be that a higher education demands a primary education specially designed as preparation and introduction to it. It is possible that an education, to be completed in three or five years, ought to be on an entirely different plan from that intended to cover ten or fifteen years. If such were found to be the case, our only remedy might be a twofold course in the public schools—a so-called "general course" and a "classical course." Where this were not feasible we might lament the fate of the public school, but could not remove its necessary evils. It would inevitably become the school of the proletariat, and the flourishing private school would draw away the children of wealth and competence and furnish them a different course of study.

This question touches most vitally our whole public school system, and especially the course of study in the high school. Let us inquire, therefore, what are the current standards of education, as set up by the public and private schools.

According to the theory on which college education rests, the preparatory schools should confine their work almost entirely to the disciplinary studies. The mathematics and Latin and Greek are the main requisites for admission. Not only is this the case, but for two years after admission there is very little deviation from this course. Harvard, by raising the standard for admission by at least a year's work, now makes Latin, Greek, and mathematics elective after freshman year, and requires physics, rhetoric, history, and elementary French as the regular studies of sophomore year. By this it will be seen that if public schools are to fit their pupils for the colleges they must adopt the same course as the academies and special preparatory schools and make thoroughness in collateral or information branches unessential for promotion. By the college system these collateral branches shall be reached only after the disciplinary course is finished. Even Harvard's recent and noteworthy changes consist in demanding another year's work in the preparatory school on Latin, Greek, and the mathematics. A small departure from this looks also in the direction of allowing previous work in French and other studies as an equivalent for required work. The natural sciences are to be included in the preparatory work at some future time.

It does not appear that any college has made so great a departure as to require for admission just what a public high school would consider a proper requirement for a diploma.

The public schools have generally adopted a course of study resting on a different theory from the one on which that of the colleges is based. The course of study in the public schools assumes the principle that it is best to unite disciplinary studies with collateral studies intended to supply information and insight. This union of discipline and knowledge must begin in the primary school and continue through the high school.

The amount of actual culture (including under this term both discipline and knowledge) represented by the public high school course is almost equal to that attained by the students who have completed sophomore year in most colleges—that is to say, a graduate of a city high school is as able to pursue independent investigations into the various branches of science and literature, native and foreign, as the college student of two years' standing. What he has been obliged to do thoroughly in history, United States and European; in geography, descriptive and physical; in English literature and the grammars of English, Latin, and French, or German; rhetoricals, writing, spelling, and reading; in physics, chemistry, or natural history; in mathematics; in mental and moral philosophy—what he has done in these studies is an equivalent for the Latin, Greek, and mathematics of freshman and sophomore years, together with the preparatory studies actually required.

Now, what are the facts as to admission to the colleges? The graduate of the high school is placed on the same basis as the specially prepared student who is really two years his junior in general culture. This injustice prevents the high-school graduate from resorting to the regular course in our colleges.

The question is narrowed down to this, Which is the correct system, that of the colleges which separates, or that of the public schools which unites discipline and knowledge? If the latter, then the colleges of the land ought to be reconstructed and adapted to the prevailing system of education here well established. If the former is right, then our public school system ought to be purged of the collateral work in its course of study. Finally, if both are right and necessary, each in its own sphere, then it is evident that there is required a system of private or public schools which occupy the place that the academy system in New England and New York occupies. Into these must be sent those pupils who expect to fit for a higher education. This latter alternative does not furnish a solution of the difficulty. There still remains, as has been stated at length, an irreconcilable conflict between the public school system and the system pursued in these preparatory schools.

The conflict lies between the systems as now established, and not between the systems as they ought to be. It seems to me that the public school system is substantially the correct one, and that the higher education of the country should adapt itself to it. This will appear evident if

I can demonstrate that the best course of study for a short school period is a section of the best course of study for a long period, and that conversely the long course of study can to best advantage take up for its preparatory studies just what the common school should teach. In brief, if the course of study is one for culture and for business or the professions, so that, whatever section of it be cut off from the beginning furnishes the best course up to that point, whether regarded as preparatory to a continuation of the course of study or a completed course—then it will be conceded that higher education and common school education should both adopt that course, and thus become mutually complementary. Then the academies and classical schools, private institutions supported as special feeders for the colleges, must perforce adopt the same course as the common schools.

That this is plausible I shall undertake to prove by a brief review of the causes that have led to the differences shown to exist, and that it is rational I shall endeavor to show by a survey of the psychological principles that should determine the selection of a course of study.

In all times nations have recognized the necessity of educating their directive intelligence. Those who are to rule are carefully educated for this purpose. Public money has never been grudged for the education of the governing classes. So soon as the State has found that its national strength depended on the education of a special class, that class has at once been provided for. The immense sums recently expended in the various countries of Europe for industrial education show that statesmanship has at last found out that political prosperity depends upon the prosperity of the civil community. In our comparatively new experiment of a "government of the people, by the people, and for the people," to educate the ruling class means to educate all the people. But in the earlier days of our history the system of education was definitely shaped toward providing a learned few to look after the highest interests, the clergy, the physicians, the lawyers. The three R's, reading, writing, and arithmetic, were for all. To these essentials the candidates for the professions added Latin, Greek, and higher mathematics, and then entered professional schools to study their specialties. A liberal education included the classics and mathematics, the common school education included only the three R's. But the newspaper and magazine, together with rapid transportation, have opened up so great possibilities to the one who possesses a common education that he continues his theoretic education after school life almost inevitably. The former standard of a liberal education is attained by the average of the community. The development and rapid growth of the sciences and of modern literature have added such immense provinces to the domain set apart for a liberal education that it now bears little resemblance to its first shape and magnitude. Hence, it happens that while our higher education demands only disciplinary studies as preparatory to it, and then proceeds to add at least two years more of disciplinary studies, the growth of realized intelligence, in the shape of science and literature, has introduced changes that have destroyed its symmetry and adaptation. In the common school the three R's have been so expanded by the contents they have received from literature and the sciences of nature, and of man, that they furnish much more than is required by the colleges, and much more than is used as a foundation for the superstructure there built. Moreover, the same causes that have operated to expand and fill up the common school course have likewise influenced the college course, but not in the same way. Their influence in the common school course is felt throughout its entire extent; in the college course its presence is recognized by an expansion during the last part of it. After discipline is obtained, then the student is prepared to apply himself to the rich contents of the modern world. Science, art, and history may then be explored. Short excursions are accordingly made into those realms, chiefly, however, by means of the oral lectures of the professor, who gives fine summaries of what has been accomplished in this or that special province. To such students as have no familiar acquaintance with a considerable number of the primitive facts and details, the generalizations of the professor are vague and meaningless. The ideal of the course of study in our higher education finds thus its type in the palm tree, which climbs nearly to its full height branchless and then expands suddenly into full foliage. If the plan which the public schools have unconsciously and undesigningly adopted were followed, its type would be a tree that expands into foliage from below up to the top. What serious obstacle is there in the way of adopting for the college course a curriculum involving a central axis of discipline studies and a complement of accessory branches yielding information and insight? To the disciplines of Latin, Greek, and the mathematics, add the sciences—both natural and social-political—and literature and civil history. The preparation for college should then demand the rudiments of science, literature, and history. This change would adapt the college to the public school course.

I do not ignore here the important consideration—once far more important than now—which goes to justify the present college course. I allude to the principle that education must involve a period of estrangement from the common and familiar. The pupil must be led out of his immediateness and separated in spirit from his naturalness, in order that he may be able to return from his self-estrangement to the world that lies nearest to him and consciously seize and master it. Without such self-alienation that which lies nearest to man and deepest in his nature does not become objective to him at all, but remains merely instinctive and implicit. Therefore there is a deep-lying ground for taking the student out of the familiar modern world and requiring him to breathe the atmosphere of the far-off and distant world of antiquity for several years of his life. When he again approaches his own world he is vividly conscious of it by reason of its obvious differences from the classic world, with which he has become familiar. Further reasons to strengthen this position will also be found in a consideration of the specific psychological import of the study of the classics, a consideration which it is necessary to undertake as a preliminary to the thorough investigation of the principles of a course of study. I will anticipate here, however, the final grounds of decision against the present system by saying that the expansion of the modern world of realized intelligence is so great that it leads the student quite irresistibly into the self estrangement spoken of above. Its art and literature portray the widest and deepest collisions of the problem of life; its science enumerates the whole range of existences, whether corporeal, like the mineral, plant, or animal, or incorporeal, like human institutions and generalizations. Besides this, the proper mastery over any province of knowledge involves three stages, and these must be separated in time long enough to allow of complete assimilation. The perceptive, the reflective, and the stage of insight can not be simultaneous. This points to the principle which requires the course of study to be exhaustive at each of its epochs—including all the representative provinces in some one of their types at all stages of progress. The mind should grow with all its windows open from the beginning. What it acquires in its early stages will be rudimentary, but will furnish a rich native store for future thought when the period of reflection sets in stronger and stronger. The roots of the sciences and literature and history should go down deep into the earliest years, so that the unconscious influence derived thence shall assist in molding the taste, will, and intellect during the most plastic period of growth. Without this thorough assimilation with the whole intellectual being—the unconscious molding of one's view of the world (*Weltvorstellung*, as the Germans call it)—a growth of years—later scientific and literary studies are likely to be barren, lacking a fruitful soil in the disposition (*Gemüth*) and phantasy. Almost everything great in the world of reason has a slow gestation, first gathering force in the disposition and then in the phantasy, coming gradually into shape and definiteness through a series of monstrous forms before it sees the light of conscious reason.

THE STUDY OF THE CLASSICS

No one who considers carefully the psychological results of classic study can help feeling some degree of dismay at the treatment such study receives at the hands of a majority of our so-called "prominent educators."

The cause of the public schools is indeed greatly injured by unwise zeal. Much of the alienation discoverable toward public schools on the part of those who conduct higher education is traceable to that feeling of distrust engendered by the tirades of naive, unconscious men, who find themselves face to face with a question that has two antithetic extremes, whose mediation reaches far down into the mysteries. With the cant of progress and reform on their tongues and a polemical flourish of the epithet "old fogy," they challenge whatever they can not justify on immediate, simple, and therefore shallow grounds. Hence they are sure to challenge pretty much all that is deep and rational. Nor are they the ones to blame. For there is little adequate justification proffered on the part of the installed professors who would seem called upon to defend their province of activity by showing its rationality.

This is partly due, again, to the isolation of higher education from common school education. Those who have prepared for college have conquered their prejudices and yielded to the demands of the higher course. Training has obliterated the traces of protest which might some time have burst forth. Hence the justification of the college curriculum is not undertaken, but left a tenet of blind faith. It is true, a few traditional grounds are stated in a somewhat mechanical manner. Discipline, culture, accuracy of thought, and expression—these are the stock arguments in favor of classical study.

With a view to a more thorough examination of these points I have ventured to discuss them here in their psychological bearings. It is essentially a psychological question. What influence on the mind have these studies? What peculiar influence arises from the study of Latin and Greek that the modern languages do not exert upon the scholar? What is the definite meaning of the words "discipline," "culture," "exactness of thought," "refining influence," when applied to the results of classical study, or what is the ground on which these languages are called "perfect"?

The Latin and Greek languages are spoken of as being "perfect" in the sense of completeness as regards further growth, or as regards etymological inflections, or as regards syntactical organism, or, finally, as regards capability of expression, whether artistic, scientific, or historical. This latter designation ("perfect") does not seem to recommend itself as a substantial reason for the prominent place Latin and Greek hold in education. In the first sense, as complete in respect to growth, they would have no advantage over the Anglo-Saxon, the old Norse, the Zend, the Sanscrit, or any other dead language. Nor is it obvious at first glance why such completeness is an advantage. Why should we not rather study a living, organic growth, wherein we can trace a process actually going on? Laws are manifested only in transitions from one stage to another. Again, if inflections are considered, what thoughtful man will assert that inflections are a mark of perfection? Is the Sanscrit more perfect than the Latin or Greek because it inflects twice as much as the latter? Does not maturity of spiritual development do away with inflections? Could the syntax of Greek or Latin do any more wonderful things than the syntax of Milton or Shakespeare? Could the language of Cicero express what that of Burke could not, or that of Plato and Aristotle express what Hegel and Schelling found German inadequate to do? It is doubtful if any of these questions could be answered in such a way as to defend Latin and Greek on the ground of a superior degree of perfection over all other languages.

But there are better grounds for the support of classical study. As subsidiary reason for the study of Latin one may name its importance to the English speaking people on account of the fact that it furnishes the root words to that part of our vocabulary which is more especially the language of thought and reflection, while the Teutonic or Gothic groundwork is the language of the sensuous experience and of common life. Hence it happens that even a little study of Latin makes a great difference in the grasp of the mind as regards generalization and principles. Without Latin the trope and metaphor underlying the abstract terms necessary to express all elevated sentiment or thought in English, and more specifically all scientific results—whether moral, legal, spiritual, or natural—is not perceived nor felt. Such trope or metaphor is the basis of abstract terms, and hence the latter have been called "fossil poetry." To gain command of the resources of a language one must revivify this poetic element, must acquire a feeling of the trope and metaphor which it contains.

This argument for the study of Latin by English-speaking people holds good in a greater or less degree for the Romanic nations of modern times. But it is not so convincing when applied to the Germanic, Norse, and Slavonic peoples. It is when we come to look the question earnestly in the face, as applied to all European culture, that we begin to see its truer and deeper psychological bearing.

I have already quoted the remark of Schopenhauer that—

A man who does not understand Latin is like one who walks through a beautiful region in a fog; his horizon is very close to him. He sees only the nearest things clearly, and a few steps away from him the outlines of everything become indistinct or wholly lost. But the horizon of the Latin scholar extends far and wide through the centuries of modern history, the middle ages, and antiquity.

Here we have the essential kernel of the matter hinted at under a figure of speech.

The object of education in the school should be to clear up the mind and give substance and discipline to its powers. To attain to clearness there is but one way—the student, engrossed in his little world of opinions and caprices, must learn the presuppositions of his being and activity. The individual looks out from his narrow environs in the now and here and sees that he is what he is mostly through conventionality. He does this or that because others do it; he acquired the habit when a child and has never questioned its rationality. His family and immediate circle of acquaintances have given him his habits of thinking and acting. He looks further and sees that the community in which he lives is governed likewise by use and wont. Tradition is the chief factor; accidental modifications of time and place enter as a less important factor; another factor in the result is the law of development or evolution, wherein he sees a gradual change ensuing from internal growth. Through observation of this latter fact—that of evolution—he is carried at once beyond his community and beyond all contemporary communities. He begins to trace the historic evolution of his own civilization out of the past. Out of the formless void of his consciousness there begin to arise some intimations of his whereabouts, and whence and whither.

Even the most materialistic science of our time hastens to caution us that we should never seek to know the individual by isolating him from his conditions. To know an individual thing scientifically, we must study it in its history. It is a part of a process. Its presuppositions are needed to make it intelligible. Only in the perspective of its history can we see it so as to comprehend it as a whole.

If a man does not know nor feel his existence, he can not be said to live it as an independent existence. The humblest piece of dirt beneath our feet pulsates with vibrations that have traveled hither from the farthest star. But the clod does not know nor feel its community with the universe of matter. That universe does not exist for the clod; consequently the clod does not exist for itself. When we learn to know our entire being it exists for us, and therein we come to exist for ourselves. It is conscious communion with one's existence that makes it one's own. The more complete the consciousness the higher and more personal the being. The man who does not know his history nor the history of his civilization, does not consciously possess himself. His existence, as involved in those presuppositions, is not for him, is hence unassimilated, and therefore exists as his fate and not as his freedom. The first requisite for directive power is knowledge. Directive intelligence, knowledge itself, may ceaselessly modify the effects of its presuppositions as it finds them on itself, and by successive acts of the will may determine itself in accordance with its pure ideal. This is freedom.

When the scholar learns his presuppositions and sees the evolution afar off of the elements that have come down to him and entered his being— elements that form his life and make the conditions which surround him and furnish the instrumentalities which he must wield—then he begins to know how much his being involves, and in the consciousness of this he begins to be somebody in real earnest. He begins to find himself. The empty consciousness fills with substance—with its own proper substance; it subsumes its particular being under the general self which it finds to be its true being; it "stands under" itself; rises from a particular special form of being to a generic, universal form thereof, which may be called culture.

Thus for ages the mind of youth has been trained in the schools on the two "dead languages," Latin and Greek. For the evolution of the civilization in which we live and move and have our being issued through Greece and Rome on its way to us. We kindled the torches of our institutions—of the watch-fires of our civilization—at their sacred flames. The organism of the State, the invention of the forms in which man may live in a civil community and enjoy municipal and personal rights—these trace their descent in a direct line from Rome and were indigenous to the people that spoke Latin. In our civil and political forms we live Roman life today. That side or phase of the complex organism of modern civilization is Roman. Our scientific and aesthetic forms come from beyond Rome; they speak the language of their Greek home to this very day, just as much as jurisprudence and legislation pronounce their edicts in Roman words. Religion points through Greece and Rome to a beyond in Judea for a still deeper spiritual presupposition.

To assimilate this antecedent stage of existence it is not sufficient to form an acquaintance with it by reading its history or literature in translations. The thorough assimilation of it in consciousness demands such an immediate contact with it as one gets by learning the languages of those people—the clothing of their inmost spiritual selves. We must don the garb in which they thought and spoke in order to fully realize in ourselves these embryonic stages of our civilization. For we know truly what we have lived through. We must live it in our dispositions or feelings, then realize the forms which it takes on in the phantasy, i.e., its art forms, and finally seize it in the abstract conceptions of the understanding and grasp its highest syntheses in the principles of the reason. The earlier stages, that of feeling and that of phantasy, can be readied best through the natural symbolism of the word. Each national spirit reveals itself to itself in its own way by its language. Translation loses this peculiar element of feeling, although it retains the higher rational element. But in the present instance it is essential to retain precisely the immediate, naive, germinal "cell growth" of those national spirits whose results we have assimilated.

From the modern scientific idea of method—even that called Darwinism—we see the absolute necessity of mastering our history in order to know ourselves. We must take up into our consciousness our presupposition before we can be in a condition to achieve practical freedom. Just as the uncultivated person feels and knows his narrow circle of sensations, desires, appetites, and volitions as his personal existence, his "ego," so the man of culture recognizes his identity with the vast complex of civilization, with the long travail of human history:

> He omnipresent is,
> All round himself he lies,
> Osiris spread abroad,
> Upstaring in all eyes.

For he looks at himself through the eyes of mankind and sees himself in mankind. History is the revelation of what is potentially in each man.

We may now inquire what aspect the question of the substitution of a modern language—say German or French—for Latin or Greek has. Is it not clear that a modern language stands to English in the relation of coordination and not in any sense in that of a presupposition? As immediate facts, German and French stand in need of explanation through evolution, just as much as the English does. Their civilizations are not embryonic stages of English civilization, but rather repetitions of it. To suggest a study of German or French as a substitute for Latin or Greek would be paralleled in the science of zoology by suggesting a study of snakes instead of tadpoles in the embryology of the frog.

Greece and Rome stand at the entrance to the modern world or the occidental phase in world history. Greece introduces the idea of individuality into history in place of the oriental idea of substance. Rome deepens the idea of individuality to that of legal person. Both nations conquered the Orient. First, Greece, under Alexander, avenged its wrongs, long suffered at the hand of Persia, by subduing Asia Minor, Syria, Egypt, Persia proper, Bactria, and western India. The Greek kingdoms in Asia Minor and Egypt were for centuries the seats of science. The Greek kingdoms in Syria and Bactria—no one knows how much the East Indians and Chinese owe to them in the way of scraps of science and art.

Then Rome brought under her yoke the western and northern barbarians, rooted out Carthage, and extended her sway to the east over Greece and the Greek empires temporarily. The great modern States were born in the Roman colonies of the west, and were nurtured under her civil code of laws and with such Greek refinement as followed in the wake of Roman wealth and might. Finally, Christianity, sheltered under the Roman eagle, found its way to all lands that were destined to enter modern civilization, and under the threefold nurture of Roman laws, Greek science, and Christianity the long education went on toward national independence and a humanitarian civilization.

Discipline, culture, exactness of thought, refining influence are, in a special sense, results of classical study, inasmuch as it alone furnishes a direct road to the conscious possession of the conventionalities of our civilization. Greek gives the presuppositions of the theoretical intelligence; Latin that of the practical (or will side) of the intelligence. Mere disciplined ability to give attention to a subject connectedly is not adequate to give culture or exactness of thought. Mathematical drill suffices for that sort of discipline, but it is accompanied with the mental habit of abstracting from and ignoring quality or the concrete relations of the most important of subjects—human life.

Why the argument in favor of Latin and Greek in education does not apply to oriental presuppositions beyond them may be asked. The reply is twofold. The most important of the presuppositions mentioned, the theoretical and practical, are indigenous with those two peoples—the former with Greece, the latter with Rome. Oriental presupposition appears in Greece as the basis of myths and of the religious mysteries. The myths represent the overthrow of the doctrine of substance by spiritual might—the Titans by the gods of Olympus—Asiatic fate by European free personality.

The Roman presupposition appears still less to be derived from the Orient. It is not in any proper sense to be regarded as a reaction against the Orient, although Greece is such a reaction. The presupposition of Christianity is, however, found in the Orient, in Judaism, and this fact is sufficiently emphasized in that part of our education which is left to the church. The spiritual elements embodied in religion are far more subtle than those we have just considered. But their discussion does not belong here.

With this hasty survey of the most important and most hotly contested question in higher education, let us approach the theme whose discussion is to throw light on the true relation of colleges and universities to the public schools.

THE COURSE OF STUDY

To discover precisely what the pupil gets from studying a particular branch—what he adds to his mental structure in the way of discipline and knowledge—is one of the problems of educational psychology. Without determining accurately the value of a given study by ascertaining what the pupil is to gain from it in the way of information that shall make clear his view of life or in the way of discipline that shall increase his strength to grapple with other problems, the educator is not in a condition to decide where it belongs in the course of study or how much time it demands. Indeed, it may be said that the want of such preliminary investigation has injured our educational system and is injuring it fully as much as all other causes combined. It is owing to the lack of psychological insight that we have so many changes in theories and systems, so much advocacy of one-sided extremes. Caprice and arbitrariness determine the choice of this or that study. The likes and dislikes of the teacher settle the course of the pupil; the whim of the parent is allowed to do the same thing.

We have just seen some of the psychological grounds for the large place classical study holds in the curriculum of our higher education. When Latin was the language of the learned, its paramount importance in education was not questioned. It is at first somewhat surprising to discover that it is still the language of the learned who speak English, for the reason that the vocabulary of science, of refined culture, and of abstract thought or generalization, is nearly all of Latin derivation. But more important than this is the subtle spiritual gain derived from the increase of mental strength to analyze and combine the elements of human interests—still more important, the clearing up of the view of human life, the certainty of conviction obtained by the contemplation of human nature in its evolution through long intervals of time.

Our inquiry will lead us to investigate the twofold division of branches in the course of study into disciplinary and information-giving ones. We shall find both classes of studies in the elementary branches taught in common schools, and likewise in the more advanced studies of the high school and college. What psychology teaches us in regard to the elementary branches must be seen first. In its light we can then discuss the continuation of the same by the high school and college. We can also decide the extent to which the desire of discipline or information should lead us in selecting the branches to be pursued. The "elementary branches" alluded to are—

    I. Reading and writing—the mastery of letters.
   II. Arithmetic—the mastery of number.
  III. Geography—the mastery over place.
  IV. Grammar—the mastery over the word.
   V. History—the mastery over time.

In order to show the exhaustiveness with which these studies occupy the field, both subjectively and objectively, let us reclassify these studies under a new order.

The theoretic survey of the world (and intellectual education must undertake to give this) reaches into two realms—the world of matter or nature, the world of humanity or spirit. Theoretically considered, nature falls into inorganic or organic, and the sciences corresponding to these are physics and natural history. Physics (including chemistry) treats of the inorganic phases of nature, all of which may be treated mathematically or quantitatively. Natural history treats nature's organic phases: meteorology, geology, botany, zoology, and ethnology. Meteorology can not strictly be called organic, neither can geology. But the former is a circular movement, a process which moves in cycles. Moreover, it conditions all organic life through its cycles, and is therefore studied in connection with the latter in physical geography. Geology may be called the "Earth organism" (the Germans thus name it), and it treats of the organic process of the globe—using organic as more general than the term "living." Mathematics determines the abstract *a priori* laws of time and space. Time and space are the abstract logical conditions of nature. Mathematics is the general preliminary science of nature, which fixes and defines the conditions of nature in the abstract. Mathematics, physics, and (organics or) natural history form the theory of nature, the first and second (mathematics and physics) treating nature analytically or by elements; the third treating nature synthetically, as exhibited in organic forms or cyclical processes.

The world of humanity or spirit is distinguished from that of nature by means of this mark or characteristic: It everywhere is self-determined by a conscious purpose, while mere nature obeys laws unconsciously. Spirit is an end to itself. Nature's forms are ruled and swayed by external ends. By "external" ends I mean purposes, designs, or objects which are not consciously formed in thought—not self-proposed by the being whose end and aim they express. Man can form for himself a purpose. He can think his own final cause, and he alone can think out and discover the final cause of a merely natural being, an unconscious being.

The theory of man includes three phases: (1) Theory of man as a practical being, a will power, a moral being acting socially and politically, a history maker. (2) Theory of man as a theoretical being, a thinking power, a rational being, giving an account to itself of the world and itself—in short, a science maker. (3) Theory of man as an artist, or as a being that represents or portrays himself, embodies his ideal in real forms, makes the visible world into his own image—in short, as the producer of art and literature. (A fourth sphere—that of religion, the obverse of art, a realm, wherein man strives to elevate himself above all visible forms to the absolute ideal through devotion and worship—will occur to the thoughtful classifier. It is so important that it belongs to an education apart from the rest, a sacred education to be found within the church, and not side by side with other branches in secular education.)

To tabulate our results, we find for the total theoretic survey of the world the following:

Nature	I. Inorganic	Mathematics. Physics (and chemistry).
	II. Organic	Natural History.[a]
Man or spirit	III. Theoretical or thinking	Logic, philosophy, philology.
	IV. Practical or will power	Civil history, social and political sciences.
	V. Aesthetic or art power	Literature and art.

[a] Including whatever is a circular movement or cyclical process; hence the stars, meteorological process, geological structure, the plant and animal.

The two worlds—the macrocosm, and the microcosm—here fall under five general divisions, as seen in the above general review.

Our elementary branches distribute according to this general survey as follows:

    I. Nature inorganic—arithmetic.
    II. Nature organic—geography.
    III. Man—theoretical—grammar.
    IV. Man—practical—history.
    V. Man—aesthetic—reading (literature).

That these branches lie at the basis, and open first and directly out of the mind upon the world, will be evident upon a little consideration. It will also become clear that these are the only branches which lie directly at the door of the uncultivated mind.

I. *Arithmetic quantifies.* By its mastery, man to a great degree obtains theoretical dominion over time and space, and by it he can formulate the entire inorganic world. The Pythagoreans valued its disciplinary significance in that it is the first elevation above what is merely sensuous— an elevation through abstraction from particular quality. The mastery over number opens the window of the mind upon the world of quantity, giving one power to a certain extent to recognize and fix theoretically all quantity. From this study branch out the higher mathematics and physics.

II. *Geography localizes.* By its mastery man comes to realize his spatial relation to the rest of the world. As civilized man the supply of his wants of food, clothing, and shelter is a perpetual geographical process realized through the division of labor and commercial exchange. By this geographical relation each individual becomes participant in the entire production of the globe and in turn contributes to all. In geography the child learns this fact of interdependence and community, which is, even when known particularly and not generalized by him, of the greatest possible importance as a category in his thinking or view of the world. It is the second window of the mind. Through it he learns the organic world and its relations to the human race and to himself individually. Climate (meteorology), surface (geology), plants (botany), animals (zoology), man (ethnology, sociology, political and religious forms to some extent) are the topics to which he is introduced, and these are general categories or "tools of thought" whose mastery give him great vantage ground; think of him as not possessed of these distinctions in his mind and see what imbecility in dealing with the world would result. Shut up the geographical window of the soul and what darkness ensues! From this study branch out in higher education the special organic sciences indicated in the parentheses above used.

III. *Grammar fixes and defines speech.* By its mastery man obtains the first mastery over his mind as an instrument. To grammar belong reading and writing considered as orthography. And grammar in this aspect is the first study in school and the most powerful lever for all development of what is human. It is the key to all that is spiritual. By the arts of reading and writing or orthography man issues forth from the circumscribed life of the senses in which he is confined to his own immediate experience and to that of his small circle of acquaintances. He issues forth into the world revealed through the printed page—a world extending as wide as the human race and deep into time, as deep as the earliest hieroglyphics will lead him. The library opens to him and he can now use all the senses of all mankind, for their observations have been reported; he can use their thoughts and feelings, for these also have been reported. His own five senses, used unaided, would take him but little way in beholding the spectacle of the universe. But by means of this auxiliary of orthography he can supplement his finite being by the human race and he thereby comes into an infinite heritage. Grammar as etymology and syntax initiates the pupil into the general forms of thought itself. Thus there branch out logic, psychology, and metaphysics, as well as the various phases of philosophy. Has it not been said indeed that the father of logic discovered its forms through grammar. Under a thin veil the pupil deals with pure thought when he studies syntax.

IV. *History deals with human progress and process.* By its mastery the child learns to recognize his presuppositions—his existence as continued into the past. The precedent conditions are a part and parcel of his existence, just as the distant spatial conditions belong to his aggregate social conditions, as he learns in geography. As family and a nation, his existence is spread out in time; as a social being, it is spread out in space. History opens the fourth important window of the soul. It looks upon deeds and events, chiefly the former. Man, as a will power, unfolds his nature in successive deeds, and thence in time, and hence in history, From history branch out the practical or will sciences—jurisprudence, politics, and sociology, in the latter sharing with descriptive geography the same theme.

V. *Reading, when carried beyond orthography, wherein it is a department of grammar, includes the mastery of literature, which is the highest realm of aesthetics.* Poetry, the drama, and prose fiction lead into all art realms. Art portrays, in one shape or another, the collisions which the individual encounters in solving the problem of life; the collision with the ethical and moral and religious, and the collision of the ethical against the moral and religious, as when the edict of the state and moral or religious conviction collide; or, finally, when the inclination of the individual (love, hate, etc.), collides with fate or circumstances.

These five elementary branches are exhaustive, so far as including an initiation into every phase of nature and spirit. No one would leave out any of these from the common school curriculum. It remains, therefore, for us, in carrying up this education to its higher spheres, to retain its exhaustiveness, and not suffer any sphere to drop away unrepresented. In the high school course, these five departments are continued and reinforced in the following manner:

I. Inorganic nature
  (a) Algebra.
  (b) Geometry and trigonometry.
  (c) Analytical geometry.
  (d) Natural philosophy.
  (e) Chemistry.
II. Organic nature
  (a) Physical geography.
  (b) Astronomy.
  (c) Botany.
  (d) Physiology.
  (e) Zoology.
III. Theoretical man
  (a) Philology, Latin and Greek, French or German.
  (b) Mental and moral philosophy.
IV. Practical man
  (a) Universal history.
  (b) Constitution of the United States.
V. Aesthetical man
  (a) History of English literature.
  (b) Shakespeare (some special author).
  (c) Rhetoricals (declamation and composition).
  (d) Drawing.

With so extended a curriculum for the high school, each one of the five departments of human culture being filled with what belongs to it most directly, it is impossible in its four years' course to accomplish as much in the departments of Latin and Greek as is required of those preparatory schools which concentrate their whole energies on the classics even to the neglect of higher mathematics. But in the mathematics greater advance will be made than is required for admission to college at present. So in natural sciences the general compends—(1) natural philosophy, including an outline of the sciences of inorganic nature; (2) physical geography, including an outline of the sciences of organic nature and of cyclical nature—these general compends will be mastered, and with them the general technics and the general ideas of all natural science. Some special sciences, like botany, zoology, or physiology, may be studied for the further investigation of methods. English literature, in its history and examples, will be studied to good purpose, and the special study of Shakespeare, the greatest of literary men, will serve to give the pupil insight into the nature of artistic work. History of the United States is studied in the district school. The outline of universal history is completed in the high school. The Constitution of the United States is the best discipline for the initiation of the pupil into the legal style and into the constitutional form for political organisms. The triune form, which there has its best example, is the type of state organisms, of municipal organisms, and to some extent even of corporate organisms. In a country where every person, without exception, is necessarily brought into relation with various forms of its realization, and is likely to be called upon to assist in organizing such, it is highly important that all should be taught thoroughly this archetype of our governmental forms. Accordingly, in the district schools, he studies its outlines with special reference to the coordination of its three separate functions. In the high school he studies it in its details and practical functions, and with it studies also parliamentary law. Some time is given to the outlines of philosophy, moral and mental, and their history, in the high school.

What is the course of study for the succeeding four years which the college and university occupy? The high school furnishes its pupils with less preparation in the classics, and considerably more preparation in all other branches. The college course that should adapt itself to the public school system must demand less preparation in the classics, but require one modern language; about the same in mathematics (i.e., all of algebra, geometry, and trigonometry); more in natural science, history, and literature. It would then be able to begin mathematics, in freshman year, with analytical geometry, and require all to take the differential and integral calculus in the regular course, leaving to the list of elective studies the remaining mathematics. In natural science there should be a continuation of the study of inorganic nature by special branches, and a more thorough application of mathematics to the same; organic nature also should be taught by special branches. The ordinary course in Greek and Latin for two years must be strictly followed, and, after that, made elective; comparative philology should be made a required study for a year. Logic, history of speculative philosophy, and the thorough study of the system of one of the greatest philosophers, together with a criticism of the latest philosophic movements of the day should belong to the required course, leaving farther studies of this class to the elective list. Lectures on the philosophy of history, of literature, art, science, etc., should begin early and continue throughout the course—not frequently, but at intervals. The practice of crowding into the senior year all of this matter does not find the students prepared by growth for philosophical generalization, nor acquainted with its technique. Advance views can not be communicated or acquired unless the basis of quiet assimilation has been prepared. Time is indispensable for the growth of the deep thinker. To use two or three years of the college course in learning Latin, Greek, and mathematics without attempting any generalization of the results does not prepare the pupil to enter into such generalizations, but rather confirms in him a doubt as to their possibility. No wonder that so many students graduate unable to refute the shallow sophisms with which the air is filled by thinkers of the second stage of culture in thought, when they ought to have mastered the third stage of thinking in college, or at least to have learned that there is such a stage and that all the greatest names in philosophy, from Aristotle down, have worked in it, and, more than all this, that on the third stage alone are found all positive justifications of institutions and all insight into their nature. The study of literature, art, social science, politics, law, ethnology, philology, universal history, and psychology should be conducted through lectures on their philosophy, and accompanied by recitation work in special provinces for the sake of illustration of practical method in investigation.

How much should be elective in the college course and what should be required of all? Those studies which have a direct bearing on the discipline and insight of the scholar should not be placed on the list of electives. At least, if it is necessary to establish the institution on a basis that permits one to choose any or all of the branches, it is very important to include all the branches essential to discipline and insight in the list required for a degree. I am in favor of excluding elective studies from the high school altogether. The "classical course," so-called, is adopted in order to meet the requirements of the college in preparatory work. A "general course" is made out side by side with the "classical" course, and neither course is in harmony with the public school system nor with sound psychological principles.

Those who are to "finish their education" with the high school course are the very ones who need a share of classical study. Classical study is not merely a preparation for higher study, as Latin might have been when it was studied in order to learn how to read the "language of the learned," who wrote all their books in it. If a pupil were to remain only one year in the high school he ought, by all means, to study Latin during that time; it will come the nearest of all his studies to endowing him with a new faculty—with a new power of insight.

In the district school course each of the branches named is essential to the culture of the child, and it does not matter whether his course is to be one year or three years or ten years or twenty years. If he attends one year he learns to read and write and count—nothing else so important as these arts to him, for they open the doors of the spiritual universe to him and the keys can never be taken away from him. In three years he perfects himself in reading, writing, the elements of arithmetic, and learns the outlines of geography. What other branch can be compared with one of these at this period? Botany? Drawing? What is botany to the boy who can not read or write or count, or who knows not his relation to the earth on which he lives? What is the art of drawing compared with the art of writing? The degree of universality is the test to apply in settling such questions. But botany and drawing need not be wholly banished from even the primary school. The branches being divided into disciplinary, insight giving, information giving, and technical-skill giving, the two former are to be regarded as essentials, and perhaps four-fifths of the time in school devoted to them; the latter deserve their place, and if one-fifth of the time be given them they reenforce the other branches. In St. Louis natural science is taught in oral lessons one hour a week—the lesson being given on Wednesday afternoon. The pupils are not required to prepare their lessons; they are only to listen attentively and participate actively when called upon by the teacher for their experience. They are to be interested, and no constraint is to be exercised except to secure respectful attention. I have found that the information obtained in these lessons makes its appearance especially in the geography lessons. The one lesson of the week that is devoid of constraint and contains a range of topics and explanations suited to gratify childish curiosity I believe to be very valuable—at least far more valuable than the same time devoted to arithmetic or reading. I can not say that two hours per week used in this way would be as valuable as one hour, while its inroads on the other studies would be felt to their injury. Confined to one lesson, it aids the others by reaction, while the information gradually amassed is of immediate value and of still greater indirect value in preparing the mind for the exhaustive comprehension of nature in the high school or college. It is the active feeling and phantasy of the child that does most; his senses and reflection are roused by those unconscious movements of his soul. Hence, what he can tell directly about the subjects of his lessons may not be very much or very coherent, yet his spirit of investigation and the conviction that all natural phenomena can be explained is of great consequence to his after life. Drawing, again, is the only study tending directly to cultivate the hand and eye—a sort of universal skill-developing study. A short time each day can be spent on drawing better than not, for it is a rest from the discipline studies.

In the high school and in the college the course of study should still be carried on in certain studies with a view to discipline the mind severely, and in others to give the first initiatory course, laying the foundation for what must grow several years before the teacher can venture to unfold the highest significance of it. It must be allowed to "soak" for its time. The philosophy of history, art, and literature can not be taught at once. Perhaps the first course is fortunate if it leaves a conscious conviction in the mind of the pupil that it is possible to have a philosophy of such things, the pupil not being able to give any rational account as yet of any piece of such philosophy. The descriptive phases of the sciences can be learned early. We have three cyclical movements in our natural science course, each traversing the same round and covering the whole field, gradually increasing in minuteness and scientific precision. The course in the high school ought to prove more interesting and fruitful for the previous preparation, and it probably will when the present pupils in our lower grades reach that school.

Is not the highest problem of education how to liberate the genius of the pupil? If genius can not be created or developed it certainly needs liberation. It seems to me that a course of study which plants first in the feeling and phantasy and then gradually brings out through the reflection and reason the ideas of its contents will come nearest to the liberation of genius.

The Relation of School Discipline to Moral Education
(1897)

Like other pre-Progressive educators, William Torrey Harris places great emphasis on moral education. This essay illustrates with clarity his views on the relationship between moral education and character-building and on the difference between the theory and practice of moral education. Harris argues that good habits are the indispensable vehicle of moral education and the foundation of good character. The school, he says, teaches moral education by its insistence on good habits, regularity, punctuality, silence, and industry.

Under the influence of Progressivist doctrine in the early decades of the 20th century, teachers were encouraged to ignore Harris's philosophy as obsolete and to promote individualism and student-chosen activities. As devotion to self-expression and self-esteem gained ground, Harris's concern for moral education and responsibility for the common good diminished. Having neglected moral education, American schools confronted a rising tide of student indiscipline and apathy. The ideals that Harris thought were so important should not have been ignored.

There is no topic related to education in the schools that excites so general discussion as that of moral education. And yet there is no topic concerning which the suggestions made are more idle and unprofitable. It is generally assumed that moral instruction is moral philosophy. Now the elementary schools do not attempt with success philosophical instruction of any kind, and in the nature of the case could not give successful lessons in moral phi-

Forgotten Heroes of American Education, pages 355–368
Copyright © 2006 by Information Age Publishing
All rights of reproduction in any form reserved.

losophy. On this account it has been supposed that there is no moral instruction in the elementary schools. To correct this, suggestions are made on every hand for the preparation of some catechism which should form an introduction to moral philosophy, or more often it is suggested that religious instruction should be introduced for this purpose. Perhaps Bible reading alone without note or comment is proposed as the best means of meeting the want that is felt.

The important question that meets us at this point is, What is the difference between intellectual education and moral education? When we consider its answer we come very soon to the conviction that moral philosophy belongs to intellectual education. For it treats of principles and causes. It belongs to theory, while the moral should relate especially to practice. Moral instruction, strictly speaking, should secure the formation of correct moral habits. The nature of morality is explained in moral philosophy. A correct habit of thinking, a correct view of the world is important enough for moral education, but it does not amount to a moral education, but is only one side of it. One side perhaps leads to the other. Possibly a correct habit of thinking regarding the moral will lead gradually towards the practice of the moral. And certainly a practice of the moral will lead towards a correct thinking as regards the moral.

Again, the more elementary the grade of education the greater the preponderance of practice over theory. It would seem that the children in the primary schools and the grammar schools should be taught moral practices and habits and that gradually as they go on through the secondary schools and into higher education they should learn the full theory of the ethical.

However this may be, as soon as one approaches the course of education as it is found realized in the existing school systems in America, he comes upon the fact that the matter of moral instruction in the schools belongs to the side known as discipline and not to the side known as instruction in books and theories.

The first thing the child learns when he comes to school is to act according to certain forms—certain forms that are necessary in order to make possible the instruction of the school in classes or groups. The school is a social whole. The pupil must learn to act in such a way as not to interfere with the studies of his fellows. He must act so as to reinforce the action of the other pupils and not embarrass it. This concerted action into which the pupil is trained may be called the rhythm of the school. The child must become rhythmical, must be penetrated by the spirit of the school order. Order is heaven's first law. Everyone has heard this statement quoted again and again. Inasmuch as the future member of the society will have two existences, an individual existence and a social existence, it is well that the school which fits him for life should be a social existence and have these two sides to it.

There are four cardinal rules that relate directly to the school discipline. The child must be regular and punctual, silent and industrious. Let us discuss the necessity of these rules in the school and see the immense importance which school discipline has for the formation of character. "Character," said Novalis, "is the completely rounded will." The human will has acted upon itself and made grooves or ruts in which it may act with efficiency and without contradicting and embarrassing itself. The will in the case of moral action is directed upon itself, the will controls itself. Self-control in the interest of reasonable deeds—self-control in the interest of performing reasonable deeds and in aiding all one's fellow men to perform reasonable deeds—this self-control is the essence of the moral.

The commencement of this subjugation of the will on the part of the child is accomplished through the principle of regularity. The child must come regularly to school day by day, must not omit a single session. He must study his lessons regularly, prepare himself for the tasks of the day without omitting any. Recitations or lessons must be attended regularly. Any tendency to yield to the feeling of the moment, any fits of indolence, any indisposition which offers itself must be inhibited by the child's will. He must vanquish his natural like or dislike and perform the reasonable task. He must sacrifice himself whenever necessary. The principle of self-sacrifice is another name for this will training which belongs to moral instruction. To theorize about self-sacrifice and self-control and habits of regularity is intellectual education, but not moral education.

The habit of regularity once confirmed, the pupil has attained some power of directing the action of his will upon his will. He has to that extent taken his will from its subjection to feeling or passion or mere unconscious habit. He does not will upon impulse, but wills rationally.

Not only regularity, but punctuality, is insisted on in the school. He must not merely attend the school, but he must attend it just at the time prescribed, say at the beginning of the morning and afternoon sessions. He must not be content with getting his lesson at some time in the day, but he must get the lesson at the proper time. He must be at the class at the proper time. He must be obedient to the word of command.

In order that there may be concerted action both regularity and punctuality are necessary. The rhythm of action by which the community of individuals is converted into an organic social whole requires punctuality as much as regularity. Without punctuality each individual is in the way of every other one and becomes an obstacle or stumbling block. There can be no movement of the whole as a whole without punctuality. This rhythm is necessary in order that there may be unity of human action. A prescribed order issues forth from the will of established authority. This prescribed order is carried out by individuals acting as a higher individual, namely, as an institution. For an institution is an individuality given to many. It is a unity of effort, an *e pluribus unum*. The school is to be taught in classes. In the class the pupil learns much more than he could learn by himself. If the teacher should devote himself to one person he could not instruct him in so efficient a manner as he could instruct twenty persons at the same time. For in class recitation each pupil learns more from his fellow pupils (from all their mistakes and failures as well as from their brilliant achievements) than he does from his teacher. Each pupil is more or less one-sided in his mind. It is, in fact, the object of education to bring out all sides of his mind so that each faculty may be reinforced by all the others. The pupil in learning his lesson understands some phases of it and fails to see what is essential in others, but the failures are not all alike; a given pupil fails in one thing and succeeds in another: his fellow pupil succeeds where he fails and fails where he succeeds. In the recitation each pupil is surprised to find that some of his fellows are more successful than himself in seeing the true significance. The pupil can, through the properly conducted recitation, seize the subject of his lesson through many minds. He learns to add to his power of insight the various insights of his fellow pupils. The skillful teacher knows his power of teaching by means of a class—knows that he can make each pupil understand much more through the aid of a class than he could make him understand if he were to attempt to do all of the explaining for an isolated pupil.

The class recitation is made possible only by regularity and punctuality. The efficiency of the school depends upon it. In the industrial civilization in which we live the same necessity exists for these school virtues. Unless there is regularity the mill cannot manufacture and the shop cannot go on; there can be no combination between the mechanics who work on a joint enterprise. The engineer or the fireman without this virtue of punctuality would endanger the lives of his fellow workmen by an explosion of the steam boiler, or bring the machinery to a stop through the neglect of its fires.

We are pushing forward in our time into an era of the use of machinery, not merely in manufacturing and transportation, but for all the multifarious uses of the household and the daily life. Man is conquering nature by means of machinery, and the citizen cannot enter into the fruits of this victory unless he adapts himself, through regularity and punctuality, to the demands of this new form of civilization.

But regularity and punctuality are not the only schoolroom virtues. I have mentioned two others, silence and industry. Regularity and punctuality are in a certain sense negative virtues. Silence also belongs to this class, while industry belongs to the positive virtues. Silence is another virtue that depends upon inhibition—upon the inhibitory act of the will.

The will acts to repress its self-activity; to guide its own utterance and to limit that utterance to the chosen province prescribed for it. It is especially a virtue that makes possible the combination of the individual with the social whole. The pupil that whispers or in any way attracts the attention of his fellows not only does something to make his own school time of no account, but he also does much to destroy the time and profit of his fellow pupils and the teacher. We shall see, further on, that even if the pupil converses with his fellow pupils by whispering for good purposes—endeavoring by that means to get information about his lesson or to give information about it—he does so much to destroy the efficiency of his own or of his fellows' work so far as silent preparation is concerned.

If it is true, as scientific men tell us, that man has descended from the anthropoid apes, we can see more clearly the significance of this moral training which suppresses the tendency to prate and chatter. The mere instinct for expression of the half-cultured child is to utter what comes first to his mind. He pours out his impressions before he has allowed them to ripen by reflection. If he can repress the utterance of one thought until he can add another and another and another to it he can deepen his power of thought, whereas if he utters the thought carelessly as it arises in his mind it passes away from him and he does not make a synthetic thought by adding to the immediate impression all other thoughts that relate to it. This is the deep significance of the school virtue of silence. It makes accessible the depths of thought and reflection. It makes possible the individual industry of each and every pupil associated in the school. Each one can detach his industry from the industry of the whole and pursue original study and investigation by himself although surrounded by a multitude. This individual industry is prevented by anything on the part of his fellows which tends to distract him.

The fourth virtue that has been named is industry. Industry may be of various kinds, but the industry of the school is essentially study of the book. The pupil is to add to his own feeble and undeveloped powers of thought and observation these faculties as exhibited in the strongest of his race. The printed page is the chief means by which he adds to his own observation and reflection what has been observed and thought by men specially gifted in these things. The pupil shall learn by mastering his text-book how to master all books—how to use that greatest of all instruments of culture, the library. He shall emancipate himself by this means from mere oral instruction. In the case of oral instruction the pupil must wait upon the leisure of the teacher, trusting to his memory or writing down the words and pondering them on some future occasion. In the presence of the book he can take the sentences one by one and reflect carefully upon the meaning of each word and each sentence. The book waits upon his leisure. The book contains the most systematic presentation of its author's ideas. Through the book the observers and thinkers of the past become present. Those of distant and inaccessible countries come to his side. This shows us the significance of the kind of labor which the pupil performs in his school industry.

I can describe the nature of the schoolroom industry best by explaining the two kinds of attention which the pupil must cultivate and exercise in the schoolroom. There is, first, the attention which the class must give collectively to the recitation and to the teacher who conducts it, and there is, second, the individual industry of the pupil working by himself. I have already mentioned some of the advantages of the class recitation in discussing the elementary virtues of regularity and punctuality. But it is in the development of these two kinds of attention that the chief value of the class recitation consists. In the recitation, as it is called by us in America (or in the *lesson,* as it is called by English educators), the teacher examines the work of his pupils, criticizes it, and discusses its methods and results. The pupils in the class all give attention to the questions of the teacher and to the answers of their fellow pupils. Each one, as I have already described, learns both positive and negative things regarding the results of his own studies of the lesson. He finds some of his fellow pupils less able than himself to grasp certain points in the subject of study. He finds others who are more able than himself, pupils who have seen farther than himself and developed new phases that had escaped his attention. He is surprised, too, at sides and points of view which the teacher has pointed out; items of information or critical points of view that had escaped his own attention and the attention of his fellow pupils in the class. The pupil gains an insight into human nature such as he never had before. He sees the weaknesses and the strength of his fellows; he sees the superiority manifested by the teacher, who is maturer than he, and who has reinforced his own observation and insight by the observation and insight of observers and thinkers as recorded in books. He measures himself by these standards and comes to that most important of all knowledge, self-knowledge.

This kind of attention which he exercises in lessons or class exercises is a kind of attention which may be called critical alertness directed outward to the expressions of other minds, namely, of his fellow pupils and teacher. Step by step he watches carefully the unfolding of the lesson, comparing what is said with what he has already learned by his own effort. After the recitation is over he takes up the work of individual preparation of another lesson, but he has improved in some respect his method, because he is now alert in some new direction. He has an intellectual curiosity in some new field that he had not before observed; what the teacher has said or what some bright pupil has said gives him a hint of a new line of inquiry which he ought to have carried on in his mind when he was preparing his lesson of the day before. Now he is consciously alert in this new direction and he reaps a harvest of new ideas that would have been passed over in neglect had he not received the benefits of the kind of attention which I call "critical alertness" in the work of recitation or "lesson."

This kind of attention is something that cannot be developed by the pupil in any other way so well as in that school invention called the "recitation" or "lesson."

Let us now consider the other kind of attention which the pupil cultivates and exercises in school. While pupils of one class are reciting, the pupils of the other class are preparing their lesson. Each individual is or should be absorbed in the work of preparation, not jointly with his fellows, questioning them or answering them, but by absorption on the part of each in his own work without reference to the other pupils in the room or the teacher; each one must be able to study his own book and resist the tendency to distraction which comes from the lesson or recitation that is going on with the other class. To shut out from one's mind all objects that do not concern it and concentrate one's thoughts and observation upon a special given subject, whether it be a scientific presentation of the text-book or whether it be the investigation of a topic by means of objects themselves or by the use of many books—this kind of attention is of the utmost importance. It is that of individual industry, while the other kind is that of critical alertness. Critical alertness follows the thoughts of others; takes an active part in the dialogue which is going on. The ancients call this business of questions and answers and critical alertness the dialectic, and this kind of attention is that which is trained in dialectic. But the attention which is absorbed upon its object is a different matter, although of equal importance. The pupil should learn how to neglect the distracting circumstances of the schoolroom, the movements of pupils in the tactics of the class, the dialectic of question and answer going on with illustrations and points of interest, and equally the work of his fellow pupils in the class preparing themselves by absorbing study like his own. He lets these all slip by him, disciplining himself to abstract his attention from them and to hold himself in utter indifference to these outside events. He brings to bear his best intellect upon the problems of his task, critically questions the meaning of his author, and applies himself to the work of verifying by his own observation and reflection what is compiled for him by the author. He is learning by this private industry how to reinforce himself by the work of his fellow men; he cannot help himself through the help of others unless he verify their results. Verification is always an act of self-activity. Memorizing the text of the book, committing to memory what has been told one—this is not self-help until the internal work of verification has been accomplished.

The second kind of attention that we are here considering has therefore its most important feature in verification. What someone else has seen and recorded the pupil must see for himself, if possible. What someone else has reasoned out by inference he must reason out himself and test the result by the activity of his own intellect.

At first the pupil finds himself with feeble will power and unable to absorb himself in his own task. He is easily distracted by what is going on around him. By using his moral will in self-control he gains strength from day to day in concentrating his attention and in neglecting all that is not essential in his individual industry.

Having enumerated these four cardinal duties in the schoolroom—regularity, punctuality, silence, and industry—let us now note their higher significance reaching beyond the schoolroom into the building of character for life. The general form of all school work is that of obedience. The will of the pupil comes into relation with the will of the teacher and yields to its sway. The will of the pupil inhibits its own wayward impulses, suppresses them, and supplants them by a higher rational will. In the act of obedience to a higher will the pupil becomes conscious of responsibility. Responsibility implies a sense of freedom. The child becomes conscious of its ability to accept or refuse—to obey or disobey. It becomes conscious of its power to originate actions and to give a new form to the chain of causation in which it finds itself. The great fact in the schoolroom is that the pupil is held responsible at each and every moment for all that he does. If he forgets himself and uses his voice, if he whispers, if he moves from his seat, if he pushes a book off his desk by accident, all these things are brought back to him at once by the presiding teacher. He is responsible not only for positive acts but also for neglect. Whatever he does or whatever he leaves undone is his business; this is justly regarded as the most potent means of ethical instruction. To use the language of the founder of the great system of ethics in modern times, Immanuel Kant, the child learns in the school to have a sense of his "transcendental freedom." He learns that he and not his environment is responsible for what he does or leaves undone. He regards himself as the author of his deed; he recognizes it as true that he is in the midst of a flowing stream of causation; he is the focus of innumerable influences, all tending to move him in this or that direction or hold him in this or that position. But he recognizes himself as an original cause, a will power that can react on any and all the influences that are flowing inwards towards himself. He can modify this stream of causation; he can hold back and inhibit the several influences which flow towards him; he can shape all of these so as to conform them to the ideals of his freedom; he can act in such a way as to extend his influence upon the external world and upon his fellow human beings; he can act so as to realize his ethical ideals. This is the sense of transcendental freedom. Transcendental freedom does not mean that any person can do or perform anything that he wishes upon the external world, for that would be not merely transcendental freedom but absolute omnipotence. Transcendental freedom is not omnipotence, but the power to originate some modifications upon the stream of causality within which one finds himself. Freedom means self-determination instead of the determination of something else. The fact that a person could not modify anything in the world would not prevent him from having a transcendent freedom in case he could inhibit the influence flowing in upon him; if he could resist external influence he would thereby prove his freedom.

These considerations relate to what I have called the "semi-mechanical duties," notwithstanding they furnish so important a training to the will.

They constitute an elementary training in morals without which it is exceedingly difficult to build any superstructure of moral character whatever.

Moral education in the school, therefore, must begin in merely mechanical obedience, and develop gradually out of this stage towards that of individual responsibility.

II

The higher order of moral duties falls into two classes—those that relate to the individual himself, and those that relate to his fellows:

(a) *Duties to self.*—These are first physical, and concern cleanliness, neatness in person and clothing, temperance and moderation in the gratification of the appetites and passions.

The school can and does teach cleanliness and neatness, but it has less power over the pupil in regard to temperance. It can teach him self-control and self-sacrifice in the three disciplines already named, punctuality, regularity, and silence, and in so far it may free him from thraldom to the body in other respects. It can, and does, labor efficiently against obscenity and profanity in language.

Duties to self include, second, that of self-culture. This duty belongs especially to the school. All of its lessons contribute to the pupil's self-culture. By its discipline it gives him control over himself and ability to combine with his fellow men; by its instruction it gives him knowledge of the world of nature and of man. This duty corresponds nearly to the one named prudence in ancient ethical systems. The Christian fathers discuss four cardinal virtues—temperance, prudence, fortitude and justice. Prudence places the individual above and beyond his present moment, as it were, letting him stand over himself, watching and directing himself. Man is a twofold being, having a particular, special self, and a general nature, his ideal self, the possibility of perfection. Self-culture stands for the theoretical or intellectual side of this cardinal virtue of prudence, while industry is its practical side.

(b) *Duties to others.*—Duties to self rest on the consciousness of a higher nature in the individual, and of the necessity of bringing out and realizing this higher nature. Duties to others recognize this higher ideal nature as something general, and hence as also the true inward self of our fellow men.

There are three classes of duties toward others:

(1) Courtesy—including all forms of politeness, good breeding, urbanity, decorum, modesty, respect for public opinion, liberality, magnanimity, etc., described under various names by Aristotle and others after him. The essence of this virtue consists in the resolution to see in others only the ideal of humanity and to ignore any and all defects that may be apparent.

Courtesy in many of its forms is readily taught in school. Its teaching is often marred by the manner of the teacher, which may be sour and surly, or petulant and fault-finding. The importance of this virtue both to its possessor and to all his fellows demands a more careful attention on the part of school managers to secure its presence in the schoolroom.

(2) Justice.—This is recognized as the chief in the family of secular virtues. It has several forms or species, as, for example, *(a)* honesty, the fair dealing with others, respect for their rights of person and property and reputation; *(b)* truth-telling or honesty in speech—honesty itself being truth-acting. Such names as integrity, uprightness, righteousness, express further distinctions that belong to this stanch virtue

Justice, like courtesy in the fact that it looks upon the ideal of the individual, is unlike courtesy in the fact that it looks upon the deed of the individual in a very strict and businesslike way, and measures its defects by the high standard. According to the principle of justice each one receives in proportion to his deeds and not in proportion to his possibilities, wishes, or unrealized aspirations. All individuals are ideally equal in the essence of their humanity; but justice will return upon each the equivalent of his deed only. If it be a crime, justice returns it upon the doer as a limitation of his personal freedom or property.

The school is perhaps more effective in teaching the forms of justice than in teaching those of courtesy. Truth-telling especially receives the full emphasis of all the power of school discipline. Every lesson is an exercise in digging out and closely defining the truth—in extending the realm of clearness and certainty further into the region of ignorance and guesswork. How careful the pupil is compelled to be with his statements in the recitation and with his previous preparation!

Justice, in discovering the exact performance of each pupil and giving him recognition for it, may become injustice in case of carelessness on the part of the teacher. Such carelessness may allow the weeds of lying and deceit to grow up and it may allow the dishonest pupil to gather the fruits of honesty and truth, and by this it may offer a premium for fraud. The school may thus furnish an immoral education, notwithstanding its great opportunities to inculcate this noble virtue of honesty.

The private individual must not be permitted to return the evil deed upon the doer, for that would be revenge, and hence a new crime. All personality and self-interest must be sifted out before justice can be done to the criminal. Hence we have another virtue—that of respect for law.

(3) Respect for law, as the only means of protecting the innocent and punishing the guilty, is the complement of justice. It looks upon the ideal as realized, not in an individual man, but in an institution represented in the person of an executive officer who is supported with legislative and judicial powers.

The school, when governed by an arbitrary and tyrannical teacher, is a fearfully demoralizing influence in a community. The law-abiding virtue is weakened and a whole troop of lesser virtues take their flight and give admittance to passion and appetites. But the teacher may teach respect for law very thoroughly, on the other hand. In this matter a great change has been wrought in the methods of discipline in later years. Corporal punishment has been very largely disused. It is clear that with frequent and severe corporal punishment it is next to impossible to retain genuine respect for law. Punishment through the sense of honor has, therefore, superseded for the most part in our best schools the use of the rod. It is now easy to find the school admirably disciplined and its pupils enthusiastic and law-abiding—governed entirely without the use of corporal punishment.

The school possesses very great advantages over the family in this matter of teaching respect for law. The parent is too near the child, too personal to teach him this lesson.

III

Higher than the properly moral duties—those duties to self and to others—or at least higher than the secular or "cardinal" virtues—justice, prudence, fortitude, and temperance—are certain ones which are called "celestial" virtues by the theologians; these are faith, hope, charity, and their special modifications.

The question may arise, Whether any instruction in these duties can be given which is not at the same time sectarian? An affirmative answer will have to show only that the essential scope of these virtues has a secular meaning and that the secular meaning is more fundamental than in the case of the so-called cardinal virtues.

(1) Faith in a theologic sense means the true knowledge of the first principle of the universe. Everybody presupposes some theory or view of the world, its origin, and destiny, in all his practical and theoretical dealing with it. Christendom assumes a personal Creator having a divine-human nature, who admits man to grace in such a way that he is not destroyed by the results of his essential imperfection, but is redeemed in some special way. The Buddhist and Brahmin think that finitude and imperfection are utterly incompatible with the Divine Being, and hence that things of the world cannot be permitted to have real existence; they exist only in our fancy. Here is no grace and no redemption. Nature is not a real existence to such a theory, and hence also there can be no natural science. Faith in the divine reason is necessary for science.

The prevailing view of the world in Christian countries is very properly called faith, inasmuch as it is not a view pieced together from the experience of the senses, nor a product of individual reflection, unaided by the deep intuitions of the spiritual seers of the race.

Faith is a secular virtue as well as a theological virtue, and whoever teaches another view of the world—that is to say, he who teaches that man is not immortal and that nature does not reveal the divine Reason— teaches a doctrine subversive of faith in this peculiar sense, and also subversive of man's life in all that makes it worth living.

(2) Hope, the second theological virtue, is the practical side of faith. Faith is not properly the belief in some theory of the world, but in that particular theory of the world that Christianity teaches, so that hope is not a mere anticipation of some future event, but the firm expectation that the destiny of the world is in accordance with the scheme of faith, no matter how much any present appearances may be against it. Thus the individual acts, upon this conviction. It is the basis of the highest practical doing in this world. A teacher may show faith and hope in the view of the world which he expresses and in his dealings with his school—in his teaching of history, in his comments on the reading lessons, in his treatment of the aspirations of his pupils. Although none of these things may be consciously traced to their source by the pupils, yet their instinct will discover the genuine faith and hope. Nothing is so difficult to conceal as one's conviction in regard to the origin and destiny of the world and of man.

(3) Finally, charity is the highest of these virtues, in the sense that it is the concrete embodiment and application of that view of the world which faith and hope establish. The world is made and governed by divine grace, and that grace will triumph in the world. Hence, says the individual, "Let me be filled with this principle and hold within myself this divine feeling of

grace towards all fellow creatures." Charity is therefore not mere almsgiving, but a devotion to others. "Sell all thou hast ... and follow me." Faith perceives the principle; hope believes in it where it is not yet visible; charity sets it up in the soul and lives it. There might be conceived a faith or insight into this principle of divine grace and a hope that should trust it where not seen, and yet there be in the possessor of the faith and hope a lack of charity. In that case the individual would acknowledge the principle everywhere, but would not admit it into himself. With charity all other virtues are implied—even justice.

While courtesy acts towards men as if they were ideally perfect and had not defects; while justice holds each man responsible for the perfect accordance of his deed with his ideally perfect nature and makes no allowance for immaturity, charity or loving kindness sees both the ideal perfection and the real imperfection, and does not condemn, but offers to help the other, and is willing and glad to sacrifice itself to assist the imperfect struggle towards perfection.

The highest virtue, loving kindness or charity, has of all virtues the largest family of synonyms—humility, considerateness, heroism, gratitude, friendliness and various shades of love in the family (parental, filial, fraternal, and conjugal), sympathy, pity, benevolence, kindness, toleration, patriotism, generosity, public spirit, philanthropy, beneficence, concord, harmony, peaceableness, tenderness, mercy, grace, long-suffering, etc. The typical form of this virtue, as it may be cultivated in school, is known under the name of kindness. A spirit of true kindness, if it can be made to pervade a school, would be the highest fountain of virtue. That such a spirit can exist in a school we know from many a saintly example that has walked in the path of the Great Teacher.

From the definition of the principle it is easy to deduce a verdict against all those systems of rivalry and emulation in school which stimulate ambition beyond the limits of generous competition to the point of selfishness. Selfishness is the root of mortal sin, as theologians tell us, and the lowest type of it is cold, unfeeling pride, while envy is the type next to it.

In closing let us call up the main conclusions and repeat them in their briefest expression.

1. Moral education is a training in habits and not an inculcation of mere theoretical views.

2. Mechanical disciplines are indispensable as an elementary basis of moral character.

3. The school holds the pupil to a constant sense of responsibility and thereby develops in him a keen sense of his transcendental freedom;

he comes to realize that he is not only the author of his deed, but also accountable for his neglect to do the reasonable act.

4. Lax discipline in a school saps the moral character of the pupil. It allows him to work merely as he pleases, and he will not reinforce his feeble will by regularity, punctuality, and systematic industry. He grows up in habits of whispering and other species of intermeddling with his fellow pupils; neither doing what is reasonable himself nor allowing others to do it. Never having subdued himself, he will never subdue the world of chaos, or any part of it, as his life work, but will have to be subdued by external constraint on the part of his fellow men.

5. Too strict discipline, on the other hand, undermines moral character by emphasizing too much the mechanical duties, and especially the phase of obedience to authority, and it leaves the pupil in a state of perennial minority. He does not assimilate the law of duty and make it his own.

The law is not written on his heart, but is written on his lips only. He fears it, but does not love it. The tyrant teacher produces hypocrisy and deceit in his pupils. All manner of fraud germinates in attempts to cover up shortcomings from the eye of the teacher. Even where there is simple implicit obedience in the place of fraud and the like there is no independence and strength of character developed.

The best help that one can give his fellows is that which enables them to help themselves. The best school is that which makes the pupils able to teach themselves. The best instruction in morality makes the pupil a law unto himself. Hence strictness which is indispensable must be tempered by such an administration as causes the pupils to love to obey the law for the law's sake.

—William T. Harris,
Bureau of Education,
Washington, D.C.

A Brief for Latin
(1899)

Until the early years of the 20th century, Latin was considered the cornerstone of a liberal education. Most students, even those who were not planning to apply to college, studied Latin. As demands for utility and vocational training increased, Latin came under fire. Harris, a great defender of humanistic studies in the schools, found it necessary to defend the presence of Latin in the curriculum.

The Latin language is by common consent an essential part of higher education as conducted in the colleges, universities, professional and technical schools of the United States. Most of these institutions require the study of Latin in the secondary or preparatory schools which fit pupils for admission to their course of study, statistics showing that public high schools and private academies teach Latin to one-third or even one-half of all their pupils. In fact the number studying Latin is much larger than the number fitting for college or higher institutions, showing a conviction in the minds of the people that Latin is not merely an ornamental study but a useful study. The total number of pupils in the public high schools of the United States was, for 1897, 409,433. The number studying Latin was 198,014, or more than 48 per cent, of the entire number. Seven years before the number studying Latin was less than 35 per cent. Thus the proportion of pupils taking Latin had increased nearly 50 per cent, within a very short period. In the private academies and preparatory schools giving secondary instruction the total number of pupils for the same year was 107,633. Of these 50,236 were studying Latin, or nearly 47 per cent, of the entire number; this number increases year by year.

Forgotten Heroes of American Education, pages 369–372

But the revival of the study of Latin has extended also to the elementary course of instruction which includes the first eight years of school work, or, loosely stated, the pupils from six to fourteen years of age. An active movement has begun in later years to give a portion of these first eight years to the study of Latin, and a large number of schools now commence Latin in the eighth year of the course and some of them begin the study of Latin either in the eighth or the seventh year: and towns of Massachusetts are reported in 1897 as pursuing the study of Latin either in the eighth or the seventh and eighth years: Braintree, Brookline, Concord, Dedham. Gardner, Milton, Winchester, Woburn. These cities have an aggregate of 12,152 pupils, of which 1153 pupils are in the seventh and eighth years' work, nearly all the pupils in those grades pursuing the study of Latin. It is true that this movement does not prevail in the other States to the same extent as in Massachusetts, but it is rapidly extending.

To the countries using the romance languages,—France, Spain, Portugal, and Italy,—this revival of the study of Latin may seem strange, but it is easily explained when one considers the composition of the English language which, tho Germanic or Teutonic in its colloquial vocabulary and in its grammatical structure, nevertheless resorts to the Latin and Greek for all of its technical words and for all those words which express fine distinctions of thought or subtle shades of sentiment. Any large dictionary of English includes in its vocabulary three words of Latin or Greek origin out of every four. While good English contains comparatively few of these Latin and Greek terms on a printed page,—rarely more than from 10 to 16 per cent.,—yet it will be found that whatever is precise and technical in expression, as well as whatever contains fine discriminations of thought or delicate shades of feeling, is expressed in words of Latin origin.

Hence the people who speak English have a specific reason for founding their secondary and higher studies of language on the Latin tongue. In order to understand and use with propriety a technical term or a word expressing fine discrimination it is necessary to understand the colloquial word which corresponds to it; this is generally a word denoting things or events perceivable by the senses. The word for the sense-object is taken figuratively for the intellectual object. Technical terms in the English language are drier and less significant to the person unacquainted with Latin than the technical terms of the German language to a German, or those of the French language to a Frenchman, because the uneducated Englishman does not know the literal or colloquial meaning of the words used figuratively. The illiterate German understands the word *Wissenschaft* because he recognizes the word *wissen* in it which he uses every day to express the act of knowing; but the Englishman uses the word *science* and cannot recognize in it the root *sci,* which means to know, unless he is acquainted with Latin. For altho he uses the word *knowledge* corresponding to the word *Wissenschaft* in its composition, yet he makes a technical distinction between the words knowledge and science. A little study of Latin, such as is given in the high schools and academies, is therefore very useful to the English thinker, because it enables him to use with certainty and precision the words which express the results of careful thinking.

In a broader sense, however, Latin is essential to secondary and higher education for all European peoples, in fact for all the peoples which have derived their civilization from the Romans. It is found that in all the modern languages of Europe the distinctions of thought regarding the acquirement and transfer of property, and the formation of individuals into corporations for municipal or for business purposes, are of Latin derivation. A lawyer who did not give some attention to the study of Latin would get very little insight into jurisprudence. He would find himself embarrassed in using its technical terms. The people other than lawyers who had pursued a course of study from which Latin had been omitted would have little insight into the trend of their civilization. They could not expect to understand the present issues if they had no insight into the history of the development of those issues.

Students who have paid most attention to the course of study in academies and colleges have been impressed with the peculiar value of the Latin language as a branch of study for English-speaking peoples. They have taken note of the difference between the colloquial vocabulary and the vocabulary used for the expression of elevated thoughts or sentiments and have understood the peculiar reason why Latin is so important in the schools of England and the United States. They have also taken note of the general reason which makes Latin essential to higher studies in all modern civilized countries. The language of the Romans is the language of the political and civil organization of individuals into institutions, and these constitute our civilization. For the most part, the words expressing civil and political relations in all the languages of Europe are Latin.

In view of these considerations it is obvious that schools for secondary and for elementary, as well as for higher instruction suffer injury if a rule excluding Latin from the course of study is rigidly enforced.

Still another consideration must, however, be borne in mind. While there are social castes in all countries of Europe, and it is comparatively easy to separate the children of these castes and educate them in different schools, this is not possible in America. The children of poor people have the same opportunities here that the children of rich people have to improve their condition and to obtain directive power if they make the same outlay of industry and intellectual preparation. It is therefore distasteful to an American public to suggest an organization of education by which one class of schools shall educate the laboring people and those intended for careers in humbler walks of life, while a different kind of school shall be provided for the rich and for the children of the powerful in the land. A system of schools professedly intended for the working classes, and a course of study omitting those branches which give directive power, would quickly and properly fall into disrepute in the United States.

—William T. Harris,
Bureau of Education,
Washington, D.C.

The Future of the Normal School
(1899)

In this work, Harris explains his views on teacher education. He praises the move toward establishing professorships of education in universities. He also praises the work that normal schools were doing to prepare teachers. Modern-day readers will need to look beyond the title to the subject of the essay. Much good work on teacher education has been ignored because normal schools were marginalized from higher education and because few people today understand what normal schools were all about. Among other points, Harris is arguing for the creation and continued support of stand-alone institutions as well as units within universities that are dedicated specifically to teaching teachers.

With his deeply philosophical outlook, Harris provides his views on the curriculum that prospective teachers—at both the elementary and secondary levels— should study. He is arguing for a curriculum for all teachers that is culturally powerful, academically rich, and that integrates the various subject matter disciplines with methods of teaching. He also does not neglect the role that moral and intellectual philosophy should play in curriculum for teacher education. Toward the end of the essay, Harris identifies and praises numerous "teachers of teachers," as he calls them, who dedicated their lives to teaching teachers. These individuals would be good models for modern-day teacher educators and professors of education to emulate.

Many years ago I set myself to the work of studying the methods of schools for the training of teachers, having noticed the superiority of their graduates over those without professional education, both in furnishing skilled teachers and in inspiring them with a professional zeal that causes them to

Forgotten Heroes of American Education, pages 373–384

improve for many years after entering the work of teaching. I have tried to set down in this paper the grounds for commending the normal school as it exists for its chosen work of preparing teachers for the elementary schools, and at the same time urging the need of training schools with different methods of preparation for the kindergarten, below, and for the secondary school, the college, and the post-graduate school, above the elementary school.

In our time a new epoch is beginning in the study of educational methods. There is a widespread movement known as "child-study," which devotes itself to learning the natural history of infancy, childhood, and youth. It will discover the laws of development. It will learn how to take the child out of a lower form of intellectual activity into a higher form; how to prevent that mischievous arrest of development which is produced at present by too much thoroness in mechanical methods. It will know the pathology of education as it has never been known before.

Besides "child-study" there is progress in the invention of devices of instruction. These relate to the discovery of ways and means whereby the child is made more self-active in the process of learning and not so dependent on the teacher's powers of illustration.

In this direction an entire new field, that of Froebel's kindergarten, has been occupied and brought under inspection. The educative effect of the child's first playthings has been to some extent measured. The lullaby of the nurse, the first sight of the moon and stars, the meaning of imitation, the relation of what is symbolic to what is conventional; how the child becomes original and outgrows the merely imitative stage of mind; how to preserve his interest from step to step in a graded system of instruction— these are kindergarten problems that furnish much that is of consequence for the study of method in normal schools. But the most important advances in the study of educational methods, those which warrant us in speaking of a new era in the training of teachers as being on its advent, have resulted from the movement of colleges and universities to establish professorships in education. The university professor, taking up the work of preparation of teachers, has been obliged to plan for himself a different line of work from that of the State normal schools and the city training schools. He has to deal with students advanced beyond elementary and secondary studies into those of the higher education, and he must plan a suitable curriculum for a class of students not easily interested in the traditional normal-school course. This difference has gradually become apparent to both classes of teachers. It has become evident that the method of instruction, and the organization of the work of training teachers, should vary according to the grade of education. There is one method for higher education and another for elementary. Within each of these there should be a further discrimination of methods, so that five stages of method should be noted.

First, that of the kindergarten, which is adapted to what I call the symbolic stage of the mind, needs a method more like that used by the mother of the family than that of the traditional primary school. In the symbolic stage of intellect the child lets one thing stand for another thing and does not think fully in the logical terms of universal, particular, and singular. He does not understand things in their process of derivation. His intellect is an activity of noting resemblances and symbolizing one thing by another; and his willpower is chiefly a process of imitation—an attempt to body forth by his own effort some event that he sees in the world; for imitation is the symbolism of action, while pure symbolism is the imitative process of the intellect. Both are crude preliminary stages in the entire process of mastering the world by learning all the necessary steps to the true actuality.

Now since play unites these two child-activities, symbolism and imitation, it is evident that the method of first education with the child, say from two to six years, must have reference to the play-activity, and the first school which the child may enter should be a school having the general characteristics of the kindergarten.

The method of the primary school and the grammar school, the two divisions of the elementary school proper, is founded on the habit of mind that follows the symbolic. For after the symbolic stage of mind comes the conventional stage wherein the child struggles for the mastery of the signs adopted by civilization for the purposes of collecting and preserving the lessons of experience. These signs are, for example, the written and the printed alphabets, the notations of arithmetic, the technical terms used in geography, grammar, and history, and such other technical vocabularies as enter the elements of natural science and sociology. The child has also a practical technique to learn in the elements of drawing, penmanship, and the limited fields of experiment that must go with the mastery of the word-and-idea technique.

We can see at a glance how different the method of instruction in the elementary school must be from that of the kindergarten. In the latter, precision is not attempted in the technical sense, for that would involve an abuse of the intellect and of the will, at the tender age of three to six years. Its work of imitation is a loose sort of production which omits the greater part of the process necessary for the reality of that which is imitated. For instance, the child mimics the farmer sowing the seed or mowing the grass, but does not use seed, or a scythe that will cut anything. In fact (if we notice carefully) he does not imitate closely even the motions of the hand or arm. In the symbolic or imitative stage one thing stands for another, and one act for another, when there is only a superficial resemblance. Hence the child arrives at only crude unities of thought and action in the kindergarten. He is trained to look for unities rather than to find them. But imitation and symbolism strengthen mightily his power of attention and his development of bodily skill, while they give him the ability to understand the feelings and motives of the human beings around him. But in the elementary school the child is not taught to seek resemblances so much as to analyze and define accurately. He must now individualize facts and events rather than gather them into loose aggregates by means of symbols.

The chief characteristic of the method of teaching in elementary schools must then be accuracy of definition. The word must be made to recall the child's experience. He must be made to verify for himself by experiment all that can be reproduced by him without costing too much time. For there are many things in the infinite concourse of particulars that do not pay to verify by experiment. The good normal school shows the elementary teacher how to select the typical facts in each department for illustration and where to require much or little practical experiment in the way of verification. But everywhere the child's experience must be drawn upon for illustration.

In order to fit the teacher to perform this work, the normal schools of this country, since the first one was opened at Lexington under Cyrus Pierce, have followed substantially the same tradition and made the chief part of their course of study a review of the elementary branches—reading, writing, arithmetic, geography, history, and grammar.

It has often been said with the air of an apology that this review would be unnecessary if it were possible to secure pupils of advanced grade, implying by this that if the secondary course of an ordinary high school had been completed, this review work in the elementary branches would be dispensed with and certain advanced studies would be undertaken instead.

But this is not borne out by experience. The teacher who is to teach these elementary branches after graduation finds no work of preparation in the normal school half so valuable as this review of those branches in the light of more advanced studies. No work that is done in the secondary school—that is to say, the high school or the academy—is an equivalent for the normal-school work done on the same studies. What is learned for the first time in the elementary or the secondary school is learned as a step to what lies beyond. Thus arithmetic is a step toward algebra and geography a step toward the organic sciences such as biology, geology, and ethnology. When the pupil has climbed to the studies beyond, he drops the elementary steps out of sight. Of course it follows that, in the high school or the college, those lower branches are not reviewed in the light of the higher branches—arithmetic is not studied anew in the light of algebra and geometry; descriptive geography is not reviewed in the light of physical geography, botany, zoology, and geology; English grammar is not reviewed in the light of studies in Latin and Greek, or in philosophy and logic; nor the history of the United States seen in its relations to that of Great Britain and the Continental nations of Europe.

But the teacher needs precisely this re-examination of all his elementary branches in their relations to the higher studies that furnish them their rules and laws.

It has happened that the American normal school has taken up just this work of review from the beginning, and has performed it well during the entire sixty years of its existence.

It has induced in the young men and women preparing for the work of teaching a habit of looking at the lower branches in the light of the higher branches from which they derive their principles. This we may call the method of construction; it takes up a branch of study and views it constructively—for to study arithmetic in the light of algebra and geometry is to study it constructively. Its rules are derived from algebraic formulae and are to be demonstrated by algebraic processes. So the details of geography have their explanation in the formative processes that shape the land and water, all of which are treated in physical geography, and in the sciences of which it is a compendium. The higher the standard of preparation in the pupils who enter the normal school, the more profitable is this work of reviewing the lower branches in the light of the higher and thus studying them constructively.

A good teacher in any grade of work requires the reflective habit fully formed. The subject when first learned cannot be seen as derivative from still higher branches. Hence the average graduate of the high school who has not reviewed the elementary branches in the light of the high-school course of study cannot teach them so well as the normal graduate who has applied the secondary course of study to the elementary course in a constructive manner.

The first learning of a subject is and must be largely a work of the memory. For how can the pupil know the derivation of an object until he has first formed some acquaintance with its present state of existence? But the real knowing begins beyond the process of memorizing; it begins with reflection upon the data given and with the discovery of inter-relations and the process of derivation from higher sources.

The fact that the standard of admission by age into the normal school is higher by two years, three years, or even four years, makes a great difference in the work of studying branches constructively. Nothing is more important than age in the preparation for a reflective habit of mind.

Hence the normal school finds it possible to conduct all of its lessons with special attention to method. While the pupil of an elementary school learns a lesson in arithmetic, geography, or grammar only with the object in view of clearly understanding it, the normal-school pupil is always to think of the method of explaining this and making it clear to boys and girls.

He not only masters the branch of study as presented in the text-book or by the professor, but he studies critically the method of presentation of book and teacher and thus acquires a critical point of view.

The class work and recitations of the normal school therefore take the student by surprise at first. He supposed himself to understand already the simple branches,—geography, grammar, arithmetic,—but he discovers now that there were a thousand phases of each lesson which he had not before noticed. He sees the importance of a full preparation on the part of the teacher if he is to be able to take advantage of the opportunities which the class exercise will give him to correct wrong views and bad methods of preparing the lesson.

He therefore studies his second lesson with many side questions in view. He improves from day to day, and in the course of a year he has formed a new ideal of the best method of study. He has passed from the method of following the lead of the text-book and committing it to memory to the better method of critical investigation. Formerly he would have been well satisfied with a pupil who repeated verbatim the words of the book and would have done little to probe the understanding. Now he would go directly behind the words of the book into the pupil's understanding and teach him how to think—how to investigate for himself. For the teacher has acquired in the normal school the habit of comparing one statement with another and with the results of his actual experience. He penetrates the plan of construction of the book itself. This makes him a shining light for his pupils.

We must not suppose for a moment that any other fine qualities, any acquaintance with educational devices or what are called "fads" or fashions, will make up for a defect in this knowledge of the constructive method. The solid foundation of successful work would be lacking.

This view, if correct, will explain to us the improvement that has come to our elementary schools from the multiplication of public normal schools supported by the State or the municipality or founded on their model by private enterprise.

The records show that in the past seventeen years the enrollment in normal schools supported by States or cities has increased from about 10,000 pupils to something over 43,000. The attendance on normal schools founded and supported by private enterprise has increased from about 2000 to 24,000, tho the increase has been very slow in the past three years. I have obtained the earlier terms of this ratio by revising the data furnished in the reports of 1880. Up to 1890 the statistics of normal schools did not carefully separate the pupils enrolled in the preparatory department from those in the regular course of study. I have therefore revised the earlier data, which show 25,736 students in public and private normal schools in 1880, and reduced that number by a little more than one-half. Thus revised, the figures stand 12,000 in 1880 and 67,380 in 1897. In 1880 there were 240 normal students in each million of inhabitants; in 1897 there were 936 in each million.

The normal school, it may be said, in view of the explanation I have just now given of its instruction, has the general effect of making its pupils observant of methods.

The ordinary person sees results, but does not take note of the methods by which they are produced. Hence the teacher who has never received instruction in a normal school may happen to be a good teacher, but it is quite unusual for him to understand how he secures his own results; and he is not often able to profit by seeing the work of other good teachers. For he cannot readily see what method they use, not having acquired the habit of looking at methods. On the other hand the normal-school graduate can seldom visit a successful school without carrying away some new idea or at least some new device of method. Hence normal-school graduates continue to grow in professional skill for ten, twenty, or even thirty years, while it is said truly that the teachers not from normal schools usually reach their maximum skill in from three to five years. After that period degeneration is apt to set in because of the fixation of methods in ruts—a mechanical habit grows on the teacher who does not readily see how his mannerisms look to other people. He becomes a pedagog in the bad sense of the word and is a living caricature of his profession.

It would be supposed that what we have called the constructive method is a final one and good for all grades of pupils above the rank of elementary. There is, however, a difference between the method of elementary instruction and that of secondary; and a further difference between the latter and higher instruction.

The elementary course of study is adapted to the eight years of school life extending from the seventh to the fourteenth year of age. The course of study deals largely with what have been called "formal studies," namely with those relating to arts such as reading, writing, and numerical calculation, and hence, as we have before seen, the acquirement of the use of technical words as tools of thought. Although the distinction between formal studies and studies with a content is a superficial one, because all studies have a content and the higher studies relate more to a content that is made up of forms—for example, higher geology relates to the laws of succession of the rock strata and to the laws of action of cosmic forces— and these laws are forms that govern the geologic facts of observation—or, for another example, in biology science pays most attention to the mode of behavior of plants and animals, and behavior concerns the form of action, and this form of action determines the particulars of all life—the zoologist would be unwise who should neglect the study of the modes of expression and communication of bees and ants or of monkeys and crows on the ground that language is a formal affair.

Yet we must admit that the child under fourteen years of age, when he has mastered the technique of knowledge in the elementary school, has not yet acquired much knowledge of human nature nor of the world of facts and forces about him. He can grasp isolated details, but cannot make large combinations nor perceive whole processes when they are complex.

It is, therefore, a necessary characteristic of elementary instruction, in comparison with secondary or higher, that it must take the world of human learning in fragments, and that after all has been done to arouse thought and reflection the memory will have more to do than the thinking power. The child cannot separate so well the personal equation from the results of his observation, nor can he help his warped views or his narrow prejudices. He is full of superstitions, and cannot discriminate readily between what he actually sees and what he believes that he sees because he expected to see it.

From these reasons it is obvious that elementary instruction is perforce obliged to deal more with facts than with broad, general principles; that it must return oftener to the immediate object and dwell less on the process of its construction by producing forces. The training of the teacher in the habit of tracing a lower order of facts constructively into the higher order from which it has been derived makes him alive to the shortcomings of the mind of the child and more skillful in finding the facts that will serve as types of the process. If one is to describe in a word the success of the elementary teacher, he will say that he is successful in bringing typical facts before the mind of the pupil and in stimulating the pupil to analyze them and find the law or principle embodied in them.

Every fact is a synthesis or combination. For every fact takes together a series of things and events and also excludes other series of things and events. Let me illustrate this by the fact of the fall of the apple and the observation of the law of gravity by Isaac Newton. The fall of the apple was at first a fact of very small compass, so small indeed that a swine could comprehend it and hasten to appease his appetite by eating the apple! But the fact of the movement of the moon in its orbit was another fact that had no apparent relation to the fall of the apple until Newton happened to notice it, just then looking to see whence the apple fell and observing the moon through the branches of the tree. But to Newton thenceforward both facts became one in the law of gravity.

It is easy to say that minds differ by the size of the facts which they are able to think. The child's mind is comparatively feeble and makes small combinations; the youth in the high school has gained in power of thought and his facts are much larger and contain more heterogeneous elements—such as moons and apples, stars and mountains, land and sea and air, all tied together by gravitation.

Again, in this reference, the young man or young woman graduating from college has learned to think still more complex facts and, from three or four observations on a comet, to map out its path in the sky, or, from the form of a word and its meaning, tell the grade of culture of the people that used it.

The post-graduate student who is concentrating all his studies on a narrow field comes in time to know it exhaustively thru his own observations, and to Cuvier a single bone of some extinct animal enables him to draw the entire skeleton, or to Agassiz a scale reveals the whole fish, or to Lyell a pebble tells the history of its formation under the glaciers.

It is perfectly obvious that the teacher must be all the time carefully observant of the power of synthesis in the pupil's mind; that is to say of the caliber of the facts which he can think, and if he would be helpful to that pupil, he must know how best to strengthen his power of synthesis.

Secondary education deals with a second order of facts as readily as elementary education deals with the first order. The second order of facts consists of a group of things and events systematically arranged so that each fact or event throws light on all the rest, and all the rest in turn explain it. Such a group is a science. The secondary pupil has for the predominating activity of his mind the connecting of facts and events into such scientific wholes, following the tradition left by investigators whose united labors have made these sciences and left them to the race.

To the elementary pupil a typical fact is the chief mental object. But to the secondary student the object is a fact of the second order, namely a science in which a whole field of facts and events has run together into a higher fact. He is to learn how to see scientific relations everywhere.

Secondary instruction, properly so-called, lays stress on this scientific unity, which swallows up the many facts of its province much in the same way that the sea swallows up its waves. Secondary teachers need deeper studies such as can be found alone in the college or university. Because they deal with a tendency in their pupils to combine all primary facts into secondary facts or systems they have to govern the spirit of their teachings by a still higher principle, and this is the unity of the sciences. We see that, as any given science is a second order of fact, so the unity of the sciences is itself a third order of fact.

It is the comparative method that dominates higher education such as is given by the college or university in its academic course which leads to the degree of bachelor of arts. For each branch of learning is studied in the light of all the others in a genuine college course; its method is the comparative method.

Recapitulating for the sake of clearness: (1) the infancy period of education in the kindergarten requires a method of instruction adapted to the symbolic and imitative stage of the mind. (2) The elementary school demands the method that can seize and analyze typical facts, these facts being of the first order, that is to say, facts that are not yet treated as organized into groups by science but are capable of such treatment. (3) Secondary education requires the method which deals with the large facts that include entire groups of facts systematically arranged, while higher education deals with a still larger fact, namely the several sciences unified into a single group by the comparative method so that each science helps explain all, and all, each.

It is obvious that the method of higher education deals from first to last with a view of the world, a theory of the unity of nature and its purpose. It is the ultimate fact of the universe, what the poet Tennyson calls the

"Far-off divine event towards which the whole creation moves."

See every fact in its group, this is the scientific view. See every group of facts in the light of every other group, and you see the trend and purpose of the whole and possess a world-view.

It is true that a world-view is one of the first things given to the child by the family. It is given in the form of religion and on simple authority. But higher education has for its chief object the intellectual vision of the unity that makes the world an image of the divine Reason. That which was blind faith is to become intellectual and moral insight, as the result of the first part of higher education. But there is a second part of the higher education; it includes what is now called post-graduate work for the degree of Ph.D. This second part of higher education is specialized work with a view to form experts. It requires the student to perform experiments in the laboratory and to undertake researches in the library, and it accompanies these with round-table discussions called "Seminaries." In the post-graduate work the student selects a province so narrow that he may explore it thoroughly and add by original research some new piece of knowledge to the stock of human learning already extant. The number of advanced students taking this course for three years in laboratory or seminary work has increased in twenty-five years from 200 to 5000 or 25 times what it was in 1872. It is the work of the university proper as contrasted with the academic or philosophic course of study lasting four years and leading to the degree of bachelor of arts. The method of instruction in this department of post-graduate work is that of free investigation, aided by the example of professors gifted in the art of original discovery. To mention examples, that of Agassiz will occur to everyone as an eminent teacher of the highest method of natural science; Joseph Henry in physics, Chauvenet in mathematics; Lotze in philosophy, and Wundt in experimental psychology; Woolsey in constitutional law; Stanley Hall in child-study; Faraday in chemistry, and Huxley in biology. The list is too long to be printed here. But one will be able by these few names to recognize the method of the teachers of specialists.

Beside, but apart from this class, stand the teachers of the college undergraduates, and the teacher of teachers here is the professor who elevates into consciousness the method of giving young men and young women an insight into the world-view. Such men as the late Thomas Hill Green of Oxford and John Caird of the University of Glasgow; Cousin of France, and Schelling and Hegel of Germany; Mark Hopkins of Williams College and Professor Minor of the University of Virginia; Hickok of Amherst College and McCosh of Princeton—these and others of the same type have shown power to train up teachers who are skilled in the method of higher education for culture,—the undergraduate course, whose object is to see intellectually the unity of knowledge in philosophy and comparative science. Among the eminent teachers of teachers in secondary education one thinks of Sturm, who may almost be said to have created the type of the academy as a fitting school for the college or university. Samuel H. Taylor of Phillips Academy, Andover, is a good example of the teacher powerful in training secondary teachers, for he impressed his method very strongly on his pupils. Cyrus Peirce, of the first normal school in the United States, was emphatically the type of the instructor of teachers in elementary methods.

This survey of the five steps or stages in education and their differences of method bring us to the further consideration of the new era that is now opening for normal schools; for it is evident that no longer can the teaching of teachers be limited to one method, that of the elementary school. It must rather be a comparative study of methods investigating the proper way of presenting a given branch to a pupil in any one of the five stages, and discussing the modifications needed to adapt the subject to any one of the other four stages. In the department of education of the university the students will be taught how to present a branch of study symbolically according to the method of the kindergarten; by typical facts as in the elementary schools; scientifically as in the secondary school; comparatively as in the college; as a specialist would investigate it, in the post-graduate course.

Most important of all these methods is the true method of the academic or undergraduate course in the college. I have described it as comparative, dealing with the unity of the several branches of human learning and laying emphasis on the world-view implied by this unity.

The greatest additions to our educational theory will be derived from this study of method in the college. For it is grounded on the history of civilization (what the Germans name *Kultur-Geschichte*). The comparative history of civilization, or as it is called more frequently the philosophy of history, furnishes the ultimate principle by which to solve the deepest questions relating to the course of study, the educational values of each of the several branches, the construction of school programs, the limits in educative power of the several component stages in the fivefold system of education beginning with the kindergarten and ending with specialization in the university, involving the much discussed question of electives and substitutes in the course of study.

The discussions of these important questions will draw into controversy the directors of the present normal schools on the one hand and the professors of education in the universities on the other, and the future history of the normal school will show the gradual adoption of the *Kultur-Geschichte* standpoint—the discussion of all educational questions in the light of the history of civilization as a court of last resort.

Section 5

SELECTED WRITINGS OF ISAAC LEON KANDEL

Isaac Kandel (1881–1965) is a forgotten hero of American education. His educational vision is deeply rooted in the liberal arts tradition, specifically the social and political philosophy of Plato and Aristotle. Born in Romania and educated in England, Kandel came to the U.S. in the early 1900s. His ambition was to use his knowledge of the classics, which he studied as an undergraduate at the University of Manchester, to further the ideals of democratic education. During the early years of his career, Kandel expressed admiration for John Dewey and the emerging tradition of Progressive education. However, Kandel began to criticize Progressive ideas and practices in the early 1930s. By 1940, he had become one of the nation's most knowledgeable, insightful, and trenchant critics of Progressivism.

After attending elementary and grammar school in Manchester, Kandel enrolled at the University of Manchester. He graduated in 1902 with a Bachelor of Arts degree in classics. He then began to study in the University's department of education and earned a Master's degree, in education, in 1905. He completed his teacher certification in 1905 as well.

In 1905, Kandel moved to Ireland, where he accepted a teaching position at the Royal Academical Institute in Belfast. In the summer of 1908, he met William Bagley while the two of them were studying at the University of Jena in Germany. Bagley convinced Kandel that he should move to the U.S. and study toward a Ph.D. degree at Teachers College, Columbia University. Kandel moved to the U.S. in 1908 and began his

Forgotten Heroes of American Education, pages 385–386
Copyright © 2006 by Information Age Publishing

coursework at Teachers College. His studies focused on the history and philosophy of education. For his dissertation, he completed a study on elementary teacher education in Germany.[1]

After working for the Carnegie Foundation for the Advancement of Teaching, Kandel was offered a faculty position at Teachers College in 1915. Kandel almost single-handedly created the field of comparative education during the next thirty years. He retired from Teachers College in 1947, at which point he accepted a position as Professor of American Studies at his alma mater, the University of Manchester. He held this position from 1947 to 1950. He continued to write books, articles, and monographs until the time of his death in 1965.

Kandel worked to spread the ideals of liberal education to all people throughout the globe—regardless of race, class, or gender. He was an outspoken advocate for teachers and the profession of teaching. He also made the history and philosophy of teacher education one of his primary areas of study. He was held in high esteem by scholars of education around the world.[2]

Kandel authored or co-authored more than forty books, monographs, and reports, edited another forty, and wrote more than three hundred articles and reviews. Kandel's scholarship, moreover, has been translated into French, German, Spanish, Italian, Portuguese, Dutch, Chinese, and Arabic. His accomplishments as an educational historian, educational philosopher, and scholar of comparative education eclipse the achievements of most scholars from his time period. Kandel's criticisms of the Progressive's ideas, however, placed him outside the mainstream of American educational thought. Having fallen afoul of the Progressivist consensus, Kandel—a towering figure in American education—was ignored by Progressive writers of the history of education.

---

1. Isaac L. Kandel, "The Training of Elementary School Teachers in Germany," unpublished Ph.D. diss., Teachers College, Columbia University, 1910.
2. Lawrence A. Cremin, "Isaac Leon Kandel (1881–1965): A Biographical Memoir," in *National Academy of Education,* Vol. I (Syracuse, NY: National Academy of Education, 1965–74), pp. 137–142; Robert G. Templeton, "Isaac L. Kandel's Contributions to the Theory of American Education," unpublished Ph.D. diss., Harvard University, 1956; Erwin W. Pollack, "Isaac Leon Kandel: A Pioneer in Comparative and International Education," unpublished Ph.D. diss., Loyola University of Chicago, 1989; Robert Ulich "In Memory of Isaac L. Kandel, 1881–1965," *Comparative Education Review* 9 (October 1965): 255–257; see, also, William W. Brickman, "I. L. Kandel, 1881–1965," *School and Society* 93 (October 30, 1965): 388–389.

The Influence of Dewey Abroad
(1930)[1]

Isaac Kandel was asked to deliver this address at John Dewey's 70th birthday celebration, which was held in 1929 at the Horace Mann auditorium at Teachers College, Columbia University. Since Kandel was internationally known at the time for his work on comparative education, he was the perfect choice for someone to discuss the question of the extent to which Dewey's ideas were impacting other countries. Kandel begins by explaining how difficult it is to assess Dewey's influence overseas. Nonetheless, he identifies several countries where Deweyan works, specifically his books and articles on educational philosophy, had been translated, read, and discussed.

What is most interesting here is the fact that Kandel did not take this opportunity to shower praise on Dewey's work like many of Dewey's followers did. Kandel, to be sure, had respect for Dewey, but, given that Dewey was in the audience when Kandel gave this address, his remarks are decidedly modest. Kandel gently criticizes many of the movements in educational theory that were popular at the time, almost all of which were being advocated by Dewey's followers. He concludes the paper by supporting Dewey's insistence that his philosophy not be reduced to a simple formula and by noting that Dewey's influence abroad will grow in the years to come.

It is difficult at a time when education throughout the world is passing through a period of unrest and transition to evaluate all the influences that

---

1. An address on the occasion of the Dewey Seventieth Birthday celebration, October 18, 1929, in the Horace Mann Auditorium, Teachers College.

Forgotten Heroes of American Education, pages 387–392

underlie so widespread a movement. Still less is it possible to estimate the influence of an individual. The character and purposes of educational systems from the second half of the nineteenth century to the close of the War were in most countries so definitely based on national aspirations and nationalistic indoctrination as to preclude any extraneous influences that seemed to challenge the claims of the governmental authorities in charge. Administrative centralization with fixed national aims and purposes, with prescribed curricula and courses of study, and with uniform methods was deliberately set against innovations. It is worth noting that the elementary school programs remained virtually unchanged in Prussia from 1872 until the post-War reconstruction and in France from 1887 to 1923. The theorist was free to theorize and dream his educational Utopias; practice followed the dictates of the authorities. Private initiative in education, if not rigorously controlled, was dominated by the indirect imposition of examination requirements and teacher certification, while teacher preparation was strictly controlled by regulations and prescriptions in order to produce a teacher of the desired pattern, the craftsman skilled in carrying the prescriptions into the classroom. It is significant that the first experiments that ushered in the new school movement began under the freer administrative atmosphere of England at Abbotsholme and Bedales and that the influence spread thence to Germany in the *Landerziehungsheime* and to France in the *Ecole des Roches*.

There were, besides, other retarding influences that militated against the introduction of new ideas in education. The traditional emphasis on knowledge and information, in many places on encyclopedism, combined with the social and economic privileges that were awarded for book learning, developed a certain attitude of mind on the part of the public that the function of the school is to impart nothing more than a definite round of knowledge. Nor did the new psychology find a sufficiently strong foothold in the institutions for the preparation of teachers to bring about any modifications of importance either in outlook or in practice. At the same time, the general attitude that has prevailed abroad toward the philosophy of pragmatism did not tend to render educators receptive to its educational implications. Further, the prevailing prejudices on American intellectual life did not predispose the European to look favorably on either American theory or American practice as models worthy of study or of imitation. Finally, it was not easy for the casual visitor from abroad to discern the influence of any particular philosophy in American education; in the field of education an ounce of practice would have had a greater effect on the practitioner than a pound of theory. It must be remembered that even in this country it is only within some twenty years that the imagination of the American schoolman has been stirred by Dewey's philosophy of education, even though it was so essentially an outcome and interpretation of American life.

No apology is necessary for this somewhat lengthy explanation of the reason for the difficulty in appraising Dewey's influence abroad. And yet, by a coincidence, interest in Dewey is developing in accordance with his own principles of thinking; if foreign educators are beginning to show an interest in his work and influence, it is in response to a felt need. Education has everywhere reached a fork in the road; the few tentative gropings in a new direction that were made before the War are becoming realities; old traditions and old practices are everywhere being questioned; and everywhere the tendencies seem to center around the same aims. This movement is marked by the following characteristics. In place of the strict centralization of educational systems with their rigid emphasis on definitely prescribed standards in methods, courses of study, and attainments, there is a demand for decentralization and freedom for local determination. In place of the rigid control of the teachers there is a movement for more freedom, for more initiative, for a greater recognition of the teacher as an educational scientist rather than as a craftsman.

Prescribed courses of study are giving way to outlines and suggestions to be adapted by the teacher in accordance with the character of the school and its environment. More general is the attack on knowledge for its own sake and especially on knowledge unrelated to the life and needs of the pupil. In place of learning as synonymous with seat and book work or assimilation at the teacher's dictation there is a demand for new methods that will put the pupil in a position to learn through his own interest in a problem, while the rigid pupil-teacher relationship is to be replaced by the class and school as a cooperative community.

Fundamentally, then, the basic principles in which these demands have their origin are three: greater respect for the individuality of the child, the school as a social institution, and activity as the process of learning. It is now recognized that the new democracies must educate not subjects but free and responsible individuals living in close relation to the world around them, able to play their parts in its everyday work and capable of interpreting it in relation to their own lives. This means first that the school must reflect society and at the same time be a society, and secondly that each pupil must be regarded as a growing personality. The walls of the school are being broken down; the school from which the regulations formerly excluded parents now recognizes that its welfare depends on closer cooperation between parents and teachers. For the present, these movements and demands are aspirations only, although there are sufficient examples of their incorporation into practice.

Up to the present, the new aims have in the main affected chiefly the education of the masses. And yet there are stirrings in the secondary field too. Everywhere there is unrest and dissatisfaction with the traditional conceptions of culture and of liberal education. The democratic strivings for secondary schools for all lead logically to a new orientation in which the narrow academic definition of culture must yield to a redefinition in the light of modern social and economic organization. What is cultural and what is vocational are being subjected to a reinterpretation, although at present the steps are somewhat tentative and uncertain.

There is still another field in which the new movements promise far-reaching changes. The attempts to impose European standards and practices on backward peoples have at last been recognized as ludicrous. Here, too, the basic starting point is the principle that education is not synonymous with book-learning but implies teaching how to live and that in relation to the environment of the peoples to be educated.

A certain similarity will be found between these tendencies and the educational philosophy of Dewey. How far these tendencies have been influenced directly by Dewey or indirectly by American pedagogy it would be hazardous to guess. To the average teachers abroad, especially in the elementary schools, the major portions of his writings have been inaccessible because of their lack of familiarity with English; the secondary school teacher and the university professor have not, as a rule, been interested in educational reform of a fundamental character. The absence of centers for the study of education as a university subject was a further limitation on the spread of his ideas. Thus there was left the individual student of educational theory who was sufficiently venturesome to explore abroad. Perhaps the only key that is available to indicate the interest in Dewey's writings is to be found in the number of translations. It is significant that more of Dewey's educational works have been translated than of his contributions to pure philosophy. Translations have appeared of practically all of his educational writings. One or more have been published in most of the European languages—French, German, Russian, Hungarian, Bulgarian, Greek, Italian, Spanish, and Swedish—and in Arabic, Turkish, Chinese, and Japanese, while special editions of his earlier works have been published in England. The literature about Dewey has been slight but it is noteworthy that of fourteen articles or books on his educational theory the majority are of recent date, although the first goes back as far as 1901, when an American student wrote a dissertation on his doctrine of interest for the doctor's degree in a German university.

There is, however, every evidence that the interest in educational reform everywhere and the search for light and leadership is directing increasing attention to the contribution of Dewey. It is admitted that the first stimulus for educational reform in Russia, which antedated the Revolution by nearly ten years, was obtained some twenty years ago by Zelenko's familiarity with Dewey's work; through Zelenko and through a study of Dewey's writings

Shatsky was inspired to undertake his educational experiment; more recent developments have tended to give to education in Russia its particular local and political coloration, and external influence is disclaimed. The reform of education in Mexico shows definite traces of the same inspiration, while in Turkey Professor Dewey has served as the official adviser on the reorganization of the educational system. In China Dewey's principles have been one of the guiding factors in the reform of education in general and in the inauguration of a number of experimental schools. His lectures delivered during his stay of two years in China were printed and passed through ten editions in a short time, so that every Chinese educator who wished to be modern adopted the slogan that "Education is life and the school is a society." Similar influences are evident in the liberal movements that are now beginning to bear fruit in Japan. In India widespread attention has been attracted to an educational experiment conducted by an American educator in the practical application of Dewey's theories, while another experiment conducted by an American disciple in Ceylon has shaken the authorities out of their complacent acceptance of tradition. In all these countries the philosophy of Dewey was carried abroad by former students influenced by him directly or indirectly by his followers; in some of them Professor Dewey has, on invitation, given series of lectures. In England we have it on the authority of Professor Nunn that Dewey has been one of the educational leaders who "did much to emancipate the professional intelligence of the present generation of teachers." So far as Germany is concerned, Erich Hylla, an official in the Prussian Ministry of Education and author of a recent work on American education, pays a tribute to the influence of Dewey's educational philosophy which reached Germany indirectly through Kerschensteiner; and Kerschensteiner himself makes the following statement in his *Autobiography:* 'Dewey's practical proposals for organization coincide to a great extent with mine, and the clarity and lucidity of his thinking on education have on many occasions given me the courage to try out my own ideas. Many of my ideas, when still somewhat obscure, have been clarified through the intensive study of his writings." But with one or two exceptions Dewey's writings have remained unknown to German students unfamiliar with English, a defect which is about to be corrected by the publication of Hylla's translation of *Democracy and Education.* The International Conferences on education, especially that of the New Education Fellowship, are focussing marked attention on American education and the forces that have made it and will inevitably lead to more widespread study of its leading philosopher and interpreter. Similar results may be expected from the growing interest abroad in American life and thought and the exchange of educational visits. Thus many of the two thousand foreign students who have passed through Teachers College will undoubtedly have been affected by Dewey's works.

When it is recalled that the realization of Dewey's theories in the practice of this country has been achieved mainly in the last fifteen or twenty years, the extent of the interest already manifested abroad in his writings is but a forecast of the influence that they will most certainly exercise in the ferment of thought on education that marks the present period. If it has been impossible to refer to this or that tangible realization in school practice, it has been because, unlike other leaders who now occupy the educational stage, Dewey has refrained from reducing his theories to a practical formula, definite and applicable under all conditions and circumstances. It is characteristic of his contributions to the philosophy of education that Dewey does not insist on the *ipsissima verba magistri* so much as on stimulating thought, on the development of a critical attitude, and on the application of individual effort to the solution of problems as they are recognized, and it is through this general ferment that his influence is most likely to be enduring, both in this country and abroad.

Is the New Education Progressive?
(1936)[1]

By 1936, Isaac Kandel was highly critical of Progressive education. This article is one example of the numerous criticisms that flowed from his pen. He begins this paper, which he delivered as a radio address, by stressing that the ideas promoted by Progressive educators are thousands of years old, despite their claims that what they had to say was revolutionary. Such ideas as pupil-initiated lessons and education for a changing civilization, Kandel notes, were put forward by Greek thinkers like Aristophanes in the 5th century B.C.E.

Kandel then provides an overview of the criticisms that American Progressive educators had leveled at schools for at least the past thirty years. Among other points, he challenges their use of the word "freedom," and then admonishes them to define specifically what they mean when they use this term. Next, he makes the argument that freedom always implies social responsibility, which Progressives often forgot. In a related point, Kandel asserts that the Progressive's theories rejected the need for an overall social philosophy for American education. With so much emphasis on individual freedom, Kandel claims, Progressives had abandoned the attempt to ground the profession of teaching in a principled social philosophy of education. Kandel also condemns Progressive educators for their rejection of content in the curriculum. Their worship of individual student interest, Kandel asserts, led them to promote a theory that gave students what they "wanted," but ultimately taught them little.

---

1. Broadcast over WEAF Radio, December 9, 1935.

Forgotten Heroes of American Education, pages 393–399

Kandel's solution to the problem that he addresses in this paper is one that he expressed hundreds of times throughout his career. The profession of teaching, he argues, should concentrate on teaching teachers. He contends that well-prepared and skilled teachers who understand the social and philosophical significance of their profession are the best hope for creating a solid, long-lasting profession of teaching.

The problem which we are discussing today is just about twenty-five hundred years old. Even though progressive educators claim to have made a new discovery, the type of education for which they stand is, except for its modern dress and scientific terminology, not very much unlike that at which the Greeks laughed when it was presented to them by Aristophanes in his play, *The Clouds*. Briefly, the issue then as now was concerned with freedom for the child, with individual initiative and choice, with the place of authority and standards in the education of the young, and with education for change. The issue has been revived over and over again in the history of education; progressive theories have been advanced; new schools have been established to put these theories into practice; they had their day, and what was good in them was incorporated in regular school practice and the rest discarded as unsound. The result has been that what the progressives choose to describe as the conservative or static school has itself advanced by the accumulation of principles and practices that proved to be sound and feasible. This has been particularly true of the American public school which in the last thirty-five years has shown a remarkable vitality and readiness to absorb new ideas. Like any other social institution the school has developed by a process of slow evolution, while progressive education has sought to transform the school by the acceptance of revolutionary innovations without taking into account whether such innovations are sound and valid.

Indeed, it is a major feature of the strategy of progressive education to begin by decrying everything that has ever been done in the past and to ignore the existence of any values, intellectual or moral, in the history of human civilization. Despite the obvious and recognized changes which have been going on in the so-called conservative or traditional school not only in this country but elsewhere, changes to which, it would be foolish to deny, progressive theories have made some contributions, the same charges and the same criticisms continue to be brought against the school. The criticisms usually assume the following forms: Education is tied to outworn traditions and fails to function. The schools continue to transmit the traditional conception of what parents and the public consider to be essentials. All the processes that enter into education are dominated by static and outworn meanings, which have been authoritatively handed down from the time when the older and more privileged sections of society were in positions of power. In this way knowledge has acquired a sort of sacred fixity and learning is the process of the acquisition and acceptance of facts and information on authority.

Under such conditions the pupils are trained to compliant conformity through a mass process which makes for standardization. Like empty jars they are filled up with useless, formal, dead material with the result that they are merely adjusted to the *status quo* of society. The educative process consists in the hard and meaningless grind of acquiring a body of solutions formulated by adults from past experience instead of preparing for a changing civilization. It is admitted that there have been some reforms and some progress, but they have been piecemeal and have not affected the actual fabric of the school. What is needed is a thoroughgoing revolution and the complete reorganization of the school in every aspect.

Now nothing is so easy and simple as destructive criticism, particularly when it is not based on facts. These wholesale charges which are brought against the traditional school may have been true generally at one time and in some places. But even if they were true, they ignore the actual transformations that have taken place and they refuse to consider the reason why society has had schools at all. Admitting that the old psychology upon which the educative process used to be based was unsound and admitting that much of the knowledge that was transmitted was formal and useless, the facts show that society's first interest in establishing schools from the earliest times down to the present has been to preserve itself and to maintain its own stability. And certainly in the United States, when public-school systems were first established, their purpose was to promote enlightenment among the citizens. Even if the charges and criticisms are taken at their face value, those who bring them have still to explain how with education, as it has been, the remarkable changes in all fields of human endeavor have taken place unless it has been through the trained intelligence of individuals.

And yet the objection is raised that the education of the traditional school trains for adjustment to society as it is instead of for change. By this the progressive educators mean that these schools train only for the acquiescent acceptance of authority instead of developing the enquiring mind and a free personality. The first principle upon which the progressive schools are based is that of freedom for the child. What do they mean by freedom? So far as one can gather they mean that the child shall be permitted to follow his own urges and drives and satisfy his own wants and bent; the child, according to this theory, will become self-directive only by discovering for himself those activities and purposes that give him satisfaction and by avoiding those things that fail to do so. No obstacles must be put in his way lest imposition from without thwart his purposes, kill his initiative, pervert his personality with maladjustments, and end by indoctrinating him with ideas and knowledge that are not his own. There seems to be inherent in this theory a concept of absolute freedom which never has been and never will be possible of attainment. For, if history teaches anything, it is that freedom has been a conquest for which man has had to struggle. Freedom is not an inherent right of the child but something which he has to learn and to acquire at the same time that he learns and acquires the meaning of duty and responsibility. If it is true that until the close of the Nineteenth Century the emphasis was placed on discipline, unquestioned and unreasoned, one would be inclined to say that progressive education has run to the opposite extreme of advocating the cult of freedom, absolute and unrestrained. And yet while the arguments for freedom, as contrasted with the old rigidity of discipline in the past, are sound, there is a tendency to forget that freedom, if it has any meaning in organized society, always implies a corresponding responsibility in its use; it implies the recognition of duty based not on unquestioned but on intelligent acceptance of authority and discipline.

What this means, in other words, is that an education which fails to recognize social aims and purposes is meaningless. Correlative with the insistence on freedom the progressive educators build their programs on the principle of growth of the child. Growth, they say, is the interaction between the child and his environment, which is true in the sense that all experience of any kind has some effect on the individual. But schools, as agencies of formal education, are established by society with certain definite aims in mind and these aims should define the direction of a child's growth. And yet as one examines the literature of progressive education there seems to be a complete absence of any attempt or any desire to define this direction except in terms of the individual's own urge to satisfy his needs and interests. An examination of this literature fails to reveal any explicit references to social aims or purposes, except that very indirectly it is hoped that the child will become socialized through shared experiences. The slogans which are most frequently reiterated are self-government, self-reliance, self-development, self-expression, self-activity, creative acts, pupil activity, pupil interests, individual initiative, pupil freedom, and free activity, but nowhere is there found any intelligible definition of direction. One is reminded of the conversation between the cat and Alice. "'Then it doesn't matter which way you go,' said the cat. '—So long as I get somewhere,' added Alice as an explanation."

Starting with a false notion of freedom and a refusal to define aims or goals for education except the self-direction of the child, and adding to these premises a little mental hygiene and psychoanalysis, progressive educators further refuse to define the curriculum and course of study. To do so would impose something set-out-to-be-learned or something fixed-in-advance for the pupil. All that is necessary is to confront the plastic pupil and his urges, drives, wants, and impulses with the environment and allow him to direct himself in the making of choices without any other standards or values than those which he develops himself by discovering what works or what succeeds or what satisfies. The function of the teacher is to guide but to guide by intruding himself as little as possible. In fact the old adage has been reversed and it is the teacher who should be seen and not heard. An American humorist, Dooley, once said that "It doesn't matter what you teach a child, so long as he doesn't like it"; the progressives appear to say that "It doesn't matter what a child learns so long as he does like it."

Such a theory seems very plausible; there is something attractive in seeing a classroom of pupils busily engaged in doing something that they think satisfies their wants—ships one year, houses another, dolls another. But if progressive education is aimless from the social point of view, it is in danger also of becoming contentless from the curriculum point of view, since nothing must be fixed in advance. The activities and the busy work in which pupils engage, the wide range of interests displayed by the children are the pride of the progressive school. It matters little that such activities or interests bear no relation to any orderly progress of the mind; the child who engages in them is learning, it is claimed, to direct himself and to meet novelly developing situations. It is sometimes forgotten that to meet novelly developing situations one must have a fund of knowledge and information with which to meet them. This the progressives refuse to accept as fixed-in-advance and inhibiting the growth of personality. And so children at the age of eleven or twelve are expected to direct themselves by grappling with such questions as "How people outside of Europe lived in the Thirteenth Century" and "How the civilizations outside Europe changed the life of the Europeans in home life, furniture, food, clothes, business, trade, art, science, etc." The result of such exercises in research, the discovery of knowledge and its interpretation is a precocity, which, if it does not lead to overstrain, may result in the stagnation of intellectual interests.

The fact is that no system of formal education is likely to succeed or to be fruitful unless it is rooted in a social culture and guided by strong social motives. Progressive education has been tried in two situations and more generally than in the United States. After the Revolution in Russia the doors of the schools were thrown wide open and every type of free experimental education was welcomed; the teacher was relegated to the position of guide and umpire; discipline was to result from shared social experiences. After nearly fifteen years of experimentation the leaders in the Communist Party admitted failure and returned to the bourgeois concept of a school with an ordered and fixed-in-advance program of studies, defined and prescribed by the authorities and administered by the teachers with full responsibility for discipline and control of progress through examinations. So too Republican Germany permitted the schools to experiment in their own way, with no stated aims other than the self-direction of the pupils through activity; each teacher was permitted to go his own way. The result of this experiment was chaos and rampant individualism which paved the way for a Revolution to subordinate the individual wholly to the State.

A sound system of education seeks to harmonize the claims of society and the interests and abilities of the individual; it must be guided to the attainment of ends and purposes, social and cultural, which society expects its schools to serve. But this does not mean that either society or its culture remains static. Those who today oppose the view that pupils should only learn those things that meet an immediately felt need in a present situation insist upon the formulation of curricula and courses of study in an orderly sequence, built upon the interests of the child at the start but making those interests over into acquired knowledge, attitudes and ideals that are socially valuable and significant. Progressive educators, starting with the unorganized and confused interests and experiences of the child, seem to expect the child to find his own way out of the confusion. Those who are charged with being conservative, however, insist that the school is an agency for carrying out certain aims and purposes, that these aims and purposes should serve as guides for the content to be learned, and that the child's interests and abilities should furnish the basis for the organization and sequence of the content. From progressive education they are willing to borrow certain principles of method, but on the understanding that a methodology is not a substitute for a well-founded social philosophy of education. It is as foolish to expect a child to grow in a right social direction along the lines of his own felt wants as it is to expect a man to find his way in unfamiliar territory, without a map or a compass. Organized subject-matter constitutes that map and compass which race experience has sifted out as the most valuable for its continued progress. But even when given the map and compass the child needs to be trained in their use and that training again he cannot acquire without direct instruction from a teacher who understands the child's needs as well as the map to be explored. To relegate the teacher to the position of a bystander ready to guide and to offer advice when called for is to degrade his position. Nothing has been more significant and striking in the story of the so-called child-centered school than the fact that the removal of a particular teacher means a change in its character. So that finally, the expectation that the problems of education can be solved by new methods and devices, by pitting child wants, drives, and urges against organized subject-matter is doomed to disappointment, for it is none of these things but the teachers that make a school. And if American society has to choose between building an education upon the self-direction of the child's wants and interests and entrusting education to a body of well-prepared and skilled teachers, the experience of centuries is strongly in favor of the second choice. There is far greater hope for social progress in the responsible freedom of a master-teacher than in the undirected freedom of progressive education. That is the only possible guarantee and hope of progress in education.[1]

---

1. Some readers of this article may be inclined to criticize the version of Progressive Education given above. Unlike advocates of progressive education who draw on their imagination for a picture of the conservative school, the author's account of progressive education is based on Professor W. H. Kilpatrick's *Reconstructed Theory of the Educative Process* and the idealized activity school in the *Thirty-third Yearbook* of the National Society for the Study of Education, Part II, pp. 72ff.

Dr. Alexis Carrel, in *Man the Unknown*, p. 21, makes the following pertinent reference to progressive education:

> There is no doubt that children are much happier in the schools where compulsion has been suppressed, where they are allowed exclusively to study those in which they are interested, where intellectual effort and voluntary attention are not exacted. What are the results of such an education? In modern civilization, the individual is characterized chiefly by a fairly great activity, entirely directed toward the practical side of life, by much ignorance, by a certain shrewdness, and by a kind of mental weakness which leaves him under the influence of the environment in which he happens to be. It appears that intelligence itself gives way when character weakens.

Prejudice the Garden Toward Roses?
(1939)

Ten months prior to the publication of this article, William Bagley and his like-minded colleagues met in Atlantic City to initiate the Essentialist movement in American education. Isaac Kandel was not present at this first meeting in Atlantic City, but he was in full agreement with the ideals advanced by the Essentialists in March of 1938. This paper is the first essay that Kandel published regarding educational theory after the founding of Essentialism. He was demonstrating publicly his support for the Essentialist's efforts. His unique title comes from a story by English poet and philosopher Samuel Taylor Coleridge. Kandel quotes Coleridge toward the end of the paper not to agree with the novelist, but rather to show the detrimental effects that bad teaching—or, in this case, no teaching—can have on society.

Kandel believed that teachers must have subject-matter, a curriculum, and a clear purpose in mind when they teach, instead of simply allowing the "garden"—their students—to grow in every possible direction. Children can grow like weeds, he maintains, unless the gardener takes care to tend and nurture them, in order to help them to develop educationally in the way they should grow. Kandel was critical of Progressive educators who thought that children should make their own choices about what to study, with little or no guidance from adults.

Kandel delivers a forceful critique of the Progressives' ideas with his usual witty, satirical, and philosophically substantive style. He ends the essay by challenging his colleagues on both sides of the controversy to shift their attention from theoretical debates about child's interests and intellectual disciplines to the practical world of the classroom teacher, whom he acknowledges is the key to goodness in any educational institution.

The conflict between the traditionalists or, as they have recently begun to be described, the essentialists, and the progressives in education is more than the batrachomyomachia which it appears to be to laymen and to a large part of the profession of teachers. It is a conflict between idealism in one form or another and pragmatism, between classicism and romanticism, between those who believe that the experience of the race has something to contribute to the enlightenment of the individual in the modern world and those who stress the primacy of immediate experiencing by the individual in and through the environment in which he lives. It is, therefore, a conflict which is more fundamental than the question whether instruction shall center round "subjects" or grow out of the "needs" of the pupil. Both the essentialists and the progressives believe in the principle of education as "growth," but the former hold that growth must have a definite direction whereas the latter advocate growth with nothing fixed in advance, or as an "on-going process" without direction; the latter concentrate their attention on change and constant reconstruction of values, while the former believe in the existence of certain eternal and permanent values which have grown out of the experience of the race. Frederick J. E. Woodbridge well summarized the nature of the conflict when he wrote, "For that complex of human performances which we call civilization turns out, as we examine it closely, to be a changing and shifting scene which has nonetheless a definable background. To discover that background, and to exhibit the varied lights and shadows as thrown up from it, is a proper task for philosophy." It may be added that this is a task for education also. The progressives stress the changing and shifting scene, the pre-cariousness of life and the unpredictable future; "the votaries of progress," as Dean Inge has pointed out, "mistake the flowing tide for the river of eternity." The essentialists start with a definable background, not because they wish to be conservative or, as the progressives charge, static, but because they believe, as Mr. Woodbridge puts it, that "the background is thus the important factor, at once conservative and propelling."

It is on the whole because of the failure to trace back to their origins the philosophical bases of the conflict between essentialists and progressives that education in the United States has reached its present state of chaos and uncertainty. The essentialists, relying on the persistence of their point of view through the ages and remembering that much that is claimed by the progressives is not new, have failed until recently to put forward a philosophical defense of their position, whereas the progressives, with the fervor of evangelists, have rallied round the new movement which, as John Dewey has recently warned, "takes its clew in practice from that which is rejected instead of from the constructive development of its own philosophy." And this has been easier in a cultural atmosphere whose chief tradition is to have no traditions and whose predominant interest is in change. It has been rejection of the past and desire for novelty rather than a clear-cut philosophy that have attracted adherents; *omne ignotum pro magnifico*. A certain sentimentality about the child, emphasis on respect for personality, and stress on activity are other factors that have appealed to the American mind. There has in addition been an active campaign which has presented a distorted picture of the traditional school to the public.

What is the picture of the traditional school which the progressive educators portray in such a way as to play upon the Slenderest feeling of parents—their desire to give their children the best possible start in life? The child, they say, goes to the traditional school unwillingly and is kept there under control until the close of the day, when he has a chance to explode into freedom. School equipment, with its long orderly rows of desks, is designed for maintenance of discipline and for the enforcement of obedience to authority. The classroom is arranged essentially for listening, for passivity rather than for movement and activity. Education is regarded as a preparation for adult life with deferred values to be appreciated and understood later and, therefore, with little or no meaning for the child in his immediate present. The child is to be shaped and molded to conform to a fixed pattern. Therefore the emphasis in the curriculum is not upon the child's immediate needs and interests but upon the social heritage, built up under an authoritarian concept of society, shaped by adult needs and logically arranged into a patchwork of compartmentalized subjects. The methods of instruction stress drill and study which mean memorization of formal material from books to be repeated or recited to the teacher. Such learning is not an active process but merely the uncritical accumulation of facts and information. In the social and moral fields the emphasis is upon accepted doctrines and upon authority as sacred and beyond question. Most of the work of the school is intellectual and displays an almost total disregard of the emotions. Individual differences are disregarded and promotion is determined by a standardized lockstep. Finally, the traditional school concentrates attention upon the past and ignores the contemporary life of and around the child.

If anyone is disposed to question this statement of the way in which progressive education has built itself up he is reminded of the "March of Time" film shown a little over a year ago. In this film the traditional school was represented exactly as described above; the teacher with cane in hand was calculated to strike terror into the hearts of his pupils who, as they entered the classroom to face a blackboard covered with arithmetic tables and spelling lists, abandoned all their happiness and joy outside. In the modern progressive school which was shown in contrast the pupils were happy, active, moving about and "doing things." Observers who watched closely noticed that the traditional school was of the vintage of about 50 years ago; whereas the progressive school was one of the most modern experimental schools.

This in essence has been the strategy of the protagonists of progressive education. They take a school which has all but disappeared, call it traditional and compare it with the best of the progressive type. Rarely is any mention made of the fact that the traditional school has itself been undergoing a process of transformation, that the number of children who go unwillingly to school has almost completely disappeared, that curricula and courses have been revised in order that the formal, useless and meaningless may be eliminated and that what is significant for understanding the world of the present should receive its due emphasis. Rarely, if ever, is the essentialist given any credit for building his educational theory and practice on a philosophy which is perfectly valid and acceptable or for having values which he believes to be as important for the welfare of society as for the education of the child for that society. To the impression which progressive educators have sought to convey— that the essentialist is simply seeking to carry on the school as he has inherited it from the past, without any adjustment to changing needs— they have more recently begun to add the argument that the traditionalist in education is by the same token reactionary in political and social affairs. By implication, therefore, progressives are radicals who advocate their educational theories and practices to reconstruct society and to change the social order.

The criticisms of the traditional school are thus manufactured out of whole cloth to make the flesh of parents creep. And as if these criticisms are not enough, some progressives have woven into their arguments a little of the jargon drawn from psychoanalysis. What parent will want, if he has a choice, to send his child to a school in which he will be unhappy and thwarted at every turn—with the added dangers of acquiring inhibitions, complexes and repressions and developing a dual personality? The parents will accept at its face value the implication that nothing happens to a child in the way of learning and education unless he is active, moving about, criticizing, discussing, solving problems and expressing himself.

Progressive education, however, has not always been concerned with social change. It started out 30 years ago with the theory that school and society must be brought more closely together, that the curriculum should be made more meaningful and significant to the learner and that the child or the learner with his needs and interests should be made the starting-point of a process through which his experience would be constantly reconstructed. Education must no longer be a preparation for life; education is life, arising out of the experiences and needs of the child and promoting his growth. Rejecting what was criticized as excessive emphasis on formal subject matter the progressives began to worship at the altar of the child. Children should be allowed to grow in accordance with their needs and interests; nothing must be interposed between them and their own direct and immediate experiences; knowledge is valuable only as it is acquired in a real situation; the teacher must be present to provide the proper environment for experiencing but must not intervene except to guide and advise. There must, in fact, be "nothing-fixed-in-advance" and subjects must not be "set-out-to-be-learned," for such a practice is imposition of external experience and authority and, therefore, opposed to free and natural development. Thus the purpose of the new movement was for very many years defined by the Progressive Education Association in the following terms: "(1) The pupils shall be allowed freedom to develop naturally; (2) interest of the child shall be the motive of all work; and (3) the teacher shall be considered a guide and not a taskmaster." No reference was ever made to the curriculum or its content. Nor is there, in the latest resolutions of the Association, any suggestion of what the curriculum should be except that it must be directed to the reconstruction of culture and the promotion of a new social order: "In order to establish integration again in our culture and to utilize our recent gains over the physical world, our next great period of progress must be in the direction of creating new institutional controls designed by the people for their common welfare." This task is to be begun in the school by "providing for pupils a selected and stimulating environment out of which may emerge purposes which will lead children and youth through relevant experiences to the understanding of the possibilities for human betterment in modern techniques providing we can design democratic institutions suited to the new conditions." There has thus been a shift in emphasis from the child with his needs and interests and education for growth with nothing-fixed-in-advance, to a speculative study of a vague form of social order which has not yet emerged.

The essentialist rejects the progressive theory of growth with nothing-fixed-in-advance, a planless education based upon the unselected experiences and needs of the child or even selected by cooperative, shared discussions of pupils and teachers. Growth cannot be self-directed; it needs direction through a carefully chosen environment to an end or ends in the minds of those who have been entrusted by society with the child's education. The problem is not new; it was first posed in modern times by Rousseau and has been the subject of controversy ever since. It was answered for all time by Coleridge nearly 100 years ago in the following story:

> Thelwall thought it very unfair to influence a child's mind by inculcating any opinions before it should have come to years of discretion, and be able to choose for itself. I showed him my garden, and told him it was my botanical

garden. "How so?" said he, "it is covered with weeds."—"Oh," I replied, "*that* is only because it has not yet come to its age of discretion and choice. The weeds, you see, have taken the liberty to grow, and I thought it unfair in me to prejudice the soil towards roses and strawberries."

What has been said of growth applies equally to the theory of building an education on the needs and experiences of the child. Such needs and experiences must be guided by and selected in the light of ends and purposes. And yet attempts have been made and are still being made to follow the needs and experiences of the child without a plan and with as little interference as possible from the teacher. Nothing must be done, according to this view, to determine the future thought and conduct of the child. The child is to grow in response to his own needs and through solving his own problems as they emerge out of his own experience. Despite this theory progressive schools do become conventionalized and adopt certain patterns—all students are exposed to one pattern of social studies, all build ships one year and the next turn out ashtrays and book-ends, all alike, and so on. The product, it is claimed, is unimportant; it *is* important that free rein be given the creative urge and self-expression— before there is anything to express or create. And this is carried over into the moral field; for since there are, for the progressive, no eternal verities or permanent values, and it is immoral for adults to impose their standards of morality on the child, the child must discover standards of conduct for himself, and what works is true.

The full weight of the progressive attack is against subject matter and the planned organization of a curriculum in terms of subjects. There are three reasons for this attack: First, the theory that the work of the school must grow out of the interests and experiences of the child; second, the objection that a subject-matter organization is in terms of facts, information and knowledge to be acquired and not in terms of problems, situations and activities in and out of which the need for knowledge arises; and third, the criticism that such subject matter is acquired through books and that education therefore becomes formal, verbal, and bookish. The child must be left to find out things for himself in order to solve a problem or meet a situation, but nothing is said as to how problems are recognizable without knowledge. What the traditionalist calls the essentials can, it is maintained by the progressive, be acquired incidentally without the waste of effort and formal drill. The teacher is not entirely discarded; he is part of the environment to guide and to give help when called upon, but he must have no long-range plan based on his greater and richer background of experience, because he cannot anticipate the situations and problems that will confront the child. Creative activity leading to more activity is the goal to be attained, but this goal is at best vague and places the emphasis on method at the expense of content. One is reminded of the conversation between the cat and Alice. "'Then it doesn't matter which way you *go*,' said the cat.—'So long as I get somewhere,' Alice added as an explanation."

It is that "somewhere" that is the crux of the present problem, for if the course is to be planless and improvised according to the immediate needs and urges of the child the result will be a patchwork as meaningless as a Surrealist or Dadaistic painting, which is also the product of nothing-fixed-in-advance except an inner urge to express oneself. But the progressives are not really as black as they would like to paint themselves. They hold up the child-centered school as the ideal, but on close investigation it is found that the child-centered school is a teacher-centered school, that when the teacher who has been successful in turning out poets leaves the school the Pierian springs dry up. In actual practice the teacher who is acclaimed for creating situations in which pupils produce poetry, music and art is the teacher who is inspired by a rich command of her subjects and who makes the pupils over into a pattern already "fixed-in-advance" in her mind. There is no spontaneous germination of poetry, music, art, or of anything else in the child-centered school, and the successful teacher does more than stand by and suggest.

The ranks of progressive educators are today splitting into a number of groups. There are those who, still stressing the child, would bring the community into the school in order to provide for growth through real experiences, to develop critical attitudes and to lay the basis for social reconstruction. This group, in general—usually concerned with young children whose experiences are still wholes and not yet organized—would extend its theory upwards through the grades and into the high school. A second group is opposed to a curriculum fixed-in-advance and seeks to build up an education on the immediate experiences of the pupils and the problems arising therefrom. Both groups are opposed to subjects as such.

The danger of chaos which threatens education from both points of view has recently been pointed out by leaders of what may become a third group. B. H. Bode in his *Progressive Education at the Crossroads* has attacked the theory of education based on the unselected needs and interests of the child and of growth without a sense of direction, and the theory that the school must "teach the child, not the subject." "To raise a hue and cry against subjects," writes Mr. Bode, "is to pour out the baby with the bath. The traditional subjects stood for an educational value, which we neglect at our peril." And again, "if we may assume that the purpose of teaching is to liberate the intelligence of the pupil, it appears that we must go into 'logical organization' and beyond it. The pupil must acquire some capacity for thinking as the specialist thinks; and, in addition, he must see the bearing of the subject on the question of absolute standards." At almost the same time Mr. Dewey sounded the same note of warning in his latest book, *Experience and Education*, and as the following quotations indicate urges a return to subject matter:

> But finding the material of learning within experience is only the first step. The next step is the progressive development of what is already experienced into a fuller and richer and also more organized form, a form that gradually approximates that in which subject matter is presented to the skilled, mature person.... That up to the present the weakest point in progressive schools is the matter of selection and organization of intellectual subject matter is, I think, inevitable under the circumstances.... The educator cannot start with knowledge already organized and proceed to ladle it out in doses. But as an ideal the active process of organizing facts and ideas is an ever-present educational process.

Thus the serious misgivings of the essentialists are being allayed and a bridge is being prepared for a reconciliation between the essentialist and progressive points of view. Certain doctrinal differences will continue to exist. The progressive will, no doubt, continue to stress the early experiences of the child; the essentialist will from the start select those experiences in consonance with a planned organization of education as a whole. The progressive is likely to emphasize the immediate and draw on the past only for illustrative purposes; the essentialist will seek to avoid a disorderly and discontinuous fumbling with needs, activities and experiences, and by inducting the pupil into what Charles A. Beard has described as "the treasures heavy with the thought and sacrifices of the centuries" and "a heritage of knowledge and heroic examples—accepted values stamped with the seal of permanence" he will endeavor to produce men and women possessing the understanding that comes through knowledge, men and women critical because they possess a mastery of facts and an ability to think objectively and free because they have disciplined themselves for a life of duty and responsibility.

The essentialist starts with the premise that the school is an institution created to achieve some definite purpose. He agrees with the general progressive formula that education is life, but believes that formal education must confront the pupil with a certain body of experiences selected from what is called life. He is no less interested than the progressive in the principle that learning cannot be successful unless it is based on the capacities, interests and purpose of the learner, but he believes those interests and purposes must be made over by the skill of a teacher who is master of that "logical organization" called subjects and who understands the processes of educational development. The essentialist no longer believes that that development is wholly intellectual: he recognizes that education must not be directed to the mind alone but to the whole human being, if this is to grow into a well-rounded personality. He welcomes the call of the progressive leaders for subjects and subject matter, for he has felt that when the lid was taken off the universe the bottom began to fall out of education. He is willing to learn and has learned much from progressive theory on methods of instruction; he believes, indeed, that the chief contribution of what is called the pragmatic philosophy has been to methodology. Finally, he is still concerned about the future of American education because adequate attention has not been given to the proper selection and professional preparation of teachers. Until this is done and until there is a shift of emphasis from both subject matter and the child to the teacher he has no reason to expect success from any theory of education. For ultimately it is the teacher with a broad liberal education, mastery of a special field, understanding of the process of learning and a strong conviction on the contribution that education can make to social welfare and progress who is the key to the situation.

Address at St. Paul's Chapel, Columbia University
(1940)

Kandel delivered this address during some of the darkest, earliest days of World War II. Five years earlier, in 1935, he published The Making of Nazis, *a book in which he detailed how Hitler was using the German public school system to spread his destructive ideology. Kandel was ahead of his time in 1935 when he accurately foresaw the evils of Hitler's Nazism.*

This short address provides readers with insight into the spiritual dimension of Kandel's life. He called relentlessly for an educational philosophy that brought people together instead of one that pulled them apart. The only way to do this, Kandel argues, is for teachers and other educators to concentrate on those common principles of humanity that unite human beings. Developing the spiritual essence of human nature, Kandel recognizes, is the only hope for holding diverse people together. He was a humanist in the best sense of the word, not a technologist. In this short, previously unpublished paper, Kandel reflects on the source of the ideals that sustained his work as a teacher, teacher educator, and scholar.

A week ago Lord Halifax, in broadcasting the British reply to Hitler, asked for the prayers of his countrymen and of men of good will throughout the world. The foundations of the world, he said, have been Christian teaching and belief in God. The reply was received in Germany with ridicule and written off and decried as one more piece of evidence of that Jewish mentality which has produced chaos in the world.

This reception on the part of the Germans is revealing. It gives the evidence which the world needed that the persecution of the Jews was due

Forgotten Heroes of American Education, pages 411–413

in part at any rate to hatred of Judaism because it was the cradle of Christian doctrine. The Germans deride the Jews for the claim to be the Chosen People; they would lay claim to the title themselves. And yet what a difference between the idea of a people which chooses as its mission the enslavement of the world and a people chosen to reveal God to the world of man. There is another cause of Nazi hatred of the Judaeo-Christian tradition because this revelation of the divine in man, this recognition of the dignity of the individual as a responsible human being, is the basis on which democracy rests. Intolerance and hatred are the foundations of the new ideologies; "Love thy neighbor as thyself" is the injunction of the Hebrew prophets and of the Golden Rule.

It is here that Jews and Christians, if they would only be true to their common tradition, can find a common cause. To paraphrase a statement of Thomas Carlyle: Why do we for the sake of differences of creed misknow each other and fight against each other instead of uniting to fight the common enemy—darkness and evil?

We have been overwhelmed by a great crisis in human affairs. We try to study the causes of this crisis, but one thing we refuse to face is that the crisis from one point of view is due to the fact that we have surrendered the guidance of any faith. The pillars of faith have been torn down one after the other; science destroyed faith in religion; standards of morality have been left to individual choice; each individual was to be his own God guided by science. And when the crisis came even faith in science began to be questioned and was found to be wanting.

Man's greatest need today is the guidance of some faith which will give him hope and guide his conduct; he cannot live on a negation; he needs values that have stood the test of time. Because this is a human need nearly half of the world in its despair has accepted false faiths, –isms, which it has adapted as substitutes for religion. This is not the place to discuss the result of these ideologies—the enslavement of the human spirit, the setting of one man's hands against his neighbor. "Do unto others as you would have them do unto you" has been perverted to "Do unto others as you would have them do unto you, but do it first," for you cannot trust your neighbor. We must search our hearts and see whether we cannot rediscover this spirit of the doctrine common to Jew and Christian alike which unites men in a common endeavor and a common hope.

You as students owe it to yourselves and to your fellows to look for light, for it is only as we approach the light of a great faith that we can lay aside our prejudices, learn to know our neighbors, develop that tolerance which comes from understanding, and have something to live for. Totalitarian ideologies claim that they have given their followers something to die for; our task is to discover something to live for and that, for men of culture, is to make the will of God prevail.

Here is the real challenge to those who enjoy the opportunities that you have. The least of these opportunities is the acquisition of knowledge. The greatest is the opportunity of living for a short time with others of different creeds and different sects, of different races and of different color, in an atmosphere where your task should be not to look for differences which divide, but for those common elements of humanity which make for brotherhood. The commonwealth of students cannot prosper in an atmosphere of prejudice, intolerance, and hate, for we are all engaged in the common task of developing sympathetic understanding and of preparing for service based on knowledge. But knowledge must be transformed into wisdom which comes from open-mindedness, tolerance, and sympathetic insight. What brings us together is a certain optimism about the worth of man as a creature of God.

Education fails, and we witness its failure in some countries today, if, while it advances knowledge, it only results in cynicism and skepticism, and does not develop a sense of a common humanity struggling toward light. Education, true education, should liberate; it should cultivate the genuinely free man, the man of moral judgment, of intellectual integrity; it should give us the power to see the other side; it should impart nobility of purpose and kindliness of spirit. It should leave with us the inescapable truth that man is a spiritual being and that the struggle for the mastery of the forces of nature is not merely for the satisfaction of human needs but is also inspired by the spiritual end of reaching out beyond our immediate lives to something eternal.

Our obligation is clear as we look back at the recent past and the progressive understanding of faith by which man may live and be inspired. A leading figure in American literature, analyzing recent trends in literature, has referred to the writers of the past generation as the irresponsibles. They have destroyed faith and have put nothing in its place. Here is our task and here is our duty—to rediscover some purpose, some reason, for man's existence, without these the material advancement of which we have until recently been so proud ceases to have meaning. Without some faith even that democracy, which we are at last girding ourselves to preserve, will fail. While others are discarding religion as outworn and obsolete, and others again are seeking to replace the great creeds which have inspired man by a return to their own paganism, we can preserve democracy not by making democracy our religion but by realizing that the basic principles of democracy are rooted in the religious traditions of Jew and Christian alike. Those who claim that religion has failed are wrong in attributing the failure to religion; it is we who have failed because we have discarded all faith and put nothing in its place. Today it is my conviction that there is no greater need than to restore the guidance of faith in our daily lives. This is not a counsel of despair; it is, today as it has always been, a yearning for the expression of the divine in us as human beings.

The Profession of Teaching
(1940)

Kandel takes this opportunity to reflect on the status of the profession to which he had dedicated his life for the past forty years. Using his typical historical and philosophical approach, he reexamines several movements that had taken place in the profession of teaching during the past few decades. Contemporary educators and teacher educators will recognize many of the historic challenges that Kandel addresses in this paper.

He argues specifically for increased attention to general cultural background on the part of all teachers, regardless of the age of students or the subjects they teach. Since he assumes that schools exist to pass down culture from one generation to the next, the need for teachers to have a strong cultural background is self-evident to Kandel. Beyond general culture, Kandel explains his views on curriculum for teaching teachers. He makes the point that knowledge of a particular subject like history is necessary but not sufficient for beginning a career in the profession of teaching. He affirms that teachers also must have a solid understanding of numerous other fields that relate to teaching—for example, political science, psychology, philosophy, and sociology. Teachers also must learn how and why to connect their knowledge to diverse groups of students. Teaching was not a simple art to Kandel.

Kandel ends the paper with a discussion of the selection, retention, and promotion of teachers—all of which are high profile issues that remain with the profession of teaching today. His attention to this matter indicates his insistence that good societies are largely the result of good schools, and that good schools, of course, are only as good as the teachers who teach in them.

Forgotten Heroes of American Education, pages 415–421

The time comes in the development of every profession when the methods of preparation for it and its status must be reexamined. This reexamination is due not merely to the expansion of the knowledge which practitioners of a profession must master, but to the changes in the practice of the profession which this advancing knowledge brings with it. This is as true of the profession of teaching as it is of medicine, law and engineering. Merely to extend in terms of years the period of preparation does not adequately meet the situation. The changes which are taking place involve more than the question of providing more time for the acquisition of the basic knowledge required for entrance into a profession. They involve increasingly a consideration of the aptitudes of prospective candidates; they require a reorganization of the curricula of the professional preparation; they demand the adaptation of curricula to the changing status and functions of a profession; they imply further provision for continued growth in understanding and skill by the practitioners.

In the profession of teaching these problems have arisen only recently. It may, indeed, be said that it is only recently that teaching has begun to be regarded a profession as distinguished from a trade. The situation was different when the only data in education were the subject to be taught and the methods of instruction under systems in which both were prescribed uniformly and in detail by the administrative authorities and teachers were carefully supervised to see that the prescribed regulations were meticulously followed and pupils were examined to discover whether they had absorbed the amount of knowledge, information and skills prescribed. The pupil as an individual was disregarded and pupil maladjustments did not exist or were ironed out by rigorous discipline. Standards for selecting prospective teachers were simple—good health and a certain amount of knowledge—and methods of preparation were equally simple—the acquisition of more knowledge sufficient to keep the teacher ahead of his class and skill in imparting that knowledge. Character-education and preparation for citizenship were not ignored, but they were expected to be the outcomes of knowledge on the two theories that knowledge is virtue and knowledge is power.

The prevailing patterns of selecting and training prospective teachers were much the same everywhere. In the field of elementary education candidates were selected if they had just a little more than elementary education, and their training consisted in the acquisition of routine skills either as pupil-teachers or in normal schools. At the secondary level the requirements consisted in the acquisition of more specialized knowledge with little or no training in methods of instruction because the pupils to be taught were nearer to the adult level and were themselves selected. At both levels the goals to be achieved were specific and clearly defined; failure to attain the goals was attributed more often than not to the pupil's inability to study or to laziness or to both rather than to the teacher. This situation was aggravated in the United States by the fact that teaching was looked upon as a stepping-stone to other careers—marriage or some other occupation. The result of this situation was to place the responsibility for success on the administrative and supervisory authorities.

Conditions are changing, and it is being realized everywhere not merely that "as is the teacher, so is the school," but "as is the school, so is society." Particularly is this realization growing stronger in democratic societies whose welfare and progress depend upon the qualities of the individuals upon whom the standards of political, social and economic life and of national culture depend. It is not, however, the social considerations as a whole which have contributed to this realization. An important contributory factor is to be found in the advances which have resulted from research into those branches of knowledge usually associated with what is called the process of education. The combination of the social demands and expectations and the advancing knowledge of more of the factors which contribute to sound education is slowly changing the concept of the teacher's functions.

One point which is becoming clearer increasingly and is accepted more generally is that he who would educate others must himself be educated and have a broad background of general cultural training. The teacher, irrespective of his special functions or the level of education to which he plans to devote himself, must have as broad a general preparation as members of other professions. This is particularly true in those countries in which the dual system of education—one system for the masses and another for the selected few—is beginning to disappear or has already disappeared. That general background of culture can be well defined and, as illustrated in the Pennsylvania Study of the Carnegie Foundation for the Advancement of Teaching, can be tested. A mastery of such a background is not only essential as the possession of every educated individual; for the teacher it is essential if he is to have a vision of the scope of education in general and of the relations of his part in the educative process in particular. A strong cultural background thus becomes for the teacher both his possession as an educated person and his equipment for professional use. It is only as he has enjoyed a broad liberal education that the teacher can avoid routine and show resourcefulness and enterprise in his daily work.

Further, it is only as he is broadly educated that a teacher can be expected to be clear and fluent in his speech and expression. It is difficult to assert categorically what it is in a teacher's equipment that exercises an influence for good on pupils. It may, however, be safely asserted that voice and speech are among the qualities which affect pupils favorably or adversely. It is not an accident that one of the important emphases in French secondary education is the cultivation of ability "to speak well and to write well." This does not mean an emphasis on affectation or style in speech or writing, but a recognition that it is impossible to speak well or to write well without having ideas to express. It is not necessary to discuss voice at this point, but it is not asking too much that teachers who are in daily contact with their pupils should meet standards of speech generally accepted among educated people. The danger that standards of speech may be separated from content or be defined as something distinct from standards of habitual speech can be avoided, if it is recognized. Here, too, while unanimity has not yet been reached, progress is being made with the development of standards.

Beyond the general background, which the teacher should share with members of other professions, he must have a mastery and command of the specific knowledge which his particular part in the educative process demands. It is at this point that some conflict arises. In the past it was considered enough if the teacher knew his subject; with such knowledge at his command he could adapt it to the needs of his pupils. The fields of knowledge, however, are not absolute; they must be adapted to the needs of time and place, to the abilities, interests and stage of development of a particular group of pupils. This is what is meant by the movement to provide professionalized subject matter in the preparation of teachers. Unfortunately this has too frequently been interpreted to mean that prospective teachers should acquire only that amount of knowledge which they will need to impart to their pupils. Such an interpretation would not carry the standards of preparation in the academic subjects much beyond the low standards which prevailed in the nineteenth century. A sounder interpretation would be that the teacher should not only acquire a mastery of the appropriate academic subjects, but should at the same time gain an understanding of the adaptations which he will be called upon to make with pupils at different levels. He must, in other words, see how a subject is to be built up in the minds of his pupils, having the advantage of seeing both the process of its growth and development and a mastery of it as a whole.[1]

The responsibilities of the teacher to-day transcend the mere imparting of subjects and subject matter. He should have a knowledge and understanding of the place and function of the subject which he professes, first, in the development of the pupil, and, second, as a contribution to the pupil as a future citizen. He must accordingly know more than his

---

1. The discussion has been conducted here in terms of subjects with a full awareness that subjects are becoming taboo and being replaced by "activities" and "experiences." But, while both terms can be used from the point of view of method, if education is to have content of real value, it will have to be continued in terms of subjects.

predecessors did about psychology, on the one hand, and sociology, political science and economics on the other. Not only must he know something about the psychology of growth, of learning and of education in general, but he must be in a position to detect and understand each of his pupils as an individual. The teacher is expected to be a diagnostician to know when advice is necessary and where it should be sought. This means further that he must know something about the health of his pupils, their environment and social background. These new requirements and responsibilities are not irrelevant at a time when the central problem in education is adequate guidance and when adequate guidance must be based on as much information as can be secured about each pupil. Here again the background of the teacher in the various fields which are implicit in these functions can be tested.

These are some of the essential backgrounds of the prospective and practicing teachers. There is, however, no guarantee that this background will ensure good teaching. It is at this point that the chief difficulties arise in the selection, appointment and promotion of teachers. Studies of the abilities and qualities that make a good teacher have been going on for more than a generation and every new study appears to cancel out those that preceded it. Character, personality, scholarship, practice teaching, intelligence—each has had its advocates; not only is there no agreement among the advocates, but the correlations between any one of these qualities and teaching ability are so low that little reliance can be placed on the measures for predicting success. No one would be disposed to deny that all those qualities are desirable, but there is as yet no adequate information on which aptitude tests of teaching ability can be based. And yet each of the qualities mentioned can be measured—personality, scholarship, skill in practice teaching and intelligence.

The difficulty at the initial stage of selection is to be found in the assumption that a candidate who has completed his preparation is a finished teacher. As a general rule, the assumption is not warranted, since in most cases practice teaching is under supervision and too frequently in isolated classes in isolated schools. That the assumption is not warranted is indicated by the fact that in most systems beginning teachers are appointed on probation. Unfortunately in most instances, the period of probation is not looked upon as a period of continued preparation under supervision and guidance analogous to the period of internship in medical training or the clerkship in a law office in legal training. Since conditions in actual school practice are not the same as in training schools and since conditions of environment and of interest of supervisors, principals and teachers vary from school to school, it is all the more important that probationary teachers should receive special care and attention from a group of supervisors specially assigned to this work. The length of the probationary period must depend upon the time necessary to produce those qualities that should be required for a permanent license.

It is during this period of probation that the records of students during their preparatory years can be tested and verified; under the care of a special corps of supervisors more uniform records of personality and teaching ability could be accumulated than are available at present. Assuming even that some principals are interested in looking after probationary teachers assigned to them, the ratings of a large number of principals are not comparable. But apart from the question of interest there is always the danger that such ratings would be perfunctory in the hope that a probationary teacher might later improve, or be assigned to another school, and always in the background there lurks the fear that more trouble than good would accrue as the result of a low or unsatisfactory rating which would bar a candidate from admission to the profession after a number of years of preparation and the cost involved thereon.

And yet permanent appointment and later advancement in the service must be dependent on adequate records of the quality of that service in any system which lays claim to placing principles of merit above all other considerations. The problem of promotions is as serious and as important as that of first selection, both because the welfare of a system depends upon the kind of leadership offered at all levels and because opportunities for advancement serve two purposes—they give teachers the desirable encouragement and additional inducement beyond normal salary increments to continue their professional growth, and they reward successful service. But, while these facts are recognized, the nature of requirements which should be established for promotion are not so clear. Should promotion depend solely on record? Under present conditions, it is still doubtful whether such records of personality, teaching competence and professional growth are sufficiently reliable. Should promotion depend on further tests adapted to the next levels sought by the candidates? Can such tests be sufficiently differentiated for the different functions in a school system? Does a good classroom teacher always make a good principal, supervisor or administrative officer? Should candidates at each stage of promotion be reexamined in general culture and in mastery of subject matter? Are attendance at courses and grades achieved in such courses adequate as a guide for promotion? Should the tests be performance tests suited to the positions sought? Finally, should all promotions be based on some form of competitive test?

Throughout this discussion there constantly arises the question of how personality and professional efficiency can be rated in such a way as to be valid, reliable and comparable—in other words so fair and just that they can not be attacked. The same question arises in judging performance tests as well as on the nature of the performance tests themselves.

These problems go beyond the scope of a local system as such. Within a single system it may be possible to solve the problems mentioned with some degree of accuracy. The difficulty arises when candidates from outside the system apply for appointment. Is it possible to establish something in the nature of national norms? A local system may work satisfactorily; those employed in that system may learn and adapt themselves to its standards and requirements better than candidates whose training and experience have been elsewhere. Under such conditions the danger of inbreeding is always present and the infusion of new blood is prevented.

There is another reason which gives new significance to the problems stated. Nowhere is the contrast between the new and the old education more striking than in the movement known as the individualization of instruction. Under the traditional system, with a uniform curriculum and the same methods of instruction applied to all, the function of the teacher was limited; he was in general assigned to teach the prescribed curriculum with prescribed methods and with text-books in the selection of which he played no part under somewhat rigorous supervision. Not only is the character of the curriculum changing to-day, but increased attention must be given by the teacher to the social background, the health and particular abilities and disabilities of each pupil. Further, the opportunities for teachers to participate in the preparation of curricula and courses of study are increasing, and increasingly they are demanding opportunities to participate in the formulation of policies and even beyond that to participate in administration.

Such a change in the status of the teachers throws into relief the problems involved in preparation, selection, appointment and promotion. If this status has changed, it is obvious that the methods employed in preparation, selection, appointment and promotion must be adapted to the new status. Hence the need of examinations, tests and other measures for securing teachers adequately qualified for the new responsibilities imposed upon them and guaranteeing the success and progress of the schools in the interests of the pupils attending them and the public supporting them.

The Fantasia
of Current Education
(1941)

In this essay, Isaac Kandel places the Progressive education movement within its larger historical, philosophical, and scientific context. He criticizes educational theorists who seek a panacea that allegedly will "fix" education once and for all. This obsession, Kandel asserts, has led them to ignore the teachers whom Kandel argues are the heart of good educational institutions. Kandel rejected simplistic solutions to complex problems. He does not criticize only one group of educational thinkers; rather, he finds fault in proposals from a variety of different perspectives. For example, he criticizes traditional education for too often supporting the status quo; at the same time, he critiques Progressive education for teaching "problem-solving skills" rather than focusing on moral and intellectual substance. Presenting students with problem-solving scenarios before they have the background knowledge to make good judgments, he holds, does more harm than good, and ultimately ends up frustrating students rather than inspiring them. In this paper, Kandel challenges all of American culture to attain high ideals in academic as well as ethical pursuits.

Kandel was well-informed about contemporary debates in educational thought and practice. He responds to almost every challenge that had been leveled against traditional ideas on curriculum and teaching. He gives his brief assessment of the well-known "Eight Year Study," which was initiated in the 1930s in an attempt to settle the debate between Progressives and Traditionalists once and for all, in accord with scientific principles. Yet, as he explains, it failed to end the debate. Kandel makes the point that the task of measurement was so onerous that the results of the Eight Year Study were inconclusive.

Like his article entitled "Prejudice the Garden Toward Roses?," Kandel here concludes by drawing the reader's attention to classroom teachers. He was convinced

Forgotten Heroes of American Education, pages 423–432
Copyright © 2006 by Information Age Publishing
All rights of reproduction in any form reserved.

that they had been forgotten in the smoke-filled rooms that were the setting for "scientific" discussions of educational philosophy. He calls for new efforts to raise the status of the teaching profession, because, in his words, "successful education can only be looked for as teachers become masters of what they teach, recognize the relation of what they teach to the society in which they teach, and have a sympathetic understanding of those whom they teach." Kandel's challenge remains as relevant in the early 21st century as it was in 1941.

Ever since some educational theorists made the profound discovery that we live in a changing world, that authoritarianism began to be undermined by Galileo and that life is precarious and the future uncertain, experimentalism has run riot and education has been bombarded with a chaotic welter of theories. Some twenty years ago C. W. Bardeen wrote an article under the title, "The Man Milliner in Education," but the educational milliner was just beginning to be active when he wrote; since that time the milliner's energies and activities have not flagged and every year produce several crops of new plans, new projects, new theories. Educational bibliographies have to be annotated with statements that the earlier works (written as long as fifteen or twenty years ago) of some authors do not represent their present views; one educator, careful not to be left behind by the rapidity of the changing cultural stream, announced in the 1939–40 catalog of one institution two courses on the "Psychology of American Culture"—the first semester to cover the period from 1860 to 1939, the second semester the period from 1860 to 1940, with an unfortunate gap of about two weeks unaccounted for.

Despite the widespread attacks upon it because of its traditionalism, American education has never been as rooted in its principles and practices as have the European systems. The first prize in a competition instituted by the American Philosophical Society in the early years of the Republic went to Samuel Knox for his An Essay on the Best System of Liberal Education Adapted to the Genius of the Government of the United States [1799]. Education since that time has been marked by constant attempts at adaptation but never with the intensity characteristic of the last two decades. There are, however, many educators who would reject the notion of adaptation as an end of education and would embark on a program of reconstructing society through the schools in an effort to meet the uncertain future.

The educator is turning his attention from the schoolroom to the community, to society, to the world at large and, discovering that everything is wrong, is ready to tear down the walls of the school so that pupils and students, seeing the ills of the world in which they live, may learn how to correct them. We have been through a World War; we are in the midst of another. We passed through a boom period; we are now in the midst of a depression. Youth has been betrayed by the older generation; it must be made wiser and be trained to solve the problems which the older generation has through complacency, indifference or ignorance allowed to accumulate. And the older generation has failed because the traditional education it received failed to develop its social or any other kind of intelligence, and predisposed it not only to accept but to be content with the status quo. This point of view was expressed in the preliminary program of the winter meeting (1940) of the Progressive Education Association:

> Schools no longer bound education. The teeming life of the community, the State and the nation are more really and vitally educative than books. In the educational experiences they give their children, how can the schools use these resources that lie all about them? And what can schools do to help children to become aware of the problems inherent in these resources, so that the children may help to solve these problems as they grow into manhood and womanhood?

The problems which experts the world over have failed to solve may now safely be left to children in the schools under the guidance of teachers who are only too ready to disprove Bernard Shaw's gibe and whose claims to expertness seem to have been overlooked in the formation of brain trusts. This is not the first time that teachers and educators, weary of the tasks they have professionally assumed, have sought new worlds to conquer. The sophists had useful recipes for the solution of the problems of their day. Comenius (whose reputation rests on the production of the first illustrated school text), when he grew weary of the *puerilia illa toties nauseata,* as he described his work as a teacher, had an ambitious plan to set the world of his day right by his pansophic scheme.

Despite the fact that educational literature is full of accounts of failures in the established routine subjects of the school, in the teaching of which teachers may be expected to have acquired some proficiency, they are now to become experts in the solution of all social problems. Despite the known fact that many college students fail because they are unable to read, despite a growing library of literature concerned with the problems of teaching reading, and despite the fact that in the field of adult education books have to be rewritten to make them readable, children in schools are to be plunged into surveys of their community, national and world resources, which "are more really and vitally educative than books." The reality of ideas is to be abandoned for contact with realities.

A little more than a year ago there was a conference at Teachers College, Columbia University, on "How Can Economic Illiteracy Be Reduced?" Seminars were held to discuss what can be done in this field at different school levels. The report on the findings of the Seminar on

"What Can Be Done in Elementary Schools?" (grades six and below) contained the following statement:

> It was agreed that to educate satisfactorily for economic literacy, the teacher must have a definite philosophy of life evolved from living a full life, and must have an orientation in economic theory. Although such orientation is now generally lacking, we cannot afford to wait to re-educate teachers, but we must proceed as that process of re-education goes on. *The materials to be used in such education are to be determined in the light of the problems to be solved. They shall be decided upon by teachers, children, specialists, and others in the situation.* It was agreed that research is needed to determine what materials are required for this type of instruction.

The italics, which are not in the original, are intended merely to draw attention to a trend which is not new—the optimistic attempt to have illiterates taught by illiterates.

If this proposal were due merely to an accident of wording or to a chance admission that teachers are not yet economically literate it would be bad enough. It is still worse when, as in an article in *School and Society,* October 21, 1939, it is justified as a principle. Here the author writes:

> A teacher does not need to have studied economics in order to give a good course in the subject. All that is needed is a teacher (1) who is alert to the problems of the day, (2) who is openminded, (3) who can stimulate pupils to bring economic problems to class for discussion, (4) who permits and encourages free and open discussion of all controversial subjects, (5) who instills into the pupils a spirit of tolerance for all views and a respect for the opinions of others, and (6) who shows in all discussion that he or she has at heart the solution of the economic ills of the day in a way which will restore prosperity and happiness to the whole people.

Only the traditionally trained academician would be disposed to criticize such frank open-mindedness.

Unfortunately the statement just quoted does not stand alone. A report published a few years ago revealed that there were about 150,000 high school teachers giving instruction in subjects they themselves had never studied. To this number should be added another large percentage of teachers who hold high school certificates but in no specific subjects. When German was ousted from the schools during the World War a crop of teachers blossomed forth overnight to teach Spanish. When the recent vogue for "social studies" was introduced there was no lack of teachers ready and willing to teach them, because "a teacher does not need ever to have studied [any subject] to give a good course in the subject." Lest those in higher educational circles take too much unction to themselves it is well to remind them of the college president who requested the dean of a well-known graduate school to send him two Ph.D.'s. When the dean inquired what fields the Ph.D.'s were to expound the answer came back that the fields did not matter; all that the president needed was "just two Ph.D.'s."

The harm done American education by the cult of such superficiality is incalculable. A number of explanations can be adduced for this situation. The first is a somewhat widespread contempt for knowledge and its mastery, or, as the educational theorists put it, the important thing is not "the what" but "the how," not content but method, not ideas but the thinking process. How the one is possible without the other is never explained. Hence the prevalent criticism of objective tests of scholastic attainments as measuring "mere knowledge." Hence the traditional emphasis on methods and pedagogy rather than content in the preparation of teachers, and the distinction between teaching "the child" and teaching "subjects." Thus, also, it is claimed that a great measure of success has been achieved in a large city school system in an experiment with the activity program; the pupils in these experimental classes excel in cooperation, initiative, experimentation, critical activities and leadership; but they are at a substantial disadvantage, when compared with pupils in traditional classes, in arithmetical computation, arithmetical reasoning, reading speed, spelling and language usage. These results are interpreted as bringing "democracy into the classroom." If it is objected that the pupils cannot compute, attention is directed to their initiative; the charge that they cannot spell or read is met by referring to their independence and experimentation; if inadequacy in subjects is mentioned it is countered by citing their critical activities and leadership. The new school thus becomes "dynamic" and is to replace the obsolescent traditional school which was "static."

The second explanation is to be found in a certain discontent with the preparation given to meet the problems of citizenship. The school must train pupils to solve the controversial issues of the day. Education can only be made "meaningful" as it deals with the immediate problems of the environment in which the pupils live. Whether the pupils realize the existence of these problems, whether they have any direct stake in their solution, whether the problems and the solutions will be the same when they in turn become adults is immaterial. Nor is it clear whether those who advocate the study of controversial issues at any school level are interested in fact-finding about the present or in the acquisition of methods of attack. No one could object, of course, to the development of techniques of argument and debate in the classroom; indeed a good case could be made out for teaching everything controversially. The position is different, however, with the controversial issues which it is proposed to inject into the school to develop social, political and economic literacy. Here, for example, are two problems taken from a social studies textbook actually used in a class of fifteen-year-old girls:

(1) If you were appointed economic dictator of the United States, what steps would you take to prevent business depressions? (2) Imagine yourself a member of the Round Table Conference on India which met in England in 1931. Give arguments for Indian independence from the point of view of an Indian Nationalist. Give arguments for England's retaining control from the point of view of an English Conservative. Outline the main points of what you consider a settlement fair to all concerned.

To avoid any objection that these questions are exceptional two others from another study guide for group and class discussion at the high school level may be cited:

(1) If purchasing power were increased to the extent of providing a high standard of living could mortgaging the future be prohibited? How? By whom? (2) Does the Fascist economic system balance production and consumption? How does this planning differ from the proposals of the scientific students, or the plans for controlled private capitalism in America?

Such is the revenge of the progressive educator on the traditional academic curriculum for transmitting "inert knowledge" and for its failure to be "meaningful," interesting and realistic!

A third explanation is to be found in the theory that the process of thinking can only be stimulated by having a problem to solve when a fork in the road is reached or when the choice of a course of action has to be made. How the existence of a problem can be recognized without a background of antecedent knowledge is not explained. Here again, since next steps are always uncertain and the future is always precarious, the experimental habit of mind must be cultivated. Habits, stereotypes and routine must be replaced by scientific methods of thinking; "life situations" must be dealt with as the scientist deals with his material. Unfortunately a cog is always slipped in the theory; the scientist's problems arise out of a background of knowledge accumulated by his predecessors and himself and when he experiments it is with a hypothesis or a set of hypotheses which have to be proved.

There is still another reason for the demand that pupils become discoverers rather than absorbers of knowledge. This is to be found in the fear of indoctrination through handing out what is called "knowledge fixed-in-advance." Hence the pupil is to be constantly confronted with problems since the only knowledge which becomes enduring is that resulting from his own quest. Thinking and the discovery of knowledge thus become "creative acts" which in turn contribute to the pupil's growth. Learning ceases to be the acquisition and becomes the discovery of knowledge to suit the particular situation in which the pupil finds himself or the problem he has to solve.

Underlying this movement is the critical attitude toward everything traditional in education and a faith that the latest is always the best. Traditional education, it is asserted, was passive; the pupil sat patiently at his desk while the teacher poured ready-made information into his unwilling mind. Traditional education did not develop the thinking powers. The traditional curriculum ignored the "needs, urges, drives, and interests" of the pupil, was remote from the realities about him, did not train him to deal with "life situations" and did not develop his creative abilities. Those who survived the prison walls of school, who became good and intelligent citizens and who even developed creative powers, did so in spite of their mis-education. The school must now devote itself to creative arts, creative music, creative writing and creative building of new social orders. The French emphasis on repetition, assimilation *et creation* is, according to this theory, completely fallacious and unsound. Psychologically every individual has an urge to express himself; it is the business of the school to encourage this urge, even though the pupil has nothing to express. In no other way can an integrated personality be developed. To thwart self-expression by a program fixed-in-advance is to thwart the integration of personality and to perpetuate inhibitions, obsessions and complexes.

And thus the next stage in the development of current theories is reached. No obstacles in the form of definite aims and purposes or of subjects must be placed in the way of the child's growth lest that growth be thwarted by the suppression of native drives, urges, needs and interests. The tradition of education with its formal curriculum and "subject-matter laid-out-to-be-learned" failed because it set up such obstacles. It failed for another reason; it was too intellectualistic; it sought to train the mind and failed to educate the whole person because it ignored the emotions which play such an important part in the development of attitudes. The teacher must now be not merely a psychologist but also a mental hygienist if the school is not to produce a host of misfits and mis-educated individuals. Hence instruction must concern itself with the unconscious and even the subconscious as well as with the conscious determinants of the thinking process. It is no longer the mind that is to be educated but the whole organism. Starting with an attack on "intellectualistic" education and stressing the part played by the emotions, the latter-day theorists, without realizing it, are promoting the retreat from reason.

Two ends are to be served by the new education. The first is to cultivate ability to solve the problems and issues arising out of pressing "life situations." The second is to develop an integrated personality. The first objective is to be achieved by what is called a "face to face confrontation" with the environment; the second by giving free play to the urge of the whole organism for creative activity. The duty of the school is to promote the happiness of the individual which comes from the proper adjustment to all the pressures and demands of life and from direct and personal experiencing and purposing. The traditional obstacles to the development of an integrated personality have been a fixed curriculum divided into compartments known as subjects. The whole organism is affected by a whole and not a compartmentalized environment. The school must be an experiencing institution with an integrated curriculum in which elements of what used to be called subjects are drawn upon as they are needed. The traditional school was formal in its aims, formal in its methods and formal in its organization. Form and formalism must be discarded; their place is to be taken by an integrated curriculum or what is coming to be more widely known as "general education," which should deal with all the major functions of human living. For subjects there are substituted "experiences" which make for esthetic living, social living, healthy living, vocational living and so on.

It will no doubt be objected that this description of current tendencies is overdrawn. That it does not apply to any one particular school is readily admitted; that each school seeks to interpret the tendencies in its own way is equally true. When, a few years ago, the eight-year experiment was undertaken whereby thirty secondary schools, public and private, were permitted to organize their work in their own way on the understanding that their graduates would be admitted to colleges on their records, an analysis of their programs revealed that they were embarking on twenty-six different plans—which rendered the task of evaluation rather onerous if not impossible.

The tendencies are, of course, rooted in the principle that "education is life and not a preparation for life," a principle which is sound but for school purposes requires much closer analysis than it has received. Since no one has seriously taken the trouble to discover what aspects of life should be selected for purposes of school education, "schools no longer bound education" and their activities are directed to the "teeming life of the community, the State and the nation." The new tendencies have their appeal, further, because they promise immediate returns in understanding and action; they are the educational analogies of the get-rich-quick notion.

Another explanation may be found in still another direction—the American tradition of having no traditions. It is interesting that tendencies similar to those described are found in countries without a strong social or cultural tradition or in countries where, as in Italy, Soviet Russia and Germany, there is an effort to make a complete break with the past; in England, France and the Scandinavian nations the new theories have their advocates but only a small body of followers. The rootlessness of American culture has been noted by many American writers. "Ideas," wrote Santayana, "are abandoned in virtue of a mere change of feeling." Van Wyck Brooks, in one of his critical essays, has dealt with the "superficiality of rootlessness." Rootlessness is the theme of Bromfield's *The Man Who Had Everything;* it appears again in Louis Adamic's *Grandsons.* One of the best characterizations of American education is that given by T. S. Stribling in *These Bars of Flesh:* "American education," he writes, "is like a man who continuously builds himself new homes and never lives in one. He perishes running here and there with his stones and his new blueprints."

This rootlessness has always left the door open for changes and adaptations in education. To rootlessness must be added the rapid tempo of change in the past generation, and to both of these the experimentalism which has affected all aspects of culture, not only in this country but everywhere else. The United States has undertaken a formidable task in attempting to provide an education to everybody on equal terms; the efforts have in too many cases resulted in failure; the failure has been attributed to the tradition of the so-called academic curriculum, and subjects rather than the poor preparation of teachers have been attacked; since the old curriculum has failed, new subjects or new integrations are being tried out—the teachers remain pretty much the same and their deficiencies are made up by more attractive textbooks. The venture into the new is justified on the ground that "education is life." There is, further, no real guidance from psychologists, who, having surrendered the mind as beyond definition, are busy developing a number of competing and conflicting theories. The American public still retains its faith if not in education at least in schooling and is willing to tolerate experimentation just as it welcomes every other new sensation. Under these conditions it is not surprising that experimentalism runs riot.

The educator will maintain that in embarking on experimentalism he is following the lead and methods of the sciences. Paradoxically enough the group sponsoring the new theories is the group most strongly arrayed against those who in the last thirty years have laid the foundations for a science of education. The experimentalism that characterizes the current trends in education is not, however, analogous to experimentalism in science. It is more similar to that in literature and art.

In its emphasis on functionalism it has some affinities with architecture. It has its parallels in the current novel which seeks to explore the hidden springs of thought and behavior, and to deal with the immediate and particular rather than with the universal and the permanent. But the closest analogies are found in music and art. An educational theory which aims at growth with nothing-fixed-in-advance is not in its organization and results unlike atonality in music. In the field of art its nearest analogies are to be found in surrealism and in Dadaism; one could even find some similarities between "college" and the "integrated curriculum." Like the modernist composer and modernist artist, the modernist educator starts off with a diatribe against the traditional. He refuses to believe that the modernist in art or in music has normally had a training first in the classics of his field. He would dismiss as unsound pedagogy the story that Picasso once tore up the canvas of a "creative" student in his atelier with the words "To paint like Picasso you must first learn to draw." The only criterion acceptable to the new educator is not unlike that prevalent among certain art and music critics—"Has the pupil fulfilled to his own satisfaction the task which he has undertaken?" The emphasis again is on "the how" and not "the what." Education thus has its counterparts in such current remarks as "The music in itself was not much but it was played beautifully" or "Of course the picture is beyond me but look at the technique" or "The play was no good but the acting was superb." As in other fields there has been a transition in education from classicism to romanticism to expressionism. And, finally, as in modernist music which always seems to require an enlarged orchestra and the use of every possible sound-making device that was ever created, the modern educator never has enough equipment or materials or he looks for them outside the school, so that "the community, the State and the nation" become his workshop.

There is, of course, another trend which merges into those preceding it: the effort to use the schools to build a new social order—for the educator, like the creative artist in art and music, does not feel he can keep aloof from the current political scene. At present there still seems to be some indecision as to whether education will become a "Fantasia of the Unconscious" or will help to build a "Brave New World." In any case experimentalism is rampant. As in contemporary art and music, some contribution may survive to enrich the permanent stream. Undoubtedly much that is called traditional in education is not adapted to the vast hordes now crowding into high schools and colleges; undoubtedly many of the criticisms leveled against traditional education merit consideration. One point can be insisted upon, however: educational salvation will not come either by discarding content as traditional or by substituting the new as the best. A successful education cannot be expected from recipes and panaceas; a successful education can only be looked for as teachers become masters of what they teach, recognize the relation of what they teach to the society in which they teach, and have a sympathetic understanding of those whom they teach. Unfortunately, while buildings, equipment, textbooks, modern methods and new curricula have been made the subjects of propaganda for the support of education, little, very little, has been done to "sell" teachers to the American public. Before that can be done the American public needs to become more aware of what is sold to it under the guise of progress in education.

The Cult of Uncertainty
(1943)

Isaac Kandel was a leading scholar of American education and a powerful critic of Progressive education. In 1942, he was invited to deliver the 15th Annual Kappa Delta Pi Lecture. His address was published one year later as a book entitled The Cult of Uncertainty, *which—though little known today—continues to be one of the most provocative works about American education ever written. The selection below is the preface and the introductory chapter to this book. In his lecture, Kandel begins by quoting and criticizing John Dewey, who delivered Kappa Delta Pi's 10th Annual Lecture in 1938. Kandel respected Dewey, but believed that Dewey's pragmatism had led to numerous problems in educational thought and practice. Kandel identifies many of these problems in this selection.*

Kandel selected the title, The Cult of Uncertainty, *as a not so subtle reference to Dewey's* The Quest for Certainty, *published in 1929. In* The Quest for Certainty, *Dewey claimed that the attempt to discover, understand, or practice eternal ideals was an impossible, hopeless task. He argued that philosophers should abandon any attempt to arrive at certainty in science, philosophy, or teaching. Teachers and philosophers should be content, Dewey believed, with efficient problem-solving as their purpose. Kandel disagreed with Dewey. As a critic of pragmatic philosophy, Kandel was a trenchant skeptic about the theory and claims of Progressive education.*

Kandel provided a devastating historical and philosophical critique of his colleagues who had been chasing educational fashions for more than 30 years. Educational theories that reject tradition, to Kandel, were sure to end up promoting rootlessness, cultivating nihilism, and increasing cultural fragmentation. To counteract these problems, Kandel calls upon teacher educators to re-emphasize moral ideals and intellectual standards, while at the same time working to raise the status of the teaching profession.

Forgotten Heroes of American Education, pages 433–446

PREFACE

In the catastrophe which has overwhelmed the world a grave responsibility rests upon the shoulders of all who are concerned with the education of children and youth. To consider the conflict of educational theories merely as one between traditionalists, essentialists, or progressives is to miss the fundamental challenge of our times. The challenge cannot be met by the easy adoption of labels and slogans. The world has been torn from its foundations and has lost its bearings. The changes produced by science may be admitted without the complete surrender of ideals and values which man has throughout his history sought to attain. Even those who have in the past quarter of a century sought to reconstruct education on a philosophy of change must admit that the present war, like the last, is a struggle to preserve ideas, ideals, and values against the onslaught of a new barbarism. Through education more than through any other social agency is their preservation made possible. To stress methods and techniques at the expense of content is to forget that content is itself a tool for new advances into the realms of the unknown. But the haphazard "creation" of content in the light of individual needs and purposes without the control of values carries with it the danger of irrationalism and anti-intellectualism. The retreat from reason which has been most apparent in the ideology of National Socialism has been accompanied by a rejection of humanism, which is also threatened by the cult of change and the rejection of inherited values. Nothing is gained by the charge that traditionalists and essentialists favor a static world or by the claim that progressives are dynamic. The fundamental issue is concerned with the source of ideals and values by which men live. To this conflict, which is not confined to the United States, the discussion in the following pages is addressed.

—I. L. Kandel
New York City
November 17, 1942

In the final paragraph of his book, *Experience and Education,* which appeared in 1938 in the Kappa Delta Pi Lecture Series, Dr. John Dewey recorded it as his firm belief that "the fundamental issue is not of new versus old education, nor of progressive versus traditional education, but a question of what anything whatever must be to be worthy of the name *education....* What we want and need is education pure and simple, and we shall make surer and faster progress when we devote ourselves to finding out just what education is and what conditions have to be satisfied in order that education may be a reality and not a name or a slogan." This is the most clearly stated challenge that has been heard in the recent history of education in the United States. There are few countries in the world in which as much time, energy, and attention are devoted to education as in the United States. There are few countries in the world in which there exist as much confusion and uncertainty about the meaning of education in all its aspects as in the United States.

This situation is not a product of the economic crisis of the past decade nor of the war emergency, which has both raised new problems and directed attention to some of the fundamental issues of education. The unrest in education antedated these two crises. Some two decades ago C. W. Bardeen already discussed in an article on "The Man Milliner in Education" the efforts to discover panaceas for the reconstruction of the theory and practice of education. Since that time the number of labels and slogans has increased with the passing of each year. The conflict in education is not new. It has become more serious since the beginning of the century when "the lid was taken off the universe." Just as soon as tradition and authority began to be questioned and criticized, everyone concerned with education became his own authority. The results may be examined in the educational literature which has appeared since 1900.

When the present century opened, the educational doctrines of Herbart held the stage, but they were soon challenged by the new theories of interest, effort, and discipline, which stemmed in part from the pragmatic approach and in part from the incipient study of child psychology. From both points of view the traditional organization of the educative process was attacked and the child was placed in the center of the educational stage, and the two data of the educative process—the child and the curriculum, or the school and society—were separated. Since that time efforts to relate the two have on the whole failed and for a long time the emphasis has been either on the child or on the curriculum, either on the school or on society, except in so far as a somewhat nebulous hypothesis of indeterminate experience has been appealed to in order to bridge the gap between the one and the other.

The word to conjure with was "growth," but any discussion of the direction of growth was frowned upon on the plea that growth is its own justification. The child was to grow along the lines of his own felt needs, his own interests, and his own experiences. The injection of an ordered program of studies or experiences came to be regarded as anathema lest growth be thwarted through external imposition. The issue was clinched just as soon as the dreaded word "indoctrination" was introduced to be replaced later by the still more terrifying word "propaganda." The presentation of any ideas to the pupil came to be regarded as a serious menace to independent thinking. In order to promote growth there was devised the project method whereby each pupil or group of pupils worked for their own educational salvation on problems arising out of their own interests; the project method led to the activity method, and the activity method led to the activity curriculum.

The gradual development of this theory of education prepared the stage for the next assault on the restricting influence of the so-called educational tradition—an assault on the organization of the curriculum in terms of subjects and on intellectual compartmentalization, which was assumed to be the result of this organization. Everything was now to be integrated; the stream of consciousness, whose flow was to be uninterrupted by rigid time-schedules, or activity leading to further activity, or the search for facts and information as the learning situation demanded was to serve as the basis of the educational program. Subsequently there were added to the learning situation the subconscious influences which determined attitudes, emotions, and drives. Subjects or such parts of them as might be needed now melted into each other; that this process resulted in producing new "subjects"—social studies or general science may be cited as examples— and new textbooks was not given serious thought. What was to be avoided was the logical organization of subjects which man had devised as tools for his survival. Knowledge was to be acquired when needed and knowledge for its own sake or the acquisition of what were referred to as "mere facts" was thrown into the discard. In its most blatant form the child-centered school was built up on the interests, needs, drives, and urges of the pupils. These interpretations of the theory of growth resulted in nihilism and anti-intellectualism.

That the situation was getting out of hand was recognized by some at any rate of the leaders who were referred to as the authorities for the new theories. When the extreme advocates of freedom for the child continued to insist that nothing must be "fixed-in-advance" for the pupils in the way of an organized curriculum or that no ends or plans should be suggested to them through fear that the progress of their sacred intellectual individuality would be inhibited or thwarted, it was Dr. Dewey and not a traditionalist who objected to this assumption of spontaneous germination of mental life. Such a method, he said, was stupid, since it attempted the impossible, misconceived the conditions of independent thinking, and was almost sure to be "casual, sporadic, and ultimately fatiguing, accompanied by nervous strain." When the attack on subjects had been under way for some time and "the curriculumless curriculum" or the integrated curriculum was receiving increasing attention, the spokesmen in favor of "subjects" were Dr. B. H. Bode and Dr. Dewey. "The traditional subjects," wrote the former, "stood for an educational value, which we neglect at our peril," while the latter stated that "the next step ('to finding the material of learning within experience') is the progressive development of what is already experienced into a fuller and richer form, a form that gradually approximates that in which subject-matter is presented to the skilled, mature person." As will be pointed out later, the consequences of the attack on subjects were to appear just as soon as the war broke out.

The protests of the leaders came too late. The child-centered school was soon to have a competitor. A movement was launched to build a new social order through the schools. Whether this movement was inspired by a feeling that the child-centered school was too individualistic and failed to develop a sense of social responsibility, or by a desire to correct the social deficiencies revealed by the depression, or by the report of socially useful activities in the schools of Soviet Russia is not clear. What is clear is that an effort was now made, even by some who had long refused to tolerate any ends "fixed-in-advance," to define the direction of the growth of pupils in schools in terms of the kind of society that the United States ought to become. Children and youth were to be educated to be critical, to discover the shortcomings of society, and to become the social engineers of their country. The blueprints of the new society which was proposed have been discarded, but the idea of social engineering, the critical survey of the community, and the search for immediately needed reforms has been taken over as the basis of school work and made the objective of the latest arrival on the educational stage—the community-centered school founded on interaction between the school and the community and building the program of studies around projects now stimulated by the environment rather than by the pupils' own interests.

These examples are cited as illustrations of the state of uncertainty and confusion which prevail in American education. Those who have protested against anything "fixed-in-advance" have succeeded in leaving nothing fixed. Starting with the education of young children they have gradually extended their theories upwards in the hope and expectation that all the colleges of the country will see the light radiating from the three or four experimental colleges. Those educators who have been responsible for what is called Progressive Education and is described as an attitude and not a set plan or method, have practiced what they preached; they have been creative; they have been imaginative; they have encouraged experimentation; they have, in fact, exemplified their own theories of growth but in so many directions that any concerted effort to develop an education without names or slogans has virtually become impossible.

The common starting-point has been found by these educators in their revulsion against tradition and authority, which they have so caricatured as to leave the impression that the world is only just witnessing the dawn of education and that the experience of the race, whose authority they reject, may be completely forgotten. Having no tradition and rejecting authority, they have fashioned the educational millinery of the recent decades on the claim that changing conditions demand changing educational adaptations and demand them immediately. In this view they have followed the popular tendency to confuse every change with progress, and have succeeded by painting the traditional school in its worst aspects. Nor in the rapidly kaleidoscopic changes of theory and practice have they assumed responsibility for consolidating their positions. Instead there has been a movement from theory to theory without putting any of them to their own pragmatic test of whether they work. Promotion campaigns are conducted; associations are organized and proliferate; yearbooks are published with little continuity of topics; and activities are engaged in too frequently for the sake of the activities themselves and with little regard to the possible results in practice.

Where the departure from the tradition of culture has not been so wide, there is a conflict between the claims of general education and the demands for vocational preparation, between learning to live and learning to earn a living. Few would deny the importance of both aspects of the problem; both are essential elements in living. The issue turns on the question of their appropriate organization—whether general education shall be completed, as though that were ever possible, before vocational preparation is begun, whether the two shall be continued side by side with an intimate relation between them, or whether vocational preparation can be given in such a way that it transcends mere training in skills. In the field of vocational preparation itself two issues have arisen. Of these the first is whether, in view of rapidly changing developments in technology, schools can ever hope to be adequately equipped to keep up with the changes; the second is whether, as a result of these conditions, some types of vocational preparation could not be better given by the revival of a system of apprenticeship, provided that arrangements can be made to keep the learners under the supervision of the educational authorities. While the problems of organization have still to be determined, the obligation of society to provide vocational preparation and training for earning a livelihood is universally acknowledged. The equal importance of education for the world in which the worker is to live as a citizen is as yet not recognized universally, although attention has begun to be given to adult education in this connection. But even the success of adult education itself is dependent not so much on the organization of facilities as on the development in schooldays of an interest in further education.

Nor can it be claimed that there is any stability of organization in education. The kindergarten does not yet enjoy an established position and may be sloughed off at any time as an economy measure; the nursery school has only recently appeared on the scene. The full significance of the educational care of the young, whether from the point of view of the child or of society, has not yet been fully recognized. Beyond this stage and before the six-three-three plan has been universally adopted there is already a movement for a six-four-four plan of organization. At the college level confusion has been injected by the announcement that the University of Chicago will award the first degree at the end of the sophomore year. There are some who anticipate that the effect of acceleration to meet the emergency situation may result in the adoption of a three-year course in place of the four-year college course, a result which may in turn affect the length of the junior college course. To the uncertainties of organization must be added the uncertainties of administration, of the size of administrative areas, of overlapping authorities, and of financial participation by the Federal Government. These uncertainties, however, are due to a desire to improve and extend the facilities of education and to give reality to the ideal of equality of educational opportunity. They are in an entirely different category from the confusion attending the educative process and the content of education discussed earlier.

From whatever point of view American education is approached there is evident unrest. As the pragmatist would say, the progress of education is blocked by innumerable forked roads which should stimulate thinking. But thinking on as fundamental a social problem as education requires concerted and cooperative action, which, in view of the wide cleavages noted by Dr. Dewey, no longer seems possible. Groups are arrayed against groups and a common meeting ground is no longer available. Success appears to rest with the largest and most vociferous groups and genuine criticism is resented. Many years ago Santayana, in discussing "The Moral Background of American Life," wrote "Ideas are abandoned in virtue of a mere change of feeling, without any new evidence or new arguments. We do not now refute our predecessors, we pleasantly bid them good-bye. Even if all our principles are unwittingly traditional we do not like to bow openly to authority.... People refused to be encumbered with any system, even one of their own; they were content to imbibe more or less of the spirit of philosophy and let it play on such facts as happened to attract their attention." Later, in *The Last Puritan,* Santayana returned to the same theme when he wrote "All that is American, or modern, is the absence of any tradition in which the born poet or God-intoxicated man could take root. He therefore simply evaporates or *Peters* out."

What is regarded as a strong feature in recent tendencies of educational thought and practice—the rejection of tradition and authority—has been described by critics who have shown a real concern for the meaning, significance, and potentialities of American life, as rootlessness. "A rootless people," writes Van Wyck Brooks in *Sketches in Criticism,* "cannot endure forever and we shall pay in the end for our superficialities in ways more terrible than we can yet conceive." Reflecting on the same theme in *The Man Who Had Everything,* Louis Bromfield concludes in the words of the American hero of this novel that "These people—his people—were nomads, from those who wandered across the vastness of their own country in broken-down Fords to those who moved restlessly from place to place in luxury over the face of the earth. When they grew roots, they were miserable. He wasn't the only American who had been practically active all his life without ever having lived at all."

Louis Adamic, surveying the American scene as an immigrant, describes rootlessness as the "American disease," which one of the characters in *Grandsons* defines as follows: "In this respect I was like most people in America. They were shadows flitting over the face of this beautiful continent. Shadows of what human life could be. Shadows of one another. They were not connected with any basic reality. They were hardly alive. There was little life, a real dynamic life in America. Only a sort of nervous, furious, superficial existingness. Scarcely anything human, at least contemporary human, in America had any depth. All was surface, sudden, baffling violence. These were the symptoms of the disease." To remedy this disease, says Adamic, calmness and strength are needed.

The development of calmness and strength, a sense of social stability, and a feeling of membership in a common culture should be one of the paramount functions of education. Educators, however, have not been concerned with roots or with stability. After paying lip service to the fact that the individual acquires a personality through the culture in which he lives, they concentrate their attention upon the immediately contemporary, upon the precariousness of life, upon the "dynamic," and upon building for the future, ignoring the past and allowing the present to take care of itself. "American education," writes T. S. Stribling in *These Bars of Flesh*, "is like a man who continuously builds himself new homes and never lives in one." In education, at any rate, the situation has not changed much since the days when Emerson described "The Young America" as "a country of beginners, of projects, of designs and expectations." Like the common man of the thirties and forties of the last century, educators seek novelty rather than perfection and call this process "adapting education to changing needs." As one Progressive educator put it recently, after admitting the prevalence of confusion and perplexity, he was not interested so much in finding out what produced them as in fighting for a future that can be brighter than the past, appealing, as Sydney Smith said of the American a century ago, not to history but to prophecy. For the educational theorist of this stamp, as for Alice in Wonderland, it doesn't matter which way he goes, so long as he gets somewhere.

Appeal to prophecy is safe, but there are children and youth to be educated for the present. Irresponsibility cannot continue for long, even if bolstered up by promises of a brighter future. An accounting is demanded at some time. That time arrived with the threat and the outbreak of the war, when the nation discovered to its cost what uncertainty in education means. The armed forces were compelled to lower their standards in recruiting an adequate personnel with a sufficient knowledge of mathematics, including arithmetic. Colleges had to provide introductory training in elementary mathematics for students who wished to study chemistry and physics. From one end of the country to the other came reports that students do not have a knowledge of their nation's history, because the subject had been displaced by the social studies and discussions of controversial issues. Geography has never had an assured place in the high school curriculum, so that it is not surprising that a knowledge of that subject was found inadequate. And when the ideals of democracy and the meaning of the democratic form of government had to face the greatest challenge in their history, it was discovered that the schools "had done little or nothing to impart a knowledge of them to several generations of pupils in the schools; manifestos and creeds on democracy had to be drafted; and books and methods had to be improvised hurriedly to make up for the time that had been lost. Book titles rang the changes on the word "democracy" just as in the previous decade they had been rung on "education for change."

On two points—on faith in education and on the provision of equality of educational opportunity—there is, as there always has been in the history of the United States, almost complete unanimity. And yet the 1940 census revealed that ten million citizens over twenty-five years of age had had only four grades of education or less, while the number of men rejected on account of functional illiteracy—inability to follow written instructions—under the Selective Service Act was enough to make up ten army divisions. In a country which has devoted as much attention to health instruction and physical education both in and out of school as the United States the number of men rejected from service in the armed forces for physical reasons could have filled fifteen combat divisions. In a country which annually spends more for education than any other country in the world teachers have left schools in such numbers that it was doubtful at the beginning of the school year 1942–43 whether many schools could be opened. The reflection is not on the teachers but on the fact that in almost any other occupation they could earn more than the average monthly salary of $77.42 received by them in an appreciable number of states. Poor salaries mean poor preparation, and poor preparation means that teachers are bound by the shackles of textbooks not much more advanced than those used by the pupils whom they try to educate. In the field of secondary education, as a consequence of the uncertainty of objectives and an ever-widening menu of subjects constantly expanded to meet the needs of the heterogeneous mass of high school pupils and included with little reference to educational values, a large number of teachers are required to teach subjects in which they have had little or no preparation. The frontier thinker in education, however, is too busy speculating about change and the brighter future to devote the time and intelligence needed to correct these admitted defects in American education.

These facts are known; attention has been directed to them by critics who wish to exercise a steadying influence on education. Criticism is resented, however, or rejected by the facile refutation that it emanates from traditionalists or reactionaries who favor the *status quo,* or that in pleading for orderly programs of instruction and for standards the critics wish to put education into a strait jacket. Any suggestion that one of the most important functions of education is the training of intelligence is rejected with the argument that intelligence trains itself if the pupil engages in something that he can do or wants to do. Sometimes the suggestion is rejected by the facile retort that the training of intelligence produces intellectuals too stupid or too aloof to carry on the work of the world; the watch-tower from which the contemporary world is to be surveyed must be substituted for that prison of the intellectual, the ivory tower.

Hence the revolt against college entrance requirements, despite their flexibility or even dilution; hence the gradual shift from the "academic" to the "practical"; hence the recent attack on the plan to secure some place for general education in the preparation of teachers by instituting a National Teacher Examination; hence the refusal to take seriously the report of the Carnegie Foundation on *The Student and His Knowledge,* because the tests used in this report dealt with "mere knowledge"; hence, finally, a failure to rebut the charge that many college graduates are illiterate, and the fact that many students in college fail because of inability to read in the sense of getting meanings from the printed page.

More dangerous for the present welfare and stability of the nation is the failure to train for an adequate understanding of the responsibilities of citizenship. This statement would no doubt be refuted by a reference to the attention devoted to the social studies and the discussions of controversial issues. The fact is, however, that the schools have failed to produce that moral fervor and sense of obligation for the preservation of American ideals of democracy which can in any way begin to compare with the fervor engendered in the totalitarian countries. That "vehement passion for democracy," to which Lord Bryce so frequently referred as characteristic of the American people, has declined. And yet the obligations of education to prepare for enlightened citizenship have been repeatedly expressed since the Republic was established, since the day when George Washington urged his fellow-citizens to promote "institutions for the general diffusion of knowledge"—not in order to insure the prosperity and success of the individual but because "in proportion as the structure of government gives force to public opinion, it is essential that public opinion be enlightened." In various forms this original challenge to the people of the United States has been reiterated from the time of

George Washington to the time of Franklin Delano Roosevelt. To remind the American people of their educational tradition the United States Office of Education reprinted the bulletin containing the statements of publicists and statesmen which first appeared in 1913 and brought it up to date under the title *Expressions on Education by Builders of the United States* (1941). The extensive literature on education for democracy which has appeared in the past five years may be cited as evidence, if any were needed, that the task of cultivating an understanding of the meaning, significance, and obligations of democracy has not been fulfilled. Even on the intellectual side the Report of the Regents' Inquiry in the State of New York found a large percentage of high school students to be socially incompetent despite the introduction of the social studies.

Faith in education is one of the most deeply rooted ideals in American culture and is ever reverently on the lips of every speaker and writer on the subject, whether lay or professional. The facts already cited—the uncertainty and confusion in educational theory and the failure to secure adequate results from what Dr. T. H. Briggs has described as *The Great Investment*—justify doubts whether that faith has been kept. Still less is there any ground for the assumption that faith in education has been translated into practical terms by providing equality of educational opportunity in all parts of the country. On the failure to make such provision evidence has been accumulating since the educational conditions of the country were revealed during World War I. The most recent investigations show that the opportunity for education is dependent upon the accidents of residence and of family circumstances. For current expenditure per pupil enrolled in schools the lowest state spent only $24 per pupil, less than one-fifth spent by the highest state and less than one-third spent in the nation as a whole. The value of school property per pupil showed a range from $81 in the lowest state to $526 in the highest, indicating a range from overcrowded, poorly constructed and obsolete school buildings to buildings which are the most modern in the world. The range of average salaries for teachers, according to the latest available figures, was from $524 a year to $2,604, figures which mean at the lower end of the scale the presence in the schools of teachers who are poorly prepared and lacking in those qualifications which can raise the occupation of teaching from a mechanical trade to the level of a profession. Here may be found the reason for the alarming drift of teachers from the schools into industry, just as soon as the opportunity presents itself, and for the readiness to accept without criticism the latest theories and practices as the best. The public, which is amused by the caricature of teachers, fails to realize that the reflection is on itself and not on the teachers. Wide discrepancies exist in the amount of schooling provided each year to the children; in the lowest state schools are open for an average number of 146 days as contrasted with the highest average of 187 days with further discrepancies between rural and urban schools. At the secondary level the number of pupils between fourteen and seventeen enrolled in high schools varied from 395 to 942 per thousand. The discrepancies in the provision of educational opportunities are due, of course, to the discrepancies in tax resources and the number of children to be educated, the poorest states also having the largest number of children. While the average income per child for the nation as a whole was $2,534, the range from the lowest to the highest state was from $698 to $5,130.

From the point of view of the nation the important issue raised by these figures is not whether the amount and quality of education provided are adequate for the development of each individual as a worker and a citizen, but whether unity, welfare, and stability can be assured in a nation in which such varieties of educational standards exist. The traditional mobility of the American people, the migrants of the depression period, and the wholesale shift of population in the current emergency all point to the inevitability of making the provision of equality of educational opportunity a national concern. The question of the control of education is not serious; in the light of the American tradition of educational administration ample precedents are available for its solution.

The important issue on the whole question of the relations between local and state authorities and between state and federal governments lies in the definition of equality of educational opportunity. If additional funds are made available for education only to be spent for more and better school buildings and equipment, for the extension of the school year, and for increased facilities for secondary education, there is no guarantee that the educational situation will be improved. The only guarantee of equality of educational opportunity is the teacher adequately prepared to meet the increasingly complex obligations of his profession and remunerated on a scale commensurate with these obligations. The principle "As is the teacher, so is the school" has long been recognized; that the principle has not been honored in practice has been too frequently revealed statistically in the reports on salaries and socially in terms of the poor esteem enjoyed by the profession. There is another reason, however, for raising and improving the status of teachers; with an adequate preparation in general culture and professional preparation and enjoying a status as high as that of any other profession, there is at least some hope that teachers may become more critical of and less ready to accept every new slogan, every new device, every proposed change in educational fashions as the last word in the progress and advancement of education. A new social and economic status, a new realization of their contribution to national welfare, and stronger convictions derived from a genuinely professional preparation and insight growing out of such preparation into the everyday problems of classroom teaching may give teachers the confidence, which they have not displayed sufficiently, to challenge the speculations of the theorist. For the uncertainty and confusion in education are due to a large extent to the propagation of educational theories for which their advocates have no responsibility in practice.

A few years ago Archibald MacLeish characterized the writers and scholars of the country as "The Irresponsibles" who refused to assume responsibility for the common culture and for its defense. Influenced by the methods of the scientist they cultivated "objectivity, detachment, dispassion." "What matters now," said MacLeish, "is the defense of culture—the defense truly, and in the most literal terms, of civilization as men have known it for the last two thousand years." Educators have been no less irresponsible. They have concentrated their attention on the immediately present and contemporary; they have refused to recognize any value, except incidentally as the need might arise, in the experience of the race; ignoring the immaturity of pupils they have stressed the study of controversial issues as each political or economic crisis arose; through fear of indoctrination they have emphasized techniques of controversy as more important than judgments or values, leaving in their place only cynicism and skepticism; and they have assumed that the study of controversial issues whose solution has defied the experts of the world is easier than the study of mathematics, languages, literature, and history. In a word, educators in their concern with change and with the precarious future have not only ignored but have even denied the value of what MacLeish has described as "enduring things," since eternal verities and the inherited forms of culture have no place in the vocabulary of those who have been the leaders of educational thought in the last quarter of a century.

The chief failure in the cult of uncertainty has been the refusal to accept any responsibility for a clear definition of values, for a clear statement of the purpose of education, for which the thousands of objectives and aims, the results of fact-finding analyses, have been no substitute. Only as the threat of war became imminent was an attempt made to define the meaning of democracy for education. By that time the evidences of disunity in the country—social, political, economic, religious, and racial— were too strong to be ignored. Nor was the disunity altogether due to the politico-economic crisis; when preachers of hatred and intolerance can make their appeals, their success must be attributed to the failure of education to inculcate faith in the ideals of democracy, at the heart of which stand tolerance and the recognition of the worth and dignity of the individual as a human being. That failure can also be attributed to an educational theory which refuses to accept anything as "fixed-in-advance," and which, with its emphasis on change and the precariousness of life, can only result, as it has done, in rootlessness. The cult of uncertainty, of an education without any values other than an exaggerated premium placed on methods and techniques without well-defined content, leads inevitably to a negation of ideals and of faith and to a repudiation of the inherited forms of culture and of humanity without which the surface changes in the stream of life are mistaken for the waves of the future.

Character Formation:
A Historical Perspective
(1959)[1]

Kandel was well-read in the classic works of social, political, and educational thought. His knowledge in these areas is evident in this historical reflection on the idea of character formation. He traces the persistence of the ideal of character formation from the Hebrew tradition through modern thinkers like Herbert Spencer and Johann Friedrich Herbart. As Kandel argues early in the essay, the one aim of education that has persisted throughout thousands of years of history is the ideal of character formation. Since teachers are the central element in a good school, character formation for teachers turns out to be the most essential ingredient in any curriculum for teaching teachers.

This work by Kandel helps 21st century teacher educators to think clearly and deeply about what moral education for teachers ought to include. Although Kandel seeks to treat all traditions in this essay equally, the influence of Aristotle on Kandel's work is evident throughout. Good character, to Kandel, is created through action and practical decision-making in a social setting. The cultivation of virtue demands more than knowledge; it requires practical action toward an ideal end. It is about doing more than knowing. It also requires a firm understanding of the difference between means and ends, both of which Kandel understands must conform to the standards of justice. Aristotelian social and political philosophy turns out to be a long-lasting, solid foundation for the profession of teaching.

---

1. Paper read before the Institute of Social and Religious Studies, New York, October 26, 1959.

Forgotten Heroes of American Education, pages 447–458

I

The one aim of education which has persisted through the ages has always been the formation of character. The form and content of education, whether formal or informal, may have changed, but the dominant aim has always been character formation. The Hebraic "Train up a child in the way he should go and when he is old he will not depart from it," has been stated or restated in different forms, but the central idea has always remained the same. In *The Republic,* Plato wrote that, "The beginning is the chiefest part of any work, especially in a young and tender thing, for that is the time at which the character is being formed and most readily receives the desired impressions." And it is significant that the Greek word from which character is derived meant that which is impressed on or stamped into something, and by an extension it also came to mean a likeness or image. These original meanings must be borne in mind in later discussions. The importance of the aim was restated by Herbart at the beginning of the nineteenth century when he maintained that, "the one task, and the whole task, of education may be summed up in the concept of morality." A little more than a century later, Dewey stated that "it is a commonplace of educational theory that the establishing of character is a comprehensive aim of school instruction and discipline."

The reason for the persistence of the emphasis on character formation becomes obvious when it is recalled that the function of education, whether in a simple primitive form of society or in a complex and advanced state of modern times, is to prepare the young to become members of their group, or community, or state. The human being is a social or political animal, as Aristotle said, and all his tendencies and capacities cannot develop and come to maturity except in a social setting. The task of education is to help the plastic immature being to become an acceptable member of society, but the requirements for that membership are defined by society and its culture. The immature child becomes a mature adult as he comes to adopt or as he is indoctrinated with the habits, thoughts, culture, and ways of life of his gradually expanding community. "Individuality," as Dewey once pointed out, "develops into shape and form only through the interactions with actual conditions." A French educator expressed the same idea when he wrote that "French philosophers, as is well known, distinguish between individuality and personality. The individual is such by virtue of the fact that he is different from others. He is a person to the extent that he represents the conscience of truths valid for all and the will to undertake duties common to all. The individual ought to become a person, that is, in a sense he should de-individualize himself, and this is the work of education and of personal effort." Character, then, represents "the color, the scent, and the shape" of the social culture in which the individual has been developed and by which he has been influenced in his growth.

Character formation is accordingly the process of impressing a certain way of life on the individual. The concept has been succinctly stated by Professor William E. Hocking in the statement that the first function of education is to communicate or reproduce the type in the society to which the individual belongs. Education must also create opportunities for growth beyond the type. The notion that education for the reproduction of the type is closely associated with the idea that education is an essential factor in the survival and perpetuation of society and its culture. The existence and stability of a society are conditioned by the dissemination of common objects of allegiance, commonly accepted standards of discourse, and commonly approved forms of conduct. These come to be manifested in the character of the members of the social group. Deviations from the common standard put the individual beyond the pale; he may come to be regarded as unreliable or eccentric; or under certain conditions he may become an outcast or an outlaw. And even when the second aim—growth beyond the type—is analyzed, it is found that a certain basis of conformity must be maintained and the growth must not be so far beyond the type that it becomes suspect or regarded as a danger to the structure of society.

II

The basic issue at all times has not been whether character can be changed, but rather what values can be discarded, modified, or altered without threatening the stability of a society. To discuss how and when values change and how long it takes for the changes to become generally accepted would be to embark on the discussion of another issue than that under consideration. As Herbert Spencer pointed out, the action of circumstances upon men is more effective than planning in advance in bringing about cultural changes. This axiom the history of Soviet ideology has amply demonstrated. It is open to question whether the plan to change human nature which the early Revolutionaries had intended to carry out has succeeded. The Soviet citizen is still expected to be in the right line, but the line is no longer as clearly marked as it was.

The kind of character that wins approval depends upon the traits or ways of behaving and thinking that society regards as most desirable for its stability and perpetuation. Values have varied through the ages; they have been religious, political, economic, cultural, and so on; and the changes of emphasis have produced changes in the types of character socially approved or acceptable. Character, then, is social in origin and its manifestations socially oriented, so that few actions of the individual can ever be regarded as self-regarding or free from impact on others.

Since the dominant aim of education has always been the formation of character, the problems concerned with its development have also persisted through the ages. What is meant by good, when it is claimed that society expects an individual to be a man of good character? How is a good character or virtue acquired—through habit, imitation, knowledge, will, emotions or feelings? How much does nature contribute to the formation of character and how much does nurture? What are the sanctions that determine character? Who has the responsibility for the development of character—parents, teachers, social institutions? Should instruction that aims at the formation of character be formal or informal, direct or indirect? Are there permanent values or ideals, eternal verities, that are always regarded as essential and fundamental for social living, no matter what external changes may take place?

Many of these questions were already answered in the Old Testament. Character or conduct or the way of life was clearly defined. Education, formal or informal, was to produce the God-fearing individual who walked in all his ways. When Israel was enjoined "to keep the commandments of the Lord and his statutes," it was for the good and the survival of the whole community. From the earliest days the responsibility of training the child was imposed on both the father and the mother ("My son, hear the instruction of thy father and forsake not the law of thy mother"). The way the child should go was frequently defined—to fear God and obey his commandments is the whole duty of man, for the fear of the Lord is the beginning of wisdom. Character was molded by direct participation in the life and activities of the community, by parental training and injunctions, and, when necessary, by reproof or corporal punishment. ("He that spareth the rod hateth his son; but he that loveth him chasteneth him betimes," and "The rod and reproof give wisdom, but a child left to himself bringeth his mother to shame.")

Since the fear of the Lord is the beginning of wisdom, the ignorant man, according to the Talmud, could not be religious, that is, he could not behave in ways acceptable to God and man. Individual differences were recognized, but the ultimate aim of character formation remained the same and methods suited to the differences were suggested. The dominant aim of Judaism was to mold character and to produce a man conscious of his duties as defined by his religion. But the important thing was not theory but practice; "great is the study of the law for it leads to action." The sanctions in a theocratic community were religious.

Among the Athenians as among the Jews character was developed by participation in public activities, which made it possible to evaluate the behavior of children and youth. Religious training was the responsibility of the home. Instruction in the ways of life and the qualities that were desirable was given first by the father, later by the pedagogues, and through the influence of older boys on the younger. Obedience met with approval, but if a boy did not obey, he was "straightened out by threats and blows like a piece of warped wood." Teachers were expected to devote more attention to training in manners than to teaching reading and music. All the subjects of the curriculum—literature, stories of famous men, music, and gymnastics, however, were expected to contribute to the development of character, for "the life of man in every part has need for harmony and rhythm." The Greeks more than any other people believed that a well-rounded character involved a proper balance of the intellectual, aesthetic, physical as well as moral backgrounds. The fate that befell Socrates provides evidence that importance was also attached to the maintenance of religious traditions.

Plato and Aristotle were in agreement on the social and political importance of character training; but they disagreed on both methods and ends to be achieved. Plato held that the training of character should start as early as possible, but he was cautious in the selection of the models in literature and music to be presented to the young. He wished to prevent them from imitating anything base or illiberal, for "imitations beginning in early youth at last sink into the constitution and become a second nature of body, voice, and mind." A child should be habituated to love the good and hate the bad, and "when reason comes, he will recognize and salute her as a friend with whom his education has made him long familiar." Knowledge of the good is acquired on the basis of habits. Virtue or good character; then, is knowledge, but such knowledge is gained only after long years of practice and contemplation, and is in the end dependent upon the social organization. For, he argues, "if a state has once started well, it exhibits a kind of circular progress. Adherence to a good system of nurture and education creates good natures, and good natures receiving the assistance of a good education, grow still better than they were."

Aristotle, however, while he advocated the teaching of the same subjects as Plato, was opposed to the idea of selection or censorship. He believed that if the young had the opportunity to learn about all aspects of life, their minds would be purged of evil and the good be strengthened in them. Nor did he accept the Socratic dictum that virtue is knowledge. Virtue, according to Aristotle, is an activity, not a matter of the intellect but of the will to choose between the right and the wrong. We must do good things before we can be good, and right habits develop right emotions and passions. But since man is a political animal, he can develop his capacities and character only by sharing in the life of the community. Hence to be a loyal citizen is the same thing as being a good man produced through habits, training, and discipline, for the better the character, the better the government. "The end of politics," wrote Aristotle, "is the highest good, and there is nothing that this science takes so much pains with as producing a certain character in the citizens, that is, making men good and able to do fine actions."

The formation of character among the Romans was for centuries by imitation of great men in their history, by loyalty to the traditions of their ancestors, and by reverence to their parents. Different from the Greeks, the Romans were more interested in practical and moral conduct, in manliness and courage, in prudence and earnestness. Unlike the Greeks they did not value the aesthetic side of life so that grace and beauty of character, harmony and rhythm had no place in their standards. Horace refers with pride to the debt he owed his father who taught him to avoid vice by examples and who superintended his education instead of leaving him to the care of a slave. Earlier, Cato, the latest survival of ancient practice, wrote *Maxims (Praecepta ad Filium)* and a versified moral textbook *(Carmen de Moribus)*. When, under Greek influence, the Romans turned their attention to formal education and especially to the training of the orator, they sought to combine the old emphasis on moral character with competence in public speaking. "To their morals doubtless attention is first to be paid," wrote Quintilian; "but let them also speak with propriety," imitating good models and standards set by their parents and teachers. The virtuous life and eloquence are combined and inseparable and "no one can be an orator who is not a good man."

III

The Middle Ages ushered in a new concept of the ends of education. The aim was no longer preparation for public activities as such but to prepare loyal followers of the faith, devoted not to the mundane interests of this world, but to the salvation of souls in the next. In the formation of character the ends that were emphasized were docility, obedience, and devoutness. Except in the service of the church there was no place for either intellectualism or aestheticism. All educational institutions were under the control or supervision of the ecclesiastical authorities. Side by side with the emphasis on religious character, there developed under the sanction of the church another emphasis which was more secularly oriented; that was the institution of chivalry which, while it placed military prowess in the service of religion, developed its own code of ideals of courage, pride, self-respect, honor, and obedience. In the preparation of the knight, physical and aesthetic activities were not neglected; courtesy and gallantry to women and consideration for inferiors were indoctrinated. A pattern of character was established which was later to play an important part in education.

The Renaissance period called for a new type of individual and according to Aeneas Sylvius (Pope Pius II) character, "our one sure possession," is developed by the study of philosophy and letters and by a religious nature. To these there were gradually added through an expanding revival of the literature of Greece and Rome the ideals of a man of the world as elaborated under the aegis of chivalry. The individual so trained would distinguish himself by service to the Church and State and to the life of his fellow-men. The ideal was summed up in the motto of Winchester College, founded in 1382, "Manners maketh man." The Platonic and Roman principle that literature, wisely selected, contributes to the moral development of character *(abeunt literae in mores)* was accepted, while from the traditions of chivalry something of the aesthetic and physical was derived. The aim of education that dominated the Renaissance period was directed to the promotion of individual distinction which comes from good carriage and deportment, eloquent and polished conversation, the proper use of leisure, and refined taste and manners combined with public spirit and religious devotion. As Vittorino da Feltre, the first modern educator, wrote "Not everyone is called to be a lawyer, a physician, a philosopher, to live in the public eye, nor has everyone outstanding gifts of natural capacity, but all of us are created for the life of social duty, all are responsible for the personal influence which goes forth from us." The sanction of character, then, was religious, on the one side, and social opinion, on the other. The ideal character was accordingly the Christian gentleman trained through piety and letters *(pietas literata).*

The new instrument of learning, and therefore for the formation of character, elaborated first in Italy, was adopted in Germany and in England during the Reformation, as the basis for moral, social, and religious reform. Individual development was directed to public service in church and state. In Germany the stress was laid upon the preparation of "well-trained, wise, learned, able, and God-fearing men" for the varied activities of public and private life. Luther protested against the "imprisonment" of youth in schools without contact with the world about them. "But it is dangerous," he wrote, "for youth to be left there alone, thus debarred from social intercourse. Wherefore we ought to permit young people to see, to hear, and to know what is taking place around them in the world. Yet so that you hold them under discipline and teach them self-respect."

Sterner and more intense was the disciplinary training of character that followed Calvin's theological views. Built on the doctrine of original sin, the aim of character training was to save the individual from hell-fire and lead him to find grace through condign punishment for transgressions. This attitude dominated the educational practices of home, school, and church wherever Calvinism prevailed (in Holland, Scotland, and New England). The *New England Primer,* which first appeared about 1690, sets the tone in the first two lines:

In Adam's Fall
We Sinned All.

The English schools followed the same pattern as the German but added an emphasis on "good and civil manners" to the intellectual and religious aims current at the time. Discipline was strict in the schools of both countries and each school had its own laws and regulation for the conduct of the pupils both in and out of school. Gambling (dice and cards are generally mentioned), indecent language and conduct, reading obscene books, drinking and haunting of Taverns and alehouses were prohibited. Punishments ranged all the way from copying or memorizing lines, fines, the rod or birch, and, in Germany, imprisonment to expulsion. Greater reliance was placed upon external sanctions and control in the formation of character and church attendance and religious instruction were required. The following statement by Adam Siber, the Rektor of a school at *Grimmu,* one of three Furstenschlen established in the sixteenth century, throws some light on the difficulties of the teachers:

> What is one to say of the morals of the boys? One of the results of the Fall of Man is that parents set a bad example for their children, swearing, making wicked jests, eating and drinking immoderately at an overladen table, wearing such clothes as even the devil himself would not wear. But it would be easier to count the waves of the troubled sea than to enumerate the whole list of sins. From such a source nothing but corrupt offspring can come; as in the sowing, so is the reaping.... The morals of pupils are bad and not to be mended, not only among those of low birth, but also among those of the highest nobility.

IV

The schools in the seventeenth and eighteenth centuries continued to sink more and more into formalism. Two lines of approach to the problem under discussion were gradually being developed. The first of these was the gradual emergence of a sense of nationalism and consequently of new objects of allegiance. The sanctions for this trend were both political and religious, since separation of church and State did not take place till much later. The second line of interest contributed the variety of approaches to the question of character formation and moral training of children and youth. Although the participation of the Church in education continued in

France, except for the years of the Revolution, until the Third Republic, the basic influence can be traced back to Descartes' emphasis on reason. When the French system of education was secularized the intellectual or rationalistic emphasis dominated the program of moral training. This was given by direct instruction through stories from which the pupils were expected to draw the moral precepts. In the last year of the secondary schools moral instruction gave way to the study of philosophy. Religious instruction in the schools was abolished but one day a week, besides Sunday, was left free so that pupils could receive the religious instruction of their respective denominations.

The strongest influence on English practice was that of John Locke who stressed discipline both in instruction or the formal work of the school and in education which he regarded as the broader and more important factor in the development of character. The disciplining of character was to be secured by habituation, by self-control, and by the sacrifice of immediate desires.

"Habits," Locke believed, "work more constantly and with greater facility than reason, which, when we have need of it, is seldom fairly consulted and more rarely obeyed." His theory of character formation or "virtue which is the hard and valuable part to be aimed at in education" was carried into practice when the secondary schools began to be reformed at the beginning of the nineteenth century under the influence of Thomas Arnold and others, and, when these schools came to be known as the Public Schools, they served as a model for secondary schools in general with their emphasis on the corporate life of the school, on pupil self-government, and on sports and athletics. In the elementary schools, the emphasis was placed on religious instruction, denominational or non-denominational, and when publicly maintained schools were established after 1870 religious instruction of a non-denominational character was included in the curriculum. At the same time rigorous discipline was characteristic of all schools. The literature for children at all ages, intended to inculcate moral precepts, was largely sentimental moralizing which exercised little influence on character.

Greater and more widespread was the influence exercised by Rousseau than by Descartes or Locke, although his theory of character formation and moral training was not accepted immediately. Rousseau's educational doctrine like his social theory started with a belief in the original goodness of the human being. Hence the task of education, according to Rousseau, must be to protect the child as long as possible from contacts that would mar his development. "The first education," he wrote, "should be negative. It consists not in teaching principles of virtue and truth, but in guarding the heart against vice and the mind against error." Since childhood is "the sleep of reason," negative education "disposes the child to take the path that will lead him to truth, when he has reached the age to understand it, and to goodness, when he has acquired the faculty of recognizing and loving it." In the interval while reason is asleep, the child is to receive his moral training by natural consequences. This doctrine was later popularized by Herbert Spencer, but without exercising any influence on school or out-of-school practices. Later still the doctrine was revived by Progressive educators in the United States—the child should be allowed to develop his own standards of conduct by learning to judge the consequences of his actions. The doctrine is clearly stated in the *Tenth Yearbook* of the Department of Superintendence, published in 1932: "The present trend in theory is to place on the child the responsibility of working out his own code of conduct with some help from teachers and other adults in analyzing situations and with such light as he can get from a study of the history of mankind's experience with similar problems. The authority of society or of any part of it is not presented to the child as a guide to conduct. Reliance is placed on the experience of each individual child. The experience of the race in discovering what line of conduct works out satisfactorily and what does not is utilized only insofar as the child sees fit to appeal to it." From extreme authoritarianism the pendulum swung to permissiveness which was characteristic of the *Zeitgeist*.

V

Another approach to character formation as well as to intellectual training emerged in the nineteenth century in Germany despite the authoritarian nature of the home, society, and government. Johann Friedrich Herbart undertook the task of psychologizing both instruction and education, that is, both intellectual and moral development. Rejecting Kant's concept of the moral imperative, an intuitive sense of the good, he believed that the will to moral conduct is trained through action and experience leading up to moral judgment and reason. "Instruction," he wrote, "will form the circle of thought and education the character. The last is nothing without the first. Herein is contained the whole sum of my pedagogy." The teacher through instruction should constantly seek to cultivate a moral sense by many-sided experiences and a union of judgment with desire. This process would ensure an all-round, just, and stable will. Moral conduct is developed, in Herbart's opinion, by seeing and reacting to moral activity in others. Hence care must be taken to select the right experiences and the right examples for instruction. Herbart's error lay in relying too much on the influence of ideas. Nevertheless, his contribution to the improvement of the curriculum from the intellectual and emotional standpoint extended widely through the latter part of the nineteenth century and the early years of the present century.

The Herbartian theory of character-building was abandoned when it was realized that moral ideas do not necessarily lead to moral conduct; in other words, that knowledge is not virtue as was shown in the extended study of character by Hartshorne and May in the twenties. Character is produced in a social atmosphere. In the words of Stendhal, "one can acquire everything in solitude except character." If it is maintained that judgment of values and emotional susceptibility to them are essential as drives to the right kind of conduct, it follows as a corollary that character can have meaning only in a social situation from which the individual acquires his code of values. But judgment implies knowledge or ability to distinguish between the essential and non-essential in behavior. And behavior cannot take place without certain emotional feelings and reactions, which in turn determine the will or force to action. Since judgment or knowledge is not the whole of the process involved in making choices between right and wrong, truth and falsehood, it is now believed that direct moral instruction is ineffective because such instruction is isolated from actual experience in a social atmosphere.

Since character is formed through social approval or disapproval in the expanding number of institutions of which the individual is a member—home, school, church, recreation groups, occupations, and the larger community—and personality is cultivated in human relations the basic difficulty is to avoid a break in gauge between the school and the other social institutions or media of communications to which the individual is exposed. Today with the declining influence of religious institutions, with the change in the nature of family life, with the mechanization of industrial occupations, and with the extension of mass media of communications, the task of character formation becomes more and more difficult. To all these conflicting influences may be added a certain relaxation of standards, both intellectual and disciplinary, which has been taking place in the schools of this and other countries, and reflects the same relaxation in other social institutions and the acceptance of a "get by" attitude. It was John Dewey who remarked on the occasion of the celebration of his 70th birthday that "Our present American ideal seems to be, 'Put it over—and make it snappy while you do it.'"

If I have only referred in a broad way to changes in types of character that followed fundamental cultural changes, it is in general because the question of changing individual manifestations of character or of changing human nature was not considered until the present century. Differences in character have always attracted writers from the day of Theophrastus and Plutarch; Bacon suggested in his *Advancement of Learning* that character might be studied, and John Stuart Mill in *A System of Logic* proposed a science of character or *Ethology*. These suggestions, however, came to nothing until the present century. I leave it to others to discuss whether, and to what extent, and by what methods human nature may be changed. So far as the past is concerned, despite the social and cultural changes that have taken place, the moral facilities considered desirable and approved by a society, are based on certain eternal verities which have not changed and which make social cohesion, stability, and survival possible. There is some danger that changes in manner and dress may be confused with changes in morals. As James Russell Lowell wrote in 1855:

> In vain we call old notions fudge,
> And bend our conscience to our dealing;
> The Ten Commandments will not budge
> And stealing will continue stealing.

The old notions—the customs, traditions, and value on which the hopes and ambitions of a collective society are built and which form the common currency of social intercourse—have not changed, although the sanctions may have shifted.

Revival of American Education
(1960)

This essay is Kandel's reflection on the state and future of American education following the tumultuous, criticism-filled decade of the 1950s. Kandel discusses these criticisms before indicating what he believes are the root problems of American education. Among other points, he reflects on the founding of Essentialism in 1938 and the subsequent discussion that took place between John Dewey, William Heard Kilpatrick, and William Bagley.

Kandel concludes the essay with a remarkable challenge to the American public. He argues that the only route to improving education lies in the establishment of the teaching profession on the dignified basis that it deserves. To do this, he claims that American educators must concentrate their efforts on giving teachers the moral, intellectual, and professional foundations that they deserve. He asserts, moreover, that these foundations will enable them to do their jobs well and, ultimately, be recognized for the essential role they play in shaping American culture. Curriculum for teaching teachers was the heart of the matter to Kandel. He states more than once that classroom teachers are the source of any school's success. Revival depends upon them.

The American public has always manifested a strong faith in the provision of education, but it is only in the last few years that it has begun to show a serious concern about the quality of education given in the schools that it has generously provided and maintained. A period of widespread unrest should offer an excellent opportunity to draw up an inventory of the weak and strong points of the institution which is the object of dissatisfaction. The characteristic attitude, however, has generally been one of compla-

Forgotten Heroes of American Education, pages 459–467

cency and a general feeling of confidence that better days are ahead and that a change—any change—will mean progress. To criticize the theory or practice of education has usually meant that the risk will be incurred of being decried as an enemy of public education, or as a conservative reactionary, or as an advocate of foreign systems and practices. When the Essentialist Committee was organized some twenty years ago, with the late Dr. William C. Bagley as its chairman and spokesman, its members were referred to as insignificant, and were compared to fundamentalists in religion and reactionaries in politics. That Dewey had advocated a program of essentials in his *Democracy and Education* in 1916 was completely forgotten even by those who professed to be his disciples. When his book, *Education and Freedom,* appeared a year ago, Admiral Rickover was charged with recommending that foreign school systems be imitated in this country. Critics are never given credit for honesty or sincerity or for having as great concern for the welfare of national education as their opponents claim to have.

It is very rare that efforts are made to correct patent errors that may be pointed out. The more usual tendency is to gloss them over by taking a new and, of course, a progressive step in another direction. Little attention was paid, for example, to the statement made by Dr. T. H. Briggs, in 1930, that, if executive officers in other fields of public service permitted such poor standards of accomplishment as he found in the high schools, they would be indicted for malfeasance of duty. Nor was any serious action taken to correct the deficiencies of the educational systems during World War II as revealed both by the Selective Draft Committees and by leaders in the Armed Services. The former found it necessary to reject thousands of young men on account of illiteracy or for physical defects. In the same period leaders in the Armed Services discovered a serious shortage of personnel for special services that required an adequate mastery of mathematics, science, or foreign languages. Similarly an opportunity was lost to examine the professional and social status of teachers when the shortage became serious. Such an examination might have brought out that other reasons than financial attractions outside the teaching profession kept young men and women from staying in the profession or from undertaking the necessary pre-service preparation. Salaries may not be the only factor that discourages teachers from continuing in the profession or deters young people from entering it. What has been called "the factory system" of administration applied to education as well as the frequent changes of pedagogical fashions may also be a deterrent.

II

An inventory of the strong and weak points of American education would certainly justify the people's pride in its faith in education and in its gradual attainment of the ideal of providing equality of educational opportunity. No other country has as many students enrolled in its educational institutions at all levels. The provision of buildings and equipment is lavish—sometimes more lavish than the educational and instructional needs require; the material fabric may in fact delude the public into confusing "schooling" with education. The per capita expenditure per student is unmatched elsewhere. Up to this point the quantitative assessment of American education should give cause for satisfaction, although it will be generally agreed that, taking the nation as a whole, the percentage of national income devoted to education is inadequate to ensure genuine equality of opportunity and a satisfactory standard of quality.

The quantitative measure of education has, however, been carried too far and has frequently been mistaken for qualitative values. The fact that a certain number of points, units, or credits is required for graduating from high school or college offers no indication whatever either of the content or of the quality of the education received. The absurdity of this quantitative measure becomes striking when foreign students, seeking to enter an American college or university, are expected to translate their educational careers into credits. It is as true of colleges as it is of high schools that in too many instances a certificate of graduation only means that a student has opened a non-interest-bearing account with the registrar of the institution attended, and kept it active until the requisite number of points or credits has been accumulated to enable him to graduate.

Statistics of enrollments in high schools and colleges may be regarded with pride but they are meaningless in the light of the low grade of achievements cited by Dr. T. H. Briggs in *The Great Investment,* and by Dr. W. S. Learned and Dr. Ben D. Wood in *The Student and His Knowledge.* That these studies did not result in any corrective actions either at the secondary or higher educational levels was proved during World War II when the inadequacy in the preparation of personnel in such subjects as mathematics, science, and foreign languages was revealed. Attention was again drawn to these deficiencies as a result of the panic caused by the launching of Sputnik and the consequent assumption of the superior training in these subjects in the educational institutions of Soviet Russia. The result of these discoveries has been to direct attention to the inadequate instruction provided in science and mathematics and to the low standards of achievements in other areas. There is a danger that both secondary and higher educational programs may be thrown out of balance as a consequence. Too much attention may be paid to science and mathematics at the expense of other subjects that are equally important both for the individual's education and for national culture. The accumulation of the information on the educational deficiencies should have stimulated an inquiry into the kind of general or liberal education to be provided in colleges and high schools, or at least the excellent reports on this subject published during the War might have been taken down from the shelves and dusted.

The situation has been further aggravated by the emphasis that has been placed on the discovery and education of the academically talented youth. This leaves the implications that all is well with the education given to the average and below average students and that their education is to be radically different from that of the academically talented. Nor has a clear case been made out whether the talented should be taught the academic subjects—mathematics, science and foreign languages—as a preparation for later study or as the core of a liberal education to which all students are entitled to the extent of their abilities. The differentiation between the talented and non-talented appears to be made in terms of the curriculum rather than in terms of the methods of instruction appropriate to their abilities. Equality of educational opportunity is not provided by making all subjects in the catalogue equal to each other. This is a surrender of educational values and at the same time fails to give all students that foundation in common understanding and common discourse as potential citizens of the nation. In the modern world it is essential that all citizens should have some awareness of the meaning of mathematics and science, and as international relations expand further they should have some familiarity with the speech and culture of other peoples, even though they may never have occasion to speak to a foreigner in his own language.

III

Some of the causes of the weaknesses of American education can be traced back to both recent and past history. One among several other reasons why Johnny can't read or do arithmetic is the practice of promoting pupils on schedule, whether they are prepared for the promotion or not. The practice began nearly fifty years ago, first, in order to avoid the mounting cost of retardation, and, later, to save children (and parents) from the alleged traumatizing effects of failure. The high schools were not seriously affected until their enrollments began to increase after World War I, partly as a consequence of raising the age of compulsory attendance and partly because of the increasing unemployability of youth. The high schools were confronted with the task of attempting to give a secondary education to pupils with fourth, fifth, or sixth grade ability in reading and probably in arithmetic. The situation served as the text of Dr. John L. Tildsley's *The Mounting Waste of the American High School* (1935). The facts have been well-known; they were mentioned in the pamphlet *What the High Schools Ought to Teach,* published by the American Council on Education (1946), and the Education Policies Commission's *Education for All American Youth* (1944). They were implied in the statement in one of the reports on Life Adjustment Education that 60 per cent of the students in high schools were gaining little from their stay. Finally, the same facts are just referred to but not dilated upon in Dr. Conant's report on *The American High School To-Day.* In all the discussions that have been published in recent years on the importance of searching for and educating the gifted and talented students, the operation of a sort of Gresham's Law in education has been ignored; to establish remedial classes in reading in high schools and colleges is no solution.

The deficiencies of the high schools, however, are not due only to the increased enrollments and the presence of students with an inadequate command of the fundamentals. There are historical, so-called philosophical, and administrative reasons that may be adduced to explain them. The blueprint for American education was drafted before 1800 in the proposals of an education adapted to the needs of a republican government. Widespread opposition was manifested against the educational tradition of Europe, which was denounced as "aristocratic." This criticism was carried over to the subjects of the traditional education which were also decried as "aristocratic," a derogatory term still applied not so many years ago to such subjects as foreign languages, mathematics and science. In the early proposals these criticisms were accompanied by a demand that the new courses should bring immediate returns, should be immediately practical, and should contribute to the nation's material and economic development. In the present century these proposals meant that whatever is taught should be "functional," a principle assumed to be sanctioned by Dewey by those who ignored what his interpretation of "function" actually was. The anti-intellectualism of the early advocates of the practical became a basic tenet of one school of educational philosophy.

Administratively the deficiencies of the high schools may be explained by the misinterpretation of the quantitative measure recommended at the beginning of the century that any subject competently taught was as good as any other subject taught for the same length of time. The fact that this measure was intended to apply to less than twenty subjects was ignored and opened the door for the admission of any subject that the public and students might desire to the consequent disappearance and abandonment of any sense of educational values. The practice served at any rate to lull the public into the belief that the high schools were ready to meet all their needs. Since education was now defined in terms of points, units and credits, continuity in the study of any subject was no longer a matter of importance so long as the number of units necessary for graduation was accumulated.

Just as subjects became interchangeable, so did teachers. For the general practice was to certificate them as high school teachers rather than as specialists in certain subjects. When appointed, they had to teach the subjects assigned to them, whether they had studied them or not. It was expected that leadership would be provided by the administrative officers and more emphasis has been placed on the "overhead" than on the teachers in the classroom. The idea is still current, as may be gathered from Dr. Conant's recent statement on the successful operation of a high school.

The academic specialists in subject-matter cannot be altogether absolved from responsibility for the decline of standards in the high schools. They abdicated from responsibility for secondary education and surrendered leadership entirely to the "generalists" or professors of education, who professed to have a better understanding of the problems at the secondary level and the demands of a changing culture, since the high schools had become non-selective and culture was rapidly changing. Their targets were the college entrance requirements and the academic tradition in general. Despite their claims, however, the generalists failed to develop a philosophy of secondary education and proceeded on the principle that "every boy and girl must be given a chance," but without a sense of direction. It did not seem to matter which way they went, so long as the necessary number of units was attained.

IV

At the risk of provoking the kind of criticism mentioned earlier, the question may be raised whether the comprehensive high school can successfully cope with the task assigned to it. The comprehensive high school furnishes an excellent example of the tendency in education to rationalize after the event. The institution was not planned but was established more or less by accident, because the public had grown accustomed to finding everything that it wanted under the same roof. It was not mentioned by Dr. Ellwood P. Cubberley in his article on "High Schools" in Monroe's *Encyclopedia of Education* (1912). In his *Public Education in the United States* (1919) Dr. Cubberley refers to the "cosmopolitan" high school, as it was then called, as one of seven different types and does not come out squarely for the type that is now regarded as essentially American. The comprehensive high school began later to be justified as genuinely democratic and capable of catering successfully to the individual differences of ability and needs, and above all of cultivating social understanding and solidarity. The last argument is based on the assumption that physical contiguity necessarily conduces to common understanding and the development of fellowship, co-operation, and social obligations. This argument is specious and not based on any other fact than that the comprehensive high school produces a certain herd-minded-ness and conformity while the students are in school. The ideal of democracy is both emotional and intellectual and can be cultivated as an essential part of education in separate schools where methods appropriate to the students' abilities can be employed.

So far as American education in general is concerned, its basic weakness has been caused by the constant change of fashions, which began to be decried before Progressive education became the dominant theory. Experimentation and pseudo-scientific methods as well as the administrative pressure to "sell" education to the public were in turn responsible for the multiplicity of cure-alls, panaceas, and half-baked ideas which flourished for a while and had their days until something new was concocted. The curriculum-revision jamboree, as the late Dr. Bagley called it, was succeeded by the child-centered school; then came *seriatim* education for technocracy, education for the air age, education for international understanding, the cult of Latin America, education for victory, education for the space age, education for the atomic age, and then the community-centered schools. The end of slogans has not yet come and there is still a chance for education for the electronic age. The electronic devices will commend themselves as aids to teachers as well as substitutes for teachers in this age of shortages. In a yearbook on *The American School Superintendency* (1952) it was admitted that "many teachers are confused by the changes in theory and practice that appear to them to be advocated in rapid and bewildering sequence." Beset by all the changes in theory and practice, the teacher is expected to be "a combination of psychiatrist, social scientist, scientist and an individual of considerable culture who was also a man or woman of action; the list might be expanded by adding that he should also be a hygienist, guidance and welfare officer, and able to participate in extracurricular activities. It is for these reasons that the Harvard Committee was justified in writing in *General Education in a Free Society* that "we are faced with a diversity of education which, if it has many virtues, nevertheless works against the good of society by helping to destroy the common ground of training and outlook on which any society depends." Dewey's suggestion twenty years ago that education be discussed without qualifying labels has never commended itself to educators.

V

Under the circumstances it is difficult to discover where the leadership, so urgently needed today, will be found. Federal leadership is feared lest the price for it may be too high and at the expense of local initiative and independence. The fear of external dictation, however, does not seem to extend to the acceptance of grants from a private foundation to put into practice ideas elaborated in the foundation's sanctum. In this way there have been subsidized the use of teachers' aides, the employment of "master-teachers," the more extensive use of TV programs, and a new scheme for the preparation of teachers. The use of teachers' aides was tried and abandoned in the early years of this century. The "master-teacher" idea recalls the Lancasterian system in which one teacher first taught a large class and monitors continued his work with smaller groups. The term "master-teacher" misrepresents the original use of the term. Educational TV is no doubt valuable as an aid or supplement, but it becomes open to suspicion when it is recommended as a method of "deploying" teachers and of solving the problem of teacher shortage. Pedagogical memories are short and the experiments with educational films and radio have already been forgotten. The personal and direct influence of the teacher cannot be replaced by broadcasting "his master's voice" into the classroom. Nor is there any substantial innovation in the scheme to prepare teachers by fastening the technical parts of education on to a completed liberal education; that is not the way that the much-needed reform of teacher preparation lies.

The heart of the problem of educational revival lies in the reform of the preparation of teachers for elementary and secondary schools and the establishment of the teaching career on as dignified a professional basis as is enjoyed by other professions. The classroom teacher should have greater opportunities for participating in leadership instead of being a "hand" in a system, even if the system is administered by a good board of education, a good superintendent, and a good principal. The success of an educational system depends on what goes on in the classroom and, therefore, on the teacher. External control of and dictation to the teachers are likely to militate against that clarity of aim and purpose which are essential to successful work. Further, other methods of rewarding successful teachers should be found than promotion away from the classroom. As the burden of administration increases and as the administration of an educational system takes on more of the characteristics of big business, other sources of leadership must be found. With increased professional preparation, the status of teachers and administration has changed markedly since the days when there may have been some justification for the "factory system" of administration.

Nor can the participation of the public be ignored. Since the end of World War II the public has voiced its concern about the quality of education at both the elementary and secondary levels. In many areas public councils have sprung up and are devoting their attention to raising the standards and quality of education. Leaders concerned with national welfare and the cultural progress of the country have frequently pointed to the importance of an adequate preparation of the nation's potential leaders and manpower. The opportunity now presents itself of capitalizing on the new-found concern of the public for the quality of education and of strengthening the American system of education at those points where the deficiencies have been revealed during and since World War II. There may be a new emphasis on the quality of education and on raising standards. Committees may devote their attention to new courses in science and mathematics. But such activities will be of no avail unless every student in every school in the country is taught by teachers who are professionally competent. And professional competence means a mastery of subject matter as well as a knowledge of the techniques of teaching. The two sides of competence have too long been separated, and the time has come to realize that they are aspects of the same single activity.

Section 6

SELECTED WRITINGS
OF CHARLES ALEXANDER MCMURRY

Charles A. McMurry (1857–1929) is a forgotten hero of American education. He was a teacher of teachers who dedicated his life to the philosophical and practical advancement of the teaching profession. For forty years, McMurry held firm to the moral foundations of teaching through his scholarship and his commitment to high-quality teacher education. The Herbartian pedagogical philosophy that McMurry studied in Germany reached its apex in the U.S. in the mid-1890s, yet McMurry remained dedicated to the ideals that he studied in the 1880s as a graduate student in Germany. During the 20th century, McMurry was written out of the profession of teaching because the Herbartian pedagogy that he subscribed to was ridiculed by the new doctrine of Progressivism.

McMurry was born on February 18, 1857, in Crawfordsville, Indiana. He received his elementary, high school, and undergraduate education in the training school of the Illinois State Normal School. He obtained his undergraduate degree in 1876. He was a graduate student at the University of Michigan from 1876 to 1880. During the 1880s, he served as a teacher and school administrator in Illinois and Colorado.

In 1887, he earned his Ph.D. degree in pedagogy at the University of Halle in Germany. He continued his studies in Germany following the completion of his doctoral degree. At the University of Jena, he studied

Herbartian pedagogy with Professor Wilhelm Rein and became an enthusiastic advocate of Herbartian pedagogy.

McMurry returned to the U.S. in 1888 to serve as a teacher and administrator at various normal schools throughout the Midwest. He was a professor of pedagogy and psychology from 1890 to 1902 at Northern Illinois State Teachers College in DeKalb. McMurry's growing prominence as a teacher educator during the early 1900s led many normal schools and teachers colleges to offer him teaching positions. He departed Northern Illinois in 1902 for a one-year leave of absence that turned into five. McMurry wrote prolifically during this five-year stretch. He returned to DeKalb to teach from 1907 to 1915. In 1915, he was offered a position at the George Peabody College for Teachers in Nashville, Tennessee. He remained on the faculty at Peabody until his death in 1929.[1]

McMurry's publications were scholarly contributions to the field of education. They were also practical in the sense that they related directly to classroom teaching. He was a master at combining theory and practice while focusing on the art and science of classroom teaching. His more than 40 published books include works such as *Some Principles in the Teaching of History* (with Lucy Maynard Salmon), *A Teacher's Manual of Geography*, *The Course of Study in History in the Common School*, and *Practical Teaching* (excerpted below).[2] McMurry's works are a vast resource of solid thinking on the moral and intellectual task of teaching teachers. Reading his contributions today makes clear that he based his philosophy on a sound body of philosophical principles. The profession of teaching would be much stronger today had McMurry's legacy not been marginalized. Reviving the ideals that McMurry believed in holds great promise for building a profession of teaching that has long-term influence for good in American culture.

---

1. John F. Ohles, Ed., *Biographical Dictionary of American Educators* 2 (Westport, CT: Green-wood, Press, 1978), pp. 844–845.

2. Charles A. McMurry and Lucy Maynard Salmon, *Some Principles in the Teaching of History* (Chicago: University of Chicago Press, 1902); Charles A. McMurry, *A Teacher's Manual of Geography* (New York: Macmillan, 1902); Charles A. McMurry, *The Course of Study in History in the Common Schools* (Chicago: University of Chicago Press, 1903); and Charles A. McMurry, *Practical Teaching* (Richmond, VA: Johnson Publishing, 1927).

How to Conduct the Recitation
(1880)

The separation of "liberal" from "professional" education within higher education curriculum is a figment of our modern imagination. This selection from McMurry draws our attention to a time and place when to be liberally educated and to focus on good teaching were one and the same activity. To McMurry, knowledge was to be gained so that it could be used for teaching purposes, as he makes abundantly clear in this selection. In his view, the moral and intellectual dimensions of knowledge drew power from one another as they were integrated toward ideal ends.

This introduction to a teacher's manual illustrates how McMurry was influenced by German philosopher and teacher educator Johann Friedrich Herbart. McMurry outlines the essential elements that teachers should include in good "recitation work." Recitation is a teaching approach that was widely criticized by Progressives during the early 20th century. They often claimed that it was harsh, unnecessarily demanding, and harmful to student self-expression. The idea of recitation that McMurry has in mind, however, is not harsh at all. He is deeply concerned about meeting the needs and interests of students; at the same time, however, he is focused on teaching them essential knowledge and developing their moral ideals. He explains the five formal steps, which he borrowed from Herbart, to explicate the philosophy behind his theory. He then provides specific examples of lessons that teachers can use.

INTRODUCTION

The Herbart School. This paper is in the main an exposition of some of the leading ideas which have been developed theoretically and practically

Forgotten Heroes of American Education, pages 471–480

by the Herbart school of pedagogy in Germany. The late Professor Ziller of the University of Leipzig was a disciple of Herbart, and an original thinker of unusual powers. He recast Herbart's ideas on education in a new mould, and sought in his practice school at the university to make these principles the basis of systematic class-room work for the public schools. Prof. W. Rein of the University of Jena and many other disciples of Ziller, since well known as practical teachers, have put Ziller's ideas into practice during the last twenty years, and have illustrated them in all the studies and grades of the common school. No attempt is made to present all the important ideas of the Herbart school, or to give an exhaustive discussion of any one. After a brief survey of certain leading ideas, there follows a fuller discussion of a definite and systematic plan of class-room teaching.

THE ESSENTIAL ELEMENTS OF GOOD RECITATION WORK

Facts and their Connection. A liberal education embraces a good many forms of study. Besides the subjects of the common school, there are history, classics and higher mathematics, the natural sciences and the fine arts, political economy, literature and philosophy. We are all naturally inclined to think that the more facts we have collected, the more information we have gathered in each of these topics, the better educated and the wiser we shall be. But this is only a half or a quarter true. The strength of an army does not consist in the *number* of men alone, as Xerxes discovered long ago, but in *the kind of men,* in their strength and courage, in their power of united action. Our knowledge is really serviceable to us only as it is combined into connected compact masses ready for varied use. The purpose of the school, then, is not simply to *accumulate* knowledge, but also to arrange and connect, to organize and energize the facts learned, to bring them into potent combination; just as a general first enlists recruits, then disciplines them into soldiers and organizes them into an effective army. The facts commonly learned in the schools are indeed the materials out of which our intellectual house is to be built, but we are concerned not only about getting these materials into the structure of the mind, but about the plan and order there is among them, and whether the walls are loose and shaky or firm and solidly built.

Digesting Knowledge. The stomach and the mind are alike in some points and unlike in others. The food that once enters the stomach is taken up and assimilated by the organs of digestion. Our chief care is to avoid overloading the stomach, and to give it a chance to perform its functions. It is self-acting. The materials which enter the mind pass through a digestive process; and this lasts longer. A cow chews her cud once; but the ideas which have entered our minds may be chewed over and over again, and that with great profit. Ideas do not assimilate so easily as the different food-materials in the body. Ideas have to be put side by side, compared, separated, grouped, and arranged into connected series. Thus they become organized for use. This sorting, arranging, and connecting of ideas is so important that it demands more time and more care than the first labor of acquisition.

Absorption and Reflection.   The process of acquiring and assimilating knowledge involves certain simple conditions which are easily stated. When some new object presents itself to the mind the attention must be first fixed upon it for a while so that there may be time to take it in as a whole and in its parts. The mind then recovers itself from this momentary absorption in the object, and begins to survey it in its surroundings and connections. Absorption and reflection! The mind swings back and forth like a pendulum between these two operations. Herbart, who has closely defined this process, calls it the mental act of breathing. As regularly as the air is drawn into the lungs and then excluded, so regularly does the mind lose itself in its absorption with an object only to recover itself and reflect upon it.

In this first simple action of the mind are reflected the two fundamental principles which control all growth in knowledge.

Observation.   The first is the inspection of things in themselves and in their details. Absorption with objects! Object lessons! The principle of observation is confirmed in its full scope. The training of the senses to the full capacity of sense of perception is primary and necessary. The contact with nature, the actual experience with things, is the only concrete basis of knowledge.

Survey.   The second principle is the act of reflecting upon the things which enter the mind, the comparison of objects. It brings together things that are alike, e.g., the river basins of North America and the river basins of South America. It throws into contrast things that differ, e.g., the desert of the Sahara and the rich moist valley of the Amazon. By a constant use of reflection and survey we classify our increasing knowledge into larger and smaller groups; causes are linked with their results, and the spirit of investigation is awakened which discovers and traces out those simple laws which underlie the complex phenomena of nature. The linking together of ideas into continuous series, the comparison of objects so as to bring out the salient features of whole classes, and the tracing of causes and results are means of organizing, of binding together, ideas which must be at the disposal of teachers in their recitation work or the higher results of education will not be reached. We may sum up the thoughts involved in this second great principle of learning as *Association of Ideas*.

Apperception.   Going back to the first simple state of the mind in learning, its absorption in a given object, the question arises, How can any new or partially new object be best understood at its first appearance? How can a full and distinct understanding of it be readily gained by the mind? We claim that if the kindred ideas already in the mind are awakened and brought distinctly to the front the new object will be more rapidly and accurately appropriated than by any other means. This is called the principle of *apperception*, i.e. the reception of a new or partially new idea by the assistance of kindred ideas already in the mind. If old friends come out to meet the strangers and throw their arms about them and lead them within, how much more quickly they will be at home! But these old friends who are already in the house, who stand in the background of our thoughts, must be awakened and called to the front, they must stand on tiptoe ready to welcome the new-comer; for if they lie asleep in the penetralia of the home, these strangers will come up and pass by for lack of a welcome. Closely allied to this is the principle of *proceeding from the known to the unknown,* which has caused so much discussion and misunderstanding. Apperception contains what is true in this idea of going from the known to the unknown. As soon as we see something new and desire to understand it, we at once begin to ransack our stock of ideas to see if we can find anything in our previous experience which corresponds to this or is like it. For whatever is like it, or has an analogy to it, or serves the same uses, will explain this new thing, though the two objects be in other points essentially different. We are constantly falling back on our old experiences and classifications for the explanation of new objects that appear to us.

Examples of Apperception. A boy goes to town and sees a banana for the first time, and asks, "What is that? I never saw anything like that." He thinks he has no class of things to which it belongs, no place to put it. His father answers that it is to eat, like an orange or a pear. Calling up these familiar objects, the whole significance of the new thing is clear to him though it differs from anything he has ever seen.[1]

---

1. We will add one other illustration of apperception. Two men, the one a machinist and one who is not, visit the machinery hall of an exposition. The machinist finds new inventions and novel applications of old principles. He is much interested in examining and understanding these new machines and devices. He passes from one machine to another, noting down new points, and at the end of an hour leaves the hall with a mind enriched. The other man sees the same machines, but does not understand them. He sees their parts, but does not detect the principle of their construction. His previous experience is not sufficient to give him the clue to their explanation. After an hour of uninterested observation, he leaves the hall with a confused notion of shafts, wheels, cogs, bands, etc., but with no greater insight into the principles of machinery. Why has one man learned so much and the other nothing? Because the machinist had previous knowledge and experience which acted as interpreters, while the other man had no old ideas and so acquired nothing new. "To him that hath shall be given."

From Simple to Complex.   The notion of going from the simple to the complex is illustrated also in the simple process of the mind which we described. First one object, then the survey of it in connection with other things, forming a complex unit. This idea has been confused with the idea of going from a whole to the parts. But there is no real contradiction. There are many objects which we first take in as a whole, and then descend to an analysis of their parts, e.g., a camel, a mountain, a flower. Almost all concrete objects are approached in this way. But there is an entirely different set of ideas which can be best approached gradually, adding part to part and comparing till the whole appears. This is the case with the general classifications in the natural sciences, and in all subjects that admit of a system of classified objects.

Excite Interest.   That the *interest* of children is to be awakened in the subject of study may now be accepted as one of the axioms of teaching. To answer the important question how a healthy and sustained interest is to be awakened in studies would be to solve many of the greatest difficulties in teaching. To interest children, not simply for the hour, but permanently; to select, arrange, and so present ideas that they awaken a steady appetite for more knowledge and create a taste for what is excellent, *this* at least is one aim that we must insist upon in recitation work. Some things already mentioned contribute to this result. Nature and natural objects have a charm for us all, children included. Story, biography, history, and poetry, each in its place and time, awakens mind and heart, and sows seed that will germinate and grow.

Compare.   In school life, also, the more serious work of study requires us to put familiar objects together and to notice how they resemble or differ, and it may excite interest to note the superiority of one or its defect. This gives children a chance to see and compare for themselves, to draw conclusions and form their own opinions. Still more the tracing of causes and their effects, the following out of analogies in botany and zoology, or in the life of great men, may contribute greatly to interest older children.

Arouse Self-activity.   We are already encroaching upon the principle of *self-activity* which we believe, with many other teachers, should be systematically encouraged from the beginning of school life. The child itself should have something to do, some aim set up to be reached, a problem to be solved, a series of objects, places, or words to develop,—not simply something to learn by heart, but something that requires thought, discovery, invention, and arrangement; e.g. first-grade children may be asked to hunt up and form a list of all the words in the lesson containing *th* or *ll* or some other combination.

Develop Will Power.   *The effort to create* a progressive and sustained interest in study and the arousing of self-activity are steps preparatory to the *growth of will power.* This is one of the root ideas of intellectual as well as of moral training. In connection with self-activity and interest there must be the pursuit of definite and clearly seen aims, i.e. definite and clear to the pupil, if will energy is to be developed.

Of course the adaptability of the materials of study to the child will have much to do with exciting interest and with the exertion of will power in their pursuit. But every step should involve a clearly seen aim, a natural sequence of subjects, so that children can see the objects they are working for at least in outline, and the means of reaching them. For we adopt the principle that there can be no exercise of will power unless the aim and the possibility of reaching it be distinctly seen.

Summary.   Summing up the essential ideas of good recitation work, we say: The training of the senses to close, accurate observation, and the process of comparing and classifying objects and ideas, constitute the fundamental action of the mind in learning. The assimilation of the new materials of knowledge by bringing old, familiar ideas into the closest contact with the new according to the principle of *apperception* is the true interpretation of the popular idea "from known to unknown."

The principle known as association of ideas requires that all our knowledge be united into firmly compacted groups and series, and bound together by the law of cause and effect. Finally, a sustained interest, self-activity, and will energy, steadily cultivated from the earliest years of school life, indicate that it is not simple knowledge or increased information which we aim at, but increase of intellectual resource, and a permanent, progressive interest in knowledge.

Lesson Unities.   It is evident that in this kind of teaching no single recitation can be viewed apart from the series of lessons to which it belongs. The subject-matter of any study should be first selected so as to be adapted to the age, spirit, and previous knowledge of children, and then it should be arranged into a succession of topics or unities each of which may be treated first separately, and then in its relation to the others. One of these methodical unities may be completed in a single recitation or it may be spread over a series of lessons.

Steps in Teaching a Lesson.   On the basis of the psychological principles already treated, the process of teaching a new topic leads through a series of steps. The Herbartian school of pedagogy in Germany has developed a plan of recitation work based upon these steps, and has applied them successfully to the teaching of common-school studies. The two main stages on the road to acquisition of knowledge have been already indicated: 1. As observation and scrutiny of individual things; 2. As the association and comparison of objects or ideas with a view to arrangement into classes or for the purpose of generalizing and formulating results.

First Stage: Presentation.   The first stage may be broken into two smaller half-day journeys. Before setting out on a journey it is well to survey the road and glance at a guide-book. Before beginning a new subject it is well to recall familiar ideas bearing upon it, to refresh our minds. This is a *preparatory* study, a making ready for the lesson. The second part is the actual presentation of the new facts, the familiarizing the mind with the new subject.

The subject-matter is now at hand, and the first stage of teaching the lesson is complete. But this newly acquired information has not yet settled to its proper place in the mind; it is not properly associated with previous knowledge.

Second Stage: Elaboration.   This elaboration of newly presented ideas and facts leads us through a series of three additional steps, which thus complete the process of acquisition: 1. The new object is compared with similar things already in the mind. In this way it finds its fitting companionship. 2. Every new object presented to the mind and then compared with others gives rise to new conclusions. The clear statement of this general result or truth focuses the main idea of the lesson. 3. This general truth may now be exemplified in new cases and applied to new circumstances.

Briefly stated the steps are as follows: 1. Preparation; 2. Presentation; 3. Association and comparison; 4. Generalization; 5. Practical application.

It is to be remembered that a subject to be treated in this manner must contain a unity of thought; that it must centre in an object which is typical of a class, so as to serve as a basis of comparison and generalization.

Analogy of the Farmer.   These steps may be fairly illustrated in their general outlines by an analogy taken from the work of a farmer. 1. The soil is ploughed, harrowed, and made ready for the seed. 2. The grain is sowed upon the ready soil and raked in. 3. The growing grain is cultivated and the weeds destroyed. 4. The harvest is brought in. 5. The grain is used for practical purposes of food.

The analogy is so complete that it scarcely calls for a commentary. The preparation is the preparing of the soil of the mind for the seed-corn of instruction. The presentation is sowing the seed upon this prepared soil of the mind. The third stage is the cultivation of the growing crop, the working over of the knowledge just acquired by means of comparison. The fourth step is the harvest time, the drawing out of the general truth or law involved in the lesson. Finally, the particular uses to which the harvest grain is put, the application of acquired knowledge to the practical uses of life.

No Royal Road in Teaching.   The five steps just outlined are based, as we believe, on general principles which make them applicable to almost every subject of study. But the manner of applying them to different studies varies greatly. The ability to apply them successfully to geography would not qualify for equal success in arithmetic or botany. The teacher must first be proficient in the study which he would desire to teach in this way. Both the concrete facts and the general truths of the subject should be familiar and logically arranged in his mind. To put it in a mild form, the teacher must have a thorough knowledge of his subject, and must have this knowledge well digested for teaching purposes. *For teaching purposes!* That is, that we have a knowledge of those psychological principles which we first outlined as a basis of the five steps, viz. observation of concrete things, apperception, comparison and association, generalization and the awakening of interest, self-activity, and will power by these means. Now it is evident that no plan based on these principles will furnish a *royal road* to success in teaching. Success along this line depends upon industry, adaptability, and continuous practice. It will be an uphill road for some time, and it is only gradually that one will acquire that mastery of the subject and that tact in the manipulation of a somewhat complex machinery that come only through toil and pains.

Dull Machine Work. It does not require a prophet to see that the five steps in careless hands will degenerate into a dry mechanical routine. It might be even worse than text-book lore, for a good text-book is always better than a poor teacher. It is not intended that this plan and these principles shall make a slave of the teacher, but that by a hard-earned mastery of their details, and by a successful application of them to the concrete materials of study, he gradually works his way out into the clear daylight of conscious power. In this way the teacher becomes a skilled architect, with clear ideas of the strength and resistance of materials.

Examples of the Formal Steps. Three simple illustrations of this succession of steps in the treatment of a subject will now be given. Some criticisms which have been raised against this plan will then be discussed.

(1) Statement of the Aim

We will examine and study the *oak trees* found in our forests.

1. (Preparation.) Let the class recall what they have seen of oak trees in the woods, size of trees, acorns. Do they remember the shape and size of the leaves? What is the appearance of the wood and what is it used for?

(The purpose of the teacher here is not to present any new facts to the class, but simply to find out what they remember from previous observation and to excite interest.)

2. (Presentation of facts.) The best plan is to visit the woods or an oak grove, notice carefully the trunk and bark, branches and leaves, acorns (food of squirrels.) On returning to school, have an accurate description of the oak tree from the class, according to definite points (e.g. trunk and bark, branches, leaves, and acorns.) Then follows a discussion of oak wood

for chairs, desks, doors and windows, beams, posts and other building purposes, bridges, walks, etc. (The teacher adds such facts as the children cannot furnish.)

3. (Comparison.) Name the different kinds of oak—white oak, red oak, burr oak. Notice the differences in leaves and acorns, size of trees, wood and uses.

4. (Classification, generalization.) Definition of the oak family. The oak is a native hard-wood tree. It has acorns, and simple leaves of nearly uniform shape. The wood is tough and strong, of varying colors, but always useful for furniture, building or other purposes. (After the previous observation and discussion, the pupils will be able to give a definition similar to this, assisted by a few questions from the teacher.)

5. (Application.) Children should be trained to recognize the different kinds of oak trees about home, and to distinguish them from other hard-wood trees. They may also notice the oak panels and furniture, and be able to tell oak finishing in public and private houses.

Note: If there is time enough for a separate study of two or more varieties of oak, and the trees are close by so as to be seen, it is well to treat each variety according to the first and second steps, and in the third compare as above.

(2) The Cotton-gin

(Aim.) We will find out how a machine was invented to remove the seed from cotton.

1. (Preparation.) Question the class on the cotton-plant, raising and picking cotton, and the uses of cotton.

2. (Presentation.) Tell or read the story of Whitney and the invention of the cotton-gin. Notice the effects of this invention on the production of cotton in the South, and upon the growth of the South.

3. (Comparison.) Name other important inventions and their effects,— sewing-machine, printing-press, steam-engine, reaper, steamboat, telegraph, etc. Which of these had the most important results?

4. (Generalization or abstraction.) Call upon the children to state the general purpose of all these inventions, to save labor, to make a better use of the forces of nature.

5. (Application.) Do any hardships result to anybody in consequence of these useful inventions? (e.g., men thrown out of employment by use of machinery.)

(3) Nouns

Suppose that a class has had oral and written language work, but no technical grammar.

(Aim.) In talking and writing you have been accustomed to use words. We propose to talk now about a class of words called *nouns*.

1. (Preparation.) Have you heard the word *noun* before? Give some words that you think are nouns. Try to point out the nouns in this sentence. "The ship sailed over the ocean."

(It may be that these questions cannot be answered by the children for lack of knowledge. But even if they show no knowledge of the subject, these questions may excite curiosity and awaken interest, and they require very little time.)

2. (Presentation.) I will give you some words that are called nouns. Stove, cherry, bat, courthouse, carpet, picture, whale, shoe, barn, mountain. Have you seen all these things?

3. (Comparison.) Notice these words and see if you can tell what they all refer to. We will take two or three words that are not nouns and see what they refer to. *Up, and, quickly.* What is the difference between these words and the nouns? Look at the nouns again and tell what they refer to.

4. (Definition.) Looking at our list of nouns again you may tell what a noun is. So far as these words are concerned every noun is the name of what? (The conclusion that the children may reach by a little good questioning is that all these nouns are the names of objects. The treatment of proper nouns and abstract nouns may be according to a similar method in the following lessons, and then the complete definition of a noun can be obtained.)

5. (Application.) Each child may make a list of nouns that we have not had. Let easy sentences be given in which they may point out the nouns.

Special Method
for Literature and History
in the Common Schools
(1894)

The idea of special methods courses for teachers is quite different from the idea of general methods. Special methods courses connect the practice of teaching with the various subject-matter areas that teachers teach. The Teaching of History, the Teaching of Literature, and the Teaching of Mathematics are examples of special methods courses.

In this excerpt from his book entitled Special Method for Literature and History in the Common Schools, *McMurry once again provides a philosophy of curriculum for teaching teachers that combines what to teach, how to teach, and why to teach. He discusses the teaching of fairy tales and the teaching of mythical stories, both of which are prized, according to McMurry, because of the moral lessons they teach to children.* Special Method for Literature and History in the Common Schools *is an example of one of McMurry's books that was widely used in normal schools and teachers colleges during the late 19th and early 20th centuries.*

What happened to McMurry's philosophy of curriculum for teaching teachers? It was eradicated by a radically new understanding of psychology that appeared in universities during the early 1900s. The psychology that supports McMurry's perspective retains a firm commitment to shaping the minds and hearts of children and youth. The rise of behavioral psychology during the early years of the 20th century, however, banished much of the traditional subject-matter that, historically, had formed the center of the fields of psychology and pedagogy. Consequently, curriculum for teacher training began to marginalize questions of essential knowledge and moral character. McMurry's work is based on this richer understanding of these fields. If his words highlight anything, it is that good stories

Forgotten Heroes of American Education, pages 481–500
Copyright © 2006 by Information Age Publishing

have a central role to play in teaching children. Stories also have an essential role to play teaching teachers.

PREFACE

This is the first of a series of small books treating of special method in each of the common school studies. The plan is to outline courses for each important branch of school work, to discuss the value of the materials and to explain the method of treatment in classes. The relation of studies to each other will receive much incidental notice.

The series of *Special Methods* is designed to carry forward to a fuller application and in definite detail the principles discussed in the *General Method*. This first of the series of *Special Methods* is a selection and discussion of those literary and historical materials which are adapted to an *oral treatment* throughout the grades. In the history work of the sixth, seventh, and eighth grades, books and references may be much used by the children.

The use of the best English classics as regular reading books in all the grades will be discussed in the second number of the *Special Methods* (now in press).

Another series of books is in preparation in which the actual materials (Fairy Tales, Robinson Crusoe, etc.) to be handled in history and literature, as here discussed, will be presented in the simple form required in the schools. Our plan, therefore, is to advance from the most general statement of principles to the most specific application to particular studies.

—Normal, Illinois, September 26, 1894.

HISTORY AND LITERATURE

The formative influence of classic literature and good reading upon young people is generally acknowledged. With many boys and girls who show a taste for it, the reading of choice books is held to be a sign of intellectual and moral progress. Such a taste once formed, is regarded as a strong protection and aid in the coming work of education. But where does this taste for literature properly begin, and how may it be fostered among average boys and girls? The schools of to-day are not in the habit of seriously meeting this problem till children are verging into manhood and womanhood, toward the close of the grammar grades. What of the years from six to fourteen, devoted especially to the common school, in which the great majority of children receive their whole school training? If there are choice stories, epics, and histories which have power to impress youthful thought, fancy, and feeling, let the early years reap the full benefit. Even those first entering the school should find something fair and attractive in the stories presented to them in the early months. In each grade the children should be led through some of the garden-plots of literature, leaving rich memories behind and gaining a culture that will abide through life.

By keeping steadily in view the leading purpose, to lift and strengthen moral character by means of materials of instruction suited to the needs of children, lesser advantages will follow. The highest aims in education, if wisely pursued, will yield much fruitage to the secondary aims. Those stories and books which reveal the best typical men and women in action, furnish also the most interesting and instructive lessons in other respects. The poet instinctively seizes what is beautiful and good for the highest manifestation of his art. If ignoble characters appear, it is as a foil to choicer spirits. To banish formalism from our schools we need the presence of interesting and stimulating characters, not simply as embodied in the teachers, but also as exhibited in the history and literature studied. Important as formal drill is, no teacher can find in this his best expression and influence. Sympathy with human life and struggle is the most inspiriting force in schools as well as outside of them. The interest awakened is a fair gauge of the value of the work done in a school, and for native interest there is nothing that can surpass the best literature. To put this literature into the hands of teachers and to cause them to feel responsible for the transmission of its best treasures to children is a thing to lend priestly dignity to our calling.

Of necessity, the school must be the first to pioneer the children into these regions of delight. Not many homes are capable of giving them a fit entrance. There should be no jealousy between school and home at this juncture, but rather mutual support. The school knows best how to open the doors and lead the children in; or at least it should be the pride of teachers to fit themselves for this duty. The school has more time and equipment for this work than the home, although it can only imitate the sympathetic qualities of the home. At the best, teachers can only make a beginning, cultivate a taste and habit, open the eyes and sympathies of children for what is beautiful and good, hoping that home, friends, libraries, and life's opportunities will do the rest. What books to select, and how to best present the stories to children, can be better judged by thoughtful educators than by parents. There is a vast amount of sham in literature, and pupils and parents, to a large extent, are not good judges of excellent, as compared with inferior, products. Few teachers, indeed, would be prepared to make a good selection of our best literary materials for children. But this is our problem, and considering the great interests at stake, the millions of boys and girls growing up to life's duties among us, it behooves us to spare neither labor nor pains to sift out the best for each school year.

American history and literature supply some choice materials, while England, Germany, Greece, and other countries furnish myths and epical stories of great culture value. We glean from broad literary fields and from the history of many lands. It may surprise us also to find that it is the profound literary artists and critics that can help us most in selecting choice products for children. At this point the university and the first primary school are drawn into the closest relation. Men of profound learning like the brothers Grimm, Herder, and Goethe have opened up to the world the treasures of literature for children. It can not but inspire and ennoble the primary teacher to know that she is cultivating her own mind on some of the best literary masterpieces, and while teaching children is only making use of what the best poetic minds have prepared.

Our purpose is to discuss a few of those literary masterpieces which may be made use of in schools, beginning with the first primary grade.

FAIRY TALES

Young children, as we all know, are delighted with stories, and in the first grade they are still in this story-loving period. A good story is the best medium through which to convey ideas and also to approach the difficulties of learning to read. Such a story, Wilmann says, is a pedagogical treasure. By many thinkers and primary teachers the *fairy stories* have been adopted as best suited to the wants of the little folk just emerging from the home. A series of fairy tales was selected by Ziller, one of the leading Herbartians, as a center for the school work of the first year. These stories have long held a large place in the home culture of children, especially of the more cultivated class. Now it is claimed that what is good for the few whose parents may be cultured and sympathetic, may be good enough for the children of the common people and of the poor. Moreover, stories that have made the fireside more joyous and blessed may perchance bring vivacity and happiness into school rooms. The home and the school are coming closer together. It is even said that well-trained, sympathetic primary teachers may better tell and impress these stories than overworked mothers and busy fathers. If these literary treasures are left for the homes to discover and use, the majority of children will know little or nothing of them. Some schools in this country and still more in Germany have been using them in the first grade in recent years with a pleasing effect.

But what virtue lies concealed in these fairy myths for the children of our practical and sensible age? Why should we draw from fountains whose sources are back in the prehistoric and even barbarous past? To many people it appears as a curious anachronism to nourish little children in the last decade of this century upon food that was prepared in the tents of wandering tribes in early European history. What are the merits of these stories for children just entering upon scholastic pursuits? They are known to be generally attractive to children of this age, but many sober-minded people distrust them. Are they really meat and drink for the little ones? And not only so, but the choicest meat and drink, the best food upon which to nourish their unfolding minds?

Fairy tales are charged with misleading children by falsifying the truth of things. And, indeed, they pay little heed to certain natural laws that practical people of good sense always respect. A child, however, is not so hum-drum practical as these serious truth-lovers. A little girl talks to her doll as if it had real ears. She and her little brother make tea-cups and saucers out of acorns with no apparent compunctions of conscience. They follow Cinderella to the ball in a pumpkin chariot, transformed by magic wand, with even greater interest than we read of a presidential ball. A child may turn the common laws of physical nature inside out and not be a whit the worse for it. Its imagination can people a pea-pod with little heroes aching for a chance in the big world, or it can put tender personality into the trunk and branches of the little pine-tree in the forest. There are no space limits that a child's fancy will not spring over in a twinkling. It can ride from star to star on a broom-stick, or glide over peaceful waters in a fairy boat drawn by graceful swans. Without suggestion from mother or teacher, children put life and personality into their playthings. Their spontaneous delights are in this playful exercise of the fancy, in masquerading under the guise of a soldier, bear, horse, or bird. The fairy tale is the poetry of children's inner impulse and feeling; their sparkling eyes and absorbed interest show how fitting is the contact between these child-like creations of the poet and their own budding thoughts.

In discussing the qualities requisite in a fairy story to make it a pedagogical treasure, Wilmann says:

When it is laid down as a first and indispensable requirement that a story be genuinely childlike, the demand sounds less rigorous than it really is. It is easier to feel than to describe the qualities which lend to a story the true childlike spirit. It is not simplicity alone. A simple story that can be understood by a child is not on that account childlike. The simplicity must be the ingenuousness of the child. Close to this lies the abyss of silliness into which so many children's stories tumble. A simple story may be manufactured, but the quality of true simplicity will not be breathed into it unless one can draw from the deeper springs of poetic invention. It is not enough that the externals of the story, such as situation and action, have this character. But the sensibilities and motives of the actors must be ingenuous and childlike; they should reflect the child's own feeling, wish, and effort. But it is not necessary on this account that the persons of the story be children. Indeed the king, prince, and princess, if they only speak and act like children, are much nearer the child's comprehension than any of the children paraded in a manufactured story, designed for the "industrious youth." For just as real poetry so the real child's story lies beyond reality in the field of fancy. With all its plainness of thought and action, the genuine child's story knows how to take hold of the child's fancy and set its wings in motion. And what a meaning has fancy for the soul life of the child as compared with that of the adult. For us the activity of fancy only sketches arabesques, as it were, around the sharply defined pictures of reality. The child thinks and lives in such arabesques, and it is only gradually that increasing experience writes among these arabesques the firmer outlines of things. The child's thoughts float about playfully and unsteadily, but the fairy tale is even lighter-winged than they. It overtakes these fleeting summer birds and wafts them together without brushing the dust from their wings.

But fostering the activity of fancy in children is a means, not an end. It is necessary to enter the field of fancy because the way to the child's heart leads through the fancy. The effect upon the heart of the child is the second mark and proof of the genuine child's story. We are not advocates of the so-called moral stories which are so short-winded as to stop frequently and rest upon some moral commonplace. Platitudes and moral maxims are not designed to develop a moral taste in the minds of young children, for they appeal to the understanding and will of the pupil and presuppose what must be first built up and established. True moral training is rather calculated to waken in the child *judgments* of right and wrong, of good and evil (on simple illustrative examples). Not the impression left by a moralizing discourse is the germ of a love of the good and right, but rather the child's judgment, springing from its own conviction. "That was good." "What a mean thing!"

Those narratives have a moral force which introduce persons and acts that are simple and transparent enough to let the moral light shine through, that possess sufficient life to lend warmth and vigor to moral judgments. No attempt to cover up or pass over what is bad, nor to paint it in extravagant colors. For the bad develops the judgment no less than the good. It remains only to have a care that a child's interest inclines toward the good, the just, and the right.

Wilmann summarizes the essentials of a good story, and then discusses the fairy tales as follows:

There are then five requirements to be made of a real child's story. Let it be truly childlike, that is, both simple and full of fancy; let it form morals in the sense that it introduces persons and matters which, while simple and lively, call out a moral judgment of approval or disapproval; let it be instructive and lead to thoughtful discussions of society and nature; let it be of permanent value, inviting perpetually to a re-perusal; let it be a connected whole, so as to work a deeper influence and become the source of a many-sided interest.

The child's story which, on the basis of the aforenamed principles, can be made the starting-point for all others, is Grimm's fairy tale of folklore. We are now called upon to show that the folk-lore fairy tale answers to the foregoing requirements, and in this we shall see many a ray of light cast back upon these requirements themselves.

Is the German fairy tale childlike? full of simplicity as well as of fancy? A deeply poetic saying of Jacob Grimm may teach us the answer. "There runs through these poetic fairy tales the same deep vein of purity by reason of which children seem to us so wonderful and blessed. They have, as it were, the same pale-blue, clear, and lustrous eyes which can grow no more although the other members are still delicate and weak and unserviceable to the uses of earth." Klaiber quotes this passage in his *Das Märchen und diè Kindliche Phantasie*, and says with truth and beauty, "Yes; when we look into the trusting eyes of a child, in which none of the world's deceit is to be read as yet, when we see how these eyes brighten and gleam at a beautiful fairy tale, as if they were looking out into a great, wide, beautiful wonder-world, then we feel something of the deep connection of the fairy story with the childish soul." We will bring forward one more passage from a little treatise, showing depth and warmth of feeling, which stealthily takes away from the doubters their scruples about the justification of the fairy tale. "It is strange how well the fairy tale and the child's soul mutually understand each other. It is as if they had been together from the very beginning and had grown up together. As a rule the child only deals with that part of real life which concerns itself and children of its age. Whatever lies beyond this is distant, strange, unintelligible. Under the leading of the fairy tale, however, it permits itself to be borne over hill and valley, over land and sea, through sun and moon and stars even to the end of the world, and everything is so near, so familiar, so close to its reach, as if it had been everywhere before, just as if obscure pictures within had all at once become wonderfully distinct. And the fairies all, and the king's sons, and the other distinguished personages, whom it learns to know through the fairy tale, they are as natural and intelligible as if he had moved his life long in the highest circles, and had had princes and princesses for his daily playmates. In a word, the world of the fairy tale is the child's world, for it is the world of fancy."

For this reason children live and move in fairyland, whether the story be told by the mother or by the teacher in the primary school. What attention as the story proceeds! What anxiousness when any danger threatens the hero, be he king's son or a wheat-straw! What grief, even to tears, when a wrong is practiced upon some innocent creature! And far from it that the joy in the fairy tale decrease when it is told or discussed over again. Then comes the pleasure of representation—bringing the story upon the stage. Though a child has but to represent a flower in the meadow, the little face is transfigured with the highest joy.

But the childish joy of fairy tales passes away; not so the inner experiences which it has brought with it. I am not affirming too much when I say that he who, as a child, has never listened with joy to the murmuring and rustling of the fresh fountain of fairyland, will have no ear and no understanding for many a deep stream of German poetry. It is, after all, the modest fountain of fairy song which, flowing and uniting with the now noisy, now soft and gently flowing, current of folk song and with the deep and earnest stream of tradition, which has poured such a refreshing current over German poetry, out of which our most excellent Uhland has drawn so many a heart-strengthening draft.

The spirit of the people finds expression in fairy tale as in tradition and song, and if we were only working to lift and strengthen the national impulse, a moral educative instruction would have to turn again and again to these creations of the people. What was asserted as a general truth in regard to classical products, that they are a bond between large and small, old and young, is true of national stories and songs more than of anything else. They are at once a bond between the different classes, a national treasure, which belongs alike to rich and poor, high and low. The common school then has the least right of all to put the fairy tale aside, now that few women versed in fairy lore, such as those to whom Grimm listened, are left.

But does the fairy tale come of noble blood? Does it possess what we called in the case of classics, an old title of nobility? If we keep to this figure of speech, we shall find that the fairy tale is not only noble, but a very royal child among stories. It has ruled from olden times, far and wide, over many a land. Hundreds of years gone, Grimm's fairy stories lived in the people's heart, and not in Germany alone. If our little ones listen intent to *Aschenputtel*, French children delighted in *Cindrillon*, the Italian in *Cenerentola*, the Polish in *Kopcinszic*. The fact that mediaeval story books contain Grimm's tales is not remarkable, when we reflect that traits and characteristics of the fairy tale reach back beyond the Christian period; that Frau Holle is Hulda, or Frigg, the heathen goddess; that 'Wishing-cap,' 'Little Lame-leg,' and 'Table Cover Thyself,' etc., are made up out of the attributes of German gods. Finally, such things as 'The Sleeping Beauty,' which is the earth in winter sleep, that the prince of summer wakes with kisses in spring-time, point back to the period of primitive Indo-German myth.

But in addition to the requirement of classical nobility, has the fairy story also the moral tone which we required of the genuine child's story? Does the fairy story make for morals? To be sure it introduces to an ideal realm of simple moral relations. The good and bad are sharply separated. The wrong holds for a time its supremacy, but the final victory is with the good. And with what vigor the judgment of good and evil, of right and wrong, is produced. We meet touching pictures, especially of good-will, of faithfulness, characteristic and full of life. Think only of the typical interchange of words between Lenchen and Fundevogel. Said Lenchen: 'Leave me not and I will never leave thee.' Said Fundevogel: 'Now and nevermore.' We are reminded of the bible words of the faithful Ruth, 'Whither thou goest I will go; where thou lodgest I will lodge; where thou diest will I die and there will I be buried.'

Important for the life of children is the rigor with which the fairy tale punishes disobedience and falsehood. Think of the suggestive legendary story of the child which was visited again and again with misfortune because of its obstinacy, till its final confession of guilt brings full pardon. It is everywhere a Christian thread which runs through so many fairy stories. It is love for the rejected, oppressed, and abandoned. Whatever is loaded with burdens and trouble receives the palm, and the first becomes the last.

The fairy story fulfills the first three requirements for a true child's story. It is childlike, of lasting value, and fosters moral ideas. As to *unity* it will suffice for children of six years (for this is, in our opinion, the age at which it exerts its moral force) that the stories be told in the same spirit, although they do not form one connected narrative. If a good selection of fairy tales according to their inner connection is made, so that frequent references and connections can be found, the requirement of unity will be satisfied.

The fairy tale seems to satisfy least of all the demand that the true child's story must be instructive, and serve as a starting point for interesting practical discussion. The fairy story seems too airy and dreamy for this, and it might appear pedantry to load it with instruction. But one will not be guilty of this mistake if one simply follows up the ideas which the story suggests. When the story of a chicken, a fox, or a swan is told it is fully in harmony with the childish thought to inquire into the habits of these animals. When the king is mentioned it is natural to say that we have a king, to ask where he lives, etc. Just because the fairy tale sinks deep and holds a firm and undivided attention, it is possible to direct the suggested thoughts hither or thither without losing the pleasure they create. If one keeps this aim in mind, instructive material is abundant. The fairy tale introduces various employments and callings, from the king to the farmer, tailor, and shoemaker. Many passages in life such as betrothal, marriage, and burial, are presented. Labors, in the house, yard, and field, and numerous animals, plants, and inanimate things are touched upon. For the observation of animals and for the relation between them and children, it is fortunate that the fairy tale presents them as talking and feeling. Thereby the interest in real animals is increased and heartlessness banished. How could a child put to the torture an animal which is an old friend in fairy story?

I need only suggest in this place how the fairy story furnishes material for exercises in oral language, for the division of words into syllables and letters, and how the beginnings of writing, drawing, number, and manual exercises may be drawn from the same source.

From the suggestions just made the following conclusions at least may be reasonably drawn. A sufficient counterpoise to the fantastical nature of the fairy tale can be given in a manner, simple and childlike, if the objects and relations involved in the narratives are brought clearly before the senses and discussed so that instruction about common objects and home surroundings is begun.—*Wilmann Paed. Vortraege.*

A selection of fairy stories suited to our first grade will differ from a similar selection for foreign schools. There has been a disposition among American teachers for several years to appropriate the best of these stories for use in the primary schools. In different parts of the country skillful primary teachers have been experimenting successfully with these materials. In Illinois there are several schools in which both teachers and pupils have taken great delight in them. The effort has been made more particularly with first grade children, the aim of teachers being to lead captive the spontaneous interest of children from their first entrance upon school tasks. Some of the stories used at the first may seem light and farcical but experiments with children are a better test than the preconceived notions of adults who may have forgotten their early childhood. The story of the Four Musicians, for example, is a favorite with the children.

The children have no knowledge of reading or perhaps of letters. The story is told with spirit by the teacher, no book being used in the class. Question and interchange of thought between pupil and teacher will become more frequent and suggestive as the teacher becomes more skilled and sympathetic in her treatment of the story. In the early months of school life the aim is to gain the attention and co-operation of children by furnishing abundant food for thought. Children are required or at least encouraged to narrate the story or a part of it in the class. They tell it at school and probably at home, till they become more and more absorbed in it. Even the backward or timid child gradually acquires courage and enjoys narrating the adventures of the peas in the pod or those of the animals in the Four Musicians.

The teacher should acquire a vivid and picturesque style of narrating, persistently weaving into the story, by query and suggestion, the previous home experiences of the children. They are only too ready to bring out these treasures at the call of the teacher. Often it is necessary to check their enthusiasm. There is a need not simply for narrative power, but for quick insight and judgment so as to bring their thoughts into close relation to the incidents. Nowhere in all the schools is there such a call for close and motherly sympathy. The gentle compulsion of kindness is required to inspire the timid ones with confidence. For some of them are slow to open their delicate thought and sensibility, even to the sunny atmosphere of a pleasant school.

A certain amount of drill in reproduction is necessary, but fortunately the stories have something that bears repetition with a growing interest. Added to this is the desire for perfect mastery and thus the stories become more dear with familiarity.

Incidentally, instructive information is gathered concerning animals and plants that are actors in the scenes. The commonest things of the house, field, and garden acquire a new and lasting interest. Sometimes the teacher makes provision in advance of the story for a deeper interest in the plants and animals that are to appear. In natural science lessons she may take occasion to examine the pea blossom, or the animals of the barnyard, or the squirrel or bird in their cages. When a few days later the story touches one of these animals, there is a quick response from the children. This relation between history and natural science strengthens both.

Many an opportunity is given for the pupils to express a warm sympathy for gentle acts of kindness or unselfishness. The happiness that even a simple flower may bring to a home is a contagious example. Kindly treatment of the old and feeble, and sympathy for the innocent and helpless, spring into the child's own thought. The fancy, sympathy, and interest awakened by a good fairy tale make it a vehicle by which consciously and unconsciously a good many advantages are borne home to pupils.

Among other things, it opens the door to the *reading lesson*; that is, to the beginning efforts in mastering and using the symbols of written language. The same story which all have learned to tell, they are now about to learn to read from the board. One or two sentences are taken directly from the lips of the pupils as they recall the story, and the work of mastering symbols is begun at once with zest. First is the clear statement of some vivid thought by a child, then a quick association of this thought with its written symbols on the board. There is no readier way of bringing thought and form into firm connection, that is, of learning to read. Keep the child's fresh mental judgment and the written statement clearly before his mind till the two are wedded. Let the thought run back and forth between them till they seem as one.

After fixing two or three sentences on the board, attention is directed more closely to the single words, and a rapid drill upon those in the sentence is followed by a discovery and naming of them in miscellaneous order in a column. Afterwards new sentences are formed by the teacher out of the same words, written on the board, and read by the children. They express different, and perhaps opposite forms of thought, and should exercise the child's sense and judgment as well as his memory of words. An energetic, lively, and successful drill of this kind upon sentences drawn from stories, has been so often witnessed, that its excellence is no longer a matter of question. Drill, however, and repetition, are essential, and this drill is a form of mental activity in which children delight if the teacher's manner is vigorous and pleasant.

When the mastery of new word-forms as wholes is fairly complete, the analysis may go a step further. Some new word in the lesson may be taken and separated into its phonic elements, as the word *hill*, and new words formed by dropping a letter and prefixing letters or syllables, as ill, till, until, mill, rill, etc. The power to construct new words out of old materials should be cultivated all along the process of learning to read.

This plan of work for learning to read is both analytic and synthetic, proceeding from sentences to words, and from words to sounds, then leading back again to the construction of words and sentences from the sounds and words mastered. The sentence, word, and phonic methods of learning to read are utilized in this general plan. It makes the *content* of interesting thought the starting point, and the power to recognize and express this thought is exercised at each step, while the purely formal and drill work of learning the symbols of writing and reading is so coupled with the child's own interests and needs as to become largely incidental.

Still other school activities of children stand in close relation to the fairy tales. They are encouraged to draw the objects and incidents in which the story abounds. Though rude and uncouth, the drawings still often surprise us with their truth and suggestiveness. The sketches reveal the content of a child's mind as almost nothing else—his misconceptions, his vague or clearly defined notions. They also furnish his mental and physical activities an employment exactly suited to his needs and wishes.

The power to *use good English* and to express himself clearly and fittingly, is cultivated from the very first. While this merit is purely incidental, it is none the less valuable. The persistence with which bad and uncouth words and phrases are employed by children in our common school, both in oral work and in composition, admonishes us to begin early to eradicate these faults. It seems often as if intermediate and grammar grades were more faulty and wretched in their use of English than primary grades. But there can be no doubt that early and persistent practice in the best forms of expression, especially in connection with interesting and appropriate thought matter, will greatly aid correctness, fluency, and confidence in speech. There is also a convincing pedagogical reason why children in the first primary should be held to the best models of spoken language. They enter the school better furnished with *oral speech* than with a knowledge of any school study. Their home experiences have wrought into close association and unity, word and thing. So intimate and living is the relation between word and thought or object, that a child really does not distinguish between them. This is the treasure with which he enters school, and it should not be wrapped up in a napkin. It should be unrolled at once and put to service. Oral speech is the capital with which a child enters the business of education; let him employ it.

A retrospect upon the various forms of school activity which spring, in practical work, from the use of a good fairy story, reveals how many-sided and inspiriting are its influences. Starting out with a rich content of thought peculiarly germane to childish interests, it calls for a full employment of the language resources already possessed by the children. In the effort to picture out, with pencil or chalk, his conceptions of the story, a child exercises his fanciful and creative wit, as well as the muscles of arms and eyes. A good story always finds its setting in the midst of nature or society, and touches up with a simple, homely, but poetic charm, the commonest verities of human experience. The appeal to the sensibility and moral judgment of pupils is direct and spontaneous, because of the interests and sympathies that are inherent in persons and touch directly the childish fancy. And, lastly, the irrepressible traditional demand that children shall *learn to read,* is fairly and honestly met and satisfied.

It is not claimed that fairy tales involve the sum total of primary instruction, but they are an illustration of how rich will be the fruitage of our educational effort if we consider first the highest needs and interests of children, and allow the formal arts to drop into their proper subordination. "The best is good enough for children," and when we select the best, the wide-reaching connections which are established between studies carry us a long step toward the now much-bruited correlation and concentration of studies.

LIST OF FAIRY TALES FOR FIRST GRADE

FALL LITERATURE—First Term

1. The Old Woman and Her Pig—Scudder's Book of Folk Stories
2. Little Red Riding-Hood—Grimm
3. The Anxious Leaf—Beecher's "Norwood," *Public-School Journal,* December 1891
4. The Three Bears—Scudder's Book of Folk Stories
5. The Lion and the Mouse—Aesop, *Public-School Journal,* March 1893
6. The Little Match Girl—Andersen

WINTER LITERATURE—Second Term

1. The Fir-Tree—Andersen, *Public-School Journal*, 1893
2. The Four Musicians—Grimm
3. The Discontented Pine-Tree—Todd and Powell's Third Reader
4. Cinderella—Grimm
5. The Straw, the Coal of Fire, and the Bean—Grimm

SPRING LITERATURE—Third Term

1. The Ugly Duckling—Andersen
2. The Proud Apple Branch—Andersen
3. The King of Birds—Grimm, *Intelligence,* June 15, 1893
4. The Pea Blossom—Andersen, *Public-School Journal,* November, 1891

We are indebted for this list to Mrs. Lida B. McMurry, who has used it in first grade. These stories, adapted to first grade, are published by the Public-School Publishing Co., of Bloomington, Ill.

THE MYTHICAL STORIES

In the third grade we wish to bring a number of the mythical stories vividly before the children. The classical myths which belong to the literature of Europe are the fund from which to select the best. Not all, but only a few of the simple and appropriate stories are chosen. Only two recitation periods a week are to be set apart for the oral treatment of these classical myths. But later in the progress of the reading lessons other stories should be treated. The few recitation periods used for oral work are rather designed to introduce children to the spirit of this literature, to get them into the appreciative mind.

This body of ancient myths comes down to us, sifted out of the early literature of the active-minded Greeks. They have found their way as a simple and charming poetry into the national literature of all the European countries. Is this the material suited to nine and ten-year-old children? It will not be questioned that these myths belong to the best literary products of Europe, but are they suited to children?

It is evident that some of our best literary judges have deemed them appropriate. Hawthorne has put them into a form designed especially for the young folk. Charles Kingsley wrote of the Greek myths for his children: "Now I love these old Hellens heartily and they seem to me like brothers, though they have all been dead and gone many a hundred years. They have come to tell you some of their old fairy tales, which they loved when they were young like you. For nations begin at first by being children like you, though they are made up of grown men. They are children at first like you—men and women with children's hearts; frank, and affectionate, and full of trust, and teachable, loving to see and learn all the wonders around them; and greedy also, too often, and passionate and silly, as children are."

Not a few other authors of less note have tried to turn the classical myths of the old Greek poets into simple English for the entertainment and instruction of children. Scarcely any of these stories have not appeared in various children's books in recent years. Taken as a whole, they are a storehouse of children's literature. The philosopher, Herbart, looked upon the poems of Homer as giving ideal expression to the boyhood of the race, and the story of Ulysses was regarded by him as the boy's book. For the child of eight or nine years he thought it the most suitable story.

Kingsley says in his introduction:

> Now you must not think of the Greeks in this book as learned men, living in great cities, such as they were afterwards, when they wrought all their beautiful works, but as country people, living on farms and in walled villages, in a simple, hardworking way; so that the greatest kings and heroes cooked their own meals and thought it no shame, and made their own ships and weapons, and fed and harnessed their own horses. So that a man was honored among them, not because he happened to be rich, but according to his skill and his strength and courage and the number of things he could do. For they were but grown up children, though they were right noble children too, and it was with them as it is now at school, the strongest and cleverest boy, though he be poor, leads all the rest.

In the introduction to the *Wonder Book* we find the following:

> Hawthorne took a vital interest in child life. He was accustomed to observe his own children very closely. There are private manuscripts extant which present exact records of what his young son and elder daughter said or did from hour to hour, the father seating himself in their play room and patiently noting all that passed. To this habit of watchful and sympathetic scrutiny we may attribute in part the remarkable felicity, the fortunate ease of adaptation to the immature understanding, and the skillful appeal to the fresh imaginations which characterize his stories for the young.

Hawthorne himself says:

> The author has long been of the opinion that many of the classical myths were capable of being rendered into very capital reading for children. No epoch of time can claim a copyright on these immortal fables. They seem

never to have been made, and so long as man exists they can never perish; but by their indestructibility itself they are legitimate subjects for every age to clothe with its own garniture of manners and sentiment and to imbue with its own morality. The author has not always thought it necessary to write downward in order to meet the comprehension of children. He has generally suffered the theme to soar, whenever such was its tendency. Children possess an unestimated sensibility to whatever is deep or high in imagination or feeling so long as it is simple likewise. It is only the artificial and the complex that bewilder them.

A brief analysis of the qualities which render these myths so attractive will help us to see their value in the education of children.

The astonishing brightness of fanciful episode and of pure and clear cut imagery has an indestructible charm for children. They can soar into and above the clouds on the shining wings of Pegasus. With Eolus they shut up the contrary winds in an ox-hide and later let them out to plague the much-suffering Ulysses. They watch with astonishment as Jason yokes the fire-breathing oxen and strews the field with uprooted stumps and stones as he prepares the soil for the seed of dragon's teeth. Each child becomes a poet as he recreates the sparkling brightness of these simple pictures. And when a child has once suffered his fancy to soar to these mountain heights and ocean depths, it will no longer be possible to make his life entirely dull and prosaic. He has caught glimpses of a bright world that will linger unfading in the uplands of his memory. And while they are so deep and lofty they are still, as Hawthorne says, very *simple*. Some of the most classic of the old stories are indeed too complete for third grade children; too many persons and too much complexity, as in the Tales of Troy. But on the other hand, many of the most beautiful of the old myths are as plain and simple to a child as a floating summer cloud. High in the sky they may be or deep in the reflection of some classic lake or spring, but clear and plain to the thought of a little child. These stories in their naive simplicity reflect the wonder and surprise with which a person first beholds grand and touching scenery, whether it be the oppressive grandeur of some beetling mountain crag, or the placid quiet of a moonlit stream. The stories selected for this grade should be the simplest and best; The Golden Touch, Chimaera of Hawthorne, the episodes of the Golden Fleece, with others similar.

In one form or another they introduce us to the company of heroes, or, at least, of great and simple characters. Deeds of enterprise and manliness or of unselfishness and generosity are the climax of the story. To meet danger and hardship or ridicule for the sake of a high purpose is their underlying thought. Perseus and Jason and Ulysses are all ambitious to prove their title to superior shrewdness and courage. When we get fairly into the mythical age, we find ourselves among the heroes, among those striving for mastery and leadership in great undertakings. Physical prowess and manly spirit are its chief virtues. And can there be any question that there is a time in the lives of children when these ideas fill the horizon of their thought? Samson and David and Hercules, Bellerophon, and Jason, are a child's natural thoughts; or, at least, they fit the frame of his mind so exactly that one may say the picture and the frame were made for each other. The history of most countries contains such an age of heroes. Tell in Switzerland, Siegfried in Germany, Bruce in Scotland, Romulus and Horatius at Rome, Alfred in England, are all national heroes of the mythical age, whose deeds are heroic and of public good. The Greek stories are only a more classic edition of this historical epoch, and should lead up to a study of these later products of European literature.

Several forms of moral excellence are objectively realized or personified in these stories.

As the wise Centaur, after teaching Jason to be skillful and brave, sent him out into the world, he said: "Well, go, my son; the throne belongs to thy father and the gods love justice. But remember, wherever thou dost wander, to observe these three things:

"Relieve the distressed.
"Respect the aged.
"Be true to thy word."
—*Jason's Quest*, p. 55.

And many events in Jason's life illustrate the wisdom of these words. The miraculous pitcher is one whose fountain of refreshing milk bubbled always because of a gentle deed of hospitality to strangers. King Midas, on the other hand, experiences in most graphic form the punishment which ought to follow miserly greed, while his humble penitence brought back his daughter and the homely comforts of life. Bellerophon is filled with a desire to perform a noble deed that will relieve the distress of a whole people. After the exercise of much patience and self-control he succeeds in his generous enterprise. Many a lesson of worldly wisdom and homely virtue is brought out in the story of Ulysses' varied and adventuresome career.

These myths bring children into lively contact with European history and geography, as well as with its modes of life and thought. The early history of Europe is in all cases shrouded in mist and legend. But even from this historically impenetrable past has sprung a literature that has exercised a profound influence upon the life and growth of the people. Not that children are conscious of the significance of these ideas, but being placed in an atmosphere which is full of them, their deeper meaning gradually unfolds itself. The early myths afford an interesting manner in which, especially for children, to come in contact with the history and geography of important countries. Those countries they must, sooner or later, make the acquaintance of both geographically and historically, and could anything be designed to take stronger hold upon their imagination and memory than these charming myths, which were the poetry and religion of the people once living there?

It is a very simple and primitive state of culture, whose ships, arms, agriculture, and domestic life are given us in clear and pleasing pictures. Our own country is largely lacking in a mythical age. Our culture sprang, more than half grown, from the midst of Europe's choicest nations, and out of institutions that had been centuries in forming. The myths of Europe are therefore as truly ours as they are the treasure of Englishmen, of Germans, or of Greeks. Again, our own literature, as well as that of European states, is full of the spirit and suggestion of the mythical age. Our poets and writers have drawn much of their imagery from this old storehouse of thought, and a child will better understand the works of the present through this contact with mythical ages.

In method of treatment with school classes, they will admit of a variation from the plan used with Robinson Crusoe. One unaccustomed to the reading of such stories would be at a loss for a method of treatment with children. There is a charm and literary art in the presentation of the stories that would make the teacher feel unqualified to present them. The children are not yet sufficiently masters of the printed symbols of speech to read for themselves. Shall the teacher simply read the stories to children? We would suggest first of all, that the teacher, who would expect to make use of these materials, steep himself fully in literature of this class, and bring his mind into familiar acquaintance and sympathy with its characters. In interpreting classical authors to pupils, we are justified in requiring of the teacher intimate knowledge and appreciative sympathy with his author. Certainly no one will teach these stories well whose fancy was never touched into airy flights—who cannot become a child again and revel in its pleasures. No condescension is needed, but ascension to a free and ready flight of fancy. By learning to drink at these ancient fountains of song and poetry, the teacher might learn to tell a fairy story for himself. But doubtless it will be well to mingle oral narrative and description on the part of the teacher with the fit reading of choice parts so as to better preserve the classic beauty and suggestion of the author. Children are quite old enough now to appreciate beauty of language and expressive, racy turns of speech. In the midst of question, suggestion, and discussion between pupil and teacher, the story should be carried forward, never forgetting to stop at suitable intervals and get such a reproduction of the story as the little children are capable of. And indeed they are capable of much in this direction, for their thoughts are more nimble, and their power of expression more apt, oftentimes, than the teacher's own.

We would not favor a simple reading of these stories for the entertainment of pupils. It should take more the form of a school exercise, requiring not only interest and attention, but vigorous effort to grasp and reproduce the thought. The result should be a much livelier and deeper insight into the story than would be secured by a simple reading for amusement or variety. They should prepare also for an appreciative reading of other myths in the following grades.

After all, in two or three recitation periods a week, extending through a year, it can not be expected that children will make the acquaintance of all the literature that could be properly called the myth of the heroic age in different countries. All that we may expect is to enter this paradise of children, to pluck a few of its choicest flowers, and get such a breath of their fragrance that there will be a child's desire to return again and again. The school also should provide in the succeeding year for an abundance of reading of myths. The same old stories which they first learned to enjoy in oral recitations should be read in books, and still others should be utilized in the regular reading classes of the fourth and fifth grades. In this way the myths of other countries may be brought in, the story of Tell, of Siegfried, of Alaric, and of others.

In summarizing the advantages of a systematic attempt to get this simple classic lore into our schools, we recall the interest and mental activity which it arouses, its power to please and satisfy the creative fancy in children, its fundamental connection with the root ideas of European history and literature, its living personification of generous feeling and instincts, the virtues of bravery, manliness, and unselfishness, and all this in a classic form that still further increases its culture effect upon teacher and pupil. It should never be forgotten that teacher and pupil alike are here imbibing lessons and inspirations that draw them into closer sympathy because the subject is worthy of both old and young.

BOOKS FOR THIRD GRADE

The Wonder Book of Nathaniel Hawthorne

The following stories are especially recommended: The Gorgon's Head, The Golden Touch, The Miraculous Pitcher, and The Chimaera.

One should preserve as much as possible of the spirit and language of the author. Perhaps in classes with children the other stories will be found equally attractive. The Paradise of Children and the Three Golden Apples. Published by Houghton, Mifflin & Co., Boston. Price, 40 cents.

Kingsley's Greek Heroes

The stories of Perseus, the Argonauts, and Theseus, especially adapted to children. It is advisable for the teacher to abbreviate the stories, leaving out unimportant parts, but giving the best portions in the fullest detail. Published by Ginn & Co., of Boston.

Jason's Quest, **by Lowell**

The story of the Argonauts with many other Greek myths woven into the narrative. This recent book is a store of excellent material. The teacher should select from it those parts specially suited to the grade. Published by Leach, Shewell & Sanborn, Chicago.

Adventures of Ulysses, **by Lamb**

A small book from which the chief episodes of Ulysses' career can be obtained. Published by Ginn & Co., Boston. Price, 35 cents.

Tales of Troy, **by DeGarmo**

The story of the siege of Troy and of the great events of Homer's Iliad. This story, on account of its complexity, we deem better adapted to the fourth grade. Published by Public-School Publishing Co., Bloomington, Ill. Price, 20 cents.

Stories of the Old World, **by Church**

Stories of the Argo, of Thebes, of Troy, of Ulysses, and of Aeneas. Stories are simply and well told. It is a book of 350 pages and would serve well as a supplementary reader in fourth grade. Published by Ginn & Co., of Boston. Price, 50 cents.

Gods and Heroes, **by Francillon**

A successful effort to cover the whole field of Greek mythology in the story form. Ginn & Co.

The Tanglewood Tales of Nathanial Hawthorne

A continuation of the *Wonder Book*. Price, 40 cents.

Tales from Spenser

An interesting prose version of the stories of Una and the Lion, Prince Arthur, Britomart, etc. Macmillan & Co. Price, 50 cents.

Heroes of Asgard

Stories of Norse mythology; simple and attractive. Macmillan & Co. Price, 50 cents.

The Elementary Schools and Civic Education
(1897)

Civic education at the elementary level requires that teachers engage children in the subject of history, the ideals of citizenship, and the virtue of fair-mindedness, claims McMurry in this short discussion of elementary teaching and civic education. He discusses the different teaching techniques that should be used when teachers teach different subject-matters, for example history and mathematics. Some fields of study, McMurry asserts, require students to make judgments that are social and cultural in nature. On the other hand, other fields of study, for example mathematics, necessitate that students hold firm to "dogmatic" beliefs, as he puts it, which are not dependent upon social and moral concerns. Among other points, McMurry argues that the subjects of history and government are especially useful in preparing students for citizenship, precisely because they require us to make informed judgments about social and ethical questions. McMurry says that this task should begin at the earliest grades.

Thoroughly educated people often seem as partisan and one-sided as the ignorant and illiterate. The tolerant, fair-minded, judicial spirit is a difficult acquirement even in an educated man. In fact a good part of education is directly opposed to it. Most of us, so far as we are educated, are trained to one-sided views, and, what is worse, to prejudiced feelings and attitudes of mind. In church, in politics, in historical views, in theories of education itself, in social problems, we have met everywhere partisan, often violently prejudiced, teachers. There is very little security against this sort of partisanship in society so long as the machinery of education moves in these

Forgotten Heroes of American Education, pages 501–505
Copyright © 2006 by Information Age Publishing
All rights of reproduction in any form reserved.

deeply cut grooves. Education itself contributes its powerful, often unconscious influence to strengthen prejudiced attitudes of mind and habits of thinking. The higher institutions of learning, as well as the common schools, by cultivating the debating, contentious, partisan spirit, produce a result the opposite to that most needful in the discussion of public and social problems. Education, therefore, in the ordinary sense of the word, is but little protection against partisanship. It depends entirely upon what kind of education it is, whether it contributes to fair-mindedness or to violent prejudice.

This difficulty seems to point clearly to the following query: How can a race of teachers be gradually educated into the spirit of a tolerant, fair-minded discussion of controverted questions? No sudden or marked change is likely to take place in the direction of tolerance because it is a question of improving the inner spirit and temper of teachers, a question of self-control and reasonableness. Growth in self-mastery and in judicial tolerance is growth in the innermost spirit of charity and good sense, and we must not expect too rapid a progress in this highest form of education either in ourselves or in others. Unconsciously we are all too deeply rooted in partial and biased views and habits to be easily capable of frank and many-sided tolerance. But the place to begin is with ourselves and with the body of teachers whose attitude of prejudice or tolerance is repeated, on the average, in the growing generation of children.

It does not seem so very difficult to set up such a standard and ideal of fair-mindedness as will appeal to the good sense of teachers. Nor is it difficult to point out numerous opportunities for exercising the spirit of candor and of suspended judgment, both in school management and in instruction. The historical materials and topics worked over in the school grades are even better for purposes of cultivating fair-minded study than those controverted, and as yet unsettled, questions of present society and government treated in the political and social science of colleges and universities. Very many of the important history topics usually handled in the sixth, seventh, and eighth grades of the grammar school, were two-sided questions, furnishing the best opportunity for a thoughtful, unprejudiced weighing of evidence. For example: the attitude of the Puritans toward the Quakers and other sects; the conflict between the French and English for the possession of North America; the Pequod War and the French wars against the Iroquois; the rights of royal governors and of the colonies; the question of taxation of the colonies by Parliament; in adopting the Federal Constitution, the conflict between state rights and federal sovereignty; the acquisition of Louisiana and Texas; the implied powers of the Constitution; the treason of Arnold; the execution of Major Andre; the important acts of leading men in important crises, as Jay's treaty with England; in fact all treaties and compromises at home and abroad, all wars, all conflicts of political parties involve difficult questions requiring impartial weighing of evidence. No just appreciation of these problems and their importance can be had except by a candid survey of the facts and arguments *on both sides.*

The common historical materials worked over now in the schools furnish, therefore, the precise occasion needed for the exercise of fair-mindedness in study.

It is in this class of historical and social problems, where exact mathematical tests and reasonings are impossible, that candor and a thoughtful weighing of reasons and even of probabilities can be cultivated. In mathematics there is no demand for candor, but absolute dogmatism is permissible. In history all important questions are problematic. They involve not only questions of right and wrong, but of expediency and necessity, of public sentiment, of prevailing opinions and prejudices. The suspended judgment is necessary in the treatment of historical controversies. Prudence, caution, open-mindedness to all sides of a question are indispensable to fair and honest study. The questions of history are good materials upon which to develop a judicial spirit because they are so interesting and so objective. We are not warped by our own interests and prejudices, and it is easier to be fair and comprehensive.

Below the high school the materials for civic training and culture for developing a patriotic American spirit are found also in reading and literature. A few out of the many selections already used in some schools for this purpose are here noted. Burke on Conciliation with America, Longfellow's Courtship of Miles Standish, Building of the Ship, and Paul Revere's Ride, Hawthorne's Stories of New England and Grandfather's Chair, Whittier's Voices of Freedom, Barbara Frietchie, National Hymn, Webster's two speeches at Bunker Hill, at Plymouth; on Washington and on Adams and Jefferson, Emerson's American Scholar, The Fortune of the Republic, The Emancipation Proclamation, Bryant's Song of Marion's Men, Our Country's Call, O Mother of a Mighty Race, Washington's Letters and Farewell Address, Holmes' Grandmother's Story of Bunker Hill, Ballad of the Boston Tea Party, Robinson of Leyden, Lexington, Lincoln's Inaugurals and Gettysburg Speech, Lowell's Under the Old Elm, Concord Ode, and Essay on Democracy, Autobiography of Franklin, Mrs. Hemans' Landing of the Pilgrims, America and other patriotic songs. The Declaration of Independence, Scudder's Essays on Literature in Schools. The best of our American poets and statesmen have given in the forms of literature a dignified and commanding expression to the best ideals of our civilization. We are waking up to the fact that hand in hand with the astonishing growth of our material resources in the last hundred years has gone a growth in culture-ideals, social, political, and religious, which is of supreme educative value for the present and the future. Our poets and true statesmen have made articulate the best experience and thought of our national life. They have winged this thought with poetry and eloquence, stirring the hearts of mature men and women and touching the sensitive life of millions of schoolchildren.

An unpleasant attendant of this genuine spirit of patriotism and true Americanism is a sentimental bombast or braggadocio which has been fully exploited in this country for many years. It is a too common counterfeit for true patriotism, exalting everything American and placing other countries in contempt. It is the exact opposite of the spirit of candor and liberality which should be willing to face and acknowledge the evils in our own society and approve and adopt the merits found in the societies of other countries. The spirit of indiscriminate praise and boastfulness in regard to all things American is not the spirit to cultivate in our American schools with our future citizens. Our best American literature does indeed reflect the self-respect of a great and free nation, proud of its past and exuberant in future hopes, but it is a pride based only in small part in our material riches and physical strength. Physical strength and resources are valuable in a nation, as they are in a man but we do not admire a giant for boasting of his bulk and muscle.

One cause of this boastful spirit is the manner in which we have selected and used selections from our patriotic literature. The brief outbursts of eloquence in Webster and our short patriotic ballads when separated from their setting in longer masterpieces of literature and in life have given a wrong impression of boastfulness. When we use Webster's speeches as wholes a body of thought will be put behind these utterances, giving them full meaning. To get at the true enlightened spirit of patriotism we need to consult Emerson, Webster, Lowell, Everett, Bryant, and Sumner in their complete poems, essays, and speeches.

Another cause of the narrow and perverted American spirit is the manner in which our history has been taught. In our treatment of the Revolutionary War, the War of 1812, and the Civil War a false pride has caused us to magnify our own virtues and successes and to minimize the worth of our enemies. It may be said that very little effort has been made in our histories to treat any of these conflicts in an impartial way, thoughtfully presenting the causes and conflicts on both sides. There is a tacit assumption in nearly all cases that we were in the right and our enemies in the wrong, certainly a very primitive and barbaric mode of getting lessons out of history.

Still another cause of partisan spirit in our education has been steadily cultivated in our debating societies, contests, and various forms of literary contention. The philosopher, John Locke, was strongly of the opinion that debate, controversy, and the love of contention were not favorable to the discovery of truth, and no matter how much we may admire skill and power in debate, we must always remember that the partisan and the advocate mast be laid aside in the search for truth.

Our present course of study certainly has a considerable influence in shaping the political ideas of children in preparation for citizenship, but there seem to be two defects which may be clearly pointed out. On the one side an exaggerated and somewhat bombastic spirit of patriotism has been cultivated which we might fairly call sentimental patriotism, and on the other side many of the facts belonging to history and civics have been taught in a spiritless way, as if facts alone constitute education. The constitution and framework of our government are important enough, but they are often taught in a listless and perfunctory way. It is not difficult to set up the ideal towards which we must work in the teaching of civics.

The golden mean between these two extremes is an interesting, instructive study of our history, government, and social life which not only gets at the important facts but constantly awakens those better sympathies and ideals which are so necessary in any true culture.

Practical Teaching
(1925)

What makes a subject of study practical? What makes for practical teaching? McMurry answers these questions in both direct and indirect ways in this selection from his book entitled Practical Teaching. *This is another work that was used widely by teacher educators in normal schools, teachers colleges, and universities during the early 20th century. McMurry combines methods of teaching with teaching subjects such as history, civics, and geography. He carefully explains his conception of a "practical philosophy of teaching," a perspective that is quite at odds with what is often considered "practical teaching" today. Practicality, to McMurry, could not be separated from morality.*

CHAPTER ONE: INTRODUCTION

The Plan of Study and Teaching

The purpose of this book is to give teachers an introduction to the art of instruction through specific illustrations of organization and of detailed method.

Four Standard Units of Instruction. In order to attain this purpose, the instruction must bring about a full mastery of the materials of study and of the teaching situation presented by classes of children. Each of the four large units[1] elaborately wrought out in this book is a campaign of

---

1. There are four pamphlets to be used by the pupils. They contain the following projects: "New Orleans, a Gulf Port," "The Salt River Project and Irrigation," "The Muscle Shoals," and "Panama Canal." For the convenience of the teacher, each project is exactly reproduced in this book after the discussion is given.

Forgotten Heroes of American Education, pages 507–519

study. Each aims to bring together into one natural, rational process of thought the materials of knowledge essential to a well-rounded unit of instruction. These four demonstrations of large, organized topics may serve as standards of carefully-planned instruction. They also suggest a similar treatment of other large topics.

A Bold Enterprise.   To provide a complete exhibit of one of these large teaching units should be recognized as one of the most difficult and serious enterprises that an experienced teacher can undertake. To make a complete and successful job of one such topic presupposes, first, a complete practical philosophy of teaching; second, a thorough grasp of the subject; and, third, an intelligent, sympathetic, and many-sided knowledge of children.

The Purpose of These Fully-prepared Topics.   When one of these large topics has been organized and developed satisfactorily, other teachers may appropriate it, master it, and handle it with success in the classroom. The purpose of working out big topics beforehand is to get them into such shape that they will be of immediate service to the rank and file of teachers. The use to be made by regular teachers of these fully-prepared topics is the main thing, the one purpose of all this preliminary work.

The Full Preparation of Such a Topic Not an Easy Task.   The problem set before teachers is not some easy method of getting large results. In fact the wise handling of a big topic in the class room is no easy task for anybody. Such a well-organized topic affords an opportunity to determine what wisely-directed effort can accomplish in the serious work of instruction. It is taken for granted that the teacher who undertakes one of these standard units of instruction in the classroom will make adequate preparation. This is mentioned by way of suggesting the necessity of thorough preparation.

Can Young Teachers Make Good Use of These Prepared Topics?   Let us suppose that one of these big units has been fully worked out beforehand by a qualified scholar who is also a master of the art of teaching. Can the young teacher accept this prepared material and master it himself so completely, both in its plan of organization and its detail of illustrative method, that he is prepared to carry it through in class with success?

Can Young Teachers Master the Technique of Instruction?   The young teacher can, no doubt, grasp the subject, so far as its organization goes, but how far, by careful preparation and forethought, can he master the technique of class instruction? If possible, the teacher should acquire beforehand this technique of recitation, illustrative device, and cooperative working with children in developing the subject. Probably the best way to approach the task is for the young teacher to observe demonstrations of such lessons by a successful teacher. In the four topics developed in this book, an effort is made to present a variety of illustrations and devices in the technique of classroom instruction. Suggestive questions are asked, maps and blackboard sketches especially appropriate to the topic are introduced, diagrams and cross sections are given to clear up special difficulties, and illustrative pictures form the dramatic setting. By a thoughtful use of these concrete reenforcements, young teachers should acquire the power of self-help and self-direction.

A Problem for a Group of Experienced Teachers. In order to understand better the emphasis we are placing upon a masterful study and treatment of a single large unit of instruction, let us weigh and consider the following statement: A whole group of scholarly, ambitious teachers could wisely concentrate their thought upon one of these large units of instruction, thoroughly wrought out on the basis of a sound scholarship and sound pedagogic organization. Such a critical discussion of a standard pedagogical organization of a great unit of study might lead to a superior conception of method and of the basic organization of studies. But at present we are chiefly concerned with the rank and file of teachers engaged in the daily tasks of instruction.

A Fit Study for Young Teachers. The well-executed project or *type study* is intelligible to young teachers and is probably the best available introduction to the materials and methods of study, because it is a clear object lesson taught through the medium of a brisk and lively treatment of an important subject. A project is not a dry homily but is like a drama staged in two acts, showing what may be designated as the objective growth of an idea in its two phases. For example, the following story of John Winthrop, the representative Puritan leader of New England, employs these two dramatic stages.

The Story of John Winthrop as an Illustration. First is given the full account of John Winthrop himself, told so as to bring out his personal qualities and his strong religious convictions. He grew into leadership as the embodiment of the resolute purpose to establish in America a Puritan commonwealth. If, as seemed probable, the Puritan ideal should be overwhelmed in England he thought it might be saved in America. His life was a serious, consistent, and successful struggle to achieve this noble end. Second, there should be included in this story a study of other Puritan leaders, such as Dudley, Harry Vane, Davenport, and Anne Hutchinson, so as to give a sufficient basis for generalizations on the Puritan character. Compare Winthrop with Roger Williams, Lord Baltimore, and William Penn, in order to note contrasts with the religious ideas of other sects. Thus, in the first place, the portraiture of the leading Puritan with his life setting in an age of religious ferment, puts him in his true place as a notable landmark in history. Then, in the second stage, a detailed comparison of Winthrop with religious leaders in New England and the other colonies brings out clearly the scope and power of the religious motive, which exercised such a strong influence in the early American settlements.

Type Studies Dramatize Ideas.   To dramatize such ideas and to make an energetic organization of knowledge and experience around dominant characters is the well-determined purpose of these projects. This plan of intensive study serves the higher purpose of education, both for teacher and pupil. These masterful ideas should have the right of way and the main directive influence in carrying children through the fields of knowledge.

Plain School Topics Lifted into Prominence and Leadership.   The four projects here presented are just ordinary school topics—with one distinctive difference. They are worked out to their full dimensions; they are given an artistic, even spectacular, setting; they are permitted to grow from small beginnings, step by step, into a national and world significance. This expansion emancipates the mind from the routine of mere facts. The child's spirit is lifted above the commonplace and allowed to breathe freely in the larger world of thought and action. Yet this dislike of the commonplace implies no scorn of the humble facts of daily experience. In truth, out of these homely elements of local experience imagination builds up a beauteous and imposing structure of thought. A union of outside information with this substratum of common daily experience supplies the spiritual soil out of which the most important ideas spring. A real project stretches its powerful roots far out into the depth and breadth of our common program of business—the *agenda* of conduct over against the *credenda* of the schools. To the expanding, organizing power of a basal type no limit can be set because growth is its function.

The Example of Self-Government.   For example, self-government was born out of the pressing needs of the early American settlements. It grew with the natural colonial expansion. It ever appropriated the new materials of its environment, and to this hour it has developed in power and effectiveness through the growth of our institutions. Still we are hardly more than well started in the movement toward the self-governing organization of society. There is much more to come.

The Example of New Orleans.   New Orleans as treated in this book is another illustration. It is one of those trite commonplaces mentioned in all the geographies in which, like hundreds of other cities, it is slightly discussed and then dismissed. But in the project it is a subject matter of great interest. It takes on large dimensions and becomes an important factor in the realm of studies. Its introduction is a nucleus around which an expanding array of world knowledge is grouped and synthesized. It is converted from a flat commonplace to a world-conquering idea. This growing, expanding, constructive quality is what gives a type study its superior place and potency, its right to prevail both in the learning process and in the curriculum.

Harbor improvement to meet the rapidly increasing needs of New Orleans as a port is the central idea around which a body of knowledge is built up and organized. With the opening of the Panama Canal, the idea of harbor improvement expands to a similar development in many other seaport cities. A study of one case grows, soon into an interpretation of many; ocean and inland commerce respond to a simple constructive idea.

What Is a Type Study? What we call the type study is a demonstration of a principle discovered to be operative in a multitude of individual cases. A type study, in its first stage, is the dramatic setting for an idea and, in its second stage, it unfolds a constructive principle of broad application. To ignore the typical element in a large unit is to shut out the light, but to give it the full right of way opens a broad highway of knowledge. After this manner what often appears in our texts as a mere commonplace is seen to be a matter of importance in world business.

The organization of knowledge in concrete units is the only visible defense against complexity and confusion in studies; schoolmasters are now turning to this large and simple plan of instruction.

Large Topics in Control. The main difficulty lies in persuading teachers to spend time enough upon one of these large topics to develop it properly and thereby demonstrate the value of the principle of large organization. Heretofore teachers have been so entangled in a forest of small facts that any larger survey of knowledge has been shut out from view. The importance of centers of thought has not been appreciated. There is now developing a better strategy in educational warfare. Thoughtful people perceive that by concentrating effort at a few strategic points control can be obtained of the knowledge comprised in the elementary curriculum. Such is the purpose of the four centers of thought selected for treatment in this book.

How to Test the Big Units. The progressive organization of knowledge, illustrating the broad scope of these everyday school topics, will serve as a test of our theory. Anyone who will take time to study one of these topics closely and master it in various relations may decide this whole question for himself. If he will try out with a class of children the larger unit in a series of connected lessons, he will settle a number of important questions that can be settled in no other way. Even the inexperienced teacher, by adequate study, can master one of three large units of instruction and then try it out with reasonable success in the classroom. It is easier to teach a single well-organized topic, rich in materials and developed naturally, than a group of simpler topics lacking these qualities. Fruitful major topics are the best for young teachers to begin with: a well-organized, interesting subject, like a good story, carries teacher and children with it. This ready adaptability of big topics to everyday classroom use fits in with our present purpose of dealing with the rank and file of teachers. We need a simple plan which all energetic teachers can adopt and carry out.

In the present book we make a determined effort to set before teachers in the clearest possible way a demonstration of the large projects. We should like to see this done with a class of children before teachers. Lesson by lesson, a large teaching unit might be worked out in a complete series. This would be not a dramatization of the teaching process but a direct demonstration, a full exhibition of the thought as it unfolds in the classroom from day to day. This would include everything essential: the direct handling of subject matter by the teacher, reproductions, blackboard sketching by teacher and pupils, questions by teacher and children, assignments, reviews, pictures and maps, models and constructions, dramatizations, outside readings and references, correction of faults and mistakes, solution of problems, correlations with other studies, debates by the children, and whatever else the socialized recitation demands. In the end it should be rounded out into a complete achievement—the full mastery of a fundamental idea in its scope and applications.

Discussion of Lessons Observed. If we were dealing with a group of would-be teachers, daily discussions would be employed, evaluated. However, as such a full demonstration before teachers is not always practicable, we are attempting to furnish as complete a substitute for it as the scope of the book allows. Each teacher will have to make up for necessary deficiencies by abundant imagination and thought.

Previous Type Studies Worked Out through Two Main Phases. The type studies, heretofore published in pamphlet form, have aimed at an orderly descriptive treatment, bringing together the detail, imagery, and related facts required to give a complete setting to the main idea. Then follows a series of comparisons by which the subject is expanded to proper scope—its later and larger dimensions—on the basis of its recognized principle.

A Criticism of the Older Type Studies. Type studies have been criticized on the ground that they fail to work out details of method, forms of questioning, graphic illustrations of individual or class treatment, and skilful devices in meeting emergencies and difficulties. In this book we are trying to silence criticism by remedying such deficiencies by enlarging the type study into real projects.

Major and Minor Method. It may be well to observe that method may fall under two heads, designated as *major* and *minor* method. The complete, orderly arrangement of subject matter in a developing process of thought is provided for in the original plan and outline of the type study. It is fundamental and may be known as major method. This method springs from the subject itself, and proceeds in logical process of development.

It is the function of minor method to make adjustments in the special emergencies and difficulties that constantly arise in the classroom. Details tax the ingenuity and resourcefulness of the teacher at every step. The methods and devices that accompany the larger thought movements, that is, reenforce them and make them effective, are what chiefly concern us in the province of minor method.

Close-up Contact with Difficulties in Special Topics.   In the present book we make a serious effort to reach into the region of special adjustment, into the particulars of illustrative method and concrete example—to reveal, as it were, the tricks of the trade as evidenced in the use of special devices. We should like to dramatize the principles of teaching in the most effective way. In fact, we are quite willing to exhaust our resources in the way of showing "how to do it." Let no one suppose that this is an easy undertaking or one suitable only to dull minds. Only those who have a certain respect for their abilities undertake such a job. If it were easily done, some one would have done it before. The hardest thing in education is to show how to teach by direct demonstration.

A Mode of Attack upon a Large Unit.   For those teachers who are interested in this plan of developing large units we suggest the following mode of procedure: Select one fully-expanded and well-illustrated type study and resolve to master it both in its organization and in its illustrative background. Go to the bottom of it, on the supposition that the bottom is not near the surface, but deep down and well worth the trouble of digging for. This implies not casual reading, but thoughtful and reflective study and ingenious forethought in framing pedagogical devices as well as such schemes of illustration and application as children can use. It is difficult to indicate how complete the teacher's mastery of the subject should be. Indeed we have in mind a superior kind of teaching that stimulates self-activity and resourcefulness in children. The teacher has felt out the subject beforehand in all its connections. He has acquired a prophetic instinct for the problems and difficulties sure to arise. He knows the pupils well enough to anticipate their needs and responses as they meet the problems of the subject. It is to some extent a game of chance with children, and he learns how to make use of his chances and even to forestall them.

All this by way of preparation, before the battle comes on, before the actual teaching begins. It is not expected that the inexperienced teachers will master all these difficulties in the first onset or even in the first campaign. But thorough preparation will go a long way and will point out clearly the main road to success.

Importance of Success in the First Big-Teaching Project. If one important type study is thus mastered and fully worked out beforehand, the standard of scholarship and pedagogical organization for the whole succeeding series of studies is set. This is the first stage on the way toward victory over the obstacles in the path of good instruction. A failure to organize and master the knowledge materials and the problems involved in this first important teaching project, that is a failure to make adequate preparation, is likely to prove disastrous. The necessary conditions for success have not been provided; other failures may follow and our whole pet scheme of instruction falls to the ground. We cannot afford, from lack of preparation, to make a failure of this first big teaching project. There may be partial failure, even with complete preparation; but a quick recovery is in sight, and there is a good outlook for final success.

The Ultimate Test of Success Is a Complete Classroom Achievement. The mastery of the first big project is not complete until the project has been tried successfully with a class of children in a connected series of lessons. This is the ultimate test and proof of efficiency, for the experienced as well as the inexperienced teacher. It is an ordeal that might well be prescribed for all teachers as a ticket of entrance to the profession. Any supervisor or leader of teachers can make this test for himself; until it has been successfully passed, all mere theorizing about teaching is relatively worthless, a mere promissory note, not a payment. Young and inexperienced teachers, by putting the necessary preparatory study and thought upon the problem, usually master and successfully teach this first unit of instruction.

To do a really good job in this first attempt at the teaching of a rounded whole, or unit of instruction, is, as noted above, a gateway into the profession of teaching. It sets up for its standard of achievement a masterpiece of pedagogical art. Not that such results are achieved all at once, even with the best effort, but an objective, tangible standard is set up as the aim and measure of future effort.

The Scope of One Clear, Demonstrated Type. Our theory of types is applied in this plan of work to the main process of teaching, which can be illustrated by one outstanding type. The chief reason for placing such emphasis upon this first teaching project is that it is the first of a kindred series of basal types and is itself the key to the entire group. Besides being openly objective and lifelike, it also has in it an element of universality. It illustrates tangibly the main principle of pedagogic organization. It is the entering wedge into a pedagogical system at once simple and universal.

It may seem incredible that by means of a full treatment of a single commonplace topic the science of teaching can be focused in this way at one point so as to bring its main secret to light. It is none the less true that the master principle of teaching is simple and universal and can be plainly shown by a single instance. Its wider applications may be made later.

No Apology Required for This Elaborate Plan of Dealing with a Single Topic. We are therefore not obliged to make any apology for the elaborate treatment of this topic. The reason why the unit of study, "New Orleans, a Gulf Port," occupies so many pages is because a generous space is required to give the central idea in this topic its full setting. More time and labor may be applied to it if needed in order to insure a good job. We are in no haste to find another task until this piece of work has been wrought out. A whole campaign of study may be profitably applied to this single topic.

The Two Stages in the Process. The New Orleans topic exhibits two main stages: first, the demonstration of harbor improvement as an outstanding example of development; and, second, the illustration of this idea by a chain of similar instances, namely, Galveston and Houston, Mobile and Pensacola, San Francisco and Portland, New York and Boston. This expansion of the main idea to show the range and variety of its application leads the children into the organizing process. It strengthens and propagates a seed thought and starts the child on a definite highway of knowledge.

The teacher must see that the children travel the road marked out by these two stages with their eyes open, with their minds on the stretch, with their thinking caps pulled down. The highways of thought opened in this manner run parallel with the main achievements of the world's progress. This is what is meant by type studies.

Three Other Demonstrations. To show a similar development of thought along other trunk lines is the purpose of the three large units of instruction that follow, namely, "The Salt River Project and Irrigation," "The Muscle Shoals," and "The Panama Canal." One convincing demonstration of such large-topic organization must be followed by another and another, until a sufficient variety of cases has been presented to make a full argument in favor of continuous growth in structural knowledge. Each of the topics named is a notable project and worthy of unstinted treatment. Any teacher who masters one of these dominating topics and organizes it into a successful schoolroom exercise deserves to be knighted for high performance.

The Salt River Project. The Salt River Project lends itself remarkably to a graphic treatment, with a full assortment of blackboard sketches and maps, diagrams and models, graphs and pictures, sand tables and constructions, appropriate to cooperative effort. The whole scheme can be laid out on the playground or in some neighboring creek valley with the placing of the dams, canals, and spillways. A score of problems, demanding thoughtful interpretation, spring up in the process of working out the original project. Some of the main difficulties can be solved convincingly by arithmetical calculations. The second stage, exhibiting the broad scope and varied application of the type to larger and smaller irrigation schemes through all the Western states, is a perfect illustration of the continuous growth and organization of knowledge in a big topic. The thought problems arising in this second stage measure up to the full capacity of children for inventive and constructive planning.

Muscle Shoals and Panama Canal. The Muscle Shoals and Panama Canal topics are surprising demonstrations in other geographic regions of this expansion of thought movements based on tangible projects. These draw children into powerful life currents that give character to our age.

The Project in Two Stages. The main purpose of this book, in demonstrating the merits of the big unit of study, is to portray on the colossal scale of these modern engineering accomplishments the two big stages of the pedagogical drama: first, the scenic objectification of the main idea; and, second, the great propaganda by which the idea is broadened to a universal meaning as a type.

The Principles of Teaching. Involved in this inductive movement and parallel with it, the principles of sound teaching may be seen in operation. This suggests the dramatizing of these principles in the elaborated studies we are engaged in. Just as a steam engine is a piece of machinery invented for harnessing and using the power of steam, so the large teaching project is a scheme for harnessing the principles of teaching and causing them to cooperate in the teaching process. The best way to do this is to dramatize principles by giving them full objective play in natural teaching situations. Such a thing occurs in the classroom when boys and girls are working out and demonstrating a large unit of study. Teacher and children are combining forces in the effort to organize a definite subject matter into a rational thought movement. A clear objective is embodied in a life situation and is staged in a natural habitat, i.e., the Panama Canal. The completeness of this dramatic action lends reality to the whole enterprise and, as it were, exposes the principles to observation. It is a question whether principles ever get a real grip upon our inner thought, so as to affect our outer actions, unless they are first demonstrated to our senses in some life-like embodiment.

Principles in Working Clothes. In introducing teachers to the principles governing instruction, it is well to see these principles in their working clothes—active on the job. On the other hand, the smooth formulation of such principles into educational dogma is a means of storing them away on a back shelf where they are almost certain to be forgotten. We want our principles harnessed to practice, governing both the material and method of teaching operative in the classroom.

The Life Energy at Work.   This whole program of instruction as it develops dramatically is full of the life energy of growing projects. It has a much stronger, deeper influence than the moving picture, stronger even than the drama, for the reason that the large, fully-developing project has a deep fundamental thought sequence as its constructive principle.

The Missing Link.   This pronounced accent upon the dramatic and descriptive part of a "knowledge-whole" directs attention to what may be called the *missing link* in our teaching procedure. In order to gain quick results in our instructions, we commonly jump at conclusions. We leave out the details of the experiences from which such results spring. We are so anxious to know the outcome that we are not willing to read the story. This premature haste to reach the goal of instruction without traveling the road is the besetting sin of much of our teaching. This proneness of educators to wake up at the end of the journey and to drop out the essential intermediate stages by which knowledge grows and matures to its natural fruition makes a bad job of the whole business. It is a method of fooling both teacher and children with the semblance of knowledge. It develops a fundamental intellectual dishonesty by pretending to know important truths for which we have no basis in experience. It leaves out the intervening stages of thought and yet pretends to be training children as thinkers. In other words, it is a fraud that has nested itself securely in our school practice and lies there at the center of our teaching process. And it openly defies progress.

When Shakespeare desires to present an idea, he impersonates it in a single character; as Othello or Macbeth; he dramatizes it in a complete series of acts in a full life setting. The teacher reads the play for the student and sums up the conclusion in a brief aphorism, because the students do not have time to read Shakespeare. This short cut to knowledge is a sure way of never reaching any knowledge of real value.

A Sound Basis for Learning.   In the large, fully-elaborated type study, an attempt is made to get back to a sound basis of knowledge by supplying what we have called the missing link in the process of thought, the enriching elements of experience in which all true knowledge is grounded. From the standpoint of our present course of study this looks like an extravagant expenditure of time on a few subjects. But from the point of view of the type, which gives a commanding survey of a broad area of knowledge, it is the essence of economy. Depth of knowledge and power to think never spring from superficial studies. We cannot be satisfied with a course of study in which big central topics are dwarfed into insignificance. They should not be reduced thus to mutilated and stunted remnants, but should stand out as the natural imposing strongholds of knowledge. The effort is here made to exhibit a few of these large topics as complete demonstrations of a sound procedure both in learning and in teaching.

The Duty of Teachers. Can teachers generally master these developed and organized topics thoroughly and appropriate them to their own uses in teaching? It would be an insult to the average teacher to say that he could not do this, because there is no serious difficulty involved. We may go a step further and say that, with a little suggestion and encouragement, children can do it. They have done it. We have no fear for the children whatever, if we can only get teachers to go ahead and use a reasonable amount of energy and persistence in mastering these subjects beforehand. It is simply a question of the willingness of teachers to help themselves.

A Basis for Self-Help. Self-help is the best tool in the teacher's possession. Without this quality of self-determination, guided along lines of sound constructive study, no important progress will be achieved. A well-organized, graphic treatment of a large topic is interesting and easy for the teacher—much easier than our usual dry and inadequate treatment in the textbook. Indeed some people have objected to putting this well-prepared treatment of the subject in the hands of the teacher, claiming that he ought to make this preparation for himself—to build up these topics.

Do Not Overload the Teacher. There are two excellent reasons why we should not lay upon the busy teacher the extra labor of preparing these big topics. One is that he has not the materials and resources at hand with which to do it; the other is that it will take all the time he has at his disposal to master the subject when it is already prepared for him and placed in his hands.

Some day when the teacher has gained experience in dealing with these big well-arranged and fruitful topics, he may try his hand at collecting material and working out the original treatment of a large type study. However, anyone who has tried it will be slow to lay so heavy a burden upon a teacher just starting out. No greater folly could be perpetrated.

An Open Door to Progress. On such a plan of deliberate study of big units already worked out, teachers engaged in school work may start and progress. They will steadily enlarge their scholarship in history, science, geography, and literature and develop a sound method of teaching based on a few main principles. In other words, there is a fundamental process of teaching involved in the productive treatment of these commanding types; anyone who devotes himself to the mastery and classroom treatment of such well-planned units will become clearly conscious of the principles involved.

A System of Self-Instruction. The four big units worked out in this book may be regarded as a system of self-instruction, organizing knowledge in big topics and applying this method of procedure to classroom instruction. It would be interesting to learn how many teachers use this plan of self-instruction and, after first learning how to teach themselves, develop into efficient teachers of children.

Most needed in the teaching profession are demonstrators who will go out among teachers and illustrate the plan of teaching the type studies in classes. As fast as we find demonstrators, we spread the contagion of this method. A certain amount of demonstration of large units of study is indispensable. We learn to do by doing and by seeing other people doing the things worth trying. But in the end all progress depends on resolute self-instruction, on the resourcefulness of the teacher and the independent use he makes of organizations, suggestions, and modes of procedure gained from any and all sources.

We would lay special emphasis on the necessity of the teacher's mastering the large organization of big topics. Until this larger conquest has been made by the teacher the road to success is not open. The larger plan in every big unit of instruction must be first clearly laid out. Then the minor devices of teaching will find their proper places.

Section 7

SELECTED WRITINGS OF WILLIAM C. RUEDIGER

Ｗilliam C. Ruediger (1874–1947) is a forgotten hero of American education. Like the other individuals in this volume, he dedicated his life to teaching teachers, a calling that he excelled at within the university environment. He was well-schooled in the theory of education and in educational psychology, but he also brought numerous years of classroom teaching experience to his work as a teacher of teachers. He taught teachers for a short time with William C. Bagley at Montana State Normal School in Dillon, Montana, but Ruediger's final institutional home was George Washington University in Washington, D.C.

Ruediger taught teachers in GWU's School of Education for nearly thirty years. Prior to World War I, he established and then maintained in downtown Washington a demonstration school for prospective teachers. He also served as Dean of the School of Education at George Washington from 1926–1934. A history of George Washington University states that, by the end of his career, Ruediger had "trained more than half of the teachers in the Washington (D.C.) public schools." GWU's history further states that students in their School of Education today "follow Dean Ruediger's model by teaching full time at the District's public schools."[1] Ruediger's work is testimony to what can be achieved for the teaching profession when

---

1. See George Washington University, "Traditions and Trendlines," www.gwu.edu.

Forgotten Heroes of American Education, pages 521–522

professors of education within universities work to connect their institutions to the children and teachers within their local communities.

Ruediger was born in Fountain City, Wisconsin, on March 29, 1874. After growing up in Wisconsin, he attended the University of Wisconsin in Madison, where he earned his undergraduate degree in 1893. From 1893 to 1902, Ruediger served as an elementary and high school teacher in various Midwestern towns, including Alma, Wisconsin; Eau Claire, Wisconsin; and Winona, Minnesota. He continued to study toward his Master's degree during this time, which he completed at Wisconsin, in psychology, in 1903.[2]

Beginning in the fall of 1903, Ruediger was a professor of pedagogy at Montana State Normal School in Dillon, Montana. After serving for two years on the faculty at Montana State from 1903 to 1905, Ruediger moved to New York City where he began his doctoral study at Teachers College, Columbia University. After earning his Ph.D. degree at Teachers College in 1907, Ruediger accepted a position as professor of education and psychology at George Washington University. He remained at GWU until his retirement in the late 1930s. He died on July 4, 1947, in Washington, D.C.[3]

In addition to his efforts as a teacher of teachers, Ruediger published numerous books and articles on educational philosophy and teacher education. His books include works such as *Teaching Procedures, The Principles of Education, Vitalized Teaching,* and *Agencies for the Improvement of Teachers in Service.*[4] Ruediger is an example of another forgotten hero who dedicated his life to teachers, teaching teachers, and to building the foundations of the teaching profession. His work merits renewed attention today.

---

2. W. Stewart Wallace, Compiler, *A Dictionary of North American Authors Deceased Before 1950* (Toronto: The Ryerson Press, 1951), p. 393.

3. *Who Was Who in America: A Companion Biographical Reference Work to Who's Who in America,* Volume 2 (Chicago: The A. N. Marquis Company, 1950), p. 462.

4. William C. Ruediger, *The Principles of Education* (New York: Houghton Mifflin, 1910); William C. Ruediger, *Agencies for the Improvement of Teachers in Service* (Washington, D.C.: U.S. Bureau of Education Government Printing Office, 1911); and William C. Ruediger, *Teaching Procedures* (New York: Houghton Mifflin, 1932).

Present Status of Education as a Science
(1912)

In this work, Ruediger presents an exhaustive survey of the content of Principles of Teaching courses at prominent institutions of higher education across the country. He was searching for the common principles that united these courses. He was disappointed to find few commonalities.

After presenting the results of his survey, Ruediger argues in favor of the unifying principles that he thinks should hold together the science of education in general and the profession of teaching in particular. Like Bagley, who was Ruediger's colleague for three years at Montana State Normal School, Ruediger asserts that the profession of teaching is as much a calling as it is a science in a restricted, modern sense.

Ruediger concludes the study by connecting the profession of teaching to the social sciences, the natural sciences, and the humanities. Throughout the work, he stresses the need for his profession to attend to history, the purpose of schooling, curriculum, and moral education. He also argues that professors of education like him must concentrate on advancing knowledge and teaching teachers.

I. INTRODUCTION

1. The phrase "the status of education as a science" is likely to prove misleading in at least one serious respect. It is likely to lead people to think that it is the aim to arrive at just one coherent and homogeneous science called "education," as we have one coherent science of chemistry or botany. This is apparently the point of view from which Dilthey, Royce (*Ed. Rev.*, I, 15 and 121), and not a few others have written and spoken.

523

Now a little observation and reflection will show that from the standpoint of science, education cannot be compared with a pure science like chemistry or botany, but that it must be compared with such concepts as medicine, engineering, and architecture. These concepts do not stand for such bodies of knowledge as we have come traditionally to call sciences, but they stand for vast fields of practice in which the results, not only of one, but of many sciences are applied for the direct benefit of mankind. They stand, not for so many sciences, but for professional callings, among which education should be included.

2. But while a profession from its theoretical side cannot be consistently looked upon as one science, it both rests upon and embraces a number of sciences. These sciences may be conveniently grouped under two heads: pure sciences and applied sciences.

3. It is the aim of the pure sciences to classify and organize the facts and principles that observation and reflection reveal in nature, art, and industry on the basis of their logical similarities and relationships. This classification and organization is prompted primarily by man's instinctive curiosity and tendency toward rationalization, and the result is to give man a consistent, satisfying, and reliable knowledge of the world in which he lives.

In the pure sciences, therefore, man views the world as a theoretical being, as a being that wants to know without necessarily any immediate reference to the use that he or his fellows may make of the knowledge that has been gathered.

But by force of circumstances man is a practical, as well as a theoretical, being. No matter how soul-satisfying theoretical contemplation may be, if it did not also contribute to man's material well-being it would have no chance for survival. The touchstone of survival is ever the objective test of usefulness, but this limit is social and hampers the individual only when in the indulgence of his powers he transgresses this limit, when he signally fails to reach it, or when society fails to grasp the significance of his performances.

The practical aspect of life gives us the applied sciences. No matter where or for what purpose knowledge may have been gained, it may be used in solving the practical problems of life, and this use, like the satisfaction yielded by insight, is facilitated by organization. The doctor does, indeed, profit by such sciences as chemistry, bacteriology, physiology, and anatomy, but this profit is largely indirect and is gained fully and directly only after the material in them that bears on the preservation and restoration of health has been selected and reorganized into the applied sciences of hygiene, *materia medica*, surgery, and the like.

The difference between the pure and applied sciences, therefore, is found, not in mutually exclusive subject-matter, but in the criteria used for the selection and classification of subject-matter. Whereas the pure sciences select facts and principles on the basis of their logical congruity, the applied sciences select them on the basis of the use to which they are put. The two, therefore, cross-classify, and in one sense are mutually exclusive.

What is true in the professions generally is true also in the profession of teaching. So far as teaching has a theoretical aspect, this aspect is represented by a group of applied sciences, and these in turn are closely related to a group of pure sciences. These pure sciences are chiefly psychology, logic, sociology, and ethics.

4. The relation that the pure sciences underlying the profession of teaching (or those underlying any other profession, for that matter) bear to the applied sciences involved in the calling is usually expressed by saying that they are basal to them. This is all right when it is interpreted to mean that the person beginning the study of the profession should have at least an outline knowledge of the sciences in order to give him an apperceptive basis and perspective in pursuing the applied sciences, but it is wrong when it is interpreted to mean that the applied sciences must get their facts and principles from the pure sciences and that they must wait upon them for their own contentful advancement.

That there is a relation of content between the pure and applied sciences cannot be denied, but this relation is largely a reciprocal one. The applied scientist may indeed turn to the pure scientist for principles, and even for facts, just as the pure scientist gets many of his facts and problems from the practitioner, but before the applied scientist can make adequate use of the data so obtained he must reorganize them and test their application. The latter step frequently not only involves experimentation, but leads to new problems that fall to the lot of the applied scientist for solution. Indeed, an applied science should certainly progress no less through the researches prosecuted within its own field than through the researches prosecuted in the related pure sciences.

5. This investigative or progressive feature of a science compels us to note still another aspect of the use of the word "science." When applied to any body of knowledge, this word has a twofold significance. It has reference to this body of knowledge either (1) as an organized system of facts and principles, or (2) as possessing an inductive and relatively exact method of investigation. Both uses of the word are justifiable and are in no way incompatible. In fact, a body or field of knowledge, to merit the name "science," should embrace both meanings of the word. Every true science includes both content and method. Physics, botany, geology, and the like would be but names for socially profitless disturbances without their bodies of knowledge, relatively established and organized and therefore available for use; and without vital and somewhat clearly conceived methods of growth the names would but stand for so much dead matter. And what is

true of the pure sciences in this respect is true of the applied sciences also. These, too, are characterized both by coherent bodies of facts and principles and by methods of research through which they maintain their growth and vitality.

II. THE PRESENT STATUS OF THE PRINCIPLES OF EDUCATION AS AN ORGANIZED BODY OF KNOWLEDGE

1. As indicated by college courses.

The status of the principles of education as a coherent and organized body of knowledge ought to be indicated both by the topics included in college and university courses in the principles of education and by the topics treated in textbooks on the principles of education.

I quote first the outlines of eighteen courses, entitled "Principles of Education," offered by eighteen different colleges and universities, and then eleven other courses, essentially similar in content to the preceding but bearing different titles, offered by nine institutions. Omitting duplications, twenty-six institutions are represented.

With the exception of New York University, whose outline was kindly furnished by Dean Balliet, all these outlines have been taken from recent catalogues and announcements, but to save space a few of them have been slightly abridged. The aim has been to select only those courses that are intended solely or largely for undergraduates, and the remarks that I have made concerning them should be taken to have reference to undergraduate work only.

Chicago, 1910–11. Principles of Education. A course of lectures and readings introducing students to the general problems of education and to the scientific methods of solving these problems.

Colorado, 1910. Science and Principles of Education. An examination of those facts and hypotheses which have significance for educational theory. Biological, physiological, anthropological, psychological, sociological, and philosophical data will be considered to the end of deciding on a working hypothesis for educational practice.

Columbia, (Monroe), 1910. Principles of Education. One third of Education B (History of Education). (This course deals with the biological, psychological, sociological, and vocational phases of education.)

Cornell, 1900–10. Principles of Education. This course is designed to be an introduction to the general theory of education, and falls into two distinct parts, one pertaining especially to the school studies and the other to the scientific methods of teaching them. The social and individual basis of education; the basis for the selection of studies; their classification; their function and relative worth; the mental discipline that each should furnish;

the organization of studies into curricula; the correlation of high-school studies; scientific basis of high-school methods; etc.

George Washington, 1911. Principles of Education. The basis, aims, values, and essential content of education as revealed by biological, psychological, sociological, and ethical principles.

Harvard, 1910. Introduction to the Study of Education—Discussion of Educational Principles. The following topics indicate the general character of the work: The scope and meaning of education; the fortuitous education of experience and environment; the school as the chief means of systematic education; the development of the individual and his adaptation to the civilization of his time; the special aims of elementary and secondary education; educational values and programs (courses) of study; the relation of psychology and ethics to educational theory and practice; the correlation of studies; general principles of method; the bearing of instruction on character; discipline and moral training; the study of children; school hygiene; vocational education; education as a function of society.

Illinois, 1910. Principles of Education. Biological principles which condition and limit education; heredity and environment; psychological principles governing the educative process, especially the laws of attention, habit, memory, and the formation of meanings; developmental principles which describe and explain the changes of childhood and youth; application of these principles to educational practice in connection with the course of study, methods of instruction and training, and school hygiene.

Iowa, 1909–10. Principles of Education. Education considered from the standpoint of (1) biology, (2) neurology, (3) psychology, (4) anthropology, (5) sociology. Representative topics: instinct, heredity, habit, culture epochs, individual differences, imitation, suggestion; training of memory, imagination, emotions, will, senses, motor activities, moral nature; formal discipline, educational values, social education, classical and contemporary theories.

Michigan, 1911. Principles of Education. The purpose of this course is to outline and examine briefly the distinguishing aspects of the educative process. An attempt is made to interrelate the industrial, biological, psychological, aesthetic, religious, and sociological points of view. The course is planned for those students who desire sufficient acquaintance with educational theory to enable them to read critically the modern literature on the subject.

Missouri, 1911. Principles of Education. The purpose of this course is to give insight into the meaning of education and thereby to reveal the fundamental principles upon which educational procedure should rest.

New York, 1911. Principles of Education. Brain localization and its bearing on education; the order of maturing of the nervous system and its bearing on educational problems; fatigue; reflex action, instinct, and habit in their bearing on educational problems; the evolution of the feelings and its application to education; the evolution of morals in the race and in the child; the principles of moral education; play; educational ideals critically studied; "formal discipline"; education from the standpoint of the state; industrial education; physical education; etc. (Course intended primarily for college and normal graduates.)

Ohio State, 1911. Principles of Education. A review of educational theory and the principles underlying teaching.

Pittsburgh, 1910. Principles of Education—An Introduction to Educational Theory. A discussion of the most important applications of psychology to education, based on the study both of child development and of the origin and organization of the subject-matter of the curriculum. The topics studied include the meaning of education, the social and individual aspects of education, the nature and function of work and play, the relation of motor and mental processes in development, true and false correlation; formal steps of the recitation, the doctrine of interest, formal discipline, educational values and motives, inductive and deductive thinking, etc.

Virginia, 1909–10. Principles of Education—A Summary of Present Educational Theory and Practice. After an introductory consideration of the method and material of educational theory, the aim of education is defined and illustrated at length. Theories of organic evolution are outlined and discussed in their influence upon theories of education. The second and third terms are devoted to a study of school hygiene, educational psychology, curricula, and general method.

Washington, (State), 1910–11. Principles of Education. The nature and development of the child as the basis of the methods and processes of education; ideals of individual and social character in determining the aim of education; physiological, intellectual, and moral training; the special tasks and methods of the school and the teacher as compared with other agencies, such as the home, the calling, the church, social intercourse; the branches of study and their values and methods; discipline, organization, and administration; the qualifications and preparation of the teacher.

Wellesley, 1910–11. Principles of Education. A study of the educative process, with a consideration of educational values, the hygiene of instruction, periods of development in the life of the child, and special problems of the high school and the elementary school in the United States.

Wisconsin, 1911. Principles of Education. The foundation of educational theory viewed in the light of contemporary thought; also practical problems of curriculum and methods of teaching, accompanied by observation in the schools of Madison.

Yale, 1910–11. Principles of Education. Education and psychology; education and ethics. The end in education, what knowledge is of most worth. The process, apperception, interest, the doctrine of formal discipline, the acquiring of knowledge, habituation.

Cincinnati, 1910–11. Philosophy of Education. The first part of the course will present an integrated view of the facts of the various sciences having educational significance, for the purpose of arriving at a philosophical definition of education as a whole. The second part of the course will deal with the organization of elementary education as determined by its philosophical meaning thus derived and as modified by practical considerations. In the appropriate connections there will be special consideration of the process of education as world-building; the historical and logical origin, meaning, and classification of studies will be briefly considered; special attention will be given to the question, What happens when we try to know? and to the place of symbolism and systems of institutional and inventional expression in education.

Columbia, (Suzzallo, 1911). Educational Sociology. A systematic presentation of the relation of education to society, being a special application of modern sociological knowledge to the problems of social welfare as achieved through educational activities. The relation of social conditions to school aims, functions, values, organizations, curricula, and methods will be noted.

Columbia, (MacVannel), 1911. Philosophy of Education. This course aims to lay the basis for a scientific theory of education considered as a human institution. The process of education is explained from the point of view of the doctrine of evolution and idealism, and the principles thus arrived at are applied from the standpoints of the typical forms of human culture, the institutional factors in the educative process, the course of personal development, and education in the school.

Indiana, (Black), 1910. Elementary Pedagogy. (A) The functions and processes of education determined by the nature of human life considered under its biological, psychological, and social aspects. (B) The science of the recitation and the principles of school management in general, deduced from the foregoing.

Indiana, (Jones), 1910. Philosophy of Education. (1) Fall term. Physical education ... A hygienic course of study to be developed. (2) Winter term. Education as individualism will be considered. The formal side of education in its relation to inhibition, facilitation, discipline, interest, and correlation will be thoroughly worked out. (3) Spring term. Education will be considered chiefly as an adjustment of the individual to an ever-changing environment, and will be shown to be a unifying of the individual and social forces for harmony and efficiency.

Kansas, 1911. Philosophy of Education. The purpose of this course is to study the distinguishing points of view of educational theory. The attempt will be made to interrelate the industrial, biological, psychological, aesthetic, ethical, and social ideals.

Leland Stanford Junior, 1911. Educational Theory. An introductory course dealing with the topics fundamental to education, such as the nature of infancy, physical and social heredity, the relation of the organism to environment, of instinct to habit, etc.

Minnesota, 1910–11. The Theory of Education. An introductory course in educational theory including a somewhat detailed study of the principles on which is based the present practice in teaching.

Nebraska, 1911. Philosophy of Education. The principles underlying all education and their influence in determining the material curricula in schools of instruction.

Peabody College, 1910. Philosophy of Education. In this course the philosophical principles upon which the methods and subject-matter of education are based will be brought out. The meaning of education in its various aspects will be defined, the relation which it bears to the natural and mental sciences indicated, and its field outlined.

Texas, 1910–11. Philosophy of Education. In this course will be studied the growth of the philosophical and psychological ideas that have underlain and conditioned the various systems of education. (Historical and psychological.)

While it would be in place at this point to compare these several courses for the purpose of discovering types, agreements, and disagreements, I shall leave these comparisons till we come to the discussion of the organization of the principles of education from the logical side. The disagreements apparently so greatly outnumber the agreements in these courses that the comparisons can be made more readily after a few fundamental principles have been at least tentatively laid down.

2. As indicated by textbooks.

Bagley, *The Educative Process*, 1905.
>   Part I. Functions of education (three chapters).
>   Part II. The acquisition of experience (three chapters).
>   Part III. The functioning of experience (three chapters).
>   Part IV. The organization and recall of experience (three chapters).
>   Part V. The selection of experiences for educational purposes: Educational values (three chapters).
>   Part VI. The transmission of experience and the technique of teaching (eight chapters).

Bagley, *Educational Values,* 1911.
> Part I. The controls of conduct. (Six chapters, one dealing with the instincts as inherited controls of conduct, four with the acquired controls of conduct, and one with heredity as limiting the educative forces.)
> Part II. The classification of functions and values. (Nine chapters, one dealing with the aim of education as the criterion of value, one with the rubrics of function and value, six with the values to be realized in fulfilling the various functions, and one with the school environment as a source of educative material.)

Bolton, *Principles of Education,* 1910.
> (The twenty-eight chapters of this book may be roughly grouped as follows: The first chapter, entitled "The New Interpretation of Education," is introductory, the next six or seven are primarily biological and neurological, and the remaining twenty or twenty-one deal with psychological topics and their relation to education.)

Boone, *Science of Education,* 1904.
> Part I. The nature of education (twelve chapters).
> Part II. Education as a science (two chapters).
> Part III. The data of educational science (two chapters).
> Part IV. Contributing sciences (eleven chapters).

Henderson. *Text-Book in the Principles of Education,* 1910.
> Introduction: Various conceptions of the aim of education.
> Part I. Education as a factor in organic and social evolution. (Three chapters devoted respectively to readjustment, heredity, and society.)
> Part II. The process of education in the individual. (Nine chapters devoted to topics in educational psychology.)
> Part III. The educational agencies. (Five chapters as follows: Analysis of educational agencies; the evolution of the school; the functions of the school; the academic and the practical; liberal and vocational education.)

Horne, *Philosophy of Education,* 1904.
> Eight chapters apportioned as follows:
> 1. The field of education: Introduction.
> 2. Biological aspects of education.
> 3. Physiological aspects of education.
> 4. 5. Sociological aspects of education.
> 6. 7. Psychological aspects of education.
> 8. Philosophical aspects of education.

Jones, *Principles of Education*, 1911.

Seven chapters as follows: The meaning of education; the subjects of study; motivation; utilization of play impulse; the teacher an influence; methods; professional criticism.

O'Shea, *Education as Adjustment*, 1903.

Part I. The present status of education as a science. (Three chapters dealing with the character of the field of education, effective method in education, and the data for a science of education.)

Part II. The meaning and aim of education. (Five chapters developing the conception and implications of education as adjustment.)

Part III. The method of obtaining adjustment. (Seven chapters dealing with topics in educational psychology.)

Ruediger, *The Principles of Education*, 1910. Sixteen chapters as follows:

1. The field of education: Introduction.
2. Biological bases of education.
3. 4. 5. 6. The aim of education and formal discipline.
7. 8. 9. The elemental educational values.
10. 11. 12. The curriculum and the values of the studies.
13. 14. The administration of the curriculum and the agencies that educate.
15. 16. The psychological bases of teaching.

These textbooks show but little more agreement in the topics treated than the outlines of the courses given in colleges. Comparisons between them will again be left till after we have discussed the organization of the fundamental courses in education from the logical side, when they can be made more readily.

3. The twofold nature of the teacher's problem.

In view of the fact that so little uniformity in the content and organization of the principles of education is found in textbooks and in college courses, it becomes necessary to inquire what this subject should contain from a logical point of view. What should be the guiding principle in the selection of data for the principles of education, and how could these data be most effectively organized? In attempting to answer these questions any one person can obviously do little more than bring up topics for discussion.

It is axiomatic that the primary function of educational theory is to assist the teacher in his work.

When the teacher in the schoolroom reduces the complex problem confronting him to its lowest terms, he finds at least two fundamental and irreducible factors. These are (1) the child that is to be taught, and (2) the subject-matter of instruction and the ideals of conduct and efficiency into which the child is to be initiated. For brevity's sake we may refer to these as (1) the child and (2) the curriculum.

The child and the curriculum are in many respects far apart. The child is immature and inexperienced, but plastic and active, while the curriculum represents the mature and sifted knowledge, ideals, and dexterity of the race. But the first need of the teacher is to understand both sides.

4. The resulting subjects of study:

a) Educational psychology. The scientific knowledge of the child may be obtained by the teacher from the study of general, genetic, child, and educational psychology. The first three may be looked upon as giving a general outline of this knowledge while the last investigates and summarizes especially those aspects of mental science that the teacher needs particularly to know. These aspects are especially the study of the child (or adult) as an educatable being and the investigation of the learning process, including not only the acquisition of knowledge, but also the formation of habits, acts of skill, ideals, and attitudes.

b) Principles of education. An adequate comprehension of the curriculum by the teacher is contributed to primarily by three sources. These are (1) an acquaintance with human life itself, (2) a knowledge of the social sciences, and (3) an understanding of the philosophy of the curriculum as related to life.

Little space can be taken here for the discussion of the first two of these sources. Unless the teacher has a direct acquaintance with life, especially with those phases that are represented by the subjects that he is teaching, he is but an example of the blind leading the blind. The greatest source of realistic and vital teaching is realistic and vital knowledge on the part of the teacher.

But even if the teacher could obtain a direct acquaintance with life in all its phases, which is out of the question, he would still stand in need of a systematic and scientific study of this life. This he may obtain from the study of history, political science (including civics), economics, sociology, and ethics. These are the fundamental social sciences, and as teaching from one point of view may be regarded as applied sociology, it is immensely to the teacher's advantage to cultivate as many of these sciences as his time and opportunity permit. Few will study them all, but too many of our teachers now end with history and civics, and perhaps a little economics.

Assuming the basis of an adequate acquaintance with life itself and of a knowledge of the fundamental social sciences, the teacher still stands in need of a subject that will give him a systematic conception of the relation of the school to life. He needs a science that will apply to education the facts and principles pertaining to human life in general. This science should give him a clear conception of the general goal he is striving for with his pupils, of the elemental values that the various phases of education should subserve, of the curriculum in outline that results from these values, and of the way this curriculum should be administered in order that these values may be realized.

It is to the subject that gives this knowledge, it seems to me, that the term "Principles of Education" should be applied. This term would be properly descriptive, just as the term "Principles of Teaching" is properly descriptive. The word "teaching" is commonly applied to the process of the teacher's work; "education," to the broader social relations and consequences of that work.

c) Principles of teaching.   Logically the principles of teaching should follow the principles of education. It was noted above that the child (which is elucidated finally by educational psychology) and the curriculum (which is elucidated finally by the principles of education) are in some respects far apart. There is a gap over to the curriculum that the child cannot well cross unaided. He needs the teacher as an intermediary whose primary function it is to lead him gradually into the cultural and vocational possessions of the race.

Now in performing this function of intermediary, the teacher needs the principles of teaching to guide him. It is the function of this subject to assist the teacher in becoming an intelligent, resourceful, and progressive worker in the immediate task of classroom instruction and of training in conduct and skill.

The principles of teaching rest primarily upon both the nature of the child and upon the forms and methods that the mind uses in acquiring knowledge. These bases are scientifically set forth respectively by psychology (general and educational) and logic. The spirit of the teaching and the devices used are, however, also profoundly influenced by the teacher's conception of the aim and values of education.

5. The contents of textbooks classified

That the objective or sociological phase of educational theory to which I have applied the term "Principles of Education" is beginning to be recognized as comprising a unit by itself is indicated both by the contents of the textbooks given above and by the outlines of the courses. Parts I and V (about one-third) of Bagley's *Educative Process;* all of Bagley's *Educational Values;* the introduction and Parts I and III (fully one-half) of Henderson's *Text-Book in the Principles of Education;* practically all of Horne's *Philosophy of Education;* chaps. I and II (over one-fourth) of Jones's *Principles of Education;* Parts I and II (about one-half) of O'Shea's *Education as Adjustment;* and all but the last two chapters (about seven-eighth) of Ruediger's *Principles of Education* fall distinctly into this field.

The remaining portions of these books and practically all of Bolton's *Principles of Education* are devoted to topics in educational psychology, save that about one-third of Bagley's *Educative Process* and one chapter in Jones's *Principles of Education* are devoted to topics in the principles of teaching. Boone's *Science of Education* is hard to classify, for it seems in the main merely to talk *about* education.

6. The contents of courses classified

Judging by the descriptions given in the outlines of courses quoted above, practically the entire courses given at Columbia (Suzzallo), Colorado, George Washington, Missouri, Nebraska, Peabody College, Washington, and perhaps Kansas, and large and distinct sections of the courses given at Cincinnati, Columbia (MacVannell and Monroe), Cornell, Harvard, Illinois, Indiana (Black and Jones), Iowa, Ohio State, Pittsburgh, Wisconsin, Virginia, and Yale fall into this field. This includes fully three-fourths of the courses quoted. Parts of the remaining courses may also belong here, but the descriptions given do not make this inference safe.

The courses given at Columbia (Monroe), Cornell, Illinois, Indiana (Black), Ohio State, Pittsburgh, Washington, Wisconsin, and Yale appear to be quite distinctly divided about equally between the principles of education and the principles of teaching (including usually educational psychology). The dividing line between educational psychology and the principles of teaching is still far from distinct, it seems.

To include both the principles of education and the principles of teaching (or educational psychology) under the direct or kindred title of "Principles of Education" appears to be a somewhat common practice. Not only these nine courses, but also, as noted above, the textbooks of Bagley, Henderson, Jones, and O'Shea, appear to follow it, while Bolton's book, under the title of *Principles of Education,* appears even to be restricted almost solely to topics in educational psychology and the principles of teaching. The more heterogeneous college courses, too, include many topics from educational psychology and the principles of teaching, and this in spite of the fact that in nearly all the schools separate courses in educational psychology are also given.

7. Criticism of college courses

Restricting ourselves now to about one-half of the college courses in the principles of education, it appears to be true that all conceivable topics in educational theory are hopelessly intermingled in them. If the title, "Principles of Education," is meant to stand for some definite and coherent phase of educational theory, these outlines of courses certainly do not show it. Apparently this title is still used by many teachers of education as a blanket phrase. Save that the material is educational, no uniform principle of selection is apparent. It would be difficult to find any topic in educational theory that is not included in one or more of these outlines, and the topics of but few of the outlines correspond to any considerable degree. In this list there are apparently as many different courses in respect to content as there are persons giving them. This shows a greater primitiveness in the organization of educational theory, if not the content as well, than one would have reason to expect.

The effect of this heterogeneous array of topics under the title "Principles or Philosophy of Education" (and other educational subjects and even the relation between subjects appear to be little, if any, better) has a number of harmful effects. It serves to disgust more students than many teachers of education realize. The average college student wants something definite; he rightly wants to cover a relatively distinct phase of subject-matter in each study that he pursues, and when he finds himself in a subject that apparently possesses no limiting principles of selection and no logical sequence of topics, he is frankly disgusted.

Now when this student goes to another educational course he is likely to find many of the same topics again treated—*and treated in a primary way*—that he has had in the principles of education. This adds to his disgust, for it not only leaves him bewildered but it wastes his time. Allowing for all adequate correlation, it would no doubt still be well within the mark to say that from one-fourth to one-half of the student's time in teachers' colleges and departments of education is wasted, and this all through lack of organization. This is undoubtedly the most regrettable result that follows the present chaotic state of educational theory.

III. A SUGGESTED LIST OF TOPICS FOR THE PRINCIPLES OF EDUCATION

What are the topics that the principles of education should include and in what order should these topics be presented?

Questions like these are deserving of the best thought of educational specialists. The effective organization of educational theory inheres in their solution, and upon this organization the effective teaching of educational theory is in turn dependent. But the solution of these questions calls for co-operative effort, and any one person can do little more than to lead off in a discussion.

1. Introduction: The field of education

Somewhere in his professional training the student of education should be orientated in his chosen field, and this, it seems to me, could well be done in the introductory chapter of the principles of education. This course should logically come early in the student's professional work, preceding the principles of teaching and following educational psychology, and so a discussion of the field of education would be in place. This is now done to a certain extent in the textbooks of Horne, O'Shea, and Ruediger, and the need of something like this is further indicated by the fact that the courses listed from Chicago, Columbia (Monroe), Harvard, Leland Stanford Junior, Michigan, Minnesota, Pittsburgh, and Indiana (Black) are either explicitly or by inference introductory to educational theory, which accounts in large part for their general nature.

But for the purpose of orientating the student it would seem that an introductory chapter would be better than an introductory course. What the beginner in educational theory needs to know is the most general character and the divisions of the field, and anything more than this is likely to take the zest away from succeeding courses. The idea of a brief, general, diversified course for general culture is not worthy of entertainment. The college student who does not wish to teach but nevertheless wishes an acquaintance with educational theory could no doubt profit most by fairly thorough courses in the principles of education, history of education, and, perhaps, educational psychology.

2. The controls of conduct

The term "conduct control" has recently been brought into educational literature by Bagley (*Educational Values*). Human life in a broad sense may be regarded as synonymous with conduct, and it may therefore be truly said that it is the function of education to supply conduct controls.

The conduct controls that are operative in human life may be divided into two classes: (1) inherited controls and (2) acquired controls.

Most of the textbooks in the principles of education discuss in some detail such topics as brain complexity and intelligence, the period of infancy, heredity, and, to a slight extent, eugenics. These topics are closely related to what the child should study, it is true, but logically it seems clear that they fall on the child side, rather than on the curriculum side, of the teacher's problem. They should therefore be discussed in detail in educational psychology, and this is done by Pyle in his *Introduction to Educational Psychology*, and also by Thorndike in his advanced *Educational Psychology*.

But even when the discussion of the biological bases of education is relegated to educational psychology, the closely related native controls of conduct deserve consideration in the principles of education. These controls are obviously the various reflexes and instincts. Of course no full discussion of these is in place here, but their relation to conduct should nevertheless be clearly brought out. Their limiting influence on education should be especially revealed to the student, for much that is of service to teachers has been disclosed by the study of heredity. Heredity forestalls some of the effects that the teacher might like to produce and it is well for his economic expenditure of energy and for his peace of mind to know this.

But even though heredity limits the influences of education, it does not eliminate these influences. It leaves open, or rather provides for, a number of very important channels through which education may have its effects.

The effects of education, to which the expression "acquired controls of conduct" may be applied, may be grouped under three heads: *(a)* habits, *(b)* knowledge, and *(c)* emotional dispositions. These are closely interrelated, for a response that is guided by knowledge or by an emotional disposition at one time may become habitual at another. In a general way we may designate these three rubrics as the "what" of education and we may say that they are imparted respectively by training, by instruction, and by inspiration.

The range of habits that should be made or influenced by education is a wide one. It includes not only acts of skill, deportment, and the mechanization of knowledge and processes frequently used, but also many phases of conduct that have an ethical significance. It is rightly expected that education should form as well as inform a person.

The knowledge that is imparted by the instructional phase of education is thought of by many as being limited to the facts, principles, and laws embodied in the textbooks on the various studies. This is a mistake, for the vital knowledge of a subject includes not only facts, principles, and laws, but also the technique and methods used in acquiring and applying these facts, principles, and laws. Knowledge is a dynamic, not a static, affair. Every subject includes both content and method, and either alone is but a dependent abstraction. Scientific culture includes the mastery of scientific method and the ability to use information certainly no less than a knowledge of scientific facts and principles. The conception of scientific method, for example, is not merely something to be acquired along with the study of zoology; it is an indispensable phase of the knowledge of zoology itself.

Through the inspirational aspect of education are imparted all those emotional dispositions that we know by such terms as ideals, standards, appreciations, prejudices, tastes, and attitudes. The life of the average person is governed by these dispositions probably more than by knowledge content, and they may be derived from all of the school studies, especially from history, social science, literature, and art, and also from methods of work and from the atmosphere of school, home, and social life. Moral and social training fall primarily under this head. It is here especially that the personality of the teacher is of first importance.

3. The generalized effects of education

If the so-called doctrine of formal discipline is to be discussed at all in the principles of education, this may logically be done immediately after considering the acquired controls of conduct. These controls function not only in the specific channels in which they have been acquired, but most, if not all, of them are to a certain extent generalized in their effects. Habits, indeed, are specific responses to specific stimuli, but a variety of situations may have present the one element that sets off a certain habit. Thus the habit of courteous deportment acquired in the home may function in the school, church, and street, and therefore may be said to be socially, even if not psychologically, generalized. The other acquired controls are all in a measure generalized through the three well-known channels of identical or common elements—content, method, and aim.

The discussion of formal discipline in textbooks is now overdone. It is found in the texts on the principles of education, the principles of teaching, educational psychology, and even general psychology (Pillsbury).

It may indeed be asked if it is not about time to relegate the phrase "doctrine of formal discipline" to the historical side of educational theory. This expression, together with the conception underlying it, rests on false psychology, and it should go the way of that psychology. In the modern conception of psychology the old notion of formal discipline only causes confusion. It is out of harmony, and the expression "the generalized effect of education" serves the purpose much better.

Logically one would think that a full discussion of the generalized effects of education belongs to educational psychology. But even so, a brief summary of this topic may well be included in the principles of education at this point. Only a brief chapter need, perhaps, be given to it, and the point of view from which it would be presented would necessarily differ somewhat from that adopted in educational psychology.

4. The aim of education

No one doubts that the consideration of the aim of education falls within the domain of the principles of education. This topic is propaedeutic to the curriculum. It gives the educational administrator a criterion for the selection of subject-matter and the classroom teacher a vision of the goal that he must endeavor to achieve.

The aim of education is a large topic and for its adequate exposition requires a number of chapters. Philosophers and educators have discussed this topic ever since the dawn of history, and if the present ideals in education are to be understood they must be considered in the light of their historical development. Not only should the principles of education be preceded by the history of education, but the historical evolution of educational ideals must be traced also within the principles of education. The history and the principles of education are necessarily closely related, and whether they are taught in succession or simultaneously, they should always be closely correlated. But insight into secular history, economics, sociology, and ethics is also highly desirable for the comprehension of the educational aim.

It is primarily from the historical standpoint that one can harmonize the social and individual elements in the aim of education. Society in Athens, where the ideal of personal culture developed, was very different from what it is now, and it is only in thoroughgoing social democracy, such as we are hopefully tending toward in America, that a genuine ideal of social service can develop. The student must be led to see, however, that there is no inherent contradiction between these two ideals, at least so far as the vast majority is concerned. They are mutually supplementary, and because man is instinctively a social animal and so cannot realize his own life except in a social medium, the two ideals are comparatively seldom in conflict. But when such conflict occurs, the individual is not necessarily always the one who is in the wrong. Witness in this respect the fate of Socrates and of Jesus. The life to which the educated person should be adjusted is progressive as well as social. This, of course, means no more than to say that not necessarily present, but ultimate, social good should be the criterion of conduct and of educational forces, which are among the determinants of conduct.

Viewed from the contentful side, there is at present a very general agreement as to how the goal of education should be achieved, but educators are not yet agreed as to the best way of defining this goal. This disagreement results from the fact that the goal may be defined from one of several points of view, of which two are now in the lead. These are the social and the biological. From the former the end of education is defined as the production of the socially efficient individual, while from the latter it is defined as the adjustment, or readjustment, of the individual to his environment. The ultimate meaning back of the definitions is approximately the same, and their relative merits are further so closely balanced that both have numerous and distinguished adherents. The biological point of view appears to have this advantage, however: it views education from a position far enough away to include positively the rights of both the group and the individual, while the social point of view regards education solely from the side of the group. In some essential respects the rights of the individual are undoubtedly subordinated to the rights of the group, but this subordination is not omitted in the biological point of view.

5. The elemental educational values

But whether the aim of education is defined as adjustment to environment or as social efficiency, we have in either case only a general definition of the goal toward which the teacher should strive. The teacher gains much by being distinctly aware of this goal, but for some of his work this is not specific enough. He needs to know in detail the value or values that ought to be derived for the pupils from each study that he is teaching. There are at least two reasons why he should have this knowledge.

In the first place, when a teacher is not clearly aware of the values that he ought to obtain from each study, it is only by chance that he will be teaching in the most effective manner; and his teaching from subject to subject is likely to be very uneven. He may hit it right in one subject but miss it in another. When literature is taught from the disciplinary, conventional, or utilitarian motive, more harm than good is likely to be done, and the motives or ends that give good results in literature may fail in mathematics.

The effectiveness of teaching depends, not only upon the methods employed, but also upon the goal in the teacher's mind. As this goal varies from subject to subject, and even among phases of the same subject, it is necessary that the teacher have a clear conception of the elemental educational values.

A second reason why the teacher should know the elemental educational values is found in the fact that he is frequently called upon to give advice on the selection of studies both by parents and by pupils. He ought to be able to give this advice in as thoroughly a scientific manner as the chemist gives advice in his field or the electrical engineer in his. Indeed, for social purposes the teacher should be an educational engineer, and for this the general conception of the aim of education is not sufficient.

For some reason, probably because they have had but little immediate contact with elementary- and secondary-school work, educational specialists have given much less attention to the analysis of the elemental educational values than this problem deserves. The problem has also been obscured by the disciplinary conception of education, for under this conception only one result, mental discipline, and perhaps personal pleasure, was thought to result from the perusal of the school studies.

In ancient times Aristotle made some inquiry into the effects of studies from the contentful side, and in modern times this problem was opened by Spencer.

The effects of education have a social conventional value because they contribute to the community of habits and ideas that make social intercourse rich and enjoyable. Others are interested in my knowledge and accomplishments from this point of view because they may derive pleasure from them. Furthermore, because society is, and for social purposes must be, divided into groups or strata, certain habits, knowledge, and accomplishments are taken as indices to the culture necessary for admission to certain groups or strata.

The sentimental and liberalizing values are personal in their reference and from the social point of view we are interested in them only indirectly. They are motives that keep the individual occupied on a higher plane in his leisure moments, thus conserving his substance and leading him into knowledge that he may later apply in economic and social situations. But the recreation that the indulgence of one's trained tastes and sentiments affords is perhaps the greatest indirect benefit that is derived. Recreation means increased buoyancy and health, which obviously have a vital bearing on economic and social efficiency.

Although the sentimental and liberalizing values are primarily personal rather than social in their reference, it is true, nevertheless, that they should be realized only through such material and activities as are not interdicted by the social good. But in realizing them the best results, as a rule, are obtained when the individual aims directly for his own enjoyment and satisfaction, leaving the ulterior effects, which may justify them ultimately, to come as by-products.

6. The curriculum

After the student or prospective teacher has gained a clear conception of the elemental educational values, he should proceed either to the consideration of the curriculum as a whole or to an analysis of the fundamental values contained in the various subjects found in the school. The order adopted may be left to the tastes of the teacher, for either order appears to be logical and compatible with good teaching. But the distinction between the content, form, and expression subjects, or, perhaps better, between the content, form, and expression phases of subjects, can be made more readily, it would seem, in organizing the curriculum, and as these distinctions are necessary in evaluating the various subjects, we have at least this much ground for considering first the curriculum as a whole. But whichever order is adopted, the teacher must bear in mind that the curriculum and the values of the studies are really but two phases of the same topic.

The curriculum bears a relation to courses of study similar to that borne by a map of the world to the courses that travelers may take in traveling around the world. A traveler needs the map in order to select his course properly and to apportion his time advantageously. Similarly the teacher needs a complete and organized view of the curriculum, which to him is a condensed chart of civilization, in order that he may miss nothing essential in guiding his pupils along courses of study, in order that he may correlate subjects properly, and in order that he may apportion the time of his pupils advantageously.

Many schemes for the classification of studies have been suggested, but, because the interrelations of studies require all three dimensions of space for their adequate exhibition, none presented on paper is entirely satisfactory. Perhaps the most satisfactory classification is the one suggested by Dr. Elmer Ellsworth Brown, which I have developed briefly on p. 179 of my *Principles of Education*. Brown's scheme, while fundamentally threefold, may also be looked upon as ninefold. The fundamental divisions are those of the humanities, the natural sciences, and philosophy. From the opposite point of view we have the content, form, and expression subjects. Into this scheme, when elaborated, it appears that all studies can be logically fitted, although all their essential interrelations are not exhibited.

7. The values of the studies

This topic needs but little space here, although it deserves much in a course on the principles of education. The elemental educational values are presented, not merely for theoretic contemplation, but for the sake of having them applied. It is surprising to find how much difficulty teachers experience in analyzing unaided the values of the subjects they are teaching. Many appear still to be blinded by the notion of formal discipline, and an apparently equally large percentage does not have a sufficiently broad acquaintance with life to realize the values that the studies should subserve. They need help at this point and the course in the principles of education is the place to give it. Something may later be expected in this respect from courses in special method, but the values of all the studies are likely to come in for consideration only in the principles of education.

8. The construction and execution of courses of study

After the studies and the curriculum in general have been discussed, there still remain a number of chapters in educational theory that logically belong to the principles of education. These pertain more or less directly to the course of study and have for their function the presentation of those principles that underlie the construction and the execution of the course of study. Ruediger's *Principles of Education* presents these principles in the chapters entitled "The Administration of the Curriculum" and "The Agencies that Educate." Henderson covers this ground in five chapters entitled, respectively, "Analysis of Educational Agencies," "The Evolution of the School," "The Function of the School," "The Academic and the Practical," and "Liberal and Vocational Education." In Bolton the chapters entitled "The Theory of Recapitulation" and "The Culture Epoch Theory" would classify here in part as laying the basis for the course of study. I say "in part" because the full discussion of these topics belongs logically to educational psychology. Only so much of them need to be reviewed here as bears on the course of study. Bagley's final chapter in his *Educational Values,* entitled "The School Environment as a Source of Educative Material," also belongs here in the main.

The title of these chapters tells what belongs to this phase of the principles of education perhaps better than any brief discussion that I myself might present. This corner of the field has been but little cultivated in a systematic way and so is not yet thoroughly organized.

9. Summary

Such, in outline, appear to me to be the leading topics that belong to the principles of education. The pivotal point of the course is the curriculum, but this must be led up to by a rounded exposition of the aim of education and by an analysis of the elemental educational values; and it must be led down from by the presentation of those principles that underlie the construction of courses of study. With this conception in mind, the class is ready to proceed to the principles of teaching whose function it is to present those principles that will assist the teacher in initiating his pupils into the studies, ideals, and activities represented by the curriculum in general and by the course of study in particular.

IV. SCIENTIFIC METHOD IN THE PRINCIPLES OF EDUCATION

1. Available sources of progress

While from the standpoint of teaching the principles of education a discussion of this subject as an organized body of knowledge is of primary importance, from the standpoint of educational progress the topic of this section is of first importance. College teachers of education, like all college and university teachers have a twofold obligation. They should assist both in preparing efficient teachers and in advancing the theory and practice of education; i.e., they should both teach and advance knowledge.

Educational progress on the side of the curriculum and the course of study, and *pari passu* in the principles of education, can be contributed to from the following four sources at least: (1) By a historical study of the relation of the school and society; (2) by utilizing the advances continually being made in the pure sciences; (3) by generalizing from existing educational practices; and (4) by formal experimentation and quantitative measurement.

2. Historical study

That the experiences of the historic past throw light on the curriculum, course of study, and the ideals that should actuate teaching does not need emphasis before a body like this. The study of history in general is justified primarily by the light that it throws upon the present, and this is true in education no less than in other lines. Indeed, many of the present activities in education, like those in religion, government, commerce, industry, and social life, cannot be understood save when viewed from the standpoint of their development, and this knowledge not only enables us to manage the present more effectively, but also to guide progress. Take the introduction of the vocational subjects into the curriculum as an example. The motives for introducing these subjects, the opposition encountered, and the schools, equipment, and tactics needed are all in part illumined by historical study. Think also of the various and even conflicting ideals that dominate education at present. Only historical study can round out the grasp of these ideals and point the way toward harmonious readjustment. But this readjustment cannot be made once for all. The continual changes in life make this an ever-present problem, thus making a continual demand on historical knowledge.

3. Contributions from the pure sciences

But this historical study at best gives us only half of the picture. The effective administration of education depends first of all upon the needs and conditions of the present, and this must be understood not only historically but also directly.

The sciences that contribute the direct comprehension of our civilization are primarily psychology, anthropology, sociology (including ethics), economics, and political science. Many of the advances made in these sciences have a bearing on the content, ideals, and administration of the curriculum, and it is the duty of the specialists in educational theory to be on the lookout for these advances and to adapt them to educational practice. In this there is nothing incongruous. The principles of education is an applied science and therefore naturally cuts across many of the pure sciences, whose data, indeed, do not function in practice until they have been taken over by the applied scientist or the practitioner. The pure and the applied scientist may often, of course, be the same person.

4. Generalizations from existing practices

When we look upon the content and practice of education as they were no farther back than at the time of Basedow and Pestalozzi and then look upon them as they are today, we are fairly struck with the amount of progress that has been made. This progress has been made less, no doubt, through formal experimentation and measurement than through informal trials and successes and through the generalizations and descriptions made on the basis of existing practices by the insight of educational leaders.

Education is a practical art as well as an applied science. It ranks in this respect with agriculture, government, navigation, and business. In all these fields practice rests at present only in part on scientific laws and principles held consciously. But all successful practice undoubtedly does rest upon such laws and principles, and it is the duty of the scientist to make them explicit. He should study the practices about him and generalize from them. It is in this way that by far the most of our principles of education and of teaching have been obtained. Nor should this method of inquiry be disparaged. Social life is the primary laboratory for the social sciences and it is abundantly in place for the scientist to make use of it as such.

5. Formal experimentation and measurement

The informal experimentation discussed in the preceding section and the formal experimentation now so much emphasized in educational circles merge into one another imperceptibly. Just where the experimental schools of Comenius, Basedow, Pestalozzi, Froebel, Dewey, Montessori, and others should be placed it is difficult to say. All these schools have been instituted for the purpose of advancing both the content and the method of education, and they have unquestionably assisted in this advance; but they have seldom, if ever, given us quantitative results. Their results have been formulated as principles rather than as exact, mathematical laws.

The importance of these non-mathematical generalizations should again not be underestimated. Ordinary practice can be guided by them very efficiently in most respects, and it is in the main only when precise comparisons of results are desirable that quantitative formulations are needed.

Educational theory is now in possession of a number of quantitative studies, but these appear to fall entirely into the domains of educational psychology, educational method, and school administration. In the principles of education, as here defined, only general studies have so far been made. But there is no reason why the effects of different curricula, ideals, and the like should not be subjected to statistical study and mathematical measurement.

The report of the University of Chicago Elementary School as given in Dewey's *School and Society* approaches this, and as laboratory schools in connection with teachers' colleges and departments of education get more common we can expect much more in this line. It is more difficult to measure precisely the social influences of education than to test methods of instruction, and so far the facilities for making such measurements have been but meagerly available; but the laboratory schools that are now being established will bring in this opportunity and we may rest assured that our college teachers of education will take advantage of it. It would be well indeed if every school system of considerable size would set apart one of its schools as a model or laboratory school with a well-trained educational expert in charge. Scientific progress in education would then begin to have the chance that its importance deserves.

Section 8

SELECTED WRITINGS
OF EDWARD AUSTIN SHELDON

Edward Austin Sheldon (1823–1897) is a forgotten hero of American education. He was a generation older than most of the individuals included in this book, and should be remembered as one of the founders of the great tradition of teaching teachers in the United States. His ambition was not fame or national prominence, but rather service to his local community, to teachers, to children, and to the profession of teaching, to which he dedicated his life. In Oswego, New York, he founded the first urban teacher training school in the nation. He also pioneered the use of practice teaching experiences in normal schools and teachers colleges.

By the time of his death in 1897, Sheldon had endeared himself to the teachers and children in New York State to such an extent that children across New York donated pennies to build a statue in his honor. Completed in 1900, the copper statue stood in the rotunda of the New York State capitol building until 1922 when it was returned to the Oswego campus. The statue now stands in a prominent location on the Oswego campus next to the institution's original building, Sheldon Hall.

Sheldon's tradition has been forgotten in higher education because the principles that he believed in—liberal education for all, high-quality teacher education, and high moral and intellectual standards for all—have been replaced by concerns with technology, vocational training, and the pursuit of professions other than the profession of teaching. His legacy also

Forgotten Heroes of American Education, pages 549–551
Copyright © 2006 by Information Age Publishing
All rights of reproduction in any form reserved.

has been hidden from history because 20th century writers of the history of education ignored Sheldon's philosophy and the tradition of teaching teachers that he embodies.

Sheldon was born in Perry Center, Massachusetts, on October 4, 1823. He grew up in rural New England, the son of devoutly Puritan parents. He began his undergraduate studies in 1844 at Hamilton College in Clinton, New York. He returned home during his sophomore year, however, due to illness. After much prayer and concern about his future, Sheldon traveled to Oswego, New York, to assist a friend who was operating a nursery and selling plants.

While in Oswego, Sheldon became concerned about the plight of poor Irish immigrants in his new town. The nursery that employed him went out of business; consequently, he was looking for a new direction in life. At one point, he planned to attend seminary and enter the ministry, but his interest in the plight of immigrant children led him to education as his calling. He launched a campaign to establish a free public school system in Oswego. He persuaded several prominent Oswego political leaders to join his cause, which led to the creation of the Orphan and Free School Association in 1848. This association established Oswego's first public school. Due to his newfound success as an educator, Sheldon abandoned his interest in seminary and became the school's first teacher in the fall of 1848. It closed its doors after only one year.[1]

In the fall of 1849, Sheldon for the first time turned his attention to teaching teachers. He opened the Oswego Seminary for teachers in 1849, but that endeavor failed after only one year as well. He then accepted a position as superintendent of schools in Syracuse, New York, a post he held from 1851–1853. While in Syracuse, Sheldon dedicated himself to educating African-American children at a time when agitation over slavery was intense. Sheldon was an ardent abolitionist.

The new public school that Sheldon helped to open in Oswego in the fall of 1848 was revived while he was serving as superintendent in Syracuse, and he was persuaded to return to Oswego in 1853 to become the school district's first superintendent. He became Oswego's most influential educational statesman, a position to which he had aspired for many years. He served Oswego in this capacity for the next forty-four years until his death in 1897.

To Sheldon, teachers were the key to a good school. Acting on this commitment, he founded the Oswego State Normal School in 1861 to prepare teachers for the Oswego schools. Sheldon served as the

---

1. Dorothy Rogers, *Oswego: Fountainhead of Teacher Education* (New York: Appleton-Century-Crofts, 1961), pp. 33–38.

institution's first president until his death in 1897.[2] Throughout his career as an educational leader, Sheldon remained devoted to children, teachers, and the spiritual element that is involved in all good teaching. He was motivated by his love of nature, his commitment to God, and his efforts to build a solid foundation for the teaching profession. He dedicated almost fifty years to teaching teachers. As much as anyone else whose work is included in this volume, Sheldon should be remembered as a deeply knowledgeable, tireless contributor to the great tradition of teaching teachers.

---

2. Garraty, John A., and Mark C. Carnes, Eds., *American National Biography*, 19 (New York: Oxford University Press, 1999): 782–782.

A Manual of Elementary Instruction

(1862)

Some of the best thought ever produced on curriculum for teaching teachers grew out of the Oswego State Normal School in Oswego, New York. Sheldon was both a teacher of teachers and a scholar of educational philosophy. Johann Pestalozzi, of Switzerland, was the influential philosophical leader whose ideas Sheldon sought to spread through his work at Oswego.

This introduction to Sheldon's book on elementary instruction indicates how his views on teacher training curriculum combine moral instruction, subject-matter learning, and methods of teaching in a seamless curriculum. Theory and practice within the school's curriculum were intimately integrated at all levels, but especially through the work of the Oswego training school. This selection provides insight into a view of teacher education curriculum that did not even consider the possibility of separating the "what" of teaching from the "how." Both were held together by the moral purpose that attracts people to become teachers in the first instance.

PREFACE

For many years there has been a growing conviction in the minds of the thinking men of this country, that our methods of primary instruction are very defective, because they are not properly adapted either to the mental, moral, or physical conditions of childhood. But little reference has hitherto been had to any natural order in the development of the faculties, or to the many peculiar characteristics of children. Memory, by no means the most important of the infant faculties, and reason, at this age but

Forgotten Heroes of American Education, pages 553–559

faintly developed, have been severely taxed, while but little direct systematic effort has been made to awaken and quicken the *perceptive faculties,* which are the first to develop themselves, and upon the proper cultivation of which we must depend for success in all our future educational processes. Even in schools where better views have prevailed, the want of some systematic exercises, with proper apparatus and facilities for putting them into practice, has been strongly felt.

The design of this work is to meet this demand: to present a *definite course* of *elementary instruction* adapted to philosophic views of the "laws of childhood."

We do not claim for it originality, either in thought or method. It is now a full half century since that distinguished educational reformer, Pestalozzi, to a great extent gave expression and embodiment to the principles and methods herein contained.

Important modifications have however been made; many errors both in principles and practice have been eradicated, and we are now able to bring to bear the suggestions of some of the most distinguished educators in Europe, based upon many years of careful study and experiment.

The work upon which this is founded, and from which, with the kind consent of its authoress, Miss Elizabeth Mayo, we have largely drawn, is, as stated in her preface, "A Manual, in two volumes, containing the essential portions of the five in which alone such help has hitherto been attainable; and this, too, with the addition of much valuable matter which is now published for the first time."

This work, entitled "Manual of Elementary Instruction," has been compiled within the past year, and brings down to us the light and experience of the best schools of Europe, where these methods have been longest and most thoroughly tested.

She further says, "The whole work has been carefully reconstructed on a plan which presents principles and practice in immediate connection, in order to illustrate their mutual dependence; all details of practice being exhibited as flowing naturally from the first truths on which they are founded."

While the general plan of this work has been followed, and some of the lessons adopted with slight changes, a large proportion of original matter has been added, and the whole arranged with special reference to the wants of our American schools.

The Lessons on Objects, Color, Moral Instruction, Lessons on Animals, and the Introduction have been made up from the original manuscripts of Miss M. E. M. Jones, with such exceptions as are indicated, and the whole arranged by her. For more than fifteen years this lady was engaged in training teachers in these methods in the Home and Colonial Training

Institution, London, and has been connected with the schools of this country sufficiently long to understand something of their wants.

Prof. Hermann Krusi[1] is the author of the Lessons on Form and Inventive Drawing. He has also rewritten and arranged the third step in Number. His suggestions on many other points have been very valuable. We can but congratulate ourselves and those engaged in primary instruction for this timely aid from one so eminently fitted for the work.[2]

Of the remaining subjects, Reading has been entirely rewritten. The Lessons on Place or Geography have been slightly changed, introducing two or three original sketches of lessons in the first step, and so changing the third step as to adapt it to our American locality. Some changes have also been made in the Lessons on Sound, Size, and Weight; new matter added, and, in two or three instances, substituted for that contained in the old volumes.

While these lessons are prepared for primary schools, they are also arranged with special reference to use in Normal and Training classes. Model lessons are given, and then subjects suggested on which similar lessons may be drawn up. The models should be carefully examined and analyzed, and, in the case of classes in training, the original sketches should in every instance be submitted to the criticism of the teacher. By individual teachers, these sketches may be written out and used as lessons in their schools. In some of the lessons, general directions only are given; in others, these directions are more particular; while many are drawn out at full length, including both questions and answers. In any case, they are only designed as suggestions and models to guide teachers in working out their *own plans and methods*. Teachers who confine themselves simply to the lessons presented in this book, and to their exact minutiae, can but fail in their work. To be truly successful, they must catch the spirit and philosophy of the system, and work it out somewhat in their *own way*, of course, always conforming to the principles upon which it is based: these we believe to be sound and philosophical, and they should never be violated.

---

1. At present teacher in the Oswego Training School.
2. Prof. K. was born, as it were, in the very school of Pestalozzi, in which his father was for twenty years a leading and active teacher. For ten years he was engaged with his father in teaching a government school for the training of teachers in Pestalozzian principles, in one of the cantons of Switzerland, his native country. After this, he was for six years engaged in the Home and Colonial Institution, working out and adapting these methods to the English schools; and it was here that he first brought out the Inventive Drawing. In this country he has been for several years engaged in teaching normal schools and teachers' institutes. He has studied carefully the characteristics of our schools and people; and is, in every way, abundantly qualified to adapt this system to our peculiarities and wants.

The lessons that have been taken with no alteration, other than an occasional verbal expression, have been indicated either in the index, or in the body of the work where they occur, by the letter *M*.

It is now more than four years since these methods were practically and thoroughly introduced into the Oswego schools, and from a constant and careful observation of their working, we feel that we are in some degree prepared to judge as to what is wanted in a book of this kind for our teachers and schools; and we trust we may not be disappointed in the hope that it will meet these wants.

The subjects are arranged into steps, simply with reference to the order of time in which it is thought various portions of the work may be accomplished. All first-step lessons are designed for children from four to five years of age, or during the first year of their school life. In the same way the second step is designed for the second year, and the third step for the third year; thus covering the time usually allotted to our primary departments in towns where the schools are graded. In some instances a fourth step is added, which is designed for the next grade. The order of succession in which the various subjects are arranged, has no reference to any order in which it may be supposed they should be taken up. While it is the design that the lessons of each step, in every subject, shall be taken up at the same stage of the child's development, it is not expected that they will all be treated simultaneously. From three to five only are taken at once, and these are carried on until the interest of the children begins to flag, when they are changed for other subjects, which in their turn are to be changed, as the children weary, for others still, until we again return to the first course, to resume it, after a rapid review, where we left it. This necessity for change with little children cannot be too carefully observed; for no matter how interesting the subject is at first, they will in time tire of it; and a lively interest can only be maintained by change. Reading, spelling, and number are the only subjects that are constant. With the youngest children the programme should change fortnightly, and with the older ones monthly. In the Appendix may be seen some programmes of the Oswego schools, which will give a very good idea of the way in which these may be arranged.

In the country schools, where no such gradation and classification are possible, where the teachers find it impracticable to take up all the topics, as they usually will, they must confine themselves to those which seem to them of the most practical importance; as, for instance, Moral Instruction, Reading, Geography, Number, Language, Form, Color, and Size.

Others might make a different selection of subjects: we only call attention to this, by way of expressing our view of the importance of doing well and thoroughly whatever is undertaken. It may seem difficult to make a selection of subjects where all are important; but it is better to leave half of them untouched than to undertake to do all, and do nothing as it should be done. Whatever is taught, let it be taught with reference to correct principles.

—E. A. Sheldon
Oswego, August 25, 1862

EXPLANATION OF ABBREVIATION

S. R.—Simultaneous repetition.
W. B.—Write on the board.
R. T.—Repeat together.

MANUAL OF ELEMENTARY INSTRUCTION

INTRODUCTION
    I. NECESSITY OF TRAINING
    II. PESTALOZZIAN PLANS AND PRINCIPLES
    III. PREPARATION OF SKETCHES
    IV. CRITICISM LESSONS
    V. REPORTS OF MODEL LESSONS
    VI. MISCELLANEOUS EXERCISES IN METHOD

I. Necessity of Training

Were we to undertake to discuss the importance of a regular apprenticeship to the mechanic who builds houses or makes machines, or of a professional education to the artist, the lawyer, or the physician, we should expose ourselves to public ridicule. It is too self-evident to admit of sober discussion. All regard it a necessity. And even when a thorough professional education has been obtained, or a complete term of service as apprentice served, we are slow to employ them until their success has been tested by long *experience*. We are slow to trust the setting of a broken bone to one who has not given *practical* demonstrations of his skill. And yet these things are important only in a physical sense—the lowest of all human wants and necessities. How much more, then, would it seem important that those to whom we intrust the moral and intellectual destiny of the race should be carefully educated and prepared with special reference to their work!

It would seem too obvious to require an argument that every teacher should clearly comprehend the character of the infant mind, and its mode of operation—the way in which each faculty stands related to the other, and the order of its evolution—as also the related order of appliances in the process of development, together with a knowledge of the many striking peculiarities and characteristics of children. It is clear that, without this knowledge, teachers go blindly at their work, and can but fall into many and grievous errors. One thing is certain, that with the principles and methods here discussed, no one can hope to succeed who does not carefully study and intelligently practise them.

II.   Pestalozzian Plans and Principles.

There are several different ways of giving a lesson.

Example—Six ways of giving a Lesson on a Plant

1. Account of the plant learned by children from a hook, and repeated to the teacher.
2. Description learned and repeated as before, teacher afterward explaining the meaning.
3. Piece first explained by the teacher, then learned by the children, and repeated.
4. Picture shown—parts pointed out by teacher. Description learned, and repeated as before.
5. Specimens given—parts examined first by teacher, then observed by the children.
6. Specimens distributed—parts found out by the children, who frame a description, which is put on the board and committed to memory.

We need not add that the latter is the correct method.

All lessons should be given in accordance with the following principles, which were laid down by Pestalozzi:

1. Activity is a law of childhood. Accustom the child to do—educate the hand.
2. Cultivate the faculties in their natural order—first form the mind, then furnish it.
3. Begin with the senses, and never tell a child what he can discover for himself.
4. Reduce every subject to its elements—one difficulty at a time is enough for a child.
5. Proceed step by step. Be thorough. The measure of information is not what the teacher can give, but what the child can receive.

6. Let every lesson have a point; either immediate or remote.

7. Develop the idea—then give the term—cultivate language.

8. Proceed from the known to the unknown—from the particular to the general—from the concrete to the abstract—from the simple to the more difficult.

9. First synthesis, then analysis—not the order of the subject, but the order of nature.

Of course, the educational teacher, in addressing a class of students, would explain and illustrate these principles.

Section 9

JOHN DEWEY'S FORGOTTEN ESSAYS

John Dewey (1859–1952) can hardly be considered a "forgotten hero" of American education, but certainly many of his most interesting writings have been forgotten or purposely ignored. We have titled this chapter "John Dewey's Forgotten Essays" to distinguish it from the other sections in the book. Dewey is remembered as a saint in many circles today, to such an extent that all other thinkers on teaching and education are completely ignored. We think this is a problem, but not to the extent that Dewey should be ignored entirely. His work is useful in some respects, but it should not be considered an end in and of itself.

John Dewey was born on October 20, 1859, in Burlington, Vermont. He grew up in a strictly Calvinist home. His father was a shopkeeper in Burlington. Young Dewey attended the University of Vermont as an undergraduate from 1875 to 1879. While at Vermont, he became intrigued with Darwinian evolution and social philosophy. He was undecided about what to do with his life following his graduation in 1879. He taught high school in Oil City, Pennsylvania, for two years. Then, he taught high school for one more year in a small town near Burlington. He began graduate study at Johns Hopkins University in 1882.

Dewey studied logic with Charles S. Peirce and experimental psychology with G. Stanley Hall while at Johns Hopkins. He was more heavily influenced, however, by philosopher George Sylvester Morris. Morris deepened Dewey's interest in Hegelian philosophy. Dewey left behind the

Forgotten Heroes of American Education, pages 561–563
Copyright © 2006 by Information Age Publishing
All rights of reproduction in any form reserved.

idealistic dimensions of Hegel's philosophy, however, during the next fifteen years. Dewey also abandoned the Christianity that influenced his early life and career.

From 1884 to 1894, Dewey taught and wrote on the philosophy faculty at the University of Michigan. He left Michigan in 1894 for a unique opportunity at the University of Chicago. At Chicago, he was a professor of philosophy, psychology, and pedagogy. He became well-known during this time for the Laboratory School that he created as part of Chicago's department of pedagogy (i.e., education). In 1904 following controversy with the Chicago administration, Dewey resigned and accepted a position at Columbia University in New York City. While at Columbia, he held appointments in the department of philosophy and at Teachers College. He remained in New York City for the rest of his life. He died on June 1, 1952.[1]

Dewey published an enormous amount of scholarship and commentary. Although he did not dedicate his career to teaching teachers like other individuals included in this volume, some of the philosophy that Dewey produced has relevance to teacher education. The following selections are essential because they are rarely cited or discussed, because (at least in two cases) they portray Dewey trying to redirect his Progressive colleagues, and because they present a view of Dewey that is at odds with the dominant contemporary view of who he was and what he had to say. His thoughts on teacher education provide an interesting contrast to the other essays included in this volume.

There are, however, real problems with Dewey's work. First of all, his writing is undeniably difficult to interpret. He used language that was vague and that could be interpreted in dozens of different ways. Moreover, he supported all sides of many issues in both education and cultural issues generally, an approach that led him to inspire divergent schools of thought. He often said everything to everyone and nothing to anyone at the same time. The result was confusion over where Dewey stood on many issues.

For example, Dewey was a good friend and admirer of William Heard Kilpatrick. Kilpatrick spent much of his career attacking organized subject-matter, belittling the idea of "subject-matter-set-out-to-be-learned," and otherwise criticizing traditional understandings of knowledge and moral education.[2] Dewey supported Kilpatrick in this endeavor. In fact, Dewey

---

1. Garraty, John A., and Mark C. Carnes, *American National Biography* 6 (New York: Oxford University Press, 1999), pp. 514–518; see, also, Robert B. Westbrook, *John Dewey and American Democracy* (Ithaca, NY: Cornell University Press, 1991).

2. See, for example, William Heard Kilpatrick, *Foundations of Method* (New York: Macmillan, 1926).

published a glowing tribute to Kilpatrick's work in a 1951 biography of Kilpatrick that was written by Samuel Tenenbaum.[3] Yet, in two of the essays we have published here, Dewey says just the opposite. He asserts that Progressives such as Kilpatrick (who is not named, but who advocated exactly what Dewey is arguing against in "Individuality and Experience" and "How Much Freedom in New Schools?") have neglected subject-matter, worshipped individualism at the expense of social responsibilities, and otherwise made a serious mistake by exalting freedom to the point of anarchy. On the other hand, Dewey recognizes that American youth need and should be provided with well-educated and well-trained teachers, teachers who seek to impart knowledge and impact young people in the direction of excellence. Teachers, Dewey remembers in these forgotten essays, were much more than mere facilitators.

---

3. Samuel Tenenbaum, *William Heard Kilpatrick: Trail Blazer in Education* (New York: Harper and Brothers, 1951; see Dewey's Introduction).

Pedagogy as a University Discipline
(1896)

This selection from John Dewey demonstrates the different philosophical visions that Dewey and William Bagley had for the profession of teaching. John Dewey wrote this article only two years after he arrived at the University of Chicago as a professor of philosophy, psychology, and pedagogy. Because of his growing interest in pedagogy, Dewey argues in this essay that pedagogy should be established as a university discipline that integrates all three fields of study.

What is most interesting about this selection is that Dewey asserts that his newly created department of pedagogy would distance itself from the "rank and file" of teachers. Instead, he and his department would focus on training "leaders of our educational systems," which sounds strikingly at odds with the democratic philosophy that he customarily espoused. His new department of pedagogy at Chicago, in other words, would be too "prestigious" to concentrate its efforts on teaching teachers (compare this perspective to what Bagley has to say, for example, in "The Status of the Classroom Teacher").

The goal of Dewey's new department was to train educational leaders who held power over the teachers who did the daily work of teaching children and youth. As everyone who studies the history of American education knows, Dewey was successful in establishing his department as well as creating an influential Laboratory School at Chicago. Not only was this model influential, but so too was the fact that Dewey's example caused many professors of education to prefer the production of modern scientific theory to the less glamorous task of teaching teachers.

Forgotten Heroes of American Education, pages 565–568

I

A distinct division of labor is indicated as regards training in the science and art of education. There must be some schools whose main task is to train the rank and file of teachers—schools whose function is to supply the great army of teachers with the weapons of their calling and direct them as to their use. It must be the province of such schools to give discipline along lines already well established rather than to undertake experiment along new lines. They must, indeed, be awake to the reception of new ideas, but in undertaking the primary preparation of teachers for the school room, it will rarely be advisable to undertake their initiation into ideas or methods not having some guarantee of time and experience back of them.

Parallel to such training schools must be those which direct their energies to the education, not of the rank and file, but of the leaders of our educational systems—teachers in normal and training schools, professors of pedagogy, superintendents, principals of schools in our large cities, many of whom have under them more teachers than a superintendent in smaller towns. Such persons are not in need of introduction to the rudiments of their work; they have already served their apprenticeship in practice and learned the elements of the theory. They are, moreover, as a rule persons who have already had a college training, and who know what disciplined scientific work is. Such students are necessarily repelled if they find work adjusted to a lower intellectual level than they have become familiar with, or carried on by less orderly intellectual methods than they have mastered. Because of these facts college graduates very rarely seek a normal or training school after having had a college education; if they become dissatisfied with their pedagogical horizon, there is, at present, very little resource save a journey to some German university which has recognized the need of advanced as well as elementary pedagogics.

Training schools of this type should and may, moreover, devote themselves more directly to the work of pedagogical discovery and experimentation. Dealing with those who know what has already been accomplished, what the existing status is, who are mature and have the balance of learning and experience, such work can be safely undertaken. There is no danger of confusion, of premature introduction to a range of truth lying beyond capacity for successful application. Such students are not only capable of initiation into the region of discovery and testing of new truths, but require it; since, as a rule, they seek after this higher type of training just because they are dissatisfied with the existing regime, or their educational environment.

It is obvious, without argument, that this higher type of training must be undertaken for the most part, if it is to be done in America at all, by universities and to a considerable extent as graduate work.

An additional, urgent reason for attempting such work in an American University may be found in our social and political traditions. These are all against any close, systematic and centralized direction and supervision of education on the part of a governmental authority. Extreme local self-government has been the rule in education even more, if anything, than in any other part of the American system. It makes little practical difference, for present purposes, whether one regret or laud this tendency. It is clear that our educational systems are in need of some kind of direction and systematization from expert sources. If the government does not furnish this, so much the greater the necessity for its being undertaken on a voluntary basis. It must be assumed with the authority of science, if without that of bureaucratic control. The universities are the natural centers of educational organization, unless the chaos of extreme centrifugal force is to continue indefinitely. It is for them to gather together and focus the best of all that emerges in the great variety of present practice, to test it scientifically, to work it out into shape for concrete use, and to issue it to the public educational system with the imprimatur, not of governmental coercion, but of scientific verification. Organization on the basis of cooperation, of free and full interaction of the various parts of our educational system is a necessity. It must accomplish what the central educational departments of Germany and France accomplish under the conditions prevailing in those countries.

One other fact may be mentioned as marking the university as the destined place assuming the responsibility of this higher training. A reorganization of the educational system is already occurring. It is impossible to undertake, here, a complete statement of the conditions meeting fulfillment in this reconstructive movement. One of these, however, is the great intellectual advance of the present century, an advance equally great in the regions of history and of science. The accumulation of knowledge has become so great that the educational system is disintegrating through the wedges of new studies continually introduced. While there is an almost constant cry that the curriculum is being too diversified, that students are distracted and congested by the wealth of material forced upon them, the demand for more studies and for more time for each of these studies never ceases. The pressure began in the college and high school. It is now finding its way into the primary grades, partly from social infiltration, partly from the continued pressure from above for such training below as will relieve the difficulties of the situation above. It is as nearly certain as any educational expectation may be that if the increased demands, as regards number of languages, range of literary study, of history and of the physical and biological sciences are to be met, even half way, in the college and high school, the response must proceed from changing the methods in the lower grades, and by beginning work along these lines in the primary school—yes, and in the kindergarten. It is not a mere question of local expedience, whether it is advisable here and there to modify the traditional "three R's" curriculum. It is a question of the right organization and balance of our entire educational system, from kindergarten to university, both in itself as a system and in its adjustment to the existing social environment.

This reconstruction may go on in a haphazard, an empirical, way, now trying this scheme, now abandoning it for that, without consciousness of the ends to be reached, without utilization of the manifold failures and successes and with all the waste of time, money and human life involved in such change. Or it may go on with some clear, if flexible, consciousness of the nature of the problem, of the ends to be met, and with some adaptation of means to these ends the latter conditions ought to be most clearly met at a university, where psychology and sociology are most systematically pursued; where scientific inquiry is at its height and where methods of work are most fully developed. In addition, it is at the university where there is the accumulation of the quantity and quality of knowledge which is trying to break through into the secondary and primary school systems. That is to say, the experiment of the introduction of science or history into lower education is a matter of subject matter as well as of method. It is reasonable to suppose that it can most fruitfully and efficiently be attempted where this subject matter is most adequately and accurately represented. One of the difficulties in introducing scientific methods and materials into lower grades is that "facts" are taught which are not facts; or facts are brought in an unrelated, relatively incoherent way; methods are used which are out of date. The child should be started on the most advanced plane, with the least to unlearn and to correct as regards both particular things and methods; with the maximum of attainable accuracy and with a selection of ideas and principles in some ratio to their importance and future fertility. Where specialists abound, where investigations are continually in progress, where the laboratory and the library are thoroughly equipped, is, if anywhere, the place where such requirements are met. On the other side, the necessity of applying a specialized range of considerations to the purposes of education is the best way of preventing the specialist from becoming narrow. Such a task necessitates looking at the special material in the light of both its adaptation to other studies and to human nature. For one danger of higher education, from the point of view of broad human interests, is that with high specialization there is increasing likelihood of the center of scholarship getting removed from the mass of men, and the things of daily life. Culture becomes tangential to life, not convergent. The problem of the application of the results of special research to educational ends compels a generalization both of subject-matter and of interest.

The Relation of Theory to Practice in the Education of Teachers
(1903)[1]

This is one of the few essays in which Dewey addresses directly the question of teacher training. He attempts to demonstrate how a professional school for training teachers can both prepare good teachers and produce educational research. He discusses the theoretical and the practical dimensions of curriculum for teaching teachers, but his answer to the question of what holds these two dimensions of curriculum together remains unclear. Teacher educators are left with the idea that their field is one to theorize about (and only theorize about), rather than one to engage in practically, morally, and philosophically. Moreover, Dewey's answer to the question of why to teach, which was so crucial to individuals like William C. Bagley, is conspicuously absent from Dewey's highly theoretic treatment of curriculum for teaching teachers.

It is difficult, if not impossible, to define the proper relationship of theory and practice without a preliminary discussion, respectively, (1) of the nature and aim of theory; (2) of practice.

---

1. This paper is to be taken as representing the views of the writer, rather than those of any particular institution in an official way; for the writer thought it better to discuss certain principles that seem to him fundamental, rather than to define a system of procedure.

A. I shall assume without argument that adequate professional instruction of teachers is not exclusively theoretical, but involves a certain amount of practical work. The primary question as to the latter is the aim with which it shall be conducted. Two controlling purposes may be entertained so different from each other as radically to alter the amount, conditions, and method of practice work. On one hand, we may carry on the practical work with the object of giving teachers in training working command of the necessary tools of their profession; control of the technique of class instruction and management; skill and proficiency in the work of teaching. With this aim in view, practice work is, as far as it goes, of the nature of apprenticeship. On the other hand, we may propose to use practice work as an instrument in making real and vital theoretical instruction; the knowledge of subject-matter and of principles of education. This is the laboratory point of view.

The contrast between the two points of view is obvious; and the two aims together give the limiting terms within which all practice work falls. From one point of view, the aim is to form and equip the actual teacher; the aim is immediately as well as ultimately practical. From the other point of view, the *immediate* aim, the way of getting at the ultimate aim, is to supply the intellectual method and material of good workmanship, instead of making on the spot, as it were, an efficient workman. Practice work thus considered is administered primarily with reference to the intellectual reactions it incites, giving the student a better hold upon the educational significance of the subject-matter he is acquiring, and of the science, philosophy, and history of education. Of course, the *results* are not exclusive. It would be very strange if practice work in doing what the laboratory does for a student of physics or chemistry in way of securing a more vital understanding of its principles, should not at the same time insure some skill in the instruction and management of a class. It would also be peculiar if the process of acquiring such skill should not also incidentally serve to enlighten and enrich instruction in subject-matter and the theory of education. None the less, there is a fundamental difference in the conception and conduct of the practice work according as one idea or the other is dominant and the other subordinate. If the primary object of practice is acquiring skill in performing the duties of a teacher, then the amount of time given to practice work, the place at which it is introduced, the method of conducting it, of supervising, criticising, and correlating it, will differ widely from the method where the laboratory ideal prevails; and *vice versa.*

In discussing this matter, I shall try to present what I have termed the laboratory, as distinct from the apprentice idea. While I speak primarily from the standpoint of the college, I should not be frank if I did not say that I believe what I am going to say holds, *mutatis mutandis,* for the normal school as well.

I. I first adduce the example of other professional schools. I doubt whether we, as educators, keep in mind with sufficient constancy the fact that the problem of training teachers is one species of a more generic affair—that of training for professions. Our problem is akin to that of training architects, engineers, doctors, lawyers, etc. Moreover, since (shameful and incredible as it seems) the vocation of teaching is practically the last to recognize the need of specific professional preparation, there is all the more reason for teachers to try to find what they may learn from the more extensive and matured experience of other callings. If now we turn to what has happened in the history of training for other professions, we find the following marked tendencies:

1. The demand for an increased amount of scholastic attainments as a prerequisite for entering upon professional work.

2. Development of certain lines of work in the applied sciences and arts, as centers of professional work; compare, for example, the place occupied by chemistry and physiology in medical training at present, with that occupied by chairs of "practice" and of "*materia medica*" a generation ago.

3. Arrangement of the practical and quasi-professional work upon the assumption that (limits of time, etc., being taken into account) the professional school does its best for its students when it gives them typical and intensive, rather than extensive and detailed, practice. It aims, in a word, at *control of the intellectual methods* required for personal and independent mastery of practical skill, rather than at turning out at once masters of the craft. This arrangement necessarily involves considerable postponement of skill in the routine and technique of the profession, until the student, after graduation, enters upon the pursuit of his calling.

These results are all the more important to us because other professional schools mostly started from the same position which training schools for teachers have occupied. Their history shows a period in which the idea was that students ought from the start to be made as proficient as possible in practical skill. In seeking for the motive forces which have caused professional schools to travel so steadily away from this position and toward the idea that practical work should be conducted for the sake of vitalizing and illuminating *intellectual* methods two reasons may be singled out:

a) First, the limited time at the disposal of the schools, and the consequent need of economy in its employ. It is not necessary to assume that apprenticeship is of itself a bad thing. On the contrary, it may be admitted to be a good thing; but the time which a student spends in the training school is short at the best. Since short, it is an urgent matter that it be put to its most effective use; and, relatively speaking, the wise employ of this short time is in laying scientific foundations. These cannot be adequately secured when one is doing the actual work of the profession, while professional life does afford time for acquiring and perfecting skill of the more technical sort.

b) In the second place, there is inability to furnish in the school adequate conditions for the best acquiring and using of skill. As compared with actual practice, the best that the school of law or medicine can do is to provide a somewhat remote and simulated copy of the real thing. For such schools to attempt to give the skill which comes to those adequately prepared, insensibly and unavoidably in actual work, is the same sort of thing as for grammar schools to spend months upon months in trying to convey (usually quite unsuccessfully) that skill in commercial arithmetic which comes, under penalty of practical failure, in a few weeks in the bank or counting-house.

It may be said that the analogy does not hold good for teachers' training schools, because such institutions have model or practice departments, supplying conditions which are identical with those which the teacher has to meet in the actual pursuit of his calling. But this is true at most only in such normal schools as are organized after the Oswego pattern—schools, that is to say, where the pupil-teacher is given for a considerable period of time the entire charge of instruction and discipline in the class-room, and does not come under a room critic-teacher. In all other cases, some of the most fundamentally significant features of the real school are reduced or eliminated. Most "practice schools" are a compromise. In theory they approximate ordinary conditions. As matter of fact, the "best interests of the children" are so safeguarded and supervised that the situation approaches learning to swim without going *too* near the water.

There are many ways that do not strike one at first glance, for removing the conditions of "practice work" from those of actual teaching. Deprivation of responsibility for the discipline of the room; the continued presence of an expert ready to suggest, to take matters into his own hands; close supervision; reduction of size of group taught; etc., etc., are some of these ways. The topic of "lesson plans" will be later referred to in connection with another topic. Here they may be alluded to as constituting one of the modes in which the conditions of the practice-teacher are made unreal. The student who prepares a number of more or less set lessons; who then has those lesson plans criticised; who then has his actual teaching criticised from the standpoint of success in carrying out the prearranged plans, is in a totally different attitude from the teacher who has to build up and modify his teaching plans as he goes along from experience gained in contact with pupils.

It would be difficult to find two things more remote from each other than the development of subject-matter under such control as is supplied from actual teaching, taking effect through the teacher's own initiative and reflective criticism, and its development with an eye fixed upon the judgment, presumed and actual, of a superior supervisory officer. Those phases of the problem of practice teaching which relate more distinctly to responsibility for the discipline of the room, or of the class, have received considerable attention in the past; but the more delicate and far-reaching matter of intellectual responsibility is too frequently ignored. Here centers the problem of securing conditions which will make practice work a genuine apprenticeship.

II. To place the emphasis upon the securing of proficiency in teaching and discipline *puts the attention of the student-teacher in the wrong place, and tends to fix it in the wrong direction*—not wrong absolutely, but relatively as regards perspective of needs and opportunities. The would-be teacher has some time or other to face and solve two problems, each extensive and serious enough by itself to demand absorbing and undivided attention. These two problems are:

1. Mastery of subject-matter from the standpoint of its educational value and use; or, what is the same thing, the mastery of educational principles in their application to that subject-matter which is at once the material of instruction and the basis of discipline and control;

2. The mastery of the technique of class management.

This does not mean that the two problems are in any way isolated or independent. On the contrary, they are strictly correlative. *But the mind of a student cannot give equal attention to both at the same time.*

The difficulties which face a beginning teacher, who is set down for the first time before a class of from thirty to sixty children, in the responsibilities not only of instruction, but of maintaining the required order in the room as a whole, are most trying. It is almost impossible for an old teacher who has acquired the requisite skill of doing two or three distinct things simultaneously—skill to see the room as a whole while hearing one individual in one class recite, of keeping the program of the day and, yes, of the week and of the month in the fringe of consciousness while the work of the hour is in its center—it is almost impossible for such a teacher to realize all the difficulties that confront the average beginner.

There is a technique of teaching, just as there is a technique of piano-playing. The technique, if it is to be educationally effective, is dependent upon principles. But it is possible for a student to acquire outward form of method without capacity to put it to genuinely educative use. As every teacher knows, children have an inner and an outer attention. The inner attention is the giving of the mind without reserve or qualification to the subject in hand. It is the first-hand and personal play of mental powers. As such, it is a fundamental condition of mental growth. To be able to keep track of this mental play, to recognize the signs of its presence or absence, to know how it is initiated and maintained, how to test it by results attained, and to test *apparent* results by it, is the supreme mark and criterion of a teacher. It means insight into soul-action, ability to discriminate the genuine from the sham, and capacity to further one and discourage the other.

External attention, on the other hand, is that given to the book or teacher as an independent object. It is manifested in certain conventional postures and physical attitudes rather than in the movement of thought. Children acquire great dexterity in exhibiting in conventional and expected ways *the form* of attention to school work, while reserving the inner play of their own thoughts, images, and emotions for subjects that are more important to them, but quite irrelevant.

Now, the teacher who is plunged prematurely into the pressing and practical problem of keeping order in the schoolroom has almost of necessity to make supreme the matter of external attention. The teacher has not yet had the training which affords psychological insight—which enables him to judge promptly (and therefore almost automatically) the kind and mode of subject-matter which the pupil needs at a given moment to keep his attention moving forward effectively and healthfully. He does know, however, that he must maintain order; that he must keep the attention of the pupils fixed upon his own questions, suggestions, instructions, and remarks, and upon their "lessons." The inherent tendency of the situation therefore is for him to acquire his technique in relation to the outward rather than the inner mode of attention.

III. Along with this fixation of attention upon the secondary at the expense of the primary problem, *there goes the formation of habits of work which have an empirical, rather than a scientific, sanction.* The student adjusts his actual methods of teaching, not to the principles which he is acquiring, but to what he sees succeed and fail in an empirical way from moment to moment: to what he sees other teachers doing who are more experienced and successful in keeping order than he is; and to the injunctions and directions given him by others. In this way the controlling habits of the teacher finally get fixed with comparatively little reference to principles in the psychology, logic, and history of education. In theory, these latter are dominant; in practice, the moving forces are the devices and methods which are picked up through blind experimentation; through examples which are not rationalized; through precepts which are more or less arbitrary and mechanical; through advice based upon the experience of others. Here we have the explanation, in considerable part at least, of the dualism, the unconscious duplicity, which is one of the chief evils of the teaching profession. There is an enthusiastic devotion to certain principles of lofty theory in the abstract—principles of self-activity, self-control, intellectual and moral—and there is a school practice taking little heed of the official pedagogic creed. Theory and practice do not grow together out of and into the teacher's personal experience.

Ultimately there are two bases upon which the habits of a teacher as a teacher may be built up. They may be formed under the inspiration and constant criticism of intelligence, applying the best that is available. This is possible only where the would-be teacher has become fairly saturated with his subject-matter, and with his psychological and ethical philosophy of education. Only when such things have become incorporated in mental habit, have become part of the working tendencies of observation, insight, and reflection, will these principles work automatically, unconsciously, and hence promptly and effectively. And this means that practical work should be pursued primarily with reference to its reaction upon the professional pupil in making him a thoughtful and alert student of education, rather than to help him get immediate proficiency.

For immediate skill may be got at the cost of power to go on growing. The teacher who leaves the professional school with power in managing a class of children may appear to have superior advantage the first day, the first week, the first month, or even the first year, as compared with some other teacher who has a much more vital command of the psychology, logic, and ethics of development. But later "progress" may with such consist only in perfecting and refining skill already possessed. Such persons seem to know how to teach, but they are not students of teaching. Even though they go on studying books of pedagogy, reading teachers' journals, attending teachers' institutes, etc., yet the root of the matter is not in them, unless they continue to be students of subject-matter, and students of mind-activity. Unless a teacher is such a student, he may continue to improve in the mechanics of school management, but he can not grow as a teacher, an inspirer and director of soul-life. How often do candid instructors in training schools for teachers acknowledge disappointment in the later career of even their more promising candidates! They seem to strike twelve at the start. There is an unexpected and seemingly unaccountable failure to maintain steady growth. Is this in some part due to the undue premature stress laid in early practice work upon securing immediate capability in teaching?

I might go on to mention other evils which seem to me to be more or less the effect of this same cause. Among them are the lack of intellectual independence among teachers, their tendency to intellectual subserviency.

The "model lesson" of the teachers' institute and of the educational journal is a monument, on the one hand, of the eagerness of those in authority to secure immediate practical results at any cost; and, upon the other, of the willingness of our teaching corps to accept without inquiry or criticism any method or device which seems to promise good results. Teachers, actual and intending, flock to those persons who give them clear-cut and definite instructions as to just how to teach this or that.

The tendency of educational development to proceed by reaction from one thing to another, to adopt for one year, or for a term of seven years, this or that new study or method of teaching, and then as abruptly to swing over to some new educational gospel, is a result which would be impossible if teachers were adequately moved by their own independent intelligence. The willingness of teachers, especially of those occupying administrative positions, to become submerged in the routine detail of their callings, to expend the bulk of their energy upon forms and rules and regulations, and reports and percentages, is another evidence of the absence of intellectual vitality. If teachers were possessed by the spirit of an abiding student of education, this spirit would find some way of breaking through the mesh and coil of circumstance and would find expression for itself.

B. Let us turn from the practical side to the theoretical. What must be the aim and spirit of theory in order that practice work may really serve the purpose of an educational laboratory? We are met here with the belief that instruction in theory is merely theoretical, abstruse, remote, and therefore relatively useless to the teacher as a teacher, unless the student is at once set upon the work of teaching; that only "practice" can give a motive to a professional learning, and supply material for educational courses. It is not infrequently claimed (or at least unconsciously assumed) that students will not have a professional stimulus for their work in subject-matter and in educational psychology and history, will not have any outlook upon their relation to education, unless these things are immediately and simultaneously reinforced by setting the student upon the work of teaching. But is this the case? Or are there practical elements and bearings already contained in theoretical instruction of the proper sort?

I. Since it is impossible to cover in this paper all phases of the philosophy and science of education, I shall speak from the standpoint of psychology, believing that this may be taken as typical of the whole range of instruction in educational theory as such.

In the first place, beginning students have without any reference to immediate teaching a very large capital of an exceedingly practical sort in their own experience. The argument that theoretical instruction is merely abstract and in the air unless students are set at once to test and illustrate it by practice-teaching of their own, *overlooks the continuity of the class-room mental activity with that of other normal experience.* It ignores the tremendous importance for educational purposes of this continuity. Those who employ this argument seem to isolate the psychology of learning that goes on in the schoolroom from the psychology of learning found elsewhere.

This isolation is both unnecessary and harmful. It is unnecessary, tending to futility, because it throws away or makes light of the greatest asset in the student's possession—the greatest, moreover, that ever will be in his possession—his own direct and personal experience. There is every presumption (since the student is not an imbecile) that he has been learning all the days of his life, and that he is still learning from day to day. He must accordingly have in his own experience plenty of practical material by which to illustrate and vitalize theoretical principles and laws of mental growth in the process of learning. Moreover, since none of us is brought up under ideal conditions, each beginning student has plenty of practical experience by which to illustrate cases of arrested development—instances of failure and maladaptation and retrogression, or even degeneration. The material at hand is pathological as well as healthy. It serves to embody and illustrate both achievement and failure, in the problem of learning.

But it is more than a serious mistake (violating the principle of proceeding from the known to the unknown) to fail to take account of this body of practical experience. Such ignoring tends also to perpetuate some of the greatest evils of current school methods. Just because the student's attention is not brought to the point of recognizing that *his own* past and present growth is proceeding in accordance with the very laws that control growth in the school, and that there is no psychology of the schoolroom different from that of the nursery, the playground, the street, and the parlor, he comes unconsciously to assume that education in the class-room is a sort of unique thing, having its own laws.[2] Unconsciously, but none the less surely, the student comes to believe in certain "methods" of learning, and hence of teaching which are somehow especially appropriate to the school—which somehow have their particular residence and application there. Hence he comes to believe in the potency for schoolroom purposes of materials, methods, and devices which it never occurs to him to trust to in his experience outside of school.

I know a teacher of teachers who is accustomed to say that when she fails to make clear to a class of teachers some point relative to children, she asks these teachers to stop thinking of their own pupils and to think of some nephew, niece, cousin, some child of whom they have acquaintance in the

---

2. There is where the plea for "adult" psychology has force. The person who does not know himself is not likely to know others. The adult psychology ought, however, to be just as genetic as that of childhood.

unformalities of home life. I do not suppose any great argument is needed to prove that breach of continuity between learning within and without the school is the great cause in education of wasted power and misdirected effort. I wish rather to take advantage of this assumption (which I think will be generally accepted) to emphasize the danger of bringing the would-be teacher into an abrupt and dislocated contact with the psychology of the schoolroom—abrupt and dislocated because not prepared for by prior practice in selecting and organizing the relevant principles and data contained within the experience best known to him, his own.[3]

From this basis, a transition to educational psychology may be made in observation of the teaching of others—visiting classes. I should wish to note here, however, the same principle that I have mentioned as regards practice work, specifically so termed. The first observation of instruction given by model- or critic-teachers should not be too definitely practical in aim. The student should not be observing to find out how the good teacher does it, in order to accumulate a store of methods by which he also may teach successfully. He should rather observe with reference to seeing the interaction of mind, to see how teacher and pupils react upon each other—how mind answers to mind. Observation should at first be conducted from the psychological rather than from the "practical" standpoint. If the latter is emphasized before the student has an independent command of the former, the principle of imitation is almost sure to play an exaggerated part in the observer's future teaching, and hence at the expense of personal insight and initiative. What the student needs most at this stage of growth is ability to see what is going on in the minds of a group of persons who are in intellectual contact with one another. He needs to learn to observe psychologically—a very different thing from simply observing how a teacher gets "good results" in presenting any particular subject.

It should go without saying that the student who has acquired power in psychological observation and interpretation may finally go on to observe more technical aspects of instruction, namely, the various methods and instrumentalities used by a good teacher in giving instruction in any subject. If properly prepared for, this need not tend to produce copiers, followers of tradition and example. Such students will be able to translate the practical devices which are such an important part of the equipment of a good teacher over into their psychological equivalents; to know not

---

3. It may avoid misapprehension if I repeat the word *experience*. It is not a *metaphysical* introspection that I have in mind, but the process of turning back upon one's own experiences, and turning them over to see how they were developed, what helped and hindered, the stimuli and the inhibitions both within and without the organism.

merely as a matter of brute fact that they do work, but to know how and why they work. Thus he will be an independent judge and critic of their proper use and adaptation.

In the foregoing I have assumed that educational psychology is marked off from general psychology simply by the emphasis which it puts upon two factors. The first is the stress laid upon a certain end, namely, growth or development—with its counterparts, arrest and adaptation. The second is the importance attached to the social factor—to the mutual interaction of different minds with each other. It is, I think, strictly true that no educational procedure nor pedagogical maxim can be derived directly from pure psychological data. The psychological data taken without qualification (which is what I mean by their being pure) cover everything and anything that may take place in a mind. Mental arrest and decay occur according to psychological laws, just as surely as do development and progress.

We do not make practical maxims out of physics by telling persons to move according to laws of gravitation. If people move at all, they *must* move in accordance with the conditions stated by this law. Similarly, if mental operations take place at all, they *must* take place in accordance with the principles stated in correct psychological generalizations. It is superfluous and meaningless to attempt to turn these psychological principles directly into rules of teaching. But the person who knows the laws of mechanics knows the conditions of which he must take account when he wishes to reach a certain end. He knows that *if* he aims to build a bridge, he must build it in a certain way and of certain materials, or else he will not have a bridge, but a heap of rubbish. So in psychology. Given an end, say promotion of healthy growth, psychological observations and reflection put us in control of the conditions concerned in that growth. We know that if we are to get that *end*, we must do it in a certain way. It is the subordination of the psychological material to the problem of effecting growth and avoiding arrest and waste which constitutes a distinguishing mark of educational psychology.

I have spoken of the importance of the social factor as the other mark. I do not mean, of course, that general theoretical psychology ignores the existence and significance of the reaction of mind to mind—though it would be within bounds to say that till recently the social side was an unwritten chapter of psychology. I mean that considerations of the ways in which one mind responds to the stimuli which another mind is consciously or unconsciously furnishing possess a relative importance for the educator which they have not for the psychologist as such. From the teacher's standpoint, it is not too much to say that every habit which a pupil exhibits is to be regarded as a reaction to stimuli which some persons or group of persons have presented to the child. It is not too much to say that the most important thing for the teacher to consider, as regards his present relations to his pupils, is the attitudes and habits which his own modes of being, saying, and doing are fostering or discouraging in them.

Now, if these two assumptions regarding educational psychology be granted, I think it will follow as a matter of course, that only by beginning with the values and laws contained in the student's own experience of his own mental growth, and by proceeding gradually to facts connected with other persons of whom he can know little; and by proceeding still more gradually to the attempt actually to influence the mental operations of others, can educational theory be made most effective. Only in this way can the most essential trait of the mental habit of the teacher be secured—that habit which looks upon the internal, not upon the external; which sees that the important function of the teacher is direction of the mental movement of the student, and that the mental movement must be known before it can be directed.

II. I turn now to the side of subject-matter, or scholarship, with the hope of showing that here too the material, when properly presented, is not so *merely* theoretical, remote from the practical problems of teaching, as is sometimes supposed. I recall that once a graduate student in a university made inquiries among all the leading teachers in the institution with which he was connected as to whether they had received any professional training, whether they had taken courses in pedagogy. The inquirer threw the results, which were mostly negative, into the camp of the local pedagogical club. Some may say that this proves nothing, because college teaching is proverbially poor, considered simply as teaching. Yet no one can deny that there is *some* good teaching, and some teaching of the very first order, done in colleges, and done by persons who have never had any instruction in either the theory or the practice of teaching.

This fact cannot be ignored any more than can the fact that there were good teachers before there was any such thing as pedagogy. Now, I am not arguing for not having pedagogical training—that is the last thing I want. But I claim the facts mentioned prove that scholarship *per se* may itself be a most effective tool for training and turning out good teachers. If it has accomplished so much when working unconsciously and without set intention, have we not good reason to believe that, when acquired in a training school for teachers—with the end of making teachers held definitely in view and with conscious reference to its relation to mental activity—it may prove a much more valuable pedagogical asset than we commonly consider it?

Scholastic knowledge is sometimes regarded as if it were something quite irrelevant to method. When this attitude is even unconsciously assumed, method becomes an external attachment to knowledge of subject-matter. It has to be elaborated and acquired in relative independence from subject-matter, and *then* applied.

Now the body of knowledge which constitutes the subject-matter of the student-teacher must, by the nature of the case, be organized subject-matter. It is not a miscellaneous heap of separate scraps. Even if (as in the case of history and literature), it be not technically termed "science," it is none the less material which has been subjected to method—has been selected and arranged with reference to controlling intellectual principles. There is, therefore, method in subject-matter itself—method indeed of the highest order which the human mind has yet evolved, scientific method.

It cannot be too strongly emphasized that this scientific method is the method of mind itself.[4] The classifications, interpretations, explanations, and generalizations which make subject-matter a branch of study do not lie externally in facts apart from mind. They reflect the attitudes and workings of mind in its endeavor to bring raw material of experience to a point where it at once satisfies and stimulates the needs of active thought. Such being the case, there is something wrong in the "academic" side of professional training, if by means of it the student does not constantly get object-lessons of the finest type in the kind of mental activity which characterizes mental growth and, hence, the educative process.

It is necessary to recognize the importance for the teacher's equipment of his own habituation to superior types of method of mental operation. The more a teacher in the future is likely to have to do with elementary teaching, the more, rather than the less, necessary is such exercise. Otherwise, the current traditions of elementary work with their tendency to talk and write down to the supposed intellectual level of children, will be likely to continue. Only a teacher thoroughly trained in the higher levels of intellectual method and who thus has constantly in his own mind a sense of what adequate and genuine intellectual activity means, will be likely, in deed, not in mere word, to respect the mental integrity and force of children.

Of course, this conception will be met by the argument that the scientific organization of subject-matter, which constitutes the academic studies of the student-teacher is upon such a radically different basis from that adapted to less mature students that too much pre-occupation with scholarship of an advanced order is likely actually to get in the way of the teacher of children and youth. I do not suppose anybody would contend that teachers really can know more than is good for them, but it may

---

4. Professor Ella F. Young's "Scientific Method in Education" *(University of Chicago Decennial Publications)* is a noteworthy development of this conception, to which I am much indebted.

reasonably be argued that continuous study of a specialized sort forms mental habits likely to throw the older student out of sympathy with the type of mental impulses and habits which are found in younger persons.

Right here, however, I think normal schools and teachers' colleges have one of their greatest opportunities—an opportunity not merely as to teachers in training, but also for reforming methods of education in colleges and higher schools having nothing to do with the training of teachers. It is the business of normal schools and collegiate schools of education to present subject-matter in science, in language, in literature and the arts, in such a way that the student both sees and feels that these studies *are* significant embodiments of mental operations. He should be led to realize that they are not products of technical methods, which have been developed for the sake of the specialized branches of knowledge in which they are used, but represent fundamental mental attitudes and operations—that, indeed, particular scientific methods and classifications simply express and illustrate in their most concrete form that of which simple and common modes of thought-activity are capable when they work under satisfactory conditions.

In a word, it is the business of the "academic" instruction of future teachers to carry back subject-matter to its common psychical roots.[5] In so far as this is accomplished, the gap between the higher and the lower treatment of subject-matter, upon which the argument of the supposed objector depends, ceases to have the force which that argument assigns to it. This does not mean, of course, that exactly the same subject-matter, in the same mode of presentation, is suitable to a student in the elementary or high schools that is appropriate to the normal student. But it does mean that a mind which is habituated to viewing subject-matter from the standpoint of the function of that subject-matter in connection with *mental* responses, attitudes, and methods will be sensitive to signs of intellectual activity when exhibited in the child of four, or the youth of sixteen, and will be trained to a spontaneous and unconscious appreciation of the subject-matter which is fit to call out and direct mental activity.

We have here, I think, the explanation of the success of some teachers who violate every law known to and laid down by pedagogical science. They are themselves so full of the spirit of inquiry, so sensitive to every sign of its presence and absence, that no matter what they do, nor how they do it, they succeed in awakening and inspiring like alert and intense mental activity in those with whom they come in contact.

---

5. It is hardly necessary to refer to Dr. Harris's continued contention that normal training should give a higher view or synthesis of even the most elementary subjects.

This is not a plea for the prevalence of these irregular, inchoate methods. But I feel that I may recur to my former remark: if some teachers, by sheer plenitude of knowledge, keep by instinct in touch with the mental activity of their pupils, and accomplish so much without, and even in spite of, principles which are theoretically sound, then there must be in this same scholarship a tremendous resource when it is more consciously used—that is, employed in clear connection with psychological principles.

When I said above that schools for training teachers have here an opportunity to react favorably upon general education, I meant that no instruction in subject-matter (wherever it is given) is adequate if it leaves the student with just acquisition of certain information about external facts and laws, or even a certain facility in the intellectual manipulation of this material. It is the business of our higher schools in all lines, and not simply of our normal schools, to furnish the student with the realization that, after all, it is the human mind, trained to effective control of its natural attitudes, impulses, and responses, that is the significant thing in all science and history and art so far as these are formulated for purposes of study.

The present divorce between scholarship and method is as harmful upon one side as upon the other—as detrimental to the best interests of higher academic instruction as it is to the training of teachers. But the only way in which this divorce can be broken down is by so presenting all subject-matter, for whatever ultimate, practical, or professional purpose, that it shall be apprehended as an objective embodiment of methods of mind in its search for, and transactions with, the truth of things.

Upon the more practical side, this principle requires that, so far as students appropriate new subject-matter (thereby improving their own scholarship and realizing more consciously the nature of method), they should finally proceed to organize this same subject-matter with reference to its use in teaching others. The curriculum of the elementary and the high school constituting the "practice" or "model" school ought to stand in the closest and most organic relation to the instruction in subject-matter which is given by the teachers of the professional school. If in any given school this is not the case, it is either because in the *training class* subject-matter is presented in an isolated way, instead of as a concrete expression of methods of mind, or else because *the practice school* is dominated by certain conventions and traditions regarding material and the methods of teaching it, and hence is not engaged in work of an adequate educational type.

As a matter of fact, as everybody knows, both of these causes contribute to the present state of things. On the one hand, inherited conditions impel the elementary school to a certain triviality and poverty of subject-matter, calling for mechanical drill, rather than for thought-activity, and the high school to a certain technical mastery of certain conventional culture subjects, taught as independent branches of the same tree of knowledge! On the other hand traditions of the different branches of science (the academic side of subject-matter) tend to subordinate the teaching in the normal school to the attainment of certain facilities, and the acquirement of certain information, both in greater or less isolation from their value as exciting and directing mental power.

The great need is convergence, concentration. Every step taken in the elementary and the high school toward intelligent introduction of more worthy and significant subject-matter, one requiring consequently for its assimilation thinking rather than "drill," must be met by a like advance step in which the mere isolated specialization of collegiate subject-matter is surrendered, and in which there is brought to conscious and interested attention its significance in expression of fundamental modes of mental activity—so fundamental as to be common to both the play of the mind upon the ordinary material of everyday experience and to the systematized material of the sciences.

III. As already suggested, this point requires that training students be exercised in making the connections between the course of study of the practice or model school, and the wider horizons of learning coming within their ken. But it is consecutive and systematic exercise in the consideration of the subject-matter of the elementary and high schools that is needed. The habit of making isolated and independent lesson plans for a few days' or weeks' instruction in a separate grade here or there not only does not answer this purpose, but is likely to be distinctly detrimental. Everything should be discouraged which tends to put the student in the attitude of snatching at the subject-matter which he is acquiring in order to see if by some hook or crook it may be made immediately available for a lesson in this or that grade. What is needed is the habit of viewing the entire curriculum as a continuous growth, reflecting the growth of mind itself. This in turn demands, so far as I can see, consecutive and longitudinal consideration of the curriculum of the elementary and high school rather than a cross-sectional view of it. The student should be led to see that the same subject-matter in geography, nature-study, or art develops not merely day to day in a given grade, but from year to year throughout the entire movement of the school; and he should realize this before he gets much encouragement in trying to adapt subject-matter in lesson plans for this or that isolated grade.

C. If we attempt to gather together the points which have been brought out, we should have a view of practice work something like the following— though I am afraid even this formulates a scheme with more appearance of rigidity than is desirable:

At first, the practice school would be used mainly for purposes of observation. This observation, moreover, would not be for the sake of seeing how good teachers teach, or for getting "points" which may be employed in one's own teaching, but to get material for psychological observation and reflection, and some conception of the educational movement of the school as a whole.

Secondly, there would then be more intimate introduction to the lives of the children and the work of the school through the use as assistants of such students as had already got psychological insight and a good working acquaintance with educational problems. Students at this stage would not undertake much direct teaching, but would make themselves useful in helping the regular class instructor. There are multitudes of ways in which such help can be given and be of real help—that is, of use to the school, to the children, and not merely of putative value to the training student.[6] Special attention to backward children, to children who have been out of school, assisting in the care of material, in forms of hand-work, suggest some of the avenues of approach.

This kind of practical experience enables, in the third place, the future teacher to make the transition from his more psychological and theoretical insight to the observation of the more technical points of class teaching and management. The informality, gradualness, and familiarity of the earlier contact tend to store the mind with material which is unconsciously assimilated and organized, and thus supplies a background for work involving greater responsibility.

As a counterpart of this work in assisting, such students might well at the same time be employed in the selection and arrangement of subject-matter, as indicated in the previous discussion. Such organization would at the outset have reference to at least a group of grades, emphasizing continuous and consecutive growth. Later it might, without danger of undue narrowness, concern itself with finding supplementary materials and problems bearing upon the work in which the student is giving assistance; might elaborate material which could be used to carry the work still farther, if it were desirable; or, in case of the more advanced students, to build up a scheme of possible alternative subjects for lessons and studies.

Fourthly, as fast as students are prepared through their work of assisting for more responsible work, they could be given actual teaching to do. Upon the basis that the previous preparation has been adequate in subject-matter, in educational theory, and in the kind of observation and practice already discussed, such practice teachers should be given the maximum amount of liberty possible. They should not be too closely supervised, nor

---

6. This question of some real need in the practice school itself for the work done is very important in its moral influence and in assimilating the conditions of "practice work" to those of real teaching.

too minutely and immediately criticised upon either the matter or the method of their teaching. Students should be given to understand that they not only are *permitted* to act upon their own intellectual initiative, but that they are *expected* to do so, and that their ability to take hold of situations for themselves would be a more important factor in judging them than their following any particular set method or scheme.

Of course, there should be critical discussion with persons more expert of the work done, and of the educational results obtained. But sufficient time should be permitted to allow the practice-teacher to recover from the shocks incident to the newness of the situation, and also to get enough experience to make him capable of seeing the *fundamental* bearings of criticism upon work done. Moreover, the work of the expert or supervisor should be directed to getting the student to judge his own work critically, to find out for himself in what respects he has succeeded and in what failed, and to find the probable reasons for both failure and success, rather than to criticising him too definitely and specifically upon special features of his work.

It ought to go without saying (unfortunately, it does not in all cases) that criticism should be directed to making the professional student thoughtful about his work in the light of principles, rather than to induce in him a recognition that certain special methods are good, and certain other special methods bad. At all events, no greater travesty of real intellectual criticism can be given than to set a student to teaching a brief number of lessons, have him under inspection in practically all the time of every lesson, and then criticise him almost, if not quite, at the very end of each lesson, upon the particular way in which that particular lesson has been taught, pointing out elements of failure and of success. Such methods of criticism may be adapted to giving a training-teacher command of some of the knacks and tools of the trade, but are not calculated to develop a thoughtful and independent teacher.

Moreover, while such teaching (as already indicated) should be extensive or continuous enough to give the student time to become at home and to get a body of funded experience, it ought to be intensive in purpose rather than spread out miscellaneously. It is much more important for the teacher to assume responsibility for the consecutive development of some one topic, to get a feeling for the movement of that subject, than it is to teach a certain number (necessarily smaller in range) of lessons in a larger number of subjects. What we want, in other words, is not so much technical skill, as a realizing sense in the teacher of what the educational development of a subject means, and, in some typical case, command of a method of control, which will then serve as a standard for self-judgment in other cases.

Fifthly, if the practical conditions permit—if, that is to say, the time of the training course is sufficiently long, if the practice schools are sufficiently large to furnish the required number of children, and to afford actual demand for the work to be done—students who have gone through the stages already referred to should be ready for work of the distinctly apprenticeship type.

Nothing that I have said heretofore is to be understood as ruling out practice-teaching which is designed to give an individual mastery of the actual technique of teaching and management, provided school conditions permit it in reality and not merely in external form—provided, that is, the student has gone through a training in educational theory and history, in subject-matter, in observation, and in practice work of the laboratory type, before entering upon the latter. The teacher must acquire his technique some time or other; and if conditions are favorable, there are some advantages in having this acquisition take place in cadetting or in something of that kind. By means of this probation, persons who are unfit for teaching may be detected and eliminated more quickly than might otherwise be the case and before their cases have become institutionalized.

Even in this distinctly apprenticeship stage, however, it is still important that the student should be given as much responsibility and initiative as he is capable of taking, and hence that supervision should not be too unremitting and intimate, and criticism not at too short range or too detailed. The advantage of this intermediate probationary period does not reside in the fact that thereby supervisory officers may turn out teachers who will perpetuate their own notions and methods, but in the inspiration and enlightenment that come through prolonged contact with mature and sympathetic persons. If the conditions in the public schools were just what they ought to be, if all superintendents and principals had the knowledge and the wisdom which they should have, and if they had time and opportunity to utilize their knowledge and their wisdom in connection with the development of the younger teachers who come to them, the value of this apprenticeship period would be reduced, I think, very largely to its serving to catch in time and to exclude persons unfitted for teaching.

In conclusion, I may say that I do not believe that the principles presented in this paper call for anything Utopian. The present movement in normal schools for improvement of range and quality of subject-matter is steady and irresistible. All the better classes of normal schools are already, in effect, what are termed "junior colleges." That is, they give two years' work which is almost, and in many cases quite, of regular college grade. More and more, their instructors are persons who have had the same kind of scholarly training that is expected of teachers in colleges. Many of these institutions are already of higher grade than this; and the next decade will certainly see a marked tendency on the part of many normal schools to claim the right to give regular collegiate bachelor degrees.

The type of scholarship contemplated in this paper is thus practically assured for the near future. If two other factors co-operate with this, there is no reason why the conception of relation of theory and practice here presented should not be carried out. The second necessary factor is that the elementary and high schools, which serve as schools of observation and practice, should represent an advanced type of education properly corresponding to the instruction in academic subject-matter and in educational theory given to the training classes. The third necessity is that work in psychology and educational theory make concrete and vital the connection between the normal instruction in subject-matter and the work of the elementary and high schools.

If it should prove impracticable to realize the conception herein set forth, it will not be, I think, because of any impossibility resident in the outward conditions, but because those in authority, both within and without the schools, believe that the true function of training schools is just to meet the needs of which people are already conscious. In this case, of course, training schools will be conducted simply with reference to perpetuating current types of educational practice, with simply incidental improvement in details.

The underlying assumption of this paper is, accordingly, that training schools for teachers do not perform their full duty in accepting and conforming to present educational standards, but that educational leadership is an indispensable part of their office. The thing needful is improvement of education, not simply by turning out teachers who can do better the things that are now necessary to do, but rather by changing the conception of what constitutes education.

Individuality and Experience
(1926)

In this rarely cited article, Dewey seeks to redirect his Progressive counterparts by making the point that subject-matter was just as essential as meeting the needs and interests of students. He criticizes the practice of allowing children to learn whatever they want to learn without regard to the end or plan that teachers and administrators have in mind for students. Dewey shockingly calls radical proponents of individual freedom "stupid" for rejecting the idea that teachers should teach a rationally-designed curriculum to children.

The interesting report of Dr. Munro in the October number of this *Journal* on the methods of picture-making employed in the classes of Professor Cizek in Vienna raises a question that has to be dealt with in every branch of instruction. The question develops in two directions, one suggested by his statement that it is impossible to exclude outside influences, and the other by his report that upon the whole the more original constructions are those of younger pupils, that older students seem gradually to lose interest, so that no prominent artist has been produced. The problem thus defined consists in the relation of individuality and its adequate development to the work and responsibilities of the teacher, representing accumulated experience of the past.

Unfortunately, the history of schools not only in art but in all lines shows a swing of the pendulum between extremes, though it must be admitted that the simile of the pendulum is not a good one, for the schools remain most of them, most of the time, near one extreme, instead of swinging periodically and evenly between the two. Anyway, the two extremes are external imposition and dictation and "free-expression." Revolt from the

Forgotten Heroes of American Education, pages 589–594

costly, nerve-taxing and inadequate results of mechanical control from without creates an enthusiasm for spontaneity and "development from within," as it is often phrased. It is found that children at first are then much happier in their work—anyone who has seen Cizek's class will testify to the wholesome air of cheerfulness, even of joy, which pervades the room—but gradually tend to become listless and finally bored, while there is an absence of cumulative, progressive development of power and of actual achievement in results. Then the pendulum swings back to regulation by the ideas, rules, and orders of some one else, who being maturer, better informed and more experienced is supposed to know what should be done and how to do it.

The metaphor of the pendulum is faulty in another respect. It seems to suggest that the solution lies in finding a mid-point between the two extremes which would be at rest. But what is really wanted is a change in the direction of movement. As a general proposition no one would deny that personal mental growth is furthered in any branch of human undertaking by contact with the accumulated and sifted experience of others in that line. No one would seriously propose that all future carpenters should be trained by actually starting with a clean sheet, wiping out everything that the past has discovered about mechanics, about tools and their uses and so on. It would not be thought likely that this knowledge would "cramp their style," limit their individuality, etc. But neither, on the other hand, have carpenters been formed by the methods often used in manual training shops where dinky tasks of a minute and technical nature are set, wholly independent of really making anything, having only specialized skill as their aim. As a rule carpenters are educated in their calling by working with others who have experience and skill, sharing in the simpler portions of the real undertakings, assisting in ways which enable them to observe methods and to see what results they are adapted to accomplish.

Such learning is controlled by two great principles: one is participation in something inherently worth while, or undertaken on its own account; the other, is perception of the relation of means to consequences. When these two conditions are met, a third consideration usually follows as a matter of course. Having had an experience of the meaning of certain technical processes and forms of skill there develops an interest in skill and "technique:" the meaning of the result is "transferred" to the means of its attainment. Boys interested in base-ball as a game thus submit themselves voluntarily to continued practice in throwing, catching, batting, the separate elements of the game. Or boys, who get interested in the game of marbles will practice to increase their skill in shooting and hitting. Just imagine, however, what would happen if they set these exercises as tasks in school, with no prior activity in the games and with no sense of what they were about or for, and without any such appeal to the social, or participating impulses, as takes place in games!

If we generalize from such a commonplace case as the education of artisans through their work, we may say that the customs, methods and *working* standards of the calling constitute a "tradition," and that initiation into the tradition is the means by which the powers of learners are released and directed. But we should also have to say that the urge or need of an individual to join in an undertaking is a necessary prerequisite of the tradition's being a factor in his personal growth in power and freedom; and also that he has to *see* on his own behalf and in his own way the relations between means and methods employed and results achieved. Nobody else can see for him, and he can't see just by being "told," although the right kind of telling may guide his seeing and thus help him see what he needs to see. And if he has no impelling desire of his own to become a carpenter, if his interest in being one is perfunctory, if it is not an interest in *being* a carpenter at all, but only in getting a pecuniary reward by doing jobs, the tradition will never of course really enter into and integrate with his own powers. It will remain, then, a mere set of mechanical and more or less meaningless rules that he is obliged to follow if he is to hold his job and draw his pay.

Supposing, again, that our imaginary pupil works for and with a master carpenter who believes in only one kind of house with a fixed design, and his aim is not only to teach his apprentice to make just that one kind of house, but to accept it with all his soul, heart and mind as the only kind of house that should ever be built, the very type and standard model of all houses. Then it is easy to see that limitation of personal powers will surely result, not merely, moreover, limitation of technical skill but, what is more important, of his powers of observation, imagination, judgment, and even his emotions, since his appreciations will be warped to conform to the one preferred style. The imaginary case illustrates what often happens when we pass from the education of artisans to that of artists. As a rule a carpenter has to keep more or less open; he is exposed to many demands and must be flexible enough to meet them. He is in no position to set up a final authority about ends and models and standards, no matter how expert he may be in methods and means. But an architect in distinction from a builder is likely to be an "authority;" he can dictate and lay down what is right and wrong, and thus prescribe certain ends and proscribe others. Here is a case where tradition is not enhancing and liberating, but is restrictive and enslaving. If he has pupils, he is a "master" and not an advanced fellow worker; his students are disciples rather than learners. Tradition is no longer tradition but a fixed and absolute convention.

In short, the practical difficulty does not reside in any antagonism of methods and rules and results worked out in past experience to individual desire, capacity and freedom. It lies rather in the hard and narrow and, we may truly say, uneducated habits and attitudes of teachers who set up as authorities, as rulers and judges in Israel. As a matter of course they know that as bare individuals they are not "authorities" and will not be accepted by others as such. So they clothe themselves with some tradition as a mantle, and henceforth it is not just "I" who speaks, but some Lord speaks through me. The teacher then offers himself as the organ of the voice of a whole school, of a *finished* classic tradition, and arrogates to himself the prestige that comes from what he is the spokesman for. Suppression of the emotional and intellectual integrity of pupils is the result; their freedom is repressed and the growth of their own personalities stunted. But it is not because of any opposition between the wisdom and skill of the past and the individual capacities of learners; the trouble lies in the habits, standards and ideas of the teacher. It is analogous to another case. There is no inherent opposition between theory and practice; the former enlarges, releases and gives significance to the latter; while practice supplies theory with its materials and with the test and check which keeps it sincere and vital. But there is a whole lot of opposition between human beings who set themselves up as practical and those who set themselves up as theorists, an irresolvable conflict because both have put themselves into a wrong position.

This suggests that the proponents of freedom are in a false position as well as the would-be masters and dictators. There is a present tendency in so-called advanced schools of educational thought (by no means confined to art classes like those of Cizek) to say, in effect, let us surround pupils with certain materials, tools, appliances, etc., and then let pupils respond to these things according to their own desires. Above all let us not suggest any end or plan to the students; let us not suggest to them what they shall do, for that is an unwarranted trespass upon their sacred intellectual individuality since the essence of such individuality is to set up ends and aims.

Now such a method is really stupid. For it attempts the impossible, which is always stupid; and it misconceives the conditions of independent thinking. There are a multitude of ways of reacting to surrounding conditions, and without some guidance from experience these reactions are almost sure to be casual, sporadic and ultimately fatiguing, accompanied by nervous strain. Since the teacher has presumably a greater background of experience, there is the same presumption of the right of a teacher to make suggestions as to what to do, as there is on the part of the head carpenter to suggest to apprentices something of what they are to do. Moreover, the theory literally carried out would be obliged to banish all artificial materials, tools and appliances. Being the product of the skill, thought and matured experience of others, they would also, by the theory, "interfere" with personal freedom.

Moreover, when the child proposes or suggests what to do, some consequence to be attained, whence is the suggestion supposed to spring from? There is no spontaneous germination in the mental life. If he does not get the suggestion from the teacher, he gets it from somebody or something in the home or the street or from what some more vigorous fellow pupil is doing. Hence the chances are great of its being a passing and superficial suggestion, without much depth and range—in other words, not specially conducive to the developing of freedom. If the teacher is really a teacher, and not just a master or "authority," he should know enough about his pupils, their needs, experiences, degrees of skill and knowledge etc., to be able (not to dictate aims and plans) to share in a discussion regarding what is to be done and be as free to make suggestions as any one else. (The implication that the teacher is the one and only person who has no "individuality" or "freedom" to "express" would be funny if it were not often so sad in its outworkings.) And his contribution, given the conditions stated, will presumably do more to getting something started which will really secure and increase the development of strictly individual capacities than will suggestions springing from uncontrolled haphazard sources.

The point is also worth dwelling upon, that the method of leaving the response entirely to pupils, the teacher supplying, in the language of the day, only the "stimuli," misconceives the nature of thinking. Any so-called "end" or "aim" or "project" which the average immature person can suggest in advance is likely to be highly vague and unformed, a mere outline sketch, not a suggestion of a definite result or consequence but rather a gesture which roughly indicates a field within which activities might be carried on. It hardly represents thought at all: it is a suggestion. The real intellectual shaping of the "end" or purpose comes during and because of the operations subsequently performed. This is as true of the suggestion which proceeds from the teacher as of those which "spontaneously" spring from the pupils, so that the former does not restrict thought. The advantage on the side of the teacher—if he or she has any business to be in that position—is the greater probability that it will be a suggestion which will permit and require thought in the subsequent activity which builds up a clear and organized conception of an end. There is no more fatal flaw in psychology than that which takes the original vague fore-feeling of some consequence to be realized as the equivalent of a *thought* of an end, a true purpose and directive plan. The thought of an end is strictly correlative to perception of means and methods. Only when, and as the latter becomes clear during the serial process of execution does the project and guiding aim and plan become evident and articulated. In the full sense of the word, a person becomes aware of what he wants to do and what he is about only when the work is actually complete.

The adjective "serial" is important in connection with the process of performance or execution. Each step forward, each "means" used, is a partial attainment of an "end." It makes clearer the character of that end, and hence suggests to an observing mind the next step to be taken, or the means and methods to be next employed. Originality and independence of thinking are therefore connected with the intervening process of execution rather than with the source of the initial suggestion. Indeed, genuinely fruitful and original suggestions are themselves usually the results of experience in the carrying out of undertakings. The "end" is not, in other words, an end or finality in the literal sense, but is in turn the starting point of new desires, aims and plans. By means of the process the mind gets power to make suggestions which are significant. There is now a past experience from which they can spring with an increased probability of their being worthwhile and articulate.

It goes without saying that a teacher may interfere and impose alien standards and methods during the operation. But as we have previously seen, this is not because of bringing to bear the results of previous experience, but because the habits of the teacher are so narrow and fixed, his imagination and sympathies so limited, his own intellectual horizon so bounded, that he brings them to bear in a wrong way. The fuller and richer the experience of the teacher, the more adequate his own knowledge of "traditions" the more likely is he, given the attitude of participator instead of that of master, to use them in a liberating way.

Freedom or individuality, in short, is not an original possession or gift. It is something to be achieved, to be wrought out. Suggestions as to things which may advantageously be taken, as to skill, as to methods of operation, are indispensable conditions of its achievement. These by the nature of the case must come from a sympathetic and discriminating knowledge of what has been done in the past and how it has been done.

How Much Freedom in New Schools?
(1930)

This article is another rarely cited work from John Dewey. Once again, he condemns his Progressive colleagues for over emphasizing individual freedom. Some of them, he claims, have trumpeted individuality to such an extent that they have begun to advocate anarchy. Dewey tries to focus his followers on the task of balancing individual freedom with social responsibility. For whatever reason, however, admonishments like this one from Dewey went ignored.

It is not easy to take stock of the achievements of progressive schools in the last decade: these schools are too diverse both in aims and in mode of conduct. In one respect, this is as it should be: it indicates that there is no cut-and-dried program to follow, that schools are free to grow along the lines of special needs and conditions and so to express the variant ideas of innovating leaders. But there is more than is suggested by these considerations in the existing diversity. It testifies also to the fact that the underlying motivation is so largely a reaction against the traditional school that the watchwords of the progressive movement are capable of being translated into inconsistent practices.

The negative aspect of progressive education results from the conditions of its origin. Progressive schools are usually initiated by parents who are dissatisfied with existing schools and find teachers who agree with them. Often they express discontent with traditional education or locally available schools without embodying any well thought-out policies and aims. They are symptoms of reaction against formalism and mass

Forgotten Heroes of American Education, pages 595–600

regimentation; they are manifestations of a desire for an education at once freer and richer. In extreme cases they represent enthusiasm much more than understanding.

Their common creed is the belief in freedom, in esthetic enjoyment and artistic expression, in opportunity for individual development, and in learning through activity rather than by passive absorption. Such aims give progressive schools a certain community of spirit and atmosphere. But they do not determine any common procedure in discipline or instruction; they do not fix the subject matter to be taught; they do not decide whether the emphasis shall be upon science, history, the fine arts, different modes of industrial art, or social issues and questions. Hence the diversity of the progressive schools, and hence the great difficulty in appraising them. Adverse criticisms may be readily and often effectively answered on the ground that they do not apply to specific schools.

Strong and weak points go together; every human institution has the defects of its qualities. Colonel Francis W. Parker, more nearly than any other one person, was the father of the progressive educational movement, a fact all the more significant because he spent most of his educational life in public rather than private schools—first at Quincy, Massachusetts, and then at the Cook County Normal School in Englewood, Chicago. I do not know whether he used the phrase which has since come into vogue, "child-centered schools." One of his most frequent statements was that teachers had been teaching *subjects* when they should be teaching *children*. He engaged in aggressive warfare against the burden of ready-made, desiccated subject matter formulated and arranged from the adult point of view—in other words, against the stock in trade of the conventional curriculum. He pleaded for subject matter nearer to the experience and life of the pupils. He strove to throw off the yoke of fixed and uniform disciplinary measures. He introduced many things, innovations in his day, which are now almost commonplaces in the public schools which lay any claim to being modern—for example, the school assemblies conducted by the pupils themselves.

Even such an inadequate statement as the foregoing brings out an antithesis which has persisted to a considerable extent in the later movement of progressive education: that between the human and personal element represented by the pupils, the children, youth, and, on the other hand, the impersonal and objective factor—the subject matter of studies, the body of knowledge and organized and skilled accomplishment. In saying that the antithesis thus set up has resulted, upon the whole, in a lack of balance, I do not mean in any way to hold the work and influence of Colonel Parker responsible. I mean that the same reaction against dead, formal and external studies which affected his early reforms has continued to operate with his successors, and to produce a one-sided emphasis—that upon pupils at the expense of subject matter.

That there was need for the reaction, indeed for a revolt, seems to me unquestionable. The evils of the traditional, conventional school room, its almost complete isolation from actual life, and the deadly depression of mind which the weight of formal material caused, all cried out for reform. But rebellion against formal studies and lessons can be effectively completed only through the development of a new subject matter, as well organized as was the old—indeed, better organized in any vital sense of the word organization—but having an intimate and developing relation to the experience of those in school. The relative failure to accomplish this result indicates the one-sidedness of the idea of "child-centered" school.

I do not mean, of course, that education does not center in the pupil. It obviously takes its start with him and terminates with him. But the child is not something isolated; he does not live inside himself, but in a world of nature and man. His experience is not complete in his impulses and emotions; these must reach out into a world of objects and persons. And until an experience has become relatively mature, the impulses do not even know what they are reaching out toward and for; they are blind and inchoate. To fail to assure them guidance and direction is not merely to permit them to operate in a blind and spasmodic fashion, but it promotes the formation of *habits* of immature, undeveloped, and egoistic activity. Guidance and direction mean that the impulses and desires take effect through material that is impersonal and objective. And this subject matter can be provided in a way which will obtain ordered and consecutive development of experience only by means of the thoughtful selection and organization of material by those having the broadest experience—those who treat impulses and inchoate desires and plans as potentialities of growth through interaction and not as finalities.

To be truly self-centered is not to be centered in one's feelings and desires. Such a center means dissipation, and the ultimate destruction of any center whatever. Nor does it mean to be egoistically bent on the fulfillment of personal wishes and ambitions. It means rather to have a rich field of social and natural relations, which are at first external to the self, but now incorporated into personal experience so that they give it weight, balance and order. In some progressive schools the fear of adult imposition has become a veritable phobia. When the fear is analyzed, it means simply a preference for an immature and undeveloped experience over a ripened and thoughtful one; it erects into a standard something which by its nature provides no steady measure or tested criterion. In some recent articles in *The New Republic* I have argued that an adult cannot attain an integrated personality except by incorporating into himself the realities of the life-situations in which he finds himself. This operation is certainly even more necessary for the young; what is called "subject matter" represents simply the selected and organized material that is relevant to such incorporation at any given time. The neglect of it means arrest of growth at an immature level and ultimate disintegration of selfhood.

It is, of course, difficult to use words that are not open to misapprehension. There may be those who think that I am making a plea for return to some kind of adult imposition, or at least to ready-made and rather rigidly predetermined topics and sequences of study. But in fact many of the current interpretations of the child-centered school, of pupil initiative and pupil-purposing and planning, suffer from exactly the same fallacy as the adult-imposition method of the traditional school—only in an inverted form. That is, they are still obsessed by the personal factor; they conceive of no alternative to adult dictation save child dictation. What is wanted is to get away from every mode of personal dictation and merely personal control. When the emphasis falls upon having experiences that are educationally worthwhile, the center of gravity shifts from the personal factor, and is found within the developing experience in which pupils and teachers alike participate. The teacher, because of greater maturity and wider knowledge, is the natural leader in the shared activity, and is naturally accepted as such. The fundamental thing is to find the types of experience that are worth having, not merely for the moment, but because of what they lead to—the questions they raise, the problems they create, the demands for new information they suggest, the activities they invoke, the larger and expanding fields into which they continuously open.

In criticizing the progressive schools, as I have indicated already, it is difficult to make sweeping generalizations. But some of these schools indulge pupils in unrestrained freedom of action and speech, of manners and lack of manners. Schools farthest to the left (and there are many parents who share the fallacy) carry the thing they call freedom nearly to the point of anarchy. This license, however—this outer freedom in action—is but an included part of the larger question just touched upon. When there is genuine control and direction of experiences that are intrinsically worth while by objective subject matter, excessive liberty of outward action will also be naturally regulated. Ultimately it is the absence of intellectual control through significant subject matter which stimulates the deplorable egotism, cockiness, impertinence and disregard for the rights of others apparently considered by some persons to be the inevitable accompaniment, if not the essence, of freedom.

The fact that even the most extreme of the progressive schools do obtain for their pupils a degree of mental independence and power which stands them in good stead when they go to schools where formal methods prevail, is evidence of what might be done if the emphasis were put upon the rational freedom which is the fruit of objective knowledge and understanding. And thus we are brought to the nub of the matter. To conduct a progressive school is much more difficult than to conduct a formal one. Standards, materials, methods are already at hand for the latter; the teacher needs only to follow and conform. Upon the whole, it is not surprising that, in history, science, the arts and other school "studies," there is still a lack of subject matter which has been organized upon the basis of connection with the pupils' own growth in insight and power. The time-span of progressive schools has been too short to permit very much to be accomplished. What may rightfully be demanded, however, is that the progressive schools recognize their responsibility for accomplishing this task, so as not to be content with casual improvisation and living intellectually from hand to mouth.

Again one needs to guard against misunderstanding. There is no single body of subject matter which can be worked out, even in the course of years, which will be applicable all over the country. I am not arguing for any such outcome; I know of nothing that would so completely kill progressive schools and turn them into another kind of formal schools, differentiated only by having another set of conventions. Even in the same school, what will work with one group of children will not "take" with another group of the same age. Full recognition of the fact that subject matter must be always changing with locality, with the situation and with the particular type of children is, however, quite consistent with equal recognition of the fact that it is possible to work out varied bodies of consecutive subject matter upon which teachers may draw, each in his own way, in conducting his own work. The older type of education could draw upon a body of information, of subject matter and skills which was arranged from the adult standpoint. Progressive education must have a much larger, more expansive and adaptable body of materials and activities, developed through constant study of the conditions and methods favorable to the consecutive development of power and understanding. The weakness of existing progressive education is due to the meager knowledge which anyone has regarding the conditions and laws of continuity which govern the development of mental power. To this extent its defects are inevitable and are not to be complained of. But if progressive schools become complacent with existing accomplishments, unaware of the slight foundation of knowledge upon which they rest, and careless regarding the amount of study of the laws of growth that remains to be done, a reaction against them is sure to take place.

Such reference as has been made to the subject matter of a worth-while and continuously developing experience is too general to be of value in actual guidance. The discovery of such subject matter, which induces growth or skill, understanding and rational freedom, is the main question to be worked upon cooperatively. The question may be raised, however, of whether the tendency of progressive schools has not been to put emphasis upon things that make schooling more immediately enjoyable to pupils rather than upon things that will give them the understanding and capacity that are relevant to contemporary social life. No one can justly decry the value of any education which supplies additions to the resources of the inner life of pupils. But surely the problem of progressive education demands that this result be not effected in such a way as to ignore or obscure preparation for the social realities—including the evils—of industrial and political civilization.

Upon the whole, progressive schools have been most successful in furthering "creativeness" in the arts—in music, drawing and picture making, dramatics and literary composition, including poetry. This achievement is well worth while; it ought to assist in producing a generation esthetically more sensitive and alive than the older one. But it is not enough. Taken by itself it will do something to further the private appreciations of, say, the upper section of a middle class. But it will not serve to meet even the esthetic needs and defaultings of contemporary industrial society in its prevailing external expressions. Again, while much has been achieved in teaching science as an addition to private resources in intellectual enjoyment, I do not find that as much has been done in bringing out the relation of science to industrial society, and its potentialities for a planned control of future developments.

Such criticisms as these are not met by introducing exercises and discussions based on what are called "current events." What is needed is something which may indeed connect intellectually in time with what currently happens, but which takes the mind back of the happenings to the understanding of basic causes. Without insight into operative conditions, there can be no education that contains the promise of improved social direction.

This fact brings us back again to the enormous difficulty involved in a truly progressive development of progressive education. This development cannot be secured by the study of children alone. It requires a searching study of society and its moving forces. That the traditional schools have almost wholly evaded consideration of the social potentialities of education is no reason why progressive schools should continue the evasion, even though it be sugared over with esthetic refinements. The time ought to come when no one will be judged to be an educated man or woman who does not have insight into the basic forces of industrial and urban civilization. Only schools which take the lead in bringing about this kind of education can claim to be progressive in any socially significant sense.

COPYRIGHT PERMISSIONS

Bagley, William C., "The Ideal Preparation of a Teacher of Secondary Mathematics from the Point of View of an Educationist," *Mathematics Teacher* 26 (May 1933): 271–276. Reprinted with permission from *Mathematics Teacher*. Copyright © 1933 by the National Council of Teachers of Mathematics.

Bagley, William C., "Teachers' Rights, Academic Freedom, and the Teaching of Controversial Issues," *Teachers College Record* 40 (November 1938): 99–108. Reprinted with permission from *Teachers College Record* and Blackwell Publishing. Copyright © 1938.

Kandel, Isaac L., "Prejudice the Garden Toward Roses?," *The American Scholar* 8 (January 1939): 72–82. Reprinted with permission from *The American Scholar*. Copyright © 1938 by the Phi Beta Kappa Society.

Kandel, Isaac L., "The Profession of Teaching," *School and Society* 52 (Oct. 5, 1940): 284–288. Reprinted with permission from *School and Society* and the Society for the Advancement of Education. Copyright © 1940.

Kandel, Isaac L., "The Fantasia of Current Education," *The American Scholar* 10 (Summer 1941): 286–297. Reprinted with permission from *The American Scholar*. Copyright © 1941 by the Phi Beta Kappa Society.

Kandel, Isaac L., Selection from *The Cult of Uncertainty* (New York: Kappa Delta Pi, 1943), pp. ix–31. Reprinted with permission from the Kappa Delta Pi International Honor Society in Education. Copyright © 1943.

Bagley, William C., "A 'Realistic' Attitude Toward the Teachers-College Problem," *School and Society* 63 (February 1946): 107–108. Reprinted with permission from *School and Society* and the Society for the Advancement of Education. Copyright © 1946.

Kandel, Isaac L., "Revival of American Education," *The Educational Forum* 24 (March 1960): 271–278. Reprinted with permission from the Kappa Delta Pi International Honor Society in Education. Copyright © 1960.

Kandel, Isaac L., "Character Formation: A Historical Perspective," *The Educational Forum* 25 (March 1961): 307–316. Reprinted with permission from the Kappa Delta Pi International Honor Society in Education. Copyright © 1961.

RECOMMENDED READINGS

Primary Sources

Bagley, William C. *Craftsmanship in Teaching*. New York: Macmillan, 1911.

Bagley, William C. *Determinism in Education: A Series of Papers on the Relative Influence of Inherited and Acquired Traits*. Baltimore, MD: Warwick and York, 1925 (Reprinted in 1969 by Ayer Publishing, Manchester, New Hampshire).

Bagley, William C. *Education and Emergent Man: A Theory of Education with Particular Application to Public Education in the United States*. New York: T. Nelson and Sons, 1934.

Bagley, William C. *A Century of the Universal School*. New York: Macmillan, 1937.

DeGarmo, Charles. *The Essentials of Method*. Boston: D.C. Heath, 1892.

DeGarmo, Charles. *Interest and Education: The Doctrine of Interest and its Concrete Application*. New York: Macmillan, 1902.

Felmley, David, Holmes, Manfred James, and Elizabeth Mavity. *The Relation Between Theory and Practice in the Training of Teachers*. Chicago: National Society for the Scientific Study of Education, 2nd Yearbook, 1903.

Harris, William Torrey. *The Theory of American Education*. Washington, D.C.: J. H. Holmes, 1871.

Harris, William Torrey. *Psychologic Foundations of Education*. New York: D. Appleton, 1898 (Reprinted in 1969 by Arno Press, New York City).

Harris, William Torrey. *Elementary Education*. Albany, New York: J. B. Lyon, 1900.

Kandel, Isaac L. "The Philosophy Underlying the System of Education in the United States," in *Educational Yearbook of the International Institute of Teachers College, Columbia University*. New York: Teachers College Bureau of Publications, 1929.

Kandel, Isaac L. *Comparative Education*. Boston: Houghton Mifflin, 1933.

Kandel, Isaac L. "Alice in Cloud-Cuckoo Land," *Teachers College Record* 34 (May 1933): 627–634.

Kandel, Isaac L. *The Making of Nazis*. New York: Teachers College Bureau of Publications, 1934.

Forgotten Heroes of American Education, pages 603–605
Copyright © 2006 by Information Age Publishing
All rights of reproduction in any form reserved.

Kandel, Isaac L. *The Cult of Uncertainty*. New York: Macmillan and Kappa Delta Pi, 1943.

Learned, William S., Bagley, William C., McMurry, Charles A., Strayer, George D., Dearborn, Walter F., Kandel, Isaac L., and Homer W. Josselyn. *Professional Preparation of Teachers For American Public Schools: A Study Based Upon An Examination of Tax-Supported Normal Schools in the State of Missouri*. New York: The Carnegie Foundation for the Advancement of Teaching, 1920.

McMurry, Charles A. *Special Method in History*. New York: Macmillan, 1903.

McMurry, Charles A. *Special Method in Arithmetic*. New York: Macmillan, 1905.

McMurry, Charles A. *How to Organize the Curriculum*. New York: 1923.

Ruediger, William C. *The Principles of Education*. New York: Houghton Mifflin, 1910.

Ruediger, William C. *Vitalized Teaching*. New York: Houghton Mifflin, 1923.

Sheldon, Edward Austin. *Sheldon's Primer Adapted to the Phonic, Word, and Alphabet Modes of Teaching to Read*. New York: Scribner, Armstrong, and Company, 1873.

Sheldon, Edward Austin, and Mary Sheldon Barnes. *Autobiography of Edward Austin Sheldon*. New York: Ives-Butler, 1911.

Secondary Sources

Chall, Jeanne. *The Academic Achievement Challenge*. New York: Guilford, 2000.

Hirsch, E. D., Jr. *Cultural Literacy*. New York: Vintage, 1988.

Hirsch, E. D., Jr. *The Schools We Need*. New York: Anchor, 1996.

Hofstadter, Richard. *Anti-Intellectualism in American Life*. Toronto: Vintage Books, 1962.

Kolesnik, Walter Bernard. *Mental Discipline in Modern Education*. Madison, Wisconsin: University of Wisconsin Press, 1958.

Macintyre, Alasdair. *After Virtue: A Study in Moral Theory*, 2nd ed. South Bend, IN: Notre Dame University Press, 1997.

May, William F. *Beleaguered Rulers: The Public Obligation of the Professional*. London: Westmister John Knox, 2001.

Milson, Andrew J., Bohan, Chara H., Glanzer, Perry L., and J. Wesley Null, Eds. *Readings in American Educational Thought: From Puritanism to Progressivism*. Greenwich, CT: InfoAge, 2004.

Null, J. Wesley. *A Disciplined Progressive Educator: The Life and Career of William Chandler Bagley*. New York: Peter Lang, 2003.

O'Donnell, John M. *The Origins of Behaviorism: American Psychology, 1870–1920*. New York: New York University Press, 1985.

Ravitch, Diane. *The Troubled Crusade: American Education, 1945–1980*. New York: Basic Books, 1985.

Ravitch, Diane. *Left Back: A Century of Battles Over School Reform*. New York: Simon and Schuster, 2000.

Ravitch, Diane, and Joseph P. Viteritti. *Making Good Citizens: Education and Civil Society*. New Haven, CT: Yale University Press, 2001.

Reid, William A. *Curriculum as Institution and Practice: Essays in the Deliberative Tradition*. Mahwah, NJ: Lawrence Erlbaum Associates, 1999.

Reuben, Julie A. *The Making of the Modern University: Intellectual Transformation and the Marginalization of Morality*. Chicago: University of Chicago Press, 1996.

Robinson, Daniel N. *An Intellectual History of Psychology*, 3rd ed. Madison, WI: University of Wisconsin Press, 1995.

Sullivan, William M. *Work and Integrity: The Crisis and Promise of Professionalism in America*. New York: HarperCollins, 1995.

Westbury, Ian, and Neil J. Wilkof, Eds. *Joseph J. Schwab: Science, Curriculum, and Liberal Education*. Chicago: University of Chicago Press, 1982.

Zoch, Paul. *Doomed to Fail*. Chicago: Ivan R. Dee, 2004.

ABOUT THE EDITORS

J. Wesley Null is a teacher educator, historian of education, and Assistant Professor in the School of Education and the Honors College at Baylor University. Before serving on the faculty at Baylor, he taught social studies in public schools in New Mexico and Texas. He earned his undergraduate and master's degrees from Eastern New Mexico University. In 2001, he completed his Ph.D. degree at The University of Texas at Austin, where he studied the history of education and curriculum. At Baylor, he teaches history and philosophy of education in the School of Education and social science and great texts in the Honors College. He also teaches teacher education courses each semester at Waco High School. He is the author of *A Disciplined Progressive Educator: The Life and Career of William Chandler Bagley* (Peter Lang, 2003) and co-editor of *Readings in American Educational Thought: From Puritanism to Progressivism* (Information Age, 2004). He serves as Editor of the *American Educational History Journal.*

Diane Ravitch is a historian of education and Research Professor of Education at New York University. She is a Visiting Senior Fellow at the Brookings Institution in Washington, D.C. and a member of the Koret Task Force at the Hoover Institution at Stanford University. She served on the National Assessment Governing Board, to which she was appointed by Secretary of Education Riley in 1997 and reappointed in 2001. From 1991 to 1993, she was Assistant Secretary of Education and Counselor to Secretary of Education Lamar Alexander in the administration of President George H. W. Bush. As Assistant Secretary, she led the federal effort to promote the creation of state and national academic standards. Before entering government service, she was Adjunct Professor of History and Education at Teachers College, Columbia University. She is the author of numerous books, including *Left Back: A Century of Battles Over School*

Forgotten Heroes of American Education, pages 607–608
Copyright © 2006 by Information Age Publishing
All rights of reproduction in any form reserved.

Reform (Simon and Schuster, 2000), *The Language Police: How Pressure Groups Restrict What Students Learn* (Knopf, 2003), and *The Troubled Crusade: American Education, 1945-1980* (Basic Books, 1983). She is a director of the New York State Council for the Humanities and has received honorary degrees from eight institutions. A native of Houston, she is a graduate of the Houston public schools. She received a B.A. from Wellesley College in 1960 and a Ph.D. in history from Columbia University's Graduate School of Arts and Sciences in 1975.

INDEX OF NAMES

Forgotten Heroes of American Education, pages 609–612
Copyright © 2006 by Information Age Publishing

INDEX OF SUBJECTS

Forgotten Heroes of American Education, pages 613–623

Copyright © 2006 by Information Age Publishing

T

Printed in the United States
200670BV00041B/28/A